AF516642

The Life and Legacy of ARUN JAITLEY

Advance Praise for the Book

Crafting a eulogy that would do justice to a truly multi-dimensional personality like Arun is a challenging task. Everyone knows that he was a remarkable leader and true statesman. His contributions to Indian politics and law are immense. Everyone knows that his eloquence and mastery of parliamentary procedures earned him respect from colleagues across party lines and that he played a pivotal role in shaping Indian's economic policies.

I think of Arun Jaitley as a seasoned orchestra conductor: he didn't just keep the tempo, he co-authored the score, blending finance, law and politics into a single resonant composition. His legacy is like a marble statue and more a living library—pages you can flip through for strategy, empathy. Politically, he was a bridge builder, who laid down planks that invited others to walk together.

On a personal note, we came to know each other from our college [SRCC] days. Both did law and we treaded the same path as lawyers for twenty years. I switched side by becoming a judge while politics remained his forte along with the legal profession. An outstanding quality in him—which many would not know—was that not only did he preach about the need for judicial integrity, he practised it as well, as he never tried to influence anyone, even when he had acquaintance with many judges. He was a man of his word, who always walked the talk. Another sterling quality in him, which I noticed, was that he encouraged and uplifted all those deserving who came to his contact, and Sumant Batra is one of them.

No wonder he is fondly remembered by one and all even today. Much has been written about him. Among all these, the present biography authored by Sumant Batra would stand tallest. I commend Sumant for his brilliant efforts in bringing about the multi-dimensional persona of Arun in a remarkable way, which is unique. What an unprecedented way to pay homage to your mentor!

~ **Justice A.K. Sikri,** *Former Judge, Supreme Court of India; International Judge, Singapore International Commercial Court*

In Indian public life, relationships are usually shaped by circumstance, but sometimes they are shaped by sheer human quality. Arun Jaitley belonged to that rare class of leaders whose friendships went beyond politics. With him, it never mattered if you were on his side of the argument or passionately opposed to it. He had a natural ability to dissolve the stiffness of political roles and reveal the human being behind them. That is why, even when we sat on opposite benches debating, disagreeing, and negotiating hard, the conversation never turned cold. It never became personal, and it never lost dignity.

Years have passed since he left us, but the sense of his absence hasn't faded. It lingers in the corridors of Parliament, in committee rooms, in Central Hall, and in private conversations among colleagues who still recall him with warmth. It is rare for a political figure to be missed by adversaries as genuinely as by allies, yet Jaitley commanded that kind of affection. Many Opposition leaders even today remark with a sigh: "If Arun were around, the strategy would have been different. The dialogue would have been smoother. The impasse wouldn't have dragged on this long." That sentiment doesn't come from politeness. It comes from the confidence he inspired.

As Leader of the Opposition, his room in Parliament was almost like a political adda, an informal saloon where MPs of every party dropped in, not just for work, but because they felt welcome. He never allowed his political role to overshadow his personal grace. When he became Finance Minister, one might have expected the atmosphere around him to change, but it didn't. He continued to host Opposition MPs for lunch, discussing the most difficult political issues with remarkable calmness and candour. The formality of office never erased the warmth of the man.

His friendships across party lines were not accidental. They were shaped by a temperament that instinctively valued dialogue over dominance. He knew that democracy isn't sustained by victories alone. It survives on conversations, on the ability to listen, and the willingness to respect the dignity of the other side. Influence came to him not because he held powerful offices, but because he was deeply trusted by friends and opponents alike.

Jaitley had a command over several languages, and I don't just mean linguistically, but culturally and politically. He understood the emotional undertones behind words and the cultural rhythms behind expressions. This gave him an extraordinary ability to sense the mood of the room, the anxieties behind demands, and the unspoken fears behind political postures. It made him one of the most effective negotiators in modern Indian politics because he didn't just argue harder, he listened better.

He was the ultimate "solution finder". When ministries clashed, when committees reached dead ends, or when parties hardened their positions, a simple suggestion would circulate: "Talk to Jaitley." More often than not, the knot would untangle. He had a way of separating ego from the problem, and noise from the substance.

During my tenure as Minister for Parliamentary Affairs, I saw this repeatedly. Weeks would pass with Parliament in stalemate, full of slogans and walkouts. Tension would build on both sides. Yet Jaitley would sit with us, calm and measured, and simply say, "Let's find a middle path." Somehow, that middle path always emerged. He had a rare political craftsmanship that made even his opponents feel that their dignity was intact, even during a compromise.

One of the finest examples was during the Anna Hazare movement, when Parliament was nearly paralysed. A draft resolution was prepared, and I took it to him. He went through it carefully, suggested changing just two words, and dictated the amended text. Nothing dramatic, no long rewrites, no ideological battles. Just two words. But those two words created the possibility of a consensus that had seemed impossible minutes earlier. That was Jaitley. Minimal noise, maximum effect.

His work on the Goods and Services Tax (GST) was just as remarkable. The country had debated GST for years, but getting consensus among states was a massive task. Each state had its own worries about revenue or autonomy. Over six months, Jaitley met every chief minister individually. He heard them out, explained the nuances, and reassured them without dismissing their concerns. Many Opposition chief ministers later acknowledged the respect he showed them. The eventual consensus wasn't just a tax reform; it was a political achievement that bore his imprint.

Cricket was another arena where his depth of understanding surprised even the professionals. Though he was deeply involved in administration, he rarely accepted top posts. He believed those roles should go to people whose primary goal was the sport itself. Only once, at my insistence, did he agree to become Vice President of the BCCI, and only because he felt the moment required his balance. His knowledge of cricket was encyclopaedic. He could recite domestic stats, recall forgotten matches, and assess young players with ease. People often joked that he could hold his own in a selection meeting, and they were not wrong.

His personal tastes were equally refined. Watches, pens, and shawls fascinated him, not as status symbols, but as stories of craftsmanship. He appreciated the engineering of a mechanical watch or the weave of a traditional shawl with the passion of a collector. It was a world he understood intimately.

One of my favourite memories is the day I took him to meet Lata Mangeshkar in Mumbai, shortly after he became a minister. Over tea, he began to speak about the origins of her songs, the composers, and the emotional tone behind the music. For nearly an hour he narrated anecdotes with such precision that Lata-ji herself sat in amazement. She said she had never heard anyone describe her own songs with such detail and affection. That moment revealed the breadth of his mind. He didn't just read widely; he remembered deeply.

Jaitley was a voracious reader, a loyal friend, and truly "a man who knew". Wherever he sat, the discussion became richer, more historical, and more informed. Many described him as a walking encyclopaedia, and they didn't say it lightly. It was the simplest way to capture a mind that absorbed everything from law to cricket, history to cinema, and global economics to Indian poetry.

Today, as politics grows louder and often more unforgiving, remembering Arun Jaitley feels like remembering a gentler era. He showed us that disagreement doesn't have to lead to hostility, and debate doesn't require disrespect. He showed us that political life at its best is the art of holding one's convictions without abandoning civility. Arguments will always be part of democracy, but bitterness doesn't have to be. He understood that distinction better than anyone.

As someone from the Opposition, I say this with complete sincerity. Arun Jaitley was a bridge, steady and strong, that connected political shores which otherwise drifted apart. His absence isn't just the absence of a leader. It is the absence of a culture that valued balance, conversation, and thoughtful engagement. Our democracy is poorer without that spirit, and I consider myself fortunate to have witnessed it up close.

Sumant has authoritatively brought out many of these dimensions of Arun Jaitley in his book.

~ **Rajeev Shukla**, *Member of Parliament, Rajya Sabha, Indian National Congress; Member, Congress Working Committee; Vice President, Board of Control for Cricket in India*

I can do better than to adopt from my two written obituaries on Arun, apart from my obituary address to a massive BJP audience, which included the PM and most of his Cabinet. I had then said: We have lost a good man in public life, a decent human being, a respected and able lawyer, a witty thinker, a lifelong student of politics, a remarkable communicator, a committed pillar of his party and a close friend to many. A book on a man of such versatility by an able professional is most welcome.

Of all the major opening debates I did during 2006–12, the maximum involved Arun on the other side. It was not uncommon for us to appear against each other in the early morning in diverse cases in the SC, after which Arun would rush to Parliament to open an important debate. I would rush shortly after him, to be the opening person to reply to him.

Arun opened the Lokpal debate in 2011 by pointing out the unimaginable coincidence that the son (me) of the man who invented and coined the words Lokpal and Lokayukta in 1962 (my father) was chairing the Standing Committee in 2011 which was going to give birth to that institution after fifty years! He was always magnanimous, large hearted, and a number of journalists told me in Central Hall how Arun had spoken highly of me behind my back, despite our legal and political opposition.

His foodie vices, circumscribed by diabetes, meant that in the old days when we did press debates in Noida TV studios, he would hesitate wistfully when offered samosa with tea. Never have the lawns of the BJP main office, allotted in his name, been put to greater public interest use than at his foodie parties! He had a great sense of humour and timing. Most know how he got Vajpayee to release a book, which the PM was unwilling to do, by a senior BJP functionary widely known to have had it ghost written. Arun supposedly told the PM that he must release the book since this would be the first book he would release which had not been read even by the author! Once, after Yechury had strongly advocated legal prohibition against any practising professional being allowed into Parliament, coincidentally both he and I crossed Sita in the lobby and together exclaimed: "Sita wants a Parliament not only of the unemployed but also the unemployable."

Whenever he saw me in Central Hall, he would say that while there was no value of the time of public servants like himself, my time was very expensive and should not be wasted in Central Hall! I used to retort by telling him that since he was collecting 42 per cent of my expensive time as taxes, it was better to make him suffer some deprivation while I gossiped in Central Hall.

Two days before his demise, an appointment had been fixed for me. It was cancelled and I guessed that the end was near. I felt saddened that we would lose a man I had known for decades as a lawyer, politician, spokesperson, minister and a great conversationalist.

~ **(Dr) Abhishek Singhvi**, *Member of Parliament; Member, Congress Working Committee; Eminent Jurist and former Additional Solicitor General of India; former Chair, Parliamentary Standing Committees on Commerce, Law & Home; senior National Spokesperson, Congress; Chair, Cong Department on Law, Human Rights & RTI*

Sumant, as always, impresses with both his writing and his choice of subjects. From banking and cinema to political history, fiction, and now a political biography of one of Bharat's most influential and towering statesmen, Arun Jaitley. He continues to expand his body of work with yet another impactful contribution. The work reflects a depth and clarity of thought that resonate profoundly with Jaitley's own intellectual legacy. It is a work that not only informs but also inspires, reflecting the statesman's enduring imprint on India's political and economic canvas.

~ **Baijayant Jay Panda**, *National Vice President, Bharatiya Janata Party*

Beyond the brilliance of his mind and his mastery of law, Arun Jaitley-ji possessed a deeply collegial and generous spirit. He was a formidable opponent and an unmatched orator, but he always offered grace, genuine wit, and profound respect across the aisle. Even when our political convictions differed, he showed us how to debate fiercely and still be friends. We really miss him in Parliament, his contribution to making the discourse collaborative was unmatched. Sumant Batra's book is a much-needed tribute to this warm-hearted parliamentary veteran.

~ **Supriya Sule**, *Member of Parliament; Working President, Nationalist Congress Party (Sharad Pawar)*

My heart fills with warmth every time I think of Arun. Kaka, as he was known to his family, was truly a man for all seasons. While his achievements as an astute lawyer and politician are well-known, having known him for a lifetime gave me insight into his personal side, which few were privy to. He was a connoisseur of shawls, pens, and kurtas. A great foodie and a generous host, he was a teetotaler himself but always offered his guests the best to imbibe.

A devoted family man, we took many trips together, both domestic and international. He never threw his weight around. He was taken from us far too soon. Alas! I am glad that Sumant Batra decided to write his biography—a befitting tribute to a great man and his even greater legacy.

~ **Mukul Rohatgi**, *Senior Advocate, former Attorney General of India*

Arun Jaitley led a remarkable life—student leader, lawyer, family man, politician, parliamentarian, minister, reformer. As someone who worked closely with him, I had hoped that someone would write a full-fledged biography documenting his extraordinary journey. I am glad, therefore, that lawyer-writer Sumant Batra took up the challenge. He knew Arun Jaitley at close quarters and the many facets of his life. In this well-written and exceptionally well-researched book, Batra brings alive the man and his times.

~ **Sanjeev Sanyal**, *Economist and Author, Member, Economic Advisory Council to the Prime Minister; was Principal Economic Advisor in Ministry of Finance when Arun Jaitley was Finance Minister*

Arun Jaitley's life comes alive in these pages as both a towering public figure and a deeply human presence. Drawing on research and rare insider vantage, Sumant Batra maps his journey from fiery student activist to reformist finance minister who steered GST, the Insolvency and Bankruptcy Code, and banking clean-up with calm conviction. This is an intimate, authoritative portrait of a jurist, strategist and consensus-builder whose intellect, civility and warmth reshaped Indian politics and governance.

~ **Amitabh Kant**, *Ex-G 20 Sherpa, Govt. of India; Ex-CEO, NITI Aayog*

Writing a book on Arun Jaitley should have been a cakewalk—so many achievements in one extraordinary life. Yet capturing the multi-dimensional man behind the legend? That's a mountain to climb. Sumant Batra scales it armed with knowledge and rare insights. Having worked with Arun Jaitley in the GST Council, I marvelled how he wove consensus from chaos, turning bitter opponents into allies with a smile, a quip, and a tea break! This isn't a flat photograph; it's a living, breathing portrait painted with deep respect, and quiet reverence. Jaitley comes across larger, warmer, and more human than ever.

~ **Dr Haseeb A. Drabu**, *Economist, Former Finance Minister of Jammu and Kashmir, who worked with Arun Jaitley in the GST Council*

Jaitley-ji was an exceptional cricket administrator, whose deep knowledge and passion for the game were matched only by his commitment to merit. At the DDCA, he was approachable, listened to players, and ensured deserving talents like me could achieve our dreams for India. His contributions were phenomenal, and I am glad Sumant Batra's book highlights this impactful aspect of his public life.

~ **Virender Sehwag**, *Former Indian Cricketer*

Arun Jaitley left early but left behind a rich legacy of public achievements, legal acumen and political goodwill, and an astonishing circle of friends and well-wishers. Sumant Batra's book makes a determined effort to capture the big moments and the little details that made Arun Jaitley so unique and so special in every field and endeavour that he embraced.

~ **Ashok Malik**, *Chair, The Asia Group, India Practice; worked with Arun Jaitley in election campaigns and later in government*

The Life and Legacy of ARUN JAITLEY

Foreword by
M. Venkaiah Naidu

SUMANT BATRA

Om Books International

First published in 2026 by

Om Books International

Corporate & Editorial Office
A-12, Sector 64, Noida 201 301
Uttar Pradesh, India
Phone: +91 120 477 4100
Email: editorial@ombooks.com
Website: www.ombooksinternational.com

Sales Office
107, Ansari Road, Darya Ganj,
New Delhi 110 002, India
Phone: +91 11 4000 9000
Fax: +91 11 2327 8091
Email: sales@ombooks.com
Website: www.ombooks.com

Cover image courtesy Getty Images

ISBN: 978-93-6395-795-4

Printed in India

10 9 8 7 6 5 4 3 2 1

Dedicated to my late father Shri G.L. Batra. He served in the Lok Sabha Secretariat for years. While serving as Additional Secretary, he was appointed Chairman of the Haryana Public Service Commission. He was a great admirer of Arun Jaitley-ji, who held my father in high esteem for his contributions particularly in setting up the parliamentary standing committees.

Contents

Part I

A Nationalist Politician, Outstanding Parliamentarian

Part II
Jaitley's Flagship Reforms

M. Venkaiah Naidu

1, Tyagraja Marg,
New Delhi, 110011

Foreword

Film historian, writer, and internationally renowned lawyer with proven expertise and worldwide experience in insolvency and bankruptcy, Sumant Batra brings alive the life and legacy of my dear departed friend, the late Shri Arun Jaitley in this compelling narrative, aptly entitled *The Life and Legacy of Arun Jaitley.* This book traces the life and career of one of the most eminent leaders of our times, portraying diverse facets of his personality and different phases of his life with authenticity.

I feel privileged to count myself among Shri Arun Jaitley's close friends. We began our careers around the same time in the turbulent decade of 1970s, and were rooted in the same ideological moorings. Over the next few decades, until Shri Jaitley's sad demise in 2019, we remained in regular touch, sharing responsibilities in the party as well as the government. His passing was a profound personal loss for me, because I lost a close friend with whom I bonded over a range of issues that were common to our lives as public figures and partymen. Additionally, ours was a close friendship predicated on trust, mutual respect and understanding. Incidentally, both of us also shared a common love for good Indian food.

Shri Jaitley will be remembered as a brilliant lawyer, an orator par excellence, an articulate parliamentarian, and a reformer endowed with exceptional foresight. Shri Arun Jaitley stood apart from the common run of political leaders. His unique combination of profound erudition, political acumen and human warmth are extremely rare in the arena of politics. Both as the BJP's master strategist, and as the nation's finance minister, and also as the fiery voice of the Opposition, Shri Jaitley lent depth, clarity, persuasive diplomacy and unimpeachable integrity to the task, as this book reveals. His tact and

email: fvpioffice@gmail.com, Tel: 011-21412080.

M. Venkaiah Naidu

1, *Tyagraja Marg,*
New Delhi, 110011

diplomacy, as also his incisive insights and knowledge, made him the bridge between diverse ideologies. All of us saw in him a man who was deeply trusted across party lines, the hallmark of a true statesman.

Shri Arun Jaitley remains one of contemporary India's most fascinating political figures, and will always be admired for the rare harmony between intellect, articulation, and humane sensibility. As a distinguished lawyer, a seasoned parliamentarian, and a respected party leader and administrator, he combined eloquence with depth, wit with dignity, and conviction with grace. We find illustrations of these qualities of his personality at different stages of his career in this book.

Shri Jaitley, even in adversarial settings, in parliament or in the court, spoke with restraint, allowing logic and structure, to prevail. His arguments were always measured, evidence-based, and delivered with rare charisma. He was endowed with the ability to simplify intricate economic, constitutional, or political issues without diluting their essence.

Shri Jaitley's speeches in parliament, which I had the privilege of listening to, were layered with nuanced reasoning. His wit was sharp yet never unkind, his rejoinders crisp but never rude. This made him an asset both to the party and to Parliament. Whether defending policy, rebutting criticism, or explaining reform, he spoke with a calm assurance, tempered with dignity, that commanded attention.

In Parliament, Jaitley stood out as a conciliator as much as a debater. He was a leader who valued institutions deeply and firmly believed, as I did, that disagreement need not lead to disrespect. As Leader of the Opposition in the Rajya Sabha, he held the government to account without personal animosity or hostility. Later, as a cabinet minister, he defended the government while respecting dissent or criticism.

email: fvpioffice@gmail.com, Tel: 011-21412080.

M. Venkaiah Naidu

1, Tyagraja Marg,
New Delhi, 110011

Legislation, especially major reforms like the Goods and Services Tax, progressed in part due to his ability to negotiate consensus across parties, combining intellect with tact.

Shri Jaitley's human qualities were deeply cherished by those who knew him. Friends across the political spectrum spoke of his generosity with time and friendship. He continued to serve the nation in spite of his illness with stoic dignity.

Shri Jaitley's analytical depth in diverse domains, be it dissecting economic structures, interpreting constitutional principles, or explaining political strategy, revealed his mastery over detail and perspective, as we see in Sumant Batra's book. He was someone who could articulate the philosophy behind taxation reform one day and break down global geopolitical shifts the next, and it is this intellectual versatility which made him not just a political leader but a public educator. Shri Arun Jaitley's life, as this book also tells us, offers an enduring reminder of what public leadership can aspire to: principled intelligence, persuasive articulation, institutional respect, and above all, humanity.

In this definitive portrait of one of India's most admired leaders, bearing the title, *The Life and Legacy of Arun Jaitley*, Sumant Batra chronicles his journey from his student activist days in the 1970s to emerging as one of the most powerful public figures in recent Indian politics.

(M. VENKAIAH NAIDU)

December 08, 2025
Hyderabad

email: fvpioffice@gmail.com, Tel: 011-21412080.

Introduction

On Monday, 8 November 2021, a sense of reverence filled the grand hall of Rashtrapati Bhavan as the announcer invited Sangeeta Jaitley to receive the Padma Vibhushan—India's second-highest civilian honour—awarded posthumously to her late husband, Arun Jaitley, in recognition of his exceptional and distinguished service to the nation. The atmosphere was imbued with solemn pride as dignitaries sat in composed silence. When Sangeeta Jaitley stepped forward with grace to accept the honour from President Ram Nath Kovind, the three leaders seated in the front row—Vice President M. Venkaiah Naidu, Prime Minister Narendra Modi, and Home Minister Amit Shah—appeared visibly moved, their expressions reflecting both the sorrow of personal loss and the nation's deep appreciation of Arun Jaitley's enduring legacy.

Throughout history, only a few individuals leave behind a legacy that transcends time, their influence shaping the very course of their nation's destiny. Arun Jaitley (28 December 1952–24 August 2019) was one such distinguished son of India, a man whose life embodied scholarship and sacrifice, diligence and discipline, and the quiet dignity of a self-made individual. His journey was a rich tapestry woven with ambition, adversity, and altruism; nothing came easily to him. From modest, middle-class beginnings, Jaitley ascended to the highest echelons of India's Executive Office, distinguishing himself as an erudite orator, a brilliant lawyer, a perceptive lawmaker, and a charismatic Leader of the Opposition who seamlessly blended legal acumen with political sagacity.

The "first satyagrahi" against the Emergency in 1975, Jaitley grew in the shadow of the legends, Atal Bihari Vajpayee and Lal Krishna Advani. He emerged as a leading figure of the bridge generation, linking the old Jana

Sangh with a new wave of leaders who articulated its ideology through the lens of modernity and the evolving post-Emergency sensibilities.

Despite his deep political involvement, his professional identity for many years remained that of one of India's most accomplished lawyers and among the nation's most distinguished jurists. For many years, he was not just one of India's best lawyers, but also one of India's highest taxpayers. Yet he excelled in his political pursuits and responsibilities given by his party, putting his heart and soul into them. While the formative years of Jaitley were shaped under the watch of Vajpayee and Advani, the later part of his life was shadowed by no one else than Narendra Damodardas Modi. He was a trusted lieutenant of Vajpayee, a faithful follower of Advani, and a good friend of Modi; and none of these clashed with each other. He alone had the ability to make them sit together and have lunch at his home. He was the go-to man of all seasons for his political party.

He was soon elevated to the role of the BJP's general secretary, and later inducted into its Central Parliamentary Board, the party's highest decision-making body. He went on to become one of India's top politicians. He was credited with successfully stitching alliances and ensuring his party's victory in many states, besides being the key strategist and trouble-shooter for the BJP at the national level and in many states.

Political pundits called Jaitley a politician who did not have a mass base, but knew how to manage the masses better than anyone else. In his forty-year-long political life, Jaitley contested only one election in 2014, which he lost. He was a four-time Rajya Sabha member, thrice elected from Gujarat and once from Uttar Pradesh.

Jaitley was an old-school politician: ambitious but not driven. Often called the half-liberal in the right-wing political party, the Bharatiya Janata Party (BJP), Jaitley was essentially a mix of many contradictory traits—a liberal among hard-core right-wingers and an ardent believer of Hindutva politics among liberals and left-wingers. But the reality was very different; when it came to hard politics, Jaitley's commitment was unflinchingly ideological. He supported every "Hindu" turn of the BJP, particularly the decision to make Ayodhya a political plank. He was a proud Indian and die-hard nationalist who masterminded the abrogation of Article 370 of the Constitution with Amit Shah and plotted the removal of Article 35-A many months before the bill was moved. He worked behind the scenes on the Ram Janmabhoomi movement with other leaders, and on the legal strategy on the dispute in the Supreme Court. He balanced his contradictions with charm and eloquence.

He rose above politics when it came to personal and humanitarian issues. Yet he was as shrewd as a politician could be, and rapidly rose in the BJP, becoming a member of its national executive at the age of thirty-nine. His politics reflected decency even though he never shied away from hitting his punches. A glib talker and suave operator in New Delhi's power circles, Jaitley thrived in television studios, election war rooms, and policy debates in Parliament.

He was a man with a mission. However, what made his mission purposeful was his indomitable courage, great eloquence, and mastery of the language. In the words of Prime Minister Narendra Modi, "Few are the people who have a natural interest in complex policy issues. Fewer still are those who can grasp them and understand them. Among these, those who can reduce complex issues and explain them in a simple manner are rarest of the rare. Arun Jaitley, in this aspect, was one of his kind."[1]

In 2009, he quit his legal career at its peak to pursue a full-time career in politics. But the image of being a technocrat, rather than a politician, never really left him.

Jaitley earned more admirers than distractors. He had an uncanny ability to connect with people from different backgrounds and parties. His trademark smile, infectious exuberance, disarming humility, and unfettered benevolence made him extremely popular amongst the members of the Bar, members of the political class across party divides, bureaucrats, entrepreneurs, diplomats, his electorate as well as the Indian gentry in general.

He was the face the nation loved. Suave, urbane, articulate, Jaitley's public face was mostly visible in television studios, aggressively defending the government on a wide range of issues, where his sharp legal brain was an obvious asset. He was undoubtedly the BJP's most popular face on television, a darling of the media, and the most well-informed politician about what was happening in the lives and politics of his colleagues (without using intelligence bureaus). His colleagues often teased him for being the "chief of bureau" among journalists.

Jaitley was an outstanding parliamentarian. As a Leader of the Opposition in the Rajya Sabha from 2009 to 2014, he put his bilingual eloquence to good

---

1. Arun Jaitley, *A New India: Selected Writings 2014–19* (Juggernaut, 2020), pp. vii–ix.

use in Parliament, particularly when in its second term the United Progressive Alliance (UPA) government[2], the UPA-II, was besieged with controversies and corruption scams and criticised for its ineffective approach to questions of national security after the 26/11 Mumbai terror attacks. He mercilessly cornered UPA-II on all these issues, laying the ground for a resounding victory of his party, and his friend Narendra Modi as the prime ministerial candidate.

In his election speeches, Modi had promised many revolutionary reforms, assuring that they would set the country on a path that would transform the lives of its citizens. Amongst the foremost of these was to rejuvenate the economy and the mood of the nation. Jaitley was Modi's Chanakya. Modi turned to Jaitley to steer the key reforms and implement his chief promises. The two carefully created a team of able ministers and officials, effecting a generational shift in the government by giving Cabinet rank to younger colleagues. Jaitley was entrusted with the most significant finance and corporate affairs ministry, where several key reforms promised by Modi were to be launched. In addition, he was entrusted with the portfolios of defence, and information and broadcasting from 2014 to 2016, becoming the first man in independent India's history to hold the finance and defence portfolios at the same time.

As Plato said, "the measure of a man is what he does with power." Jaitley hit the ground running immediately. An ambitious programme of reforms was launched to revitalise the economy and regain investor's confidence, and make India attractive to foreign and domestic investors once again. The next five years became a transformative decade, marking a significant chapter in India's economic history. Jaitley lived up to Modi's expectations. Every budget he delivered was deeply thought through, far sighted, and aimed at creating history.

As Modi's confidante, Jaitley was at the forefront of the transformation. As a young minister of law, corporate affairs, commerce, and disinvestment in the Vajpayee government from 1999 to 2004, Jaitley steered many reforms for economic liberalisation. He spearheaded several key reforms promoting good

---

2. The UPA is an alliance of political parties in India whose largest and predominant constituent is the Indian National Congress. The UPA was in power from 2004 to 2014 under Prime Minister Manmohan Singh. It served its second term (2009–14), again under Manmohan Singh.

corporate governance, facilitating smoother market entry, and enhancing the ease of doing business, advocating for competition laws that nurtured a free-market economy and insolvency laws that ensured efficient exits. A decade later, as India's finance minister, he would bring these reforms to their logical culmination.

When Modi appointed Jaitley as finance minister in 2014, Jaitley took over from where he had left in 2004 and championed many key reforms needed in the rapidly changing global geopolitical landscape and accelerated India's economic growth. His efforts completed a crucial phase in Indian economic reform, which had previously addressed freedom of entry and operation, but lacked a robust mechanism for business closure. He was determined to destroy the system which heavily favoured those who defaulted on loans.

He heralded the Goods and Services Tax (GST), a blue-chip reform that will go down in history as one of the most ground-breaking economic reforms in Indian taxation. Implementing GST would not have been possible without his persistence and persuasive skills.

When Jaitley entered North Block, the banking sector was on the brink of crisis. Together with the Reserve Bank of India (RBI), he took many bold decisions to restore the health of the ailing public sector banks. Under his leadership, the Indian government overcame its dismal track record on the implementation of laws by deploying unprecedented political will for an effective rollout of the Insolvency and Bankruptcy Code, 2016 (IBC). Another epic reform of the Modi government, the IBC proved to be an effective tool in dealing with non-performing loans, revitalising the credit market, and boosting growth. I had the opportunity to work with Jaitley's ministry on this reform.

The National Democratic Alliance (NDA) government's anti-corruption agenda leaned heavily on the finance ministry under Jaitley. The war against black money was driven by him. He institutionalised the monetary policy framework, a reform that made the process of setting interest rates by RBI more transparent. He convinced Prime Minister Modi to support the Electoral Bonds Scheme for increased transparency in electoral funding. He led the transformation to the digital economy. His tenure as defence minister saw the clearance of a number of big-ticket reform measures. He advocated for a comprehensive approach to judicial reforms, including the establishment of clear criteria for judicial appointments and addressing the issue of post-retirement appointments for judges.

Jaitley was a steadfast advocate of judicial independence, consistently raising his voice to uphold and protect the integrity of the institution. He was, however, critical of the collegium system for the appointment of judges to the Supreme Court and high courts. He supported the 99th Constitution Amendment to establish a National Judicial Appointments Commission, highlighting the BJP's consistent support for such a commission. The Supreme Court, however, struck down the amendment. "It is difficult to hold that the wisdom of appointment of judges can be shared with the political-executive. The expectation from the judiciary, to safeguard the rights of the citizens of this country, can only be ensured, by keeping it absolutely insulated and independent, from the other organs of governance," Justice J.S. Khehar, the presiding judge on the five-judge Constitution Bench, explained in his individual judgment. In his blog criticising the judgment, Jaitley wrote that Indian democracy cannot be "a tyranny of the unelected".

Jaitley left an indelible mark in whichever room he was asked to sit, in the North or South Block or Shastri Bhawan. Informally called "scholar minister" in political circles, he could be the man Friday of anyone at the helm. He was often considered the third-most powerful man in the party, after Prime Minister Narendra Modi and BJP president Amit Shah. All party spokespersons flocked to him for advice.

History will ultimately judge Jaitley for his tenure as the finance minister from 2014 to 2019. However, historians should note that many of his accomplishments were not immediately apparent, nor has he been fully recognised for the reforms enacted during his leadership. I have observed, often from close quarters, Jaitley's contribution to India's economic trajectory and his path-breaking reforms in the diverse spheres of life he traversed. His nationalism was marked by a quiet determination—focused on strengthening India, fostering self-reliance, and building an economic powerhouse—expressed without rhetoric or hyperbole. His superb four-decade-long political career was sadly cut short by failing health, depriving him of the opportunity to present the final budget of Modi's first term. Citing health issues, he opted out of any responsibility when Modi returned to power in 2019.

Jaitley seamlessly juggled many other roles. He was not only a passionate cricket lover, but a part of it as well. Cricket administration was among the many hats Jaitley wore in public life. His deep commitment to cricket was evident in the many improvements made in the game's administration during his stint as the longest-serving president of the Delhi and District Cricket Association (DDCA) for close to thirteen years (1999–2013), as vice president of the Board of Control for Cricket in India (BCCI), and as a member of the Governing Council of Indian Premier League (IPL).

Jaitley was versatile like few others. He was like a living encyclopaedia who knew everything from politics and economics to sports, watches, and pens to fashion and food. He was an institution in himself.

Despite his demanding career, Jaitley was a family man, a dependable friend, and a compassionate human, supporting everyone who turned to him for help, whatever their political loyalties. Countless people, including me, have been beneficiaries of his mentorship and guidance. Everyone who knew or knows of him, even remotely, has a compelling Arun Jaitley story to tell. He will be remembered for many reasons, but those who have worked with him in any capacity will recall him for his unfettered commitment to India.

This committed son of India passed away on 24 August 2019, leaving a void in the party, government, politics, profession, and lives of his family and innumerable friends. His passing created a profound vacuum in both political strategy and economic policymaking. It is worth reflecting on how the course of decisions taken by the BJP-NDA government during its second term—and especially in the initial years of its third—might have differed had Arun Jaitley been there. His nuanced understanding of markets, credibility within the business community, legal acumen, and the respect he commanded in the judiciary would have ensured a more coherent strategy for many complex issues. His voice would have provided a robust, persuasive defence of government policies, both inside and outside Parliament, potentially altering the narrative on key reforms.

A lot has been written about Jaitley. There are anthologies of his speeches and writings, but there is no single comprehensive chronicling of his contributions in public life. This book seeks to fill that void. It seeks to trace the transformative reforms introduced by Arun Jaitley—reforms that have left an enduring imprint on India's business, economic, and political landscape—firmly establishing his legacy as a visionary reformist minister. A Herculean task, if not impossible.

As I explored the archives, conducted interviews, and pieced together the fragments of his remarkable journey, I was struck by the many defining moments that revealed the essence of Arun Jaitley's character. While the focus of this work is on the transformative reforms he championed, it also traces the events—both personal and political—that shaped his life and influenced the man and leader he became. In doing so, the book journeys into Jaitley's past, reconstructing the contexts that moulded him and following his life from childhood onward. At its heart, this biography portrays a politician who stood apart—a reformer, leader, and administrator who left a lasting imprint on India's economic, political, and judicial landscape. His life—both as an individual and as a statesman—was an inspiring story long waiting to be told.

It is often said that the true measure of a person's greatness lies in the length of the shadow he casts over posterity. By that measure, Arun Jaitley's legacy stands tall. The politics he practised, marked by dignity, restraint, and civility, will continue to inspire generations of young leaders across party lines. While his political career, like that of any public figure, remains open to scrutiny and debate, few would dispute that he was an able administrator and a dedicated public servant who worked tirelessly for the nation's progress. The structural reforms implemented under his leadership will have a lasting impact, upholding the freedom to start, to sustain, and to exit enterprises, the three vital pillars of economic liberty. To those who knew him closely, he will forever remain a shining example of friendship, grace, and humanity.

Part I

A Nationalist Politician, Outstanding Parliamentarian

1

An Inheritance of Loss

In August 1947, India's long-awaited independence was paradoxically accompanied by its hasty and ill-conceived partition into Hindu-majority India and Muslim-majority Pakistan. The arbitrary, crooked red line drawn by Sir Cyril Radcliffe tore through rivers, villages, fields, and homes, triggering a violent upheaval. For millions of Indians, the division was a brutal affront. They endured sudden displacement while grappling with a profound sense of betrayal, as political leaders conceded vast portions of their motherland to Pakistan, a state founded on religious ideology.

West Punjab witnessed an exodus of Hindus and Sikhs moving eastward, while Muslims from East Punjab travelled westward. Amidst the chaos, millions fled for their lives—many barefoot, leaving behind their land, homes, belongings, and a part of their hearts. Bengal met a similar fate, split into East Pakistan (now Bangladesh) and West Bengal. This mass exodus, one of the largest migrations in recorded history, unfolded against a backdrop of relentless violence, arson, and devastation.

Millions were uprooted from ancestral homes, and an estimated three million perished due to violence, hunger, suicide, or disease. Families were shattered as homes were destroyed and loved ones killed. Refugees travelled by any means available—on foot, by bullock cart, train, or makeshift boats. Trains packed beyond capacity became easy targets for armed mobs, resulting in gruesome massacres. Refugee convoys were attacked, leaving trails of corpses along the routes. Families were torn apart, children orphaned, and women subjected to abductions, rape, sexual violence, and forced conversions.

The twinning of Independence with Partition forever disrupted any sense of celebration for millions of displaced Indians.[1]

Among those who survived the genocide and managed to escape from Lahore were thirty-eight members of the Jaitley parivar, including the twenty-nine year-old Maharaj Kishen Jaitley, his young wife Ratan Prabha—barely nineteen year old, their two month old daughter Madhu—and Maharaj's many siblings.[2] The couple had married in 1946, less than a year earlier. Prabha had just returned to Lahore only a few weeks before, after giving birth to Madhu at her parent's house in Amritsar. A fragile bundle of innocence and hope amid the surrounding despair, Madhu brought much-needed joy to the family and lightened the burden of grief weighing on the parivar.

The large Punjabi Brahmin family sought shelter in the home of Ratan Prabha's father, Ruldu Ram Trikha, in Bazaar Khoo Sunarian, within the walled city.[3]

For Hindus and Sikhs, the decision to partition the country was excruciating enough, but ceding Lahore to Pakistan came as an even greater shock. Lahore was home to powerful Hindu and Sikh merchants, businessmen, and intellectuals—lawyers, doctors, and teachers—many of whom occupied prominent positions in the civil services. They formed nearly half the city's population and owned close to 80 per cent of its property.[4] Monuments, businesses, and institutions—including Sir Ganga Ram Hospital, Gulab Devi Hospital, Janki Devi Hospital, Dr. Khera Government Hospital, Dayal Singh College, and Dayal Singh Library—were largely managed by Hindus.[5]

---

1. Sumant Batra, *Kafila: A Jhangi Family's Partition Memoir* (Om Books International, 2025). *See*, Preface.
2. Arun Jaitley, My Journey, "Family Background", accessed 25 May 2025, https://www.arunjaitley.com/my_jounry/family-background/,
3. Neeraj Bagga, "With Jaitley's Passing Away, Amritsar Loses Connection to One of BJP's Tallest Leaders", The Tribune, accessed 25 May 2025, https://www.tribuneindia.com/news/archive/punjab/with-jaitley-s-passing-away-amritsar-loses-connection-to-one-of-bjp-s-tallest-leaders-822217/.
4. Pran Nevile, *Lahore: A Sentimental Journey* (Penguin, 1993). *See*, Introduction.
5. Kirti Pandey, "Bloodshed and Independence Day: How India Suddenly Lost Lahore to Pakistan at the Eleventh Hour of Partition", Times Now News, accessed 25 May 2025, https://www.timesnownews.com/india/article/bloodshed-and-independence-day-how-india-suddenly-lost-lahore-to-pakistan-at-the-eleventh-hour-of-partition/468922.

Punjabi Brahmin families also had deep roots in Lahore. Many worked in government service or teaching, while others practiced Ayurveda as vaids, the most famous being Pandit Thakur Dutt Sharma of Amrit Dhara fame. Brahmins rarely ventured into business—Anarkali Bazaar had only one Brahmin-owned shop, Lall Bros. Cloth Merchants. On Lahore's Mall Road, the city's commercial and cultural hub, one of the earliest Brahmin enterprises was Vasudeva Radios, opened in the late 1930s. Lahore was truly the beating heart of Punjab.[6]

It was in this vibrant city that Maharaj Kishen's father, Pandit Ram Ratan Jaitley, grew up, married Kunti Devi, and raised a family. In the 1920s, he held a senior position with the railways under British administration. His untimely death left behind a young widow with eight children. Maharaj was only eight years old when he lost his father. Despite hardships, his mother persevered and ensured that all her children were educated. Four of her sons became lawyers, and, unusually for that time, she was equally determined that her daughters be educated—a remarkable stance in the 1920s.

The Jaitleys were among Lahore's most prominent Punjabi Brahmin families. While Maharaj's father was a senior government officer, three of his uncles were eminent lawyers. Maharaj and several cousins followed suit, taking up law. Another uncle was a professor of physics, one served as an army psychologist, the first to be employed by the army. The extended Jaitley family lived together in a large ancestral home, well-known in the city as the *vakeelan vali haveli*—the grand house of lawyers, located in Vacho Wali near Shahalami. Immersed in Lahore's rich literary culture, Maharaj himself became a lawyer and had just begun establishing his practice at the bustling high court and district court.[7] Punjab, notorious for disputes over land, water, money, and women—the proverbial Persian "three Zs": *zar* (gold), *zan* (woman), and *zamin* (land)—saw more lawsuits filed than any other province. The Lahore district courts, near Government College, bustled like a mela each day with litigants, witnesses, and lawyers. It was here that Maharaj dedicated himself to his profession.[8]

---

6. Pran Nevile, *Lahore: A Sentimental Journey* (Penguin, 1997). *See*, Introduction.
7. Lahore was the seat of High Court for Punjab Province and Delhi since 1919.
8. Pran Nevile, *Lahore: A Sentimental Journey* (Penguin, 1997), pp.167–68.

Like most Lahoris, the Jaitleys cherished their city and its vibrant culture. The notion of Lahore becoming part of Pakistan was unimaginable. Only when they saw Congress leaders quietly moving their families eastward did reality sink in—the unthinkable had come to pass. Lahore had been handed over, largely to ensure Pakistan was given a major city, much like Calcutta had been allocated to India. Without warning, Hindus and Sikhs were forced to flee. Hundreds lost their lives in Lahore.[9] Overnight, the Jaitleys' beloved hometown had become a foreign land. For Maharaj, Partition meant the loss of the workplace he was deeply devoted to. For the young couple, Maharaj and Ratan Prabha, life was uprooted before they had even settled into marriage.

★

The ordeal of the Jaitley family did not end with their safe arrival in Amritsar. Partition was not merely a political event; it was a profound human tragedy. It forged a new social order, leaving behind a collective wound and an enduring inheritance of grief and suffering. Like countless others, the Jaitleys were branded as "refugees" in their own country. They were forced to abandon their accustomed way of life and confront the daunting task of rebuilding everything from scratch. Yet, the Punjabis of West Punjab were known for their resilience and enterprise. Even amidst turmoil, they displayed remarkable courage and carved new paths forward. Slowly but steadily, the Jaitleys began to stitch their lives together with unyielding determination.

Heartbroken though they were, the Jaitleys refused to succumb to despair. After Partition, the high court for East Punjab was set up in Simla on 15 August 1947. But like most displaced people of West Punjab, the Jaitleys did not see the hill town as a place to rebuild their future. Each group of refugees sought resettlement according to their roots: families from Jhang and Muzaffargarh settled in Rohtak; Multanis gravitated to Hisar; agriculturists from Lahore and Montgomery received land in Ferozepur; those from Rawalpindi, Sheikhupura, and Gujranwala went to Karnal, Patiala, and PEPSU; migrants from Shahpur

---

9. Haroon Khalid, *In Search of Shiva: A Study of Folk Religious Practices in Pakistan* (Rupa, 2015); Haroon Khalid, *A White Trail: A Journey Into the Heart of Pakistan's Religious Minorities* (Vintage Books, 2023).

and Gujarat settled in Ambala; from Dera Ghazi Khan and Mianwali in Gurgaon; and from Sialkot in Hoshiarpur, Gurdaspur, and Amritsar.[10] The enterprising and intellectual Lahoris, however, moved wherever opportunities beckoned.

Maharaj and Ratan Prabha chose Delhi—then a city of sprawling refugee camps—as their new home. At the peak of Partition, Delhi had absorbed nearly half a million refugees. Monuments and open grounds became makeshift shelters. Camps mushroomed across the city, and many of today's Delhi neighbourhoods grew out of these refugee settlements. By the mid-1950s, refugees had moved into empty flats in Lodhi Colony and built homes around Nizamuddin and Jangpura. In 1951, Khan Market was established, with shops and flats entirely owned by refugees. By 1956, southern Delhi began taking shape with the development of Lajpat Nagar and Defence Colony. To the west, refugee colonies transformed open land into new neighbourhoods—Rajinder Nagar, West Patel Nagar, Moti Nagar, and Rajouri Garden—areas that would become quintessentially Punjabi Delhi.

For Hindus and Sikhs arriving from West Punjab, the government faced the urgent challenge of providing alternative properties, livelihoods, and employment. The Ministry of Relief and Rehabilitation, set up in September 1947, introduced a series of laws to address these needs. Under the East Punjab Evacuees (Administration of Property) Act, 1947—later replaced by the Administration of Evacuee Property Act, 1950—all properties abandoned by Muslims were declared evacuee property and redistributed to displaced families. Shops, houses, industrial sites, and even *kholas* (dilapidated houses) were initially allotted on rent.

The Resettlement of Displaced Persons (Land Acquisition) Ordinance, 1948, empowered the government to acquire land for new townships like Faridabad, Nilokheri, and Kalyan, while extending existing suburbs to absorb refugees. By 1950, the government had also moved to compensate displaced persons. Under the Displaced Persons (Claims) Act, 1950, families were asked to file claims for their abandoned properties. Compensation was to be derived from a central "compensation pool" comprising Muslim evacuee properties left in India, amounts expected from Pakistan, and government contributions.

---

10. Sumant Batra, *Kafila: A Jhangi Family's Partition Memoir* (Om Books International, 2025), pp. 170–78.

Carrying both hope and uncertainty, Maharaj and Ratan Prabha moved into a refugee colony with their two young daughters. Their second child, Manju, was only two months old when they arrived in Delhi. Maharaj was allotted a house near Azad Market, as compensation for his Lahore property.[11] He deliberately chose the locality because of its proximity to the civil courts—his future workplace. Though housed in a crumbling British-era building at the time, plans were already underway to relocate the court to a new court complex at Tis Hazari, literally "thirty thousand". Tis Hazari, which was to become Maharaj's Karam Bhoomi, had a long and layered history. Some say its name came from the 30,000 trees planted there by Shah Jahan; Sikh records suggest it was a garrison of 30,000 cavalrymen during the uprising of 1857. The site had once been a royal garden, owned in turn by Aurangzeb's daughter Zeb-un-Nisa and Muhammad Shah Rangeela's queen, both of whom were buried there. Damaged during the Revolt of 1857, it nevertheless remained steeped in history and was now destined to become the nucleus of Delhi's judiciary.[12]

Many of Maharaj's extended family, including his lawyer uncles, also migrated to Delhi. But the luxury of the sprawling *vakeelan vali haveli* of Lahore was lost; cramped refugee accommodations left no room for joint-family living. Other family members moved to Hoshiarpur or Dehradun. The family remained united in spirit, though scattered by circumstance.

Maharaj joined the Delhi Bar Association, a body with deep roots dating back to 1888.[13] The Partition had reshaped its membership: many prominent Muslim lawyers had moved to Pakistan, while Hindu lawyers from Lahore and Rawalpindi swelled its ranks in Delhi. Maharaj quickly established himself, securing offices in Chandni Chowk close to Tis Hazari, and began the arduous task of rebuilding his legal practice. He also continued to operate a small office from his residence.

---

11. Kumkum Chadha, *The Marigold Story: Indira Gandhi & Others* (Westland, 2019), p. 321.

12. Ziya Us Salam, "How Did Tis Hazari Get Its Name?", *The Hindu*, accessed 25 May 2025, https://www.thehindu.com/news/cities/Delhi/watch-how-did-tis-hazari-get-its-name/article65503255.ece.

13. Delhi Bar Association, "History", accessed 25 May 2025, https://delhibarassociation.in/history.

It was in Azad Market, on a freezing December morning of 28 December 1952 just before midnight, that a son was born to Maharaj Kishen and Ratan Prabha. They named him Arun, meaning "dawn" or "the first ray of sunlight". He was the youngest of their three children, joining sisters Madhu and Manju.

True to his Brahmin heritage, Maharaj consulted astrologers for his son's horoscope. The predictions foretold that Arun would achieve fame and livelihood through his oratory. Signs of his charisma appeared early: by the age of two, he was already articulate and confident, answering questions clearly and charming all around him. His precocious talent won him an award from then Health Minister Sushila Rohatgi, a first public recognition of qualities that would only grow stronger with time.

★

The Delhi Bar Association at the time was dominated by local lawyers—mainly Banias and Kayasths, with a small number of Muslims. Newcomers often found it difficult to establish themselves, which eventually led to the formation of a separate "refugee bar". Maharaj worked tirelessly to provide for his family. Over the years, he built a thriving legal practice and eventually rose to become president of the Bar.[14] At the same time, he remained deeply committed to supporting displaced people in need.

His three children were largely raised by his wife, Ratan Prabha, a strong-willed woman typical of many Punjabi women from Amritsar. She grew up in a large household with four sisters and two brothers. Her father, an affluent businessman, imported textiles from England and sold them in India. Arun Jaitley often heard stories of how his maternal grandfather would sail to Manchester to procure *lathha* (rolls of fabric).[15]

Ratan Prabha not only encouraged her children to face life's challenges with resilience but also set high standards for them. Education was valued in the Jaitley family, and she herself stood out among women of her generation for

---

14. Arun Jaitley, *Articles & Speeches by Arun Jaitley: A Compilation* (Universal Law Publishing Co. Pvt. Ltd., 2014). *See*, Arun Jaitley's introduction on the last page.

15. Kumkum Chadha, *The Marigold Story: Indira Gandhi & Others* (Westland, 2019), p. 320.

being literate in both Hindi and English. Academically gifted, she completed a pre-university course in Fine Arts and consistently excelled in school.[16] Her picture was even featured in the newspaper when she topped her tenth-grade class. Recognising the importance of quality education, she ensured her children attended the best schools. Madhu and Manju were admitted to Queen Mary School near Kashmiri Gate. Arun Jaitley was admitted to Noble School, run by a family friend. In January 1957, he was admitted to St. Xavier's Senior Secondary School, a prestigious missionary institution in Delhi's Civil Lines.

As Azad Market grew increasingly crowded, the family relocated from Old Delhi to a rented house in Model Town. Yet Ratan Prabha longed for a home of her own, rather than one that was rented or provided by the government. She was never fully satisfied with the "refugee allotment" house her family had been given. In the 1960s, her dream was realised when Maharaj Kishen successfully bid for a plot at a Delhi Development Authority (DDA) auction in Naraina Vihar, West Delhi, and built a house there. For Ratan Prabha, this was the fulfilment of a long-cherished aspiration. At the time, Delhi had not yet developed the clear distinction between south and north; Maharaj chose the location simply because it was affordable.[17]

★

The traumatic experiences of Partition left deep and lasting scars on Maharaj Kishen. He never reconciled with the idea of being a refugee in his own country, and the wounds of being forced out of Lahore never truly healed. He carried the pain of Partition almost like an inherited family heirloom. Though he did not hold individuals responsible for his loss and suffering, he remained angry and resentful towards the political leadership of the time for conceding to Partition. What he missed most, however, was Lahore itself. Delhi had its share of fine food, but for him, nothing compared to Nikoo Shah's puris near Dyal Singh High School, Bhagwan Singh's lassi at Anarkali, the savouries at Bhan Shah's shop in Chowk Chakla, or Nahar Singh's milkshake.

16. Ibid.

17. Ibid., p. 320.

Arun Jaitley grew up in a close-knit, middle-class household where he constantly witnessed his parents' struggles and the lingering weight of Partition on the faces of his elders. He held deep respect for his parents, and their relationship reflected the dynamics typical of Punjabi Khatri families. Sons in such families rarely expressed dissent directly to their fathers, leaving their mothers to mediate differences of opinion. This silence was born not of fear but of reverence, an unspoken understanding that bound fathers and sons together. In the Jaitley family too, this delicate balance of reverence and affection defined the bond between Maharaj Kishen and Arun.[18]

Arun Jaitley's early years unfolded in a refugee community where anti-Congress sentiment ran deep, a political climate that would leave a lasting imprint on his worldview. Like many displaced Punjabi families, the Jaitleys gravitated towards the Bharatiya Jana Sangh (BJS), founded in 1951 by Syama Prasad Mookerjee. Though Maharaj Kishen himself was not directly active in politics, his unwavering commitment to justice and fairness profoundly shaped his son's political thinking and ideological leanings.[19]

★

Arun Jaitley was a bright and curious child who excelled in both academics and extracurricular pursuits. He was immensely fond of cricket, a love that would last a lifetime. In 1961–62, the English team was touring India. They had played one Test match in Pakistan, then travelled to India for an entire five-match Test series, then went back to Pakistan for two more Tests in Pakistan, and finally a tour match in Sri Lanka. The first three Test matches in India were played at Bombay, Kanpur, and Delhi. All these Tests were a draw. The Indian men led by Nari Contractor won the series against a major nation, England, for the first time.

Maharaj Kishen would drop his ten-year-old son at Feroz Shah Kotla grounds, then one of the oldest cricket stadiums in India, in the morning to

---

18. From conversations with a member of the Jaitley family.

19. Ashok Malik, "Arun Jaitley's Demise, An Irreplaceable Loss to the Nation", in *The Discussant: Journal of Centre for Reforms, Development, and Justice*, Special Edition, An Obituary to Arun Jaitley, Vol. VII, No. 3 (July–September 2019), pp. 56–59.

watch the Delhi Test match. Ratan Prabha would pack him a lunch of aloo parathas and other snacks. Jaitley would ride back home on a tanga, the horse cart, on his own, in the evening. The Indian team was put up at the Imperial Hotel during the Delhi Test match. Jaitley would insist that his father take him to the hotel, to meet the team. The stadium where Jaitley once spent days watching his favourite sport would later benefit from his patronage as a successful lawyer and politician—and, after his death, would even be renamed in his honour.

In school, Jaitley quickly gained recognition for his debating skills, a talent that would later become the defining hallmark of his political career. His years at St. Xavier's Senior Secondary School played a crucial role in shaping his thinking and nurturing his early political vision. Though he initially aspired to become an engineer, he eventually enrolled at Delhi University's prestigious Shri Ram College of Commerce (SRCC) in January 1969 as a B.Com (Hons) student.[20]

Maharaj Kishen was a man of strong principles He instilled in his children values of discipline, hard work, and integrity. Known for his humility and simplicity, his only mission was to give a good future to his children, which in those times meant, marrying the daughters into a respectable family as soon they turned eighteen, and providing a worthy career for the sons. He believed his son was brilliant enough to pursue engineering at the newly established Indian Institute of Technology, Delhi (set up in 1961 as the College of Engineering). He was saving money for his son's coaching classes. But Jaitley's fascination with commerce grew steadily, and his interest ultimately evolved into a passion for law after he became deeply involved in student politics. Manju aspired to become a doctor, but Maharaj was keen she complete her graduation and get married.

By the 1960s, good times had returned for Maharaj and Ratan Prabha. Their son had secured admission into SRCC, one of Delhi's most reputed colleges, and was already gaining notice for his sharp intellect and eloquence. Maharaj could now afford to take the family for holidays. Every year, the family travelled to Mussoorie, one of the most famous hill stations in India, for

---

20. Praveen Donthi, "Talk of the Town", *Caravan Magazine*, accessed 25 May 2025, https://caravanmagazine.in/reportage/talk-town.

a month-long vacation. A bath in the holy Ganga, on the way to Mussoorie, was an annual ritual.

Madhu got married in 1968 at the age of twenty-one, and plans were underway for Manju's marriage to a prospective groom from Mumbai.

In many ways, Arun Jaitley lived the life of a typical college student. He wore his hair long, dressed casually in jeans, and sported John Lennon–style glasses that his peers jokingly called "Gandhi goggles".[21] With friends, he often visited The Cellar, Delhi's only discotheque in Connaught Place, or Rambles across the street. While others went to dance, Jaitley focused on the food, especially the sandwiches; dancing never interested him, and he never learned how. Girls noticed him, but he remained elusive and shy.[22]

Academically, Jaitley was a B-plus student, but his brilliance shone in oratory. He could speak extemporaneously on virtually any subject without notes and won several gold medals in debates.[23] He rose to become captain of the debate team and also served as president of the Rotaract Club, where his leadership emerged through intellectual discussions. On stage, he was a commanding speaker who could hold audiences for hours, yet offstage, he was reserved and withdrawn.[24]

It was during these years that Jaitley's association with the Delhi University Students' Union began—an engagement that would eventually chart the course of his political journey.

---

21. Kumkum Chadha, *The Marigold Story: Indira Gandhi & Others* (Westland, 2019), pp. 321–22.
22. Revealed by Jaitley's close family friend.
23. Praveen Donthi, "Talk of the Town", *Caravan Magazine*, accessed 25 May 2025, https://caravanmagazine.in/reportage/talk-town.
24. Kumkum Chadha, *The Marigold Story: Indira Gandhi & Others* (Westland, 2019), p. 322.

2

The Political Beginning

Arun Jaitley entered student politics at the age of nineteen. His reputation as a sharp, articulate public-school boy was further honed at SRCC, one of India's premier institutes for commerce and economics, established in 1926. These formative years shaped the course of his political career.

Growing up, Jaitley absorbed the stories of displacement and loss that marked his refugee family's life. Living in unstable housing, watching his parents adapt to unfamiliar cultural norms, and enduring the trauma of losing their homeland instilled in him resilience and strength. The children of refugee families were not just survivors; they grew into young men carrying the legacy of their parents' struggles as a source of courage. Yet, beneath that resilience, simmered silent anger against the political establishment, whom they held responsible for their families' suffering. Arun Jaitley, too, carried this anger. His early political engagement was not only part of the wider wave of anti-government student politics of the 1970s but was also fuelled by a personal bitterness towards the Congress, an outlook he inherited from his father.

By the early 1970s, India's university campuses had become crucibles of dissent against Prime Minister Indira Gandhi's increasingly authoritarian style of governance. Born in Allahabad on 19 November 1917 to Jawaharlal and Kamala Nehru, Indira Gandhi had grown up in Anand Bhavan, the sprawling family estate that pulsed with the energy of the national movement. From early childhood, her life was interwoven with India's freedom struggle. She was only two when her father was jailed for the first time. Her political involvement began long before she held any official title.

On 26 March 1942, she married freedom fighter Feroze Gandhi, with whom she had two sons, Rajiv and Sanjay. By 1955, she had entered the Congress Working Committee (CWC), the party's apex decision-making body, which became her launchpad for active politics. Three years later, she was appointed to the Central Parliamentary Board, and in 1959, she rose to the presidency of the Indian National Congress (INC). Between 1964 and 1966, she served as Minister for Information and Broadcasting.

Her life took a dramatic turn on 11 January 1966 when Prime Minister Lal Bahadur Shastri died suddenly in Tashkent, just hours after signing a peace accord with Pakistani President Ayub Khan. Within the Congress, the old guard leaned towards Morarji Desai for leadership. However, twelve of the fourteen Congress chief ministers rallied behind Indira Gandhi and persuaded their MPs to support her. She won decisively, securing 355 votes against Desai's 169. Accepting defeat gracefully, Desai pledged his cooperation. Indira Gandhi humbly described herself as a *"Desh Sevika"* (servant of the nation) and became India's first and to date only woman prime minister.[1]

Within a year, she faced her first electoral test in the 1967 Lok Sabha and Assembly elections, leading Congress to victory. In a shrewd political move, against the advice of her close aides, she offered Morarji Desai the post of deputy prime minister along with the finance portfolio, which he accepted. This diffused tensions and prevented another leadership battle.[2]

Her initial years in office were turbulent. India's economy was weakening, foreign exchange reserves were depleting, imports of essential goods were restricted, and exports were faltering. The aftershocks of the 1965 Indo-Pak war strained both stability and the economy. China's hostility sharpened, the Mizo rebellion spread in the Northeast, and demands for a Punjabi Suba grew louder. On top of this, a devastating drought in 1966 triggered severe food shortages and spiralling inflation. During her first visit to the United States, President Lyndon Johnson offered conditional food aid, which spurred her to push forward the Green Revolution. Though its results would take three years, it eventually made India self-sufficient in food production—one of her

---

1. Capt. Praveen Davar, Indira Gandhi's four Tenures as PM, Indian National Congress Website, accessed 2 September 2025, https://inc.in/congress-sandesh/tribute/indira-gandhi-s-four-tenures-as-pm.

2. Ibid.

landmark achievements in the early years of governance. Rebuilding relations with the USA which had suffered in the aftermath of 1965 Indo-Pak conflict, was an important milestone in the country's foreign policy.[3]

In July 1969, she introduced a new economic policy, laying the foundation for the nationalisation of banks. When she took over the finance ministry from Desai, he resigned in protest. The old guard, still resentful, engineered a split in the Congress later that year. While the CWC expelled her, the Congress Parliamentary Party reaffirmed confidence in her leadership. Out of 268 Congress MPs, 220 sided with her. Thus emerged Congress (R)—first "Requisitionists," later "Ruling"—while her rivals formed Congress (O) for "Organisation".[4] Though still prime minister, Indira Gandhi had to rely on smaller parties for support.

Refusing to lead a fragile minority government, she recommended dissolution of the Lok Sabha in December 1970, paving the way for fresh elections in March 1971. The opposition parties—including Congress (O), Jana Sangh, Swatantra Party, and the Samyukta Socialist Party—formed a *mahagathbandhan* (Grand Alliance) under the slogan "*Indira Hatao*" (Remove Indira). Indira Gandhi countered with a simpler but more powerful call: "*Garibi Hatao*" (Remove Poverty).[5] The people responded with overwhelming support, giving her 330 seats out of 536.

Barely had she consolidated her authority when the Bangladesh crisis erupted. In 1970–71, Pakistan's eastern wing revolted against domination by the western elite. After Sheikh Mujibur Rahman's Awami League swept the elections, he was denied the prime ministership, arrested, and East Pakistan was subjected to brutal military suppression. Indira Gandhi opened India's borders to 10 million refugees, provided arms and training to the Mukti Bahini, and built global support for Bangladesh's independence. When Pakistan launched pre-emptive air strikes on 3 December 1971, India formally entered the war. Within two weeks, Pakistan surrendered, and Bangladesh was born.

The victory transformed Indira Gandhi's stature. Once dismissed as a "*goongi gudiya*" (dumb doll) by Ram Manohar Lohia and derided as "*yeh chokri*" (this

---

3. Ibid.

4. Ibid.

5. Shakti Sinha, *Vajpayee: The Years That Changed India* (Penguin, 2020), p. 2.

chit of a girl) by Morarji Desai, she was now hailed as Durga.[6] Though President Nixon derisively called her an "old witch",[7] she was celebrated globally as the "Empress of India".

I remember being taken with my schoolmates to meet her one winter afternoon. Among the crowd of students, my short height hid me from her view until she noticed and gently pulled me forward. That small gesture of warmth remains etched in my memory.

After the triumph of 1971, her stature towered over the political landscape. Opposition parties, demoralised and divided, failed to mount any real challenge. For a time, protests against her government virtually disappeared. Yet, her increasingly authoritative style of governance sowed the seeds of future unrest.

★

Established in 1922, Delhi University (DU) was one of the most politically vibrant campuses in the early 1970s. During India's struggle for independence from British rule, DU and its affiliated colleges were hotbeds of political activity, with students and faculty often collaborating with revolutionaries and participating in initiatives led by freedom movement leaders.[8] At the time, the Delhi University Students Union (DUSU) served as the official student body, recognised by the university as the representative of student interests. Each college elected ten councillors, who in turn selected the DUSU president and vice president. Over the years, DU had become a training ground for future political leaders, with student groups representing diverse ideologies vying for positions on its prestigious panels.[9]

---

6. Neerja Chowdhury, *How Prime Ministers Decide* (Aleph, 2023), p. xiv.
7. Ibid.
8. Fareeha Iftikhar and Risha Chitlangia, "DU at 100: The Nursery of Political Luminaries", *Hindustan Times*, accessed 25 May 2025, https://www.hindustantimes.com/cities/delhi-news/duat-100-the-nursery-of-political-luminaries-101651689599323.html.
9. Ibid.

Arun Jaitley—already an "angry young man"—added his voice to the chorus critical of Congress governance.[10] However, he was not initially inclined towards active politics. At SRCC, Jaitley was content winning medals for debates and showcasing his oratory skills. It was Sri Ram Khanna, a senior at SRCC and a leader in the Akhil Bharatiya Vidyarthi Parishad (ABVP), who first persuaded Jaitley to consider politics. Having witnessed Jaitley's debating prowess, Khanna recognised his potential as an articulate leader.[11] Jaitley was initially hesitant, but Khanna's persistence eventually led him to join the ABVP in 1971 and contest SRCC's union elections. Khanna nominated him for the post of DU's supreme councillor—one of ten electors responsible for indirectly voting for the DUSU president. This marked Jaitley's formal entry into SRCC politics and the beginning of his association with the ABVP, the student wing linked to the Rashtriya Swayamsevak Sangh (RSS), a right-wing Hindutva organisation.[12]

The ABVP's early history distinguished it from other student political groups, which were typically affiliated with political parties and had limited autonomy.[13] Although connected to the RSS, the ABVP functioned as a largely independent organisation, with the RSS providing guidance rather than direct control. The ABVP was formed in the wake of the RSS ban following Mahatma Gandhi's assassination on 30 January 1948. Most RSS cadres at that time were young, and after the ban, they began meeting under the banner of ABVP. Its formal status was confirmed months later at a meeting in Ambala on 13 June 1948,[14] and it was officially established on 9 July 1949.[15] Its constitution,

---

10. Praveen Donthi, "Talk of the Town", *Caravan Magazine*, accessed 25 May 2025, https://caravanmagazine.in/reportage/talk-town.

11. Fareeha Iftikhar, "One Student, One Vote: How Arun Jaitley Helped Change DU Polls", *Hindustan Times*, accessed 25 May 2025, https://www.hindustantimes.com/gurugram/how-arun-jaitley-helped-change-du-polls/story-WrInT3JDag3SU0SDuRjhKJ.html.

12. Praveen Donthi, "Talk of the Town", *Caravan Magazine*, accessed 25 May 2025, https://caravanmagazine.in/reportage/talk-town.

13. Priyanka Dubey, "Student Days", *Caravan Magazine*, accessed 25 May 2025, https://caravanmagazine.in/reportage/age-of-abvp.

14. Ibid.

15. ABVP celebrates the day as *rashtriya chhatra diwas*, or national students' day to commemorate the anniversary of its founding, https://caravanmagazine.in/reportage/age-of-abvp.

drafted by RSS ideologue Eknath Ranade, emphasised the organisation's mission as being for the glory of the nation, an aspect that resonated with the nationalist-minded Jaitley.[16]

By the late 1950s, the ABVP was placed under the leadership of Yashwant Rao Kelkar, an RSS pracharak who strengthened the organisation's Mumbai unit and set up state-level operations in Maharashtra. By the mid-1960s, the ABVP had expanded across Maharashtra and Madhya Pradesh, and by 1970, it had built a loose national network of student activists.[17]

★

Khanna and Jaitley proved to be a formidable team. Shri Ram Khanna was a charismatic leader, widely popular, and had defeated Deepak Malhotra, another prominent student leader, in the 1972 DUSU elections. Jaitley, a natural leader himself, was equally charismatic, easily drawing attention with his fluent English, compelling oratory, and fiery speeches that resonated in the university's political circles. Together, they not only reshaped Delhi University politics but also played a key role in pushing the administration to reform the election process, organising protests against what they viewed as an undemocratic system.

At the time, the DUSU had four main office bearers—president, vice president, secretary, and assistant secretary—elected annually by the members of the supreme council. Students could not vote directly for the president or vice president. The rules restricted eligibility for the vice president and assistant secretary to students not appearing for final university examinations that year, though oddly, this restriction did not apply to the president and secretary, who carried greater responsibilities. The union had a quasi-federal structure: its membership included students from various faculties, departments, and affiliated colleges, though only twenty-eight of the forty-eight DU colleges were linked to DUSU.

16. Priyanka Dubey, "Student Days", *Caravan Magazine*, accessed 25 May 2025, https://caravanmagazine.in/reportage/age-of-abvp.

17. Ibid.

The supreme council, composed of student representatives from affiliated colleges—one for every hundred students—was the highest decision-making body. It had ten councillors, who then elected the DUSU president and vice president. The executive committee, consisting of twenty-four members, conducted the union's day-to-day activities. At least one-fourth of the executive committee comprised presidents of affiliated college unions, serving as ex-officio members. The DUSU president had the authority to nominate 50 per cent of the committee, allowing significant influence over its composition. The vice-chancellor could nominate up to three non-voting associate members from the teaching staff. While the supreme councillors primarily voted for office bearers and passed the budget, decision-making largely rested with a few student leaders led by the president.[18] Jaitley would later spearhead a historic protest to reform this electoral system.

In 1972, Jaitley was elected president of SRCC while Khanna became the DUSU president. Together, they led protests against the undemocratic election process. In response, Vice-Chancellor Dr Sarup Singh rusticated Khanna, Deepak Malhotra, Vijay Mehta, and Prithipal Singh.[19] The move ignited a massive student agitation, which Jaitley helped lead, organising a strike that lasted fifty days, from November 1972 to January 1973, arguably the longest in DU's history. Tens of thousands of students joined, including those from non-affiliated colleges. Jaitley demanded direct elections for union executives and the revocation of the rustication orders. The university was forced to shut down indefinitely.[20]

Eventually, the administration conceded, forming a committee to review reforms in the electoral process. In 1973, Delhi University transitioned to direct elections, allowing all students to vote, a change in which Jaitley played a pivotal

---

18. T.K. Oommen, "Student Politics in India: The Case of Delhi University", *Asian Survey*, Vol. 14, No. 9 (1974), pp. 777–94, https://www.jstor.org/stable/2642743.

19. Pankaj Vohra, "Delhi University's Iconic Leaders", *The Sunday Guardian*, accessed 25 May 2025, https://sundayguardianlive.com/opinion/delhi-universitys-iconic-leaders.

20. Fareeha Iftikhar and Risha Chitlangia, "DU at 100: The Nursery of Political Luminaries", *Hindustan Times*, accessed 25 May 2025, https://www.hindustantimes.com/cities/delhi-news/duat-100-the-nursery-of-political-luminaries-101651689599323.html.

role.[21] This reform marked a turning point, linking DUSU closely with national politics, with student leaders from diverse ideologies vying for its positions. Ironically, both Khanna and Malhotra later became academics—Khanna as dean of the DU commerce department and Malhotra as principal of Dyal Singh College. Jaitley, who joined the Bharatiya Janata Party (BJP) in 1980, went on to become one of its most influential leaders, holding key ministerial portfolios in both the Vajpayee and Modi governments. Decades later, he even helped my sister-in-law Jyoti Barmola Mamgain gain admission to Dyal Singh College when she moved from Imphal to Delhi for higher education.[22]

Despite his active political involvement, Jaitley never neglected his studies. He remained a diligent student, excelling in debates and developing a lifelong affection for SRCC. Even after rising to national prominence, he maintained humility, respect for his teachers, and a willingness to support his alma mater. Later, he joined SRCC's governing body, participating actively in its affairs. In 2013, he facilitated Narendra Modi's campaign launch at SRCC, marking the beginning of Modi's journey as the BJP's prime ministerial candidate for the 2014 elections.

★

Although deeply involved in student politics, Jaitley was also contemplating his future career. Initially, he had aspired to become a chartered accountant, but he ultimately chose to pursue law. His father, a successful lawyer practising at the Tis Hazari courts, had earlier encouraged him to become an engineer. Observing his son's active engagement in politics, he believed that a career in law would suit him better.[23]

Jaitley enrolled in the Campus Law Centre at Delhi University, following in the footsteps of his father and his granduncles. Among his peers, friends like Raian Karanjawala had also decided to pursue law. It was during this period

21. T.K. Oommen, "Student Politics in India: The Case of Delhi University", *Asian Survey*, Vol. 14, No. 9 (1974) 777–94, https://www.jstor.org/stable/2642743.

22. Jyoti is now a celebrated author and married to a high-ranking Indian army officer.

23. As told by a long-standing friend of Arun Jaitley.

that Jaitley was persuaded to reconsider his professional path and embrace the legal profession.

By now, Jaitley had become a well-known figure not only in Delhi but across the country. His role in reforming the DUSU electoral system had significantly boosted his popularity among students. In 1973, he was widely seen as the natural choice for the ABVP's presidential candidate for the DUSU elections. Surprisingly, however, the position went to Alok Kumar, an RSS member who later became a BJP MLA in Delhi. Kumar himself later acknowledged that Jaitley had been the more deserving candidate.[24]

The decision to overlook Jaitley was not due to doubts about his electability but stemmed from a strategic concern within the ABVP. The organisation had recently faced the defection of its first elected DUSU president—Khanna's predecessor—to the Congress-affiliated National Students' Union of India (NSUI). Reeling from this shock, the RSS chose Kumar, a candidate perceived as more ideologically loyal, over Jaitley, who was relatively new to the ABVP and had yet to demonstrate his commitment. Nevertheless, Jaitley was given the vice-presidential ticket.

Undeterred, Jaitley contested the DUSU vice-presidency in 1973. The ABVP swept all positions, and Jaitley won decisively, securing an impressive majority. He maximised the influence of this key secondary position. Fluent and persuasive in both Hindi and English, Jaitley played a crucial role in making the ABVP appealing to the urbane, English-speaking student population nationwide. His abilities gained particular recognition in ABVP conferences, where the charismatic young Jaitley made his presence felt by his articulate interventions.[25]

The following year, Jaitley was elected DUSU president, while Ravi Shankar Prasad became the assistant general secretary of the Patna University equivalent. During this period, Jaitley began formal interactions with Atal Bihari Vajpayee. Having first heard Vajpayee speak in 1967 while at St. Xavier's Senior Secondary

---

24. Praveen Donthi, "Talk of the Town", *Caravan Magazine*, accessed 25 May 2025, https://caravanmagazine.in/reportage/talk-town.

25. Ravi Shankar Prasad, "In Remembrance: Arun Jaitley Was an Affectionate Elder Brother to Me and Leaves Fond Memories", *The Times of India*, accessed 25 May 2025, https://timesofindia.indiatimes.com/blogs/toi-edit-page/in-remembrance-arun-jaitley-was-an-affectionate-elder-brother-to-me-and-leaves-fond-memories/.

School, Jaitley had been profoundly inspired by his eloquence, wit, and mastery of language.[26] Vajpayee's ability to explain complex issues in simple terms, his instant responsiveness, and his poetic touch in speeches greatly influenced Jaitley, who began to adopt many of these traits in his own oratory.[27] This was also likely the moment when Vajpayee recognised the potential in the young, fiery leader emerging within the ABVP.

★

It was the turbulent events of the early 1970s that awakened Jaitley's natural leadership abilities and drew him deeper into politics. University campuses across India had become increasingly volatile, with students protesting against the governance of the Congress party in various states. These protests were often spontaneous and disorganized, involving university students, union leaders, the ABVP, and the Samajwadi Yuvjan Sabha. Grievances ranged from "amenities on campuses, reduction in fees, concession in cinema tickets",[28] hostel fee, mess bill, unemployment, price rise and corruption.[29]

In December 1973, a seemingly minor incident ignited widespread unrest: Lalbhai Dalpatbhai College of Engineering (LDCE) in Ahmedabad refused to roll back increased mess fees. Food prices had doubled that year, and hostel bills had surged by 40 per cent in December alone.[30] Students at Gujarat University erupted in protest, demanding the dismissal of the Congress government in

---

26. "Atal Bihari Vajpayee—India's Greatest Orator Since Independence: Arun Jaitley", NDTV, accessed 25 May 2025, https://www.ndtv.com/india-news/atal-bihari-vajpayee-indias-greatest-orator-since-independence-arun-jaitley-717951.

27. Arun Jaitley, "Atalji, The Quintessential Gentleman—How He Made a Difference", accessed 25 May 2025, https://www.arunjaitley.com/atalji-the-quintessential-gentleman-how-he-made-a-difference/.

28. Ghanshyam Shah, *Protest Movements in Two Indian States: A Study of the Gujarat and Bihar Movements* (Ajanta Publications, 1977), p. 85.

29. Rupak Kumar, "The Making of India's Resilient Opposition in the 1970s", *South Asian Survey*, Vol. 31, No. 1 (2024), pp. 102–23, available at https://journals.sagepub.com/doi/10.1177/09715231241264933#bibr16-09715231241264933.

30. Vinay Sitapati, *Jugalbandi: The BJP Before Modi* (Penguin, 2020), pp. 82–83.

the state. What began as scattered demonstrations in Gujarat soon escalated into large-scale agitations in Bihar and other states. Student marches, met with police repression, sparked nationwide criticism of state governments. Over 100 people were killed, more than 3,000 injured, and 8,000 arrested during the unrest.[31]

The Congress government in Gujarat underestimated the crisis, dismissing it as a routine student strike. Yet the movement quickly spread nationwide. Inspired by the Gujarat protests, students in Bihar—frustrated by corruption, inflation, and unemployment—took to the streets against their own Congress-led state government. Key student leaders in Bihar included Lalu Prasad Yadav, Sushil Kumar Modi, and Nitish Kumar.

On 17 February 1974, student leaders such as Lalu Prasad Yadav, Arun Jaitley, Sushil Kumar Modi, and Ram Vilas Paswan formed the Chhatra Sangharsh Samiti.[32] The ABVP was the main constituent of this body, holding one-third of its twenty-four-member governing committee. Four members were socialists, two were from the Gandhian Tarun Shanti Sena, and two represented Congress (O).[33]

The Samiti launched a mass movement in Bihar, where police brutality escalated tensions. On 18 March 1974, police fired on unarmed student demonstrators, killing eight people.[34] This movement came to be known as the Navnirman Andolan—or the movement for regeneration. Students appealed to Jayaprakash Narayan (JP) to lead the effort.[35]

---

31. Ibid.

32. Rupak Kumar, "The Making of India's Resilient Opposition in the 1970s", *South Asian Survey*, Vol. 31, No. 1 (2024) fn 6, available at https://journals.sagepub.com/doi/10.1177/09715231241264933#fn6-09715231241264933.

33. Christophe Jaffrelot, "Who Mainstreamed BJP?", *The Indian Express*, accessed 25 May 2025,https://indianexpress.com/article/opinion/columns/who-mainstreamed-bjp/.

34. Rupak Kumar, "The Making of India's Resilient Opposition in the 1970s", *South Asian Survey*, Vol. 31, No. 1 (2024) 102–23, available at https://journals.sagepub.com/doi/10.1177/09715231241264933#bibr16-09715231241264933.

35. Christophe Jaffrelot, "Who Mainstreamed BJP?", *The Indian Express*, accessed 25 May 2025,https://indianexpress.com/article/opinion/columns/who-mainstreamed-bjp/.

A freedom fighter and respected leader, JP had retired from active public life in Patna. Born on 11 October 1902 in Sitabdiara, Saran district, he had been deeply involved in India's independence movement, spending considerable time in jail, and later played a key role in the Congress Socialist Party. Despite offers to join government posts after Independence, JP's Gandhian principles led him to decline office, earning him widespread respect.

In March 1974, JP agreed to lead the movement, aided by Nanaji Deshmukh, a dedicated RSS pracharak.[36]

Born on 11 October 1916 at Kadoli, a small town in Maharashtra, Chandikadas Amritrao Deshmukh (affectionately called Nanaji) worked as a vegetable seller to pay for his early education. Through hard work and dedication, he later graduated from the prestigious Birla Institute of Technology and Science in Pilani, Rajasthan. His family was in touch with K.B. Hedgewar, the founder of the RSS. Inspired by freedom fighter Lokmanya Tilak and his thoughts on nationalism, Nanaji joined the RSS as a pracharak around 1940. Nanaji went to Gorakhpur as a pracharak to expand organisational work in eastern Uttar Pradesh. In a span of three years, over 250 RSS shakhas were established in the region. He also played a key role in establishing India's first Saraswati Shishu Mandir School at Gorakhpur in 1952. Today, there are more than 20,000 such schools running across the country and catering to over three million students. In 1947, the RSS decided to launch two journals *Rashtra Dharma* and *Panchjanya* as well as a daily named *Swadesh*. Atal Bihari Vajpayee was appointed as the editor, Deendayal Upadhyaya as the margdharshak (mentor), and Nanaji as the managing director. Nanaji played a crucial role in setting up a strong base for the BJS in Uttar Pradesh. By 1957, the party had presence in every district of the state, with Nanaji as the organising secretary of its state unit. He later also worked as the party's treasurer.[37]

---

36. Janata Dal (Secular), "Jayaprakash Narayan: Founder of Janata Dal Party", accessed 25 May 2025, https://jds.ind.in/en/founder-of-jds-jpnarayan.php.

37. Arun Anand, "Nanaji Deshmukh—Key Architect of Janata Party, Who Quit Politics to Transform Rural India", *The Print*, assessed 25 May 2025, https://theprint.in/indiananaji-deshmukh-key-architect-of-janata-party-who-quit-politics-to-transform-ruralindia/521300/.

Nanaji enjoyed JP's confidence and worked in close contact with JP's associates in the Sarvodaya Movement[38] and the Gandhi Peace Foundation.[39] JP's close friends like Ramnath Goenka and Ganga Sharan Singh also supported the movement. Together they mobilised the entire non-communist opposition in support of the movement led by JP.[40]

JP toured India, urging citizens to rise against Indira Gandhi's increasingly authoritarian rule. On 8 April 1974, he led a silent procession in Patna, which was met with police lathi charges. The movement rapidly gained momentum, combining student activism with the largest working-class mobilisation in Indian history.

George Fernandes, a firebrand trade union leader, a socialist politician, and an incredibly powerful orator, led the All India Railwaymen's Federation (AIRF) strike in May 1974. Fernandes was a man with a mind of his own. He believed in militant opposition to the government. Many felt that the idea of a militant opposition was misconceived but he believed that this was the only course. The Indian Railways was the largest employer in India, and one of the largest in the world; it was the network of veins through which administration flowed across the country. The entire country resonated with the slogan "*Rail ka chakka jaam karenge*" (We will block the railway tracks).[41] The strike would immobilise India.[42]

On 5 June 1974, JP addressed a massive gathering at Gandhi Maidan in Patna, declaring:

---

38. The Sarvodaya Movement is a socioeconomic and political philosophy started by Mahatma Gandhi, emphasising the principles of non-violence, self-reliance, and the well-being of all. The term "Sarvodaya" translates to "the welfare of all" in Sanskrit. It aimed at bringing his vision of an ideal society to reality. He inspired several prolific leaders, such as Vinoba Bhave, Jayaprakash Narayan, and Jai Jagat, to carry forward this movement in post-independence India.

39. The foundation was established on 31 July 1958 to preserve and spread Mahatma Gandhi's philosophy.

40. Arun Jaitley, *Articles & Speeches by Arun Jaitley: A Compilation* (Universal Law Publishing Co. Pvt. Ltd., 2014), pp. 227–28.

41. Arun Jaitley, "George Saheb as I Knew Him", accessed 25 May 2025, https://www.arunjaitley.com/george-saheb-as-i-knew-him/.

42. Rakesh Ankit, "Janata Party (1974–77): Creation of an All-India Opposition", *History and Sociology of South Asia, Vol.* 11, No. 1 (2016), pp. 39–54, 53.

> This is a revolution, friends! We are not here merely to see the Vidhan Sabha dissolved. That is only one milestone on our journey. But we have a long way to go ... After 27 years of freedom, people of this country are wracked by hunger, rising prices, corruption ... oppressed by every kind of injustice ... it is a Sampoorna Kranti (Total Revolution) we want, nothing less![43]

JP called for colleges and universities to close for a year, urging students to devote themselves to rebuilding the nation.[44] Indian campuses became political crucibles, and JP's Sampoorna Kranti movement inspired participation from multiple political parties. The anthem of the Bihar movement, "*Jayaprakash ka bigul baja toh jaag uthi tarunai hai, tilak lagane tumbe jawano, kranti dwar par aayi hai*" (Jayaprakash's bugle has awoken the youth, for revolution now stands at your doorstep and beckons you), reverberated through the Bihar countryside in 1974–75, as JP crisscrossed the length and breadth of the state. He urged the youth to create a casteless society for social transformation to take place.[45] The slogans JP raised—against nepotism, elitism, exclusionary politics, authoritarianism, and those in favour of people's democracy, socialism, participatory rule, and the social audit of politics—continue to reverberate in Indian polity, even though their colour and character have changed in unrecognisable ways.

The ABVP played a key role in mobilising students and youth in alignment with JP's vision. Its disciplined, cadre-based approach helped sustain the movement despite harsh government crackdowns, including arrests and censorship. In Bihar and Gujarat, the protests were organised by ABVP leaders alongside other student groups, trade unions, and political parties. Leaders like K.N. Govindacharya in Bihar and a young Narendra Modi in Gujarat were instrumental in guiding the movement locally.

---

43. Janata Dal (Secular), "Jayaprakash Narayan: Founder of Janata Dal Party", accessed 25 May 2025, https://jds.ind.in/en/founder-of-jds-jpnarayan.php.

44. "Jayaprakash Narayan: A Rebel Always", Press Information Bureau, Government of India, Special Service and Features, accessed 25 May 2025, https://www.pib.gov.in/newsite/printrelease.aspx?relid=148928.

45. Neerja Chowdhury, *How Prime Ministers Decide* (Aleph, 2023), p. 41.

Twenty-year-old Jaitley, then DUSU vice president, was drawn into the JP Movement. He became convener of the Loktantrik Yuva Morcha (committee for youth), travelling with JP across the country as the movement gained momentum. He attended conventions in Patna and Ahmedabad, working alongside future BJP leaders such as M. Venkaiah Naidu, Nitin Gadkari, Shivraj Singh Chouhan, Devendra Fadnavis, Jagat Prakash Nadda, Ravi Shankar Prasad, Vijay Goel, and Anant Kumar.[46]

Jaitley's involvement in the JP Movement shaped his political ideology, aligning him with the BJS (later BJP). It strengthened his commitment to democratic principles and laid the foundation for his future role as a key strategist in Indian politics. His early activism reflects a lifelong dedication to civil liberties and opposition to authoritarianism.

★

JP's call for *parivartan*, or change, quickly became a rallying cry among students. Ahead of the DUSU election, Jaitley declared that if elected, he would invite JP to address the university. Jaitley went on to win the election, defeating the NSUI candidate Brij Mohan Bhama by a substantial margin. His victory as an ABVP candidate marked a watershed moment in student politics, as Congress-affiliated organisations then dominated most campuses. The win represented a breakthrough for the ABVP and cemented Jaitley's growing reputation as a student leader.

In 1973, Jaitley enrolled in the three-year postgraduate law program at DU's Campus Law Centre. By 1974, Indira Gandhi had addressed a massive youth rally at the India Gate boat club lawns, inspiring the young Jaitley to promise that he would hold an even larger rally for JP if elected DUSU president.[47] By this time, his popularity within DU had peaked, and he was widely regarded as the inevitable next DUSU president. His poised, articulate, and more liberal image of the ABVP attracted attention even from Congress, which attempted

46. Priyanka Dubey, "Student Days", *Caravan Magazine*, accessed 25 May 2025, https://caravanmagazine.in/reportage/age-of-abvp.

47. Sonia Singh, *Defining India: Through Their Eyes* (Penguin, 2019), p. 25.

to woo him into joining the NSUI.[48] Prominent Congress leaders Bahadur Singh and Kulbir Singh reportedly tried to convince him to contest on the NSUI ticket, but Jaitley remained firmly loyal to his party.[49]

This time, the RSS supported Jaitley's candidacy on the advice of Rajkumar Bhatia. Campaigning with characteristic energy, he rode pillion on Prabhu Chawla's scooter, canvassing for votes. Some accounts suggest that had the ABVP not chosen him, he might have considered joining the NSUI; Jaitley consistently denied this, stating, "There was no question of this happening. I hated the Congress, and this suggestion is absurd."[50]

After his election, Jaitley invited JP to the DU campus. JP had earlier been hosted for lunch by Ramnath Goenka at the Indian Express guesthouse in Delhi, where student leaders were also invited to meet him. Seizing the opportunity, Jaitley invited JP to inaugurate a student leaders' conference at the DUSU office. Their association deepened as Jaitley met JP on multiple occasions, including at the Gandhi Peace Foundation in Delhi and at JP's home in Kadamkuan, Patna.[51]

Later, Jaitley organized a mass rally on the university campus, drawing an unprecedented turnout. Students filled every visible space—from hostel and building rooftops to trees and streets—creating a highly charged political atmosphere. In March 1974, he also hosted a two-day student conference attended by leaders from across India, including Lalu Prasad Yadav, Sushil Modi, Satyapal Malik, and Venkaiah Naidu.[52]

During Jaitley's tenure as DUSU president, the ABVP transformed into a more assertive and rebellious organisation, emphasising anti-leftist positions rather than extreme Hindu nationalism. Jaitley's strong managerial skills made

---

48. Praveen Donthi, "Talk of the Town", *Caravan Magazine*, accessed 25 May 2025, https://caravanmagazine.in/reportage/talk-town.

49. Pankaj Vohra, "Delhi University's Iconic Leaders", *The Sunday Guardian*, accessed 25 May 2025, https://sundayguardianlive.com/opinion/delhi-universitys-iconic-leaders.

50. Kumkum Chadha, *The Marigold Story: Indira Gandhi & Others* (Westland, 2019), p. 324.

51. Arun Jaitley, *Articles & Speeches by Arun Jaitley: A Compilation* (Universal Law Publishing Co. Pvt. Ltd., 2014), pp. 219–20.

52. Ibid.

him an effective leader. He also displayed an early hallmark of his political style: the ability to maintain cordial relations with ideological opponents, a trait that would define his later national career.

Campus politics remained heated, with the ABVP and NSUI often exchanging accusations. Shashi Tharoor, then president of St. Stephen's College Union, later acknowledged that despite ideological differences, Jaitley held no personal animosity towards his opponents.[53]

Amidst his political activities, Jaitley continued to focus on his legal career. He had completed his second-year law exams and had one year remaining before he could practise professionally. He devoted his available time to working in his father's chamber and interning with senior lawyers. However, the events of the following year were poised to dramatically alter the trajectory of his life.

53. "'My Friend and Delhi University Senior': Shashi Tharoor Mourns Arun Jaitley", *Hindustan Times*, accessed 25 May 2025, https://www.hindustantimes.com/india-news/my-friend-and-delhi-university-senior-shashi-tharoor-mourns-arun-jaitley/story-FQY62HRyPvfUXLH8kNl4MJ.html.

3

The First Satyagrahi

On 12 June 1975, Justice Jagmohan Lal Sinha of the Allahabad High Court annulled Indira Gandhi's election, invalidating her Lok Sabha membership. This verdict followed an election petition filed by Raj Narain, a flamboyant wrestler-turned-politician and leader of the Samyukta Socialist Party, recognizable by his signature green bandana. Indira Gandhi had originally defeated Narain in the Rae Bareli constituency of Uttar Pradesh on 10 March 1975 by 110,000 votes. However, Narain challenged the result, alleging electoral malpractice.

The court found that Indira Gandhi had engaged in corrupt practices, including misusing government resources for her campaign. An officer on special duty in the Prime Minister's Secretariat was found to have arranged rostrums, loudspeakers, barricades, and police postings to support her election tours. Furthermore, the court ruled that Yashpal Kapur, a gazetted officer serving in the PM's Secretariat, had unlawfully acted as her election agent. Although Kapur resigned on 13 January 1971, his resignation was officially notified only on 25 January 1971. Since he actively campaigned for Gandhi before this notification, he remained a government employee, violating Section 123(7) of the Representation of the People Act, 1951.[1] Justice Sinha granted Gandhi a fortnight to appeal the decision.

---

1. Sub-section (7) of Section 123, to the extent material for our present purpose, reads: The obtaining or procuring or abetting or attempting to obtain or procure by a candidate or his agent or, by any other person with the consent of a candidate or his election agent, any assistance (other than the giving of vote) for the furtherance of the prospects of that candidate's election, from any person in the service of the

By the evening of 12 June 1975, large demonstrations erupted outside the prime minister's residence, demanding that the high court's judgment be rejected. The Congress party rallied behind her.[2]

Indira Gandhi appealed the verdict to the Supreme Court, which was then on summer vacation. She engaged Nani Palkhivala to represent her. Justice V.R. Krishna Iyer, serving as the vacation judge, was to hear the appeal and consider an interim order against the high court ruling. Prior to the hearing, Law Minister H.R. Gokhale requested a meeting with Justice Krishna Iyer to discuss the case. Upon learning the purpose, the judge politely declined. This was later disclosed in his memoirs.[3] A former judge of Bombay High Court, Gokhale resigned in 1962 and successfully contested the 1971 general election. Indira Gandhi appointed her law minister in her Cabinet.

Meanwhile, pressure mounted on Indira Gandhi to resign. The Opposition was consolidating, and in the Gujarat Assembly elections, the newly formed Janata Front—a coalition including the Jana Sangh—secured a majority, ending Congress's dominance in the state.[4]

On 20 June 1975, Indira Gandhi staged a massive rally at the Boat Club lawns near India Gate to display her strength. Her sons, Rajiv and Sanjay, and daughters-in-law, Sonia and Maneka, joined her on stage. Haryana Chief Minister Chaudhary Bansi Lal mobilized an estimated one million people from his state, instructing police stations to provide trucks and buses for transport. Journalist Coomi Kapoor described the scene as "a sea of humanity covering the lawns on either side of Rajpath". In her speech, Gandhi accused powerful

---

Government and belonging to any of the following classes, namely:— (*a*) gazetted officers.

2. Arun Jaitley, "The Emergency Revisited – Part – I (3-Part Series): The Circumstances Leading to the Imposition of Emergency", accessed 25 May 2025, https://www.arunjaitley.com/the-emergency-revisited-part-i-3-part-series-the-circumstances-leading-to-the-imposition-of-emergency/.

3. Ibid.

4. T. Ramakrishnan, "The 1975 Gujarat Assembly Election", *The Hindu*, accessed 25 May 2025, https://www.thehindu.com/elections/ gujarat-2017/the-1975-gujarat-assembly-election/article21262462.ece.

vested interests, backed by the press, of attempting to oust her and physically harm her, spreading lies to achieve their goals.[5]

On 22 June 1975, a nationwide Janata Front was formed to demand Gandhi's resignation, with an action plan drafted by Nanaji Deshmukh.[6] The JP Movement had reached monumental proportions. Facing disqualification, Gandhi decided to revive a plan for imposing the Emergency, originally suggested by her confidante, West Bengal Chief Minister Siddhartha Shankar Ray, months earlier. In January 1975, concerned about the growing JP Movement, Ray and other Congress leaders had proposed the Emergency to curb Opposition influence. Gandhi initially agreed but later hesitated after officials warned of accusations of repression.[7] Although *The Indian Express* received a tip about the plan, it was dropped due to lack of verification.[8] However, *The Motherland*, a Jana Sangh–RSS daily edited by K.R. Malkani, published a front-page article on 30 January 1975 predicting the Emergency, the arrest of JP, the RSS ban, and the closure of the newspaper.[9] The newspaper claimed the story was based on an astrological prediction by Vasanth Kumar Pandit, a Jana Sangh Member of Parliament and astrologer.[10] The *Motherland* report about the impending arrests, which was dismissed as far-fetched and unsubstantiated by most in the media at that time, in retrospect appears to have been based on solid evidence.[11]

Following the Allahabad High Court verdict, JP convened urgent meetings with Opposition leaders in Delhi to plan the next steps. At these meetings,

---

5. Coomi Kapoor, *The Emergency: A Personal History* (Penguin, 2015, 2016), pp. 14–18.
6. Vinay Sitapati, *Jugalbandi: The BJP Before Modi* (Penguin, 2020), pp 81–96.
7. Coomi Kapoor, *The Emergency: A Personal History* (Penguin, 2015, 2016), pp. 1–18.
8. Kuldip Nayar, who was the editor of Express News Service at *The Indian Express*, wrote in his autobiography that he was tipped about the likelihood of an Emergency by Ramnath Goenka, the owner of *The Indian Express*, but since the tip could not be authenticated the story was dropped. *See*, Kuldip Nayar, *Beyond the Lines: An Autobiography* (Roli Books Pvt. Ltd., 2012).
9. "KR Malkani: When the Journalist Who Predicted Emergency Became Its First Victim", *Organiser*, accessed 25 May 2025, https://organiser.org/2025/06/25/131710/bharat/kr-malkani-and-emergency/.
10. Kuldip Nayar, *Beyond the Lines: An Autobiography* (Roli Books Pvt. Ltd., 2012).
11. Arun Jaitley, *A New India: Selected Writings 2014–19* (Juggernaut, 2020), pp. 284–85.

Arun Jaitley attended as convener of the Sangharsh Samiti.[12] It was decided to hold a massive rally in Delhi on 24 June, demanding Gandhi's resignation. This increased the pressure on her, prompting a reconsideration of the Emergency plan, including the arrest of Opposition leaders. Consequently, JP postponed the rally by a day, and Gandhi delayed the arrests.

On 24 June, the situation worsened for Gandhi. Justice Krishna Iyer heard Palkhivala for Gandhi and Shanti Bhushan for Raj Narain, admitting the appeal but rejecting Palkhivala's request to stay the high court judgment. While Gandhi could attend Parliament, she could only speak as prime minister, not as an elected member.[13]

This Supreme Court order weakened Gandhi's position, intensifying calls for her resignation. Opposition leaders met JP at the Gandhi Peace Foundation. As the convener of youth and student organizations, Jaitley sat in the back row, observing the national leaders chalking out the strategy.[14]

On the morning of 25 June 1975, the Opposition leaders met again at JP's house to plan further action. A People's Struggle Committee, the Lok Sangharsh Samiti, was formed with Morarji Desai as president and Nanaji Deshmukh as general secretary.[15] That evening, a massive rally was held at Ramlila Maidan in North Delhi, with over 100,000 participants.[16] Leaders such as Vajpayee addressed the crowd, but it was JP who electrified the audience, declaring Gandhi's prime ministership illegal and urging the police and army to defy her orders.[17] JP recited Ramdhari Singh Dinkar's poem, "*Singhasan khaali karo / ke janata aati hai*" ("Surrender your throne, for the people are coming"),

---

12. Sonia Singh, *Defining India Through Their Eyes* (Penguin, 2019), pp.19–34.

13. Arun Jaitley, "The Emergency Revisited – Part – I (3-Part Series): The Circumstances Leading to the Imposition of Emergency", accessed 25 May 2025, https://www.arunjaitley.com/the-emergency-revisited-part-i-3-part-series-the-circumstances-leading-to-the-imposition-of-emergency/.

14. Arun Jaitley, *A New India: Selected Writings 2014-19* (Juggernaut, 2020), p. 280. https://www.arunjaitley.com/the-emergency-revisited-part-i-3-part-series-the-circumstances-leading-to-the-imposition-of-emergency/.

15. Abhishek Choudhary, *Vajpayee: The Ascent of the Hindu Right 1924-1977* (Picador India 2023), p. 297.

16. Bipan Chandra, *In the Name of Democracy: JP Movement and the Emergency* (Penguin, 2003), p. 131.

17. Vinay Sitapati, *Jugalbandi: The BJP Before Modi* (Penguin, 2020), p. 86.

to thunderous applause. Prominent leaders including Morarji Desai (Congress O), Raj Narain, Nanaji Deshmukh, and Madan Lal Khurana were present.[18] As ABVP and DUSU president, Jaitley played a key role in mobilizing the crowd.[19] JP announced an all-India satyagraha starting 29 June to compel Gandhi to resign. In what was seen as an extra-constitutional overreach, he urged public-sector employees, police, and the armed forces to defy government orders given Indira Gandhi's refusal to step down.[20]

★

Indira Gandhi set her plan into motion, taking a drastic political step to shield herself from the consequences of an unfavourable court verdict. At 10 p.m. on 25 June 1975, she informed her press secretary, H.Y. Sharada Prasad, saying, "I have decided to declare an Emergency. The President has agreed. I will have to inform the Cabinet tomorrow."[21] Just before midnight, President Fakhruddin Ali Ahmed signed a brief Proclamation declaring the Emergency under Clause 1 of Article 352 of the Constitution of India.

The following morning, at 5 a.m. on 26 June 1975, Cabinet ministers were abruptly woken and summoned for a meeting. Around 6 a.m., Home Secretary S.L. Khurana, who had also been kept in the dark until the last moment, read out the Proclamation to the stunned ministers.[22] Not a single question was raised, except by the mild-mannered defence minister, Swaran Singh. Gandhi justified the Emergency by citing the deteriorating law-and-order situation, claiming that JP's incitement of the army and police the previous night, combined with

---

18. Coomi Kapoor, *The Emergency: A Personal History* (Penguin, 2015, 2016), pp. ix–xvi.
19. Sonia Singh, *Defining India Through Their Eyes* (Penguin, 2019), pp. 19–34.
20. Abhishek Choudhary, *Vajpayee: The Ascent of the Hindu Right 1924-1977* (Picador India 2023), p. 297.
21. B.N. Tandon, *PMO Diary-I: Prelude to the Emergency* (Konark Publication, 2002), pp. 414–16.
22. D.R. Mankekar and Kamla Mankekar, *Decline and Fall of Indira Gandhi* (Vision Books, 1977).

the chaos caused by his movement, threatened national security.[23] In truth, the only threat was to her own political power.[24] The ministers, bleary-eyed and compliant, said nothing—the decision had already been executed: electricity to newspaper presses was cut, and Opposition leaders were set to be arrested. By 8 a.m., Gandhi announced on All India Radio, in a solemn voice, that the Emergency had been declared.[25]

Later, *Shankar's Weekly*, the era's only cartoon periodical, published Abu Abraham's famous cartoon depicting President Fakhruddin Ali Ahmed in a bathtub, telling an aide handing him documents, "If there are any more ordinances, just ask them to wait."[26]

Within her own family, Gandhi received little support. Rajiv Gandhi and his wife, Sonia, reportedly distanced themselves from political discussions, confining themselves mostly to their room. Vijayalakshmi Pandit openly criticized the Emergency and is said to have confronted Gandhi in an unpleasant meeting, voicing her concerns. However, she did not campaign for the Janata Dal when repeatedly requested during the elections.[27]

India had already been under a declared Emergency since the 1971 war with Pakistan, citing external aggression. Alongside the Proclamation, another declaration under Article 359 suspended fundamental rights guaranteed under Articles 14, 19, 21, and 22 of the Constitution. Every citizen was effectively stripped of their basic rights. Press restrictions were imposed: electricity was cut to Delhi's Press Street at Bahadur Shah Zafar Marg, and an official from the censor department was sent to sit in the office of every newspaper.

The young democracy, barely three decades old, plunged into crisis. Police arrests of political leaders had begun even before Gandhi's 8 a.m. address on 26 June. K.R. Malkani, editor of *The Motherland*, was among the first arrested in

23. P.N. Dhar, *Indira Gandhi, the 'Emergency', and Indian Democracy* (Oxford University Press, 2000).

24. Vinay Sitapati, *Jugalbandi: The BJP Before Modi* (Penguin, 2020), p. 87.

25. L.K. Advani, *My Country, My Life* (Rupa, 2008), p. 274.

26. N.P. Ullekh, Politics, "The Cartoons of Abu Abraham Savaged the Pieties and Pretences of Politics", accessed 25 May 2025, https://ullekhnp.com/2024/11/15/the-cartoons-of-abu-abraham-savaged-the-pieties-and-pretences-of-politics/

27. Kuldip Nayar, *Beyond The Lines: An Autobiography* (Roli Books Pvt. Ltd., 2012), p. 228.

Delhi. He was awakened before 1 a.m. by policemen banging on his Rajendra Nagar bungalow gate, surrounded by officers in his garden. When his alarmed wife, Sundari, asked for an explanation, the response was simply, "Malkani sahib knows."[28]

Fearing for his safety, Malkani negotiated to be accompanied to the police station by a trusted neighbour as a witness. He also alerted *The Motherland* office, the RSS, BJS, and news agencies like the Press Trust of India and United News of India immediately, enabling many to evade arrest. The *Hindustan Times* reported his arrest in a small front-page box—the only Emergency-related news published the next day.

At Civil Lines police headquarters in Old Delhi, detainees such as Biju Patnaik, Piloo Mody, Raj Narain, Chandra Shekhar, Samar Guha, and Ram Dhan were brought in. They were transported in police vans without being told their destination. Raj Narain, a veteran of numerous jail terms, remained composed, using his holdall as a pillow and sleeping on three planks in the van. The prisoners were ultimately taken to Rohtak jail, with Madhu Dandavate of the Socialist Party arrested shortly after.[29]

Malkani, however, was held in a guest house in Haryana for three days before being sent to jail. During this time, intelligence agencies interrogated him about the source of his article predicting the Emergency, suspecting a government leak. Malkani maintained that it was purely an astrological prediction.[30]

JP was arrested around 3 a.m. on 26 June from the Gandhi Peace Foundation and taken to a guest house in Sohna, Haryana, where Morarji Desai, also arrested, was held separately. Rumours circulated about JP's health, prompting Gandhi's principal secretary, P.N. Dhar, to check on him. JP's cryptic reply was, "You can go and tell your prime minister that I shall outlive her."[31] He opposed the personality cult forming during the Emergency and later wrote Gandhi a

---

28. "KR Malkani: When the Journalist Who Predicted Emergency Became Its First Victim", Organiser, accessed 25 May 2025, https://organiser.org/2025/06/25/131710/bharat/kr-malkani-and-emergency/.

29. Ibid.

30. Arun Jaitley, *A New India: Selected Writings 2014–19* (Juggernaut, 2020), pp. 284–85.

31. Arun Jaitley, "Jayaprakash Narayan", in *Articles & Speeches by Arun Jaitley: A Compilation* (Universal Law Publishing Co. Pvt. Ltd., 2014), pp. 219–20.

firm letter rebuking the slogan, "Indira is India and India is Indira," stating, "Do not equate yourself with the Nation; this country is immortal, you are not."[32]

On 25 June, Atal Bihari Vajpayee, Lal Krishna Advani, and Congress (O) MP Shyam Nandan Mishra had travelled to Bangalore for a Joint Parliamentary Committee meeting. At 7:30 a.m. on 26 June, Advani received word from the local Jana Sangh office that Opposition leaders were being arrested. The Bangalore police soon arrived to detain them.[33]

The maharanis of Gwalior and Jaipur, Vijayaraje Scindia and Gayatri Devi, were arrested under COFEPOSA and lodged in Tihar Jail.[34] RSS chief Madhukar Dattatreya Deoras (Balasaheb) was detained a few days later, and Kuldip Nayar was arrested on 24 July.

While most Opposition leaders were detained, some evaded arrest and continued the satyagraha. Nanaji escaped and travelled in disguise, holding secret meetings to mobilise protests—only to be arrested a few weeks later.[35] Until his arrest, he led the underground movement against Indira Gandhi and her regime for the restoration of democracy.[36] Subramanian Swamy, an MP from the BJS, too, escaped the police during a visit to Ahmedabad railway station, disguised as a Sikh, where he was received by a twenty-five-year-old pracharak Narendra Modi, also disguised, as a Sikh.[37] Later, Swamy managed to sneak out of the country. He built public opinion based on the Emergency from the United States.[38]

---

32. Ibid.

33. Abhishek Choudhary, *Vajpayee: The Ascent of the Hindu Right 1924–1977* (Picador India, 2023).

34. Vinay Sitapati, *Jugalbandi: The BJP Before Modi* (Penguin, 2020), p. 87.

35. Arun Jaitley, *Articles & Speeches by Arun Jaitley: A Compilation* (Universal Law Publishing Co. Pvt. Ltd., 2014), pp. 227–28.

36. Arun Anand, "Nanaji Deshmukh—Key Architect of Janata Party, Who Quit Politics to Transform Rural India", *The Print*, assessed 25 May 2025, https://theprint.in/india/nanaji-deshmukh-key-architect-of-janata-party-who-quit-politics-to-transform-rural-india/521300/.

37. "When NaMo, Swamy Played Hide and Sikh", *The Times of India*, accessed 25 May 2025, https://timesofindia.indiatimes.com/india/when-namo-swamy-played-hide-and-sikh/articleshow/47838942.cms.

38. Coomi Kapoor, *The Emergency: A Personal History* (Penguin, 2015, 2016), pp. 127–52.

Four days later, on 4 July 1975, the RSS was banned for the second time.

★

Unaware of the Proclamation and the arrest of political leaders, Jaitley was fast asleep on a cot in the open courtyard at the back of his Naraina residence in Delhi on the night of 25 June 1975. June was a hot and humid month in Delhi, and in those days, when air and noise pollution were minimal, people preferred sleeping outdoors. After a hectic day organizing the rally, he had quickly fallen asleep upon returning home.

Around 2 a.m., Delhi police knocked at his door. His father opened it, rousing Jaitley with the commotion. Peering out, he saw his father arguing with the police. He overheard his father assert that Jaitley had not returned home that night and, as a lawyer, question how the police could arrest his son without an FIR or detention order.[39]

Jaitley assumed that the police were making preventive arrests ahead of the planned national satyagraha on 29 June 1975. He quietly slipped out through the back entrance into the service lane and spent the night at his friend Anil Bhargava's house in the same colony.[40] Later, he learned that the police had taken his father to the local thana, releasing him with a warning that Jaitley should report to them if he returned home.[41]

The morning of 26 June saw no newspapers delivered. The electricity supply to Bahadur Shah Zafar Marg—Delhi's Press Street—had been cut to prevent publication. By 10 a.m., censorship had been imposed, with officials from the Censor Department stationed in every newspaper office.[42] It was only

39. Arun Jaitley, "Emergency" in *Articles & Speeches by Arun Jaitley: A Compilation* (Universal Law Publishing Co. Pvt. Ltd., 2014), pp. 221–24.

40. Coomi Kapoor, *The Emergency: A Personal History* (Penguin, 2016), pp. 34–36.

41. Arun Jaitley, *A New India: Selected Writings 2014–19* (Juggernaut, 2020), pp. 281–82.

42. Arun Jaitley, "The Emergency Revisited – Part – I (3-Part Series): The Circumstances Leading to the Imposition of Emergency", accessed 25 May 2025, https://www.arunjaitley.com/the-emergency-revisited-part-i-3-part-series-the-circumstances-leading-to-the-imposition-of-emergency/.

through Indira Gandhi's address on All India Radio that Jaitley learned of the Proclamation.[43]

Fortunately, the power was briefly restored that afternoon. During this window, the editorial and press team of *The Motherland*, despite the previous night's arrest of editor K.R. Malkani, managed to publish a two-page issue. Although pre-censorship had been enforced, the newspaper defied the order by reporting the arrests. As soon as the copies hit the stands, people rushed to buy them. A newspaper that normally cost 10 annas started selling for 1 rupee, and in some areas, prices surged to 5–10 rupees. Police caught hawkers across the city, confiscating newspapers and, in some cases, beating them or seizing their sales proceeds. By evening, the offices of *The Motherland* were sealed with government locks.[44]

By then, news of JP and other leaders' arrests was emerging. Jaitley finally understood why police had come to his house the previous night. Unafraid of arrest, he decided to advance the satyagraha planned for 29 June and stage a protest against the leaders' arrests and the newspaper shutdown. Colleges were closed for summer vacation, and the admission process for the next academic year had begun. With the help of his close friends Vijay Goel and Rajat Sharma,[45] Jaitley went from college to college on scooters, mobilizing students to join the protest.[46] By late morning on 26 June, he had gathered around 200 students, mostly ABVP members.

BJP leader Vijay Jolly, who would later become DUSU general secretary in 1978 and president in 1980, recalled: "I was about to board a No. 6 double-decker bus from Maurice Nagar to Tilak Nagar when I saw a student protest at an intersection of the campus. I was drawn to it as students were vocally

43. Arun Jaitley, "Emergency" in *Articles & Speeches by Arun Jaitley: A Compilation* (Universal Law Publishing Co. Pvt. Ltd., 2014), pp. 221–24.

44. Krishnanand Sagar Sharma, "Emergency Days: Triumph of 'The Motherland'—Read the Diary of a Swayamsevak", *Organiser*, accessed 25 May 2025, https://organiser.org/2023/07/09/182719/bharat/triumph-of-the-motherland-read-the-diary-of-a-swayamsevak/

45. Vijay Goel went on to become a senior leader of the BJP and a minister in the government. Rajat Sharma did not continue in politics. Today he is a journalist and editor-in-chief of India TV.

46. Arun Jaitley, "Emergency" in *Articles & Speeches by Arun Jaitley: A Compilation* (Universal Law Publishing Co. Pvt. Ltd., 2014), pp. 221–24.

protesting against Prime Minister Indira Gandhi."[47] Jaitley later wrote, "We organized the first, and perhaps the only, protest of the day. We marched from college to college, shouting slogans against the government. The march ended at the coffee house behind the vice-chancellor's office."[48]

Jaitley addressed the crowd, protesting the arrests and censorship, while the students burned an effigy of Indira Gandhi.[49] Aware that the police would soon arrive, he had planned an escape to continue organizing protests. He had even arranged for his friend Prabhu Chawla, who later went on to become a prominent journalist, to meet him with a scooter at a little-known side entrance of a university building. However, when the police, led by Deputy Inspector General P.S. Bhinder, arrived in force, Jaitley found his friend absent.[50] Scared of getting arrested, the "friend" had fled. At that moment, Jaitley resolved to offer himself for arrest while instructing Goel and Sharma to go underground and participate in the satyagraha.[51] Strangely, Chawla, who had abandoned Jaitley in that crucial hour, had the audacity to go to Jaitley's house. He pleaded he be given sanctuary in the house, without disclosing that he had abandoned their son who may have likely got arrested. Not only did he enjoy the protection of the house but also the hospitality of Jaitley's family for many days.

Jaitley was arrested and taken to North Delhi's Alipur police station, where he was served a detention order under the Maintenance of Internal Security Act, 1971 (MISA).[52] The order, pre-signed by an additional district magistrate, had blank fields that were later filled with his personal details.[53] MISA, enacted by the Indian Parliament in 1971, granted extensive powers to law enforcement,

---

47. Vijay Jolly, "TRIBUTE: Arun Jaitley, the Go-Getter", *The Week*, accessed 25 May 2025, https://www.theweek.in/news/india/2019/08/28/arun-jaitley-the-go-getter.html.

48. Arun Jaitley, "Emergency" in *Articles & Speeches by Arun Jaitley: A Compilation* (Universal Law Publishing Co. Pvt. Ltd., 2014), pp. 221–24.

49. Ibid.

50. As told by a friend of Arun Jaitley.

51. Arun Jaitley, *A New India: Selected Writings 2014–19* (Juggernaut, 2020), p. 296.

52. Ibid., 284–85.

53. Ibid.

including preventive detention, searches, seizures, and wiretapping, ostensibly to counter civil unrest, sabotage, terrorism, and threats to national security.[54]

In the early evening, Jaitley was swiftly transported in a police van to Delhi's notorious Tihar Jail and placed in Ward No. 2 with other detainees. He held a unique distinction: by organizing the sole protest on the morning of 26 June 1975 before his arrest, he became, in a sense, the first satyagrahi to stand defiantly against the Emergency—a bold, solitary voice of resistance at the dawn of one of India's darkest chapters.[55]

★

Jaitley was lodged in Delhi's overcrowded Tihar Jail, which had a capacity of 1,273 inmates but housed 2,669 prisoners on 26 June 1975. By March 1976, this number would rise to 4,250. Water and sewage facilities were designed for only 750 people, creating dire living conditions.[56]

After a week, Jaitley and nineteen other detainees were summoned with their belongings to the jail office and transported in a Black Maria, the prison van, to Ambala Central Jail in Haryana. Haryana's Chief Minister, Chaudhary Bansi Lal, was known for his strictness, and the state's jails were notoriously harsh. Jaitley spent the next three months there. Meanwhile, his family remained in the dark. Rumours circulated that he had been sent to Kala Pani (Andamans) or killed.[57]

Ratan Prabha was grief-stricken. Every time any update was received about Arun, many unconfirmed, about the state of jail and prisoners, she would break down, crying unstoppably. Often, news they received suggested that prisoners were being tortured in jail. Maharaj tried to keep such stressful news away

---

54. During the Emergency, MISA was used to suppress political dissent. MISA was eventually repealed in 1977 following Indira Gandhi's defeat in the general elections and the subsequent rise to power of the Janata Party.

55. Arun Jaitley, *A New India: Selected Writings 2014–19* (Juggernaut, 2020), p. 284–85.

56. Coomi Kapoor, *The Emergency: A Personal History* (Penguin, 2016), p. 38.

57. Rohan Jaitley, "The Emergency: A Political Battle and a Personal Story", *Hindustan Times*, accessed 25 May 2025, https://epaper.hindustantimes.com/Home/ShareArticle?OrgId=377741a993.

from his wife, but her health deteriorated. She spent days and nights praying for her son's return. There was hardly any gurudwara and temple in town she did not visit to ask for her son's well-being.

Despite the uncertainty, Ratan Prabha drew strength from her faith in her son's resilience, while Jaitley endured his ordeal with remarkable courage. Maharaj Kishen struggled between anguish and duty, using every resource to locate his son and facilitate his transfer back to Delhi.[58]

Three months later, Jaitley was fortuitously transferred back to Delhi. Seven false FIRs had been filed against him for speeches calling for the overthrow of the government and participation in various agitations. Courts in Delhi summoned him, and one magistrate insisted on his personal presence, leading to his return to Tihar under a court order.

Back in Tihar, Jaitley was placed in Ward No. 1, known as the "Approvers Ward" because it housed approvers who were kept separate from the main accused,[59] although none of them was an approver. This ward had a large garden and five small rooms accommodating numerous inmates, including K.R. Malkani, journalist Virendra Kapoor, former MP Kanwar Lal Gupta, Hansraj College professor Ram Nath Vij, IIT Delhi lecturer Suresh Upadhyaya, JNU Students' Union president D.P. Tripathi, Delhi University Teachers' Association president O.P. Kohli, and Balbir Tokas, a student with no political affiliation who happened to have been persuaded to stand for election to his college union by the ABVP.[60]

D.P. Tripathi had emerged as the face of protests in JNU. He was believed to have infamously stopped Maneka Gandhi—Indira Gandhi's daughter-in-law, a JNU student studying German—from attending classes. This was to force her to join the anti-Emergency class boycotts. Jaitley and Tripathi had an excellent relationship. They had worked closely to lead protests at JNU and become close friends. Their imprisonment deepened their friendship. Tripathi would later

---

58. Ibid.

59. Arun Jaitley, *Articles & Speeches by Arun Jaitley: A Compilation* (Universal Law Publishing Co. Pvt. Ltd., 2014), p. 223.

60. Coomi Kapoor, *The Emergency: A Personal History* (Penguin, 2015, 2016), pp. 110–11.

rise to prominence as a national leader.[61] Both maintained a lifelong cordial relationship, in spite of their sharp political divides.

Many wards housed about 200 detainees,[62] exemplifying the appalling conditions prevalent in most jails: severe overcrowding, inadequate sanitation, and water shortages. Pipes were rusted and leaking, tanks and toilets had been broken for nearly two decades, and twenty-eight inmates shared a single fan and three non-flush latrines. Prisoners bathed outdoors, relying on a single tap that ran dry by 9 a.m., while hand pumps provided only a feeble trickle.[63] Despite these hardships, periodic protests led to small concessions, such as the right to use heating rods for bathing water in winter, play badminton, and receive basic utilities like soap, toothbrushes, toothpaste, and writing materials from outside.[64] Jaitley often wrote to his father, and a DU friend and ABVP colleague Inderjit Nagpal to send these items, sharing them with fellow inmates who had no external support.

Daily routines were organized according to the jail manual. Atal Bihari Vajpayee was responsible for cooking;[65] as a lover of food, he relished this role. In his autobiography, Advani recalls, 'The food he cooked was simple but wholesome'.[66] The British-era manual prescribed exact caloric intake, protein count, firewood usage, and rations. With Rs 3 allotted per detainee per day, inmates had to manage all meals within strict limits.[67] Dal was watery, chapatis undercooked, and flies floated in food. But, over a period of time, prisoners got used to fishing the flies out and eating without a qualm.[68]

---

61. "JNU's Tryst with Indira's Emergency", *Hindustan Times*, accessed 25 May 2025, https://www.hindustantimes.com/education/jnu-s-tryst-with-indira-s-emergency/story-6WdaILFxj1LPCIEeR1OboJ.html.

62. Arun Jaitley, *Articles & Speeches by Arun Jaitley: A Compilation* (Universal Law Publishing Co. Pvt. Ltd., 2014), p. 223.

63. Coomi Kapoor, *The Emergency: A Personal History* (Penguin, 2015, 2016), pp. 39–43.

64. Ibid.

65. LK. Advani, *My Country, My Life* (Rupa, 2008), p. 213.

66. Ibid.

67. Sonia Singh, *Defining India Through Their Eyes* (Penguin, 2019), pp. 19–34.

68. LK. Advani, *My Country, My Life* (Rupa, 2008), p. 213.

Jaitley, who appreciated good food, had a disappointing experience with meals in the prison. As the person overseeing the kitchen, he discussed the issue with fellow inmates, leading to a protest. Following the agitation, the food allowance was raised to Rs 5—a modest but somewhat better amount for that time.[69] Sometime, Jaitley was able to organize parathas for breakfast. Additionally, he used various techniques to improvise. He often faked illness so he could get a medical diet of eggs, bread, and butter which used to suffice as breakfast. The jail staff were usually sympathetic. Doctors and dispensing staff came daily to distribute medicine, and they often prescribed a more "palatable medical diet". For the non-vegetarians, some money was slipped quietly to the jail guard, who would bring some lamb or chicken, which was then cooked in the jail kitchen.[70] Malkani and Jaitley loved good food, although Jaitley could just about cook. Malkani once remarked to Jaitley, "I have rarely seen in anybody a combination of a glutton and a gourmet. You are both."[71]

Life in prison remained challenging. Access to outside information was limited, but when newspapers and transistors were allowed, detainees eagerly awaited the morning BBC news.[72] Despite restrictions, they carved out routines: morning badminton, reading from the jail library and underground literature, political discussions in the afternoons, volleyball in the evenings, and card games such as Sweep or Seep favoured by leaders like Charan Singh.[73]

The families endured their own ordeals. Once, Maharaj Kishen received a phone call, informing him that his son had had an accident and was breathing his last at the All India Institute of Medical Sciences.[74] Maharaj Kishen, who

---

69. Arun Jaitley, "The Emergency Revisited – Part – I (3-Part Series): The Circumstances Leading to the Imposition of Emergency", accessed 25 May 2025, https://www.arunjaitley.com/the-emergency-revisited-part-i-3-part-series-the-circumstances-leading-to-the-imposition-of-emergency/.

70. Sonia Singh, *Defining India Through Their Eyes* (Penguin, 2019), pp. 19–34.

71. Ajay Singh, "When Jaitley Asked Me to Guess His Age…", *Governance Now*, accessed 25 May 2025, https://www.governancenow.com/news/regular-story/when-jaitley-asked-me-to-guess-his-age.

72. LK. Advani, *My Country, My Life* (Rupa, 2008).

73. Ibid.

74. Rohan Jaitley, "The Emergency: A Political Battle and a Personal Story", *Hindustan Times*, accessed 25 May 2025, https://epaper.hindustantimes.com/Home/ShareArticle?OrgId=377741a993

until then had maintained composure through insurmountable moments of anxiety, could bear it no longer and suffered a heart attack. The rumour was untrue, but neither the first nor the last of its kind. Relatives would describe the torture of political prisoners in excruciating detail, which caused family members to withdraw. Friends quietly distanced themselves fearing consequences, and loyal staff quit, as police constantly circled the house, tormenting those who offered support. "No one," Jaitley's eldest sister Madhu recalled, "no one wanted to be associated with us."[75] Even the servants had left, intimidated by the police questioning them every time they stepped out of house. With Ratan Prabha debilitated and Maharaj Kishen dedicating himself to ensuring their son's survival, it fell to Jaitley's eldest sister, Madhu, to manage her own home in Bikaner, as also that of her parents. She would travel by train weekly, along with her cook, and prepare as much food as possible for her parents before returning home.[76]

After months of separation, families were allowed brief monthly visits, later extended to weekly. Friday was visitor's day. Two visitors per detainee were permitted, bringing not only love but also extra food.[77] Madhu recalled bringing food parcels and fulfilling Jaitley's whimsical requests, including once arranging Chinese food for fifteen inmates from Majnu ka Tila.[78] During court appearances in cramped vans, his mother anxiously waited outside, carrying homemade meals. These meals, shared among prisoners, became a small but vital connection to home—a taste of comfort and freedom amid the harsh, dehumanizing conditions of incarceration.[79]

★

75. Ibid.

76. Ibid.

77. Coomi Kapoor, *The Emergency: A Personal History* (Penguin, 2015, 2016), p. 113.

78. Rohan Jaitley, "The Emergency: A Political Battle and a Personal Story", *Hindustan Times*, accessed 25 May 2025, https://epaper.hindustantimes.com/Home/ShareArticle?OrgId=377741a993

79. Kumkum Chadha, *The Marigold Story: Indira Gandhi & Others* (Westland, 2019), pp. 318–38.

Several detainees filed petitions challenging their detention, but like most leaders, Jaitley chose not to seek bail in the false cases against him, allowing the trials to drag on indefinitely. Maharaj Kishen petitioned to enable his son to appear for his final-year examinations from jail, but Delhi University was instructed to enforce its rule requiring students' physical presence at the examination centre. Jaitley offered to be escorted under police custody to take the exams, but the government denied the request, citing concerns that his appearance might disrupt public order. Consequently, his nineteen-month detention caused him to miss one academic year, with the risk of losing another.[80]

Determined to make the best of his time as a political prisoner, Jaitley turned to reading and writing. Books were sent by family members and Inderjit Nagpal, or borrowed from the jail library, whose librarian was Delhi's renowned ophthalmologist Dr N.S. Jain, who was himself facing trial for murder. In jail, Jaitley developed a deep habit of reading extensively and writing regularly—a passion that stayed with him throughout his life. Notably, he read the entire Constituent Assembly Debates during this period, immersing himself in India's constitutional history.[81]

★

Arun Jaitley's imprisonment as a political detainee became a defining chapter in his life. He approached "jail as a state of mind", deliberately refusing to let despair dominate him. Instead, he channelled his energy into resisting the Emergency. The disruption of his academic year weighed heavily, as it did on other students, yet Jaitley faced uniquely harsh treatment. While Delhi University accommodated another student by setting up an exam centre just a mile from Tihar Jail, Jaitley was denied the same opportunity, forcing him

80. Arun Jaitley, "The Emergency Revisited – Part – I (3-Part Series): The Circumstances Leading to the Imposition of Emergency", accessed 25 May 2025, https://www.arunjaitley.com/the-emergency-revisited-part-i-3-part-series-the-circumstances-leading-to-the-imposition-of-emergency/.

81. Sonia Singh, *Defining India Through Their Eyes* (Penguin, 2019), pp. 19–34.

to forfeit an entire academic year.[82] This only strengthened his resolve to fight against the Emergency. Reflecting on this period, he later said:

> If you have a lot of liabilities outside, like family, livelihood issues and so on, then it worries you and kills you. We were young students; we had no such problems. Both my sisters were married, my father was a lawyer, and my parents lived by themselves. So, I thought either I live with my parents and complete my studies, or I live here in jail. If you have nerves of steel, you can take it. At that time, we lived as a middle-class family in an India where the living conditions had not made us very vulnerable. If you feel like you're a part of an ideological struggle and you're fighting for democracy, then that gives you a sense of pride about what you're doing. It also gives you an opportunity to shape your own ideas.[83]

Jaitley devoted himself to political education in jail, building on friendships he had previously formed with RSS workers, ABVP members, and socialists from across the country.[84] He befriended individuals from various Opposition parties and fellow MISA detainees, spending time with leaders such as Atal Bihari Vajpayee, L.K. Advani, K.R. Malkani, and Nanaji Deshmukh.[85] After his arrest, Nanaji was also imprisoned in Tihar, in Ward No. 17, where Jaitley and several detainees had by then been moved.

In one of his articles, Jaitley recounts a memorable anecdote about Nanaji. When Nanaji entered the ward, he decided to play a prank on the young wards. He did not disclose his identity as his appearance had changed beyond recognition. He had discarded his customary kurta and dhoti for a bush shirt

---

82. Ashok Malik, "Arun Jaitley's Demise, An Irreplaceable Loss to the Nation", in *The Discussant, Journal of Centre for Reforms, Development, and Justice*, Special Edition, An Obituary to Arun Jaitley, Vol. VII, No. 3 (July–September 2019), pp. 56–59.

83. Sonia Singh, *Defining India Through Their Eyes* (Penguin, 2019), pp. 19–34.

84. Praveen Donthi, "Talk of the Town", *Caravan Magazine*, accessed 25 May 2025, https://caravanmagazine.in/reportage/talk-town.

85. Kumkum Chadha, *The Marigold Story: Indira Gandhi & Others* (Westland, 2019), pp. 318–38.

and trousers, and acquired a moustache and a thick crop of dyed black hair on his head and a different pair of eyeglasses. It took the wards some time after hearing his voice to realize that he was the Nanaji they all revered. Nanaji told them that he had managed to escape arrest and continued the satyagraha as secretary of the Sangharsh Samiti. He changed his appearance beyond recognition and toured the entire country organizing underground activities. His stay in several houses was organized by his political colleagues. He was able to evade arrest and organize protests across the country until the day he got arrested accidentally while staying in a safe house in Delhi's Safdarjung Development Area.[86]

Even his host was unaware of his presence. Punjab BJP leader Krishan Lal Sharma, along with another colleague, came to meet Nanaji secretly, unaware they were being trailed by Punjab intelligence. With support from Delhi police, the house was raided to arrest Sharma, and the officers stumbled upon Nanaji, failing to recognize him. He was taken to the police station, where a voice test confirmed his identity despite his changed appearance.

Jaitley learned much from Nanaji simply by observing him. Nanaji remained calm, read extensively, analysed the political situation, and even coordinated financial support for the families of ultra-left activists imprisoned alongside them. In jail, Jaitley also discovered Nanaji's enjoyment of good food as a form of relaxation—a habit that would influence him in later years.[87]

During his imprisonment, Jaitley was tasked with writing pamphlets, which were translated into Hindi and circulated. It was here, amid these responsibilities, that Jaitley underwent his political baptism.[88] He was no longer an outsider; the jail experience cemented his role within the RSS and marked the beginning of his formal journey into active political life.

★

86. Arun Jaitley, "Nanaji Deshmukh" in *Articles & Speeches by Arun Jaitley: A Compilation* (Universal Law Publishing Co. Pvt. Ltd., 2014), pp. 227–28.

87. Ibid.

88. Praveen Donthi, "Talk of the Town", *Caravan Magazine*, accessed 25 May 2025, https://caravanmagazine.in/reportage/talk-town.

At first, the general public struggled to comprehend the full implications of the Emergency; many were stunned and bewildered. Political workers were intimidated—some chose inactivity, while others even issued statements in support of the Emergency. The central government assumed dictatorial control, and the entire system began to crumble. Most institutions, including the judiciary, the media, and civil services, succumbed. Even the Supreme Court yielded to authority, and the press largely became servile. Over 200,000 false FIRs were filed, with almost no police officers objecting, and thousands of detention orders were issued without justification. Barely any collector refused to endorse unlawful detentions. Gradually, people realised that the democratic system they had trusted for over twenty-five years was being dismantled: fundamental rights were suspended, judicial authority weakened, and close to 100,000 individuals were detained. What followed was a wave of illegal and unjust actions, spreading immense suffering and hardship. Outside, fear and terror gripped the nation, and political activity ground to a halt.

The press was completely intimidated. Pre-censorship was imposed across all media, requiring government approval before publication. A censor officer was stationed at every major newspaper. Opposition activities were blacked out, while newspapers carried only government propaganda. Many editors and journalists reconciled themselves to living under dictatorship. The Congress party's *National Herald* editorially suggested that India should evolve into a single-party democracy, and Indira Gandhi herself advocated for a "disciplined democracy".[89]

There were, however, notable dissenters. *The Indian Express* and *The Statesman* became symbols of press freedom, with figures like Ramnath Goenka, C.R. Irani, and editor Kuldeep Nayar gaining legendary status for resisting censorship. *Shankar's Weekly*, in contrast, chose to shut down voluntarily. In its final editorial, titled "*Farewell*" (31 August 1975), the editor reflected on the role of humour in society and the corrosive effects of dictatorship:

---

89. Arun Jaitley, "The Emergency Revisited – Part – I (3-Part Series): The Circumstances Leading to the Imposition of Emergency", accessed 25 May 2025, https://www.arunjaitley.com/the-emergency-revisited-part-i-3-part-series-the-circumstances-leading-to-the-imposition-of-emergency/.

In our first editorial we made the point that our function was to make our readers laugh—at the world, at pompous leaders, at humbug, at foibles, at ourselves. But, what are the people who have a developed sense of humour? It is a people with certain civilized norms of behaviour, where there is tolerance and a dash of compassion. Dictatorships cannot afford laughter because people may laugh at the dictator and that wouldn't do. In all the years of Hitler, there never was a good comedy, not a good cartoon, not a parody, or a spoof.

From this point, the world and sadly enough India have become grimmer. Humour, whenever it is there, is encapsuled. Language itself has become functional, each profession developing its own jargon. Outside of the society of brother-economists, an economist is a stranger, floundering in uncharted territory, uncertain of himself, fearful of non-economic language. It is the same for lawyers, doctors, teachers, journalists and such-like.

What is worse, human imagination seems to be turning to the macabre and the perverse. Books and films are either on violence or sexual deviations. Nothing seems to awaken people except unpleasant shocks. Whether it is the interaction of the written word and the cinema on society or not, society reflects these attitudes. Hijackings, mugging in the dark, kidnappings and plain murder are becoming everyday occurrences and sometimes lend respectability by giving it some kind of political colouration.

But *Shankar's Weekly* is an incurable optimist. We are certain that despite the present situation, the world will become a happier and more relaxed place. The spirit of man will in the end overcome all death-dealing forces and life will blossom to a degree where humanity will find its highest purpose discharged. Some call this God. We prefer to call it human destiny. And on that thought we bid you good-bye and the best of luck.[90]

---

90. L.K. Advani, "Emperor Has No Clothes, Says a Child", Bharatiya Janata Party, accessed 25 May 2025, https://www.bjp.org/hi/pressreleases/shri-lk-advanijis-latest-blog-emperor-has-no-clothes-says-child.

Despite these outliers, the majority of political opposition was silenced. Bold activists protested at the risk of imprisonment.[91] Meanwhile, the Constitution of India (1950) and the Representation of the People Act were amended retrospectively to validate Indira Gandhi's election, overturning each legal ground on which it had been challenged. During the Emergency, the government issued forty-eight ordinances, including five amendments to the MISA, granting authorities sweeping powers to detain individuals without a warrant.[92] Opposition MPs were detained, reducing Parliament's numerical strength and enabling the government to pass constitutional amendments with a two-thirds majority.

The amendments were challenged in the Supreme Court. Shanti Bhushan argued that free and fair elections were part of the Constitution's basic structure, and validating an invalid election violated that principle. Meanwhile, the three senior-most judges of the Supreme Court were superseded.[93] The Court ruled that the basic structure doctrine applied only to constitutional amendments, not ordinary laws, striking down the 39th Amendment but upholding retrospective amendments to the RPA.[94] Consequently, Indira Gandhi's election was legally validated.

Lawyers and judges began resisting. Thousands of political prisoners filed petitions challenging their detention without trial. In April 1976, five Supreme Court judges ruled on these cases: four held that illegally detained individuals had no judicial recourse during the Emergency.[95] Justice H.R. Khanna dissented, asserting that such rights could never be extinguished by law. He observed:

---

91. Arun Jaitley, *A New India: Selected Writings 2014–19* (Juggernaut, 2020), pp. 327–28.

92. PTI, "Ordinance Raj During Emergency: 48, Including 5 to Amend MISA, Promulgated", *The Economic Times*, accessed 25 May 2025, https://economictimes.indiatimes.com/news/india/ordinance-raj-during-emergency-48-including-5-to-amend-misa-promulgated/articleshow/122002414.cms?from=mdr.

93. Arun Jaitley, "The Emergency Revisited – Part-2 (3-Part Series): The Tyranny of Emergency", accessed 25 May 2025, https://www.arunjaitley.com/the-emergency-revisited-part-2-3-part-series-the-tyranny-of-emergency/.

94. In *Indira Nehru Gandhi vs Shri Raj Narain*, AIR 1975 SC 2299.

95. *DM Jabalpur vs Shivkant Shukla*, AIR 1976 SC 1207.

> It has been argued that suspending the right of a person to move any Court for the enforcement of right to life and personal liberty is done under a constitutional provision and therefore it cannot be said that the resulting situation would mean the absence of the rule of law…
>
> …In one sense, it might in that event be argued that even if lives of hundreds of persons are taken capriciously and maliciously without the authority of law, it is enforcement of the above enacted law. Thus, in a purely formal sense, any system or norm based on a hierarchy of orders, even the organized mass murders of Nazi regime, can qualify as law.

Khanna was referencing Article 21, which guarantees both the right to life and personal liberty.[96] Following his dissent, he was superseded, and Justice Beg was appointed Chief Justice of India. Khanna resigned, with Nani Palkhivala remarking that the post of Chief Justice had become "too small for Justice Khanna".[97]

★

At the height of the Emergency, public anger against Indira Gandhi was widespread. Yet she appeared convinced that she was the real victim. Observers noted that her deep-seated insecurity and mistrust—traits that had been evident since her father's death—sometimes manifested as paranoia.[98] Noted journalist Khushwant Singh, a strong supporter of Indira Gandhi during the Emergency, later remarked:

---

96. Vinay Sitapati, *Jugalbandi: The BJP Before Modi* (Penguin, 2020), p. 92; PTI, "Advani Compares the Emergency to Germany's Nazi Rule", *Deccan Herald*, assessed 25 May 2025, https://www.deccanherald.com/content/125686/advani-compares-emergency-germanys-nazi.html.

97. "Arun Jaitley takes dig at left parties for supporting 1975 Emergency by Indira Gandhi", *The New Indian Express*, accessed 2 September 2025, https://www.newindianexpress.com/nation/2018/Jun/26/arun-jaitley-takes-dig-at-left-parties-for-supporting-1975%E2%80%8B-emergency-by-indira-gandhi-1833952.html.

98. L.K. Advani, *My Country, My Life* (Rupa, 2008), pp. 248–49.

> In her insecurity, she destroyed the institutions of democracy. She packed Parliament with her supporters with loyalty being more important than ability. She believed India was under threat from foreign powers. She made periodic insinuations, even before the declaration of the Emergency that her life was in danger.

L.K. Advani recalled an instance when Indira Gandhi accused the BJS of plotting to assassinate her. The BJS was outraged by the unfounded allegation, and a delegation confronted her. According to Advani, she neither substantiated nor retracted the claim, nor did she suggest that she had been misquoted—she simply said nothing.[99]

Meanwhile, JP's health deteriorated in custody. Diagnosed with kidney failure, he required regular dialysis, which imposed a significant financial burden. Supporters decided to raise funds from the public, collecting Re 1 per person to finance a portable dialysis machine, deliberately avoiding government assistance. When news of JP's condition spread, support poured in from across India and abroad, though progress was slow. In a gesture that might have reflected concern or political strategy, Indira Gandhi quietly contributed Rs 90,000 towards his treatment. JP initially accepted the amount but later returned it following his supporters' advice. In a letter to Indira Gandhi on 11 June 1976, he wrote:

> I had given my consent without knowing that the money would be from the Prime Minister's Relief Fund. I took it for granted that it would be from your personal account, though a little thought on my part should have shown that it was not possible for you to contribute personally such a large amount. Be that as it may, the position is that before the contribution from your Fund was received, more than three lakh rupees had already been collected from the public in response to the appeal. I do fervently hope that you will not misunderstand me and

99. Ibid.

think me ungrateful and discourteous. There is no discourtesy meant at all and I am grateful for the concern shown by you for my health.[100]

A global appeal eventually raised Rs 5 lakh (around USD 65,000 at the time) to purchase and maintain JP's portable dialysis machine.[101]

As the Emergency continued, Indira Gandhi faced international scrutiny. World leaders and media outlets were aghast that Nehru's daughter had abandoned democracy and embraced authoritarianism. She repeatedly assured international audiences that the Emergency was temporary. Encouraged by intelligence agencies and advisors, she decided on a snap election, confident that the absence of a fully organized Opposition would allow the Congress to win easily.[102]

On 18 January 1977, she announced elections, surprising the nation. The date was reportedly set by her astrologers.[103] Opposition leaders were still imprisoned, the Emergency continued, and intelligence reports predicted a comfortable Congress victory. Polling was scheduled for March 1977. Censorship was partially relaxed, and orders were issued for the release of some detainees.

Jaitley's release came on 25 January 1977, nearly nineteen months after his arrest. Stepping out of Tihar Jail with a bag in hand, he hailed a taxi home, arriving at the *Amritvani Sankirtan*[104] organized by his mother—an event dedicated to enhancing faith, spreading divine blessings, and celebrating the

---

100. Sugata Srinivasaraju, *The Conscience Network: A Chronicle of Resistance to a Dictatorship | Untold History of India's Emergency Resistance | US Solidarity, Indian Diaspora & Gandhi-Inspired Civil Rights* (Penguin, 2025), pp. 200–05.

101. Ibid.

102. Arun Jaitley, "The Emergency Revisited – Part-3 (3-Part Series): How it Ended?", accessed 25 May 2025, https://www.arunjaitley.com/the-emergency-revisited-part-3-3-part-series-how-it-ended.

103. Neerja Chowdhury, *How Prime Ministers Decide* (Aleph, 2023), p. 37.

104. Amritvani sankirtan is a gathering of Lord Rama devotees for selfless invocation to the "God of Gods" Sri Ram, praying for abiding faith and knowledge of the all-pervasive godliness, goodness, and well-being—and see that true spirituality permeates the universe and the "holiest of the holy" Ram Ñaam transcends (rises above) all barriers!

wisdom of Sanatan Dharma. Ratan Prabha, aware of his imminent release but unprepared for his sudden arrival, could not contain her emotions and thanked God for answering her prayers. Soon, friends gathered at Inderjit Nagpal's house, where Jaitley was welcomed with stories from the past nineteen months and a lavish meal prepared by Nagpal's mother.[105]

Barely twenty-five at the time, Jaitley had become part of history, a national hero. On 27 January 1977, ABVP friends led him in a large procession across every college in the university campus. That evening, released political leaders convened at 7 Jantar Mantar, which would eventually become the Janata Party headquarters.[106]

Imprisonment had transformed Jaitley. He had put on weight, shed his lanky college-boy appearance, and assumed the persona of a seasoned politician. A close friend of Jaitley observed that his jail term had impacted him to such an extent that he just wasn't the same man. His close friend Anip Sachthey recalled, "Arun had become withdrawn."[107]

During his incarceration, the Delhi University administration had dissolved the elected DUSU body and appointed nominees.[108] Upon release, Jaitley was appointed national secretary of the ABVP, fully committing to politics.[109] His attire shifted from shirt and trousers to the kurta-pyjama and sling bag typical of RSS pracharaks—an outward sign that he had firmly stepped onto the path that would define his political career.[110]

---

105. Arun Jaitley, *Articles & Speeches by Arun Jaitley: A Compilation* (Universal Law Publishing Co. Pvt. Ltd., 2014), p. 224.

106. Arun Jaitley, "The Emergency Revisited – Part-3 (3-Part Series): How it Ended?", accessed 25 May 2025, https://www.arunjaitley.com/the-emergency-revisited-part-3-3-part-series-how-it-ended/.

107. Kumkum Chadha, *The Marigold Story: Indira Gandhi & Others* (Westland, 2019), p. 320.

108. Coomi Kapoor, *The Emergency: A Personal History* (Penguin, 2015, 2016), p. 146.

109. Praveen Donthi, "Talk of the Town", *Caravan Magazine*, accessed 25 May 25, https://caravanmagazine.in/reportage/talk-town

110. As told by Arun Jaitley's close family friend.

4

1977 Elections: A Missed Ticket

With the 1977 general elections announced, opposition leaders quickly gathered to strategize. With barely forty-five days to prepare, events moved at a rapid pace. Ramnath Goenka and Jayaprakash Narayan took the initiative. On 19 January 1977, the day after Indira Gandhi's announcement, they convened leaders of the original Janata Front—the Congress (O), Bharatiya Lok Dal (BLD), Socialist Party, and Bharatiya Jana Sangh (BJS).[1]

The Congress (O), a faction that had attempted to expel Indira Gandhi in 1969, had been largely sidelined by her dominance. The BLD, led by the rustic farmer leader Charan Singh, primarily represented the peasantry of North India. It had earlier absorbed C. Rajagopalachari's Swatantra Party, which had championed free enterprise and free trade. Rajagopalachari, a former Congressman, was also the last Governor-General of India before it became a republic in 1950. The Socialist Party had emerged from the socialist caucus within the Congress, while the BJS, founded in 1951 by Dr Syama Prasad Mookerjee with the help of RSS pracharaks such as Rajendra Singh, Balasaheb Deoras, Nanaji Deshmukh, Deendayal Upadhyaya, and Atal Bihari Vajpayee, represented the Hindu nationalist stream.

These were diverse groups with strong-willed leaders, and earlier attempts to unite them in 1976 had failed. On 4 January 1976, some of them—Charan Singh, Parkash Singh Badal of the Shiromani Akali Dal, Nanaji Deshmukh,

---

1. Rakesh Ankit, "Janata Party (1974–77): Creation of an All-India Opposition", *History and Sociology of South Asia*, Vol. 11, No. 1 (2017), pp. 39–54.

and Surendra Mohan of the Socialist Party—met in Ward No. 2 of Delhi's Tihar Jail, where they were imprisoned under MISA, to discuss unity. George Fernandes, held in Ward No. 17, and Arun Jaitley, then in Ward No. 1, also joined these consultations. While most leaders supported contesting elections, Fernandes dissented. He argued that participating in what he saw as a sham election would legitimize Indira Gandhi's dictatorship. Though in a small minority, Fernandes held firmly to his stance.[2]

Nineteen months of imprisonment together had fostered camaraderie among these leaders, yet differences persisted. Charan Singh pushed for a complete merger of the parties, while others preferred a federal alliance. Talks stalled. Singh, however, could not be ignored: born in 1902 in Meerut, he had built a formidable mass base among farmers and rural communities in North India, and his influence extended to Muslim voters as well. Jaitley, watching these negotiations closely from Tihar, noted Singh's uncompromising stand.

Eventually, JP intervened, warning that if unity was delayed, the opportunity would be lost. His words broke the deadlock.[3] Four days later, a united Janata Party was announced. Even then, fissures appeared—most visibly over the party flag. Singh wanted it green to honour farmers, but Sikander Bakht of Congress (O), who later joined the BJP, objected, arguing it echoed Pakistan's flag. L.K. Advani suggested saffron, the Hindu sacred colour.[4] The compromise was a two-thirds saffron and one-third green flag, with a plough-bearing farmer symbol on the saffron side.[5]

On 23 January 1977, the leaders of the Congress (O), BLD, BJS, Socialist Party, and a group led by Chandra Shekhar met again at Morarji Desai's residence in Delhi.[6] Shekhar, born in 1927 in Uttar Pradesh's Ballia district to a farming family, had been a fiery socialist since his student days.[7] After earning a master's degree in political science from Allahabad University, he

2. Arun Jaitley, *A New India: Selected Writings 2014–19* (Juggernaut, 2020), pp. 327–28.
3. Kuldip Nayar, *Beyond the Lines: An Autobiography* (Roli Books Pvt. Ltd., 2012), p. 254.
4. L.K. Advani, *My Country, My Life* (Rupa, 2008), p. 264.
5. Vinay Sitapati, *Jugalbandi: The BJP Before Modi* (Penguin, 2020), p. 94.
6. Neerja Chowdhury, *How Prime Ministers Decide* (Aleph, 2023), pp. 38–39.
7. "Shri Chandra Shekhar", PMIndia, accessed 25 May 2025, https://www.pmindia.gov.in/en/former_pm/shri-chandra-shekhar/.

joined the Praja Socialist Party (PSP) before shifting to the Congress in 1967. Known as a "Young Turk" for his courage and integrity, Shekhar had pressed Indira Gandhi's Congress to adopt radical socialist policies. His group of young radicals, nicknamed the "Ginger Group", evolved into the well-known "Young Turks", who initially supported Indira against the party old guard.[8]

After long deliberations and JP's persuasion, the parties finally agreed to merge into the Janata Party. Their momentum grew stronger when, on 2 February 1977, Indira Gandhi's trusted lieutenant Jagjivan Ram, along with Hemwati Nandan Bahuguna and Nandini Satpathy, resigned from the Congress and launched the Congress for Democracy (CFD).[9] Though the CFD contested elections separately, it aligned with the Janata Party and merged with it later.[10] Jagjivan Ram, a veteran leader and champion of Dalit rights, dealt a heavy blow to Indira by denouncing both the Emergency and the erosion of internal party democracy. His departure was expected to pull significant Dalit support away from the Congress, particularly in Bihar, Uttar Pradesh, and Odisha.

Morarji Desai was chosen chairman of the new party, with Charan Singh as deputy.[11] L.K. Advani, who had earlier been general secretary of the Janata Front, was reinstated, alongside Madhu Limaye, Ram Dhan, and Surendra Mohan.[12] Neither Indira Gandhi nor the Intelligence Bureau had foreseen how quickly the opposition would consolidate into a single force.

Jaitley, though not part of the negotiations, found his name on the list of the Janata Party's national executive the next day, recommended by Nanaji

---

8. Harivansh and Ravi Dutt Bajpai, "When Chandra Shekhar's Young Turks Beat Congress Old Guard with Indira Gandhi's Support", *The Print*, accessed 25 May 2025, https://theprint.in/pageturner/excerpt/when-chandra-shekhars-young-turks-beat-congress-old-guard-with-indira-gandhis-support/263491/.

9. "Jagjivan Ram's Exit from Congress Adds New Dimension to the Opposition", *India Today*, accessed 25 May 2025, https://www.indiatoday.in/magazine/indiascope/story/19770228-jagjivan-rams-exit-from-congress-adds-new-dimension-to-the-opposition-818729-2015-03-09; Jitendra Tuli,"We are Confident About Getting a Two-thirds Majority: Jagjivan Ram", *India Today*, assessed 25 May 2025, https://www.indiatoday.in/magazine/interview/story/19770331-we-are-confident-about-getting-a-two-thirds-majority-jagjivan-ram-823634-2014-08-01.

10. L.K. Advani, *My Country, My Life* (Rupa, 2008), p. 263.

11. Ibid., p. 262.

12. Ibid.

Deshmukh on JP's insistence.[13] JP had been impressed by Jaitley's leadership and oratory during the student movement, while Nanaji had witnessed his energy in Tihar Jail. Neither the ABVP of which he was general secretary nor Jaitley himself had been consulted before including Jaitley's name in the list of office bearers. Jaitley was excited and thrilled at the prospects of being part of the functionaries of the newly formed political outfit. His friends started planning a grand announcement and celebration.[14] However, Jaitley, unsure of who had proposed his name and mindful of organisational discipline, declined the post, saying it was for the RSS and ABVP to decide representation.[15] Had he known it was Nanaji's recommendation, with tacit RSS approval, he might have accepted—potentially altering his political trajectory.

★

The next challenge for the Janata Party was to allocate seats among its constituents and finalise candidates within a very short span of time. JP entrusted this task to L.K. Advani, Chandra Shekhar, Charan Singh, and Jagjivan Ram before stepping aside. Predictably, each ensured that their own supporters were fielded.[16]

Advani, however, chose a different path. Following instructions from Vajpayee, he worked quietly behind the scenes to ensure Janata candidates' success, deciding not to contest the Lok Sabha polls himself and instead continuing in the Rajya Sabha.[17] George Fernandes was chosen to contest from Bihar, but he initially refused to sign his nomination papers. It finally took Morarji Desai, who visited him at the Tis Hazari courts (where George

---

13. As told by a close family friend of Arun Jaitley.
14. As told by a college friend of Arun Jaitley and an ABVP activist in those days.
15. Praveen Donthi, "Talk of the Town", *Caravan Magazine*, accessed 25 May 2025, https://caravanmagazine.in/reportage/talk-town.
16. Kuldip Nayar, *Beyond the Lines: An Autobiography* (Roli Books Pvt. Ltd., 2012), p. 254.
17. Vinay Sitapati, *Jugalbandi: The BJP Before Modi* (Penguin, 2020), p. 95.

was appearing for trial), personally persuading him and presenting the papers. Only then did George relent and sign, enabling him to contest from prison.[18]

For the BJS, Arun Jaitley was the natural choice to contest against Sanjay Gandhi. His eloquence and organisational skills had impressed Vajpayee in the pre-Emergency months. Vajpayee summoned him and asked him to prepare for the campaign. To his astonishment, Jaitley explained that he had been born in December 1952 and was therefore a year short of the minimum age requirement—twenty-five years—to contest a Lok Sabha election.[19] Under Articles 84 and 173 of the Constitution of India, the minimum age to contest parliamentary or assembly elections is twenty-five. Thus, at just twenty-four, Jaitley missed the chance to contest what might have been a defining election in 1977. Ironically, his first electoral contest came only thirty-seven years later, in 2014, though unsuccessfully.

In an interesting twist, nearly half a century later, in 2023, the Parliamentary Standing Committee on Personnel, Public Grievances, Law and Justice recommended lowering the minimum age for contesting Lok Sabha and assembly elections to eighteen—the same as the voting age. The Committee argued that young people could be "reliable and responsible" participants in politics, drawing on evidence from international practices in countries such as Canada, the UK, and Australia, as well as rising political awareness among youth in India. However, the Election Commission of India opposed the idea, calling it "unrealistic" to expect eighteen-year-olds to have the maturity and experience required of legislators.[20] The irony remains that in a country where 68 per cent of the population is between fifteen and sixty-four years of age, and where citizens are deemed responsible enough to vote at eighteen, they must still wait until twenty-five to contest elections.[21]

---

18. Arun Jaitley, *A New India: Selected Writings 2014–19* (Juggernaut, 2020), pp. 327–28.

19. Praveen Donthi, "Talk of the Town", *Caravan Magazine*, accessed 25 May 2025, https://caravanmagazine.in/reportage/talk-town.

20. Sreeparna Chakrabarty, "House Panel Bats for Lowering Minimum Age to Contest Polls; Election Commission Differs", *The Hindu*, accessed 25 May 2025, https://www.thehindu.com/news/national/house-panel-bats-for-lowering-minimum-age-to-contest-polls-election-commission-differs/article67158744.ece.

21. Statista, "India: Age Distribution from 2013 to 2023", available at https://www.statista.com/statistics/271315/age-distribution-in-india/.

★

Jaitley's stature within the ABVP grew enormously after being considered—at such a young age—for both the Janata Party national executive and a possible Lok Sabha candidature. His decision to resign from the national executive out of respect for his own organisation's discipline reaffirmed his loyalty to the party over personal ambition—a quality he would demonstrate repeatedly throughout his political career. Earlier, during the DUSU elections, he had shown the same instinct by refusing to switch to the NSUI when denied a presidential ticket. Instead, he had accepted his party's decision and contested as vice president.

Although Jaitley lost the chance to serve on the Janata Party's national executive and to contest the election, his energy and commitment remained undiminished. Soon, the youth and student wings of the Jana Sangh, Congress (O), Socialist Party, and Swatantra Party came together to form the Loktantrik Yuva Morcha, with Jaitley as its convenor. His home became a hub of political activity. Maharaj Kishen, distanced from politics, was not enthused by his son jumping into active politics. He wanted his son to focus on his studies. Ratan Prabha too shared his disapproval but, in the face of his determination, could not bring herself to tell her son to stop. She decided to support her son and actively hosted meetings. In her heart, she carried anger against the Congress for keeping her son imprisoned for nineteen months without cause.[22]

Too young to stand for election, Jaitley threw himself into campaigning. As a rising youth leader, he travelled across the country with seasoned figures like Vajpayee, Charan Singh, Advani, Jagjivan Ram, George Fernandes, Madhu Limaye, Piloo Mody, Nani Palkhivala, and Rajmata Vijayaraje Scindia. His popularity soared, and he emerged as a household name among India's youth.[23] He toured extensively across North India, spending the final week in Rae Bareli and Amethi—where Indira Gandhi and Sanjay Gandhi were contesting.

---

22. Kumkum Chadha, *The Marigold Story: Indira Gandhi & Others* (Westland, 2019), p. 324.

23. Vijay Jolly, "TRIBUTE: Arun Jaitley, the Go-Getter", *The Week*, accessed 25 May 2025, https://www.theweek.in/news/india/2019/08/28/arun-jaitley-the-go-getter.html.

His campaign trail stretched from Uttar Pradesh to Rajasthan, Mumbai, and finally Pune.[24]

The Janata Party's rallies were unlike anything the country had seen. From Delhi's Ramlila Maidan to Chennai's Marina Beach and Kolkata's Maidan, crowds turned out in massive numbers. Supporters often stayed till dawn to hear opposition leaders speak. Across northern India, university students campaigned vigorously, and lawyers' associations in even the smallest towns mobilised in support, sometimes staging dramatic demonstrations in cities.

On 6 February 1977, the Janata Party held its first major rally at Ramlila Maidan. Initially, permission had been sought for Chandni Chowk, but the police, citing fears of a stampede, diverted it to Ramlila grounds.[25] Jaitley and ABVP workers plastered posters across Delhi.[26] The press was cautious at first, but curiosity soon gave way to bold coverage of the growing Janata wave. Journalist Tavleen Singh, in her book *Durbar*, recalls how many reporters initially dismissed the posters as a prank. Even if genuine, they thought, few would attend; the fear of the Emergency still loomed, and most believed Indira Gandhi was invincible. She wrote, "It was widely believed that Gandhi was undefeatable, it would make no difference even if there was going to be an opposition rally, as Indira wouldn't have gone for elections if she had any doubts about winning."

But the rally stunned everyone. It drew record crowds, with Jaitley once again at the forefront of mobilising attendees. For the first time, he addressed the largest audience of his life as the opening youth speaker before stalwarts like Bahuguna and Jagjivan Ram. The mood was electric.

Congress leader V.C. Shukla tried to sabotage the rally by scheduling a telecast of the hit film *Bobby* at the same time on Doordarshan. Yet people preferred to walk miles—since bus services were suspended—to hear the

---

24. Arun Jaitley, "The Emergency Revisited – Part-3 (3-Part Series): How it Ended?", accessed 25 May 2025, https://www.arunjaitley.com/the-emergency-revisited-part-3-3-part-series-how-it-ended/.

25. Ibid.

26. As told by a friend of Arun Jaitley.

opposition speak.[27] The scale and passion of the gathering sent ripples across the nation: a Janata wave was unmistakably building.

Journalist Tavleen Singh, who was present at the rally, described the scene vividly:

> When we got to the grounds we noticed that people were streaming in from all sides. But not even this prepared us for what we saw when we got inside. There were more people than I had ever seen at a political rally. The crowd stretched all the way to the end of the Ram Lila grounds and beyond.
>
> At about 6 p.m., the opposition leaders arrived in a convoy of white Ambassadors. One by one they rose to make long, boring speeches about their travails in jail. … It was past 9 p.m. and the night had got colder although the rain had stopped.
>
> … It was well past 9.30 p.m. when Atalji's turn finally came and as he rose to speak the huge crowd stood up and started to clap. Softly, hesitantly at first, then more excitedly, they shouted, "*Indira Gandhi murdabad! Atal Behari zindabad!*" He acknowledged the slogans with hands joined in a namaste and a faint smile. Then, raising both arms to silence the crowd and closing his eyes in the manner of a practiced actor, he said, "*Baad muddat ke mile hain deewane.*" (It has been an age since we whom they call mad have had the courage to meet.) He paused. The crowd went wild.
>
> When the applause died he closed his eyes again and allowed himself another long pause before saying, "*Kehne sunne ko bahut hain afsane.*" (There are tales to tell and tales to hear.) The cheering was more prolonged, the last line of a verse that he told me later he had composed on the spur of the moment. "*Khuli hawa mein zara saans to le lein, kab tak rahegi aazadi kaun jaane.*" (But first let us breathe deeply of the free air for we know not how long our freedom will last.) The crowd was now hysterical.

---

27. Arun Jaitley, "The Emergency Revisited – Part-3 (3-Part Series): How it Ended?", accessed 25 May 2025, https://www.arunjaitley.com/the-emergency-revisited-part-3-3-part-series-how-it-ended/.

The crowd erupted into frenzy, yet listened in pin-drop silence as Vajpayee continued, weaving poetry into politics.[28] Despite the cold drizzle, nobody left. His speech struck a chord so deep that when party workers circulated drenched sheets to collect donations, even rickshaw pullers and labourers contributed whatever they could.

Reflecting on that night, Tavleen Singh wrote: "On that cold January night, as I watched rickshaw-wallas and those who lived on a pittance from manual labour donate what they could, I got my first inkling that Indira Gandhi could lose the election."[29]

★

Elections were finally held in March 1977. The Election Commission of India (ECI) did not grant the Janata Party formal recognition before the polls, so its candidates contested under the Bharatiya Lok Dal (BLD) symbol. The birth of the Janata government became a lesson in defending democracy, while its later downfall would serve as a cautionary tale about the ease with which power-hungry leaders can erode democratic gains.[30]

The results, announced on 21 March 1977, stunned the nation. All India Radio (AIR), the only official source of information, continued to broadcast cautiously under the lingering shadow of the Emergency. In the early tallies, AIR reported a neck-and-neck contest: fifty seats each for the Congress and the Janata Party. In reality, it was deliberately holding back results from constituencies where the Congress was losing by large margins. Journalist Prannoy Roy, listening closely, noted that the reported numbers masked a much larger wave. "Based on the Butler Theory of Uniform Swing, it was clear that even though AIR was reporting an initial fifty seats each, the end

---

28. L.K. Advani, "*Durbar*: An Extremely Interesting Book", *Times of India*, accessed 25 May 2025, https://timesofindia.indiatimes.com/blogs/lkadvanis-blog/durbar-an-extremely-interesting-book/.

29. Ibid.

30. L.K. Advani, *My Country, My Life* (Rupa, 2008).

result was going to be very different, with the swing to Janata Party pointing to many other victories elsewhere."[31]

The verdict was emphatic. The Janata Party inflicted a crushing defeat on Indira Gandhi. Despite fears that she might rig the election, the outcome demonstrated that the polls had been free and fair. The Janata Party secured 298 Lok Sabha seats and 43.4 per cent of the popular vote. Together with allies—the Shiromani Akali Dal (9), DMK (2), CPI(M) (22), RSP (4), AIFB (3), Peasants and Workers Party (5), and Republican Party of India (Khobargade) (2)—the tally reached 345. Jagjivan Ram's Congress for Democracy (CFD) added another 28. Within the Janata fold, the Jana Sangh emerged as the largest bloc with 93 seats.[32]

The Congress, which had once led India to Independence and ruled uninterruptedly for thirty years, was decimated. Its strength fell from 350 seats in 1971 to just 153. The party was wiped out across North India: it won nothing in Uttar Pradesh, Bihar, Punjab, Haryana, or Delhi. For the first time since Independence, the Congress failed to win a single seat in Uttar Pradesh. Both Indira Gandhi and Sanjay Gandhi were defeated. Indira lost Rae Bareli by 55,000 votes to Raj Narain, despite desperate last-minute appeals for a re-poll.

In all of North India and the Hindi heartland, the Congress managed just one seat each in Madhya Pradesh and Rajasthan, 3 in West Bengal, 4 in Odisha, and 10 each in Assam and Gujarat. Meanwhile, George Fernandes won his seat with a landslide.[33] The Janata wave, however, faltered in the South: it secured only one seat each in Andhra Pradesh, Tamil Nadu, and Karnataka. The difference reflected the relatively fewer Emergency excesses in the South and the limited spread of atrocity tales.[34]

In one stroke, the electorate ended three decades of Congress dominance, eleven years of Indira Gandhi's prime ministership, and nearly twenty-one months of authoritarian rule under Emergency. The mandate was unequivocal: Indians demanded the restoration of personal freedom and democratic

---

31. Prannoy Roy and Dorab R. Sopariwala, *The Verdict: Decoding India's Elections* (Penguin, 2019), pp. 16–18.

32. Vinay Sitapati, *Jugalbandi: The BJP Before Modi* (Penguin, 2020), p. 95.

33. Arun Jaitley, "George Saheb as I Knew Him", accessed on 25 May 2025, https://www.arunjaitley.com/george-saheb-as-i-knew-him/.

34. Kuldip Nayar, *Beyond the Lines: An Autobiography* (Roli Books Pvt. Ltd., 2012), p. 256.

rights. The poor, in particular, proved that they valued liberty as deeply as the privileged classes. By voting, they reclaimed their sovereignty, reminding politicians that the people were the true masters of India.[35]

Years later, Indira's aide R.K. Dhawan blamed the Emergency on Siddhartha Shankar Ray, then chief minister of West Bengal. In an interview, Dhawan claimed that Indira was shaken only when Jagjivan Ram deserted her. His departure convinced her that the campaign ahead would be difficult. In response, she sought to shore up loyalty by granting tickets mainly to senior Congress leaders, restricting Sanjay's loyalists to just twenty nominations.[36] Yet she never believed defeat was possible. Even the Muslim electorate, long a solid Congress vote bank, turned away.[37]

On 20 March 1977, as results poured in, it became clear that the Congress was collapsing. That evening, Dhawan informed Indira she was trailing badly in Rae Bareli, with the margin widening steadily. When her close friend and biographer Pupul Jayakar visited her at 1 Safdarjung Road around 8 p.m., she found Indira sitting alone. "Pupul, I have lost," she admitted quietly. They sat together in silence.[38] Defeat had shocked her, yet Dhawan observed that there was also a flicker of relief—freedom, at last, from relentless political pressures, and time for herself and the family.[39]

Late that night, Indira convened a Cabinet meeting at her residence. Amidst the sounds of celebration on Delhi's streets—drums, dancing, and the distribution of sweets—she informed her colleagues that she and her ministers would resign. The Cabinet also decided to revoke the Emergency. Cabinet Secretary B.D. Pande and Home Secretary S.L. Khurana prepared the formal notification. Pande got the note approved by Indira after 1 a.m. on 21 March. He then rushed to the vice president's house at 6 Maulana Azad Road.

---

35. Ibid.

36. Neerja Chowdhury, *How Prime Ministers Decide* (Aleph, 2023), pp. 38–39.

37. Christophe Jaffrelot (ed.), *India Since 1950: Society, Politics, Economy and Culture*, (Yatra Books, 2012), p. 581.

38. Neerja Chowdhury, *How Prime Ministers Decide* (Aleph, 2023), p. 4.

39. "Indira Gandhi was Relieved She Lost 1977 Election: RK Dhawan", *India Today*, accessed 25 May 2025, https://www.indiatoday.in/india/story/indira-gandhi-emergency-rule-rk-dhawan-congress-259245-2015-06-23.

It was 2 a.m. by the time he was done.[40] B.D. Jatti, who had been officiating as the President after the death of President Fakhruddin Ali Ahmed on 11 February that year, signed in the early hours of 21 March. On 22 March, Indira Gandhi resigned as prime minister after eleven years in office. India breathed freely again.

Her residence at 1 Safdarjung Road, once the nerve centre of power, suddenly looked abandoned—like a battlefield after defeat. The prime minister of yesterday was today not even a Member of Parliament. Furniture and papers lay scattered, the visitors and crowds had disappeared.[41] Stripped of staff, official cars, and even a working telephone operator, Indira found herself unable to recall the phone numbers of friends. For decades, others had managed her life. Now, files no longer came to occupy her hours. She faced, for the first time in years, an empty day.[42]

The 1977 election was transformative. From 1952 to 1977, most large and medium states had repeatedly voted the same ruling party back to power—Andhra Pradesh, Assam, Bihar, Gujarat, Haryana, Karnataka, Maharashtra, Madhya Pradesh, Rajasthan, and Uttar Pradesh. Only Kerala, Odisha, Punjab, Tamil Nadu, and West Bengal had shown periodic changes.[43] That pattern was shattered in 1977. In the state assembly polls of June that year, the Congress was annihilated, losing Bihar, Madhya Pradesh, Rajasthan, Tamil Nadu, Uttar Pradesh, West Bengal, Delhi, Haryana, Kerala, Odisha, and Punjab.[44]

★

The sixth Lok Sabha was constituted on 23 March 1977, marking a historic break in Indian politics. For the first time, a non-Congress leader—Morarji Desai—became the prime minister of India. His Cabinet reflected the broad coalition

---

40. Neerja Chowdhury, *How Prime Ministers Decide* (Aleph, 2023), p. 4.

41. Kuldip Nayar, *Beyond the Lines: An Autobiography* (Roli Books Pvt. Ltd., 2012), p. 257.

42. Neerja Chowdhury, *How Prime Ministers Decide* (Aleph, 2023), pp. 3–4.

43. Prannoy Roy and Dorab R. Sopariwala, *The Verdict: Decoding India's Elections* (Penguin, 2019).

44. Ibid.

that had come together under the Janata Party banner. It included two deputy prime ministers: Charan Singh, who took charge of home affairs, and Jagjivan Ram, who held defence. Senior Jana Sangh leaders also secured key positions—Atal Bihari Vajpayee became Minister of External Affairs, Lal Krishna Advani was appointed Minister of Information and Broadcasting, and Brijlal Verma was given the Industry portfolio. The Industry Ministry had initially been offered to Nanaji Deshmukh, but in keeping with the Sangh Parivar's strategy, he declined, choosing instead to focus on organisational work.[45]

George Fernandes, ever the rebel, at first refused to join the Cabinet, misjudging the political mood. Jaitley later recalled how a crowd of 500 workers gheraoed him, raising hostile slogans, until he finally relented and accepted a ministerial berth.[46]

By this time, Arun Jaitley had become a devoted disciple of Jayaprakash Narayan. He firmly believed that JP's leadership had provided the moral and ideological foundation for the anti-Emergency struggle. The unprecedented upsurge of the 1977 election, he felt, was the direct outcome of JP's movement. JP inspired an entire generation of youth with a spirit of idealism and, during the Emergency's tyranny, instilled in them a freedom from fear.[47]

Jaitley also held Nanaji Deshmukh in high regard. A key organiser of the JP Movement, Nanaji remained central to the Sangh Parivar's strategy even after the Janata victory. Despite being offered a Cabinet post by Morarji Desai, he chose to remain outside government, devoting himself to organisational work. However, the disunity within the Janata Party, where leaders of different ideologies clashed endlessly over leadership, left him disillusioned. At the age of sixty, he surprised the nation by announcing his political sanyas.

Nanaji spent the remaining thirty-four years of his life dedicated to rural transformation, guided by two central ideas—*gramodaya* (rise of the village) and *swawalamban* (self-reliance). He worked tirelessly to build model villages, educational institutions, and centres for rural reform in Gonda, Balrampur, and

---

45. Abhishek Choudhary, *Vajpayee: The Ascent of the Hindu Right (1924–1977)* (Picador India, 2023).

46. Arun Jaitley, *A New India: Selected Writings 2014–19* (Juggernaut, 2020), pp. 327–28.

47. Arun Jaitley, "Jayaprakash Narayan" in *Articles & Speeches by Arun Jaitley: A Compilation* (Universal Law Publishing Co. Pvt. Ltd., 2014), pp. 219–20.

Chitrakoot.[48] In 1991, he established India's first rural university—Chitrakoot Gramodaya Vishwavidyalaya in Satna, Madhya Pradesh—which was later renamed Mahatma Gandhi Chitrakoot Gramodaya Vishwavidyalaya.

In recognition of his lifelong service, Nanaji was nominated to the Rajya Sabha in 1999 and awarded the Padma Vibhushan the same year. He passed away on 27 February 2010 in Chitrakoot. In 2019, he was posthumously honoured with the Bharat Ratna, India's highest civilian award.

★

With democracy restored and the ban on the RSS revoked, the ABVP decided to step away from student elections for a few years to focus on strengthening its organisation, returning to electoral politics only in 1982. During this interlude, Jaitley resumed his studies and sat for his final-year law examinations in April–May 1977.

That year, his friends Vijay Goel and Rajat Sharma contested the DUSU elections for the offices of president and general secretary, and Jaitley campaigned enthusiastically for both. Fellow student Vijay Jolly later recalled his first impression of Jaitley:

> I was fascinated by Jaitley, who was eloquent in both English and Hindi. He was the smartest of the three—wearing a brown leather jacket and black goggles—though I still remember Rajat Sharma's speech, "*ghaas kaisi bhi ho, chashma hara hona chahiye*" (whatever the colour of the grass, one should see it through green glasses). This was my first contact with the "Jaitley & Company" in 1977.[49]

After Goel and Sharma's victory, the new office-bearers turned to Jaitley for advice on whom to invite for the DUSU inauguration ceremony. Jaitley

---

48. Arun Jaitley, "Nanaji Deshmukh" in *Articles & Speeches by Arun Jaitley: A Compilation* (Universal Law Publishing Co. Pvt. Ltd., 2014), pp. 227–28.

49. Vijay Jolly, "Tribute: Arun Jaitley, the Go-Getter", *The Week*, accessed 25 May 2025, https://www.theweek.in/news/india/2019/08/28/arun-jaitley-the-go-getter.html.

suggested none other than Prime Minister Morarji Desai. To their surprise, Desai accepted the invitation and attended the function, which Jaitley presided over—a remarkable moment linking campus politics with the national stage.[50]

Upon completing his law degree in 1977, Jaitley shifted focus to building his legal career. He began practising at the Tis Hazari courts, alongside his father, Maharaj Kishen Jaitley, who specialised in cases involving the Municipal Corporation of Delhi (MCD) and the Delhi Development Authority (DDA).[51] Following his father's path, the younger Jaitley quickly established himself as a promising lawyer.

Although he now stood on the threshold of a legal career, politics never left him entirely. He continued to guide and mentor ABVP's student leaders at Delhi University, helping craft Vijay Jolly's victory as DUSU general secretary in 1978 and as president in 1980. Many future leaders in the ABVP owed their grooming and early success to Jaitley's organisational skills, strategic mind, and quiet mentoring.[52]

What he could not have foreseen was how his early legal specialisation in DDA cases would soon catapult him into the national spotlight—providing him with a high-profile brief, media recognition, and, eventually, a renewed acceleration of his political journey.

---

50. Rajat Sharma, "Arun Jaitley: My Friend, Guardian and Guide", assessed 25 May 2025, https://rajatsharma.in/arun-jaitley-my-friend-guardian-and-guide/.

51. Praveen Donthi, "Talk of the Town", *Caravan Magazine*, accessed 25 May 2025, https://caravanmagazine.in/reportage/talk-town.

52. Vijay Jolly, "TRIBUTE: Arun Jaitley, the Go-Getter", *The Week*, accessed 25 May 2025, https://www.theweek.in/news/india/2019/08/28/arun-jaitley-the-go-getter.html.

5

Early Strides in Law and Politics

While Jaitley's political initiation took place during his imprisonment, his formal entry into politics began with the split in the Janata Party and the formation of the present-day BJP in April 1980, marking his transition from the ABVP to the BJP in the same year.

The 1980s were a defining decade for India, one that shaped the nation's political landscape and destiny. The Janata Party, which had come to power in March 1977, split and collapsed in less than three years. On 23 June 1980, Sanjay Gandhi, the younger son of Prime Minister Indira Gandhi, died in a plane crash in New Delhi. Indira Gandhi returned to power in 1980 and swiftly reasserted her dominance over both national and state politics. The BJP was born the same year, emerging from the remnants of the Bharatiya Jana Sangh (BJS).

The year 1984 proved especially calamitous for India. Punjab was in turmoil, culminating in the army's assault on the Golden Temple in Amritsar in June during Operation Blue Star. This was followed by Indira Gandhi's assassination by her Sikh bodyguards in October and the horrific anti-Sikh riots that ensued. In December, the Bhopal gas tragedy struck when methyl isocyanate (MIC) leaked from the Union Carbide plant, killing at least 4,000 people.[1] Rarely

1. Just after midnight on 2 December 1984, a storage tank at the Union Carbide chemical plant in Bhopal began leaking a gas called MIC. The plant, in Bhopal, Madhya Pradesh, India, was equipped with six safety systems designed to detect such a leak—none of which were operational that night. Twenty-seven tons of MIC gas spread throughout the sleeping city. As an engineer was flushing water through a corroded pipe in the MIC production complex, a series of valves failed,

before had India faced three such catastrophic events within a single year, each making global headlines.[2]

That same year, on 7 April 1984, the Vishwa Hindu Parishad (VHP) convened its first *dharma sansad*, gathering 600 religious leaders from various sects. The assembly urged gurudwaras to reject extremist elements and declared that there was "no direct clash between Hindus and Sikhs in Punjab", blaming politically motivated interests for fomenting hatred. The meeting also resolved to "liberate" Lord Ram in Ayodhya from what it termed Muslim control.[3]

Although Sikh militant Jarnail Singh Bhindranwale was killed during Operation Blue Star, violence continued to plague Punjab. In 1985, Sikh terrorists bombed an Air India flight from Canada, killing 329 passengers. In August 1986, Lieutenant General Kuldip Singh Brar, who had led Operation Blue Star, was shot dead, and two months later, a Sikh assassin fired at the President and prime minister during their visit to Mahatma Gandhi's samadhi.[4]

---

allowing the water to flow freely into one of the three-storey tanks holding the toxic chemical in a liquid state. This caused a rapid and violent reaction. The tank shattered in its concrete casing and spewed a deadly cloud of MIC, hydrogen cyanide, monomethylamine, and other chemicals. As the toxic cloud blanketed much of Bhopal, people began to die. Many people died in the stampedes through narrow alleyways. The crush of fleeing crowds wrenched children's hands from their parents' grasp. Families were literally ripped apart. MIC, used in the production of pesticides, is highly corrosive if inhaled. Half a million people were exposed and suffered from disorders caused by the accident and the subsequent contamination—respiratory diseases, kidney and liver disorders, cancers and gynaecological issues. No one knows exactly how many thousands of people died. Union Carbide put the number at 3800. Municipal workers who collected bodies, loading them on to lorries to be buried in mass graves or burned on funeral pyres, say they handled at least 15,000 corpses. *See*, Judah Passow and Tim Edwards, "The Long, Dark Shadow of Bhopal: Still Waiting for Justice, Four Decades On", *The Guardian*, accessed 25 May 2025, https://www.theguardian.com/global-development/2023/jun/14/bhopal-toxic-gas-leak-chemical-environmental-disaster-waiting-for-justice-union-carbide-dow.

2. Prannoy Roy and Dorab R. Sopariwala, *The Verdict: Decoding India's Elections* (Penguin, 2019).

3. L.K. Advani, *My Country, My Life* (Rupa, 2008), p. 363.

4. Tania Midha, Inderjit Badhwar and Prabhu Chawla, "Attempt to Assassinate Prime Minister Rajiv Gandhi Exposes Chinks in his Security Armour", *India Today*, accessed 25 May 2025, https://www.indiatoday.in/magazine/cover-story/story/19861031-

In 1986, Prime Minister Rajiv Gandhi overturned the Supreme Court's verdict in the Shah Bano case to appease orthodox Muslim groups. Attempting to regain Hindu confidence, he subsequently ordered the opening of the Babri Masjid's locks for Hindu worshippers. That same year, leadership within the BJP shifted, with L.K. Advani succeeding Atal Bihari Vajpayee as party president.

In April 1987, Swedish Radio reported that Bofors had paid kickbacks to senior Indian politicians and defence officials to secure an arms deal. Defence Minister V.P. Singh rebelled against Rajiv Gandhi, gaining immense public support. Riding the anti-corruption wave, V.P. Singh defeated Rajiv Gandhi in 1989 to become prime minister.

In June 1989, the BJP's Palampur session in Himachal Pradesh formally endorsed a firm stance on the Ram Mandir issue. Then, on 7 August 1990, Prime Minister V.P. Singh announced the implementation of the Mandal Commission's recommendations, granting 27 per cent reservation in government jobs and educational institutions to Other Backward Classes (OBCs). The decision triggered widespread unrest and political upheaval. Within a single decade, India had witnessed extraordinary political and social turbulence.

Jaitley's own life during this decade was equally eventful, particularly in its latter half. After joining the legal profession, he dedicated himself to building his practice while continuing his involvement with Janata Party activities. His diligence soon earned him recognition as a sought-after lawyer and a visible political figure. By the late 1980s, Jaitley had emerged as one of the most articulate and sharp young leaders—first within the ABVP, and later, the BJP—working initially under Vajpayee and subsequently under Advani.[5]

The sequence of events that would shape his political path began with the disintegration of the Janata Party government and the decision of the BJS to part ways and form the BJP in early 1980. The Janata Party, led by Morarji Desai, had risen to power in 1977 on a massive wave of popular hope following

attempt-to-assassinate-prime-minister-rajiv-gandhi-exposes-chinks-in-his-security-armour-801365-1986-10-30.

5. Nitin Gadkari, "Arun Jaitley Helped BJP Set the Narrative", in *The Discussant, Journal of Centre for Reforms, Development, and Justice*, Special Edition, An Obituary to Arun Jaitley, Vol. VII, No. 3 (July–September 2019), pp. 20–22.

the Emergency. Its members even took an oath of honesty and transparency at Rajghat.[6] Yet, this initial enthusiasm quickly gave way to internal discord.

Rivalries surfaced during the contest for the prime minister's post, with Jagjivan Ram, Morarji Desai, and Charan Singh vying for leadership. Despite the Jana Sangh's numerical strength, its claim to key positions was unacceptable to others. In reality, the Janata Party functioned less as a unified entity and more as a loose federation of factions, each led by its own "chieftain".[7] Jayaprakash Narayan and Jiwatram Bhagwandas Kripalani (Acharya Kripalani) were called upon to mediate. A well-known Gandhian and a socialist, Acharya Kriplani had turned into a critic of the Congress party after it agreed to the Partition of India. Born in Hyderabad, Sindh, in 1888, he became the Congress president in 1946, but resigned from his position in 1947.[8] In the absence of consensus, they chose Morarji Desai after consulting the party's elected members.[9]

Morarji Desai, born on 29 February 1896 in Bhadeli village (now in Gujarat's Valsad district), was the son of a schoolteacher from an Anavil Brahmin family. A 1918 graduate, he served as a deputy collector for twelve years before resigning in 1930 to join the freedom movement. He was imprisoned thrice. Desai was detained in the individual satyagraha launched by Mahatma Gandhi, released in October 1941, and detained again in August, 1942 at the time of the Quit India Movement. He was released in 1945. Earlier, in 1931, he joined the All India Congress Committee and was secretary of the Gujarat Pradesh Congress Committee until 1937. When the first Congress government assumed office in 1937, Desai became the minister for revenue, agriculture, forest and cooperatives in the ministry headed by B.G. Kher in the then Bombay Province. The Congress ministries went out of office in 1939 in protest against India's involvement in the World War without the consent of the people. After the elections to the state assemblies in 1946, he became the minister for home and revenue in Bombay. In 1952, he became the Chief Minister of Bombay.

---

6. Kuldip Nayar, *Beyond the Lines: An Autobiography* (Roli Books Pvt. Ltd., 2012), p. 259.

7. Vinay Sitapati, *Jugalbandi: The BJP Before Modi* (Penguin, 2020), p. 95.

8. Kritika Sharma, "Acharya JB Kripalani: Congress Chief in 1947 Who Became a Harsh Critic of Nehru & Indira", *The Print*, accessed 25 May 2025, https://theprint.in/theprint-profile/acharya-jb-kripalani-the-congress-chief-in-1947-who-turned-harsh-critic-of-nehru-indira/148144/.

9. L.K. Advani, *My Country, My Life* (Rupa, 2008), pp. 269–70.

After the reorganisation of the states, Desai joined the Union Cabinet as the minister for commerce and industry on 14 November 1956. Later, he took the finance portfolio on 22 March 1958. In 1963, he resigned from the Union Cabinet under the Kamraj Plan. Lal Bahadur Shastri, who succeeded Nehru as the prime minister, persuaded him to become chairman of the Administrative Reforms Commission for restructuring the administrative system.[10]

Jagjivan Ram had not opposed the resolution supporting the imposition of the Emergency under Indira Gandhi. This may have counted against him in the leadership race. Had JP been given a free hand, he might have preferred Chandra Shekhar as prime minister, but the latter lacked sufficient parliamentary support and was instead made Janata Party president.

Within a year of taking office, the Janata government began to unravel. Morarji Desai, Charan Singh, and Jagjivan Ram pursued conflicting agendas, squandering a historic opportunity.[11] Desai, upright but rigid, struggled to hold the coalition together. By mid-1979, the government collapsed under the weight of its contradictions and clashing egos. This disintegration paved the way for the creation of the BJP—an organisation that, three decades later, would become the world's largest political party. JP's deteriorating health left him unable to restore order within the fractious Janata ranks.

★

The Desai government assumed office on 23 March 1977, beginning on a promising note. Its foremost task was to reverse the excesses committed by Indira Gandhi during the Emergency and to revive the democratic institutions she had weakened to centralize power. It rolled back the constitutional amendments enacted during the Emergency and made it more difficult for any future government to impose a national Emergency. Through the Constitution (44th Amendment) Act, 1978, the Janata government effectively nullified most provisions of the 42nd Amendment, tightening the conditions required for such proclamations.

---

10. "Shri Morarji Desai", PMIndia, accessed 25 May 2025, https://www.pmindia.gov.in/en/former_pm/shri-morarji-desai-2/.

11. Neerja Chowdhury, *How Prime Ministers Decide* (Aleph, 2023), p. 40.

Soon after taking charge, the Cabinet—urged on by Home Minister Charan Singh—resolved to dismiss the Congress governments in nine states, arguing that they too had lost their mandate following Indira Gandhi's electoral defeat. Acting President B.D. Jatti accepted the Cabinet's recommendation and dissolved the assemblies. By April 1977, the Janata government had established eight commissions of inquiry, led by retired judges, to investigate alleged misconduct by Indira Gandhi, Sanjay Gandhi, and senior Congress leaders such as Bansi Lal, V.C. Shukla, and Pranab Mukherjee.

Pranab Mukherjee, an experienced Congressman and administrator, had entered full-time public life after his election to the Rajya Sabha in 1969. Under Indira Gandhi's mentorship, his political ascent was swift—he served as deputy minister for industry, shipping and transport, and steel and industry, and later as minister of state for finance between 1973 and 1974. He went on to become Finance Minister in 1982 and Leader of the House in the Rajya Sabha in 1980.

Among the commissions, Justice H.R. Khanna was tasked with probing the misuse of state resources and agencies by Sanjay Gandhi in his Maruti project. Another commission examined the treatment of Jayaprakash Narayan during his imprisonment, which had caused the kidney ailment that ultimately led to his death. The government even ordered an inquiry into the death of socialist leader Ram Manohar Lohia in 1967, a long-standing source of suspicion among socialists. But the most high-profile of all was the commission led by former Chief Justice of India J.C. Shah, mandated to investigate "the excesses, malpractices, and abuse of authority" during the Emergency, extending even to "the highest political authority".

Indira Gandhi denounced the Shah Commission as an act of political vendetta. She ignored two summons before finally appearing in January 1978, asserting that decisions during the Emergency were collective Cabinet responsibilities and denying personal knowledge of any wrongdoing.[12]

Meanwhile, serious discord brewed within the Janata Party. Charan Singh resented being passed over for the prime ministership in favour of Desai. Socialist leader Madhu Limaye repeatedly objected to Vajpayee and Advani's continued association with the RSS, a sensitive issue given the Jana Sangh faction's origins.[13] The eighty-one-year-old Morarji Desai, principled yet rigid,

12. Neerja Chowdhury, *How Prime Ministers Decide* (Aleph, 2023), pp. 8–9.

13. L.K. Advani, *My Country, My Life* (Rupa, 2008), pp. 300–04.

struggled to manage the fractious coalition. Charan Singh, impatient and abrasive, often acted unilaterally as home minister, alienating colleagues with his temper and unilateral decisions.

In the aftermath of her crushing defeat, Indira Gandhi briefly contemplated withdrawing from public life. "I will take a place somewhere, maybe where there are trees all around and a spring. I can spend the rest of my life there reading books," she reportedly confided to a friend.[14] Suddenly, she smelt an opportunity to bounce back.[15]

The turning point came on 3 October 1977, when Charan Singh ordered her arrest. Many Janata leaders supported the move, unwilling to forgive her for the Emergency. Although Desai and Indira Gandhi had been rivals for years—Desai had served as her deputy prime minister in 1967—he opposed vindictive action. "We must take action only according to the law," he advised. Chandra Shekhar, president of the Janata Party, also dissented, arguing that the electorate had already punished her at the polls.

However, Charan Singh grew increasingly insistent on prosecuting her. Morarji Desai had promised Indira Gandhi that her family would be physically safe, although Sanjay Gandhi would not be let off the hook for his crimes during the Emergency.[16] He was under immense pressure to do so from his home minister Charan Singh, George Fernandes, and other ministerial colleagues. Charan Singh demanded a Nuremberg type of trial against her.[17] Finally, Morarji Desai relented, and it was decided to arrest her.

Indira Gandhi, tipped off in advance by loyalists within the CBI and Intelligence Bureau, prepared for the moment with characteristic calculation. When officers arrived at her residence at 12 Willingdon Crescent, she and Sanjay Gandhi were playing badminton. Calmly, she stepped forward and declared, "Handcuff me. I will not go until you handcuff me." The police wireless crackled, "King five to queen four, king five to queen four…"; back in the home ministry, an anxious Charan Singh paced up and down the room keeping a minute-by-minute track of the drama that was unfolding at 12

14. Neerja Chowdhury, *How Prime Ministers Decide* (Aleph, 2023), pp.1–2.

15. Ibid., p. 40.

16. Ibid., pp. 8–9.

17. Ibid.

Willingdon Crescent.[18] Indira Gandhi then sat down on a cane chair on the veranda. And she demanded an arrest warrant. The CBI did not have one. She was playing for time.

Meanwhile, Sanjay mobilized the Youth Congress to organize street protests. R.K. Dhawan alerted the press: "If you want a big story, come quickly to 12 Willingdon Crescent." As cameras and crowds gathered, Indira Gandhi emerged to address reporters, distributing her prewritten statement. Her security guard lay in front of the jeep meant to take her away, shouting that it would have to drive over his body. A convoy of cars and buses followed her as she was taken away, transforming her arrest into a spectacle.[19]

As journalist Neerja Chowdhury recounts in *How Prime Ministers Decide*, the CBI was taking her to Bhatkal Lake in Haryana when they were stopped at a closed railway crossing. Indira got out, sat on a culvert, and refused to leave Delhi's jurisdiction. The team was forced to turn back. She spent the night at the Police Lines in North Delhi, accompanied by Nirmala Deshpande, and appeared before a magistrate the next day. Outside, the streets were in turmoil—some crowds shouted "Indira Gandhi zindabad," others "murdabad". Tear gas filled the air, seeping even into the courtroom. Standing in the dock, Indira asked for water. Sanjay brought her a glass, and she used her handkerchief to wipe her tear-stung eyes—a moment that displayed her instinctive understanding of optics.

The magistrate released her unconditionally. Overnight, the "villain" of the Emergency had become a martyr. Charan Singh's attempt to humiliate her instead restored her political stature.[20]

Her release made the government look weak and indecisive, effectively resurrecting Indira Gandhi's career. Meanwhile, infighting within the Janata Party deepened. Raj Narain publicly questioned Chandra Shekhar's leadership, while Charan Singh accused the government of failure.[21] Corruption charges against Desai's son Kantilal—accused of profiteering—further damaged the prime minister's image. There had been distressing stories about the suicides

---

18. Ibid., pp. 46–49.

19. Ibid.

20. Ibid.

21. Shantanu Gupta, *Bharatiya Janata Party: Past, Present and Future: Story of the World's Largest Political Party* (Rupa, 2020), p. 241.

that had earlier taken place in his family. He feared that firmness with his son might lead to yet another tragic consequence.[22]

Despite JP's best efforts, harmony within the Janata Party proved impossible. Chandra Shekhar could only watch as senior leaders turned on one another. Eventually, Morarji Desai resigned as prime minister.

Instead of calling for fresh elections, President Neelam Sanjiva Reddy invited Charan Singh to form a government. With Congress support, he was sworn in as prime minister, but Indira Gandhi withdrew her backing before he could prove his majority. On 20 August 1979, he resigned, bringing the sixth Lok Sabha to an early end on 22 August 1979—two years ahead of schedule.

India went to the polls again in January 1980. The Congress had split into Indira Gandhi's Congress (I) and Y.B. Chavan's Congress (U). Charan Singh revived his Bharatiya Lok Dal (BLD). Indira's campaign slogan was simple and powerful: *Vote unhein dein jo kaam kar sakein*—"Vote for those who can deliver". The Janata Party, plagued by infighting, was decimated. It won only 31 seats, down from 298 in 1977; the BJS faction secured just 16, compared to 93 earlier. In contrast, Congress (I) won 353 of 492 contested seats, including 51 of Uttar Pradesh's 85. Indira triumphed in Rae Bareli and Medak, and Sanjay regained Amethi.

Overall, although Charan Singh did not fare too badly in UP, winning 29 of the 34 seats the Congress (I) lost, its nationwide tally was just 41 seats. The other Congress, which contested in alliance with the Janata Party (S), won but 13 of the 212 seats it fought, and over the next few years, withered away, with most of its leaders, in ones and twos, trickling into Indira's party.[23] The electorate punished the Janata Party for betraying the 1977 mandate.

The electoral debacle intensified the rift within the Janata Party. Jagjivan Ram raked up the issue of the BJS section continuing with their RSS membership, which they termed as the dual membership. It was decided to discuss the issue at the RSS Pratinidhi Sabha on 21–22 March 1980. Instead of waiting, the Janata Party Parliamentary Board, on 19 March 1980, prohibited its functionaries from joining RSS activities. On 4 April, the national executive of the Janata Party was scheduled to hold a crucial meeting in Delhi to take a final decision on the

---

22. L.K. Advani, *My Country, My Life* (Rupa, 2008), p. 299.

23. Debashish Mukerji, *The Disruptor, How Vishwanath Pratap Singh Shook India* (HarperCollins, 2021), p. 140.

dual membership issue. In anticipation of the outcome of this meeting, the former members of the BJS decided to hold a national convention in Delhi on 6 April. Morarji Desai and some others made a last-ditch effort to retain the BJS within the Janata Party on the basis of a mutually acceptable compromise. But the die had been cast.[24] On 4 April, the Janata Party executive decided to expel all former Jana Sangh members from the party.[25] Jagjivan Ram quit the Janata Party to join the Congress (U) on 5 April.

On 6 April 1980—Easter Sunday—over 3,500 delegates gathered at Delhi's Feroz Shah Kotla Grounds to form a new political organization: the Bharatiya Janata Party (BJP). Atal Bihari Vajpayee was elected president, with L.K. Advani, Sikander Bakht, and Suraj Bhan as general secretaries.

Atal Bihari Vajpayee, born on 25 December 1924 in Bateshwar (Uttar Pradesh), was the fifth child of Krishna Bihari and Krishna Devi. His grandfather, Shyamlal, a priest and astrologer, named him Atal—meaning firm and fearless.[26] The Vajpayees of Bateshwar owned some land, but were not adept at farming. Despite his expertise, Shyamlal struggled to make a living. In the end, his only stable source of income was the occasional recital of the Bhagavad Gita in and around Bateshwar.

Krishna Bihari broke the age-old cycle. After passing his middle-school exams, he decided that instead of going to Banaras to study Sanskrit, he would go to Agra for high school and teach himself English. After matriculation, he did some odd jobs in Agra and Etawah. Later, he took up the position of a Hindi teacher and found himself a job in Gwalior. In Gwalior, Vajpayee was deeply influenced by the RSS's ideology and attended shakhas. In mid-1934, Krishna Bihari was promoted and sent off to be the headmaster of a school in Barnagar near Ujjain. The parents took Atal along, and enrolled him into the AVM school: he was christened Atal Bihari Lal Vajpayee.[27]

After some time, Vajpayee moved to Kanpur aspiring to become a journalist. Sometime in mid-1947, M.S. Golwalkar (known as Guruji) visited Kanpur. At

---

24. L.K. Advani, *My Country, My Life* (Rupa, 2010), pp. 307–14.

25. L.K. Advani, *My Take* (Prabhat Prakashan, 2014), p. 183.

26. Abhishek Choudhary, *Vajpayee: The Ascent of the Hindu Right, 1924–1977* (Picador India, 2023), p. 44.

27. Ibid., pp. 5–8. Whereas Vajpayee was born in Bateshwar in 1924, the school certificate proclaimed he was born in Gwalior on 1 May 1926.

the function held in his honour at a shakha, Atal recited a poem especially prepared for the occasion. Golwalkar vaguely recalled the face of the *"baal swayamsevak"*. But Atal had never had a chance to talk to Guruji at length. Golwalkar asked Atal to accompany him; the RSS was considering launching a Hindi press at Lucknow.[28] Atal moved to Lucknow to join the *Rashtradharma* office. The main brain behind the mouthpiece was the provincial organiser of the RSS in Uttar Pradesh, Bhaurao Deoras.[29] Thus began Vajpayee's journey as a staunch nationalist inspired by the ideals of the RSS.

Vajpayee's formal political career took shape in 1951 when he joined the newly formed BJS. A brilliant orator, he quickly rose through the ranks and became a prominent voice for conservative and nationalist politics. In 1957, he was elected to the Lok Sabha for the first time from Balrampur, Uttar Pradesh, marking the beginning of his parliamentary legacy. As the BJP's first president, he went on to steer the party towards moderate politics, emphasising democracy and development. He also created a second line of leaders both in the Centre and the states.

Claiming to be the real Janata Party, the Vajpayee faction submitted affidavits to the ECI in its support from a few Lok Sabha members. Even the Chandra Shekhar group filed its own counterclaims. After considering all the claims, the ECI, on 24 April 1980, froze the original party symbol. It granted interim recognition to the Vajpayee faction as a national party with the prefix 'Bharatiya' to the original Janata Party name. It also allotted the newly minted BJP the lotus symbol. The lotus had been planted. While its green shoots would emerge over the next decade, it would blossom only in the 1990s.

As Advani wrote in one of his blogs in April 2013, in 1980, on Good Friday, the Jana Sangh was crucified by the Janata Party resolution and on Easter Sunday the BJP was resurrected.[30]

★

---

28. Ibid., 37–38.

29. Ibid., 44.

30. L.K. Advani, "BJP, and Easter Sunday", Bharatiya Janata Party, accessed 25 May 2025, https://www.bjp.org/pressreleases/shri-lk-advanijis-latest-blog-bjp-and-easter-sunday.

Jaitley joined the Bharatiya Janata Party (BJP) in the same year it was founded, in 1980. Atal Bihari Vajpayee appointed him as the president of the Bharatiya Janata Yuva Morcha (BJYM), the party's youth wing. Though the BJP was newly formed, its Yuva Morcha had been established two years earlier, in 1978, to represent the voice and aspirations of India's young generation.

Jaitley was also made secretary of the BJP's Delhi unit—a natural extension of his long-standing association with the city since his ABVP days. Thus began his remarkable four-decade-long journey within the BJP. He initially focused on strengthening the party's organisation in Delhi, which at the time was still a union territory.

The governance framework of Delhi had evolved gradually over the years. The Delhi Municipal Corporation Act of 1957 created a unified municipal corporation for the entire city. (The New Delhi Municipal Council, in one form or another, had existed since 1913, but its jurisdiction was confined to what is now known as Lutyens' Delhi.) Later, the Delhi Administration Act of 1966 established a Metropolitan Council—a partly democratic body with fifty-six elected members and five nominated by the President. However, this council had only recommendatory powers. The real administrative authority in Delhi continued to rest with the Centre, exercised through the lieutenant governor or administrator appointed by the President.

The first council elections were held in 1966. Veteran freedom fighter and Congressman Mir Mushtaq Ahmed became the first chief executive councillor (CEC) of Delhi—equivalent to the post of chief minister—for the 1966–67 term. After the Jana Sangh's victory in the 1967 elections, Vijay Kumar Malhotra became the CEC while L.K. Advani was chosen as chairman of the council. In the 1972 elections, the Congress returned to power with forty-four seats; freedom fighter and Gandhian Radha Raman became the CEC, and Mir Mushtaq Ahmed served as chairman. The 1977 elections brought another shift, with the Janata Party winning forty-six seats. RSS veteran Kedarnath Sahni became the CEC, and BJP leader Kalka Dass was appointed chairman. Around this time, L.K. Advani represented Delhi in the Rajya Sabha.

Jaitley's deep involvement in the BJP's organisational work in Delhi brought him into close contact with Advani, a relationship that would play a defining role in his political journey in the years to come.

★

The turbulence of the Emergency years had finally subsided. Indira Gandhi was firmly back in power, seemingly having learned her lessons from the debacle of 1977. Political activity in Delhi was minimal, with elections to the council and corporation still more than three years away.

At this time, Jaitley turned his attention to building his law practice. Although Delhi had its own high court since 1966, he chose to begin prudently at the Tis Hazari Courts—an environment he knew well. He had practically grown up there, spending time around his father, and often walking through the nearby Azad Market where the family once lived. Joining his father's chamber in the Tis Hazari Court Complex, Jaitley began appearing before the courts.

Practising in the lower courts gave him a strong foundation, exposing him to a wide range of cases—civil, criminal, land disputes, and more. Before long, he developed a specialisation in cases involving the Municipal Corporation of Delhi and the Delhi Development Authority. He also began appearing occasionally before other courts, including the Delhi High Court, and would often spend time after work with close friends and fellow lawyers Raian Karanjawala, Mukul Rohatgi, and Rohinton Nariman.

Interestingly, Jaitley never learned to drive. He had deliberately decided neither to buy nor to operate a car himself. Mukul Rohatgi once told journalist Sunetra Choudhury in a podcast that he used to drop Jaitley at either the Indian Institute of Technology or Dhaula Kuan, from where Jaitley would take an autorickshaw to Naraina.[31]

On 24 May 1982, Jaitley married Sangeeta (Dolly to her friends), the elder daughter of veteran lawyer and Congress leader Girdhari Lal Dogra and Shakuntala Dogra. Girdhari Lal Dogra, a towering figure in Jammu and Kashmir politics, had the rare distinction of presenting twenty-six consecutive budgets as the state's finance minister. The Jaitley and Dogra families already knew each other—Maharaj Kishen Jaitley and Girdhari Lal Dogra had studied law together. The match was suggested by a member of the Punjabi community, and once the families met, they readily agreed it was an ideal alliance.

Respecting his parents' choice but wishing to meet his prospective bride, Jaitley arranged through a friend to meet at the National Sports Club of India. Later, he came to see her at the New Delhi railway station before she boarded

31. "On the record with Sunetra Choudhury", *Hindustan Times*, accessed on 5 September 2025, https://www.htsmartcast.com/news-podcasts/on-the-record

a train to Jammu.[32] The Dogras divided their time between Delhi and Jammu. The meeting was brief, but the two instantly took a liking to each other—and, as they say, the rest is history.

Their wedding, held at the Dogra residence on Kamaraj Lane[33] in New Delhi, was a grand affair Political stalwarts from across party lines attended, and guests dined on the famed cuisine of Delhi's iconic Kwality restaurant in Connaught Place.[34] Both Vajpayee and Advani were present—and so was Indira Gandhi.[35]

Marriage brought Jaitley a streak of good fortune. His legal career began to rise rapidly afterward. Over the next few years, his clarity of thought, logical precision, and razor-sharp courtroom arguments earned him a reputation as an outstanding lawyer. His debating background, articulate oratory, and keen intellect accelerated his ascent. At this time, the family owned a Fiat. Before long, he bought his second car—a red Maruti 800.[36] True to form, he still didn't drive; Sangeeta did. A generous host, Jaitley's home—run under Sangeeta's warm supervision—became known for its hospitality, always ready to welcome a dozen guests at short notice.

Jaitley's first major legal breakthrough arrived soon after. Despite having mellowed, Indira Gandhi had not forgotten those she blamed for her defeat in 1977. Among them was Ramnath Goenka, the fiery publisher of *The Indian Express*, whose paper had been fiercely critical of her during the Emergency. Determined to retaliate, she allegedly pressured the DDA to revoke a building permit issued to the newspaper. Acting on these directions, the lieutenant governor of Delhi cancelled the lease of *The Indian Express* building and ordered parts of it demolished, citing construction violations.

Goenka approached his friend and prominent litigator Raian Karanjawala for help. Karanjawala, in turn, enlisted Jaitley—by then well-versed in DDA

---

32. As narrated by a family friend of the Jaitleys.

33. Formerly called Dupleix Road, after Governor General of French India Joseph François Dupleix.

34. Kwality had been founded in 1940 by P.L. Lamba and his brother-in-law I.K. Ghei.

35. Praveen Donthi, "Talk Of the Town: How Arun Jaitley wins friends and influences people", *The Caravan*, accessed on 3 September 2025, https://caravanmagazine.in/reportage/talk-town.

36. As told by Arun Jaitley's friend.

cases—to represent *The Indian Express* in its legal challenge. Jaitley argued the case forcefully, and the court granted a stay order, preventing the demolition.[37] His victory safeguarded the newspaper's headquarters and marked one of the early triumphs of his legal career.

★

Jaitley was rising swiftly in his legal career, but he continued to work for the party as a karyakarta, mastering the art of political strategy, organisation, and public mobilisation. He honed the sharp legal and oratory skills that would later define his stature as a formidable BJP leader. In 1983, elections were held for both the Delhi Metropolitan Council and the Municipal Corporation. The BJP fielded fifty candidates, while the Congress contested fifty-six seats. Jaitley played a prominent role in leading the BJP's campaign.

However, the results were disappointing. The BJP won only nineteen seats with a vote share of 36.99 per cent, while the Congress secured thirty-four seats with 47.5 per cent of the votes. The BJP lost control of both the metropolitan council and the municipal corporation.[38] The outcome was significant—and unsettling. Delhi, once considered the Jana Sangh's stronghold with its large base of Punjabi Hindu refugees, had shifted its support to Indira Gandhi's Congress.[39]

The only consolation for the BJP was that the Janata Party had been completely decimated, winning just one of the thirty-seven seats it contested. In the aftermath, Vajpayee offered to resign as party president, but his resignation was rejected.[40]

Eight months later, in October 1983, Jammu and Kashmir went to the polls. In the previous election, BJP candidates—then contesting under the

---

37. Praveen Donthi, "Talk Of the Town: How Arun Jaitley wins friends and influences people", *The Caravan*, accessed on 3 September 2025, https://caravanmagazine.in/reportage/talk-town

38. Christophe Jaffrelot, *The Hindu Nationalist Movement in India* (Columbia University Press, 1998), p. 328.

39. Ibid.

40. Vinay Sitapati, *Jugalbandi: The BJP Before Modi* (Penguin, 2020), p. 126.

Bharatiya Jana Sangh banner—had won twelve seats from the Hindu-majority Jammu region.[41] This time, both the BJP and Indira Gandhi sought to appeal to Hindu voters, pledging to protect their interests against perceived threats from the Muslim-majority Kashmir Valley. The strategy backfired. Farooq Abdullah's National Conference swept the Muslim vote in the Valley, while the Congress captured most of the Hindu vote in Jammu.[42] The BJP failed to win a single seat.[43]

In 1984, while pursuing his M.Com at Delhi University's South Campus, student leader Vijay Jolly—then DUSU president—organised the *Chhatra Shakti Awards*. Among those honoured were Arun Jaitley (as Youth Icon), actor Dev Anand (Evergreen Film Star), Maneka Gandhi (Political Leader), and Prabha Dutt, *Hindustan Times'* Chief Reporter.[44]

★

On 27 June 1983, Arun Jaitley and Sangeeta Dogra were overjoyed at the birth of their daughter, Sonali. Although Jaitley's professional commitments as a lawyer and his growing involvement in politics kept him increasingly busy, he made every effort to balance his demanding schedule with his role as a devoted father. His social media posts over the years—filled with pictures of him playing with Sonali—capture how deeply he cherished those early moments with his first child. Despite his hectic life, he ensured that her upbringing was filled with love, warmth, and attention. Sonali's own posts in recent years reveal how profoundly she continues to miss her father.

---

41. Sumit Mitra, "J&K Assembly Polls: National Conference Poised to Sweep Valley, Congress (I) Eyes Jammu", *India Today*, accessed 25 May 2025, https://www.indiatoday.in/magazine/indiascope/story/19830531-j-k-assembly-polls-national-conference-poised-to-sweep-valley-congressi-eyes-jammu-770698-2013-07-19.

42. Ibid.

43. "Statistical Report on General Election, 1983 to the Legislative Assembly of Jammu & Kashmir", Election Commission of India, New Delhi, available at https://old.eci.gov.in/files/file/3792-jammu-kashmir-1983/.

44. Vijay Jolly, TRIBUTE: Arun Jaitley, the go-getter. "Jaitley was my DU senior whom I always referred to as the Big Boss", *The Week*, accessed on 4 September 2025, https://www.theweek.in/news/india/2019/08/28/arun-jaitley-the-go-getter.html.

★

The tectonic plates of Indian politics shifted dramatically over the next few years. On 31 October 1984, Prime Minister Indira Gandhi was assassinated by two of her bodyguards as she walked through the wicket gate connecting her residence at 1, Safdarjung Road, with 1, Akbar Road—the venue of her daily darbar, or public meeting. Her killing was an act of revenge by radical Sikh extremists in response to Operation Blue Star.[45]

Just hours after her death, Indira's elder son, Rajiv Gandhi, was sworn in as India's seventh prime minister. In the aftermath, horrific anti-Sikh violence broke out in several parts of the country, with Delhi being the worst affected. Sikh homes were burned, their businesses looted, and their places of worship desecrated. Thousands of innocent men, women, and children were brutally killed.

During the violence, the RSS came forward to protect members of the Sikh community.[46] The relationship between the RSS and Sikhs had deep historical roots. During the Partition of India in 1947, the RSS had saved many Sikh lives and played a crucial role in protecting Punjab's population from attacks by

---

45. Operation Blue Star was a military operation ordered by Indira Gandhi in June 1984 to remove militant Jarnail Singh Bhindranwale from Sri Harmandir Sahib, the Golden Temple. Bhindranwale was a leader of the Sikh educational organisation Damdami Taksaal. He planned to secede Punjab from India and had the backing of Pakistan's Inter-Services Intelligence (ISI). ISI also supplied his group with arms and ammunition. He believed himself to be above the law of the land who had been chosen by God for a mission. His ambition was to wield so much power that all the police and troops of India would not dare challenge him. By July 1982, he had taken up residence inside Sri Harmandir Sahib (the Golden Temple), the most important pilgrimage site of the Sikhs. It was from there that he led the terrorist campaign in Punjab. He heavily fortified Akal Takht, one of the five seats of power of the Sikhs, located inside the Golden Temple complex. After repeated negotiations between the Government of India and Bhindranwale to evict him failed, Indira Gandhi permitted the army to use tanks and heavy artillery to flush out the militants. The militants responded with anti-tank and machine-gun fires. Bhindranwale was killed. Akal Takht was damaged, hurting Sikh sentiments.

46. "RSS Swayamsevaks Protected Sikhs During the 1984 Anti-Sikh Riots", *Organiser*, accessed 25 May 2025, https://organiser.org/2021/02/18/25963/bharat/rss-swayamsevaks-protected-sikhs-during-the-1984-anti-sikh-riots/

Muslim League-led mobs. It had also helped relocate Sikhs to safer areas and defended the sacred Darbar Sahib (Golden Temple) in Amritsar when it came under attack that year.[47]

Decades later, on 25 June 1989, tragedy struck again when Khalistani terrorists attacked RSS swayamsevaks during their daily shakha in Moga's Nehru Park, killing twenty-seven volunteers. The attack was intended to provoke communal clashes between Hindus and Sikhs. However, the RSS and BJP took the lead in maintaining peace. Advani visited Moga soon after and praised both Hindu and Sikh residents for their restraint and maturity in the face of such grave provocation.[48]

Arun Jaitley openly blamed the Congress party and its leaders for orchestrating the 1984 anti-Sikh riots, accusing Congressmen of leading the mobs.[49] He called Operation Blue Star a "historic blunder" of the Congress government—poorly planned and executed without proper intelligence—which resulted in the deaths of many innocents and severe damage to the revered Sri Harmandir Sahib and Akal Takht, deeply wounding the psyche of the patriotic Sikh community. At the same time, he described Indira Gandhi's assassination as one of the most tragic and condemnable acts in India's history.[50] Later, as a Member of Parliament, Jaitley frequently raised the issue and played a key role in setting up a special investigation team (SIT) to probe the 1984 riots.

Indira Gandhi's assassination created a massive sympathy wave that gravitated the nation towards the Congress. On 9 November 1984, Rajiv Gandhi called for early general elections, hoping to capitalise on that sentiment. The polls were held between 24 and 28 December, and the results were staggering. Rajiv Gandhi secured an unprecedented mandate—greater than any achieved by his grandfather or mother—with the Congress winning 403 of 515 Lok Sabha

---

47. Arun Anand, "How RSS Helped Save 'Darbar Sahib' Twice and Upheld Hindu-Sikh Unity", *The Print*, accessed 25 May 2025, https://theprint.in/india/how-rss-helped-save-darbar-sahib-twice-and-upheld-hindu-sikh-unity/633599/?amp.

48. L.K. Advani, *My Country, My Life* (Rupa, 2008), p. 432.

49. Arun Jaitley, "The Legacy of 1984", accessed 25 May 2025, https://www.arunjaitley.com/the-legacy-of-1984/.

50. Ibid.

seats.[51] The BJP, by contrast, won only two seats—the lowest tally ever for the Jana Sangh or the BJP. Vajpayee himself lost from Gwalior to Madhavrao Scindia. A dismayed Advani described it as an election to the *shok sabha*—a "house of mourning"—driven purely by sympathy.[52]

The BJP was left stunned. Vajpayee remarked that the verdict gave the party an opportunity to introspect and to project younger faces such as Pramod Mahajan and Arun Jaitley.[53] At the party's national executive meeting in Calcutta on 15 March 1985, he offered to resign, taking "full moral responsibility" for the debacle. However, other leaders persuaded him to stay on.

A year later, in May 1986, a significant leadership change took place. At the party's plenary session in New Delhi, L.K. Advani was appointed the new BJP president. Born on 8 November 1927 in Karachi (now in Pakistan), Advani had begun his political journey in the 1940s when he joined the RSS. After Partition, he migrated to India and became an active member of the Bharatiya Jana Sangh (BJS) in the 1950s, rising through the ranks as a disciplined organiser and articulate leader. His election to the Rajya Sabha in 1970 marked his formal entry into national politics.

As president, Advani prioritised infusing the party with young and energetic leadership. He appointed Pramod Mahajan—then only thirty-seven—as one of four general secretaries, alongside senior leaders Kedarnath Sahni, Krishan Lal Sharma, and Murli Manohar Joshi. Mahajan's appointment, backed by Vajpayee, reflected his growing reputation for organisational acumen and persuasive oratory.[54] Advani also brought into his team a new generation of leaders, including Sushma Swaraj, M. Venkaiah Naidu, Arun Jaitley, Narendra Modi, Rajnath Singh, K.N. Govindacharya, and Jaswant Singh.[55]

While Vajpayee admired Mahajan's political sharpness, Advani developed a fondness for the Delhi boy, Jaitley. Under Advani's leadership, Jaitley began

---

51. "India: Dates of Elections: 24, 27 and 28 December 1984", available at http://archive.ipu.org/parline-e/reports/arc/INDIA_1984_E.PDF.

52. Vijai Trivedi, "Haar Nahi Manoonga: Ek Atal Jeevan Gatha" (HarperCollins Hindi, 2016), p. 73.

53. Praveen Donthi, "Talk of the Town", *Caravan Magazine*, accessed 25 May 2025, https://caravanmagazine.in/reportage/talk-town.

54. Vinay Sitapati, *Jugalbandi: The BJP Before Modi* (Penguin, 2020), pp. 136–53.

55. L.K. Advani, *My Country, My Life* (Rupa, 2010), pp. 324–26.

to take long strides, swiftly emerging as a promising party strategist who combined political insight with legal brilliance.

★

Meanwhile, Jaitley's legal career continued its upward trajectory. The *Indian Express* case had travelled from the high court to the Supreme Court, where Jaitley argued that freedom of expression—a cornerstone of democracy and the lifeblood of a free press—must be protected from oppressive forces seeking to suppress dissent. In October 1985, the Supreme Court overturned the lieutenant governor's order. Jaitley's defence of *The Indian Express* building became a landmark case.[56]

The victory significantly boosted his professional and political standing. If his imprisonment during the Emergency had launched the young Jaitley into national political prominence, the *Indian Express* legal battle firmly established him in the legal world—at just thirty-three. It also brought him into close association with Ramnath Goenka, the newspaper's formidable owner, a relationship that would prove invaluable throughout his career.

In 1987, Jaitley once again represented *The Indian Express*—this time leading the newspaper's plea before the Delhi High Court for injunctions against striking employees accused of resorting to violence and obstruction. The court granted the injunction, restricting picketing within a fifty-metre radius of the Express building. The employees challenged the order, arguing that their strike was lawful under the Trade Unions Act, 1926, and the Industrial Disputes Act, 1947, and that a civil court had no jurisdiction in the matter. They further contended that the fifty-metre restriction effectively nullified their right to strike.

The crux of the dispute lay in whether the strike constituted legitimate labour action or unlawful coercion, and whether the court was empowered to issue such injunctions. Jaitley contended that under Section 151 of the Code of Civil Procedure, 1908, the court indeed had the authority to direct police enforcement of its orders, even if the police were not parties to the suit—citing

56. *Express Newspapers Pvt. Ltd. & Ors vs Union of India & Ors* on 7 October 1985, *Indian Kanoon*, available at https://indiankanoon.org/doc/1902038/.

precedents to substantiate his position. The court accepted Jaitley's arguments, holding that a distance restriction was necessary to prevent violence and that the suit was maintainable. It also affirmed that the court could, as Jaitley had argued, direct police to enforce its injunction.[57]

The *Indian Express* cases were only episodes in a larger confrontation unfolding through the 1980s—an era marked by growing tensions between politicians, industrialists, and media barons. Jaitley found himself repeatedly at the heart of these legal battles—sometimes assisting senior counsels, often leading from the front.

He was also drawn into a politically sensitive series of cases involving the Enforcement Directorate and Fairfax, an American detective agency reportedly hired by Finance Minister V.P. Singh to investigate illicit Indian funds stashed abroad. Jaitley, alongside senior advocate Ram Jethmalani, successfully defended S. Gurumurthy—RSS ideologue and financial advisor to Goenka—against accusations of leaking classified information to Fairfax. The charges had arisen soon after Gurumurthy published a series of hard-hitting *Indian Express* articles critical of the Congress and Reliance.[58]

Jaitley's sharp legal mind and courtroom composure soon made him one of the most sought-after advocates among top industrialists and multinational corporations. His growing stature in the legal field naturally brought him closer to the BJP's inner circle, strengthening both his professional reach and political influence.

★

Then came the breakthrough that would propel Jaitley's legal and political career to new heights. In 1987, V.P. Singh walked into Jaitley's office with Raian Karanjawala to seek his counsel. Singh had recently resigned as Rajiv Gandhi's defence minister and was facing an inquiry by Supreme Court

57. *Indian Express Newspapers (Bombay) vs T.M. Nagarajan and Ors* on 4 December 1987, *Indian Kanoon*, available at https://indiankanoon.org/doc/728395/.

58. Praveen Donthi, "Did Arun Jaitley do Enough to Investigate the Bofors Scam?", *Caravan Magazine*, accessed on 25 May 2025, https://caravanmagazine.in/politics/did-arun-jaitley-do-enough-investigate-bofors-scam.

judges M.P. Thakkar and S. Natarajan for allegedly bypassing established procedures and engaging a foreign detective agency—Fairfax, led by Michael Hershman—to investigate black money stashed abroad. Singh vehemently denied any wrongdoing.[59]

When Rajiv Gandhi became prime minister, he had appointed V.P. Singh as finance minister, a move that surprised many. His predecessor, Pranab Mukherjee, had been widely expected to retain the post after the Congress's landslide victory in December 1984. However, Rajiv excluded both Mukherjee and Arjun Singh from the Cabinet, reportedly because they had not displayed enough enthusiasm for his elevation. Explaining his decision, Rajiv remarked, "I thought we needed a change. The finance minister has to be very tough. He can't be goody-goody. I don't think he (Mukherjee) was tough enough."[60]

As finance minister, V.P. Singh lived up to Rajiv's expectations—perhaps too well. He launched an unprecedented crackdown on tax evaders and black money. Under his watch, income-tax officers, Enforcement Directorate officials, and the Directorate of Revenue Intelligence carried out widespread raids.[61] In two years, his ministry conducted nearly 6,000 raids, searched over 100,000 premises, and questioned half a million people. The drive, dubbed Operation Ketu, shook India's corporate world.[62] Singh also refused to meet industrialists privately, saying, "I did not have to raise funds for the party, so I could do what I wanted. When Rajiv Gandhi gave me the job, he knew I was incapable of raising funds."

---

59. Pankaj Pachauri, "Fairfax issue: Thakkar-Natarajan Commission report adds little to what was already known", *India Today*, accessed 25 May 2025, https://www.indiatoday.in/magazine/indiascope/story/19871231-fairfax-issue-thakkar-natarajan-commission-report-adds-little-to-what-was-already-known-799678-1987-12-30.

60. Debashish Mukerji, *The Disruptor: How Vishwanath Pratap Singh Shook India* (HarperCollins, 2021), pp. 221–22.

61. "HT This Day: April 13, 1987—V. P. Singh Resigns", *Hindustan Times*, accessed 25 May 2025, https://www.hindustantimes.com/india-news/ht-this-day-april-13-1987-v-p-singh-resigns-101649694857800.html; Ajay Singh, "An Eerie Shadow: With the Return of Raid Raj, the Spectre of VP Haunts Modi", *Governance Now*, accessed 25 May 2025, https://www.governancenow.com/news/regular-story/an-eerie-shadow-with-the-return-of-raid-raj-the-spectre-of-vp-haunts-modi.

62. Debashish Mukerji, *The Disruptor: How Vishwanath Pratap Singh Shook India* (HarperCollins, 2021), p. 224.

For his clean-up drive, Singh needed officers as firm and upright as himself and, as in his previous positions, set about finding them.[63] His biographer Debashish Mukerji later noted that Singh encouraged his officers to act freely: "He told Bhure Lal that no one was sacrosanct, that he could raid anyone—but only after thorough homework."[64]

The backlash was swift. Rajiv Gandhi, under pressure from his party and corporate allies, transferred Singh to the defence ministry, a move Singh resented but accepted dutifully. In his new role, he uncovered irregularities in a defence deal and ordered an inquiry. His decision was perceived as an attempt to embarrass Rajiv, who had previously held the defence portfolio. Soon after, the government appointed a commission led by two Supreme Court judges to investigate Singh's engagement of Fairfax. On 11 April 1987, Singh resigned as defence minister, declaring he would face the inquiry without the privileges of office.

The tide turned against the Congress within days. On 16 April 1987, Swedish Radio reported that Bofors had paid kickbacks to top Indian politicians and defence officials to secure an artillery gun contract. Rajiv Gandhi denied the allegations, but the scandal quickly snowballed into a political firestorm.

At this time, Jaitley was advising V.P. Singh—the man who would, within two years, become India's next prime minister. While representing Singh before the Thakkar–Natarajan Commission, Jaitley also capitalised on the political opportunity presented by the Bofors revelations. Alongside Ram Jethmalani and S. Gurumurthy, he was instrumental in *The Indian Express*'s bold "Ten Questions a Day" campaign, which publicly challenged Rajiv Gandhi to respond to the corruption charges.[65] When the paper doubled the list to twenty, the Congress neither sued for defamation nor issued a convincing reply.[66] The Opposition dubbed Bofors "India's Watergate"—a metaphor meant to place Rajiv in the same frame as US President Richard Nixon, who had resigned

63. Ibid., 228.

64. Ibid., 225–26.

65. Nalini Gera, *Ram Jethmalani: The Authorized Biography* (Penguin, 2003).

66. "Counsel calls it a day", *Sunday*, Vol. 21, No. 39, 25 September–1 October 1994, p. 42.

over the Watergate scandal in 1975.[67] Rajiv, however, maintained that neither he nor his family had received any payment from Bofors.[68]

Jethmalani and Jaitley's legal acumen helped V.P. Singh weather the Fairfax inquiry. The commission's report, released in December 1987, uncovered no fresh evidence but predictably indicted Singh and bureaucrats Vinod Pande and Bhure Lal for procedural lapses. It even claimed—without basis—that appointing Fairfax had endangered national security. For Jaitley, the case was another major legal success and a political windfall, further elevating his standing as a lawyer and strategist in anti-Congress circles.

A few months later, V.P. Singh rebelled. On 15 July 1987, while addressing a rally in Haridwar, he heard a Doordarshan bulletin announcing the expulsion of Arun Nehru, Arif Mohammad Khan, and V.C. Shukla from the Congress for "anti-party activities".

Arun Nehru, Rajiv's powerful cousin and former minister of state for internal security, had been one of his closest advisers. He was the great grandson of Motilal Nehru's brother Nandlal Nehru, and therefore Rajiv's third cousin. All intelligence agencies reported to him. He conceptualised the Special Protection Group for the security of the prime minister and his family members. Along with Arun Singh, another confidante of Rajiv Gandhi, Arun Nehru introduced new government departments and merged many into one.

Arif Mohammad Khan, a principled politician known for his resignation over the Shah Bano controversy, had long been at odds with the party's appeasement politics. He became an MLA on a Janata Party ticket from Siana in Uttar Pradesh at the age of twenty-six and was a deputy minister, but resigned soon over the government's handling of the Lucknow riots between Shias and

---

67. In 1972, US President Richard Nixon was caught spying on his political rivals. *The Washington Post* reporters Bob Woodward and Carl Bernstein broke the story. In June 1972, five men were arrested for breaking into the Democratic National Committee's offices at the Watergate Complex in Washington DC. At the time, sitting President Richard Nixon was running for re-election. The burglars turned out to be members of Nixon's Committee to re-elect the President, and, it would later emerge, were there to steal documents and tap the office phones. The burglars were caught red-handed by a building security guard. Nixon swore he had nothing to do with the break-in. Campaigning proceeded, then the polls. He was re-elected for his second term, in a landslide victory.

68. Aditi Phadnis, "Behind The Cover-Up", *Sunday* (Vol. 24, No. 8, 22 February–1 March 1997), p. 21.

Sunnis. He later joined the Indira faction of the Congress. In 1980, Khan—who was then an AICC joint secretary—entered Parliament for the first time and found a place in the Indira Gandhi Cabinet too, as the deputy minister in charge of information and broadcasting. The defining moment of his career came in 1986, when Khan was the minister of state in the Rajiv Gandhi-led Congress government, holding the portfolios of energy, industry and company affairs, and home. The young minister resigned after the government brought in legislation to overturn the Supreme Court judgment in the Shah Bano case.[69] Khan's stand endeared him to those on the right and a section among the progressives, but angered the Muslim clergy and his own party colleagues.

V.C. Shukla, a veteran Congressman from Madhya Pradesh, notorious for his stint as information and broadcasting minister during the Emergency, also fell out with the leadership.

The bulletin expelling Arun Nehru, Arif Mohammad Khan, and V.C. Shukla made no mention of V.P. Singh. That night and the following morning, long discussions ensued on his next step. Singh decided to quit. During a lunch stop at a colleague's home in Muzaffarnagar, he locked himself in a room, wrote his resignation from both the Congress and the Rajya Sabha, and had it cyclostyled for immediate distribution to the press. Rajiv refused to accept it, but within four days, Singh was expelled from the party.[70]

The Opposition sensed an opening. In V.P. Singh, the fragmented anti-Congress forces saw a leader who could unite them. By late 1988, Singh's breakaway group merged with the Lok Dal to form the Janata Dal. Regional parties like the Telugu Desam Party (TDP), Dravida Munnetra Kazhagam (DMK), and Asom Gana Parishad soon joined hands, forming the National Front, with N.T. Rama Rao as president and Singh as convener.[71]

When general elections were announced in November 1989, the Congress faced widespread disillusionment. The results marked a seismic political shift. The Congress was reduced from 421 to 197 seats. The Janata Dal won

---

69. Arif Mohammad Khan biography, accessed on 24 August 2025, https://indianexpress.com/about/arif-mohammad-khan/

70. Debashish Mukerji, *The Disruptor: How Vishwanath Pratap Singh Shook India* (HarperCollins, 2021), pp. 272–74.

71. L.K. Advani, *My Country, My Life* (Rupa, 2008), pp. 768–71; Kuldip Nayar, *Beyond the Lines: An Autobiography* (Roli Books Pvt. Ltd., 2012).

143, and the National Front coalition secured 146. The CPI(M) won 33 seats; and the Communist Party of India (CPI) got 12 seats.[72] The BJP, meanwhile, stunned observers by winning 85 seats from just two seats in 1984. Its vote share rose to 11.36 per cent.[73] Jaitley, who played a key role in the BJP's publicity campaign and fundraising efforts, was credited as one of the architects of this resurgence.[74]

Rajiv Gandhi, though still leading the single largest party, chose to sit in the Opposition. The BJP extended support to the National Front, and in December 1989, V.P. Singh was sworn in as India's prime minister.

★

By now, Jaitley had largely shifted his legal practice to the Supreme Court, while continuing to appear regularly before the Delhi High Court. He had bought a bigger car and hired a driver, and soon rented an apartment on Prithviraj Road in Delhi, sharing the space with senior lawyer Dushyant Dave. Around this time, he also acquired a chamber in the Delhi High Court. It was in Chambers 435 and 439—one belonging to Jaitley and the other to Rohatgi—that the two young lawyers would meet for lunch every day without fail.[75]

On 31 January 1989, Sangeeta and Arun Jaitley were blessed with their second child—a son who bore a striking resemblance to his father. They named him Rohan.

---

72. Walter K. Andersen, "Election 1989 in India: The Dawn of Coalition Politics?", *Asian Survey, Vol.* 30, No. 6 (June 1990), pp. 527–40.

73. Shantanu Gupta, *Bharatiya Janata Party: Past, Present and Future: Story of the World's Largest Political Party* (Rupa, 2020), p. 286.

74. Praveen Donthi, "Did Arun Jaitley do Enough to Investigate the Bofors Scam?", *Caravan Magazine*, accessed on 25 May 2025, https://caravanmagazine.in/politics/did-arun-jaitley-do-enough-investigate-bofors-scam.

75. Kumkum Chadha, *The Marigold Story: Indira Gandhi & Others* (Westland, 2019), p. 329/

Over the next two years, Jaitley became a trusted confidant and a "great favourite" of V.P. Singh.[76] In December 1989, when V.P. Singh became prime minister, he decided to appoint Jaitley as the additional solicitor general of India.

Jaitley already had a thriving practice but had not yet been designated a senior advocate. Although there was no legal requirement for such designation, conventionally, the post of additional solicitor general was held by a senior advocate. Mukul Rohatgi advised Jaitley to request the prime minister to delay the notification of his appointment by a day. Rohatgi then approached five senior judges of the Delhi High Court, requesting that Jaitley be designated a senior advocate—a matter of pride for the local Bar since a Delhi High Court lawyer was being appointed to such a prestigious position. The judges agreed to take it up with the Chief Justice. The Delhi High Court decided to hold a Full Court meeting by circulation—a process involving all sitting judges—to approve Jaitley's designation. By the end of the day, Arun Jaitley was a senior advocate.[77]

In January 1990, at the age of thirty-seven, he became the youngest lawyer to be appointed as a senior law officer of the country. The speed of the process was unprecedented—he had been designated a senior advocate and appointed additional solicitor general within a single day.[78] Maharaj was elated. His son had made him proud. Ratan Prabha did not understand what being designated as senior advocate or appointment as additional solicitor general meant, she did not understand these titles, but she was happy to see her husband feeling proud, and their son having earned the recognition for which congratulations were pouring in from everywhere.

By the late 1980s, Jaitley had firmly established himself as a top-tier lawyer and one of the BJP's most prominent young faces—a leader deeply rooted in the ideology of the RSS and Jana Sangh, yet capable of articulating that

76. Praveen Donthi, "Did Arun Jaitley do Enough to Investigate the Bofors Scam?", *Caravan Magazine*, accessed on 25 May 2025, https://caravanmagazine.in/politics/did-arun-jaitley-do-enough-investigate-bofors-scam.

77. On the record with Sunetra Choudhury, *Hindustan Times*, accessed on 5 September 2025, https://www.htsmartcast.com/news-podcasts/on-the-record.

78. Kumkum Chadha, *The Marigold Story: Indira Gandhi & Others* (Westland, 2019), p. 329.

philosophy in the idiom of modernity and post-Emergency politics. He had also earned the trust and respect of Prime Minister V.P. Singh. No one knew more about the Bofors pay-off scandal—or the network surrounding the alleged middleman Ottavio Quattrocchi—than Jaitley. Jaitley was appointed by Singh to lead a high-powered investigation team probing the alleged kickbacks in the 155-mm howitzer gun deal, travelling to Switzerland and Sweden in 1990 to trace the complex financial transactions. Former Enforcement Director Bhure Lal and CBI Deputy Inspector General M.K. Madhavan were also part of the team.[79] Jaitley was also called upon by Singh to advise him on an issue of national importance that was going to alter the course of Indian politics.

---

79. Pankaj Pachauri, "Bofors Inquiry: Despite Running into Unexpected Glitches, CBI Makes Considerable Progress", *India Today*, accessed 25 May 2025, https://www.indiatoday.in/magazine/special-report/story/19900831-bofors-inquiry-despite-running-into-unexpected-glitches-cbi-makes-considerable-progress-812972-1990-08-30.

6

The Ram Janmabhoomi Ordinance

V.P. Singh's political journey was nothing short of extraordinary. Born on 25 June 1931 to Bhagwati Prasad Singh and his third wife, Braj Raj Kanwar, he was the third of five sons and three daughters. Bhagwati Prasad came from a modest landowning family within the Daiya estate. However, the previous Raja of Daiya, Digvijay Singh, had named Bhagwati Prasad as his successor in his will. Following the Raja's death in 1923, his widow adopted Bhagwati Prasad, fulfilling the late Raja's wish. At that time, Daiya was a mid-sized estate, comprising seventy full villages and parts of sixty others, paying an annual revenue of Rs 40,915 to the British government in the mid-1940s. For the first five years of his life, V.P. Singh lived the typical life of a privileged child.

On 11 December 1936, he was adopted by the Raja of Manda, Ram Gopal Singh, whose estate was considerably larger than Daiya, comprising 209 villages and shares in another 187, paying an annual revenue of Rs 106,853. Manda had the largest population among the estates of Allahabad district. Despite the grandeur of Manda Fort and the sprawling Aish Mahal, V.P. Singh found himself isolated, surrounded by servants but without warmth or affection—especially a mother figure. He later described this period simply: "I was insecure, very insecure."[1]

A staunch loyalist of Indira Gandhi, Singh remained committed even after her 1977 electoral defeat, at a time when many senior Congress (R) colleagues,

---

1. Debashish Mukerji, *The Disruptor: How Vishwanath Pratap Singh Shook India* (HarperCollins, 2021), pp. 5–19.

convinced she had become a political liability, spoke against her. Singh faced personal challenges too—he had to vacate 19 Safdarjung Road after losing ministerial office. His elder son, Ajeya, had moved to London for chartered accountancy studies, while his younger son, Abhay, was preparing for the pre-medical exam at home. Singh requested an extension to stay in the house until Abhay completed his preparations, but the request was denied. The family stayed temporarily with relatives and friends, yet Singh continued to support Indira Gandhi unwaveringly. He often remarked, "We should have raised this when we were sharing power with her, and not when she has lost power… If we shared power with her during the Emergency, we should also share defeat with her. If and when she is back in power, we could take up the issue again. But when she is out of power, we should not leave her." He repeated his view at a meeting in the house of a Congress leader from Kerala, where many spoke against Indira Gandhi. "If you had integrity, you should have said all this when the Emergency was on," he told one of the Congressmen.[2]

During this period, Singh also became a source of encouragement for Indira Gandhi, urging her to resume political activity. "People are angry with you, but you are still in their hearts. Start meeting people, don't sit back," he advised. Their meetings became more frequent once Singh purchased a flat in South Delhi's Kailash Colony to provide stability for Abhay.[3] Coincidentally, Arun Jaitley would later also settle in Kailash Colony.

Within a decade in the 1980s, Singh rose from chief minister of Uttar Pradesh to holding key Union Cabinet portfolios—commerce, finance, and defence—before ultimately becoming prime minister. Between October 1974 and March 1977, he served as deputy minister and later minister of state for commerce, albeit briefly. Yet, even though his tenures were short, his impact as finance minister and defence minister under Rajiv Gandhi, and later as prime minister, along with his two-and-a-half-year period out of office, left a lasting imprint on India's political trajectory.

Singh transformed the political landscape on 7 August 1990 by implementing the recommendations of the Mandal Commission,[4] granting 27 per cent

---

2. Ibid.

3. Ibid., 126–28.

4. The Janata Party government had, in January 1979, set up a commission to identify socially or educationally backward classes of India. The commission, called the

reservation to Other Backward Classes (OBCs). While the Constitution had already provided for reservations for Scheduled Castes and Scheduled Tribes, OBCs had been excluded. This historic affirmative action policy sparked intense backlash, with upper and intermediate castes protesting for months, even resorting to self-immolation over perceived lost opportunities. Singh, though shocked by the extremity of the protests, remained steadfast: "I was prepared for the protests, not the self-immolations."[5] By 1993, OBC reservations were formally adopted, reshaping India's social and political landscape. The term "Mandalisation" emerged as a symbol of declining elitism and rising egalitarianism, empowering a new generation of backward caste leaders.

Singh's decision to implement the Mandal Commission Report was also shaped by internal political dynamics, particularly his long-standing friction with Deputy Prime Minister Devi Lal. The seventy-five-year-old Devi Lal, a powerful and independent-minded politician, frequently embarrassed Singh with controversial remarks and unilateral actions. He once described himself metaphorically: "Tau (elder uncle) is the driver if the BJP is the accelerator and the Left parties the brakes." The day before the National Front government was to introduce a Bill in Parliament to extend the period for reservation for SCs, he said: "Reservations should favour only economically weaker sections." Congress (I) MPs gleefully raised this in Parliament, much to the chagrin of the embarrassed government.[6]

Devi Lal also demanded equal say in key appointments and discretionary powers typically reserved for the prime minister, even threatening to mobilize massive crowds at India Gate. To counter this pressure, Singh decided to

---

Socially and Educationally Backward Classes Commission (SEBC Commission), was headed by an MP, B.P. Mandal, after whom it became famous as the "Mandal Commission". The commission submitted its report in December 1980, but it was not implemented by the subsequent Congress governments headed by Indira Gandhi and her son Rajiv Gandhi.

5. Debashish Mukerji, *The Disruptor: How Vishwanath Pratap Singh Shook India* (HarperCollins, 2021), p. 401.

6. Harinder Baweja, "Devi Lal Creates Controversies and Causes Embarrassment for V.P. Singh Govt", *India Today*, accessed 25 May 2025, https://www.indiatoday.in/magazine/special-report/story/19900215-devi-lal-creates-controversies-and-causes-embarrassment-for-vp-singh-govt-812362-1990-02-14.

announce the implementation of OBC reservations, a move that solidified the support of the backward classes for his minority government.[7]

L.K. Advani requested him not to announce implementation of the Mandal Commission Report before discussing its implications in the informal coordination committee comprising the leaders of the National Front, the BJP, and the Opposition parties. V.P. Singh did not agree. He could not wait, he said.[8] His minority government survived. No member of the National Front could risk being accused of pulling the rug from under V.P. Singh for the fear of losing OBC support.

The Mandal decision catalysed the rise of a new generation of OBC leaders who dominated Indian politics for the next twenty-five years, including Lalu Prasad Yadav, Mulayam Singh Yadav, Nitish Kumar, Kalyan Singh, Uma Bharti, Akhilesh Yadav, Shivraj Singh Chouhan, Ashok Gehlot, and ultimately Narendra Modi, who became the first OBC prime minister of India in 2014.

As prime minister, Singh initiated several reforms whose full potential remained unrealised due to his brief tenure. He sought to make All India Radio and Doordarshan autonomous, citing decades of government-biased reporting. In his first speech as prime minister on 3 December 1989, he promised to make them autonomous and, sure enough, in September 1990, he had the relevant Bill passed by Parliament, creating the public broadcaster Prasar Bharati to run them both. But with his government falling soon after, Prasar Bharati was eventually set up only in November 1997. Similarly, he passed the Act setting up the National Commission for Women, which became functional in January 1992. Singh also laid the groundwork for the Right to Information Act, sending officials to Sweden and Finland to study models of transparency. In his first speech as prime minister, he had declared: "Right to information will be enshrined in our Constitution … If the government functions in full public view, wrongdoings will be minimized."[9]

★

7. Kuldip Nayar, *Beyond the Lines: An Autobiography* (Roli Books Pvt. Ltd., 2012), p. 335.

8. L.K. Advani, *My Country, My Life* (Rupa, 2008), p. 446.

9. Debashish Mukerji, *The Disruptor: How Vishwanath Pratap Singh Shook India* (HarperCollins, 2021), p. 360.

It is widely believed that without the implementation of the Mandal Commission recommendations, the BJP might not have successfully leveraged the politics of the Ram Janmabhoomi movement. Or as was commonly said those days, without the politics of Mandal there would have been no politics of *kamandal*.[10] While this interpretation holds some truth, it only tells part of the story. In reality, the RSS had decided to launch the Ram Janmabhoomi campaign long before the political actions of Rajiv Gandhi or V.P. Singh created a backdrop for Hindu voters to gravitate towards the BJP. The party merely followed suit shortly thereafter.

If 1984 was a year of despair for India, 1985 initially promised hope, albeit briefly. Rajiv Gandhi, who assumed power in the aftermath of his mother's assassination, had genuine intentions of modernising India and tackling corruption—the most persistent criticism of the previous Congress government.[11] His early governance was marked by the introduction of the anti-defection law and several measures to promote integrity in public service. He sought to rejuvenate the Congress (I) with fresh talent, restructure ministries for efficiency, and retrain the bureaucracy. Economically, he pursued industrial and trade liberalization, preparing India for a prosperous twenty-first century. His administration also rolled out a new education policy, revitalised family planning initiatives, and emphasised anti-poverty programmes.

V.P. Singh's tenure as finance minister further contributed to this optimism—not through transformative economic measures but through a vigorous anti-corruption drive targeting some of India's most established corporations. By 1985, the forty-year-old, tech-savvy Rajiv Gandhi was being seen as a new star on the country's horizon. The media had hailed 1985 as the "Year of Hope" for India. Rajiv Gandhi had calmed the nation after the traumatic assassination of Indira Gandhi, addressed insurgencies in Assam and Mizoram, and sought to modernise India through technology and governance reforms. He lowered the voting age to eighteen, promoted computerisation and public call offices (PCOs)

---

10. A reference to the Ram Janmabhoomi Movement. The kamandal is a traditional Indian water pot used by ascetics, mendicants, and sages for carrying water, associated with religious figures and practices.

11. In 1985, on a visit to the drought-affected Kalahandi district in Odisha, he famously said that out of every rupee spent by the government for welfare of the downtrodden, only 15 paise actually reached the persons for whom it was intended.

in villages, and launched technology missions aimed at national development. Yet, the deep-rooted caste and community dynamics of India remained beyond his comprehension, foreshadowing political challenges ahead.[12]

Rajiv Gandhi signed accords in Punjab and Assam in 1985, followed by one in Mizoram in 1986, to address longstanding insurgencies. Punjab had been gripped by militancy, aiming for a separate Khalistan; Assam faced anti-foreigner agitations led by students demanding the deportation of illegal Bangladeshi migrants; and Mizoram's insurgency had persisted for sixteen years. In Assam, the All Assam Students' Union (AASU), led by Prafulla Kumar Mahanta and Bhrigu Phukan, directed the agitation. Their leadership was marked by remarkable integrity, guiding state-wide protests that were largely non-violent. Curfews imposed by the government were ignored by the population in obedience to AASU's directives, demonstrating the movement's discipline. When Neerja Chowdhury went to Guwahati to cover the agitation on behalf of *The Indian Express*, she was struck by their integrity and dedication. So non-violent was the agitation that at their call hundreds would line up peacefully outside the deputy commissioner's office to violate Section 144, a ban on the assembly of over five persons. The government appreciated the point that people from across the border should not be allowed to enter India without valid documents but the border between Bangladesh and India was so porous that it could be crossed at many points. The Border Security Force were also partly to blame, allowing many to infiltrate in return for a paltry bribe.[13] The Assam Accord, signed in the early hours of 15 August 1985 by the Union government, AASU, and the All Assam Gana Sangram Parishad, ended six years of agitation (1979–1985). It outlined measures to detect, disenfranchise, and deport "illegal" residents, while safeguarding Assamese cultural, social, and linguistic identity. Clause 5 specified that persons who arrived before 1 January 1966 would be regularised, those arriving between 1966 and 24 March 1971 would face a ten-year electoral exclusion, and those arriving on or after 25 March 1971 would be expelled. Clause 6 assured constitutional, legislative, and administrative safeguards for the Assamese people. The subsection 8 of Clause 5 stated: "Foreigners who came to Assam on or after March 25, 1971 shall continue to be detected, deleted and expelled in accordance with

12. Neerja Chowdhury, *How Prime Ministers Decide* (Aleph, 2003), p. xv.

13. Ibid., 114.

law. Immediate and practical steps shall be taken to expel such foreigners." Integral to Clause 5, Clause 6 of the Accord assured constitutional, legislative and administrative safeguards to "protect, preserve and promote the cultural, social, linguistic identity and heritage of the Assamese people".[14]

In Punjab, the Rajiv-Longowal Accord was signed on 24 July 1985 between Prime Minister Rajiv Gandhi and SAD president Harchand Singh Longowal, ending four turbulent years. The eleven-point agreement addressed the transfer of Chandigarh, territorial disputes between Punjab and Haryana, Ravi–Beas water disputes, referring the controversial Anandpur Sahib Resolution to the Sarkaria Commission, investigations into the 1984 anti-Sikh riots, rehabilitation of army deserters, and compensation for victims of violence since August 1982. The memorandum was tabled in the Lok Sabha within twenty minutes of its signing by a beaming prime minister, who expressed the hope that this "will bring to an end a very difficult period through which the nation has passed". Although the accord promised significant concessions to Sikhs, most were not implemented. Longowal's assassination on 20 August 1985 dealt a severe blow to peace efforts in Punjab.[15]

In 1986, the Mizoram Peace Accord resolved the insurgency by the Mizo National Front (MNF), allowing the state to move towards lasting peace and development.[16]

Rajiv Gandhi also established six technology missions under advisor Sam Pitroda—covering drinking water, immunization, literacy, oilseeds, dairy production, and telecommunications. The telecommunications mission, in particular, had a transformative impact. PCO booths proliferated across the country, connecting villages to the rest of India. In 1986, the Mahanagar Telephone Nigam Limited expanded phone access, and railway reservations were computerised, laying the groundwork for mobile telephony. By 1988, the voting age was lowered to eighteen, and initiatives were launched to devolve

---

14. Team Frontline, "1985: Assam Accord signed", *Frontline*, assessed on 24 August 2025, https://frontline.thehindu.com/politics/india-at-75-epochal-moments-1985-assam-accord-signed/article65721984.ece.

15. Jupinderjit Singh, "A Moderate, Signed Rajiv-Longowal Accord", *The Tribune*, accessed May 25, 2025, https://www.tribuneindia.com/news/punjab/a-moderate-singed-rajiv-longowal-accord/.

16. Neerja Chowdhury, *How Prime Ministers Decide* (Aleph, 2023), p. 113.

power to panchayati raj institutions, preparing a generation of women leaders for larger political roles. These bills could not be passed during Rajiv Gandhi's term.[17] Over the years, this helped create a pool of women who had acquired experience of governance in local governments—and were ready for a larger role. Rajiv Gandhi also gave the go-ahead to get India ready for nuclear testing; this was finally executed by Atal Bihari Vajpayee in 1998. Above all, Rajiv Gandhi envisioned taking India into the twenty-first century as a modern, scientifically-oriented, tech-savvy, and forward-looking nation.[18]

Despite these efforts, the early optimism began to wane. The Congress lost most assembly elections after its March 1985 victories; several chief ministers underperformed, provoking dissidence; Punjab remained volatile with militants controlling parts of the Golden Temple; tensions between Rajiv Gandhi and President Zail Singh intensified; Hindu–Muslim relations deteriorated; and India's intervention in Sri Lanka's civil war backfired.[19] Rajiv Gandhi also became overly reliant on a close-knit coterie, including his Doon School friend Arun Singh and cousin Arun Nehru. Arun Singh, from the Kapurthala royal family, and Arun Nehru, a successful young corporate leader, exerted disproportionate influence over governance and administration.

Three major controversies further undermined his premiership. First was the Shah Bano case of 1985, in which the Supreme Court ordered her husband, Mohammad Ahmed Khan, to provide maintenance.[20] The episode unfolded when Shah Bano and her five children were thrown out of the house by her husband Mohammad Ahmed Khan. Shah Bano then knocked at the doors of courts demanding maintenance. The case reached the Supreme Court. The Supreme Court directed that the Muslim divorcee be paid maintenance by her husband under the Criminal Procedure Code, 1973 (CrPC) (now

---

17. These were enacted during P.V. Narasimha Rao's premiership as the Constitution (73rd Amendment) Act, 1992 and the Constitution (74th Amendment) Act, 1992—and provided for reservation of one-third of positions in local governments for women.

18. Neerja Chowdhury, *How Prime Ministers Decide* (Aleph, 2023), pp. 113–14.

19. Debashish Mukerji, *The Disruptor: How Vishwanath Pratap Singh Shook India* (HarperCollins, 2021), p. 246.

20. Mohd. Ahmed Khan vs Shah Bano Begum And Ors on 23 April 1985, *Indian Kanoon*, available at https://indiankanoon.org/doc/823221/

Bharatiya Nagarik Suraksha Sanhita, 2023). Orthodox Muslim religious leaders and intellectuals opposed the Supreme Court verdict on the grounds that it interfered with Islamic laws. On advice from his coterie, Rajiv Gandhi enacted the Muslim Women (Protection of Rights on Divorce) Act, 1986, overturning the Court's ruling. This alienated Hindu voters and helped the BJP gain traction.

Second, realising that the Congress's response to the Shah Bano judgment had angered Hindus, Rajiv Gandhi decided to appease them. He opened the Babri Masjid gates to Hindu worshippers on 1 February 1986,[21] following a district court injunction, triggering the formation of the Babri Masjid Action Committee among Muslims. According to historical and religious accounts, Ayodhya is the Ram Janmabhoomi—the birthplace of Lord Rama. The original temple was destroyed in 1528 by Mir Baqi, a general of Babur, and the Babri structure was built on the site.[22] Hindu rituals continued around the site despite the mosque's presence, and an idol of Ram Lalla was installed under the central dome on 22 December 1949. In 1989, legal proceedings led to the unlocking of the inner courtyard gates for Hindu worshippers.

The two decisions—the revocation of the Shah Bano verdict and the reopening of the gates to the temple in Ayodhya—cost the Congress both the Hindu and Muslim vote base. However, it was the third controversy, the Bofors scandal in 1987 that tarnished Rajiv Gandhi's "Mr. Clean" image. Though no direct evidence implicated him, connections between his family and middlemen like Italian businessman Ottavio Quattrocchi raised suspicions of kickbacks in the sale of Swedish Bofors howitzers. V.P. Singh relentlessly attacked Rajiv Gandhi on Bofors during the 1989 general elections, contributing significantly to the Congress's electoral defeat.

★

---

21. "Ram Mandir Inauguration: A Look at 500-year Timeline, from Babri Masjid to Lalla Virajman", *Livemint*, accessed 25 May 2025, https://www.livemint.com/news/ram-mandir-inauguration-a-look-at-500-year-timeline-from-babri-masjid-to-lalla-virajman-11705903028037.html.

22. Arun Anand and Vinay Nalwa, *Ramjanamabhoomi: Truth, Evidence, Faith* (Prabhat Prakashan, 2020).

Unlike the relatively late entrant BJP, the RSS and the VHP had long maintained that constructing a Ram temple in Ayodhya was a matter of faith, not one for the courts. Founded in 1964 by M.S. Golwalkar, Shivaram Shankar Apte, and Swami Chinmayananda Saraswati, the VHP's mission was to "organise and consolidate Hindu society and serve and protect Hindu Dharma".[23] Over the years, it had led efforts to construct and renovate temples, prevent cow slaughter, counter religious conversions, and assert Hindu claims over Ram Janmabhoomi.[24] The VHP sought to create a central religious authority capable of mobilizing Hindus, though from 1967 to 1981, it largely receded from public view.[25]

The RSS began laying the groundwork for the Ram temple movement after the BJP's precursor, the BJS, suffered defeats in the 1980 general elections, in Delhi in 1983, and in Madhya Pradesh and Uttar Pradesh local body polls. By 1983, the VHP resurfaced, becoming increasingly active. Between November and December that year, it organised a nationwide procession, carrying pots of Ganga water across the country.[26] Water was distributed in villages along the way and replaced with local river or temple water at each stop—a symbolic effort to unite diverse Hindu rituals and geographies.[27] This marked the formal beginning of the Ayodhya movement. The procession was so successful that it became the blueprint for L.K. Advani's famous yatra seven years later. On 7 April 1984, the VHP held a dharma sansad, deciding among other things to "liberate" Ram in Ayodhya from Muslim control.[28]

The BJP's decisive engagement began after its humiliating defeat in the 1984 general elections following Indira Gandhi's assassination. The RSS interpreted the results as evidence that the Hindu vote had swung to Congress, providing it a "massive Hindu mandate". "It was a conscious Hindu vote, consciously

---

23. Swagatam, Vishva Hindu Parishad, https://vhp-kashiprant.org/Home.

24. Shantanu Gupta, *Bharatiya Janata Party: Past, Present and Future: Story of the World's Largest Political Party* (Rupa, 2020), p. 263.

25. Vinay Sitapati, *Jugalbandi: The BJP Before Modi* (Penguin, 2020), p. 128.

26. Manjari Katju, *Vishva Hindu Parishad and Indian Politics, 2nd Ed.* (Orient Blackswan, 2010), p. 38.

27. Peter Van Der Veer, "'God Must be Liberated!' A Hindu Liberation Movement in Ayodhya", *Modern Asian Studies*, Vol. 21, No. 2 (1987), pp. 283–301, at 292.

28. L.K. Advani, *My Country, My Life* (Rupa, 2008), p. 363.

and deliberately solicited by the Congress party as a Hindu party." And this is what "decimated the 'revisionist' BJP and reincarnated Congress (I) as BJP".[29] Determined to reclaim this constituency, the RSS and BJP sought to advance the Ram temple cause. In November 1989, the VHP performed a shilanyas (foundation-laying) ceremony at the Ram temple site, supported by the BJP. Holy bricks, known as Ramshilas, were brought from across India in preparation for constructing a granite temple costing Rs 55 crore. The permission was granted by the Congress government. At a Haridwar meeting in June 1990, the VHP announced 30 October 1990 as a "non-negotiable" date for the temple's construction.[30]

Between 1986 and 1989, the BJP gradually aligned with the Ayodhya movement. Initial resistance within the party, including scepticism of Advani's Hindu-centric approach, gave way when the BJP national executive met in Palampur, Himachal Pradesh, in June 1989. The party passed a resolution supporting the Ram Janmabhoomi movement, asserting that the dispute could not be resolved by courts alone.[31] The resolution called upon the Rajiv Gandhi government to respect Hindu sentiments, akin to the approach taken for Somnath, and to hand over the site—preferably through negotiation or legislation:

> The BJP holds that the nature of the (Ayodhya) controversy is such that it just cannot be sorted out by a court of law. ... The BJP calls upon the Rajiv Gandhi government to adopt the same positive approach in respect of Ayodhya that the Nehru government did with respect to Somnath. The sentiments of the people must be respected, and Ram Janmasthan [Ram's birthplace] handed over to the Hindus—if possible through a negotiated settlement, or else by legislation. Litigation certainly has no answer.[32]

---

29. "A Massive Hindu Mandate", *Organiser*, Vol. 36, 34 (6 January 1985), p. 1.
30. "BJP's White Paper on Ayodhya & The Ram Temple Movement", April 1993, accessed on 3 September 2025, www.liberalpartyofindia.sabhlokcity.com.
31. Kanchan Gupta, "A Chariot in History", *Open*, accessed on 3 September 2025, https://openthemagazine.com/cover-stories/a-chariot-in-history/.
32. Bharatiya Janata Party, accessed on 3 September 2025, https://www.bjp.org/files/kamal-sandesh-documents/ks-oct-e-02-2010_1.pdf.

The BJP emphasised that Hindus had long lived with the hope of a temple at the site, and historical circumstances, including Mughal and British interference, had prevented it from being realised. The party contended that during the War of Independence against the British in 1857, Muslims had accepted the Hindu claim to build a temple on the site in view of their sentiments and that the British, who believed in the policy of divide and rule, did not let the agreement fructify. The BJP's resolution also said Muslims should forgo their claim on the Ram Janmabhoomi, keeping in mind Hindu sentiments. The party declared that it would take the matter of the temple in its own hands. The BJP attacked the Congress for having a callous attitude towards the sentiments of the overwhelming majority in this country—the Hindus. The party demanded that the Ram temple be built at the site and included the temple construction on its agenda.[33] While advocating temple construction, the party insisted it should not hurt Muslim sentiments.

The Palampur session marked a turning point, setting the stage for a nationwide agitational program. In the 1989 general elections, contesting 226 of 529 seats, the BJP's tally rose from two to 85 seats, signalling the growing resonance of its Hindutva message. After V.P. Singh took the Mandal decision in August 1990, the BJP started recalibrating its strategy. In September 1990, Advani launched the Ram Rath Yatra, starting on 25 September—coinciding with Pandit Deendayal Upadhyaya's birth anniversary—from Somnath in Gujarat, a site historically associated with the eleventh-century plunder by Mahmud Ghaznavi and symbolically rebuilt in 1950 by Sardar Vallabhbhai Patel. The yatra was designed to culminate in Ayodhya for the VHP's planned temple ceremony on 30 October 1990.[34]

Advani's rath, a Toyota truck converted into a chariot and fitted with loudspeakers, travelled through ten states, with devotional music and messages broadcast along the way. Lata Mangeshkar recorded a bhajan and Manoj Kumar recorded messages. Both were played on the loudspeakers as the rath trundled through districts and villages of India's hinterland, entering cities and towns to thunderous applause by ecstatic crowds. The campaign drew

---

33. Prabhat Jha (Ed.), "Kamal Sandesh" (October 2010), available at https://www.bjp.org/files/kamal-sandesh-documents/ks-oct-e-02-2010_1.pdf.

34. "Ram Rath Yatra", Bharatiya Janata Party, assessed 25 May 2025, https://www.bjp.org/ram-rath-yatra.

massive crowds, evoking the imagery of Ramanand Sagar's televised *Ramayan*. The movement became India's largest mass mobilization since Independence, cementing Ayodhya as a non-negotiable symbol of Hindu aspirations.[35] BJP leaders, workers, and sympathisers showed up in force to amplify the impact of the yatra. As the rath rolled on, it became increasingly clear that the question of building a Ram temple deeply touched the emotional chords of the majority of the community.[36] The yatra succeeded in mobilising the Hindutva forces.[37]

Narendra Modi and Arun Jaitley emerged as key organisers—Modi managing the route through 600 villages in Gujarat, and Jaitley preparing daily press briefings.[38] The yatra received a rousing reception in rural parts of Gujarat, with crowds thronging the way. Surrounded by a sea of saffron flags and lakhs of supporters, Advani couldn't hear his own voice, such was the din.[39] Modi's team had spread the word effectively. The BJP succeeded in capturing the imagination of the print media which played up the significance of this yatra. Modi and Jaitley came in the limelight for their excellent management of the yatra. The yatra captured widespread media attention, amplifying its impact and demonstrating the BJP's growing political clout.

Simultaneously, the VHP launched the Shri Ram Jyoti Yatra. That year Vijayadasami was on 28 September. The VHP took out various rallies and reached out to people in almost every nook and corner of India. Then the Diwali festival followed on 18 October, and the VHP gave a call to light a lamp for Shri Ram Lalla of Ayodhya in every home, a Ram Jyoti. Devotthan Ekadasi of 1990 would fall on 30 October. Sants and sadhus resolved to commence the construction of the temple at the location where the sacred idols of Ram

---

35. Kanchan Gupta, "A Chariot in History", *Open*, accessed on 3 September 2025, https://openthemagazine.com/cover-stories/a-chariot-in-history/.

36. Atal Bihari Vajpayee, *Four Decades in Parliament*, Vol. 1, ed. N.M. Ghatate (Shipra Publications, 1996), p. xxxi.

37. "1990: Lal Krishna Advani embarks on rath yatra", Frontline, accessed on September 3, 2025.

38. Ajay Singh, "The first sightings of an organiser: How Modi surprised Advani with his organisational skills", *First Post*, accessed on 3 September 2025, https://www.firstpost.com/opinion/the-first-sightings-of-an-organiser-how-modi-surprised-advani-with-his-organisational-skills-10917931.html.

39. Rahul Shrivastava, "BJP Journeys On, Forgets Yatri Advani", NDTV, accessed on 3 September 2025.

Lalla were placed on that day. Advani had already announced that the Rath Yatra would culminate at Ayodhya on 30 October. The combined energy of the Advani Rath Yatra and VHP campaigns created a euphoric "Rama wave", galvanizing Hindu sentiment across India.[40]

★

Alarmed by the momentum the Rath Yatra was gaining, V.P. Singh and his National Front colleagues began trying to curtail it. The Ayodhya issue had become the focal point of national debate, with many Hindus and Muslims believing it should be resolved through dialogue between religious leaders, without political interference.[41]

On 15 October 1990, V.P. Singh called Jaitley—whom he trusted—to discuss the matter. He also summoned Swaminathan Gurumurthy, a longtime RSS member who had worked with Singh when the latter was finance minister. Gurumurthy flew from Madras (now Chennai) to Delhi for the meeting.[42] After intensive consultations with party bosses and the RSS, Jaitley and Gurumurthy proposed a three-point solution.

First, of the approximately 70 acres of the proposed temple complex, only 2.5 acres were disputed; the remaining 67 acres, on which shilanyas had been performed in 1989 with the approval of the Rajiv Gandhi government, were undisputed. It was proposed that the central government acquire the entire 70 acres, handing over the undisputed 67 acres for kar seva.

Second, the disputed structure would remain under central government control in its current state, along with a 30-foot surrounding area.

Third, the government would make a single-point reference to the Supreme Court under Article 143 of the Constitution to determine if a temple had historically existed on the site. A question of faith, such as whether Lord Ram

---

40. Aravindan Neelakandan, "Ayodhya: Everything That Happened Before 30 October 1990", *Swarajya*, accessed 25 May 2025, https://swarajyamag.com/politics/ayodhya-everything-that-happened-before-30-october-1990.

41. L.K. Advani, *My Country, My Life* (Rupa, 2008), p. 380.

42. Debashish Mukerji, *The Disruptor: How Vishwanath Pratap Singh Shook India* (HarperCollins, 2021), p. 412.

was born there, would be excluded.[43] On 30 October, a symbolic kar seva could be performed near the disputed structure, involving prayers and laying a few bricks without commencing construction. Singh accepted this proposal, and Gurumurthy communicated the plan to the temple leaders, and relayed back their acceptance to the prime minister.[44]

Advani was in Delhi for a Diwali break during the Rath Yatra. He arrived on 14 October, planning to resume from Dhanbad on 20 October, travelling there by train, with the rath having already been transported beforehand.[45] V.P. Singh spoke to Advani and requested him to halt the yatra pending the ordinance. Advani, who was to leave on the evening of 18 October 1990, agreed.[46] He had intended to spend a day in Calcutta (now, Kolkata) before resuming his yatra from Dhanbad on 20 October, but cancelled the visit.[47]

Over the next four days, marathon meetings took place between government representatives, the RSS, the BJP, the VHP, and Hindu and Muslim leaders, with intermediaries like Jaitley and Gurumurthy shuttling between them. On 17 October, an all-party meeting convened by the prime minister was boycotted by the BJP (on ideological grounds) and the Congress (due to Rajiv Gandhi's animosity towards V.P. Singh).[48]

After much persuasion, V.P. Singh agreed to promulgate an ordinance on the three-point solution agreed earlier with Gurumurthy and Jaitley. A draft ordinance was finalised at the Cabinet secretary's residence at 5 a.m. the following day. Jaitley and Gurumurthy approved the draft. At 10 a.m., the Cabinet met at the prime minister's residence and approved the ordinance and the three-point solution.[49] But the ordinance was not promulgated despite its

---

43. L.K. Advani, *My Country, My Life* (Rupa, 2008), pp. 380–85.

44. Debashish Mukerji, *The Disruptor: How Vishwanath Pratap Singh Shook India* (HarperCollins, 2021), pp. 411–20.

45. Ibid.

46. L.K. Advani, *My Country, My Life* (Rupa, 2008), pp. 380–85.

47. Debashish Mukerji, *The Disruptor, How Vishwanath Pratap Singh Shook India* (HarperCollins, 2021), pp. 411–20.

48. Aravindan Neelakandan, "Ayodhya: Everything That Happened Before 30 October 1990", *Swarajya*, accessed 25 May 2025, https://swarajyamag.com/politics/ayodhya-everything-that-happened-before-30-october-1990.

49. L.K. Advani, *My Country, My Life* (Rupa, 2008), pp. 380–85.

approval by the Cabinet. On 18 October, disappointed with V.P. Singh's dilly-dallying, Advani boarded the Rajdhani Express from Delhi to continue the Rath Yatra in Bihar.

Lalu Prasad Yadav, Bihar's chief minister, initially planned to halt the Rajdhani Express and arrest Advani, but Singh dissuaded him.[50] Vajpayee, considered a moderate, was asked by the Intelligence Bureau to persuade Advani to stop. In their presence, Vajpayee phoned Advani via landline, announcing after a brief discussion that Advani would not halt the Rath Yatra.[51]

Jaitley and Gurumurthy were summoned again to Delhi to resolve further complications. When Gurumurthy spoke to Singh on telephone on his arrival in Delhi, Singh's tone was markedly different from before. "He said that not just the disputed structure, but all the land taken over would remain with the government and would not be handed over to the Ayodhya movement," recounted Gurumurthy to Singh's biographer Debashish Mukerji.[52] This time, V.P. Singh was assisted by four senior ministers—George Fernandes, Arun Nehru, Ajit Singh—the president of the Rashtriya Lok Dal (RLD) and son of Charan Singh—and Dinesh Goswami. Goswami, who was then the law minister, argued that it was not possible to issue the ordinance because of the multiplicity of lawsuits and hundreds of contentious issues involved.

Once again, it required Gurumurthy and Jaitley "to rescue the kernel from the welter of inessential information". The "hundreds of contentious issues", they explained, fell under just three heads: one, whether Lord Ram was born at the disputed site; two, whether a Hindu structure existed at the disputed site; and three, to whom did the different lands adjacent to the disputed site belong.

The first question, Jaitley explained, was not capable of judicial solution or even legislative determination. The second question lent itself to judicial opinion or verdict, based on an examination of the evidence and records available. The third aspect was capable of legislative action under the government's undisputed power of compulsory acquisition. This explanation

50. Aravindan Neelakandan, "Ayodhya: Everything That Happened Before 30 October 1990", *Swarajya*, accessed 25 May 2025, https://swarajyamag.com/politics/ayodhya-everything-that-happened-before-30-october-1990.

51. Ibid.

52. Debashish Mukerji, *The Disruptor: How Vishwanath Pratap Singh Shook India* (HarperCollins, 2021), p. 415.

was so logical and irrefutable that the prime minister and his colleagues had no arguments against it. The government decided to go ahead with the ordinance and informed the nation of its decision to issue the ordinance through a late-night press release.[53]

N.T. Rama Rao—who was no longer Andhra Pradesh chief minister, having lost the 1989 assembly elections, but remained as the National Front chairman—had also arrived in Delhi to help resolve the crisis. He personally met Advani to urge him to halt the yatra. Advani refused, and Rao staged a sit-in outside his house until health complications forced him to be hospitalised.[54]

The Ram Janmabhoomi Ordinance was finally promulgated on 19 October 1990, taking over the 70 acres, including the disputed structure. Arif Mohammad Khan expressed scepticism about Muslim acceptance, but Singh assured him that key Muslim leaders, including Syed Shahabuddin, had been consulted.

A diplomat by career, Shahabuddin took premature retirement in the 1970s to enter politics. As a diplomat, he had lobbied for the creation of Bangladesh and rallied support in Latin America, where he was posted at that time, for Indian intervention. Although considered to be in the good books of the then Prime Minister Indira Gandhi, he was one of the few diplomats who were openly anti-Emergency. Within eight months of relinquishing service, Shahabuddin was elected to the Lok Sabha in 1979 from Kishanganj in Bihar, a Muslim-majority constituency that sent him to Lok Sabha multiple times. He was at the forefront of the movement from the Muslim side.[55]

Events took a dramatic turn within forty-eight hours. According to Singh's biographer Debashish Mukerji, a meeting of the Babri Masjid Action Committee leaders was convened in Delhi. Muslim leaders had all come to Delhi from different parts of the country and checked into hotels, which the government had arranged for them. They opposed the idea vehemently. Uttar Pradesh Chief Minister Mulayam Singh Yadav warned that his government

---

53. L.K. Advani, *My Country, My Life* (Rupa, 2008), pp. 380–85.

54. Debashish Mukerji, *The Disruptor: How Vishwanath Pratap Singh Shook India* (HarperCollins, 2021), pp. 413–15.

55. "Ex-diplomat and former MP Syed Shahabuddin dies at 82", *India Today*, accessed on 24 August 2025, https://www.indiatoday.in/india/story/mp-syed-shahabuddin-dead-963955-2017-03-04.

would not allow the Centre to take possession of the area around the disputed structure. V.P. Singh was shocked at the volte-face.[56]

On the evening of 19 October 1990, immediately after Advani left Delhi, Mulayam had telephoned V.P. Singh to say he was set to halt the Rajdhani Express at Rura, 55 kilometre short of Kanpur, which it would reach around 8.30–9 p.m., and detain Advani forthwith.[57] Mulayam mulled the decision with the state police chief and chief secretary. Both understood the mood of their political boss and agreed that the state government could arrest Advani.

Mulayam sent for Nripendra Misra, the then principal secretary in his government to seek his advice. Misra, to the surprise of the three men, disagreed. He said the government had no "cause" to arrest Advani because the leader had not explicitly preached disharmony. Mulayam was enraged, but before he could reprimand the bureaucrat, the phone rang, with the Janata Dal leader and Mulayam's mentor, Chandra Shekhar, on the line.[58] He too advised Mulayam against arresting Advani. Mulayam relented.[59]

V.P. Singh realised that if the Babri Masjid's surroundings were transferred to the VHP, as he had earlier agreed to, and did so against the wishes of both the Muslim leaders and Mulayam, his own Muslim support would ebb drastically. By the morning of 21 October 1990, V.P. Singh decided that there was no point in the government keeping the land either, and convened another Cabinet meeting to get its consent to take back his own ordinance.[60] "I thought, what is the point of the ordinance if neither Hindus nor Muslims are happy about it, when it has not built confidence on either side? So I withdrew it,"[61]

---

56. Debashish Mukerji, *The Disruptor: How Vishwanath Pratap Singh Shook India* (HarperCollins, 2021), pp. 413–15.

57. Ibid., 298–317.

58. Modi appointed Nripendra Misra as his principal secretary when he became the prime minister in 2014. He was later appointed as the chairman of the Ram Temple Construction Committee by Shri Ram Janmabhoomi Teerth Kshetra Trust.

59. Archis Mohan, "Modi's Handpicked Men", *Business Standard*, accessed 25 May 2025, https://www.business-standard.com/article/specials/modi-s-handpicked-men-114060601120_1.html.

60. Debashish Mukerji, *The Disruptor: How Vishwanath Pratap Singh Shook India* (HarperCollins, 2021), pp. 298–317.

61. Ibid.

Singh is stated to have told Mukerji. V.P. Singh government's withdrawal of the Ordinance on 21 October, within forty-eight hours of its promulgation, came as a big disappointment and betrayal to the leaders and followers of the temple movement.[62]

In the meantime, the BJP national executive met in Delhi on 17 October 1990—which Advani also attended. It was decided if Advani was arrested, support to the V.P. Singh government would be withdrawn.

Meanwhile, the yatra had moved on from Dhanbad and Gaya and reached Patna on 22 October. Advani addressed a mammoth crowd at Gandhi Maidan. As he was addressing the meeting, there was a public address broadcast by V.P. Singh. He said that the nation was in a communally dangerous situation. The speech was dark and ominous. It was clear what the intention was. There was also an indirect appeal to the Congress MPs to support him if the BJP were to withdraw its support. It was evident that Lalu Prasad and, consequently, V.P. Singh would claim credit for halting the Rath Yatra. However, there was no indication of Advani's arrest.[63]

A day earlier, Lalu Prasad Yadav sought V.P. Singh's consent to detain Advani. V.P. Singh asked Lalu to make all preparations for Advani's detention, without actually taking the step, and then called him again on 22 October 1990 directing him to go ahead, advising only that the arrest be carried out after 2 a.m. In that pre-internet age, with television being state-controlled, V.P. Singh hoped, thus, to prevent news of the arrest from appearing in the morning's newspapers, since all newspapers would have closed their editions by then. This would give state governments enough time to make security arrangements to meet possible protests before RSS/BJP/VHP supporters found out and reacted.[64]

Soon after 2 a.m. on 23 October 1990, the Bihar police stopped Advani as his yatra was approaching Samastipur town, taking him away immediately by helicopter to a guesthouse on the Bihar–Bengal border. Advani was presented with an arrest warrant by the district magistrate. He requested a few minutes,

---

62. L.K. Advani, *My Country, My Life* (Rupa, 2008), pp. 380–85.

63. Aravindan Neelakandan, "Ayodhya: Everything That Happened Before 30 October 1990", *Swarajya*, accessed 25 May 2025, https://swarajyamag.com/politics/ayodhya-everything-that-happened-before-30-october-1990

64. Debashish Mukerji, *The Disruptor: How Vishwanath Pratap Singh Shook India* (HarperCollins, 2021), pp. 298–317.

during which he wrote a letter to the President of India declaring that the BJP was withdrawing its support from the V.P. Singh government.[65] Hours later, Vajpayee submitted the letter to the President, signalling party unity despite personal opposition to the move.[66] Street protests, which began only in the late afternoon and were not as large as V.P. Singh had feared, were quickly contained.

The yatra continued unabated. On 26 October, Keshubhai Patel, Narendra Modi, and other BJP leaders resigned from Gujarat's coalition government and marched to the governor's residence, shouting slogans like '*Bharat mata ki jai*', displaying a large picture of L.K. Advani in chains, pledging before Sardar Vallabhbhai Patel's statue that "Ram Mandir Shall Be Built!"[67] Despite Advani's arrest, the movement's momentum grew, with Mulayam Singh ordering the detention of 150,000 activists heading towards Ayodhya.[68]

★

V.P. Singh did not resign immediately, expecting Congress support while trying to sustain secularism. However, the Congress did not oblige, and he lost the vote of confidence in Parliament on 7 November 1990. Isolated—dumped by the BJP and outside the Congress ecosystem—V.P. Singh slipped into political wilderness, largely neglected in public memory. Even his political heirs—leaders of Janata Dal splinter parties such as Mulayam Singh Yadav (Samajwadi Party, SP) and Lalu Prasad Yadav (Rashtriya Janata Dal, RJD), who reaped enormous benefits from the Mandal politics—did little to commemorate him. His legacy thus remains paradoxical: a transformative political leader,

---

65. Aravindan Neelakandan, "Ayodhya: Everything That Happened Before 30 October 1990", *Swarajya*, accessed 25 May 2025, https://swarajyamag.com/politics/ayodhya-everything-that-happened-before-30-october-1990.

66. Vinay Sitapati, *Jugalbandi: The BJP Before Modi* (Penguin, 2020), p. 162.

67. Modi Archive on X, https://x.com/modiarchive/status/1748925220998508602.

68. Shyma Rauf, "Advani's Ram Rath Yatra: The Chariot of Chaos on the Road to Disorder", *Deccan Herald*, accessed 25 May 2025, https://www.deccanherald.com/india/advanis-ram-rath-yatra-the-chariot-of-chaos-on-the-road-to-disorder-2858918#google_vignette.

yet barely remembered by the very forces he helped unleash. Despite this, V.P. Singh remained an admirer of Arun Jaitley, and they stayed in touch personally.

On 10 November 1990, Chandra Shekhar became prime minister with outside support from the Congress. Jaitley resigned as additional solicitor general on 22 November 1990 after the BJP withdrew support from the National Front. Chandra Shekhar lasted only seven months before Rajiv Gandhi pulled the rug from under his government. While Chandra Shekhar continued to be elected from his Ballia constituency in Uttar Pradesh, his relevance in national politics diminished.

Jaitley had been at the centre of the events preceding the fall of the V.P. Singh government. He and his BJP colleagues had persuaded Singh to promulgate the Ram Janmabhoomi Ordinance, paving the way for temple construction—a move the government later withdrew, estranging relations with the BJP. The withdrawal disappointed millions of Hindus and altered the course of history; had the ordinance persisted, the Ram Janmabhoomi Temple and Babri Masjid might well have stood next to each other today.

The year 1990 also became a landmark for the BJP. Assembly elections were held in ten states and union territories: Bihar, Gujarat, Madhya Pradesh, Himachal Pradesh, Maharashtra, Manipur, Odisha, Puducherry, Arunachal Pradesh, and Rajasthan. Except for Arunachal Pradesh, the BJP contested all, improving its tally in Bihar, Gujarat, and Maharashtra. The party formed governments in Madhya Pradesh, Himachal Pradesh, and Rajasthan—securing absolute majorities in Madhya Pradesh (220 seats) and Himachal Pradesh (56 seats). In Rajasthan, the BJP won 85 seats, while Congress fell to 50 seats, and Janata Dal won 55; the BJP formed the government with allied support. In Maharashtra, the BJP increased its tally from 14 in 1980 to 42 seats, but it failed to win any in Manipur or Puducherry. With these victories, the stage was set for the BJP's rise: it now had governments in three states, while Janata Dal held power in five, including Rajasthan in alliance with the BJP.[69]

By this time, Jaitley had completed a decade in the BJP, already making a mark as a party worker, legal professional, and negotiator. Serving as the country's law officer at the young age of thirty-seven, his efforts in the Ram Janmabhoomi Ordinance negotiations showcased his astute legal acumen and

69. Shantanu Gupta, *Bharatiya Janata Party: Past, Present and Future: Story of the World's Largest Political Party* (Rupa, 2020), p. 269.

established him as a key strategist within the party.[70] It was time to climb the ladder in the party ranks.

But Jaitley suffered a setback in his personal life. Ratan Prabha passed away in February 1991, leaving an everlasting void in Jaitley's life. Every time, he crossed a milestone, Jaitley missed his mother. There is no joy greater for a child, however old the child may have grown, than watching the exhilaration in a mother's eyes on learning of her child's accomplishments.

---

70. Nilanjan Mukhopadhyay, "Jaitley: Modi's valued friend who wore many hats", *Deccan Herald*, accessed on 3 September 2025, https://www.deccanherald.com/opinion/jaitley-modis-valued-friend-who-wore-many-hats-756694.html.

7

Emergence of the Young Turks (1991–99)

As the BJP moved into the 1990s, another phase of hard work started for its leaders. The decade proved to be eventful for the country and its politics. In 1991, India faced a foreign reserves crisis, forced to pledge its gold to secure a bailout from the International Monetary Fund (IMF). The Congress Prime Minister P.V. Narasimha Rao introduced big-ticket reforms, opening the country's economy to globalisation, liberalisation, and privatisation. The BJP witnessed a steady rise since its formation in 1980. Between 1990 and 1996, it formed governments in many states and also increased its tally in the Lok Sabha all this while.

The BJP did fabulously in Uttar Pradesh, winning 221 out of 424 seats in 1991, with Kalyan Singh taking the oath as the BJP's first chief minister in the state.[1] In between, the country witnessed the demolition of the Babri Masjid in December 1992 leading to the arrest of Advani, Murli Manohar Joshi, and other senior BJP leaders. The discovery of a businessman S.K. Jain's diary created a political storm, the Hawala scandal, leading to the resignation of Advani from the Lok Sabha in 1996 followed by the appointment of Madan Lal Khurana as the chief minister of Delhi. Advani vowed not to enter Parliament till his name was cleared.

The BJP formed its first government in the Centre in 1996 under Vajpayee albeit for thirteen days. The United Front formed a government led by H.D.

---

1. Shantanu Gupta, *Bharatiya Janata Party: Past, Present and Future: Story of the World's Largest Political Party* (Rupa, 2020), p. 269.

Deve Gowda for one year (1996–97) and the next by I.K. Gujral (1997–98) which too lasted a year. Vajpayee became the prime minister for the second time in March 1998 for thirteen months.

India conducted five nuclear tests in Pokhran (Rajasthan) on 11–13 May 1998. Pakistan incursion in the Kargil sector—the highest battlefields in the world, in May 1999—led to the three-month-long war; it ended on 26 July 1999 with India reclaiming its territories. Finally, the BJP formed a government at the end of the decade in 1999 with Vajpayee as prime minister on 13 October 1999, which was to last a full term of five years with Vajpayee becoming the first non-Congress prime minister to complete a full five-year term. In October 1999, Jaitley was handed over his first ministerial assignment.

An Indian Airlines flight, IC 814, with 178 passengers on board travelling from Kathmandu to Delhi was hijacked on 24 December 1999 and finally landed in Kandahar in Taliban ruled Afghanistan. The Indian government had to release three terrorists in exchange for passengers.

From the grind of the 1990s emerged the Young Turks of the party—Pramod Mahajan, Arun Jaitley, M. Venkaiah Naidu, and Sushma Swaraj. All four, with extraordinary individual political attributes, went on to become ministers under Vajpayee in this decade. The rise of Mahajan and Jaitley in the party ranks was exponential. Jaitley also emerged as one of the finest speakers of the party and went on to become the BJP spokesperson. Modi was, in the meantime, assigned to strengthen the party all over the country. He would go on to become the chief minister of Gujarat at the start of the next century.

This was also the decade when Jaitley lost his father. He passed away on 23 May 1994. Maharaj was very proud of his son but chose to remain in the background even as Jaitley rose to national prominence. His life was marked by perseverance and quiet dedication, virtues that he passed on to his children.

★

Jaitley's instrumental role in boosting the BJP's tally from just two seats in 1984 to 85 in 1989, his effective management of Advani's Rath Yatra, and his negotiations on the Ram Janmabhoomi Temple Ordinance solidified his reputation as a formidable strategist, alongside Pramod Mahajan.

Chandra Shekhar had just begun consolidating his government when the Congress withdrew support, leading to its collapse after only seven months. General elections were announced for May 1991, to be held in three phases—on 20, 23, and 26 May. In January 1991, Advani appointed Jaitley to the BJP national executive. Headed by the party president, the national executive included various office-bearers—one general secretary (organisation), one treasurer, up to nine general secretaries, fifteen secretaries, and thirteen vice presidents nominated by the president. At thirty-nine, Jaitley became part of the party's key decision-making body at a time when the leadership was largely composed of the old guard, with Pramod Mahajan as the only other young leader, promoted to general secretary at thirty-seven. Jaitley now assisted senior leaders in drafting political and economic resolutions.

Advani was impressed by Jaitley's eloquence. Urbane and versatile, with fluency in English and Hindi, Jaitley could connect with both English-speaking audiences and the aspirational middle class emerging after economic liberalisation. Later that year, Advani appointed him as the party's spokesperson for the elections. Jaitley articulated arguments sharply and succinctly, often coining phrases that made compelling headlines. His points were well-structured, often infused with wit and humour, and he maintained dignity without resorting to personal attacks,[2] earning the admiration of media and public alike—a reputation he retained until his death in 2019.

The 1991 Lok Sabha elections were conducted against the backdrop of the Ram Rath Yatra. Advani decided to contest from both New Delhi and Gandhinagar in Gujarat. The Congress fielded the former Hindi cinema superstar Rajesh Khanna against Advani in New Delhi—a last-minute move that surprised Advani. Previously, Ambika Soni had been considered, but Rajiv Gandhi insisted on Khanna. Despite preferring to contest from Thane in Bombay, Khanna agreed to Delhi, requiring Advani to recalibrate his campaign strategy.[3] Jaitley, with his strong connections in the city, was appointed a key campaign manager.

---

2. Nitin Gadkari, "Arun Jaitley Helped BJP Set the Narrative", in *The Discussant: Journal of Centre for Reforms, Development and Justice*, Special Edition, An Obituary to Arun Jaitley, Vol. VII, No. 3 (July–September 2019), pp. 20–22.

3. Pankaj Vohra, "Rajesh Khanna: The Politician and the Phenomenon", *Hindustan Times*, assessed 25 May 2025, https://www.hindustantimes.com/delhi/rajesh-

Jaitley admired both Advani and Vajpayee. While he respected Vajpayee's democratic spirit, liberal outlook, and exceptional oratory that could simplify complex issues, he was equally impressed by Advani's Hindu nationalist vision, shaped by the extremities of Partition and his personal experiences as a young refugee. Drawing inspiration from Vajpayee's communication style, Jaitley developed his own sharp, witty, and impactful approach. Like Jaitley, Advani had also benefited from his good command of English. He was, perhaps, the only senior party leader in those days who could expertly handle the English media and represent his party on forums outside their Hindu nationalist milieu.[4] Both Advani and Jaitley shared fluency in English, love for books, cricket, good food, and movies.

On 21 May 1991, the day after the first polling phase, Rajiv Gandhi was assassinated in Sriperumbudur, Tamil Nadu, by an LTTE suicide bomber. The remaining two phases of the elections were held under the shadow of this tragic event, generating a sympathy wave for the Congress. Ultimately, Congress won 232 seats, while the BJP emerged as the main opposition with over 120 seats, and Janata Dal secured 69. The BJP's vote share nearly doubled from 11.36 per cent in 1989 to 20.11 per cent in 1991, proving the effectiveness of its new strategies. In Uttar Pradesh, where Ram temple sentiments ran high, the BJP won 51 of 85 seats.[5]

Jaitley worked tirelessly to ensure Advani's victory. Khanna performed well, claiming some assembly segments like Minto Road and Gole Market, but Advani retained key areas such as Lajpat Nagar, Sewa Nagar, and Amar Colony.[6]

---

khanna-the-politician-and-the-phenomenon/story-6or0NKQnVDNXgb7JPlvdQJ.html.

4. Bhaskar Roy, "Advani's Wife Told Him She Won't Marry Him if He Came Wearing Dhoti-Kurta", *The Print*, accessed 25 May 2025, https://theprint.in/pageturner/excerpt/advanis-wife-told-him-she-wont-marry-him-if-he-came-wearing-dhoti-kurta/1973532/.

5. Shyamlal Yadav, "Held after Rajiv Gandhi's assassination, how the 1991 elections heralded change for India under PV Narasimha Rao", *The Indian Express*, accessed 21 August 2025, https://indianexpress.com/article/explained/explained-politics/how-the-narasimha-rao-years-changed-india-9336116/.

6. Vivek Shukla, "Recalling the Bollywood Showdown for New Delhi: Kaka vs Shotgun", *Patriot*, accessed 25 May 2025, https://thepatriot.in/reports/recalling-the-bollywood-showdown-for-new-delhi-kaka-vs-shotgun-48551#google_vignette/

Khanna initially refused to accept his narrow defeat, alleging foul play, though he later won the seat in a by-election.[7] Advani retained Gandhinagar, vacating New Delhi, and asked Shatrughan Sinha to contest the subsequent bypoll against Khanna. Jaitley again played a key role in campaign management, although Sinha lost by nearly 27,000 votes. "It was a triple whammy for me. First, a popular superstar like Rajesh Khanna was fielded by the Congress from the prestigious New Delhi seat. Secondly, post-Rajiv Gandhi's assassination, there was a bit of sympathy for Congress. And thirdly, but most importantly, I faced a hostile New Delhi electorate, who had voted for Advani-ji, my friend, philosopher and guide, during the 1991 polls, but he vacated the seat while retaining Gandhinagar," Shatrughan said later. Despite the loss, Sinha's political standing within the BJP soared, and he became one of the party's top star campaigners, with helicopters and private jets ready to deploy him across constituencies. Jaitley and Sinha developed a strong personal and professional rapport during this period.[8]

★

The Congress Working Committee (CWC), presided over by P.V. Narasimha Rao, initially elected Sonia Gandhi as party president. However, she declined to become prime minister the very next day. The offer then went to Vice President Shankar Dayal Sharma, who politely refused due to age and health concerns.[9] A subsequent CWC meeting, presided over by H.K.L. Bhagat, saw strong support from MPs elected from peninsular India for a South Indian leader. Consequently, P.V. Narasimha Rao, a towering figure in undivided Andhra Pradesh who had nearly retired from politics, was elected and sworn

---

7. Abhay Kumar, "'Shatru' made poll debut against 'dost' Rajesh Khanna", *Deccan Herald*, accessed 20 August 2025, https://www.deccanherald.com/india/shatru-made-poll-debut-against-dost-rajesh-khanna-725771.html.

8. Ibid.

9. C.L. Manoj, "Sharma, not Rao was Sonia's PM choice, says Natwar", *The Economic Times*, accessed 20 August 2025, https://economictimes.indiatimes.com/news/politics-and-nation/sharma-not-rao-was-sonias-pm-choice-says-natwar/articleshow/5426283.cms?from=mdr.

in as India's ninth prime minister on 22 June 1991. He appointed economist Manmohan Singh as finance minister.

Born on 26 September 1932 in Punjab, Singh completed his Economic Tripos at Cambridge in 1957 and a D.Phil. in economics at Oxford in 1962. He taught at Punjab University and the Delhi School of Economics before joining the Indian government as economic advisor in the commerce ministry in 1971. He quickly rose to chief economic advisor in the finance ministry in 1972. Singh also served at UNCTAD in Geneva, as Secretary General of the South Commission (1987–90), and held key posts including finance ministry secretary, deputy chairman of the Planning Commission, RBI governor, prime minister's advisor, and UGC chairman.[10]

Together, Narasimha Rao and Manmohan Singh transformed India's fortunes. Rao became prime minister at a time of severe economic crisis. In 1991, amid a foreign reserves crunch, his government introduced landmark economic reforms—globalisation, liberalisation, and privatisation. These measures represented the most radical shift in India's economic policy since Nehru's Industrial Policy Resolution of 1956, moving away from a "socialistic pattern of society" towards unleashing private enterprise.

Despite leading a minority government, Rao restored political stability, redefined national politics, and demonstrated that leadership could exist beyond the Nehru–Gandhi dynasty. His decisive vision laid the foundation for India's ongoing economic liberalisation, making him one of the few leaders after Lal Bahadur Shastri to exercise independent historical judgement, even while managing the dominant Nehru–Gandhi influence.

Meanwhile, the BJP continued the Ram Janmabhoomi movement. In 1992, the movement faced a critical juncture. On 6 December, the VHP and BJP organised a rally in Ayodhya attended by 150,000 kar sevaks. The rally turned violent, and the crowd overwhelmed security forces, demolishing the Babri Masjid. The demolition triggered widespread communal riots across the country. Taking moral responsibility, Kalyan Singh resigned as Uttar Pradesh chief minister, while Rao dissolved the state assembly and dismissed BJP governments in Rajasthan, Madhya Pradesh, and Himachal Pradesh, imposing

---

10. "Dr. Manmohan Singh", Indian National Congress, accessed 25 May 2025, https://inc.in/our-inspiration/dr-manmohan-singh.

President's Rule. Prominent leaders like Advani and Murli Manohar Joshi were subsequently arrested.[11]

The Babri Masjid demolition reshaped India's political landscape, deepening communal divisions and bolstering regional parties. The BJP expanded nationally, while Uttar Pradesh and Bihar saw the rise of caste-based parties. In Uttar Pradesh, the BSP, led by Mayawati, mobilised Dalits and marginalised communities, while Mulayam Singh Yadav's SP gained traction among Yadavs and other backward castes. Regional parties leveraged local, linguistic, and religious identities, reshaping Indian politics, while the Congress gradually lost its status as the natural party of governance.

As a member of the national executive, Jaitley became a key strategist in state elections. In 1993, the BJP won a clear majority in Delhi with 49 of 70 seats, appointing Madan Lal Khurana as chief minister. In Rajasthan, the party captured 95 seats, forming the government under Bhairon Singh Shekhawat. Non-Congress parties in Rajasthan had till then held the reins of power only twice. And each time, Shekhawat was the chief minister. The first time was in 1977, when in the post-Emergency anti-Indira Gandhi wave, the Janata Party was swept to power and Shekhawat of the BJS became the chief minister. His government was dismissed in 1980 when the Congress returned to power at the Centre. Shekhawat suffered a similar fate twelve years later, after helping the BJP come to power in 1990 following the Ram temple wave. The Congress had imposed President's Rule in Rajasthan on 15 December 1992 following the Babri Masjid demolition.

In Uttar Pradesh, the BJP failed to secure a majority, with the SP (109 seats) and BSP (67 seats) forming the government. The party also won four seats in Goa (none in 1989) and rose from 39 to 41 seats in Bihar. In 1995, the BJP achieved a two-thirds majority in Gujarat (121 seats, up from 67) under Keshubhai Patel. In Maharashtra, the BJP's tally increased from 42 to 64 seats; together with Shiv Sena (73 seats), it formed a coalition government with Manohar Joshi as chief minister. In Odisha, the party grew from two seats in

---

11. Shantanu Gupta, *Bharatiya Janata Party: Past, Present and Future: Story of the World's Largest Political Party* (Rupa, 2020), pp. 271–72.

1990 to nine in 1995. In the Northeast, the BJP secured its first seat in Manipur, though it failed in Arunachal Pradesh.[12]

In 1996, eight states held elections. The BJP emerged as the largest party in Uttar Pradesh (174 seats) and formed a government in alliance with the BSP (67 seats). It improved performance in Haryana (11 seats, up from two), Jammu and Kashmir (eight seats, up from two), while dipping in Assam (four seats, down from ten). Its vote share improved in Kerala, West Bengal, and Puducherry, though no seats were won.[13] In Madhya Pradesh, the Congress retained power, with Digvijaya Singh as chief minister, a position he held until 2003. Jaitley spent years studying Madhya Pradesh politics and later became the poll strategist who helped the BJP capture power in 2003.

In 1994, Advani proposed Jaitley for a Rajya Sabha seat from Delhi, though the nomination was dropped at the last moment. Undeterred, Jaitley continued his tireless party work.[14] In the South, the BJP won its first seat in Tamil Nadu in 1996.

In Punjab, the BJP allied with the Shiromani Akali Dal (SAD) for the 1997 assembly elections. The alliance leveraged SAD's rural Sikh base and BJP's urban Hindu constituency. Madan Lal Khurana orchestrated the coalition with Jaitley's support. The SAD contested 94 seats, BJP 23, and together they won a landslide, capturing 93 of 117 seats (SAD 75, BJP 18). The alliance's decisive victory marked a turning point in Punjab's political landscape. Jaitley closely observed state politics and later assumed responsibility for managing the alliance.

Karnataka became another state where Jaitley focused his long-term efforts. By 2002, he had positioned himself as the key strategist behind the BJP's emergence as the dominant party in the state, establishing it as the party's gateway to the south.

---

12. Vijay Kumar Malhotra and J.C. Jaitli, *Evolution of BJP, Party Documents*, Vol. 10 (New Delhi, 2006).

13. Shantanu Gupta, *Bharatiya Janata Party: Past, Present and Future: Story of the World's Largest Political Party* (Rupa, 2020), pp. 272–75.

14. Praveen Donthi, "Talk of the Town", *Caravan Magazine*, accessed 25 May 2025, https://caravanmagazine.in/reportage/talk-town.

★

Indian politics was shaken in February 1994 when fourteen politicians, including five former ministers, were implicated in the Hawala case. The case traced back to 1991, when a student's arrest revealed a Hawala money trail, prompting a Central Bureau of Investigation (CBI) probe. During a raid on industrialist S.K. Jain's farmhouse, police recovered a diary allegedly detailing payments made to 115 politicians and bureaucrats between 1988 and 1991, recording recipients' names or initials.

In October 1993, two journalists filed a public interest litigation with the Supreme Court, which issued a landmark order requiring the CBI to report monthly on its progress. The investigation caused political tremors. On 16 January 1996, the CBI filed a chargesheet accusing L.K. Advani of accepting a bribe of Rs 60 lakh, prompting him to resign from Parliament on moral grounds. The diary also implicated Delhi Chief Minister Madan Lal Khurana for Rs 3 lakh, leading him to step down on Advani's advice.[15]

Like Jaitley, Khurana's family had migrated to Delhi following Partition in 1947, when he was only twelve.[16] A key architect of the BJP's rise in the capital and a deeply rooted RSS leader, Khurana had served twice as a metropolitan councillor before becoming Delhi's chief minister in 1993.[17] He proposed Jaitley as his interim replacement, but this did not materialise despite Advani's willingness. A BJP troika in Delhi suggested Sushma Swaraj, the party's affable spokesperson, but that too fell through.[18]

---

15. Ruhi Tewari, "Madan Lal Khurana: BJP's Punjabi Face Who Opposed 'Pseudo-Hindutva'", *The Print*, accessed 25 May 2025, https://theprint.in/politics/madan-lal-khurana-bjps-punjabi-face-who-opposed-pseudo-hindutva/141460/.

16. Asian News International, "Madan Lal Khurana, the man who gave new vision in death", *Hindustan Times*, accessed 25 May 2025, https://www.hindustantimes.com/delhi-news/madan-lal-khurana-the-man-who-gave-new-vision-in-death/story-hJhYXfCkb1yX8Q2xCkoeRK.html.

17. Ibid.

18. N.K. Singh, "Demoralisation at the Top Leaves BJP Open to Pressure Tactics of State Leaders", *India Today*, accessed 25 May 2025, https://www.indiatoday.in/magazine/special-report/story/19960315-demoralisation-at-the-top-leaves-bjp-open-to-pressure-tactics-of-state-leaders-834764-1996-03-14.

Ultimately, Sahib Singh Verma, a prominent local Jat leader and then education minister in Khurana's Cabinet, staked his claim. Verma's political career began in 1977 as a councillor in the Delhi Municipal Corporation. He had lost the 1991 Lok Sabha elections to Congress leader Sajjan Kumar—who, in February 2025, was convicted and sentenced to life imprisonment for the murder of a man and his son during the 1984 anti-Sikh riots. Verma won the 1993 Delhi Assembly elections from Shalimar Bagh by 21,000 votes.

After deliberations, the BJP legislative party elected Verma as Delhi chief minister. He took office on 26 February 1996, marking a significant shift in the capital's political landscape. Khurana was appointed chairman of the Delhi BJP legislative party. Verma asked to work with the existing Cabinet.[19] Months later, Khurana was acquitted, having received a clean chit. His counsel, Arun Jaitley, successfully argued that there was no independent evidence against him and that his name had not been clearly mentioned in the Jain diaries, which by then had lost any evidentiary value.

★

Jaitley served as the BJP's key legal representative, becoming L.K. Advani's primary counsel in October 1993, after the CBI filed cases against BJP leaders in connection with the Babri Masjid demolition. He frequently sought advice from senior lawyer Ram Jethmalani.

On 8 April 1997, the Delhi High Court acquitted Advani, ruling that the CBI had failed to present any material that could be deemed legally admissible evidence.[20] The court rejected the prosecution's claim that entries in the diary maintained by the Jain brothers were admissible under the Indian Evidence Act, 1872. In its seventy-page judgment, the high court acquitted Advani along with the Jain brothers, noting that there was no evidence to show that any money had been disbursed. The verdict sparked jubilant celebrations: Advani's wife Kamla and BJP leader Uma Bharti danced on the lawns, while Advani likened his acquittal to the resurrection of Christ. BJP workers burst crackers, marking

19. Ibid.

20. Vinay Sitapati, *Jugalbandi: The BJP Before Modi* (Penguin, 2020), p. 199.

the political storm's end. Elated at his release, S.K. Jain sent bouquets to Arun Jaitley in gratitude.[21] A year later, on 2 March 1998, the Supreme Court also acquitted Advani.

Jaitley continued to represent the BJP and its senior leaders in the Babri Masjid demolition case, cementing his reputation as a formidable legal strategist.

★

The Narasimha Rao government completed a full five-year term, strengthened by several opposition members joining through party splits and mergers. The next general elections were held in 1996, with results announced on 9 May. The Third Front—a coalition of non-Congress and non-BJP parties including the Janata Dal, Left parties, and the DMK—won 173 seats. The Congress was reduced to 140 seats, while the BJP emerged as the single-largest party with 161 seats, 111 short of the 272 required to form a stable government.[22] The BJP staked its claim to form the government, and Atal Bihari Vajpayee became the country's first BJP-led prime minister, though his government lasted only thirteen days.

Meanwhile, the United Front—a thirteen-party coalition later supported by the National Conference—took shape. For the first time, a left party, the CPI, shared power at the Centre, while the CPI(M), AIFB, and RSP supported it from outside. The Congress offered outside support with its 140 MPs. Several candidates were considered for the prime minister's post, including Narasimha Rao, Ramakrishna Hegde, V.P. Singh, and Jyoti Basu. Although Lalu Prasad Yadav had campaigned in his home state of Bihar in order to become India's prime minister, his name did not figure in the post-election parleys. Efforts were made to convince V.P. Singh to become the prime minister, but he refused.[23]

---

21. Harinder Baweja, "Jain Hawala Case: Acquittals of Advani, Shukla Bring Cheer to Chargesheeted Politicians", *India Today*, accessed 25 May 2025, https://www.indiatoday.in/magazine/nation/story/19970430-jain-hawala-case-acquittals-of-advani-shukla-bring-cheer-to-other-chargesheeted-politicians-831309-1997-04-29.

22. Vinay Sitapati, *Jugalbandi: The BJP Before Modi* (Penguin, 2020), p. 194.

23. Debashish Mukerji, *The Disruptor: How Vishwanath Pratap Singh Shook India* (HarperCollins, 2021), pp. 406–40.

Finally, Jyoti Basu was invited to become the prime minister. Jyoti Basu was a man of towering political stature, India's pre-eminent and most charismatic communist leader, and one of its most illustrious statesmen of the past century. His political career, representing the second-generation communist experience, spanned an astonishing seven decades. As the longest-surviving of the nine founding members of the CPI(M) politburo and as independent India's longest-serving chief minister by far (21 June 1977 to 6 November 2000), he made game-changing contributions at the political, ideological, and administrative levels in West Bengal. The qualitative impact made by him at the national level, transcending the regional limitations of the left's base and influence, won him the offer of the prime minister's job in 1996.[24]

The political economist Lord Meghnad Desai said, "Jyoti Basu was the best prime minister India never had." Later, Jyoti Basu famously characterised his decision to turn down the offer as a historic blunder. His subsequent public explanations made it clear that this was not on account of any personal disappointment but because he reckoned that having a communist veteran, even for a while, at the helm in New Delhi would have been a real opportunity (which would probably never arise again) to introduce and project the party's programme and policies to the people of India. However, experts believe that given the left's, and the United Front's, modest numbers in Parliament and the total dependence on the Congress party for support, Basu's decision to turn down the offer was well-reasoned and sound; India's pre-eminent communist leader would have ended up becoming a sacrificial prime minister.[25]

The United Front finally chose Karnataka Chief Minister H.D. Deve Gowda, who was sworn in on 1 June 1996. Less than a year later, the Congress withdrew support, leading to I.K. Gujral becoming prime minister in April 1997. This too proved short-lived.

Sonia Gandhi, until now a private citizen, decided to join the Congress as a primary member in August 1997. Two months later, on 9 November 1997, the media leaked portions of an interim report by a judicial commission investigating Rajiv Gandhi's assassination. The leaks suggested that the commission had indicted the DMK. This put the Congress party in a bind,

---

24. N. Ram, "The Genius of Jyoti Basu", *Frontline*, accessed 25 May 2025, https://frontline.thehindu.com/cover-story/the-genius-of-jyoti-basu/article64755648.ece.

25. Ibid.

since the Dravidian party was part of the United Front government they were propping up. Any attempt to resolve the situation was sabotaged by pressure groups that had formed within both the United Front and the Congress, each determined to pursue self-interest even if it meant sinking the government. They succeeded, and on 28 November 1997, the Congress once again withdrew its support from the United Front.[26] Fresh elections were called for, and the BJP prepared for the battle once more.

In the 1998 Lok Sabha elections, the BJP forged the National Democratic Alliance (NDA)[27] with regional partners like the TMC, AIADMK, Shiv Sena, and BJD. The BJP won 182 seats, surpassing the halfway mark with coalition support. But both Vajpayee's favourites, Jaswant Singh and Pramod Mahajan, lost the elections.

Vajpayee became prime minister on 19 March 1998. In April 1998, Advani handed over the reins of the party to Kushabhau Thakre, one of the most revered leaders of the BJP in its earlier avatar, the Jana Sangh.[28] He was a staunch RSS man and had been a leader in the BJS since 1956, and later in the BJP.

---

26. Sanjay Ruparelia, *Divided We Govern: Coalition Politics in Modern India* (Oxford University Press, 2015), pp. 272–75.

27. The name was a hat-tip to Syama Prasad Mookerjee whose Jana Sangh had fought the 1951 elections as part of the "National Democratic Front". Vinay Sitapati, *Jugalbandi: The BJP Before Modi* (Penguin, 2020), p. 205.

28. Born on 15 August 1922, at Dhar in the then Madhya Bharat, Thakre was educated at Victoria College in Gwalior, where Prime Minister Atal Bihari Vajpayee too studied. As a young man he became a pracharak of the RSS. In 1942, he became a swayamsevak and was put in charge of RSS affairs in the Malwa region of Madhya Pradesh. He was associated with founder-members of the BJS since 1951, and became the party secretary (organisation) for the south. In 1956, when Madhya Pradesh state was formed, he became the Jana Sangh secretary (organisation). In 1974, he was made the all-India secretary of the Jana Sangh and oversaw party affairs in Orissa and Gujarat. When the Jana Sangh merged with the Janata Party in 1977, Thakre was appointed as the president of the Madhya Pradesh unit of the Janata Party. He was jailed for nineteen months during the Emergency. In 1979, he contested and won a by-election to the Lok Sabha from Khandwa, the only election he has contested. In 1980, when the BJP was founded, Thakre was appointed as its all-India secretary and was placed in charge of party affairs in Gujarat, Madhya Pradesh, and Orissa. In 1984, he was made the national vice president, and in 1991, he became the all-India general secretary and was put in charge of party affairs in Madhya Pradesh.

The government soon conducted five secret nuclear tests at Pokhran in May, asserting India as a nuclear power. It was only the second time India had tested its nuclear strength; the earlier tests were in 1974.[29]

Vajpayee then embarked on a mission for peace with Pakistan (which, too, had become a nuclear power soon after). This was a subject very close to his heart. He started pushing for a comprehensive diplomatic peace process with his Pakistani counterpart Nawaz Sharif. The historic Delhi–Lahore bus service, aimed at increasing people-to-people contact, was inaugurated on 20 February 1999. Vajpayee undertook a journey from Amritsar to Lahore. He was received by the Pakistani prime minister at the Wagah Border. The next day, on 21 February 1999, the two prime ministers signed the Lahore Declaration, whereby the two countries agreed to a peaceful resolution of bilateral disputes, which included Kashmir, and encouraged friendly commercial and cultural exchanges with each other.

The peace momentum was sabotaged by the Pakistani incursion in the Kargil sector. Pervez Musharraf was the chief of their army staff at that time. India launched Operation Vijay on 26 May 1999 to clear the infiltrators. It ended on 26 July 1999, with India successfully reclaiming the Kargil post and clearing out infiltrators from other regions. This incident, however, shook Vajpayee's belief in the Pakistan government's sincerity for peace with India.[30]

★

Pramod Mahajan was now without a job. His key role in mediating and negotiating with allies was over. Vajpayee needed help with retail political management, so he appointed Mahajan as "political adviser to the "prime minister", with the rank of Cabinet minister. This set off a major controversy, since the move was unprecedented. Was Mahajan a minister or a civil servant? Would he attend Cabinet meetings? To settle these issues, Mahajan was sworn into office by Vajpayee himself, as is done for the deputy chairman and members of the Planning Commission. Mahajan started sitting in a room at

---

29. Kingshuk Nag, *Atal Bihari Vajpayee: A Man for All Seasons* (Rupa Publications, 2015).

30. Shantanu Gupta, *Bharatiya Janata Party: Past, Present and Future: Story of the World's Largest Political Party* (Rupa, 2020), p. 292.

7 Race Course Road, the prime minister's official residence. His appointment raised many eyebrows.

Jaitley meanwhile remained active with party affairs. Vajpayee chose him as the Indian government's delegate to the United Nations General Assembly's twentieth special session on countering the drug problem held in June 1998 where the Declaration on Laws Relating to Drugs and Money Laundering was approved. In the session held in New York, Jaitley said:

> The special session, also known as the "Drug Summit", was convened to assess the international drug problem and develop a forward-looking strategy for the next century, based on a balanced approach between demand and supply reduction. The Assembly approached the world drug problem by focusing on the following crucial issues: elimination of illicit crops and alternative development; amphetamine-type stimulants; precursor chemicals; money-laundering; and judicial cooperation. A high-level debate on the world drug problem was held in plenary. Simultaneously, an Ad Hoc Committee met to finalise negotiations on the texts, which were then submitted to the Assembly for adoption. A total of 158 speakers took part in the general debate, including 23 Heads of State, 8 Prime Ministers, one Vice-President, as well as seven observers.[31]

The Vajpayee government faced instability when the AIADMK withdrew support, causing it to lose a confidence vote by a single vote—a record in Indian parliamentary history. The Vajpayee government lasted thirteen months from 19 March 1998 to 17 April 1999. Vajpayee had the numbers on his side but the Congress played a masterstroke by getting Giridhar Gamang, its Odisha chief minister, to vote. Although Gamang was chief minister of Odisha, technically he was still an MP having been appointed as the chief minister less than six months ago, and was yet to resign from his parliamentary seat.

---

31. United Nations, "Assembly Special Session on Countering World Drug Problem Together Concludes at Headquarters, 8-10 June", Press Release, GA/9423, available at https://press.un.org/en/1998/19980610.ga9423.html.

While the Congress managed to pull down the Vajpayee government, it had suffered a significant blow after decades of exercising absolute control over Indian politics. Its support base, especially among Hindus, grew progressively thinner as the BJP came to be regarded as the party with Hindu interests at heart. The Congress's inability to prevent the demolition of the Babri Masjid dented its position with Muslims while regional parties walked away with the backward caste vote bank. The party had a hard time getting back on track and adjusting to the shifting political environment. The BJP was able to firmly establish itself as a national player by overtaking the Congress in the Hindi belt states. The electoral gains for the BJP came largely at the cost of the Congress, which, post-1989, has never been able to cross 30 per cent vote share in the region.

Sonia Gandhi became Congress president in 1998, attempting to revitalize the party. Meanwhile, the BJP went to the 1999 Lok Sabha elections under the NDA pre-poll alliance, winning an absolute majority with 306 out of 545 seats, including 182 on its own. The Congress was rejected by voters, securing only 114 seats. It was clear that the public was happy with the performance of the last NDA government and thus voted it back to power.[32]

In 2000, *Asiaweek* recognized Jaitley as one of India's most promising young political leaders, calling him "the modern face of India, a brilliant man with a clean image".[33] But one of the most defining moments of this decade was his meeting with Narendra Modi. Their acquaintance was to develop into a strong bond of friendship over the next decade.

---

32. Shantanu Gupta, *Bharatiya Janata Party: Past, Present and Future: Story of the World's Largest Political Party* (Rupa, 2020), p. 293.

33. Praveen Donthi, "Talk of the Town", *Caravan Magazine*, accessed May 25, 2025, https://caravanmagazine.in/reportage/talk-town.

8

Vajpayee's Young and Reformist Minister (1999–2004)

With a large and diverse set of parties in the NDA, Vajpayee had to carefully balance representation among his allies. The 1999 NDA Cabinet reflected this diversity, both regionally and culturally. Its initial members included L.K. Advani; Ananth Kumar, a prominent leader from Karnataka; Sikander Bakht, a senior BJP leader and influential Muslim figure; Surjit Singh Barnala, former chief minister of Punjab; George Fernandes; Murli Manohar Joshi; Kashiram Rana, MP from Surat; BJD supremo Naveen Patnaik; Pramod Mahajan; governance expert Suresh Prabhu; P.R. Kumaramangalam, whose father and grandfather had served as ministers under Indira Gandhi and Nehru; firebrand lawyer Ram Jethmalani; former Karnataka chief minister Ramakrishna Hegde; economist-journalist Arun Shourie; Army Major turned politician Jaswant Singh; Bihar leader Nitish Kumar; and former civil servant Yashwant Sinha.[1]

Arun Jaitley, despite being a deserving candidate, had to wait seven months after Vajpayee assumed office to be inducted into the council of ministers. In October 1999, he was appointed Minister of State for Information and Broadcasting with independent charge—his first ministerial role. Two months later, on 10 December 1999, the NDA government established the Department of Disinvestment under the Ministry of Finance, tasked with handling the disinvestment of central public sector enterprises (CPSEs). Jaitley was given

1. "List of Council of Ministers (as on the 5th May, 1999)", available at https://cabsec.gov.in/writereaddata/councilofministers/english/1_Upload_2139.pdf.

independent charge of this department. In 2001, it was upgraded to the Ministry of Disinvestment.

Jaitley smoothly transitioned from the Supreme Court corridors to the bustling offices of Shastri Bhawan, initially as a junior minister and later as a Cabinet minister, handling key portfolios from the start. To continue as a minister, he had to secure a seat in Parliament within six months. He made his parliamentary debut as a Rajya Sabha member from Gujarat in 2000, before Narendra Modi became the state's chief minister.

In June 1999, Ram Jethmalani resigned as minister of law, justice and company affairs, and Vajpayee entrusted Jaitley with the additional charge of the ministry on 23 July 2000. By November that year, Jaitley became a full Cabinet minister.

On 30 June 2001, the AIADMK government in Tamil Nadu, led by Jayalalithaa, arrested former chief minister M. Karunanidhi, Union ministers Murasoli Maran (Karunanidhi's nephew) and T.R. Baalu, former municipal administration minister Ko. Si. Mani, and former chief secretary K.A. Nambiar.[2] The post-midnight arrests triggered a political storm. Television footage broadcast on Sun TV showing Karunanidhi being shoved and lifted by police created a groundswell of public outrage against the AIADMK government, effectively benefiting the DMK and the BJP-led central government. Following Murasoli Maran's arrest, his commerce portfolio was also handed over to Jaitley.

Through articulate communication and dedicated effort, Jaitley quickly established himself as a significant minister, despite being at least two decades younger than Vajpayee and Advani. Journalist Swapan Dasgupta wrote in *India Today* that "in a party plagued by an image problem, he made the BJP respectable among the chattering classes and was rewarded", predicting that as the BJP evolved into a liberal right-wing party, the Sangh Parivar would view Jaitley as "a winning face for the next century".[3]

---

2. L.R. Jagadheesan and Arun Ram, "Karunanidhi Out of Jail, But Retribution Continues to Define the Statecraft of Jayalalitha", *India Today*, accessed 25 May 2025, https://www.indiatoday.in/magazine/states/story/20010716-karunanidhi-out-of-jail-but-retribution-continues-to-define-the-statecraft-of-jayalalitha-773799-2001-07-15.

3. Praveen Donthi, "Talk of the Town", *Caravan Magazine*, accessed 25 May 2025, https://caravanmagazine.in/reportage/talk-town.

★

As a young minister in the Vajpayee government, Arun Jaitley played a pivotal role in advancing major economic reforms aimed at improving the ease of doing business. He focused on competition law to promote a free market economy and on insolvency law to ensure efficient exits—a reform he would later carry to fruition a decade later as India's finance minister under Modi.

Vajpayee assumed office during a period marked by regional financial instability. The Asian Financial Crisis, triggered by Thailand in July 1997, had slowed or reversed capital flows across East Asia, put banks under stress, and pushed several countries into deep recessions. While India remained largely insulated, the slowdown in trading partners raised domestic concerns.

Domestically, the pace of reforms initiated in 1991 by Prime Minister Narasimha Rao and Finance Minister Manmohan Singh had slowed. Rao and Singh had faced stiff opposition within the Congress, with multiple MPs and ministers resisting liberalisation measures such as opening markets to foreign investment, privatising public sector firms, and reducing subsidies. They emphasised a shift from the post-independence belief that the public sector could do everything, advocating instead a market-friendly approach inspired by global trends—such as China under Deng Xiaoping and the collapse of the Soviet Union. Meanwhile, Deng Xiaoping had revolutionised China with market-friendly reforms. Succeeding the great Mao Zedong, Xiaoping took a U-turn from the theoretical position of his predecessor in pursuing the western line of development initiating economic reforms in China in 1978 with his unique plea that "it doesn't matter whether the cat is black or white, as long as it catches mice".[4]

Reforms included abolishing industrial licensing, relaxing MRTP Act requirements, allowing up to 51 per cent foreign equity in various sectors, and initiating disinvestment of government stakes in CPSEs. Fifty-five MPs opposed the liberalisation of trade policies, including seven ministers such as Union Minister for Agriculture Balram Jakhar and Madhavrao Scindia; many Congress MPs opposed the entry of multinationals, including leading

---

4. S.B. Kumar, "P.V. Narasimha Rao: The Precursor of the Era of Economic Reforms in India", *Indian Journal of Public Administration*, Vol. 63, No. 4 (2017), pp. 616–30, available at https://journals.sagepub.com/doi/10.1177/0019556117726824.

industrialist K.K. Birla; privatisation of public sector firms faced opposition from eighteen MPs; twenty MPs resisted the reduction of fertiliser subsidy; and twenty-two MPs were against the Congress–BJP understanding on reforms, including Union Minister for Human Resource Development Arjun Singh and Madhya Pradesh Chief Minister Digvijaya Singh.[5]

Rao and Manmohan Singh urged the Congressmen to have a new mindset—a shift from the four-decade policy that the public sector can do everything. Manmohan Singh propagated that 'market is God', a typical Thatcherite–Reaganite approach. By 1994–97, these measures resulted in record GDP growth of 7.5 per cent and laid the foundation for India's emergence as a major services exporter, especially in IT and call centres.

When the reforms began, all opposition parties had slammed them as a sellout to the IMF and swore to reverse these policies when they came to power. But gross domestic product (GDP) picked up so well that all subsequent governments of different political stripes stayed in the same economic direction. After 2003, the cumulative impact of years of reform and globalisation helped Indian GDP to average more than 7 per cent, making India a "miracle" economy. Remarkably, India has become a major exporter of services, leapfrogging richer developing countries to become a services exporter. This started with call centres and computer software in the late 1990s, leading to a swift rise up the value chain.[6]

The most consequential example of Rao's micro-management of opposition to reforms was the telecom policy and the mobile phone revolution. By 1994, the Indian government was actively considering a telecom policy to deal with the emerging mobile phone technology. Narasimha Rao—who collected electronic gadgets and in his spare time fixed computers—took a personal interest. He underlined each policy draft with comments on the side of the draft. The key debate was whether foreign and private players should be allowed. Rao's telecom minister Sukh Ram seemed to oppose this, but Rao

---

5. Vinay Sitapati, "IB Gave Narasimha Rao List of Congmen, Ministers Against 1991 Reforms", *The Indian Express*, accessed 25 May 2025, https://indianexpress.com/article/india/india-news-india/intelligence-bureau-ib-narasimha-rao-congress-manmohan-singh-sonia-gandhi-2874380/.

6. Swaminathan S. Anklesaria Aiyar, "Globalization Has Propelled India to Prosperity", Cato Institute, accessed 25 May 2015, https://www.cato.org/publications/globalization-has-propelled-india-prosperity#globalization-trade.

was unwavering. When a note on the telecom policy was sent to Rao stating, "We are going to put a condition that they should go to rural areas also," Rao commented with understated wit in the margins of the note, "Who goes to rural areas? The phones or foreign operation personnel?"

In July 1995, when the first mobile phone call was ready to be made, Narasimha Rao could have easily taken credit; instead he receded into the background while cleverly co-opting his political rivals. He let Sukh Ram revel in the glory of India's first mobile phone call. On the other line was Rao's implacable opponent, Jyoti Basu of the CPI(M).[7]

Globally, economic thinking was evolving. Western nations were moving away from pure Thatcherite or Reaganite models, and the World Bank and Asian Development Bank began recognising the role of state intervention in driving industrial growth. John Major, the prime minister of the United Kingdom, was by 1991–92 quietly moving the country away from the Thatcherite mindset and Bill Clinton's victory as the President of the United States in 1992 marked the burial of the Reaganite way. The World Bank, the intellectual powerhouse of economic ideas, realised which way the wind was blowing. It too started conceptualising the experience of Asian giants, reinforced the Japanese lesson that intelligent state guidance, direct and indirect intervention in markets, and sometimes direct physical intervention through the public sector can achieve economic turnaround.[8] In the late 1990s, Prof. Charles Booth, an eminent academic then based in Hong Kong, and I were hired by the Asian Development Bank to advise on the revival and strengthen the governance of state-owned enterprises (SOEs) in the People's Republic of China.

Under President Clinton, the state had taken it upon itself to play an active leadership role in promoting frontier projects and increasing its intervention in the social sector. The universal health care scheme was, perhaps, the highest on Clinton's agenda. This emboldened the Congressmen opposed to reforms

---

7. Vinay Sitapati, "IB Gave Narasimha Rao List of Congmen, Ministers Against 1991 Reforms", *The Indian Express*, accessed 25 May 2025, https://indianexpress.com/article/india/india-news-india/intelligence-bureau-ib-narasimha-rao-congress-manmohan-singh-sonia-gandhi-2874380/.

8. M.N. Birdsall et al., "The East Asian Miracle: Economic Growth and Public Policy", (Vol. 1 of 2): Main Report (English), A World Bank policy research report, 26 September 1993, available at https://documents.worldbank.org/en/publication/documents-reports/documentdetail/975081468244550798/main-report.

in India. Stiff opposition from the Congress made Rao slow down on reforms. The year 1997 was a watershed. In particular, three marker events occurred within a six-month period to check the momentum of growth.

In March, the instability inherent in the coalition governments became manifest in a political crisis, which ended the Deve Gowda government and ushered in the Gujral version of the United Front government. In July, the Thailand financial crisis raised the curtain on the Asian crisis saga, which dominated the international economic arena for next eighteen months. Finally, in September, the Gujral government announced its decisions on the Fifth Pay Commission report—decisions which were to prove costly for both the fiscal and economic health of the country.[9]

When Jaitley was inducted in the council of ministers and later the Cabinet, the nation was still debating the virtues of liberalisation. The young minister had huge responsibilities on his shoulders as the minister in charge of important portfolios. Jaitley's main task was to push for India's growth and continue economic reforms despite the slowdown in the region.

Disinvestment Reforms

One of Jaitley's most significant contributions was driving disinvestment in CPSEs, despite resistance from within the BJP and beyond. Post-independence, Nehru had championed a state-led model with CPSEs serving socio-economic objectives.[10] At the time of Independence, India was an agrarian economy with a weak industrial base, low level of savings, inadequate investment, and lack of infrastructural facilities. There also existed considerable inequalities in income and levels of employment, and glaring regional imbalances in economic development. In view of the manifold problems faced by the country on the economic, social, and strategic fronts, CPSEs were set up as instruments of the government to serve as crusaders of socioeconomic objectives, spearheading

9. Shankar Acharya, "India: Crisis, Reforms and Growth in the Nineties", Working Paper No. 139 (July 2002), available at https://kingcenter.stanford.edu/sites/g/files/sbiybj16611/files/media/file/139wp_0.pdf.

10. Sumant Batra, *Corporate Insolvency: The Road to Viksit Bharat: Law, Policy and Practice* (Eastern Book Company, 2025).

planned development in India, promoting rapid industrial development, balancing regional development, generating employment, and creating basic infrastructure network.

The government took up the work of setting up and running several companies—from airlines and telecom to bread and cars; that in most countries would be run by the private sector.[11] A whopping Rs 200,000 crore had been invested in these SOEs.[12] The public sector was made to provide a leading role in moulding and accelerating the process of industrialisation within the framework of a "mixed economy". It assumed a strategic role in the economy over years. While many of these enterprises successfully expanded production, opened up new areas of technology, built up a reserve of technical competence in a number of areas, and emerged as important players in the market, others failed. Yet the government kept bailing them out, repeatedly, over years, rather than changing the course of the economy and policies.

In a performance audit on revival of sick CPSEs carried out by the Comptroller and Auditor General of India (CAG) in March 2011, for which I acted as a consultant, it was found that out of 406 CPSEs (including 131 deemed government companies) only 378 were in operation with a total government equity investment of about Rs 188,661 crore, of which 251 earned net profit of Rs 127,141 crore, whereas 127 registered loss of Rs 23,264 crore.[13] Forty-five CPSEs with accumulated losses of Rs 63,828 crore were insolvent as of March 2010. The aggregate losses of insolvent CPSEs had mounted steadily, from Rs 6845 crore in 2005–06 to Rs 15,842 crore in 2009–10. Out of a total of 406 CPSEs, equity capital of 67 had been completely eroded by their accumulated losses. The accumulated losses in these 67 companies were Rs

11. Vinay Sitapati, *Jugalbandi: The BJP Before Modi* (Penguin, 2020), p. 249.

12. Swapan Dasgupta, "Government Must Grasp that Disinvestment is Good Politics", *India Today*, accessed 25 May 2025, https://www.indiatoday.in/magazine/guest-column/story/20000207-government-must-grasp-that-disinvestment-is-good-politics-777045-2000-02-06.

13. "Performance Audit on Revival of Sick Central Public Sector Enterprises", Report of the Comptroller and Auditor General of India, Report No. 30 of 2011–12, available at https://cag.gov.in/webroot/uploads/download_audit_report/2011/Union_Performance_Commerical_Revival_Sick_Central_Public_Sector_Enterprises_30_2011_Chapter_1.pdf.

82,477 crore against equity investment of Rs 14,660 crore.[14] Considering their inherent potential, the government kept bailing out these insolvent CPSEs through revival schemes which were nothing but induction of fresh capital, debt forgiveness, or deferment of payment of debt by state-owned banks for a whopping amount of Rs 39,658.72 crore. The taxpayer was, quite literally, being looted.[15]

Despite being provided assistance of Rs 39,658.72 crore (cash and non-cash) for their revival, the CPSEs could not reap the intended benefits of the revival schemes (more as bailouts). This resulted in a substantial loss of revenue for the government and an increase in public expenditure. Several committees were constituted in the process of disinvestment to address issues like valuation of shares, handling labour problems, reviewing of the financial health of public firms, and creating a better policy approach towards the disinvestment programme.[16] In August 1991, a committee for valuation of shares was constituted, headed by the secretary of the Department of Public Enterprises (DPE). This was popularly known as the Suresh Kumar Committee.[17]

Disinvestment was carried out in two rounds in December 1991 and February 1992 which received nine and nineteen bids respectively. Individuals were not allowed to participate in these two rounds of disinvestment, and shares were offered to only public sector mutual funds and financial institutions. This was done because it was felt that such investments would be risky for individuals. The first disinvestment target of Rs 2500 crore was achieved.[18]

---

14. Ibid.

15. Vinay Sitapati, *Jugalbandi: The BJP Before Modi* (Penguin, 2020), p. 249.

16. Sudipto Banerjee, Renuka Sane, Srishti Sharma, and Karthik Suresh, "History of Disinvestment in India: 1991-2020", NIPFP Working Paper Series, No. 373 (March 2022), available at https://www.nipfp.org.in/media/documents/WP_373_2022.pdf.

17. The Valuation Committee consisted of the secretary, Department of Chemicals and Petrochemicals, Department of Electronics, and Department of Petroleum and Natural Gas. Also, it included the heads of the public firms—chairman-cum-managing director of Maruti Udyog Ltd., Bharat Petroleum Corporation, Andrew Yule & Co. Ltd., and Indian Petrochemicals Corporation Ltd. Strategic Consultants Pvt. Ltd. was appointed to advise on pricing of shares.

18. Sudipto Banerjee, Renuka Sane, Srishti Sharma, and Karthik Suresh, "History of Disinvestment in India: 1991-2020", NIPFP Working Paper Series, No. 373 (March

By 1996, disinvestment had taken root in Indian policy thinking. The seed for disinvestment was sowed by Chandra Shekhar when he headed the government for a short period in 1990–91. It was he who propounded that the government should disinvest 20 per cent equity in CPSEs.[19] In the financial year 1996–97, only one firm, Videsh Sanchar Nigam Limited (VSNL), could be divested through a Global Depository Receipt (GDR) issue, and the disinvestment target was again missed. This was the first GDR issue of a public firm and VSNL's shares were listed on the London Stock Exchange. In the financial year 1997–98, while the budget speech set a target of Rs 4800 crore and plans were made for GDR issues in several CPSEs, only one GDR issue of MTNL could take place.[20]

In 1996, the BJP emerged as the largest party and Vajpayee was sworn in as the prime minister. However, he failed to prove his majority on the floor of the House and the government collapsed in thirteen days. With the support of the Congress, a coalition consisting of thirteen parties, the United Front, formed the government with H.D. Deve Gowda as the prime minister. The common minimum programme of the new government promised that "the United Front government will identify public sector companies that have comparative advantages and will support them in their drive to become global giants". The political intention was clear—profit-making entities would not be sold to private players, rather they would be strengthened. The government lasted for only ten months. The Congress withdrew its support to Deve Gowda in early 1997.

In April 1997, I.K. Gujral was appointed as the new prime minister who continued the United Front government with the support of the Congress party. However, he resigned soon after, and in 1998, within a span of two years, the country went through another general election.

2022), available at https://www.nipfp.org.in/media/documents/WP_373_2022.pdf.

19. Bharatiya Janata Party, "Short Discussion on Disinvestment Policy: Shri Arun Jaitley: 01.08.2000" (9 February 2013), available at https://www.youtube.com/watch?v=28hqd_EUmLc.

20. Sudipto Banerjee, Renuka Sane, Srishti Sharma, and Karthik Suresh, "History of Disinvestment in India: 1991-2020", NIPFP Working Paper Series, No. 373 (March 2022), available at https://www.nipfp.org.in/media/documents/WP_373_2022.pdf.

Meanwhile, in September 1997, the first approval of strategic disinvestment was given when the government decided to dilute 50 per cent stake in Modern Food Industries (India) Limited (MFIL). Also, the process of strategic disinvestment in Bharat Aluminium Company Limited (BALCO) was initiated towards the end of 1997. By August 1999, the Disinvestment Commission had given recommendations on fifty-three CPSEs, out of which no decision was communicated or taken in thirty cases. Out of thirty-two strategic/trade sales, no decision was taken/communicated in twenty-two cases. Even where decisions were taken, the progress was slow. In August 1998, the Disinvestment Commission recommended a sale of 40 per cent stake in Air India followed by an immediate infusion of Rs 1000 crore. This, however, did not materialise until the year 2021.[21]

As a first major step, on 10 December 1999, the government set up a separate department, Department of Disinvestment (DOD), whose mandate was to deal with disinvestment of CPSEs. For this, the DOD was vested with the power to decide on the recommendations of the Disinvestment Commission and take all steps like appointment of advisers and pricing of shares, for implementing the decisions.

Since 1991, the Department of Public Enterprises (DPE) was the nodal body to handle disinvestment activities, and from April 1999 till the formation of DOD, the Department of Economic Affairs (DEA) managed the affairs. For the first time a full department was dedicated for the work of disinvestment. Vajpayee entrusted this responsibility to the young Jaitley by making him the minister of state holding independent charge of DOD.

Vajpayee asked Jaitley to speed up the disinvestment process. Jaitley decided to accord the highest priority to turning huge industrial assets into productive assets that would spur industrial growth to a new level. He set a target of selling its stake in twenty-seven government-owned companies.[22] Vajpayee wanted the

---

21. Sudipto Banerjee, Renuka Sane, Srishti Sharma, and Karthik Suresh, "History of Disinvestment in India: 1991-2020", NIPFP Working Paper Series, No. 373 (March 2022), available at https://www.nipfp.org.in/media/documents/WP_373_2022.pdf.

22. Swapan Dasgupta, "Don't Let Secrecy and Cronyism Jeopardise the End of Socialism", *India Today*, accessed 25 May 2025, https://www.indiatoday.in/magazine/guest-column/story/20010312-dont-let-secrecy-and-cronyism-jeopardise-the-end-of-socialism-775570-2001-03-11.

government to release the huge funds blocked in CPSEs for investment in the social and infrastructure sectors.[23] Earlier, in 1996, in his short tenure, Vajpayee had announced two major policy decisions. First, in the budget of the financial year 1998–99, an announcement was made to bring down the government shareholding generally to 26 per cent, however, the implementation was to take place only on a case to case basis. Second, in March 1999, his Cabinet passed a resolution classifying strategic and non-strategic sectors for the purpose of disinvestment. Possibly this was done to streamline the earlier classification of industries on the basis of strategic group, core group, and non-core group. The constitution of the Disinvestment Commission in 1996 reflected the government's intention to promote disinvestment. For the first time, the President, during the address to the joint session of Parliament, explicitly announced that disinvestment of public sector firms in non-strategic sectors was no longer a choice but an "imperative".[24]

Jaitley set out on the task with full vigour, taking charge of delivering his prime minister's vision of this economic reform, and playing a key role in settling regulatory and political issues arising from the sale of PSUs. In July 2001, a new Disinvestment Commission was constituted under the chairmanship of R.H. Patil. The commission had new members but with the same terms of reference as the previous commission. Since the government had decided to refer all non-strategic firms to the Disinvestment Commission except the oil majors, that is, Oil and Natural Gas Corporation Limited (ONGC), Indian Oil Corporation Limited (IOCL), and Gas Authority of India Limited (GAIL), the government had to prioritise firms to be taken up first.

The decision was made to select firms that could fetch maximum revenue for the government with minimum impediments and where the bleeding of government resources had to be stopped immediately. Compared to the approach of the previous commission, the newly constituted commission did not venture into the appraisal of the disinvestment programme, but confined itself to specific recommendations on the identified firms. The commission

---

23. Ibid.

24. Sudipto Banerjee, Renuka Sane, Srishti Sharma, and Karthik Suresh, "History of Disinvestment in India: 1991-2020", NIPFP Working Paper Series, No. 373 (March 2022), available at https://www.nipfp.org.in/media/documents/WP_373_2022.pdf.

gave recommendations on a total of thirty-nine firms. It recommended immediate outright or phased strategic sale in seventeen firms.[25]

In 2001, after DOD was given the status of ministry of disinvestment, Jaitley became the minister of state with independent charge. To bring transparency and accountability in disinvestment, in July 2001, Jaitley wrote India's first disinvestment procedure manual and policy document "Disinvestment: Policy and Procedures".[26] This was a compendium of policy statements of past budget speeches and other policy announcements. It spelt out guidelines on eligibility of bidders, valuation, and advisors. While the disinvestment programme was initiated in 1991, India lacked a "documented framework or manual" on how to carry out disinvestment. The announcements in budget speeches mostly constituted the disinvestment policy.

On his ministry's recommendation, the government announced the setting up of a "disinvestment proceeds fund" to utilise the proceeds for targeted social sector reforms and the generation of employment opportunities; however, no such fund was created. In the absence of such a mechanism, it was not possible to map the utilisation of proceeds to the targeted expenditure like the social sector or retiring of public debt.[27] Faced with stiff opposition and multiple litigation, Jaitley used this document as an opportunity to offer its justification for why privatisation was needed and what it had done to privatise.

In November 2001, Jaitley was elevated as Cabinet minister. He now had more power to drive reforms. But Vajpayee and Jaitley's zeal divided his Cabinet, with George Fernandes, Union Minister of Petroleum and Natural Gas Ram Naik, and Murli Manohar Joshi all opposed to disinvestment. Advani was also

---

25. Sudipto Banerjee, Renuka Sane, Srishti Sharma, and Karthik Suresh, "History of Disinvestment in India: 1991-2020", NIPFP Working Paper Series, No. 373 (March 2022), available at https://www.nipfp.org.in/media/documents/WP_373_2022.pdf.

26. "Report No. 17 of 2006 for the period ended March 2005 Performance Audit of Disinvestment of Government Shareholding in Selected PSUs during 1999-2003", available at https://cag.gov.in/en/old-audit-reports/view/13768.

27. Sudipto Banerjee, Renuka Sane, Srishti Sharma, and Karthik Suresh, "History of Disinvestment in India: 1991-2020", NIPFP Working Paper Series, No. 373 (March 2022), available at https://www.nipfp.org.in/media/documents/WP_373_2022.pdf.

not a supporter.[28] Jaitley waded through the opposition and managed to sell Bharat Aluminium Company Limited (BALCO), Computer Management Corporation (CMC) Limited, Hindustan Zinc Limited, Hindustan Teleprinters Limited (HTL), Indian Petrochemicals Corporation Limited (IPCL), MFIL, Paradeep Phosphates Limited (PPL), VSNL, Maruti Udyog Limited (MUL), a few hotel units of Hotel Corporation of India (HCI) Limited, and seventeen hotel units of the Indian Tourism Development Corporation (ITDC) Limited to private firms, while IBP Co. Limited was acquired by IOCL.

This phase is often referred to as the "golden period of privatisation" in India, but this was not without opposition—from both within the party and outside the party. Disinvestment of Maruti faced resistance from the heavy investment ministry. The then petroleum ministry along with other Cabinet colleagues had strongly opposed the disinvestment of oil marketing companies Bharat Petroleum Corporation Limited (BPCL) and Hindustan Petroleum Corporation Limited (HPCL).[29]

In August 2000, he defended the government decision to set up the Disinvestment Commission and disinvestment policy.[30] Jaitley argued that to keep investing tax payers' money in loss-making businesses is not good economics. A politician should not oppose sale of a unit just because it falls in his constituency; national interest should govern such decisions. Sale of units under disinvestment policy is not for shutting them but passing them on in hands of able managers for the benefit of the unit and its employees; this, in fact, generates more employment. One of the repeated allegations the government had to face was undervaluation of firms and selling national assets at a throwaway price. Jaitley rejected the criticism of lower valuation. He

---

28. Rohit Parihar and Rajeev Deshpande, "How Politics, Corporate Rivalry Led Vajpayee Government to Undo Privatization", *India Today*, accessed 25 May 25, https://www.indiatoday.in/magazine/economy/story/20020923-how-politics-corporate-rivalry-led-vajpayee-government-to-undo-privatisation-796265-2002-09-22.

29. Sudipto Banerjee, Renuka Sane, Srishti Sharma, and Karthik Suresh, "History of Disinvestment in India: 1991-2020", NIPFP Working Paper Series, No. 373 (March 2022), available at https://www.nipfp.org.in/media/documents/WP_373_2022.pdf.

30. Bharatiya Janata Party, "Short Discussion on Disinvestment Policy: Shri Arun Jaitley: 01.08.2000", accessed 25 May 2025, https://www.youtube.com/watch?v=28hqd_EUmLc.

defended the valuation methodology citing adherence to international norms and claimed that the final price was decided by market forces.

Citing examples of the sale of the shares of MFIL, he said that the value of the shares as per valuation was Rs 1000 per share, but they were sold at Rs 11,090 per share.[31] Besides, the government argued that unlike the erroneous policy of minority stake sale in the past, privatisation in non-strategic sectors was necessary to revive economic efficiency of the public sector firms. He argued that selling minority shareholding as done in the past does not fetch good value. The value of shares comes in strategic sales with the transfer of management so that new investors can turn around the business and, thereby, get better returns for themselves and for minority shareholders.[32]

Some relief came in 2001, when the Supreme Court in the BALCO deal held that the courts cannot interfere in economic policy matters like disinvestment.[33] Similarly on the aspect of valuation, the Supreme Court took the position that unless there was an error in complying with the valuation procedures, it did not have the jurisdiction to question the facts of valuation. The apprehension of job loss was associated with most of the deals, and major labour unrest broke out during the sale of BALCO, when almost 7,000 workers went on a strike for sixty-seven days. But the Supreme Court's decision clarified that neither the transfer of management control to private players can be equated with job loss nor the right of job protection can prohibit the government from disinvesting a firm. However, to address the concern of job loss, every strategic deal imposed a contractual prohibition on the strategic partners not to retrench workforce for one year from the date of execution of agreement, unless certain conditions were met.

While there was no retrenchment due to privatisation, the government declared several Voluntary Retirement Scheme (VRS) packages. As of March 2005, 5.53 lakh employees had opted for VRS. Jaitley termed the VRS scheme

---

31. WildFilmsIndia, "Arun Jaitley, Indian Politician on Disinvestment Policy in India", accessed 25 May 2025, https://www.youtube.com/watch?v=procAaf_suA.

32. Bharatiya Janata Party, "Short Discussion on Disinvestment Policy: Shri Arun Jaitley: 01.08.2000", accessed 25 May 2025, https://www.youtube.com/watch?v=28hqd_EUmLc.

33. AIR 2002 SC 350, *Balco Employees Union (Regd.) vs Union of India & Ors.*

as one of the most liberal retirement schemes.[34] The Supreme Court's decision in BALCO was expected to pave a way for future strategic decisions. However, earlier in 2003, the government missed an opportunity to disinvest HPCL and BPCL when the Supreme Court held that a public sector firm created out of nationalisation under a statute cannot be privatised, unless the concerned statute was amended through parliamentary nod.

Between 1999 and 2004, the Vajpayee government privatised twelve CPSEs generating Rs 29,990 crore equivalent to US dollar 4.6 billion[35], in which the control and management of the company were transferred to the private sector in ten firms. Rest of the sales included two CPSE-to-CPSE sales and a slump sale of twenty hotel properties belonging to the ITDC and HCIL.[36] This was against the target of Rs 58,500 crore fixed for the period. The trend of one CPSE buying shares of another CPSE continued in the future phases of disinvestment.

Opposition from Parliament and even from Vajpayee's own Cabinet was unrelenting. What halted this juggernaut was the government's attempts to sell its stake in BPCL and HPCL. Unlike Centaur Hotel or even Air India, these oil companies were seen as profit making. After several years of breakneck disinvestment, disinvestment had slowed to a crawl in 2003.[37] When he was the civil aviation minister for a brief period during 1999–2000, Jaitley pitched

---

34. WildFilmsIndia, "Arun Jaitley, Indian Politician on Disinvestment Policy in India", accessed 25 May 2025, https://www.youtube.com/watch?v=procAaf_suA.

35. Jyotindra Dubey, "Disinvestment Got Boost under Vajpayee-led NDA Govt. Here's How Public Sector Companies Fared Post-Privatisation", accessed 25 May 2025, *India Today*, https://www.indiatoday.in/diu/story/disinvestment-got-boost-under-vajpayee-led-nda-govt-here-s-how-public-sector-companies-fared-post-privatisation-1563694-2019-07-06.

36. Sudipto Banerjee, Renuka Sane, Srishti Sharma, and Karthik Suresh, "History of Disinvestment in India: 1991-2020", NIPFP Working Paper Series, No. 373 (March 2022), available at https://www.nipfp.org.in/media/documents/WP_373_2022.pdf.

37. Vinay Sitapati, *Jugalbandi: The BJP Before Modi* (Penguin, 2020), p. 250.

for disinvestment of Air India arguing that if it was not done, "nothing will be left to disinvest. That was around 18 years ago."[38]

The Standing Committee on Finance, 2002, recommended improvements in the policy. In February 2003, the DOD issued a revised disinvestment manual which laid down a detailed process and steps to be followed in every disinvestment transaction. Although most of the privatisation deals were completed between 1999 and 2003 before the revised document was released, the revised manual was expected to provide clarity to policymakers both at the central and state level for future disinvestment. Some of the primary objectives set out in the revised document were to release scarce public resources locked up in non-strategic sectors, so it can be used in high priority sectors; unlock taxpayers' money in the public sector by transferring the commercial risk to the private sector; unlock workforce in managing PSUs to utilise them in social sectors; and curb further investment in non-viable firms.[39]

Jaitley had his own share of problems and controversies, some of which continued for more than a decade—this is the only phase in the history of Indian disinvestment when privatisation was carried out. The Economic Survey 2019-20 stated that over the years the productivity of these privatised firms improved significantly which substantiates the economic rationale behind privatisation.[40] Since labour overheads and productivity remained a major concern in the public sector firms, transferring ownership to private players also witnessed positive effects on labour productivity. Despite these benefits, the apprehension of political costs associated with disinvestment was probably the reason why "strategic sale" to took a back seat in the next phase of disinvestment. Interestingly, the NDA is the only government which carried

---

38. PTI, "Arun Jaitley Pitches for Air India Disinvestment", *Mint*, accessed 25 May 2025, https://www.livemint.com/Politics/OY9E6zRiEeaYfItn9xMhIP/Arun-Jaitley-pitches-for-Air-India-disinvestment.html.

39. Sudipto Banerjee, Renuka Sane, Srishti Sharma, and Karthik Suresh, "History of Disinvestment in India: 1991-2020", NIPFP Working Paper Series, No. 373 (March 2022), available at https://www.nipfp.org.in/media/documents/WP_373_2022.pdf.

40. "Economic Survey 2019-20", Vol. 1, Government of India (January 2020), available at https://www.indiabudget.gov.in/budget2020-21/economicsurvey/doc/echapter.pdf.

out privatisation, the transfer of controlling interest to private parties under the disinvestment programme.

★

A competitive market guarantees three fundamental corporate freedoms: the freedom to enter a market (start a business), the freedom to operate and continue business under a level playing field, and the freedom to exit or discontinue business efficiently. While entry reforms were introduced in 1991, the freedom to operate without restrictions remained largely unaddressed. The state continued to control several strategic sectors, and the Monopolies and Restrictive Trade Practices (MRTP) Act of 1969—designed for an era dominated by public sector enterprises—was still in force.

On 23 July 2000, Arun Jaitley assumed charge of the Ministry of Law, Justice and Company Affairs following Ram Jethmalani's sudden resignation. Several crucial economic legislations aimed at enhancing the ease of doing business were pending in the ministry. Under Jaitley's stewardship, these measures successfully passed through Parliament.

Competition Act, 2002

One key reform initiated by the Rao–Singh duo had been to open the market to competition. By 1991, India had removed nearly all industrial licensing restrictions, except the MRTP Act. As minister of state for law in the Rao Cabinet, Rangarajan Kumaramangalam, popularly known as Ranga, was emotionally stressed when he was given the task of amending the MRTP Act, a legislation authored by his father, S. Mohan Kumaramangalam. Ranga's father, who died in an air crash in 1973, had begun as a part of the communist party "barristocracy" of the 1940s but later became Indira Gandhi's minister and her philosopher and guide for the socialist programmes she undertook in the 1970s. Ranga's grandfather P. Subbarayan was a member of the Nehru Cabinet. His uncle General P. Kumaramangalam was the chief of army staff and one of the last Sandhurst-trained officers of the Indian Army. His mother, Kalyani, was the niece of Ajoy Mukherjee, the first non-Congress chief minister of West

Bengal. Ranga's parents' wide circle of friends brought him a rich harvest of highly placed "uncles": Jyoti Basu, Indrajit Gupta, I.K. Gujral, P.V. Narasimha Rao and Arjun Singh. Finance Minister Manmohan Singh, who understood his agony, called him aside and asked him to do "what your father would have liked to do in the changed circumstances". Ranga promptly signed on the amendment that did away with state control on the growth of private business.

Globally, countries that liberalised in the early 1990s, like Malawi, had already enacted competition laws, while developed nations such as the US and Canada had such frameworks in place for over a century. India still held on to the archaic MRTP Act. In his 1999 budget, Finance Minister Yashwant Sinha announced the government's intention to introduce a modern competition law suitable for India, shifting focus from curbing monopolies to promoting healthy competition. S.V.S. Raghavan, then heading the State Trading Corporation, chaired a high-level committee, which submitted its report in 2000 highlighting the need for a competition law to curb anti-competitive practices and protect consumers amidst growing foreign competition.[41]

After assuming office, Jaitley introduced the Competition Bill in Parliament on 6 August 2001. The Bill sought to establish a commission to prevent anti-competitive practices, promote fair competition, and protect consumer interests.[42] It faced opposition from Congress and Left MPs, who feared exposing Indian industries to harmful international competition and undermining existing protections under the MRTP Act. Jaitley robustly defended the bill, emphasizing that its purpose was to prevent market abuses, regulate harmful mergers, and safeguard consumer interests without disadvantaging Indian companies. He said:

> The Bill seeks to check practices which may come about as aberrations in a market economy. Therefore, the Bill is intended to protect the consumer interest. The Bill in no way says that it is going to encourage competition of the kind which is going to put any Indian company

---

41. Shaji Vikraman, "In fact: How India Learnt to Promote, and Regulate, Competition", *The Indian Express*, accessed 25 May 2025, https://indianexpress.com/article/explained/in-fact-how-india-learnt-to-promote-and-regulate-competition-2829625/.

42. Lok Sabha Debates, Introduction of Competition Bill, 2001, on 6 August 2001, *Indian Kanoon*, available at https://indiankanoon.org/doc/1881609/.

> to a disadvantage. The Bill seeks to check anti-competitive practices. The Bill seeks to prevent any abuse of dominance. The Bill seeks to prevent such amalgamation which will have an appreciable adverse effect on competition itself. Therefore, the Bill seeks to protect those very factors about which my learned friend is concerned.[43]

The bill was reviewed by the Parliamentary Standing Committee on Home Affairs (covering law, justice, and company affairs) over a year and 13 sittings. Ultimately, the Competition Act was enacted in 2002, providing a modern legal framework to promote fair competition in India.

Companies (Amendment) Act, 2002

Jaitley then turned his attention to the freedom to exit or discontinue business efficiently. While the freedom to start a business or to continue doing business was already amply recognised in the Indian legal and regulatory landscape, the journey of the Indian insolvency reforms however remained painfully slow and incremental.[44] The legal framework for insolvency remained ineffective for decades, even as reforms in other areas of economic laws advanced rapidly after the liberalisation of the Indian economy in 1991. To attract foreign investment, policymakers focused heavily on reforming entry laws but neglected improvements in exit law, underestimating the role the insolvency system plays in winning investor confidence. Only some incremental measures were taken which led to a fragmented and fractured insolvency regime.

The RBI issued a number of one-time schemes for settlement of dues between lenders and borrowers from time to time.[45] Some of these failed to produce the desired result as lenders were scared that writing off loans may

---

43. Lok Sabha Debates, Introduction of Competition Bill, 2001, on 6 August, 2001, Indian Kannon, available at https://indiankanoon.org/doc/1881609/.

44. Sumant Batra, *Corporate Insolvency: Law and Practice* (Eastern Book Company, 2017).

45. Sumant Batra, "Developing the Asian Markets for Non-Performing Assets: Developments in India", 3rd Forum for Asian Insolvency Reform (2003), available at http://www.sumantbatra.com/pdf/papers/forum_for_asia.pdf.

cause investigating bodies to come after them and question the merits of each waiver. In 1993, the Government of India decided to set up special Debt Recovery Tribunals (DRTs) for the effective and speedy recovery of bad loans through a summary procedure.[46] Only banks and certain specified financial institutions can access the DRTs. However, the DRT also could not speed up the recovery of bad loans as expected. The total number of cases filed in the DRTs by scheduled commercial banks (SCBs) as a whole amounted to Rs 150,503 with the amount involved being Rs 2601 billion. Only Rs 427 billion (constituting 16.43 per cent) were recovered till March 2014. The expectations from the DRTs were very high. But within less than a decade, it became clear that the DRTs had failed to serve their purpose.[47] Non-performing assets (NPAs) continued to rise in banks and financial institutions in the absence of an effective insolvency law, and no substantial recovery could be made through the DRT.

At the same time, the capital adequacy requirements on risk-weighted assets, together with strict provisioning and income recognition norms for loan assets, were also causing stress on banks' balance sheets and profit and loss accounts. Expert committees were set up by the government and RBI again to suggest reforms. This prompted the enactment of the SARFAESI Act[48] in 2002. Taking a cue from many countries in Asia post the Asian Financial Crisis,[49] the government decided to provide a framework for the establishment of private sector asset reconstruction and securitisation companies through the SARFAESI Act.

The winding up of companies took even longer in India. An application for winding up on any ground including pursuant to recommendation made under the Sick Industrial Companies (Special Provisions) Act, 1985 (SICA) was

---

46. The Recovery of Debts Due to Banks and Financial Institutions Act was enacted in 1993 and DRTs were established consequent to the passing of this law. DRTs continue to operate in different parts of the country. The Bill has since been amended, from time to time.

47. R. Gandhi, "Banks, Debt Recovery and Regulations: A Synergy", Reserve Bank of India (2014), available at https://www.rbi.org.in/scripts/BS_SpeechesView.aspx?id=931.

48. Securitisation and Reconstruction of Financial Assets and Enforcement of Security Interest Act, 2002.

49. Sumant Batra, *Corporate Insolvency: Law and Practice* (Eastern Book Company, 2017).

required to be filed under the Companies Act, 1956 (now 2013 Act).[50] Even as of 31 October 2015, only about 955 (out of 4636) and 163 (out of 545) cases of court and voluntary winding up were resolved within five years. A significant number of such cases had been pending for more than twenty years.[51] The lengthy process kept substantial corporate assets unrealised and undistributed. The inordinate delay in liquidation proceedings marred the possibilities of rapid use of productive assets lying dormant in these proceedings throughout the country.

Due to the inefficiency of the SICA and winding up under the 1956 Act, the government set up a high-level committee in 1999 headed by Justice V.B. Eradi, a superannuated judge of the Supreme Court of India to examine and make recommendations with regard to the desirability of changes in law relating to insolvency of companies. The Eradi Committee recommended that the jurisdiction, power, and authority relating to winding up of companies should be vested in a National Company Law Tribunal (NCLT), a specialised bankruptcy tribunal. Noting the various reasons for the failure of the SICA in the revival and rehabilitation of sick industrial companies, the Eradi Committee recommended the repealing of the SICA. It suggested that the revival and reconstruction procedures in the SICA be made part of the 1956 Act in a suitably amended form to provide for a composite law. Appointment of professionals as liquidators was also recommended.

Based on the recommendations of the Eradi Committee, the 1956 Act was amended by way of the Companies (Second Amendment) Act, 2002. The SICA was repealed in 2003, but the repealing law could not be notified as the NCLT proposed by the 2002 Amendment got entangled in litigation. The 2002 Amendment was later perceived as inadequate and not notified in any case.

---

50. The Companies Act, 1956, has been replaced by the Companies Act, 2013.

51. "Report of the Joint Committee on the Insolvency and Bankruptcy Code, 2015" (April 2016), pp. 76–77, citing data from the Department of Financial Services, available at https://ibclaw.in/report-of-the-joint-committee-of-parliament/.

World Trade Organisation Negotiations

As mentioned earlier, when Murasoli Maran resigned as minister of commerce and industry following his arrest on 30 June 2001, Arun Jaitley was given charge of the ministry, which he held from July 2001 to May 2004. This was a crucial period for India. In 2001, the World Trade Organisation (WTO) had launched the Doha Round negotiations. These negotiations aimed at minimising tariffs on agricultural and industrial goods, removing agricultural and farm subsidies, and relaxing non-tariff barriers. Developed and developing countries have had dissenting positions on subsidies for food and agricultural sectors, non-agricultural market access, and trade facilitation provisions. India made significant progress during the Fourth WTO Ministerial Conference held in Doha, Qatar, between 9 and 13 November 2001. Beginning with the Declaration on the Trade-Related Aspects of Intellectual Property Rights (TRIPS) Agreement and Public Health, India pushed for measures to protect public health and promote access to medicines for all.

Following the Doha Round, the Fifth WTO Ministerial Conference was held in Cancun, Mexico, between 10 and 14 September 2003. Jaitley led India into the Cancun ministerial meeting. The mandate for the Cancun ministerial meeting was to review the progress made with respect to negotiations concerning agriculture, non-agricultural market access, and the four Singapore issues that were still ongoing since the Doha Round concluded. Even though two years had passed since Doha, deadlines on all core issues concerning developing nations, namely, the Declaration of TRIPS Agreement and Public Health, implementation issues, and special and differential treatment, were not met. Jaitley stayed firm on getting a commitment from the European Union to reduce trade-distorting agricultural subsidies. He had support from countries like China, Brazil, and Australia. The Cancun ministerial meeting ended without consensus on various issues, in particular on the four Singapore issues, because the draft ministerial declaration that the ministers had been asked to approve did not reflect the concerns of the developing and least developed countries.

There was no headway even after the European Commission, the main proponent, offered to take its proposal for negotiations on multilateral agreements on investment and competition policy permanently out of WTO. Certain countries refused to agree on negotiations on trade facilitation on the ground that uniform customs procedures would impose heavy costs and require administrative skills that were beyond their ability. On the other hand, some other countries opposed the removal of investment and competition policy from the WTO Work Programme.[52] The Fifth WTO Ministerial Conference concluded with the ministerial statement which recognised that more work needed to be done in some key areas to enable WTO member countries to proceed towards the conclusion of negotiations under the Doha mandate. The ministerial statement instructed the officials to continue working on outstanding issues with a renewed sense of urgency and purpose and taking fully into account all the views expressed in the ministerial conference. The chairman of the General Council of the WTO, working in close coordination with the director general, was asked to coordinate this work and to convene a meeting of the general council at senior officials level no later than 15 December 2003 to enable successful and timely conclusion of the negotiations.[53]

Jaitley was lauded for his firm negotiations at Cancun. On return from Cancun, Jaitley expressed deep disappointment at the lack of progress in resolving development issues. He said that India would have preferred a declaration addressing its concerns, but this did not happen. Had the draft ministerial declaration better reflected the concerns of developing countries, the conference would have had a chance of success. Lack of political will on part of certain developed countries to reduce distortions in trade of agricultural products coupled with onerous demands on developing countries to make steep market access commitments was another reason for collapse of the trade talks, Jaitley added. In this perspective it was better not to have an agreement rather than a bad one which would haunt all countries in future.[54] "We actively engaged in the negotiations and brought the concerns of developing countries

---

52. "Ignoring the Concerns of Developing Countries Was the Cause for Failure of the Cancun Ministerial Conference: Jaitley", Ministry of Commerce & Industry and Law and Justice, available at https://archive.pib.gov.in/release02/lyr2003/rsep2003/20092003/r20092003.html.

53. "Day 5: Conference Ends Without Consensus", World Trade Organization, accessed 25 May 2025, https://www.wto.org/english/thewto_e/minist_e/min03_e/min03_14sept_e.htm.

54. "Ignoring the Concerns of Developing Countries Was the Cause for Failure of the Cancun Ministerial Conference: Jaitley", Ministry of Commerce & Industry and Law and Justice, available at https://archive.pib.gov.in/release02/lyr2003/rsep2003/20092003/r20092003.html.

at the centre stage of the trade talks. The two coalition of developing countries on agriculture and Singapore issues were active during the entire Ministerial Conference and succeeded in collectively projecting and protecting their interests till the end of the Conference. The developed countries would now find it difficult to ignore these concerns, if the Doha Work Programme has to make any meaningful progress," he said.[55]

On Singapore issues, Jaitley highlighted that ignoring concerns of the developing countries, the draft ministerial declaration proposed the launch of negotiations in trade facilitation and transparency in government procurement. He proposed that these issues should now be removed from the WTO agenda as suggested by the European Commission. The section on investment assumed that negotiations would commence on the basis of a general council decision to be taken later. The text on competition policy on the other hand referred to possible negotiations, an obvious attempt to accommodate the interest of some developed countries. Further there was no reference to explicit consensus either in the paragraphs on investment or competition policy.[56]

Justifying India's position at Cancun, Jaitley stated that the draft ministerial declaration would not only perpetuate the existing distortions, but would also introduce a slew of new measures that would increase market distortions. The continuation of blue box[57] in an enlarged form without any commitment to significantly reduce and phase out these subsidies in future was a case in point. India also opposed the continuation of distorting subsidies in the amber box, which would otherwise result in the developed countries subsidising export of agricultural items. India expressed concern at the heightened ambition on market access pillar which ironically provided for special and differential treatment in favour of developed countries and was viewed to be extremely insensitive to the large number of people living in poverty in developing countries.

---

55. Ibid.

56. Ibid.

57. In WTO terminology, subsidies in general are identified by "boxes" which are given the colours of traffic lights: green (permitted), amber (slow down—need to be reduced), red (forbidden). *See*, WTO, "Domestic support in agriculture: The boxes", accessed on 25 August 2025, https://www.wto.org/english/tratop_e/agric_e/agboxes_e.htm.

India's position on agriculture found broad-based support among other developing countries. Giving details of subsidies and domestic support provided by the developed countries in agriculture, Jaitley pointed out that these subsidies are not targeted to keeping small struggling family farms in business but to provide hefty rents to large farmers or corporates. In many developed countries, the average income of farmers is higher than the national average, reaching almost 200 per cent of the average in certain cases. Subsidies to cotton growers in a developed country totalled US $ 3.7 billion last year, which is three times that country's foreign aid to Africa. The net effect of subsidising agriculture in developed countries at the expense of products of relatively poor farmers in developing countries is to aggravate global income inequalities. Elaborating on market access in non-agricultural products, Jaitley emphasised that India supported the formula devised by the chairman of the negotiating group as it recognised and incorporated certain elements for the developing countries as mandated by the Doha Declaration, while achieving significant reduction in the tariffs of all members. India opposed the proposal for mandatory tariff harmonisation and elimination as this would entail substantial contribution by the developing countries. On sectoral proposals, India expressed the view that not all the seven sectors were of export interest to all developing countries. It was also expressed that being at different stages of development, developing countries did not have the capacity to undertake binding obligations in all the seven sectors.

Looking to the future, Jaitley was cautiously optimistic about the completion of the ongoing work programme at the WTO. He informed that India had now sought resolution of all outstanding implementation issues by March 2004. "There is never a last day as far as the calendar of trade negotiations are concerned. India has been engaging constructively in the negotiations and is optimistic that in spite of the failure of the Cancun Ministerial Conference, it would be possible to move ahead in the weeks to come. Agriculture has been the core of the negotiations. It is important that the negotiations in this area are concluded in a manner which not only leads to increased market access but also removes the distortions and inequities in the trade of agricultural commodities caused by the extremely high levels of subsidies in the developed world. The onus is now on the developed countries to deliver on their promise of the WTO Work Programme being a 'development agenda', if the negotiations are to conclude by the end of 2004. This can be achieved through a process of decision-making at the WTO which is both transparent and inclusive without ignoring the sensitivities of the developing countries," he added.[58]

As the commerce and industry minister, Jaitley also pushed for the relaunch of the India–US Commercial Dialogue. On 11 June 2003, he delivered the keynote address at the India–US Commercial Dialogue organised by the US-India Business Council (USIBC) in collaboration with the Federation of Indian Chambers of Commerce and Industry (FICCI) and Confederation of Indian Industry (CII). He cited many areas of convergence underlining relations between the United States and India, the world's two largest democracies, which are committed to the rule of law, to upholding universal peace and security of open democratic and free societies. He reiterated the Vajpayee government's commitment to the economic reform process and said that the reform process initiated in 1991 had transformed the Indian economy. Economic reforms had contributed to the present strong fundamentals of the Indian economy—a rate of growth of 6 per cent registered over the last decade, low levels of inflation, and comfortable foreign exchange reserves.

In 2002, the Indian economy grew at more than 5 per cent despite a poor monsoon and a sluggish global economy. India's exports grew by 18 per cent during 2002, Jaitley said. He attributed this robust growth in the face of various internal and external adversities to the competitiveness of the Indian economy. The reform process had also contributed to significant reductions in the poverty levels in the country. He further emphasised the government's commitment to the reform process with special focus on the infrastructure such as roads, power, telecom as also the ports including connectivity in terms of roads and telecom in rural areas.[59]

58. "Ignoring the Concerns of Developing Countries Was the Cause for Failure of the Cancun Ministerial Conference: Jaitley", Ministry of Commerce & Industry and Law and Justice, available at https://archive.pib.gov.in/release02/lyr2003/rsep2003/20092003/r20092003.html.

59. "Mr. Arun Jaitley, Minister of Commerce & Industry visit to Washington, DC", Embassy of India, Washington D.C., USA, accessed 25 May 2025, https://www.indianembassyusa.gov.in/ArchivesDetails?id=444.

Freedom of the Press

As the information and broadcasting (I&B) minister (1998–2000), Jaitley championed press freedom, becoming a favourite of the media and its consumers. Jaitley opened up the broadcasting sector in May 2000 for participation by private FM broadcasters, which changed the listening habits of people. He also launched a TV channel in Kashmiri language from Srinagar to further integrate the state with the rest of the country. "He would take the long-term view to most situations. He strongly believed in free and fair news," recalled Dipankar Mukherjee, Jaitley's officer on special duty in the ministry who had a four-decade-long association with Jaitley.[60]

Press Information Bureau officials assigned to him recall how releases issued by Jaitley's office were easy to draft as the minister himself would be succinct in his instructions. "He made life so much easier for information officers that releases got drafted within minutes. He had mastered the art of writing and the complexities of communication. He was an expert in delivery and I do not think there is or will be another genius at communication like him," recalled a senior information officer of the Government of India, who did not wish to be named.[61]

★

Vajpayee was the first non-Congress prime minister to complete a full five-year term in office. But that was not his only claim to fame. Vajpayee also pioneered economic reforms, which laid the foundation for several major steps.[62] Vajpayee was the first prime minister to set up a separate disinvestment

---

60. "Bureaucrats Remember Arun Jaitley As Master of Complexities of Communication", News 18, accessed 8 November 2025, https://www.news18.com/news/india/bureaucrats-remember-arun-jaitley-as-master-of-complexities-of-communication-2282533.html

61. Ibid.

62. "The Legacy of Atal Bihari Vajpayee: 12 Key Reforms the Former PM Rolled Out", *Business Today*, accessed 25 May 2025, https://www.businesstoday.in/

ministry. Despite facing political obstacles and internal conflicts, the Vajpayee government successfully divested many PSUs. He lavishly sanctioned funds to the Railways to strengthen the railway tracks—a policy which paid dividends for the future performance of the Railways.

The Golden Quadrilateral project, launched in 2001, was the longest road project in India and the fifth-longest highway in the world, connecting four major cities—Delhi, Mumbai, Chennai, and Kolkata. The highway project provided a huge boost to manufacturing activity and productivity in districts located within 10 km of the road network. The new road infrastructure facilitated growing young firms to move out of congested big cities in search of cheaper land and buildings. The project resulted in a 49 per cent increase in overall output for the average district located along the Golden Quadrilateral network. In 2000, a parallel programme to the Golden Quadrilateral, the Pradhan Mantri Gram Sadak Yojana (PMGSY), was launched to provide all-weather road connectivity to every rural habitation with a minimum population of 500 in the plains and 250-plus in hill states, tribal districts, and desert areas. The biggest impact of the project was on productivity.[63]

In May 1998, Vajpayee's Prime Minister's Office (PMO) notified the appointment of a National Task Force on Information Technology and Software Development headed by Jaswant Singh, who was then the deputy chairman of the Planning Commission. With this, the Vajpayee government brought about a telecom revolution in the country by replacing fixed licence fees for telecom firms with a revenue-sharing arrangement. The task force was asked to draw up a national policy on informatics aimed at helping India become an IT superpower within ten years.[64] His initiatives in the telecom sector in correcting the initial aberrations of the policy by replacing high licence fees with revenue sharing and allowing multiple technologies laid the foundation for a telecom revolution. But for his initiatives, the telecom success story would not have been there. His rural roads programme added to the rural infrastructure. Users willingly paid for the construction of the national highways, a programme that he conceived and which still bears his imprint.

---

panorama/photo/legacy-of-atal-bihari-vajpayee-key-reforms-rolled-out-nda-modi-5698-2018-08-16/13.

63. Ibid.

64. Ibid.

The new Electricity Act of 2003 was his initiative. But for the changed regime, some recent improvements in the power sector would not have taken place. Vajpayee rationalised interest rates in order to make the industry competitive. He pursued the rationalisation of the tax structure, both direct and indirect, to give an impetus to the economy. He emphasised on port construction both in the state and in the private sector. Wherever necessary in national interest, he increased the Foreign Direct Investment limits in order to attract more investments. He had realised the intrinsic link between investments, economic activity, growth, infrastructure, jobs, and additional revenue. He was aware of the political resistance to reforms. He, therefore, moved steadily and periodically announced one step after another. He provided decisive political leadership for reforms.

The Fiscal Responsibility and Budget Management (FRBM) Act was introduced in 2003 with the aim to check fiscal profligacy. The decision was taken on the back of India's mounting debt burden, which in turn affected the country's fiscal deficit and financial health of the states. The move resulted in public sector savings, which surged from 0.8 per cent of the GDP in the fiscal year 2000 to 2.3 per cent in 2004–05.

While the NDA government's second term (NDA-II) will always be credited for the implementation of the Goods and Services Tax (GST), former Prime Minister Vajpayee had first proposed the indirect tax regime. It was during a meeting between Vajpayee and his advisors that the GST was discussed. Three former RBI governors, I.G. Patel, Bimal Jalan and C. Rangarajan, were also part of the team that envisaged the tax reform.

In 2000, Vajpayee had formed a committee headed by CPI(M) leader and then West Bengal finance minister Asim Dasgupta to design a GST model. It is said that Vajpayee had personally called the then West Bengal chief minister and CPI(M) stalwart Jyoti Basu requesting him to spare Dasgupta to draft the policy.

India's Northeast policy took a new turn under Vajpayee. He made several departures from the past by setting up several autonomous councils in the region and a separate ministry for development of the region, and earmarked 10 per cent of the funds from each ministry for the development of the north-eastern states. The Bodo Peace Accord in Assam was also signed during his term as the prime minister.

Vajpayee's Cabinet was democratic; it discussed various issues extensively and then looked up to him, awaiting his direction or his nod. Invariably, it was pro-reform. If there was a stalemate, he would constitute a group of ministers composed of individuals loaded in favour of the reforms and give them a timeframe. Jaitley once famously said, "Vajpayee inherited an economy of shortages and left behind a legacy of surplage."[65]

65. Arun Jaitley, "Arun Jaitley Speech in New Jersey on 10 October 2013", in *Articles & Speeches by Arun Jaitley: A Compilation* (Universal Law Publishing Co. Pvt. Ltd., 2014), pp. 269–70.

9

Jaitley and Modi: An Everlasting Friendship

Arun Jaitley maintained a wide network of relationships, but the most defining connection in his life was with Narendra Modi. He was among Modi's earliest and most enthusiastic supporters, dating back to 1999.

Jaitley and Modi went back a long way. Modi had joined the RSS in 1972 as an RSS pracharak. Jaitley had just joined the ABVP and become active in DUSU politics. Both were at the core of the anti-Emergency movement in 1975. It was during the post-Emergency years that they came to form an important friendship, one that would last a lifetime and prove crucial to their fortunes as well as those of the BJP. What started as a bond between two party colleagues working together for the party's growth developed into mutual respect and a formidable friendship, with each standing with the other through good and troubled times.

The year 2001 was the litmus test for Modi's friends including Jaitley. In February 2002, riots broke out in Gujarat killing thousands. Modi had barely assumed the office of chief minister, the first government office ever held by him. There was a call for his replacement as chief minister. Jaitley defended Modi against those seeking his resignation. Their relationship was cemented during this period when Jaitley weighed in on Modi's side at the risk of alienating himself from his prime minister and senior party members.

Modi was born on 17 September 1950, in the ancient town of Vadnagar, about 100 kilometres north of Ahmedabad. His father Damodardas Modi was a small-time grocer. Modi was one among five brothers and a sister. At the age of twenty, Modi became a swayamsevak and later a full-time pracharak. The then prant pracharak of the RSS, Laxman Rao Inamdar, popularly known as Vakil Saheb, took Modi under his wings. Modi rose quickly within the RSS. Starting as an RSS pracharak in Gujarat, Modi played a significant role in the campaigns and expansion of the BJP in the state.[1] In 1987, Modi was appointed as the organisation secretary for Gujarat—the person within the state RSS responsible for overseeing the BJP. Unlike the BJP state or national presidents, who are public figures, the organisation secretary is supposed to operate privately, directing the party from behind the scenes and serving as a "bridge" between the RSS and its political affiliate.

In 1987, Modi was given the responsibility of organising the party campaign for the Ahmedabad municipal elections. His methodical planning helped the BJP win two-thirds of the seats in the Ahmedabad municipality.[2] The eight years that Modi spent as organisation secretary in Gujarat coincided with an era of rapid growth for the state BJP. Its strength in the state assembly went up from 11 seats in 1985 to 121 a decade later. Though there were two very senior leaders at the helm of the state party—Keshubhai Patel and Shankarsinh Vaghela, both former Gujarat BJP presidents—Modi became a third power centre, exerting influence over the formation of alliances and the selection of candidates for state and national elections.[3] He was the force behind organising the successful Nyay Yatra undertaken by Advani in 1987 and the Lok Shakti Yatra in 1989.

Modi rose within the party ranks to be named as a member of the BJP's national election committee in 1990. The same year, he was roped in to help organise Advani's Ram Rath Yatra. He facilitated the first stretch of the Somnath–Ayodhya yatra undertaken by Advani. It was during this time that Jaitley and Modi got the opportunity to work together. Jaitley was to prepare

---

1. Bhupender Yadav and Illa Patnaik, *The Rise of the BJP: The Making of the World's Largest Political Party* (Penguin, 2022).

2. PTI, "I am About Mission, Not Ambition: Modi", accessed 25 May 2025, *Hindustan Times*, https://www.hindustantimes.com/india/i-am-about-mission-not-ambition-modi/story-20w77ry9ogsOWODngscerM.html.

3. Vinod K. Jose, "Modi's Quiet Campaign Against his Predecessor and Former Ally, Gujarat CM Keshubhai Patel", *Caravan Magazine*, accessed 25 May 2025, https://caravanmagazine.in/excerpt/modis-quiet-campaign-against-his-predecessor-and-former-ally-gujarat-cm-keshubhai-patel.

the media briefing notes, the material for which was provided by Modi. The two stayed in touch after the yatra. Modi made it a point to meet Jaitley every time he visited Delhi. During their long conversations, Jaitley started gaining an understanding of Gujarat's complex politics and Modi's commitment towards the state and its people, while Modi learnt the capital's way of politics from Jaitley.

★

Modi was soon caught on the wrong side of the power struggle between Vaghela and Patel. In September 1995, Vaghela flew forty-seven MLAs to Khajuraho in Madhya Pradesh and staked his claim to the chief minister's post with their backing. This happened when Patel was in the United States. The revolt led by Vaghela was the culmination of a struggle dating back to 1992 when Modi, then a relative newcomer and newly promoted state BJP general secretary, antagonised Vaghela, an RSS veteran for thirty years.[4] In 1995, Modi masterminded BJP's win—the party scored a majority of 121 legislators out of a 182-member legislative assembly. Modi supported Patel for chief ministership. Vaghela could not accept Patel being preferred over him. A crisis erupted and as soon as Patel returned from the United States, the central leadership had to step in to handle the fallout.

Vajpayee suggested a resolution: Vaghela could not replace Patel. Instead, they would have a compromise chief minister—Suresh Mehta. But Vaghela and Patel wanted something more. They demanded that the BJP expel Modi from Gujarat because he was the one, they alleged, fanning discontent.[5] Modi was appointed as the BJP national secretary and given charge of Haryana and Himachal Pradesh.

---

4. Uday Mahurkar, "BJP Leaders Became Oblivious to the Rot That Had Set Within the Party in Gujarat", *India Today*, accessed 25 May 2025, https://www.indiatoday.in/magazine/cover-story/story/19951031-bjp-leaders-became-oblivious-to-the-rot-that-had-set-within-the-party-in-gujarat-808652-1995-10-14.

5. N.P. Ullekh, *War Room: The People, Tactics and Technology Behind Narendra Modi's 2014 Win* (Roli, 2015), pp. 83–104.

Modi moved to Delhi in 1995. Dileep Sanghani, who was then the Lok Sabha member from Amreli, Gujarat, offered him a room in his official residence on Harish Chandra Mathur Lane.[6] Out of Gujarat, Modi grew in the ranks of the party on the strength of his performance. Under his watch, the BJP's tally rose to eleven in 1996 from just two in the 1991 Haryana Assembly polls. In the Himachal Pradesh Assembly, where the BJP had just eight seats when Modi assumed charge, the tally reached thirty-one in 1998.[7] In May 1998, Modi was appointed as BJP national general secretary (organisation). Once again camping in a room in a friend's house and living nomadically out of a single suitcase,[8] Modi worked to build a wide network in Haryana, Himachal Pradesh, Madhya Pradesh, Chhattisgarh, Rajasthan, Bihar, Jharkhand, and Maharashtra. Party leaders he had befriended during this time would prove to be extremely helpful later in his race to become the prime ministerial candidate of his party.[9]

All this time, while Modi travelled all over the country, his anchor in Delhi was Jaitley. The two were, on the face of it, rather different. Modi could be reticent in contrast to Jaitley's gregarious ways. But the two hit it off.[10] Modi aspired to get a toehold in national politics. The capital city was new to Modi who was not familiar with the ways of Delhi and the politics of Lutyens' Delhi. Jaitley was rapidly emerging on the national political scene. He had played a key role for the party in the 1991 general elections. He was also representing the BJP and its top leaders in the Babri Masjid demolition and Hawala cases. Jaitley was close to both then party president Advani and veteran leader Vajpayee.

---

6. Ajay Singh, *The Architect of the New BJP: How Narendra Modi Transformed the Party* (Penguin, 2022).

7. N.P. Ullekh, *War Room: The People, Tactics and Technology Behind Narendra Modi's 2014 Win* (Roli, 2015, 2019), p. 93.

8. Andy Marino, *Narendra Modi: A Political Biography* (HarperCollins, 2014), p. 94.

9. N.P. Ullekh, *War Room: The People, Tactics and Technology Behind Narendra Modi's 2014 Win* (Roli, 2015, 2019), p. 93.

10. Diwakar and Rajeev Deshpande, "Arun Jaitley: A Politician and a Gentleman", *The Times of India*, accessed 25 May 2025, https://timesofindia.indiatimes.com/india/arun-jaitley-a-politician-and-a-gentleman/articleshow/70824103.cms.

Both young leaders—Modi and Jaitley—exchanged their learning and craft with each other on their long walks together in Lodhi Garden.[11]

Soon Modi shifted base to Chandigarh spending more time in the beautiful city on the foothills of the Shivalik hills, which provided him proximity to the mountains.[12] Between 1996 and 2001, Modi began to travel abroad on missions of international diplomacy on behalf of the party. He travelled to more than forty countries that provided him good exposure which expanded his horizons.[13] The two remained in touch. BJP leader Vijay Jolly, recalls that in 1999, he accompanied Jaitley to the Raymond (M&N Sons) showroom at Regal Building in Connaught Place to buy a cream-coloured kurta-pajama material for Modi. Jaitley personally inspected a dozen materials before he selected two of the best cream colours for Modi—the prime minister of today but, off-course, an incognito Sangh Pracharak toiling hard in the BJP then. 'I witnessed it twenty years ago," Jolly wrote.[14] Jolly had by then become a member of Delhi Legislative Assembly.

Modi and Jaitley continued to impress the Delhi hierarchy and, by 1999, Modi won the full confidence of Vajpayee, who made him the party spokesman.[15] Modi appeared more frequently in front of television cameras and proved himself adept at handling questions from journalists. He was now seen in the Delhi BJP headquarters as an astute tactician and a dependable worker.[16]

In the same year, Jaitley was inducted as a minister in the Vajpayee government. He was allotted a bungalow at 9 Ashoka Road, adjacent to the BJP's national headquarters. Jaitley had only the year before moved into his new house in South Delhi; he decided not to occupy the bungalow for residence and instead let his party colleagues use it. He held his party meetings there.

---

11. Diwakar and Rajeev Deshpande, "Arun Jaitley: A Politician and a Gentleman", *The Times of India*, accessed 25 May 2025, https://timesofindia.indiatimes.com/india/arun-jaitley-a-politician-and-a-gentleman/articleshow/70824103.cms.

12. Andy Marino, *Narendra Modi: A Political Biography* (HarperCollins, 2014), p. 90.

13. Ibid.

14. Vijay Jolly, TRIBUTE: Arun Jaitley, the go-getter. "Jaitley was my DU senior whom I always referred to as the Big Boss", *The Week*, accessed on 4 September 2025, https://www.theweek.in/news/india/2019/08/28/arun-jaitley-the-go-getter.html.

15. Andy Marino, *Narendra Modi: A Political Biography* (HarperCollins, 2014), p. 95.

16. Ibid., p. 90.

Modi moved into 9 Ashoka Road and stayed there till 2001 whenever he was in Delhi until he was sent to Gujarat as the chief minister. He used to eat in the mess that Govindacharya (then, a BJP secretary) used to run for party workers.[17] On 17 May 2014, a day after his historic victory, Narendra Modi returned triumphantly to his old home at 9 Ashoka Road where he lived as the party general secretary in the late 1990s.

★

In the 2000 municipal elections, the BJP lost control in Ahmedabad and Rajkot cities and was almost wiped out across the panchayats, losing twenty-one of twenty-three districts. Its vote share fell from 80 per cent to 20 per cent. It lost the precious Sabarmati Assembly seat and the Sabarkantha Lok Sabha seat, one of the twenty-six Lok Sabha seats. In 2000–01, the party lost every single by-election in the state. BJP leaders in Delhi were deeply concerned by the electoral setbacks in Gujarat. Losing the 2003 assembly elections suddenly looked a possibility. But still the central leadership did not act.

In January 2001 came the calamitous Kutch earthquake which killed about 20,000 people. In Ahmedabad, 400 kilometres away from the quake's epicentre, nearly 200 tall buildings, shoddily constructed allegedly in return for kickbacks, collapsed causing 750 deaths. Patel's health was failing. Relief operations were seen to be tardy. The administration seemed at first paralysed by the natural disaster, and then plain incompetent. Official stonewalling and a reluctance to part with information marked the first five days after the earthquake. When Patel at last came on television to warn of possible aftershocks, his clumsy articulation triggered a panic. It emerged later that many new buildings that were reduced to rubble in Ahmedabad and elsewhere in the state were shoddily built by unscrupulous builders who enjoyed Patel's patronage.[18] An incipient mood of anti-incumbency began to set in. Voter disgruntlement spiralled.

---

17. A. Ganesh Nadar, "When Modi was BJP General Secretary in Delhi", Rediff, accessed 25 May 2025, https://www.rediff.com/news/report/ls-election-when-modi-was-bjp-general-secretary-in-delhi/20140519.htm.

18. N.P. Ullekh, *War Room: The People, Tactics and Technology Behind Narendra Modi's 2014 Win* (Roli, 2015, 2019), pp. 83–104.

On 28 June 2000, Modi made one of his brief visits to Gujarat. There was a groundswell of enthusiasm building for Modi.[19] The political aftershocks were too intense to ignore.

It was in these trying times that Jaitley proposed to Advani that Modi be sent to Gujarat as the chief minister. Advani readily concurred. The only problem was that Modi had no administrative experience.[20] Sanjay Joshi, the powerful organising secretary of the Gujarat BJP, opposed Modi's candidature. He was in favour of elevating Vallabhbhai Kathiria, a leader from Patel community.[21] But as Modi's political mentor, Advani was also fully aware of his mentee's abilities; he was also very fond of him. Advani agreed to speak with Prime Minister Vajpayee.

On 1 October 2001, Vajpayee called Modi and suggested he take over from Keshubhai Patel and prepare the state for the next assembly polls[22]—a major decision at that time as Modi was the first full-time RSS pracharak to be directly inducted into mass politics. Modi declined the offer initially, but agreed to spend ten days a month in Gujarat working among the people. When Modi returned to Gujarat in 2001, six years after he was told to leave the state, the government, led by an ailing Patel, was hurtling from crisis to crisis, buffeted by corruption charges and nepotism. Modi realised within days that Patel's misrule had left the state BJP in disarray. Preparing the party for the elections in December 2002 was not going to be easy. He was, however, reluctant to take over as the chief minister. Advani and Jaitley stepped in. Modi heeded their advice and was sworn in as the chief minister of Gujarat on 7 October 2001, six days after Vajpayee's call. He had turned fifty-one only a few days earlier. Then came the riots of February 2002.

★

---

19. Andy Marino, *Narendra Modi: A Political Biography* (HarperCollins, 2014), pp. 96–97.
20. Ibid., p. 100.
21. Saba Naqvi, *The Saffron Storm, From Vajpayee to Modi* (Penguin, 2024), p. 122.
22. Andy Marino, *Narendra Modi: A Political Biography* (HarperCollins, 2014), p. 98.

On 27 February 2002, barely a few months after Modi took charge, a train with several hundred passengers was set on fire near Godhra by a mob, killing approximately sixty people. At 7.42 a.m., a train—9166 UP, known as the Sabarmati Express—nearly five hours behind schedule, carrying 2300 passengers, pulled into the platform of Godhra in Gujarat. Most passengers were Gujarati kar sevaks returning from Ayodhya after performing a religious ceremony, some singing and chanting slogans. The train was to terminate its journey in Sabarmati.

The train stopped for approximately five minutes at Godhra Junction. Then, as it pulled away from the platform, stones began to be pelted at the coaches by a crowd. A few minutes later, and after only 700 metres of travel, the train halted again a little way down the line at Signal Falia that runs parallel to the Godhra railway station. Allegedly somebody had pulled the emergency chain, applying the brakes. Suddenly a large crowd surrounded the train. Electric light bulbs filled with acid were thrown in after stones had shattered the glass. The pilgrims pressed suitcases against the window but Coach S6 was soon well alight. A few passengers managed to shelter beneath the carriage, but those trapped in the compartments were quickly burned to death. Those who escaped were butchered by the crowd outside.[23] In a matter of minutes fifty-nine people, including twenty-six women and ten children, perished.

The VHP gave a call for a bandh on 28 February. During the bandh riots broke out.[24] Thousands were killed in the riots. There was a clamour for Modi's resignation from opposition parties, and by many in the BJP. The Opposition accused the Modi government of inaction and allowing violence against a particular community. Jaitley was perhaps the first Delhi leader in the BJP who openly supported Modi through ups and downs during his chief ministership. Never in the history of India has there been misinformation propaganda against any political leader as it has been against Modi, Jaitley argued for Modi.[25] He defended Modi vehemently stating that propaganda cannot be a substitute

---

23. Ibid., 104–05.

24. Bhupender Yadav and Illa Patnaik, *The Rise of the BJP: The Making of the World's Largest Political Party* (Penguin, 2022).

25. "2002 Guj riots: many misled into retaliatory action: Jaitley", *Deccan Herald*, accessed on 4 September 2025, https://www.deccanherald.com/india/2002-guj-riots-many-misled-2316212.

for evidence.[26] Advani, then the home minister, visited Gujarat and defended Modi's performance in tackling the situation during the post-Godhra riots.[27] Advani rejected allegations of inaction on the part of the state government on the floor of Parliament.[28] As the clamour for Modi's resignation increased, Advani offered him his unflinching support. While Vajpayee reportedly insisted on Modi's resignation, Advani and Jaitley rallied the whole party behind Modi, forcing the then PM to back down.

Vajpayee visited the state on 4 April and apologised for not having been able to visit earlier.[29] He had a message for Modi that the chief minister should "follow his rajdharma", which of course means that a ruler should treat all of his subjects equally and without prejudice. Modi quietly replied, "*Hum bhi wahi kar rahe hain, sahib*" (That is what we are also doing, sir). Vajpayee, who used to speak with long pauses, said, "I am sure Narendrabhai is also doing the same."[30] Vajpayee implied in his avuncular way that if Modi were to survive politically, he would have to ensure peace in the state. There was no other option.[31] "Rajdharma" was, in the context, a loaded term, and for somebody in a position of power, it meant not discriminating among the higher and lower classes of society or people of any religion.[32]

---

26. TNN, "Our Stand Has Been Vindicated, Says BJP", *The Times of India*, accessed 25 May 2025, https://timesofindia.indiatimes.com/india/our-stand-has-been-vindicated-says-bjp/articleshow/9962034.cms.

27. Shantanu Gupta, *Bharatiya Janata Party, Part, Present and Future: Story of the World's Largest Political Party* (Rupa, 2026), p. 310.

28. "Shishya's coup: How Modi, Advani fell apart", *The Times of India*, accessed on 4 September 2025, https://timesofindia.indiatimes.com/india/shishyas-coup-how-modi-advani-fell-apart/articleshow/20512839.cms

29. Andy Marino, *Narendra Modi: A Political Biography* (HarperCollins, 2014), p. 142.

30. N.P. Ullekh, "How AB Vajpayee Was Foiled in His Bid to Have Narendra Modi Removed as Gujarat Chief Minister", *Scroll.in*, accessed 25 May 2025, https://scroll.in/article/826433/ how-ab-vajpayee-was-foiled-in-his-bid-to-have-narendra-modi-removed-as-gujarat-chief-minister.

31. Andy Marino, *Narendra Modi: A Political Biography* (HarperCollins, 2014), p. 142.

32. N.P. Ullekh, "How AB Vajpayee Was Foiled in His Bid to Have Narendra Modi Removed as Gujarat Chief Minister", *Scroll.in*, accessed 25 May 2025, https://scroll.in/article/826433/how-ab-vajpayee-was-foiled-in-his-bid-to-have-narendra-modi-removed-as-gujarat-chief-minister.

The BJP's national executive was scheduled to be held in Goa later that month on 12 April 2002, where Modi's continuance was likely to come up. Modi was "sad" about the 2002 Gujarat riots but had no guilt. Yet he was increasingly beginning to feel that his presence as the chief minister of Gujarat was not helping his people and was considering quitting. "There is a need for a free and frank discussion. To enable this, I wish to place my resignation before this body. It is time we decided what direction the party and the country should take from this point onwards."[33] Before the BJP national executive, Jaitley was dispatched to Gujarat to discuss the matter with Modi.[34] Jaitley knew Modi well and was convinced of his friend's innocence. In Ahmedabad, he was closeted with Modi for a few hours. The two later flew together to Goa. When asked by the media, he denied that Modi's resignation had nothing to do with the visit. "My visit was entirely for a different purpose. I am a Member of Parliament from Gujarat. I had to attend a meeting for my MP development fund. It got emphasised out of proportion that I had gone to suggest something to Mr Narendra Modi. Frankly, the mood within the party was also not to expect Mr Modi to resign," he said.[35] As events unfolded over the next two days, it became clear that Jaitley had persuaded Modi not to quit and in fact planned how to avert the demand for resignation. Meanwhile, on a plane journey from New Delhi to Goa, Vajpayee and Advani were also discussing Modi's resignation.[36]

At the executive meeting in Goa, Modi rose to speak before Vajpayee was to address the delegates. Modi offered to step down as chief minister.[37] There was an uproar. Speaker after speaker rose to speak in favour of Modi, presenting

---

33. Andy Marino, *Narendra Modi: A Political Biography* (HarperCollins, 2014), p. 142.

34. Kingshuk Nag, "How Arun Jaitley paved the way for Narendra Modi's ascent as prime minister", CNBC TV 18, https://www.cnbctv18.com/politics/how-arun-jaitley-paved-the-way-for-narendra-modis-ascent-as-prime-minister-6717251.htm.

35. The Rediff Interview/Arun Jaitley, Rediff, accessed 25 May 2025, https://m.rediff.com/news/2002/jul/08inter.htm.

36. Kingshuk Nag, "How Arun Jaitley paved the way for Modi's ascent as prime minister", CNBC TV 18, accessed on 24 August 2025, https://www.cnbctv18.com/politics/how-arun-jaitley-paved-the-way-for-narendra-modis-ascent-as-prime-minister-6717251.htm.

37. Andy Marino, *Narendra Modi: A Political Biography* (HarperCollins, 2014), p. 143.

him as the hero of Gujarat and the BJP.[38] Such was the sentiment in favour of Modi, BJP national president K. Jana Krishnamurthi proposed a resolution appreciating Modi's administrative swiftness in controlling and stopping the riots.[39] It said that "[in] a democracy there is only one way to put the issue, and the calumny to rest: the people are the ultimate arbiters, and so the people of Gujarat are the ones who can and must decide. Accordingly, the BJP's national executive unanimously rejects Shri Modi's offer to resign his post. It is confident that Shri Modi can meet every challenge, that by effective action he can counter every canard."[40]

★

After Goa, Modi decided to seek a fresh mandate by calling for a midterm election in the state, seeking to either exit or obtain legitimacy through elections. The internal assessment was that the so-called anti-incumbency against the BJP had been forgotten in the heightened communal atmosphere, and the sooner Modi went to the people, the better it would be for the party in Gujarat. Modi dissolved the assembly on 19 July 2002. Governor S.S. Bhandari accepted the recommendation. The last sitting of the assembly was held a few months earlier, on 3 April 2002. Article 174 provides that the governor shall from time to time summon the House or each House of the state legislature to meet at such time and place as he thinks fit, but six months shall not intervene between its last sitting in one session and the date appointed for its first sitting in the next session.[41] Article 176 provides for the address of the governor of a

---

38. Prem Shankar Jha, "When Vajpayee Failed to Stand Up to Modi in 2002, He Changed the Course of Indian History", *The Wire*, accessed 25 May 2025, https://thewire.in/politics/atal-bihari-vajpayee-narendra-modi.

39. Bhupender Yadav and Illa Patnaik, *The Rise of the BJP: The Making of the World's Largest Political Party* (Penguin, 2022).

40. Rajnath Singh, "Resolution on Godhra and its aftermath", Bharatiya Janata Party, accessed 25 May 2025, https://www.bjp.org/hi/speeches/resolution-godhra-and-its-aftermath.

41. Article 174(1) says that "[the] Governor shall from time to time summon the House or each House of the Legislature of the State to meet at such time and place as he

state to the state legislature at the commencement of the first session after each general election to the legislative assembly and also at the commencement of the first session of each year. Article 324 deals with superintendence, direction, and control of elections to be vested in the ECI. As there cannot be a gap of more than six months between two sittings of the House, Gujarat's governor was advised that polls were required to be held and results declared before 3 October 2002. Modi was thus ready to face the first electoral battle of his life.

There was, however, a problem. The ECI was not in agreement. The ECI received advice from the former Prime Minister I.K. Gujral, and former Chief Justice of Delhi High Court Justice Rajinder Sachar, that Article 176 did not apply in this case. There was apprehension that Article 356 may be invoked to impose President's Rule in Gujarat.

At this stage Arun Jaitley took over from Modi. He met James Michael Lyngdoh, the then chief election commissioner, on 21 July and emphatically argued that the provisions of Article 356, which relates to imposition of President's Rule in a state, did not apply as the dissolution had been done voluntarily by the state government and not followed a breakdown of the constitutional machinery. Jaitley told Lyngdoh that in his opinion, Article 324, which relates to the powers of the ECI in the conduct of polls, was circumscribed by Article 174, which says that there cannot be a gap of more than six months between two sittings of the assembly. In other words, since the last session was in April, the next had to be in October, and therefore the elections had to be held before that.[42]

Lyngdoh decided to take his two other commissioners on a tour of Gujarat in the second week of August 2002 so that the ECI could assess first-hand whether free and fair elections were possible in a riot-ravaged state. In Vadodara, he publicly accused the district administration of lying to him, calling the district collector Bhagyesh Jha and his team "a bunch of jokers".[43] On returning to

---

thinks fit, but six months shall not intervene between its last sitting in one session and the date appointed for its first sitting in the next session".

42. TNN, "Arun Jaitley Pulls Out Rulebook on Elections", *The Times of India*, accessed 25 May 2025, https://timesofindia.indiatimes.com/india/arun-jaitley-pulls-out-rulebook-on-elections/articleshow/16700264.cms?utm_source=contentofinterest&utm_medium=text&utm_campaign=cppst.

43. "Gujarat BJP Workers Take on Election Commissioner J.M. Lyngdoh", *India Today*, accessed 25 May 2025, https://www.indiatoday.in/magazine/nation/

Delhi, in a forty-page order passed on 16 August, Lyngdoh refused to announce dates before October 2002, saying that the ECI would review the situation in November–December before coming to a decision.

Jaitley launched a frontal assault on Lyngdoh. He was convinced that Article 174 made it binding on the ECI that the gap between the last sitting of the assembly in one session and the first sitting in the next session cannot be more than six months. If elections could be held in the terrorist-infested state of Jammu and Kashmir, why not in Gujarat where normalcy had returned, Jaitley argued.

As advised by the Union Cabinet, the President of India A.P.J. Abdul Kalam sent a reference to the Supreme Court on 19 August 2002 under Article 143 of the Constitution which provides that "if at any time it appears to the President that a question of law or fact has arisen, or is likely to arise, which is of such a nature and of such public importance that it is expedient to obtain the opinion of the Supreme Court upon it, he may refer the question to that court for consideration and the court may, after such hearing as it thinks fit, report to the President its opinion thereon". The Supreme Court shall, after such hearing as it thinks fit, report to the President its opinion thereon. The President's opinion as to the question being of public importance is not open to question.

The questions posed by then President A.P.J. Abdul Kalam were:

1. "Is Article 174 subject to the decision of the Election Commission of India under Article 324 as to the schedule of elections of the Assembly?
2. "Can the Election Commission of India frame a schedule for the elections to an Assembly on the premise that any infraction of the mandate of Article 174 would be remedied by a resort to Article 356 by the President?
3. "Is the Election Commission of India under a duty to carry out the mandate of Article 174 of the Constitution, by drawing upon all the requisite resources of the Union and the State to ensure free and fair elections?"

The Supreme Court bench, comprising Chief Justice B.N. Kirpal and Justices V.N. Khare, K.G. Balakrishnan, Ashok Bhan, and Arijit Pasayat directed the Centre, all the states, and the six national political parties—the BJP, the Congress (I), the CPI(M), the CPI, the Nationalist Congress Party (NCP), and

---

story/20020826-gujarat-bjp-workers-take-on-election-commissioner-jm-lyngdoh-796491-2002-08-25.

the BSP—to file submissions by 16 September 2002, and posted the matter for hearing from 17 September 2002. The bench also issued notice to the Centre, the Gujarat government, and Chief Minister Narendra Modi, on a public interest litigation (PIL) petition questioning the legality of Modi continuing as caretaker chief minister even after the dissolution of the assembly.

Jaitley argued in the Supreme Court for the BJP.

In its opinion tendered by the five-member Constitution bench—the main opinion, written by Justice V.N. Khare on behalf of Chief Justice B.N. Kirpal and Justice Ashok Bhan, and the two concurring opinions by Justices Arijit Pasayat and K.G. Balakrishnan—on 28 October 2002, the Supreme Court held the basic premise on which questions were faulty, but proceeded to answer the reference. The bench sought to explain why it could not answer any of the three queries, as posed by the President, because his basic assumption was wrong. Article 174(1), the bench opined, relates to an existing, live, and functional legislative assembly and not to a dissolved one. Articles 174(1) and 85 (the corresponding provision for Parliament) were not intended to provide any period of limitation for holding elections in order to constitute a new House, the bench said.

After explaining why it could not answer any of the three questions posed by the President, the bench, however, sought to answer a hypothetical question, which was not posed in the reference but was articulated during the hearing of the case. The bench found that the RPA has not provided any period of limitation to hold elections to constitute a fresh assembly in the event of a premature dissolution of an assembly. Examining related provisions in the Constitution and the RPA, the bench concluded that upon the premature dissolution of an assembly, the ECI was required to initiate immediate steps to hold elections in order to constitute a legislative assembly within six months from the date of such dissolution. "Ordinarily, law and order or public disorder should not be an occasion for postponing the elections, and it would be the duty and responsibility of all concerned to render all assistance, cooperation, and aid to the ECI for holding free and fair elections," the bench concluded.

Justice Pasayat, in his concurrent opinion, suggested that the reasons for deferring elections beyond six months after the dissolution of an assembly should normally bear relation to acts of God and not the acts of man. But the main opinion tendered on behalf of three judges makes no such distinction.

Yet, Chief Justice B.N. Kirpal also had some stern words for the ECI, which appeared to have inquired whether President's Rule could be imposed after a period of six months without a sitting of the state assembly. The Supreme Court bench observed that as there was no infraction of mandate to hold elections within six months of the latest sitting of the assembly, the application of Article 356 of the Indian Constitution did not arise. The bench also thundered that Article 324 of the Indian Constitution casts a responsibility and duty on the ECI to hold polls "at the earliest", adding that timely elections were the essence of democracy and that law and order should not be grounds for deferring them.[44] Within an hour of the Supreme Court verdict, the ECI announced that the assembly elections in Gujarat would be held on 12 December 2002.[45]

In the meantime, *Outlook* delivered a sensational story that went without a byline, but as a boxed special in the cover story headlined "Unhappy Atal Thinks of Quitting".[46] The story maintained that the prime minister was particularly upset at his party's continuous campaign against the ECI. And it was with Jaitley's role that the prime minister was particularly unhappy. Modi would never have tried to pull off this stunt of resigning in between assembly terms if Jaitley had not advised him to do so, the story said. Normally calm, Jaitley was enraged. He was not the sort of person to take things lying down. He protested. The *Outlook* story created huge problems. Vajpayee's principal secretary was uncomfortable projecting the prime minister as targeting Jaitley. Jaitley was aware of the source of the story, being very well-entrenched into the media.[47]

The PMO denied everything, saying the magazine's record as a BJP-baiter needed no belabouring. Brajesh Mishra called *Outlook* and accused its editor Vinod Mehta of printing a concocted report. Vinod Mehta later revealed in his autobiography that Arnab Dutta, the young correspondent who wrote the inbox story, was hired by *Outlook* at the instance of Ashok Saikia, a bureaucrat

---

44. Under Article 143(1) of the Constitution of India, 28 October, 2002, *Indian Kanoon*, available at https://indiankanoon.org/doc/308516/.

45. V. Venkatesan, "The Supreme Court's View", *Frontline*, accessed 25 May 2025, https://frontline.thehindu.com/other/article30246686.ece

46. Saba Naqvi, *The Saffron Storm: From Vajpayee to Modi* (Penguin, 2024), p. 143.

47. Ibid., 144.

in the PMO, who was close to Vajpayee and his forty-two-year-old foster son-in-law Ranjan Kishore Bhattacharya.[48]

Even in the past, many attempts had been made to plant suspicion about Jaitley in Vajpayee's mind. In June 2002, in the aftermath of the failed India–Pakistan talks at Agra the previous year, *Time* magazine ran a cover story on Vajpayee titled "Asleep at the Wheel?".[49] After a colourful description of the prime minister's dietary habits and ill health, it stated that he "is given to interminable silences, indecipherable ramblings and, not infrequently, falling asleep in meetings … an unusual candidate to control a nuclear arsenal". Vajpayee was very angry. Several pointed a finger at Jaitley. When the *Time* article appeared, Jaitley had been the minister of law and justice for two years—he took over the position from Ram Jethmalani. The same month, June 2002, there was a Cabinet reshuffle, and Jaitley was removed from his post. Jaitley was, however, brought back as the law minister after six months, in January 2003; the government needed its best legal brain.[50]

The election campaign was tense as the Delhi media targeted Modi for the riots. Unfazed, Modi positioned himself deftly as a victim of a conspiracy, even as human rights lawyers, non-governmental organisations (NGOs), and members of civil society kept raising questions about the 2002 riots in Gujarat. Even that worked to his advantage.[51] Modi romped home. The BJP secured 126 seats (which eventually rose to 127) and 49.85 per cent votes, against 117 seats and 44.81 per cent votes garnered in 1998. The Congress won 51 seats and 39.28 per cent votes in 2002, against 53 seats and 34.8 per cent votes polled in 1998. Modi was sworn in as the chief minister on 22 December 2002.

★

48. Vinod Mehta, *Lucknow Boy: A Memoir* (Penguin, 2011), p. 213.

49. Alex Perry, "Asleep at the Wheel?", *Time*, accessed 25 May 2025, https://time.com/archive/6645123/asleep-at-the-wheel/.

50. Praveen Donthi, "Talk of the Town", *Caravan Magazine*, accessed 25 May 2025, https://caravanmagazine.in/reportage/talk-town.

51. Saba Naqvi, *The Saffron Storm: From Vajpayee to Modi* (Penguin, 2024), pp. 218–21.

Having won the political battle, Modi prepared to face a long legal battle. Once again, Jaitley took charge and crafted the strategy. Jaitley strategised on the legal issues that Narendra Modi faced in Gujarat. Finally, in 2012, Modi was given a clean chit by a Special Investigation Team (SIT) appointed by the Supreme Court. It said that the then Gujarat chief minister took all possible steps to control the 2002 post-Godhra riots. In its closure report, the SIT mentioned:

> Law and order review meetings were held by Modi and all the things were done to control the situation … the Army was called on time to contain the communal violence … Modi was busy with steps to control the situation, establishment of relief camps for riot victims and also with efforts to restore peace and normalcy … In view of the detailed inquiry and satisfactory explanation of the person involved, no criminal case is made out against Narendra Modi.[52]

Later, in 2013, a local court upheld the SIT report and rejected a petition seeking prosecution of Modi over allegations he intentionally failed to protect Muslims during religious violence in his state.[53]

With the 2002 elections and political and legal vindication, two things became clear—Modi enjoyed mass popularity, and Jaitley was both a great political and legal strategist. Jaitley also established that he stood by his friends through thick and thin. This was to become one of Jaitley's strongest traits. He went on to have several good friends across the political spectrum which gave him the rare edge in the party in managing alliances and crises for his government, which became the hallmark of his career.

---

52. "How SIT Report Exonerates Modi: The Highlights", News18, accessed 25 May 2025, https://www.news18.com/news/india/how-sit-report-exonerates-modi-the-highlights-473243.html.

53. Niharika Mandhana, "Court Clears Narendra Modi in Riots Case", *The Wall Street Journal*, accessed 25 May 2025, https://blogs.wsj.com/indiarealtime/2013/12/26/court-clears-narendra-modi-in-riots-case/.

10

From Young Turk to Frontline Leader (2004–14)

Atal Bihari Vajpayee built on the reforms introduced by Narasimha Rao and Manmohan Singh. GDP was growing at 8.5 per cent in 2003–04, the IT sector was booming, mobile phones had brought the telecom revolution to the hands of the common man, and the media was thriving. A new sense of self-confidence and empowerment manifested itself in the urban Indian middle class.[1] India was improving on all parameters—the economy was doing well, several government schemes were taking shape, and internationally, too, India's diplomatic standing had improved. The BJP was gearing up for the upcoming Lok Sabha elections of 2004.

As president of the BJP, Venkaiah Naidu's had steered the party to win many elections. After Naidu took charge of the party in 2002, the party faced assembly elections in several states over the next two years. While there were a few setbacks, the party did manage to record some splendid performances in the assembly elections. In December 2003, the party won assembly elections in three states, wresting power from the Congress in Rajasthan, Chhattisgarh, and Madhya Pradesh. Pramod Mahajan, who was in charge of the poll campaign in Rajasthan, was credited with pulling off a miracle of sorts in Rajasthan. Jaitley steered his party's campaign successfully in the difficult state of Madhya Pradesh. He was lauded for overseeing Uma Bharti's campaign in Madhya

1. Vinod Mehta, *Lucknow Boy: A Memoir* (Penguin, 2011, 2013), pp. 218–20.

Pradesh.[2] Congress leader and Chief Minister Digvijaya Singh's ten-year reign came to a crashing end. The BJP contested 230 seats and won 173, with Uma Bharti becoming the chief minister.

A BJP win in these elections, the first after Chhattisgarh was carved out of Madhya Pradesh, stunned even the BJP. The year before, Jaitley had steered his party's campaign successfully in the difficult state of Gujarat. For the Congress, the only saving grace was Delhi, where Chief Minister Sheila Dikshit comfortably beat the challenge posed by the BJP's Madan Lal Khurana. The veteran Congress leader went on to serve as India's longest-serving woman chief minister.

The win in December 2003 convinced many in BJP that the mood of the nation was with the party and that people were invested in the leadership of Vajpayee, and that the NDA would easily secure a renewed mandate if parliamentary elections were to be held soon enough. A buoyant Pramod Mahajan believed India was shining; the BJP had won comfortably in three assembly elections without raising the spectre of masjid–mandir or orchestrating communal riots. Mahajan proposed that the general elections be advanced to April 2004 from September that year. Others chipped in, seeing great merit in the argument. RSS ideologue S. Gurumurthy concurred: Why not cash in and have early elections? The situation is in our favour, Mahajan and Gurumurthy argued.[3] Eventually, the elections were advanced.

Only two men in the party had serious reservations about both early elections and the India shining strategy. Vajpayee, an experienced politician, was too experienced to fall for marketing gimmicks. But no one in the party would listen to him.[4] The other was Jaitley although he went along with the popular sentiment in the party. Everyone in the party was convinced that the BJP-led NDA government had worked hard to bring about a change in India and paced up development in urban as well as rural parts of the country.[5]

Vajpayee was persuaded by the party colleagues. He, in turn, convinced NDA allies for early elections. The BJP decided to go in for early polls, by five

---

2. Saba Naqvi, *The Saffron Storm: From Vajpayee to Modi* (Penguin, 2024), p. 153.

3. Vinod Mehta, *Lucknow Boy: A Memoir* (Penguin, 2011), pp. 218–24.

4. Ibid.

5. Shantanu Gupta, *Bharatiya Janata Party: Past, Present and Future: Story of the World's Largest Political Party* (Rupa, 2020), p. 314.

months, firmly believing in their campaign tagline "India Shining"[6]—a term coined by Mahajan. The Lok Sabha was dissolved on 26 February 2004, almost nine months before schedule. The ECI, however, said it needed more time, and, subsequently, the next general elections were scheduled in April–May 2004.

The BJP decided the NDA would seek a mandate for Vajpayee's continued leadership of India. The BJP was convinced that the infrastructure had improved and they should go to the general elections with the development pitch. They even came up with a clever little acronym "BSP" (bijli sadak paani). It was also decided that all the constituents of the NDA would have a common election manifesto. The BJP would, however, prepare a separate vision document of its own to present its commitments and ideological perspectives on various issues. Jaitley chaired the committee that produced this document. Pramod Mahajan was made in charge of the election management committee[7] and the BJP's Lok Sabha election campaign "India Shining". Leaders of the BJP-led alliance, especially Pramod Mahajan, offered morning interviews while walking on their treadmills and were extremely confident of a victory.

The BJP unleashed India Shining, arguably one of the biggest ad campaigns—political or otherwise—that India has ever seen; it spent Rs 150 crore in a span of 120 days. The average yearly spend of advertising by cola companies to promote their brands was then around Rs 100 crore. Rs 150 crore is the kind of number that Hindustan Unilever Limited (HUL) would spend on brands like Sunsilk, Closeup, Lifebuoy, Rin, and Lux combined. Seldom, if ever, has a creative idea been backed with this kind of money. Conceived by Grey Worldwide, the India Shining campaign claimed to be a reflection of the mood of the nation and was expected to help the NDA return to power with an enhanced majority.[8]

The term "India Shining" was borrowed from an advertisement released on 14 October 2003 by the finance ministry on the health of the nation. When picked for the 2004 elections, India Shining had three competitors—*India Alive*,

6. Saba Naqvi, *The Saffron Storm: From Vajpayee to Modi* (Penguin, 2018, 2024).

7. L.K. Advani, *My Country, My Life* (Rupa, 2008), pp. 762–64.

8. "BJP Spends Rs 150 cr on 'India Shining' Campaign", *The Economic Times*, accessed 25 May 2025, https://economictimes.indiatimes.com/brand-equity/advertising/bjp-spends-rs-150-cr-on-india-shining-campaign/articleshow/684246.cms?from=mdr.

India Rising, and *India Dazzling*.[9] Some accounts suggest Advani selected India Shining,[10] and others insist it was Pramod Mahajan.[11]

Such was the force and momentum of India Shining and such was its illusory potency that a mood of gloom and doom descended even on the Congress.[12] On 13 May 2004, exit and opinion polls predicted a victory for the BJP.[13]

Jaitley perhaps was one of the few BJP strategists who was not completely in sync with the idea of India Shining and had a different opinion from Mahajan. He believed that the development propaganda missed an important undercurrent which can connect with the voters and was firm that India Shining would not connect with the rural masses.

Mahajan and Jaitley shared a relationship that was both collaborative and competitive, reflecting the complexities of political friendships. Their bond was rooted in a shared vision for the BJP and mutual respect that transcended political differences. Both rose through the ranks of the BJP during the 1980s and 1990s—a period when the party was transitioning from a marginal political entity to a dominant force in Indian politics. They complemented each other. Mahajan, known for his strategic mind and organisational skills, played a key role in shaping the BJP's media and communication strategies. Jaitley, a lawyer by profession, contributed his expertise on economic policies and articulate debating skills to the party's growth and policy agenda, while also showing his skills at coalition management. Mahajan was close to Vajpayee, but he also relied on Jaitley's legal and political advice. Jaitley admired Mahajan's ability to connect with grassroots workers and his knack for political manoeuvring. Both held significant positions during the Vajpayee-led NDA government (1998–2004). The two were part of a young, dynamic leadership group of leaders like Sushma Swaraj and Narendra Modi, who were fast becoming central figures in Indian politics.

9. Vinod Mehta, *Lucknow Boy: A Memoir* (Penguin, 2011), pp. 218–19.

10. Ibid.

11. "The BJP's Campaign Calculus", *The Caravan*, accessed on 4 September 2025, https://caravanmagazine.in/editors-corner/bjps-campaign-calculus.

12. Vinod Mehta, *Lucknow Boy: A Memoir* (Penguin, 2011, 2013), pp. 218–24.

13. Ibid.

There were moments of political tension between the two. Both were seen as potential future leaders of the BJP, and their ambitions occasionally led to behind-the-scenes competition. Mahajan, with his mass appeal and organisational strength, was often seen as a natural successor to the older leadership, while Jaitley's intellectual prowess made him indispensable in policymaking. However, their rivalry never turned bitter. They maintained a cordial relationship, often seen together at social gatherings and party meetings. Colleagues recall their witty exchanges and mutual admiration, even when they disagreed on political strategies.

The BJP entered the campaign in 2004 feeling supremely confident. It hoped that a bountiful monsoon that year, rising growth rates, and a reviving peace process with Pakistan would have persuaded voters to give Vajpayee another five years in office.[14] Its members began to chant that there was a "feel-good" factor, claiming they would cruise to an easy victory by pitting the charismatic and a great orator Vajpayee against the Congress president Sonia Gandhi, who read her speeches haltingly in public meetings.

★

The BJP's confidence was proved wrong. On 13 May 2004, when the results were declared, the BJP was shocked into silence. Neither the mega media budget nor the images of proud Indians giving a thumbs up to 'India Shining' had gone down well with the target audience. The NDA suffered a crushing blow in the 2004 elections. While 'India Shining' became a popular catchphrase with the English-speaking target audience and was praised in the advertising and marketing circles, it did more damage to the NDA than good. In a surprising result, the NDA alliance's seat numbers declined. It secured only 187 seats. The BJP could manage only 138 seats, a lower tally than it had in 1999. It had slid by 44 seats from its last tally of 182. The BJP's tally was even lower than its 1996 score, which was 161.

In contrast, the UPA managed to get 221 seats, with the Congress securing 145 seats, 7 more than the BJP. In all, twenty-six members in the Vajpayee

---

14. N.P. Ullekh, *War Room: The People, Tactics and Technology Behind Narendra Modi's 2014 Win* (Roli, 2015), pp. 36–51.

council of ministers were defeated. Veterans like Yashwant Sinha and then Lok Sabha Speaker Murli Manohar Joshi lost the elections.

Though in comparative terms the BJP secured just seven Lok Sabha seats fewer than the Congress, the results of the 2004 Lok Sabha elections were nothing short of a shock for the NDA government. The onward march of the BJP from 2 seats in 1984 to 182 seats in 1999 was halted. Moreover, it was no longer the largest party in the Lok Sabha, a position it had been holding since 1996.[15] The BJP, which had claimed 29 in Uttar Pradesh in 1999, was down to a dismal 10 in the 2004 polls. In Delhi, where the party had held all seven seats, it won only one.

In Karnataka, the state under Jaitley's charge, the BJP had increased its tally from 7 to 18, a remarkable leap, although he was disappointed that in Gujarat the number had dropped from 20 to 14. The only silver lining was that it got a foothold in the North-East winning both seats in Arunachal Pradesh. Some of the NDA allies such as the Janata Dal (United) [JD(U)] and the TDP blamed the Gujarat riots for their defeat and warned against reverting to a hardline agenda. The BJP accepted the defeat and decided to sit in the Opposition.

Pramod Mahajan was "half-stunned and half heart-broken". The results from Mumbai, the industrial capital of India, were perhaps even more shocking, where the BJP had a pre-poll alliance with the Shiv Sena, an arrangement for which Mahajan was credited. Actor Govinda of the Congress unseated Union Petroleum Minister Ram Naik from Mumbai North, which he had won five times with record margins.[16] Thankfully, the BJP was able to retain 13 seats in Maharashtra, the same number it had won in 1999.

It is widely believed that "Feel-Good Factor" and "India Shining" hurt the BJP. These phrases, though valid in themselves in a particular context, were inappropriate for the BJP's election campaign. There had indeed been a "feel-good" atmosphere in the country over the past one year prior to the 2004 elections, on account of a combination of factors: accelerating economic growth; sound macroeconomic management; a good monsoon yielding an all-time high food production; praise for India on account of her shining achievements in sectors such as IT; a sharp dip in incidents of cross-border

---

15. Shantanu Gupta, *Bharatiya Janata Party: Past, Present and Future: Story of the World's Largest Political Party* (Rupa, 2020), pp. 314–22.

16. Saba Naqvi, *The Saffron Storm: From Vajpayee to Modi* (Penguin, 2024), p. 159.

terrorism; the long-hoped-for turnaround in the situation in Jammu and Kashmir and the North-East; and anticipation of a new chapter of peace and cooperation with Pakistan.

However, by making the "Feel-Good Factor" and "India Shining" the verbal icons of the BJP's election campaign, the BJP gave an opportunity to its political opponents to highlight other aspects of India's contemporary reality—poverty and uneven development, unemployment among the youth, problems faced by farmers, etc., which questioned the BJP's claim.[17]

Some believed that even while the BJP seemed assured of triumph and even while Vajpayee soared in the national consciousness as a leader who stood above his party and enjoyed nationwide appeal, the BJP's election campaign had been unnecessarily vicious. It zeroed in on Sonia, Rahul, and Priyanka; not their inexperience, but their foreign origin became the core issue. That alienated a lot of voters.

The BJP national leadership was now low on morale. Many leaders were unable to reconcile with the defeat, which till a few months ago seemed a certainty under the Indian Shining campaign. Many in the party including Jaitley did not approve of the defeatist reaction to defeat.[18] He defended the India Shining campaign and argued that BJP scored wherever political and social factors were in its favour. He refused to hold any person or persons responsible for defeat. "In BJP, if we win, it is collective credit, if we lose, it is collective responsibility."[19] Mahajan sounded a confident note. "No war is lost till the last warship is sunk," he responded to a concerned BJP activist on the morning of 13 May 2004, as it became clear that the NDA was hurtling towards a shock defeat.[20]

Senior BJP leaders admitted that an argument could be made that there was no correlation between good work and getting re-elected. In his book, Yashwant Sinha, former BJP leader, who was a minister in the Vajpayee government, admitted that the Indian Shining campaign was a misjudgement.

---

17. L.K. Advani, *My Country, My Life* (Rupa, 2008), pp. 768–71.
18. Saba Naqvi, *The Saffron Storm: From Vajpayee to Modi* (Penguin, 2024), pp. 160–61.
19. Arun Jaitley in *Aap Ki Adalat*, accessed on 4 September 2025, https://www.youtube.com/watch?v=jVAbPUTr1dY
20. Venkitesh Ramakrishnan, "A Fighter and A Leader", *Frontline*, accessed 25 May 2025, https://frontline.thehindu.com/other/obituary/article30209515.ece.

Any correlation is the first fallacy of punditry. Voting is only marginally connected to the work one might have done, or the government one was a part of. It is dependent on many other factors which may or may not work in one's favour. The biggest factor is managing voter perception, and perceptions can't be managed only by slick slogans. "Feel-Good" and "India Shining" backfired on NDA-I, probably because wrong slogans were chosen, he wrote. "Perhaps we needed different slogans?" he added.[21]

The Congress-led UPA of twelve parties won 225 seats in Parliament.[22] The UPA did not enjoy a simple majority on its own in Parliament; rather it relied on external support similar to the formula adopted by the previous minority governments. An informal alliance had existed prior to the elections as several of the current constituent parties had developed seat-sharing agreements in many states. However, it was only after the elections that the results of negotiations between parties were announced. Although the mandate was a fractured and indecisive verdict as the UPA had won only 225 seats, the Congress cobbled together a coalition of eight parties to join hands with the UPA. These parties included the CPI(M) with 43 seats; SP with 36; BSP with 19; CPI with 10; and the AIFB, RSP, RLD, and Janata Dal (Secular) [JD(S)] with 3 seats each. This added another 120 seats to the UPA's 225, taking their total in the Lok Sabha to 341.[23] The party made a claim to form the government.

The UPA government was formed. Sonia Gandhi declined the post of the prime minister, choosing to appoint Manmohan Singh instead. She remained the party president and headed the National Advisory Council (NAC).

★

Over the next ten years, Jaitley rose exponentially in the party. Having lost a sure-win election in 2004, the BJP had much to introspect. There was a change

---

21. Yashwant Sinha with Aditya Sinha, *India Unmade, How the Modi Government Broke the Economy* (Juggernaut, 2018), p. 16.

22. "2004 Lok Sabha / Parliamentary Election Results", India Votes, accessed 24 August 2025, https://www.indiavotes.com/lok-sabha/2004/all-states/14/0.

23. Shantanu Gupta, *Bharatiya Janata Party: Past, Present and Future: Story of the World's Largest Political Party* (Rupa, 2020), pp. 314–22.

of leadership in the BJP, with Advani taking over from Naidu in 2004. A year later, Rajnath Singh took over from Advani. Both presidents made significant changes in the organisation during their terms. Both gave bigger responsibilities to Jaitley who immersed himself in party work. Soon he would transition from a Young Turk to become the BJP's frontline leader and chief strategist stitching alliances and strategising wins in key states while also becoming a prominent party voice in Parliament. When the BJP announced a week-long Satyagraha in September 2004, Arun Jaitley and Sushma Swaraj courted arrest on the fifth day of the BJP's week-long Satyagraha.[24]

Naidu resigned as the president of the BJP on 18 October 2004, citing personal reasons for doing so. He also added that, although collective responsibility was the accepted mantra in the BJP, he had taken "full responsibility as the party president" for the BJP's defeat in the Lok Sabha polls. He had been experiencing considerable inner turmoil, which was exacerbated by the unbecoming conduct of certain party colleagues.[25] Though the RSS has made plain its preference for former Uttar Pradesh Chief Minister Rajnath Singh, the consensus in the BJP was that Naidu should get the job. Advani himself was known to favour Naidu and many second-rung leaders, too, had agreed to see him appointed for a year before the party settled on a "long-term" candidate. But the former BJP chief was apparently miffed at being projected as a "stop-gap" arrangement.[26]

Finding a successor to Naidu became an excruciating task. In his biography, Advani writes that he was strongly in favour of a colleague from the second rung of leadership to take on the reins of the party. There were capable leaders from the younger generation: Pramod Mahajan, Arun Jaitley, Narendra Modi, and Sushma Swaraj, to name a few.[27] Indeed, it had been a conscious decision of Vajpayee and Advani since the 1980s to groom a new crop of promising young

---

24. Mayank Singh, "How Defence Took a Leap Under Late Former Finance Minister Arun Jaitley", *The New Indian Express*, accessed 25 May 2025, https://www.newindianexpress.com/thesundaystandard/2019/Aug/25/how-defence-took-a-leap-under-late-former-finance-minister-arun-jaitley-2023854.html.

25. L.K. Advani, *My Country, My Life* (Rupa, 2008), pp. 774–76.

26. "Naidu Pulls Out, BJP Race Opens Up", *The Telegraph Online*, accessed 24 August 2025, https://www.telegraphindia.com/india/naidu-pulls-out-bjp-race-opens-up/cid/831758.

27. L.K. Advani, *My Country, My Life* (Rupa, 2008), pp. 774–76.

leaders. But almost all of them felt that the party needed a senior leader at the helm at the stage. Advani was reluctant. He had no desire to become the BJP president again. Vajpayee urged Advani to accept the proposal. Ananth Kumar, the influential BJP leader from Karnataka, and Jaitley persisted with him to take up the post.[28] He relented.[29] On 27 October 2004, the BJP appointed the seventy-nine-year-old Advani as the president for the fifth time, and also the Leader of the Opposition in Lok Sabha.

Vajpayee was finally in a semi-retirement mode. He presented a garland to Advani. As Murli Manohar Joshi was not pleased with the decision, he walked out halfway through Advani's speech. Uma Bharti returned from her retreat in the hills and also to the party. She sat next to Advani's daughter, Pratibha Advani.[30] Mahajan and Jaitley sat next to each other and exchanged pleasantries, dispelling any media speculation of a rift over the India Shining campaign.[31]

With a new leadership in place, the BJP set on the path to reinvent itself. Jaitley was appointed general secretary and put in charge of many poll-bound states. Despite the failure of several of his initiatives, Mahajan continued to sustain his position, and from time to time even increased his clout in the BJP hierarchy.

Arun Jaitley, Sushma Swaraj, Pramod Mahajan, and Jaswant Singh continued to raise the party's voice in the Rajya Sabha. They became prominent faces of the party in Parliament. Jaitley immersed himself in party work, earning accolades for strategising the party's victories in several states.

A year later, Advani quit as the president. In 2005, he earned the wrath of the RSS when he went to Pakistan and praised its founder Mohammad Ali Jinnah as "secular". His comment, recorded in the mausoleum of Jinnah in Karachi, undermined the Sangh's doctrine that Jinnah was responsible for the Partition.

On 31 December 2005, Rajnath Singh was elected BJP national president, at a time when the party's morale was low, following the electoral loss of 2004.[32]

---

28. Saba Naqvi, *The Saffron Storm: From Vajpayee to Modi* (Penguin, 2018, 2024), p. 164.

29. L.K. Advani, *My Country, My Life* (Rupa, 2008), pp. 774–76.

30. Saba Naqvi, *The Saffron Storm: From Vajpayee to Modi* (Penguin, 2024), p. 168.

31. Ibid.

32. Bhupender Yadav and Ila Patnaik, *The Rise of the BJP: The Making of the World's Largest Political Party* (Penguin, 2022), p. 125.

Rajnath Singh represented the next generation of the BJP politicians, when compared with Vajpayee (born in 1924) or Advani (born in 1927). In this sense, his elevation was an important milestone, establishing a new leadership team for the BJP after the 2004 debacle. Alongside him, the next generation of BJP politicians such as Arun Jaitley (b. 1952), Sushma Swaraj (b. 1952), Pramod Mahajan (b. 1949), and Vasundhara Raje Scindia (b. 1953) started coming to the fore. Rajnath Singh's new team had Pramod Mahajan, Rajiv Pratap Rudy, Dharmendra Pradhan, Ananth Kumar, Mukhtar Abbas Naqvi, Smriti Irani, and many other young leaders. As many as 80 per cent of the people in his team were below sixty years of age.[33]

The beginning of Singh's tenure also highlighted the role of the Young Turks—Arun Jaitley, Sushma Swaraj, M. Venkaiah Naidu, and Pramod Mahajan—in the greater scheme of things. Singh had begun to look at Mahajan in the same light that Vajpayee had defined him—as the "jagat" or "everyone's Lakshman" Mahajan was poised to play a significant part in taking the party to new heights. For many in the BJP it was Mahajan's acumen as a tireless strategist that made him a fast-rising leader of his generation, but for Singh, Mahajan offered the right mix of a traditionalist and a moderniser. Unlike most politicians, he did not shy away from owning up to failures and took the blame for the way the India Shining campaign, which was his idea, had backfired.

In a way Rajnath Singh was the next generation's Vajpayee, albeit without the latter's verbal lyricism, while Mahajan, with his legendary organisational skills mixed with charismatic oratory, was a hybrid of Vajpayee and Advani. As a true party man and team player, Mahajan had underplayed his so-called coronation by Vajpayee during the BJP's December 2005 national convention in Mumbai and enjoyed a great working relationship with Rajnath Singh. Already there were indications of the BJP cadre getting back into the groove for the civic polls in Uttar Pradesh, followed by assembly elections in Goa, Himachal Pradesh, Punjab, Uttaranchal, and Uttar Pradesh. For the press and political commentators, this was being seen as Singh's acid test following his elevation to the post of the BJP national president. Singh, however, could not be bothered with the intricacies and focused on recovering lost ground. He

33. Ibid., p. 126.

held fast to the belief that the 2004 verdict was more of a defeat of the BJP than a decisive victory of the Congress.[34]

On 22 April 2006, Pramod Mahajan was shot thrice at point-blank range by his forty-six-year-old younger brother Pravin Mahajan; he died thirteen days later. After shooting his brother, Pravin walked into the Worli police station with the pistol and surrendered. Dixit has narrated the shocking incident in his book:[35]

> That morning around 7.30 a.m., Pravin reached Pramod's living room when the latter was engrossed in reading a newspaper. Pramod's wife Rekha and servant Harish, who were also present in the room till then, went to the kitchen to prepare tea for them. Pravin wanted to talk to Pramod, but while he spoke, Pramod didn't acknowledge his presence and continued to be engrossed in the newspaper. In a spur of the moment, an enraged Pravin took out his licensed F.N. Browning 0.32 bore pistol and fired three shots at Pramod's abdomen. After injuring Pramod, Pravin straightaway went to the nearby Worli police station and surrendered. His confession left the officers numb, and they took a while to decide their response. Meanwhile, Pramod Mahajan was rushed to the PN Hinduja Hospital by his brother-in-law and a senior BJP leader Gopinath Munde who stayed in the same building. On his way to the hospital, a conscious Mahajan asked Munde, *"Mi kaay chook keli Pravin ne mala marla?"* (What was my mistake that Pravin shot me?) Soon, he lost consciousness. The bullets had damaged his liver and pancreas. A police team reached the hospital to record Pramod's statement, but the doctors informed them of his precarious situation. After battling for his life for 12 days, Pramod finally gave up and was declared dead at 4.10 p.m. on May 3, 2006. His last words to Munde were taken as his dying declaration. Despite getting the best medical treatment available in the country, he couldn't be saved. Mahajan's death marked an end of an era in the BJP history.

---

34. Gautam Chintamani, *Rajneeti: A Biography of Rajnath Singh* (Penguin, 2019).

35. Jitendra Dixit, *Bombay After Ayodhya: A City in Flux* (HarperCollins, 2022).

An associate of Mahajan likened his twelve-day-long battle with death as yet another illustration of the grittiness of the man.[36]

Pramod Mahajan's tragic death shocked the nation and left a void in the BJP. Jaitley was deeply affected by the loss. In his heartfelt tribute to Mahajan, Jaitley called him a "master strategist" and a "friend who could light up any room with his presence". Jaitley also acknowledged Mahajan's contributions to the BJP's growth and often reminisced about their shared political battles.

After the premature death of Pramod Mahajan in 2006, Jaitley became the main pointsman for veteran leader L.K. Advani to deal with political challenges. Atal Bihari Vajpayee, who was not very fond of Jaitley, had by then moved towards near retirement due to his failing health. Jaitley continued to play a pivotal role in the BJP, eventually becoming one of the most influential finance ministers under Prime Minister Narendra Modi. However, he often credited leaders like Mahajan for shaping the party's modern identity.

★

Many schemes started by the Vajpayee-led government were taken forward by Dr Manmohan Singh. This, in a way, was a validation of his development initiatives.[37] The UPA started on a sound note, but it had its share of problems. The Telangana Rashtra Samithi (TRS), renamed later as the Bharat Rashtra Samithi (BRS), was the first party to quit the alliance, first when its ministers quit the Andhra Pradesh government, and finally when an official withdrawal was done at the national level by its president K. Chandrashekar Rao. The Marumalarchi Dravida Munnetra Kazhagam (MDMK) began its drift when it tied up with the UPA's rival AIADMK during the Tamil Nadu elections. On 16 March 2007, the MDMK officially withdrew its support from the UPA government. The Congress–BSP relations took a downturn in Uttar Pradesh. On 21 June 2008, the BSP, with eighteen seats, announced withdrawal of its

---

36. Venkitesh Ramakrishnan, "A Fighter and A Leader", *Frontline*, accessed 25 May 2025, https://frontline.thehindu.com/other/obituary/article30209515.ece.

37. Shantanu Gupta, *Bharatiya Janata Party: Past, Present and Future; Story of the World's Largest Political Party* (Rupa, 2020), p. 314.

support after the Congress started opposing the Uttar Pradesh government where the BSP was the ruling party.

Though the Congress and the Left Front had a tension-filled relationship, thanks to the overarching Left Front umbrella, UPA-I never once went into the danger zone. The Left Front kept the government going for four years. It was only in July 2008 when the Left Front finally withdrew its support over the Indo-US civil nuclear deal, that UPA-I felt the heat of its dwindling numbers. On 4 January 2009, the Jammu and Kashmir's Peoples Democratic Party (PDP) withdrew its support from the UPA government stating that the Congress had decided to support Omar Abdullah's National Conference government in Jammu and Kashmir after the 2008 state elections.

The UPA's first and only serious test came towards the end of its term, with just eight months left for the general elections. Often perceived as a "docile" leader, Manmohan Singh shocked critics and political observers in 2008 when he boldly stood his ground to push through the landmark Indo-US civil nuclear deal. Faced with fierce opposition from the Left Front, particularly the CPI(M) led by Prakash Karat, Singh's decisive actions during the crisis revealed a side of him that many had underestimated. The result was not just the successful implementation of the nuclear deal, but also Singh's emergence as a "strong leader" in his own right, defying expectations and securing his place in history.[38]

The Indo-US civil nuclear deal, which promised to bring India into the global fold of nuclear energy commerce, was fiercely contested by the Left Front, which had drawn a hard line against it. The Left parties threatened to withdraw their crucial support from the UPA government, potentially toppling Singh's administration. In a meeting on 7 August 2007, Singh refused to buckle under pressure.[39] Following a series of negotiations, the International Atomic Energy

---

38: "Manmohan Singh Risked His Position as Prime Minister to Help Seal the Landmark Indo-US Nuclear Deal", *The Economic Times*, accessed 25 May 2025, https://economictimes.indiatimes.com/news/india/manmohan-singh-risked-his-position-as-prime-minister-to-help-seal-the-landmark-indo-us-nuclear-deal/articleshow/116738104.cms?from=mdr.

39. "Manmohan Singh Risked His Position as Prime Minister to Help Seal the Landmark Indo-US Nuclear Deal", *The Economic Times*, accessed 25 May 2025, https://economictimes.indiatimes.com/news/india/manmohan-singh-risked-his-position-as-prime-minister-to-help-seal-the-landmark-indo-us-nuclear-deal/articleshow/116738104.cms?from=mdr.

Agency (IAEA) approved the safeguards agreement with India on 1 August 2008 following which the United States approached the Nuclear Suppliers Group (NSG) to grant a waiver to New Delhi to commence civilian nuclear trade. The NSG granted the waiver to India on 6 September 2008, allowing it to access civilian nuclear technology and fuel from other countries. The agreement was signed by then external affairs minister Pranab Mukherjee and his US counterpart Condoleezza Rice, on 10 October 2008.[40]

Despite the odds, the Singh government won the numbers game, securing the passage of the deal. The Congress's frantic search for a replacement after the Left Front withdrew its support brought the SP to its doors. Though Amar Singh and Mulayam Singh bailed out the government during the 22 July vote of confidence, their support came at a huge cost. Predictably the Congress–SP pact came undone before the April–May 2009 general elections. On 26 March 2009, the Pattali Makkal Katchi (PMK) withdrew from the UPA government.

The nuclear deal was a defining moment that reshaped Singh's image from a technocratic economist to a political leader capable of navigating intense parliamentary battles and making tough calls. Despite the coalition problems, Manmohan Singh completed his full term. Manmohan Singh emerged stronger, newspaper headlines screamed "Singh is King".[41] His decisive leadership in the nuclear deal was a key factor in the Congress party's landslide victory in the 2009 general elections.

★

The Congress fought the 2009 Lok Sabha election on Manmohan Singh's achievements, particularly the nuclear deal. The BJP's election campaign, however, lacked focus. The party laid claim to possessing the best tactical brains

---

40. PTI, "India-US Civil Nuclear Deal: Crowning Glory of Manmohan Singh's Leadership", NDTV, accessed 25 May 2025, https://www.ndtv.com/india-news/crowning-glory-of-manmohan-singhs-prime-ministership-india-us-civil-nuclear-deal-7338960.

41. Sandeep Phukan, "Manmohan Singh, Gentleman Politician Who Opened Up India's Economy in 1991", *The Hindu*, accessed 25 May 2025, https://www.thehindu.com/news/national/manmohan-singh-a-gentleman-politician/article69030747.ece.

in the land, but they made a hash of things. One day it was Mr Q, then black money in Swiss banks, then bijli-sadak-pani, then soft state and internal security lapses, then dynastic rule, then Manmohan Singh running to 10 Janpath. The strategy-a-day approach met its expected end.

A week before polling date, *Outlook* produced a forecast which suggested a slight hawa for the Congress and its allies which was by no means a wave. It gave the Congress 165 seats and its allies 36. According to its estimates, the BJP would get 136 seats and its allies 39. Thus, the UPA would have 201 versus the NDA's 175, give or take a few seats. Needless to say, *Outlook* and the rest of the media got it wrong. Again, on 16 May 2009, when the results were announced, the UPA gobbled up 260 seats, with the Congress getting 205. *Outlook* wrote, "The pseudo-secularists have won. And won stunningly."[42]

For the first time, someone who was not a member of the Nehru–Gandhi family went on to become the prime minister for two successive terms; and for the first time since 1980, a Congress government returned to power. Sonia and Manmohan did not need the fickle communists for government formation.

In a newspaper column, Jaitley outlined the reasons for the party's defeat in the elections, noting that the BJP failed to read the voter's desire for stability free of roadblocks and obstructions. The manner in which the Congress stood firm when the Left Front walked out of the alliance made the voters reaffirm their mandate in Manmohan Singh's favour. In the same piece, Jaitley wrote that with the change in the profile of the Indian voter, both the Indian politician and the political parties also needed to change.[43]

Journalist Ashok Malik, a BJP sympathiser wrote, "For the BJP to call the results disappointing would be something of an understatement. They are catastrophic."[44]

★

---

42. Vinod Mehta, *Lucknow Boy: A Memoir* (Penguin, 2011), p. 239.

43. Arun Jaitley, "Triumph of the Moderate", *Indian Express*, 27 May 2009, accessed on 6 September 2025, archive.indianexpress.com/news/triumph-of-the-moderate/466421/0.

44. Vinod Mehta, *Lucknow Boy: A Memoir* (Penguin, 2011), p. 240.

After the BJP's defeat, the fifty-two-year-old Nitin Gadkari replaced Rajnath Singh as the party president in December 2009; Rajnath Singh had been acting as the president since December 2005. Just two months before the general elections in 2009, Mohan Bhagwat, a Maharashtrian Brahmin, succeeded K.S. Sudarshan as the *sarsanghchalak* as the RSS ushered in a generational change in leadership. As the BJP faced a fresh choice of leadership, Bhagwat, in August 2009, gave a television interview in which he expressed his displeasure at the party's infighting and factionalism. "It's said there are four options before the BJP—Arun Jaitley, Venkaiah Naidu, Sushma Swaraj and Narendra Modi," said Bhagwat's interviewer Arnab Goswami. Bhagwat responded, "The BJP should look beyond these four." By November, Gadkari was being spoken of as the RSS's choice for the post. Narendra Modi, then chief minister of Gujarat, "was the first choice, but he didn't want to come to the centre before the 2012 assembly elections" in his state. It came down to Gadkari and Manohar Parrikar, a former chief minister of Goa—both of them Maharashtrian Brahmins.[45]

Sudhir Pathak, formerly the editor of the RSS mouthpiece *Tarun Bharat*, said that it was Advani who first suggested Gadkari's elevation, which the RSS happily accepted. Dilip Deodhar, a veteran RSS ideologue, said that "Advani thought Gadkari would be under his control as he had made him the state party president". In December 2009, Gadkari became the BJP's youngest-ever president.

Gadkari announced the party national executive which comprised 121 members, including thirteen vice presidents, ten general secretaries, fifteen secretaries, and a treasurer. As provided for in the BJP constitution, the office bearers included as many as thirteen women—33 per cent of the total number. In all, there were forty women members. Besides, the president had also constituted the BJP's Parliamentary Board. Jaitley was appointed as a member of the Parliamentary Board.[46] Gadkari shifted to Delhi after taking over as the party president. He was new to national politics and needed guidance. As the

---

45. Praveen Donthi, "Son of the Sangh", *The Caravan*, accessed 24 August 2025, https://caravanmagazine.in/reportage/son-of-the-sangh.

46. "BJP President Shri Nitin Gadkari Announces National Office Bearers, Members, Permanent Invitees, Special Invitees and Parliamentary Board", Bharatiya Janata Party, accessed 25 May 2025, https://www.bjp.org/pressreleases/bjp-president-shri-nitin-gadkari-announces-national-office-bearers-members-permanent.

Maharashtra BJP president, Gadkari often interacted with Jaitley on various issues, though frequent meetings were not possible.[47]

In Delhi, Gadkari found a trusted friend and senior associate in Jaitley whom he could trust blindly and speak his heart out to without any hesitation. There were occasions when Gadkari confessed he was confronted with a tricky issue, but Jaitley was always there for Gadkari in such situations with his suggestions and guidance. Jaitley came well-prepared for the party's internal meetings. He would have in-depth analyses of the issues on the agenda ready with him.[48] In fact, during Gadkari's term as the party president, Jaitley served as the Leader of the Opposition in the Rajya Sabha. "I would follow (Jaitley's) speeches in Parliament closely," Gadkari wrote once.[49] He considered Jaitley an intellectual reservoir.

Jaitley's areas of expertise were so vast that often the range of his knowledge surprised Gadkari. Law, finance, and defence were subjects in which Jaitley had special expertise. He rated Jaitley better than the best that India had ever produced in these fields. As the party president, he trusted Jaitley completely when it came to media strategy or setting the intellectual narrative.[50]

While Gadkari was trying to consolidate himself in Delhi, the Congress was facing its own trouble. After it breached the 200 seats mark in the May 2009 elections without the support from many parties and the Left Front, it appeared that UPA-II would be free of trouble. But the reality turned out different. All external supporters had had a bitter falling out with the Congress. The main parties supporting UPA-II—the SP, BSP, and RJD—were rooted in the Hindi heartland, where the imperatives of upcoming state elections would soon outweigh the politics of give-and-take at the Centre, making even a medium-term understanding with the Congress untenable. But that lay in the future. For the moment, the Congress was content to bask in the glow of an overwhelming show of hands. The illusion of solid outside support triumphed over the hard reality of numbers.

---

47. *The Discussant: Journal of Centre for Reforms, Development and Justice*, Special Edition, An Obituary to Arun Jaitley, Vol. VII, No. 3 (July–September 2019).

48. Nitin Gadkari, "Arun Jaitley Helped BJP Set the Narrative", ibid.

49. Ibid.

50. Ibid.

In April 2011, fresh trouble surfaced for the Congress when social activist Anna Hazare started an indefinite hunger strike in New Delhi to demand drafting of a Lokpal bill with more stringent penal provisions, giving more independence to the Lokpal (ombudsman) by a committee that would feature both the government and a civil society representative. The fast was a reaction to the rejection of his demand by Manmohan Singh and it caught the attention of not just the media but also thousands of supporters, some of whom also joined Hazare in his protest. Hazare was supported by Magsaysay Award winner Kiran Bedi, the former IPS officer known for her no-nonsense attitude and her jail reforms; Arvind Kejriwal, who was then recognised for his involvement in the grass-roots movement Parivartan, using the right to information legislation in a campaign against corruption; and Medha Patkar, the founder member of the thirty-two-year-long Narmada Bachao Andolan (NBA) movement that opposed the construction of dams across the Narmada. The movement was also supported by spiritual leaders Sri Sri Ravi Shankar, Swami Ramdev and Swami Agnivesh, and yoga guru Baba Ramdev. Hazare's protest attracted the common citizen in droves and the mass movement spread to Bangalore, Mumbai, Chennai, Ahmedabad, Guwahati, Shillong, Aizawl and other Indian cities.[51] Around 5 June, the Delhi Police swooped down on Baba Ramdev. A little after midnight, the police resorted to a lathi charge on Ramdev and his followers and fired tear gas shells at the gathering.[52] The BJP opposed the police action against Ramdev. Arun Jaitley sat on a day-long protest at Rajghat, along with other senior BJP leaders.[53]

Meanwhile, Gadkari soon found himself in the middle of a storm. In August 2011, Gadkari told a gathering of BJP leaders from Uttar Pradesh that he was appointing Sanjay Joshi as the party's coordinator for an assembly election

---

51. "Indian Activist Anna Hazare Begins Anti-Graft Fast", BBC News, 5 April 2011, www.bbc.com/news/world-south-asia-12968151; "Northeast Support to Hazare", *Times of India*, 9 April 2011, accessed on 6 September 2025, timesofindia.indiatimes.com/city/guwahati/Northeast-support-to-Hazares/articleshow/7921183.cms?referral=PM.

52. Bindu Shajan Perappadan. "Rajbala, Seriously Injured in Ramlila Crackdown, Dies", *The Hindu*, 26 September 2011, accessed on 6 September 2025, www.thehindu.com/news/cities/Delhi/rajbala-seriously-injured-in-ramlila-crackdown-dies/article2486713.ece.

53. Gautam Chintamani, *Rajneeti, a Biography of Rajnath Singh* (Penguin, 2019), p. 177.

which was some eight months away.[54] Joshi, who was forced out in 2005, was now reinstated to the party's national executive. In March 2012, Gadkari backed Anshuman Mishra, a London-based businessman, to take a vacant Rajya Sabha seat in place of S.S. Ahluwalia, a BJP veteran awaiting re-election into the Upper House. Mishra, a close friend of the Gadkari family, was the party's de facto treasurer through Gadkari's tenure. Many BJP leaders protested, and the party eventually nominated Ahluwalia after voting for the seat was countermanded over alleged attempts to buy the election. Mishra, upset, hit out at BJP leaders. Gadkari had to step in to defend them, and eventually Mishra apologised. The fiasco exacted a lasting cost. Jaitley and other senior leaders didn't take it too well for having lost their say in such important matters.[55] Gadkari, who had reinstated Joshi, asked him to resign.[56]

Jaitley now started preparing the ground for Modi's candidature as the prime minister for the 2014 elections. Jaitley was a key Advani loyalist, but to him his party's interest was above his personal loyalties. He was convinced that Modi alone could lead the party to victory in the 2014 elections. He persuaded Gadkari to realise Modi's potential. A month after taking over as the president of the party, Gadkari announced on the sidelines of the 9th India Today Conclave in Delhi that Modi has tremendous potential to be a good prime minister. "Modi has the ability, capacity and potential to lead the country. ... He is a role model for development politics. Look at what he has done for Gujarat. A decision on the party's prime ministerial candidate will be taken by senior leaders and the parliamentary body, but Modi is fully competent," he said. This was the first time that such an unequivocal note of support had come from a BJP president.[57] When he completed his term as the president,

---

54. Praveen Donthi, "Son of The Sangh", *Caravan Magazine*, accessed 25 May 2025, https://caravanmagazine.in/reportage/son-of-the-sangh.

55. Ibid.

56. Ibid.

57. Rahul Kanwal, "Modi Can Be a Good PM: Gadkari", *India Today*, accessed 25 May 2025, https://www.indiatoday.in/latest-headlines/story/modi-can-be-a-good-pm-gadkari-69259-2010-03-11.

Gadkari ruled himself out as his party's prime ministerial candidate, favouring Modi for the top job and promised to back his candidature as the party chief.[58]

In 2012, the party's constitution was amended to allow him a second term—although that term never came to pass.[59] Gadkari's bid for re-election had suffered a setback with his bête noire Yashwant Sinha planning to contest the election against him. Mahesh Jethmalani, who resigned from a party post after falling out with Gadkari, alleged that he had been denied a nomination paper for the election. Allegations of corruption against Gadkari surfaced in newspapers leading to the income tax department conducting searches at the offices of companies linked to Gadkari.[60]

A hurt Gadkari resigned on 22 January 2013, and proposed as his successor the RSS's preferred replacement, Rajnath Singh.[61] RSS chief Mohan Bhagwat refused to comment on the matter, calling it an internal matter of the BJP.[62] However, in his blog, senior RSS ideologue M.G. Vaidya suggested there was a conspiracy against Gadkari. He said:

> There seems to be an internal political conspiracy over the turn of events preceding Gadkari's resignation. The way the Jethmalani father–son duo started a campaign against Gadkari sometimes back, shows something. At that time Gadkari had not even received a single notice from any of the authorities, but to the Jethmalanis, Gadkari appeared

58. PTI, "Gadkari favours Modi as PM", *The Hindu*, accessed 25 May 2025, https://www.thehindu.com/news/national/Gadkari-favours-Modi-as-PM/article13377022.ece.

59. Praveen Donthi, "Son of The Sangh", *Caravan Magazine*, accessed 25 May 2025, https://caravanmagazine.in/reportage/son-of-the-sangh.

60. Sahil Makkar, "Gadkari Steps Down as BJP President, Rajnath Singh Emerges as Front-runner", *Mint*, accessed on 24 August 2025, https://www.livemint.com/Politics/lnHCZ90VLlJAnMTF61ltHN/Gadkari-out-of-race-for-BJP-president-Rajnath-seen-as-front.html.

61. Praveen Donthi, "Son of the Sangh", *Caravan Magazine*, accessed 25 May 25, https://caravanmagazine.in/reportage/son-of-the-sangh.

62. "Nitin Gadkari's Corruption Charge Is BJP's Internal Matter, but RSS Tells Him to 'Come Clean'", *Indian Express*, 24 October 2012, archive, accessed on 6 September 2025,indianexpress.com/news/nitin-gadkaris-corruption-charge-is-bjp-s-internal-matter-but-rss-tells-him-to--come-clean-/1021466/.

> as *"kalankit"* [tainted]. But this *kalank* [taint] was not proved. After that Shatrughan Sinha and Yashwant Sinha also demanded Gadkari's resignation. When all this was going on and I wrote it in my blog, I received a letter from Washington. The first line in that letter was "I am saddened by your support for Gadkari". That letter cleared my doubts and made it clear that this was an internal conspiracy against Gadkari.

In November 2012, Vaidya had created a sensation by blaming Gujarat Chief Minister Narendra Modi for running a campaign against Gadkari. Congratulating Gadkari on not seeking re-election for the presidentship of the saffron party, Vaidya said:

> Despite having the opportunity to become BJP president [for] the second time in a row, Gadkari decided to stay away from the election [for the post of BJP president]. Had there been an election, Gadkari would have won by 70 per cent votes but that would have exposed the rift in the party. It's true that Gadkari is related to the Purti group and played an important role in its establishment and progress. But suddenly, one section of the media started reporting news regarding irregularities in the Purti group. The government acted swiftly and announced that the alleged irregularities in the Purti group will be probed. Gadkari welcomed the probe but out of the blue Ram Jethmalani demanded Gadkari's resignation. He did not think it wise to wait for the inquiry to complete.

Vaidya also expressed his hunch that all this "masala" (material against Gadkari) was provided (to media and government) by some senior BJP leader or leaders. Blaming the media for the campaign against Gadkari, Vaidya wrote:

> The media is the first winner [in ousting Gadkari] and the second position goes to the conspirators against Gadkari. The BJP was known to be a party with a difference but all this [activities against Gadkari] has given it an image of a party with differences. The new president of BJP has an opportunity to reform this image of the party. I hope

> everyone will help him [Rajnath Singh] now and the party will prepare for the election with unity.[63]

Jaitley had by now graduated from being a Young Turk to a frontline leader of the party, driving key decisions, with many senior leaders aligning with his views and strategies. His influence had grown in the party which started giving him more responsibilities. He put his might behind Rajnath Singh. Before the 2012 assembly elections in Uttar Pradesh, BJP undertook two Jan Swabhiman Yatras to raise the issue of poor law and order and loot of public money. Covering sixty-one districts and 370 assembly constituencies, the two yatras were led by Rajnath Singh and BJP leader Kalraj Mishra.[64] Arun Jaitley was present as the two yatras were flagged off from Mathura and Varanasi to mobilise support to bring about a political change in the state.[65] He had rapidly become his party's key strategist and alliance stitcher.

---

63. Pavan Dahat, "Gadkari's Exit Was Due to Internal Political Conspiracy, Says Vaidya", *The Hindu*, accessed 24 August 2025, https://www.thehindu.com/news/national/gadkaris-exit-was-due-to-internal-political-conspiracy-says-vaidya/article4358239.ece.

64. Mishra later became a national vice president of the party and lieutenant governor of Jammu and Kashmir.

65. Atiq Khan, "BJP in Yatra Mode, Galaxy of Party Leaders to Descend on U.P. This Week", *The Hindu*, 9 October 2011, accessed on 6 September 2025, www.thehindu.com/todays-paper/tp-national/bjp-in-yatra-mode-galaxy-of-party-leaders-to-descend-on-up-this-week/article2522676.ece/.

11

Election Strategist, Stitching Alliances (2004–14)

In the ten years that the BJP was out of power, the party's reliance on Jaitley grew rapidly. He was made in charge of elections in many states. Jaitley played a pivotal role in stitching key alliances and ensuring electoral victories in states like Punjab, Bihar, Karnataka, and Madhya Pradesh. His approach combined pragmatic coalition building and election strategy, which expanded the party base.

In Punjab, Jaitley recognised the BJP's limited base and forged an alliance with the SAD, despite ideological differences. He ensured seat-sharing adjustments, allowing the SAD to dominate rural Sikh constituencies while the BJP focused on urban Hindu areas.

Jaitley played a big role in the formation of the NDA government in Bihar in 2005. Nitish Kumar of the JD(U) left the NDA after Modi was declared BJP's prime ministerial candidate for the 2014 general elections; Jaitley reworked alliances by bringing back Nitish Kumar's JD(U) in the NDA. He leveraged anti-RJD sentiment and positioned the BJP as the dominant partner while accommodating Nitish's leadership, leading to a sweeping NDA victory in 2019.

In 2004, Jaitley was appointed as the general secretary of the BJP. He was put in charge of Karnataka when the state faced simultaneous assembly and Lok Sabha elections in 2004. He guided the party and led it in all assembly elections since 2004, particularly in 2008. In Karnataka, his backchannel negotiations and legal expertise ensured that the BJP formed its first government. With that started the BJP's "southern sojourn" and B.S. Yediyurappa became Karnataka's chief minister. Jaitley also played a crucial role in the transition of power from Yediyurappa to BJP leaders D.V. Sadananda Gowda and Jagadish Shettar during the BJP regime of 2008–13, and stayed involved in the state's strategy till 2019.

In Madhya Pradesh, Jaitley was instrumental in laying the foundation of the BJP's fifteen-year-rule in the state; Jaitley was the BJP's poll manager for the assembly elections in 2003, during which the ten-year-old Congress government was evicted in a carefully orchestrated campaign. Displacing traditional caste politics, Jaitley went for the long-overlooked issues of bijli, sadak, and pani.

BJP's Trouble-shooter in Karnataka

Jaitley was the undisputed architect of the BJP's capture of Karnataka. Karnataka was an important state for the BJP; the party considered it as a gateway to the south—the region's outlier. Karnataka, Tamil Nadu, Andhra Pradesh, Telangana, Kerala, and the union territory. of Puducherry account for 130 seats in southern India—over one-fifth of the Lok Sabha's 543 seats. From the beginning of the coalition era in 1989, the southern states have often tilted the balance of power in Delhi. The BJP, for example, lost power in 2004 largely because the allies—the AIADMK in Tamil Nadu and the TDP in Andhra Pradesh—were routed. Conversely, Vajpayee's two national electoral triumphs in 1998 and 1999 were linked to having the right winning ally in Tamil Nadu (the DMK) and a winning political arrangement in Andhra Pradesh.

Jaitley was put in charge of Karnataka in 2002. The BJP's selection of Jaitley for Karnataka was evidence of the party's growing confidence in him. This was the beginning of Jaitley's lifelong relationship with the state. Jaitley became a regular visitor to Karnataka and also made use of the opportunity to travel to all regions of the state. He became well-known not only in party circles, cadres, and leaders but amongst people of all hues enthusiastic in public affairs and matters that concerned the average common man and the nation as a whole.[1]

The 2004 elections became a turning point for the BJP. The party improved its tally from 44 to 79 seats in the state assembly election. Although the BJP

1. Manohar Yadavatti, "Arun Jaitley's Contribution to BJP's Growth in Karnataka", My Articles, accessed 25 May 2025, https://www.myarticle.in/2019/08/arun-jaitleys-contribution-to-bjps.html.

emerged as the single largest party, the Congress and JD(S) of former prime minister, H.D. Deve Gowda, cobbled together an alliance, and a government was formed under Dharam Singh. In 2006, Deve Gowda's son H.D. Kumaraswamy joined hands with BJP and brought down the Dharam Singh government. Under a rotational chief ministership arrangement, Kumaraswamy became the chief minister and B.S. Yediyurappa his deputy.

Yediyurappa became CM for the first time in November 2007, sworn in as Karnataka's twenty-fifth but his term lasted just seven days as Kumaraswamy reneged on a power-sharing pact and walked out of the alliance. Although the government did not last long, it was a historic moment for the saffron party as it fulfilled its ambition of installing its first-ever government in the south. Later, in 2008, the BJP swept the state assembly election. Once again, Jaitley was the key strategist behind the win. A win in Karnataka boosted the BJP's national profile.

Karnataka is a complex state politically. Two traditionally powerful caste groups, the Lingayats and the Vokkaligas, virtually controlled state politics between 1956 and 1972. For several decades, every second Karnataka legislator belonged to one of these two castes. This also reflected in the choice of chief ministers. Before the 1956 reorganisation of states, two of Mysore state's first three chief ministers were the Vokkaligas (1947–56). After the reorganisation, the first four chief ministers were all Lingayats (1956–71). Thereafter, leaders from other caste groups started occupying the seat of power in Bengaluru as new caste coalitions began to challenge the traditional structures of power.[2] But Lingayat leaders still made up nine of twenty of all state chief ministers between 1956 and 2021.[3]

Lingayat regional satrap S. Nijalingappa (chief minister in 1956–58 and then 1962–68) broke away from the Congress in the great split of 1969 between Indira Gandhi and the old Congress guard. Congress leaders wove together a new rainbow caste coalition. In 1972, Chief Minister D. Devaraj Urs sought to break the stranglehold of the Lingayats and the Vokkaligas by giving political

2. Nalin Mehta, "Explained: The Lingayat-Vokkaliga Factor in Karnataka Elections", *Firstpost*, accessed 25 May 2025, https://www.firstpost.com/india/explained-the-lingayat-vokkaliga-factor-in-karnataka-elections-12510752.html.

3. Nalin Mehta, *The New BJP: Modi and the Making of the World's Largest Political Party* (Westland, 2022), pp. 407–11.

representation to other caste groups that had so far been relatively marginalised. He coined a new acronym for this fresh social coalition: AHINDA. This was a Kannada acronym for Alpasankhyataru (minorities), Hindulidavaru (backward classes), and Dalitaru (Dalits).

In 1980, when the BJP was formed, some Lingayat leaders remained with the Janata Party, others had returned to the Congress. In the decade that followed, the Congress tried to woo Lingayat voters. As part of this outreach, when it came back to power in Karnataka in 1989, Veerendra Patil was appointed chief minister—the first time such apex leadership was given to a Congress Lingayat leader in two decades, thus signalling a shift in the Congress strategy.[4] Patil was credited with mobilising the Lingayats back to the Congress and was instrumental in its biggest ever victory in 1989 (179 of the 224 seats). It was after a full eighteen years that a Lingayat had become the chief minister of the state.[5]

The BJP's rise in Karnataka owed a great deal to the Lingayat vote shifting away from the Congress and moving towards the BJP from the 1990s after Rajiv Gandhi removed Patil unceremoniously.[6] The dismissal of the Patil government through a letter sent from an airport, alienated the Lingayat community from the Congress. This resulted in its most humiliating defeat in the 1994 elections. Its tally collapsed from 179 to just 36 and it faced a 17 per cent loss of vote share, which was shared predominantly by the BJP and the Janata Dal. The BJP's vote share in 1994 increased from 4 per cent to 16.95 per cent and Janata Dal's from 27.08 per cent to 33.54 per cent. Yediyurappa and Ananth Kumar forged a new social combination, expanding into new geographies. While both Ananth Kumar and Yediyurappa played key roles in expanding the party, their intense rivalry also undermined some of its gains. Yediyurappa became

---

4. "Veerendra Patil—"The Gentleman Chief Minister" in *Political History of Karnataka: Part Nine*, KarnatakaHistory, accessed 25 May 2025, https://karnatakahistory.blogspot.com/2014/09/political-history-of-karnataka-part-nine.html.

5. "Cost of dismissing Veerendra Patil", *The Hindu*, accessed on 24 August 2025, https://www.thehindu.com/news/national/karnataka/cost-of-dismissing-veerendra-patil/article23688341.ece.

6. Akram S, "S Nijalingappa and Veerendra Patil: Lingayat stalwarts PM Modi cited for his 'insult of leaders' barb at Congress", *The Indian Express*, accessed on 24 August 2025,https://indianexpress.com/article/political-pulse/s-nijalingappa-veerendra-patil-lingayat-stalwarts-pm-modi-congress-8480116/.

the Leader of the Opposition in 1994. In 1996, Ananth Kumar became an MP. From there, their differences started.

When the state faced simultaneous assembly and general elections in 2004, Jaitley, now in-charge of the state, united both factions and formed a strategy to win the election in the state assembly and get maximum seats for the Lok Sabha. He knew Ananth Kumar from the JP revolution days. The two clicked soon. Yediyurappa greatly admired Jaitley's strategic skills. The two decided to drop their differences and work together with Jaitley. The BJP won 79 seats, its highest ever tally till then, and emerged as the single largest party.[7] This was the first time the BJP became an important party in the south. But the party was far behind the magical 113 numbers in a House of 224 to form a government of its own.[8]

The regional JD(S) outfit acted swiftly to share power with the Congress, which they claimed was necessary to "keep the communal forces in check".[9] This once again was reminiscent of the political isolation that the BJP had been facing since the days of the Jana Sangh. The Opposition parties wanted to brand the BJP a communal force and make it a political pariah.[10] N. Dharam Singh of the Congress became the chief minister while Siddaramaiah of the JD(S) was sworn in as the deputy chief minister of the first-ever coalition government in the state, which however also earned the dubious distinction of being a short-lived one. Jaitley once again used his equation with Ananth Kumar for Yediyurappa's appointment as the Leader of the Opposition, which Ananth Kumar opposed.

---

7. Bhupender Yadav and Illa Patnaik, *The Rise of the BJP: The Making of the World's Largest Political Party* (Penguin, 2022).

8. Manohar Yadavatti, "Arun Jaitley's Contribution to BJP's Growth in Karnataka", My Articles, accessed 25 May 2025, https://www.myarticle.in/2019/08/arun-jaitleys-contribution-to-bjps.html.

9. On forming a coalition government with the Congress, Deve Gowda said, "We joined hands to keep the communal forces in check." See, Stephen David, "Congress-JD(S) Coalition Government in Karnataka Fights Over Cabinet Berths", *India Today*, accessed 25 May 2025, https://www.indiatoday.in/magazine/states/story/20040614-congress-jds-coalition-governmentin-karnataka-fights-over-cabinet-berths-789807-2004-06-14.

10. Bhupender Yadav and Illa Patnaik, *The Rise of the BJP: The Making of The World's Largest Political Party* (Penguin, 2022), p. 129.

As stated earlier, the BJP formed its first government in Karnataka in 2006 albeit for a very short period. The Congress–JD(S) government fell in 2006 after the JD(S) withdrew support from the Dharam Singh-led government. Jaitley rushed to Karnataka. Ananth Kumar was then the state president and his rapport with Jaitley worked well. The BJP formed an alliance with the JD(S). H.D. Kumaraswamy was sworn in supported by the BJP. The new arrangement between the JD(S) and the BJP lasted twenty months. Karnataka was placed under the Centre's rule for thirty-four days and the state assembly was kept under suspended animation.

On 12 November 2007, a five-member BJP-led coalition ministry headed by Yediyurappa was sworn in bringing to an end to the President's Rule imposed on the state in the wake of political turmoil. The JD(S) was its partner. However, the government lasted only a week. A crisis was triggered by the BJP's refusal to accept the JD(S)'s demands to sign a new power-sharing deal allotting plum ministerial portfolios to it. After the JD(S) refused to vote for the BJP, Yediyurappa announced his decision to quit in the House and submitted his resignation to the governor, who then recommended the imposition of President's Rule in the state.

Jaitley was again roped in as a strategy planner for the BJP in the 2008 assembly elections. He chalked out every detail of the election. Jaitley strategised that the BJP should fight the contest on a three-point agenda: "betrayal, inflation, and terrorism". It went hammer and tongs against the Congress for failing to check soaring food prices—and the idea clicked. The BJP, which tasted power for just a week in November 2007 before being toppled by the JD(S), swept large parts of Karnataka, winning 110 of 224 seats. This was its first outright win in one of India's four southern states, dealing a major blow to the Congress. The backbone of the BJP, the Lingayats, backed the party in 2008 and helped it form the government.

With the victory in Karnataka, the BJP now ruled seven of the country's twenty-nine states and was part of ruling coalitions in five others. Advani promptly claimed that 2008 would prove to be a year of political change for India. A national parliamentary election was due next year.

In October 2009, there was a stand-off between Yediyurappa and three ministers, who were up in arms over his style of functioning. Jaitley was rushed in to defuse the crisis. Hours before Jaitley's arrival, Yediyurappa cracked his whip by abruptly ordering the transfer of five officials including deputy commissioner and superintendent of police of Bellary (now Ballari) district, a move seen as striking at the Reddy brothers—tourism minister G. Janardhana Reddy and revenue minister G. Karunakara Reddy, who hail from the mine-rich district. Yediyurappa's move came amid reports that Janardhana Reddy had taken a group of supporting legislators to Hyderabad and was planning to take another group to Goa to "protect" them from being won over by the Chief Minister.

On 6 October 2010, sixteen MLAs submitted letters to the governor withdrawing their support, following which the governor advised the chief minister to prove his majority. The vote of confidence was slated for 12 October 2010. Sixteen MLAs—including eleven from the BJP and five independents who had supported the government—said they would not support the chief minister during his trust vote. The day before the trust vote was scheduled, on 11 October 2010, the sixteen MLAs were disqualified by the Speaker under anti-defection laws. The strength of the 224-member assembly was reduced to 208 and the half-way mark to prove majority dropped to 105. One member was nominated from the Anglo-Indian community. Yediyurappa narrowly survived the trust vote. Governor H.R. Bhardwaj sent his report to the Centre within a few hours after the BJP government won the confidence motion by a voice vote, calling the events and the vote in the assembly "unconstitutional" and "farce". He recommended that the state be brought under President's Rule. He is understood to have noted that Speaker K.G. Bopaiah's action in disqualifying sixteen MLAs was unconstitutional. The Centre decided not to act on Bhardwaj's recommendation.

Alarmed by developments in the state, in December 2010, the BJP effected a change in the command structure of its affairs in Karnataka, replacing Shanta Kumar and appointing the party's general secretary Dharmendra Pradhan in his place. At the peak of the turmoil in Karnataka, Shanta Kumar was away in the United States to attend a United Nations conference. Pradhan, who was then one of the young faces of the BJP, was expected to be more active than his predecessors in Karnataka. Till then, he was the co-in-charge of Bihar which was under Ananth Kumar. With a spectacular victory of JD(U)–BJP combine in the just-concluded election in the state, the party decided to elevate Pradhan. Jaitley was given a special advisory role in the party's affairs in trouble-torn Karnataka. The press release said Jaitley would be giving "special attention" to Karnataka.

On 29 October 2010, the Karnataka High Court upheld the Speaker's decision disqualifying the sixteen MLAs. Aggrieved by the order, the disqualified legislators moved the Supreme Court. On 11 May 2011, the Supreme Court quashed the disqualification. The court decision came hours before Yediyurappa was to seek the confidence vote in the assembly. The Supreme Court made scathing observations about the role of the Speaker and the chief minister in the process of disqualification.[11]

Jaitley, the then Leader of the Opposition in the Rajya Sabha, wrote on the party's official website:

> … the adverse consequences it [the order] has on the functioning of the Tenth Schedule of the Constitution. An interpretation of this kind gives enough play of joints to potential defectors to misuse the provisions of the Tenth Schedule, play games with political morality and then put on an innocent expression and allege that they have done nothing wrong. The Tenth Schedule was legislated by the government headed by late Shri Rajiv Gandhi with a noble intention. It was further strengthened by the NDA government. Some provisions have been weakened by this judgement. I am sure on a future date this judgement will be re-visited.
>
> The Supreme Court is final. It is not infallible. Even erroneous views of the courts are binding. The Governor now seeks to rely on this reasoning in his recommendation to the Centre. These are the consequences that an erroneous judgement can inflict on the democracy. We don't have to merely learn to live with these errors. An erroneous judgement is a challenge to the future to correct the error in to which the judgement has fallen.[12]

---

11. BJP, "The Supreme Court's Judgement dealing with the case of the 11 Karnataka MLAs", accessed on 24 August 2025, https://www.bjp.org/interviews-and-articles/supreme-courts-judgement-dealing-case-11-karnataka-mlas.

12. Arun Jaitley, "The Supreme Court's Judgement Dealing With the Case of the 11 Karnataka MLA's", Bharatiya Janata Party, accessed 25 May 2025, https://www.bjp.org/interviews-and-articles/supreme-courts-judgement-dealing-case-11-karnataka-mlas.

Karnataka Governor Bhardwaj once again recommended President's Rule be imposed in the state based on the Supreme Court order. Led by Jaitley, the BJP mounted a campaign against the recommendation. A day after the Supreme Court quashed their disqualification, the eleven rebel BJP legislators met Jaitley to take up their issues with the central leadership. They expressed opposition to Yediyurappa. The source said that the MLAs were ready to vote for the BJP in a possible vote of confidence. The BJP, meanwhile, kept up the pressure in its battle against Governor Bhardwaj and decided to parade 121 MLAs before the President to show that the party has a majority on the floor of the House.

On 26 July 2011, Yediyurappa was forced to quit when state Lokayukta Santosh Hegde came out with a report implicating Yediyurappa in the mining scam.[13] Intense lobbying and hectic negotiations by the two main factions of the Karnataka BJP started for the office of next chief minister. Jagadish Shettar was supported by the anti-Yediyurappa faction led by Ananth Kumar, former Union minister and BJP MP from Bangalore South. Once again, responsibility fell on Jaitley to ensure smooth election of the next chief minister. There were several names floating as possible candidates, but it finally narrowed down to D.V. Sadananda Gowda, an MP from Udupi-Chikmagalur constituency. The BJP Parliamentary Board members Rajnath Singh and Arun Jaitley travelled to Bangalore. They spent three days together in Bangalore talking to 118 MLAs individually to resolve the deadlock on who should succeed Yediyurappa. The two leaders decided to hold a secret ballot to determine the preference of the MLA after their efforts to push for a compromise formula faced hurdles. All MLAs were given a plain sheet of paper to write down their chief ministerial choice. Finally, D.V. Sadananda Gowda was elected as the new chief minister. On 4 August 2011, D.V. Sadananda Gowda was sworn in as the twenty-sixth chief minister of Karnataka. The Karnataka crisis saw Jaitley emerge as the BJP's new trouble-shooter.

Soon there was a fresh storm brewing for the party in Karnataka. Gowda's shaky tenure ended in a mere eleven months, in July 2012. The caste divide between the Lingayats, to which Yediyurappa and Shettar belong, and the Vokkaligas, from which community Sadananda Gowda hails, manifested in full

---

13. Devesh Kumar, "History Set to Repeat in the South", *India Today*, accessed, 25 May 2025, https://www.indiatoday.in/opinion/devesh-kumar/story/bjp-debacle-history-set-to-repeat-in-the-south-karnataka-bs-yediyurappa-123822-2012-12-09.

form culminating in the leadership change. Jaitley and Rajnath Singh headed to Bangalore to oversee the transition from Sadananda Gowda to Jagadish Shettar. In July 2012, Shettar became the state's third chief minister in four years,[14] barely ten months before the assembly elections.[15]

Jaitley was roped in for state assembly elections to be held in 2013 and the Lok Sabha elections contest in Karnataka in 2014. By now, the BJP was in a mess in Karnataka. B. Sriramulu, once a close aide of mining baron Janardhana Reddy, had left the BJP in November 2011 and formed the BSR Congress (Badavara Shramikara Raithara Congress). Yediyurappa cut ties with the BJP and formed a new party—Karnataka Janata Paksha (KJP)—in 2012.

In March 2013, Jaitley initiated a change in party leadership in the state. The state unit chief, K.S. Eshwarappa, resigned. Assisted by BJP general secretary and Karnataka party affairs in-charge Dharmendra Pradhan, Jaitley briefed party president Rajnath Singh on the choice of new leader. At least five names were making the rounds in BJP circles to succeed Eshwarappa—former party chief and former chief minister D.V. Sadananda Gowda, Deputy Chief Minister R. Ashoka, minor irrigation minister Govind Makthappa Karjol, and the Lok Sabha members, Pralhad Joshi and Nalin Kumar Kateel. On Jaitley's recommendation, Joshi was picked by Rajnath Singh as Eshwarappa's successor. The appointment of Joshi, representing Dharwad, was announced by the Karnataka BJP just a day after the ECI declared the poll schedule.[16]

The BJP contested the election with the BSR Congress and the KJP feeding into its votes. The electorate was fed up with the infighting in the BJP ranks in the state which had seen three BJP chief ministers in five years. Sending out a powerful signal for change, Karnataka voted the BJP out of power in the election held on 5 May 2013, giving the Congress an unambiguous mandate

14. Maya Sharma, "Jagadish Shettar to be Formally Elected as Karnataka Chief Minister Today", NDTV, accessed 25 May 2025, https://www.ndtv.com/india-news/jagadish-shettar-to-be-formally-elected-as-karnataka-chief-minister-today-491652.

15. "Jagadish Shettar Sworn in K'taka CM and in a First, Two Dy CMs Too", *The Indian Express*, accessed 25 May 2025, https://indianexpress.com/article/political-pulse/jagadish-shettar-sworn-in-ktaka-cm-and-in-a-first-two-dy-cms-too/.

16. PTI, "Pralhad Joshi Appointed Karnataka BJP President", *The New Indian Express*, accessed 25 May 2025, https://www.newindianexpress.com/states/karnataka/2013/Mar/21/prahlad-joshi-appointed-karnataka-bjp-president-460768.html.

to rule, with 122 seats in the 224-strong legislative assembly. The BJP, which was elected to power in 2008 with 110 seats, managed to win only 40 seats, the same number as the JD(U). The JD(S) upped its tally to 40 from 28 in 2008 sharing the second spot with the BJP.[17]

An unexpected but significant outcome of the election was the strong showing by the JD(S), led by former chief minister H.D. Kumaraswamy. The KJP won in six constituencies, falling far short of its own double digit expectation. Yediyurappa had ensured that the BJP didn't come to power. The BSR Congress won in four seats. The remaining twelve constituencies were won by independents. Senior Congress leader Siddaramaiah was sworn in as the chief minister of Karnataka. The defeat of the BJP in the only south Indian state where it had managed to establish a solid presence marked a stunning reversal for a party that has tried hard to grow beyond the Hindi-speaking areas of the country.

Jaitley did not give up. Ahead of the 2014 Lok Sabha polls, the BSR Congress merged with the BJP. Yediyurappa too returned to the BJP and merged his outfit KJP into his former party. Sushma Swaraj, a senior BJP leader, however, opposed the BSR Congress merger and the giving of a ticket to Sriramulu for Parliament election. Jaitley defended the merger. He and many BJP state leaders felt that the BSR Congress could garner over 3 per cent votes. He countered the opposition by saying that "relatively marginal issues such as declaration of candidates" should not divert the attention from the core issues of governance. Jaitley published his blogpost "Where do we Stand",[18] on the day the BJP was finalising the list of candidates for the Lok Sabha polls and a day after the senior leader's public opposition.

"The BJP needs to concentrate on consolidating its gains. The country's mood is to install a BJP led government. Between now and the polling date all BJP leaders and cadres must work towards the goal of adding an additional two percent votes across the country. Every incremental percentage vote is capable of adding a significant number of seats to our kitty," Jaitley said. "Relatively marginal issues such as declaration of candidates particularly who is in and

17. "Karnataka Assembly Election Results in 2013", Elections.in, available at https://www.elections.in/karnataka/assembly-constituencies/2013-election-results.html.

18. Arun Jaitley, "Where Do We Stand", Bharatiya Janata Party, accessed 25 May 2025, https://www.bjp.org/pressreleases/article-shri-arun-jaitley-where-do-we-stand.

who is out cannot be allowed to dominate the political agenda in the BJP. These issues divert the attention from the core issues of governance."

The BJP Parliamentary Board was not in favour of the merger, but decided to work together with Sriramulu following several rounds of discussions with Jaitley and other party leaders. The BJP Parliamentary Board, which discussed the issue at length, overruled Swaraj's opposition, clearing the decks for the admission of Sriramulu. It was decided to field him as a candidate for the Bellary Lok Sabha seat.

The Lok Sabha polls in Karnataka were held in a single phase on 17 April 2014. A total of 28 seats went into polls. The BJP won 17, the Congress 9, and the JD(S) only 2. The Congress secured 40.8 per cent of the votes as against the BJP's 43 per cent, up from 41.63 per cent in the 2009 Lok Sabha polls. Riding on the Modi wave, a 2.2 per cent swing in its favour propelled the BJP to outperform the ruling Congress. In the backdrop of its rout a few months back in the assembly elections, this was a marvellous comeback for the BJP.

The 2018 assembly elections held in Karnataka threw up a hung House. When the election results were announced on 15 May 2018, the BJP returned as the single largest party by winning 104 seats. The Congress won 78 seats and the JD(S) 37 seats, and others 3. Soon after the results, the BJP was called to form the government as the single largest party. Yediyurappa was to be sworn in as the chief minister the next day. The decision of the governor triggered public controversy, as the BJP, while having emerged as the single largest party, fell short of commanding a majority in the Karnataka legislature. The Congress party and the JD(S) filed a petition at the Supreme Court of India to stay the swearing-in ceremony of Yediyurappa. The court admitted and heard the petition around midnight. The Supreme Court directed the production of the letter written by Yediyurappa on 16 May to the governor. The court refused to stay the swearing-in. The matter was scheduled to be heard next on 18 May 2018.[19]

On 18 May 2018, the Supreme Court reduced the fifteen-day window given by the governor to Yediyurappa to prove his majority and ordered it to be done within twenty-four hours. Two days later, the BJP government was toppled by

---

19. Satya Prasoon, "Karnataka Election Case Explained", Supreme Court Observer, accessed 25 May 2025, https://www.scobserver.in/journal/karnataka-election-case-explained/.

the Congress–JD(S) coalition government. H.D. Kumaraswamy became the chief minister on 23 May 2018.

By now Jaitley was ailing and was not in a state of health to save the government. But within one year, the Congress–JD(S) government was toppled when seventeen MLAs from the ruling coalition resigned from their assembly constituencies and joined the BJP. B.S. Yediyurappa once again became the BJP chief minister in Karnataka on 26 July 2019.

Jaitley made a significant contribution in fostering an unprecedented growth of the BJP in the state. His novel way of putting forth the ideology to strengthen the party from grassroots in an amicable manner had many takers on the ground. Being a thorough professional pleader, he made the best use of his oratory to convince his audience. He succeeded in mesmerising his listeners to subscribe to his thoughts of the party ideals and the inevitability of a commitment towards a liberal approach for developmental politics with the basic Hindu tenets in mind. One could disagree with him but it was equally difficult to negate and disprove his ideas and thoughts.[20] Senior BJP leader and Member of the Karnataka Legislative Council Lahar Singh Siroya gave the credit for the BJP's rise in the state to Jaitley.[21] "Jaitley introduced corporate style electioneering in Karnataka, roping in an ad agency to design the campaign," Siroya said.

"His [Jaitley's] approach was that of a marketing head—he believed in promotional strategy and visualisation. The BJP learnt modern ways of electioneering which the Modi—[Amit] Shah duo took to a higher level," said M.P. Kumar, former BJP state secretary and software entrepreneur.[22] Minister S. Suresh Kumar, who also served in the BJP ministry during 2008–13 period, described Jaitley as "one of the sharpest minds that emerged in

---

20. Manohar Yadavatti, "Arun Jaitley's Contribution to BJP's Growth in Karnataka", My Articles, accessed 25 May 2025, https://www.myarticle.in/2019/08/arun-jaitleys-contribution-to-bjps.html.

21. B.V. Shiva Shankar, "Arun Jaitley Helped BJP Capture Karnataka, Make It Gateway to South", *The Times of India*, accessed 25 May 2025, https://timesofindia.indiatimes.com/city/bengaluru/arun-jaitley-helped-saffron-party-capture-karnataka-make-it-gateway-to-south/articleshow/70823269.cms.

22. Ibid.

the post-Emergency era in the BJP".[23] Jaitley continued to stay involved in Karnataka till his death. As finance minister, Jaitley was one of the key speakers at the "Invest Karnataka" event conducted by the Congress regime in February 2016 for attracting investments to the state. Jaitley believed that Karnataka could surpass the national growth rate as it has vast potential. As defence minister, he inaugurated a first-of-its-kind 4200-acre Aeronautical Test Range in Chitradurga district in May 2017.

BJP's Go-to Man in Punjab

Jaitley was appointed as the in-charge of BJP affairs in Punjab in 2006, taking over from Madan Lal Khurana before the 2007 assembly elections set to be held on 13 February 2007. Punjab was his Karam Bhoomi. As a committed son of the soil he was always concerned about the progress of the state. He was a keen observer of the state's politics and stayed involved irrespective of who was the party affairs in-charge in the state. He knew Punjab so well that he invariably had the last word on the party's Punjab affairs, and the central leadership of the party respected his advice on crucial issues. Sitting in Delhi, he oversaw the alliance with the SAD from a distance, viewing it as a partnership of greater social than political significance, given the deep fault lines in Punjab's polity. During election time in Punjab, he would go into micromanagement of individual seats and fine-tune things.[24] Jaitley anchored the SAD–BJP alliance till the 2019 Lok Sabha elections.

The BJP had a complex "love–hate" relationship with the Akalis. There is a long history behind this complex relationship. In April 1952, the Jana Sangh supported the Akali Dal-led United Front government in the Patiala and East Punjab States Union (PEPSU), the first non-Congress government in

23. "Arun Jaitley Played a Key Role in the Rise of BJP in State", *The Hindu*, accessed 25 May 2025, https://www.thehindu.com/news/national/karnataka/arun-jaitley-played-a-key-role-in-the-rise-of-bjp-in-state/article29248545.ece.

24. I.P. Singh, "Arun Jaitley: Go-To Man of SAD-BJP Alliance in Punjab for 13 Years", *The Times of India*, accessed 25 May 2025, https://timesofindia.indiatimes.com/city/ludhiana/arun-jaitley-go-to-man-of-sad-bjp-alliance-in-punjab-for-13-years/articleshow/70824361.cms.

the country after the first general elections. Congress Chief Minister Colonel Raghbir Singh was sworn in despite the party being short of majority, but had to resign on the first day over the election of the Speaker after which Akali Dal's Gian Singh Rarewala became the chief minister. The Congress government at the Centre sacked the state government in March 1953 and invoked President's Rule after quickly dissolving the assembly.[25]

This was when the Akali Dal had launched the Punjabi Suba Movement demanding reorganisation of Punjab on linguistic basis. The Congress was against the demand for a Punjabi Suba, leading to a lot of bitterness between the Congress and the Akalis. The RSS was also opposed to the demand. In 1956, a compromise was struck; Punjab was divided into two regions on a linguistic basis—Punjabi and Hindi, obviating the need to reorganise the state. The PEPSU was merged into Punjab under this formula.

There were differences between the Akalis and the Jana Sangh over many issues. The Jana Sangh was part of the "Save Hindi Agitation" launched in May 1957 by the Hindi Samiti, under the overall direction of the Arya Pratinidhi Sabha. A coalition government was nevertheless formed by the Akali Dal in 1967 and then in 1969 with the Jana Sangh and Left parties supporting the government to keep the Congress out. Disagreements over the jurisdiction of Guru Nanak University concerning the Arya Samaj-controlled Dayanand Anglo Vedic (DAV) institutes prompted the Jana Sangh ministers to resign from the Badal government in June 1970.

The Congress achieved victory during the 1972 assembly elections. In 1977, the SAD formed a government in alliance with Jana Sangh legislators, who had contested as Janata Party candidates, with Badal once again serving as chief minister. Thereafter, the Congress and the SAD alternated in power until 2012.

During the insurgency in Punjab, the state politics went through a major churn with moderates in Sikh politics sidelined. Insurgency, Operation Blue Star, and Indira Gandhi's assassination kept the state in turmoil. After 1984, violent counterinsurgency eliminated the militants, marginalised the radicals, and ultimately succeeded in strengthening the moderates. The Congress's

25. I.P. Singh, "Akali Dal and Jan Singh-BJP: Long History as Adversaries & Friends", *The Times of India*, accessed 25 May 2025, https://timesofindia.indiatimes.com/india/akali-dal-and-jan-singh-bjp-long-history-as-adversaries-friends/articleshow/110703828.cms.

Beant Singh became the chief minister on 19 February 1992 after assembly elections were held in the state after five years of President's Rule. The fortunes of the Congress (I), however, declined sharply in the late 1990s after the party lost its tallest leader Beant Singh to an assassination on 31 August 1995.

Between 1985 and 1987, and again from 1992 to 1994, the struggle for dominance among Sikh factions was largely played out within the Shiromani Gurdwara Parbandhak Committee (SGPC). Confronted by Chief Minister Beant Singh's aggressive policies, the radicals and the SGPC leadership under Gurcharan Singh Tohra sought to build a united Sikh political front. In this effort, they enlisted the support of the Jathedar (head priest) of the Akal Takht, the highest seat of temporal authority in Sikhism.

Under the Jathedar's aegis, six moderate and radical Akali factions came together in May 1994 to form the Akali Dal (Amritsar). This unification was followed by the issuance of the Amritsar Declaration, which called for an independent Sikh homeland where the community could freely practise and propagate its faith without external interference.

The main moderate faction, the Akali Dal (Badal), distanced itself from the separatist stance. Demonstrating his political shrewdness, Parkash Singh Badal soon emerged as the foremost political representative of the Sikh community. In February 1995, Tohra and Badal reached a compromise: Tohra would confine his role to religious affairs, while Badal would lead the political front.

These developments significantly strengthened the position of the Akali Dal (Badal) and, coupled with its success in the May 1996 Lok Sabha elections, seemed to vindicate its slogan—"*Panth, Punjab, and Punjabiyat*" (the Sikh community, Punjab, and Punjabi identity).[26]

In May 1996, when the BJP emerged as the largest single political party in the general elections, the Akali Dal (Badal) (SAD) made a public declaration of support for the BJP's claim. Parkash Singh Badal extended "unconditional support" to Vajpayee when he formed the government for thirteen days. Before that, an even more important change was that Badal had announced that the identity of the SAD would change from "Panthic" to "Punjabi party". In 1997, the BJP and the SAD decided to fight the elections together. The SAD's base in the Sikh peasantry nicely complemented the BJP's urban Hindu constituency.

---

26. *Sunday Tribune*, 16 February 1997.

BJP leader Madan Lal Khurana was the architect of the SAD–BJP alliance in 1996–97. He played a crucial role in stitching up the alliance before the 1997 assembly elections; the SAD contested 94 seats and the BJP the remaining 23 seats in the 117-member House. The seat-sharing arrangement was to continue till the 2017 assembly elections. An alliance was stitched carefully manoeuvring differences around many key issues.

The SAD's manifesto for the elections was a mixture of rural populism and a reassertion of the demands predating the Rajiv–Longowal Accord, tempered with the need to emphasise Hindu–Sikh unity. The party pledged to fight for true federalism as contained in the Anandpur Sahib Resolution of 1973.[27] This commitment included the repudiation of all previous accords on the adjudication of interstate river waters, the postponement of the Sutlej–Yamuna Link project, the transfer of Chandigarh and other Punjabi-speaking areas to the state, and the proposal to set up a human rights commission in the state. At the same time, the manifesto concluded with the need to "maintain peace in Punjab at all costs".[28]

The BJP's election manifesto differed in one significant respect: while maintaining its opposition to the Anandpur Sahib Resolution, the BJP proposed instead to implement the report of the Sarkaria Commission to increase powers to the states and stop the misuse of Article 356 of the Constitution. In place of decentralisation and federalism, the BJP document spoke of "devolution" consistent with the "unity and integrity of the country".

---

27. The Anandpur Sahib Resolution, 1973, originally drafted by Sikh leader Sardar Kapur Singh, demanded that the Government of India hand over Chandigarh to Punjab; to also hand over other Punjabi-speaking areas presently with other states; and to increase the proportion of Sikhs in the Army. It criticised the foreign policy of India framed by the Congress party as "worthless, hopeless, and highly detrimental to the interests of the Country, the Nation and the Mankind at large". Asking for a recasting of the Indian Constitution on "real federal principles", it said that "in this new Punjab and in other states the Centre's interference would be restricted to defence, foreign relations, currency, and general administration; all other departments would be in the jurisdiction of Punjab (and other states) which would be fully entitled to frame own laws on these subjects for administration". The original draft of the Anandpur Sahib Resolution was written by Sikh leader Sardar Kapur Singh in his own hand.

28. *The Tribune* (Chandigarh), 28 January 1997.

The BJP agreed to work with the SAD as it had, after all, committed itself to "guaranteeing peace, national integrity, and communal harmony".[29] The SAD–BJP alliance won a landslide victory, capturing 93 of 117 assembly seats and almost 48 per cent of the votes polled. The SAD did particularly well in rural (70) and semi-rural (24) constituencies, making a virtual clean sweep of the Malwa region and with a strong showing in the Majha and the Doaba regions. The BJP also did better than was expected, winning its highest seats since the linguistic organisation. The SAD's share of the popular vote was slightly less than the record 38 per cent achieved by Akali Dal (Longowal)[30] in the elections of 1985. The BJP performed strongly in urban and semi-urban constituencies where traditionally it competed with the Congress (I) and the BSP. As the Hindu vote swung behind the BJP, the Congress (I)'s position was undermined by competition from the BSP.

The emphatic victory of the SAD–BJP alliance marked a decisive turning point in the configuration of political forces involved in the Punjab problem. Earlier attempts by the SAD and its predecessors to forge a regional anti-Congress coalition had repeatedly faltered—undermined both by the defection of smaller allies such as the Left parties and the BSP, and by the Congress (I)'s success in penetrating Akali ranks through factional manipulation. For the first time, the SAD's alignment with a powerful anti-Congress (I) national party closed off the possibility of such disruptions, while offering the BJP a model it could replicate in other states.

For the BJP, however, endorsing Punjab's regional demands posed serious challenges. The party was at odds with the SAD on key issues such as Centre–state relations and the Anandpur Sahib Resolution, and it also had to balance the interests of its own government in Rajasthan and coalition partners in Haryana and Himachal Pradesh—states that stood to lose from any settlement favouring Punjab. The Congress (I), for its part, had long delayed the implementation of the Rajiv–Longowal Accord, wary of unsettling its own governments in these neighbouring states.

The 2002 elections for the 117-member Punjab Legislative Assembly were held on 30 January. In the poll results, the Congress–CPI alliance defeated

---

29. Ibid., 29 January 1997.

30. SAD (Longowal) was formed on 20 August 2009 as a splinter group of the Parkash Singh Badal-led SAD.

the SAD–BJP coalition. The Congress–CPI won 64 seats of which the CPI won 2, the SAD–BJP combine won 44 seats (SAD 41 and BJP 3). Independent candidates got an unprecedented victory on 9 seats. Ahead of the polls, the Congress ran a high-decibel poll campaign against the SAD–BJP combine, focused on levelling allegations of corruption by the incumbent SAD–BJP coalition government. It accused the government of irregularities in recruitment in different government departments and in the Punjab Civil Services and judicial services. The Congress blamed the Punjab Public Service Commission chairman for openly receiving kickbacks for selecting candidates. The SAD–BJP was on the defensive. Captain Amarinder Singh led the Congress to victory.[31]

★

When Jaitley took over the party affairs in 2006, the first decision he took was to upgrade the one-room BJP office in Amritsar. He told then president of Amritsar unit Bakshi Ram Arora to expand it. When he was told of lack of finance, Jaitley directed Arora to make the plan and leave the rest to him. He arranged for the funds from the BJP headquarters. Construction started in 2008, the new office building was ready in 2011.[32]

Jaitley was confident that the anti-incumbency factor against the Congress would benefit the SAD–BJP combine in the 2007 elections. In a press conference held in Jalandhar on 28 January 2007, less than a month from polling dates, he predicted that elections would be a reversal of those in 2002. Talking "about the arithmetics of the assembly elections", he told the media that in the previous elections, because of Shiromani Gurdwara Parbandhak Committee (SGPC) chief Gurcharan Singh Tohra fielding his candidates and the Congress stitching

---

31. "2002 Punjab Legislative Assembly Elections", *Outlook*, accessed 25 May 2025, https://www.outlookindia.com/opinion/india-news-2002-punjab-legislative-assembly-elections-news-305309.

32. Kamaldeep Singh Brar, "Jaitley Remained Involved in Punjab Politics at Ground Level Much Before Contesting from Amritsar", *The Indian Express*, accessed 25 May 2025, https://indianexpress.com/article/india/arun-jaitley-death-demise-punjab-politics-contesting-amritsar-punjab-5933649/.

an alliance with the Left Front parties, the SAD–BJP suffered electoral setback. But, in 2007, he said that the Congress was contesting elections on its own and also facing anti-incumbency sentiment and his political acumen told him that "this would benefit the SAD–BJP combine and it would form its government in Punjab".[33]

When results were announced on 27 February 2007, the SAD had won 48 seats, the Congress 44, the BJP 19, and others 5. Under Jaitley's command the BJP gave its best-ever performance in the 2007 assembly elections—bagging 19 out of 23 seats.

The 2007 elections threw up a brand-new order in the legislative leadership. As many as forty-four first-time MLAs entered the portals of the 117-member Vidhan Sabha, a record-high in its sixty-year-old history. More significantly, thirty-nine MLAs—one-third of the total strength—were less than forty-five years old. Educated at some of the best institutes in India and abroad, they were driven more by ideas than ideology. Many of them had a well-heeled political lineage, but they preferred to swear by their sharp learning curves, spawning a new hope for the state in desperate need of recovery on key indices of socioeconomic development.

In 2012, confident of the SAD and the BJP returning to power, Jaitley once again stitched an alliance with the SAD. There was a new player in the election scene this time—the Sanjha Morcha which comprised the newly formed People's Party of Punjab (PPP) led by Parkash Singh Badal's estranged nephew and former finance minister Manpreet Singh Badal, the CPI, the CPI(M), and the Akali Dal (Harchand Singh Longowal). The elections were held on 30 January 2012. When results were declared on 6 March 2012, the SAD–BJP alliance created history in Punjab by storming back to power for a second consecutive term, breaking a forty-six-year-old jinx.

The SAD-BJP won 68 seats (SAD 56, BJP 12) this time as against 67 seats (SAD 48, BJP 19) five years back.[34] While the SAD improved its tally from 48, the BJP suffered a loss of 7 seats. The Congress could win only 46 seats

---

33. Dharmendra Joshi, "Anti-incumbency to Benefit SAD-BJP: Jaitley", *Jalandhar Online Edition*, accessed 25 May 2025, https://www.tribuneindia.com/2007/20070129/jal.htm#1.

34. "List of Winners" under Home—Punjab 2012, MyNeta, available at https://www.myneta.info/pb2012/index.php?action=show_winners&sort=default.

even though it improved its performance by 2 seats as compared to 2007 and gained in terms of vote percentage. While the SAD's vote share in this election declined to 34.75 per cent as compared to 37.09 per cent in 2007, the BJP's vote share came down to 7.13 per cent this time as against 8.28 per cent in the previous elections. The vote percentage of the SAD fell by 2.34 per cent whereas its ally BJP's vote percentage dropped by 1.15 per cent. The prime factor which impacted the vote share of the SAD–BJP alliance and the Congress appears to be the PPP.

It was Jaitley who initiated former cricketer Navjot Singh Sidhu into politics and the latter has always acknowledged him as his "political guru". After him, Jaitley is said to have brought in Hindi cinema actor Sunny Deol who successfully contested the 2014 Lok Sabha polls from the Gurdaspur Lok Sabha seat in Punjab.

In January 2016, Manpreet Singh Badal merged the PPP with the Congress. When Punjab went to polls on 4 February 2017, BJP vice president Prabhat Jha was made the in-charge of Punjab. Jaitley was focused on stabilising the Indian economy as the finance minister. But he continued to guide Jha and even launched the party's election campaign in Punjab by addressing the media in Amritsar.[35] At a public meeting later, he attacked Punjab Congress chief Amarinder Singh, in his usual inimitable style, over his family's Swiss bank accounts. *The Indian Express* heading on 21 January 2017 read: "Punjab polls: BJP joins campaign with Jaitley's 'Swiss' knife".[36] The Congress came back marching winning 77 seats. The Aam Aadmi Party (AAP) made significant inroads with its 20 seats eating into non-Congress votes. The SAD could muster only 15 seats, the BJP was left with 3.[37]

---

35. "Punjab: Confident of Doing Well, Visualise that We'll Bring Development, says Arun Jaitley", *The Indian Express*, accessed 25 May 2025, https://indianexpress.com/elections/punjab-assembly-elections-2017/punjab-assembly-polls-bjp-arun-jaitley-amarinder-singh-congress-4485286/.

36. Navjeevan Gopal, "Punjab Polls: BJP Joins Campaign with Jaitley's 'Swiss' Knife", *The Indian Express*, accessed 25 May 2025, https://indianexpress.com/elections/punjab-assembly-elections-2017/punjab-polls-bjp-joins-campaign-with-jaitleys-swiss-knife-4484535/.

37. "2017 Vidhan Sabha / Assembly Election Results Punjab", India Votes, available at https://www.indiavotes.com/vidhan-sabha/2017/punjab/251/7.

In September 2020, a year after Jaitley passed away on 24 August 2019, the SAD announced its decision to quit the NDA over the farm bills issue, breaking the four-decade-long alliance.[38] A day later, SAD leader Naresh Gujral said that after Arun Jaitley's demise, no one in the BJP understood the psyche of Punjab.[39] Parkash Singh Badal forecasted the trouble in alliance when Jaitley passed away. He said, 'Although the loss of every great leader is always untimely, yet nowhere will this be felt more acutely and painfully than in the case of Jaitley's departing from us. He has left us at a time when the world is in a crying need of the values he practiced and symbolised."[40] In the twenty-three years of the alliance, the SAD–BJP government was in power in the state for fifteen years. Jaitley remained in charge of Punjab affairs for only four years but he had a strong relationship with the state and the Badal family. He believed that the BJP–SAD partnership was not only a political alliance, but a social one aimed at strengthening the bonds of peace, communal harmony, amity, and brotherhood in Punjab. He played peacemaker whenever relations between the alliance partners became strained. Jaitley believed that after terrorism in Punjab ended, it was the alliance forged between the SAD and the BJP which provided a healing touch to the people of the state. "The Congress was responsible for the rise in terrorism and fought the 1984 elections on the plank of communalism," Jaitley said. He believed that the Congress pitted the people of Punjab against one another and that the SAD–BJP alliance worked towards healing the wounds of the people and brought back normalcy to the state.[41]

---

38. Vikas Vasudeva, "Akalis Quit NDA, Say Centre Ignored Farmers' Sentiments", *The Hindu*, accessed 25 May 2025, https://www.thehindu.com/news/national/shiromani-akali-dal-bjps-oldest-ally-leaves-nda-over-farm-bills/article32704939.ece.

39. PTI, "After Arun Jaitley, None in BJP Understands Psyche of Punjab: SAD MP Naresh Gujral", *The Hindu*, accessed 25 May 2025, https://www.thehindu.com/news/national/other-states/after-arun-jaitley-none-in-bjp-understands-psyche-of-punjab-sad-mp-naresh-gujral/article32708142.ece.

40. "Jaitley Transformed Politics into Statesmanship: Parkash Singh Badal", *Business Standard*, accessed 25 May 2025, https://www.business-standard.com/article/news-ani/jaitley-transformed-politics-into-statesmanship-parkash-singh-badal-119082401036_1.html.

41. PTI, "Congress Responsible for Terrorism in Punjab: Arun Jaitley", *The Economic Times*, accessed 25 May 2025, https://economictimes.indiatimes.com/news/politics-and-nation/congress-responsible-for-terrorism-in-punjab-arun-jaitley/articleshow/56407177.cms?from=mdr.

When the then Chief Minister Bhupinder Hooda of Haryana wanted a role for the Haryana government in the SGPC, Parkash Singh Badal got very perturbed. Jaitley first advised caution, pointing out that a friendly BJP government at the Centre would not allow any harm to be done to him or to the SAD. But when the Hooda government persisted in trying to divide the SGPC, Jaitley requested Attorney General Mukul Rohatgi to take the matter to the Supreme Court. A stay was obtained.[42]

On 26 September 2020, SAD announced that it was ending its alliance with the NDA as farmers' protests continued across Punjab over the proposed farm sector laws. On 5 June 2020, the Modi government promulgated ordinances to bring in force three laws: The Farmers' Produce Trade and Commerce (Promotion and Facilitation) Bill, 2020; The Farmers (Empowerment and Protection) Agreement of Price Assurance and Farm Services Bill, 2020; and The Essential Commodities (Amendment) Bill, 2020, ostensibly for transformation of agriculture in the country and raising farmers' income. Later, on 14 September 2020, bills were introduced in the Lok Sabha to replace the ordinances. Indian farmers started mass protests against the laws at the end of September 2020. The biggest activities centred on New Delhi.

Direct action by farmers in India is not new, but nothing of this scale or duration had been seen for decades. SAD's lone representative in the Union Cabinet, Harsimrat Kaur Badal, quit the government against the bills. In her resignation letter to Prime Minister Narendra Modi, Harsimrat Kaur Badal wrote, "In view of the decision of the Government of India to go ahead with the Bill on the issue of marketing of agricultural produce without addressing and removing the apprehensions of the farmers and the decision of my party, Shiromani Akali Dal, not to be a part of anything that goes against the interests of the farmers, I find it impossible to continue to perform my duties as a minister in the Union Council of Ministers."[43]

---

42. Jyoti Malhotra, "What Makes the Finance-Defence-Company Affairs Minister the Go-To Man in the Narendra Modi Government", *India Today*, accessed 25 May 2025, https://www.indiatoday.in/magazine/cover-story/story/20141110-arun-jaitley-narendra-modi-finance-defence-company-affairs-minister-805687-2014-10-30.

43. Vikas Vasudeva, "Akalis quit NDA, say Centre ignored farmers' sentiments", *The Hindu*, accessed on 24 August 2025, https://www.thehindu.com/news/national/shiromani-akali-dal-bjps-oldest-ally-leaves-nda-over-farm-bills/article32704939.ece.

SAD tied up with the BSP and contested 20 seats in 2022. The AAP swept the polls winning 92 seats. The Congress was reduced to 18. The SAD managed to win only 3, while the BJP was now at 2 from 3 seats won in 2017.[44]

On 19 November 2021, after nearly a year of mass protests against the laws, the Prime Minister Narendra Modi, made a surprise announcement that his government would repeal the farm laws.

Dislodging Digvijaya Singh from Madhya Pradesh

The state of Madhya Pradesh was created in the heart of India in 1956 with the merger of five different regions—Central Provinces and Berar with its capital in Nagpur; Madhya Bharat, which included the prominent princely states of Gwalior and Indore; Vindhya Pradesh, which comprised Bundelkhand and Baghelkhand; the princely state of Bhopal; and the Sironj tehsil of southeastern Rajasthan's Kota district (which is currently part of Vidisha, Madhya Pradesh). Congress leader Ravishankar Shukla, who belonged to Raipur, became the first chief minister of the state on 1 November 1956.

Both the Congress and BJP-RSS have deep roots in Madhya Pradesh. From Bundelkhand to Baitul, Rewa to Ratlam, the political geography of the state is diverse and complex. It has always seen a straight fight, with no third force in the picture. Though the Congress dominated, the BJS, BJP's precursor, was active in the state from the beginning.[45]

The Congress suffered a setback in the assembly polls of 1962. Katju lost in Jaora to the young BJS candidate Laxminarayan Pandey. The Congress won only 142 seats. Senior Congress leader Bhagwatrao Mandloi, an educationist from Khandwa, became the chief minister. In 1963, he resigned under the Kamaraj Plan—a suggestion by K. Kamaraj that all senior Congress leaders give up their ministerial posts and devote their energies to the organisation.

---

44. "2022 Vidhan Sabha / Assembly Election Results Punjab", India Votes, available at https://www.indiavotes.com/vidhan-sabha/2022/punjab/286/7.

45. Shyamlal Yadav, "A Political History of Madhya Pradesh, Set for Another Straight BJP vs Congress Fight", *The Indian Express*, accessed 25 May 2025, https://indianexpress.com/article/explained/explained-politics/a-poltical-history-of-madhya-pradesh-set-for-another-straight-bjp-vs-congress-fight-9020839/.

Veteran leader D.P. Mishra[46] succeeded Mandloi. In the years that followed, Mishra—a man who had once left the Congress following differences with Nehru—grew increasingly close to Indira Gandhi who had become the prime minister in 1966. Mishra was among those who had helped her fight off the challenge from the party old guard.

Meanwhile, the BJS was becoming stronger, and some socialists and erstwhile royalty like Gwalior's Vijayaraje Scindia, who had serious differences with Mishra, had joined the party. The Congress survived the opposition wave of 1967—when non-Congress governments were formed in more than a dozen other states—but the BJS won 78 of the 296 seats in the Madhya Pradesh Assembly.

In the assembly elections of 1980, the Congress won 246 of the 320 seats. The BJS had reinvented itself as the BJP, and the new party won 60 seats. Indira Gandhi chose Arjun Singh, the MLA from Churhat in Sidhi district, as chief minister. From 1980 to 1989, Madhya Pradesh had five Congress chief ministers—Arjun Singh and Motilal Vora occupied the post twice each before Shyama Charan Shukla came back as the chief minister for a short third stint. Arjun Singh and Motilal Vora remained active in Central politics until their deaths.[47]

In the assembly elections held in early 1990, the Congress lost. The BJP got a historic mandate, winning 220 of the 320 seats, and Sundarlal Patwa became the chief minister. In the elections of 1993, the BJP was reduced to 117 seats. The Congress won 174. The position of chief minister went to Digvijaya Singh of the erstwhile royal family of Raghogarh. Digvijaya remained in power for two full terms until 2003. By then, Arjun Singh had quit the Congress, and the NDA government under Vajpayee had split Madhya Pradesh into two.

The BJP uprooted the Congress from Madhya Pradesh in 2003. Jaitley's abilities as a poll manager were widely hailed. He brought the development agenda at the forefront of political discourse by focusing the campaign on

---

46. D.P. Mishra was the father of Indian Foreign Service (IFS) officer Brajesh Mishra, who was to go on to play a very important role in the government of Prime Minister Atal Bihari Vajpayee from 1998 to 2004.

47. Shyamlal Yadav, "A Political History of Madhya Pradesh, Set for Another Straight BJP vs Congress Fight", *The Indian Express*, accessed 25 May 2025, https://indianexpress.com/article/explained/explained-politics/a-poltical-history-of-madhya-pradesh-set-for-another-straight-bjp-vs-congress-fight-9020839/.

basic and long overlooked issues like bijli, sadak, paani. Jaitley played the development plank against the Congress's Dalit agenda. He projected firebrand leader Uma Bharti as the BJP's chief ministerial candidate, and the star campaigner. As the BJP's campaign strategist, Jaitley used data to challenge the Congress's rule of ten years in Madhya Pradesh and fifty years at the Centre. He confronted Digvijaya Singh in newspaper and television interviews, took on the Congress government for its failures on infrastructure, basic amenities, and other developmental issues.

In 2003, the BJP won a majority of 173 seats in what was now, after the new state of Chhattisgarh was carved out, a 230-member assembly. The Congress was reduced to just 38 seats, even though Digvijaya himself managed to win. Uma Bharti, who had shot to prominence during the Ram Janmabhoomi movement, became the chief minister. Even Uma Bharti was stunned by the overwhelming victory and admitted that she did not see it coming. Neither did the Congress. Stunned by the rout, Digvijaya vowed not to take any organisational post in the Congress for ten years.[48]

However, an old case forced Bharti to give up the post in August 2004. Leaders of the BJP wanted her to hand the baton to Shivraj Singh Chouhan, but she opposed Chouhan's appointment. On Bharti's insistence, the septuagenarian Babulal Gaur was appointed as chief minister. He had been the Leader of the Opposition in Madhya Pradesh Vidhan Sabha from 4 September 2002 to 7 December 2003.[49]

In a little more than a year, on 26 November 2005, the BJP's nine-member Parliamentary Board met and decided to replace Gaur with Chouhan, who was then the state party chief. Knowing that the decision would not go down well with Bharti, Pramod Mahajan and fellow general secretary Jaitley were deputed to inform Bharti. The two called Bharti to Mahajan's residence in Delhi. She was offered the party's general secretaryship. But she refused to accept the party's decision to replace Gaur with Chauhan. An incensed Bharti then stormed out of Mahajan's house, warning the duo of dire consequences.

---

48. Rajendra Sharma, "Arun Jaitley: Master Strategist Who Beat Caste Politics with Bijli-Sadak-Paani", *The Times of India*, accessed 25 May 2025, https://timesofindia.indiatimes.com/city/bhopal/master-strategist-who-beat-caste-politics-with-bijli-sadak-paani/articleshow/70823401.cms.

49. Bharatiya Janata Party, accessed on 24 August 2025, https://mp.bjp.org/node/63512.

Later that night she phoned Jaitley and repeated her warnings. But Jaitley did not succumb to the pressure. Even Vajpayee advised Bharti to accept the offer of general secretaryship, pointing out that this way she would be in charge of more states than just Madhya Pradesh.[50] When the Parliamentary Board met again on 30 November, the decision to expel Bharti was unanimous. She was suspended from the primary membership of the party.[51] She accused the BJP of trying to isolate leaders from backward communities in the party. "Her allegation is baseless as the BJP is not a casteist party," Jaitley responded.[52]

During the BJP's fifteen-year rule under three chief ministers—Uma Bharti, Babulal Gaur, and Shivraj Singh Chouhan—Jaitley continued to be active in elections in Madhya Pradesh. He would strategise campaigns against the Congress and counter-Congress strategies. Ahead of the 2018 assembly elections and 2019 Lok Sabha elections, Jaitley came to Madhya Pradesh to campaign for the BJP; he clearly strategised and strongly confronted the Congress charge on issues like demonetisation. Chouhan went on to serve continuously from 2005 to 2018.

In the closely fought elections of 2018, the Congress won 114 seats, and the BJP 109. After losing the Lok Sabha election in 2019, Jyotiraditya Scindia left the Congress, the party his father Madhavrao Scindia had served, and subsequently joined the party that his grandmother, Vijayaraje Scindia, had co-founded. This brought down the Congress government of Kamal Nath, and Shivraj Singh Chouhan returned as the chief minister in March 2020.

---

50. Priya Sahgal, "BJP Hardens Stand on Indiscipline, Expels Uma Bharati from Party", *India Today*, accessed 25 May 2025, https://www.indiatoday.in/magazine/nation/story/20051212-bjp-hardens-stand-on-indiscipline-expels-uma-bharati-from-party-786410-2005-12-11.

51. Venu Gopal Narayanan, "Madhya Pradesh 2004-2009: Symbol of a Fumbling, Confused BJP of the Era", *Swarajya*, accessed 25 May 2025, https://swarajyamag.com/politics/madhya-pradesh-2004-2009-symbol-of-a-fumbling-confused-bjp-of-the-era.

52. S. Satyanarayanan, "Uma's Expulsion from BJP Imminent", *The Tribune*, accessed 25 May 2025, https://www.tribuneindia.com/2005/20051204/main6.htm.

Getting Nitish Kumar on Board in Bihar

It was Jaitley who managed the BJP alliance with Nitish Kumar's JD(U) in Bihar. Though Jaitley was not a native of Bihar, he had a special affinity with the state and its people. In all these years, it was Jaitley who willingly assisted Nitish Kumar on his way to 1 Aney Marg, the chief minister's residence in Patna. "He had a feeling of respect for Bihar," Nitish Kumar said.[53] Jaitley knew Nitish Kumar from the JP Movement days. They became good friends when both served in the Vajpayee Cabinet. Whenever Nitish Kumar was in Delhi, he met Jaitley who would listen with sharp attentiveness and offer advice.[54]

Bihar is an important state for the BJP for many reasons. It sends forty members to the Lok Sabha. Between 1990 and 1995, Bihar was the only state in the Hindi heartland where the BJP's vote share declined. This decline was because of the rise of OBC politics.

Not a single person belonging to the "lower" castes was a member of the Bihar Pradesh Congress Committee between 1934 and 1946. Brahmins, Rajputs, Bhumihars, and Kayasthas made up over 40 per cent of Congress legislators from 1952 to 1962 and controlled "vote-banks" of SCs and the Muslims. While the Bihar Land Reforms Act of 1950 produced a "new class of people" from among "occupancy tenants" which affected the traditional social pyramid, this led mostly to patronage networks and caste alliances, with the reins still in the hands of the "upper" castes.[55]

Following Ram Manohar Lohia's efforts, the political landscape changed in Bihar. He was a powerful voice against social injustice, class and caste discrimination, and gender bias. In the four years after 1967, Bihar had five chief ministers from the backward castes, and two chief ministers from SCs.

53. Madan Kumar, "Jaitley Played a Big Role in Formation of NDA Govt in Bihar in 2005, says Nitish Kumar", *The Times of India*, accessed 25 May 2025, https://timesofindia.indiatimes.com/india/jaitley-played-a-big-role-in-formation-of-nda-govt-in-bihar-in-2005-says-nitish-kumar/articleshow/70925907.cms?utm_source=contentofinterest&utm_medium=text&utm_campaign=cppst.

54. Ibid.

55. Rakesh Ankit, "Caste Politics in Bihar: In Historical Continuum", *History and Sociology of South Asia*, Vol. 12, No. 2 (2018), pp. 115-36.

The 1974 JP Movement proved a watershed in Bihar's politics. Almost all of the later political leaders of the 1990s were a product of this movement. In 1974, Jayaprakash Narayan had said, "Caste is the biggest political party in Bihar." The seeds of the politics of the 1990s were sown in this social movement of the 1970s.

The issue of backward empowerment became even more important in the 1990 Vidhan Sabha elections. The Janata Dal emerged victorious with 121 seats, leaving behind the Congress (71), BJP (39), CPI (23), CPI(M) (6), and Jharkhand Mukti Morcha (JMM) (19). Independents also emerged as a major force winning thirty seats. Lalu Prasad Yadav was sworn in as the chief minister on 10 March 1990 after high drama centring around caste politics. In 1997, in the wake of the fodder scam, Lalu Prasad formed the Rashtriya Janata Dal (RJD), parting ways with the Janata Dal. He was on a sticky wicket and the Opposition hoped that he could be defeated. But they squabbled and squandered away their chance.

Nitish Kumar, whose Samata Party had allied with his former socialist colleagues Ram Vilas Paswan and Sharad Yadav's JD(U) just months ago for the Lok Sabha elections, parted ways ahead of the 2000 assembly polls. Kumar formed an alliance with the BJP. The Samata Party, which merged into the JD(U) in 2003, was the BJP's third alliance after the Shiromani Akali Dal in Punjab and the Shiv Sena in Maharashtra. It marked a new style of BJP alliances, going beyond traditional partnerships grounded in religious outlook, with the Akali Dal and the Shiv Sena, while reaching out to a respected secular/socialist partner in the form of George Fernandes.

Arun Jaitley, then BJP's Bihar in-charge, and Nitish crafted a campaign highlighting the lawlessness during the twenty years of RJD. In February 2005, Bihar elections were held for 325-member assembly[56] in three phases. The NDA started the 2005 Bihar campaign without a CM face. After the first phase, at Jaitley's insistence, Nitish was declared as the CM face.[57] When BJP announced

56. After the creation of Jharkhand, the strength of the House was adjusted to the present 243.

57. Chakshu Roy, "How a phone call to Moscow led to Nitish's first full stint as CM", *The Indian Express*, accessed on 9 November 2025, https://indianexpress.com/article/opinion/columns/how-a-phone-call-to-moscow-led-to-nitish-kumars-first-full-stint-as-the-chief-minister-of-bihar-10354269/.

Nitish Kumar as the chief ministerial candidate of the NDA, a murmur of protest came from George Fernandes. When Jaitley went to meet Fernandes, he realised, because of failing health, he had not realised the full implication of his reaction. George Fernandes's parliamentary tenure in Lok Sabha ended in 2009. He needed official accommodation for some more time. Nitish Kumar graciously put him up as a candidate in a by-election for the Rajya Sabha. George entered the Upper House for the first time. His oath-taking showed his state of health. He could no longer contribute politically. He needed help and assistance at every stage. The tiger had been tamed.[58]

The move to declare Kumar as the CM face did sway some Bihar voters, but not enough to give the NDA a majority: RJD was the single-largest party with 75 seats, followed by JD(U) with 55 MLAs, BJP with 37 seats, Ram Vilas Paswan's Lok Janshakti Party (LJP) with 29 seats and 17 independents. With an inconclusive mandate, the focus shifted to Bihar Governor Buta Singh, a Congress veteran. The RJD staked a claim, but without the support of 122 MLAs, the majority required in the assembly. The NDA staked claim in Bihar and appointed Nitish Kumar as the chief minister. The LJP told Singh that they would not support the RJD or the B.JP.

In his first report to President Abdul Kalam, Singh recommended keeping the newly elected assembly in suspended animation. His second report noted that the JD(U) and BJP were trying to secure a majority by winning over the LJP MLAs and splitting the Congress. In his final report, he informed Kalam that 17-18 LJP MLAs were moving to the JD(U), a move that would "distort the verdict of the people". He recommended fresh elections. Things moved quickly after his final report was received in Delhi on 22 May 2005. Prime Minister Manmohan Singh's Cabinet met at I1 p.m. and recommended dissolution of the newly elected Bihar Assembly. The PM called then President Kalam, who had barely arrived in Moscow on a multi-country tour, to inform him of the Cabinet's recommendation, followed by another call to answer Kalam's questions. A little later, Kalam brought the state under President's Rule. Nitish, Jaitley and other NDA MPs raised the matter in Parliament repeatedly.

Elections were held again in October that year. Ten days before the repoll, the Supreme Court held the President's decision as "unconstitutional". This time, Bihar gave the NDA a majority: JD(U) increased its share from 55 to 88

58. Arun Jaitley, *A New India, Select Writings 2014-2019* (Juggernaut, 2020), p. 329.

and the BJP's from 37 to 55 MLAs. The RJD was reduced from 75 to 54 and the LJP ended with just 10 seats. In November 2005, Nitish was sworn in as Bihar CM. Through the alliance with the JD(U), the BJP was able to wean away Lalu Prasad's traditional voter base comprising backward classes. Political scientist Milan Vaishnav noted:

> The BJP–JD(U) alliance forged a powerful political coalition that exploited the BJP's popularity among Hindu upper castes and the JD(U)'s constituency made up of the lower rungs of the OBCs, a new grouping that came to be known as Extremely Backward Castes (EBCs). The construction of the EBC identity was a savvy attempt to strip votes of non-Yadav backward castes from the RJD. Kumar's JD(U) also fractured the vote of Bihar's Dalits by again targeting the most backward among them, fashioning a new Mahadalit category and directing welfare benefits to this new group.[59]

The events of 2005 would have consequences beyond Bihar. The SC would indict Governor Singh, leading to his resignation. Kalam would also consider resigning, the judgment recasting his relationship with the government.

In 2010, riding a massive wave on the theme of development, Nitish Kumar led the JD(U)–BJP alliance to a landslide four-fifth majority in the assembly elections routing Lalu Prasad's RJD–LJP combine and a weak Congress to return to power for a second consecutive term. The BJP got 91 seats, the JD(U) got 115, the RJD got 22 and the Congress got 4, out of a total of 243 seats.[60] Nitish Kumar was sworn in as chief minister of Bihar for the second consecutive term.

The souring of ties began in 2013 when Nitish Kumar broke up with the BJP, ending the JD(U)–BJP's seventeen-year alliance. He was reportedly displeased with the announcement of Narendra Modi's name as the prime ministerial candidate. In June 2013, just a week after Modi was named the

---

59. Bhupender Yadav and Illa Patnaik, *The Rise of the BJP, The Making of The World's Largest Political Party* (Penguin, 2022), pp. 130–31.

60. "Statistical Report on General Election, 2010 to the Legislative Assembly of Bihar", Election Commission of India.

campaign committee chief of the BJP for the 2014 Lok Sabha elections, Nitish Kumar snapped his ties with the BJP. JD(U) contested the 2014 Lok Sabha elections alone and managed to bag only two seats as opposed to eighteen in 2009. Taking responsibility for his party's downfall in the 2014 polls, Nitish Kumar stepped down as Bihar chief minister and placed Jitan Ram Manjhi in his post. Manjhi was minister for Scheduled Castes and Scheduled Tribes Welfare in Nitish Kumar's Cabinet. From 1996 to 2005, he served under the RJD government with Lalu Prasad Yadav and Rabri Devi. Manjhi survived the floor test with the support of Lalu Prasad Yadav's RJD, his arch-rival.

Nitish Kumar saw Manjhi as a caretaker who would merely keep the seat warm. But the unassuming Manjhi quickly shattered those expectations. Within two months, he boldly stepped out of Kumar's shadow, asserting his independence with a defiance that shocked many. This audacity prompted Nitish to oust Manjhi and reclaim the CM's chair in February 2015, just months before the assembly polls. Refusing to be sidelined, Manjhi dramatically split from the JD(U) and formed his own party, HAM(S), aligning with the BJP-led NDA.[61]

Nitish Kumar was back in talks with Lalu Prasad and the RJD. In June 2015, the two, caught in an awkward embrace, announced their alliance for the coming assembly elections in the state. Bihar continued the ongoing trend of giving decisive verdicts as the Grand Alliance of the RJD, the JD(U), and the Congress won 178 out of the 243 seats in the state. The BJP faced a second successive defeat after Delhi and was reduced to just 53 seats. Its allies—the Lok Janshakti Party, the Hindustani Awam Morcha, the Rashtriya Lok Samata Party—won just 5 out of the 86 seats that they had contested. In terms of seats, the three parties which formed the Grand Alliance to contest the 2015 elections surpassed their 2014 Lok Sabha election performance. Manjhi's party secured only one seat, stripping him of any significant leverage with the BJP.

Kumar was appointed chief minister. However, his displeasure grew again. This time, he couldn't stand that his party came out to be a smaller force in a larger coalition, with the RJD enjoying the people's majority mandate.

61. "Jitan Ram Manjhi's extraordinary rise to central minister at the age of 80", *The New Indian Express*, accessed on 24 August 2025, https://www.newindianexpress.com/nation/2024/Jun/09/jitan-ram-manjhis-extraordinary-rise-to-central-minister-at-the-age-of-80,

Fissures in the *mahagathbandhan* (Grand Alliance) started to emerge after Kumar openly backed the BJP on demonetisation and GST. He was concerned about his "clean" image after the CBI charged Lalu Prasad and his family in a corruption case. In July 2017, when fissures developed in the JD(U)–RJD government in Bihar, the BJP sensed an opportunity to fish in troubled waters. Though Chief Minister Nitish Kumar had walked out of the NDA in 2013, protesting the BJP's decision to make Narendra Modi its prime ministerial candidate, the saffron party decided to court him again. Jaitley had stayed in close contact with the JD(U) chief after he walked out of the NDA alliance ahead of the 2014 Lok Sabha elections. After Kumar broke over Modi in 2013, the two didn't meet that much anymore, even though Jaitley is believed to say to both sides: "*Aisi bhi karvahat nahin honi chahiye*" (The big picture should not be forgotten because of personal bitterness).

Jaitley then used his good equations with Kumar to stitch together a JD(U)–BJP government within hours. On the sidelines of the farewell dinner for the then outgoing President, Pranab Mukherjee, on 22 July 2017, Jaitley tipped Bihar Chief Minister Nitish Kumar about the plan of his then ally Lalu Prasad to break Kumar's party JD(U) and possibly engineer his ouster. At the dinner itself, Jaitley convinced Prime Minister Narendra Modi for the reinduction of the JD(U) into the NDA. Nitish Kumar's return to the NDA was considered one of the biggest coups in the recent political history of the country, which not only strengthened the government but also stole the biggest names out of the opposition's cavalry. As one of the top JD(U) leaders explained, only Jaitley could have managed this.[62] Nitish Kumar resigned as the chief minister in 2017, only to be restored to the position after he switched back to the NDA and regained a majority in the assembly.

Being a junior partner in the coalition has been a matter of concern for Kumar. The same happened in the 2020 assembly polls. He was concerned about his diminished autonomy after the BJP overpowered his party in the seat tally. The coalition fell apart in 2022. The JD(U) accused the BJP of plotting to split the party and severing ties. His party gained a majority in the assembly

62. Anilesh S. Mahajan, "Arun Jaitley: Master of the Art of Making Friends and Influencing People", *Business Today*, accessed 25 May 2025, https://www.businesstoday.in/latest/economy-politics/story/obituary-arun-jaitley-master-of-the-art-of-making-friends-and-influencing-people-224783-2019-08-24.

once again with the RJD's support and Kumar has been holding onto his chief minister's post since then.

In 2022, Kumar quit the NDA to form a government in coalition with the RJD and the Congress, accusing the BJP of engineering a split in his party, the JD(U). In the absence of Jaitley, tensions between him and the BJP were growing. By the time Bihar faced the next assembly elections in November 2020, there was no Jaitley to broker peace and put the house in order. The BJP was no longer satisfied with playing a supporting role. In a Machiavellian move, they deployed Chirag Paswan of the Lok Janshakti Party to take on the JD(U).

★

While Jaitley was stitching alliances and propelling the party in Karnataka, Punjab, Madhya Pradesh, and Bihar, he was also fashioning the party's strategy in many other states like Jammu and Kashmir, Uttar Pradesh, Gujarat, and Haryana.

Uttar Pradesh

When the BJP came to power in 1998, it was largely on the back of an extraordinary performance in Uttar Pradesh, where the party garnered 57 of its 181 seats. In a move clearly aimed at the 2009 general elections, Arun Jaitley, then BJP general secretary, was given charge of its unit in Uttar Pradesh. The states of Jammu and Kashmir and Punjab were removed from under Jaitley, with Jammu and Kashmir handed over to senior BJP leader Shanta Kumar and Punjab to Sahib Singh Verma. "Jaitley's record in elections in Madhya Pradesh, Karnataka, Gujarat, Bihar, Punjab, and even Delhi (municipal elections) has been excellent. Thus, it was natural that he would be given charge of UP, which was crucial for the 2009 General Election," said a BJP office-bearer then.[63]

---

63. "BJP Gives UP Charge to Jaitley", *Business Standard*, accessed 25 May 2025, https://www.business-standard.com/article/economy-policy/bjp-gives-up-charge-to-jaitley-107053001091_1.html.

Jammu and Kashmir

On 28 July 2008, after his stints as the BJP election in-charge in Gujarat and Karnataka saw it registering convincing wins, Jaitley, the BJP general secretary, was appointed as the in-charge for Jammu and Kashmir assembly polls due in 2008.[64] Jaitley also has a personal connection with the state, being the husband of veteran Jammu and Kashmir politician Girdhari Lal Dogra's daughter Sangeeta.

In the December 2014 elections in the state, the electorate returned a fractured mandate with no party getting a clear majority. The BJP and the Peoples Democratic Party (PDP) emerged as the main players with 25 and 28 seats respectively. The Congress won 12 seats and others 5.[65] The BJP decided to increase its bargaining power with the other political parties in the state. Hoping to get support from more MLAs including some independents, the BJP's highest Parliamentary Board appointed Jaitley and party secretary Arun Singh[66] as observers for Jammu and Kashmir to travel to the state and explore alliances with other parties.

The choice before the BJP was the PDP and the National Conference.[67] Jaitley was the only top BJP leader in the BJP's then dispensation who knew the Mufti family personally. Jaitley reached out to the senior PDP patriarch, Mufti Mohammad Sayeed. Sayeed's term as the chief minister of the state between 2002 and 2005 had led to significant steps like opening of Srinagar–Muzaffarabad road, initiation of trade and travel across the Line of Control

---

64. PTI, "Jaitley Appointed BJP Election Incharge for J&K Polls", *Hindustan Times*, accessed 25 May 2025, https://www.hindustantimes.com/india/jaitley-appointed-bjp-election-incharge-for-j-k-polls/story-YnzWqeiYt4j4gcS84W3umJ_amp.html.

65. "Jaitley Heads for J&K to Explore BJP's Options", *The Pioneer*, accessed 25 May 2025, https://www.dailypioneer.com/2014/page1/jaitley-heads-for-jandk-to-explore-bjps-options.html.

66. Arun Singh served as BJP's national secretary, National Convenor of Investor Cell, national vice president and treasurer of BJYM and various other organisational responsibilities of the party since 1996.

67. Pratul Sharma, "BJP to Send Arun Jaitley to Jammu and Kashmir, to Keep All Options Open", *The New Indian Express*, accessed 25 May 2025, https://www.newindianexpress.com/nation/2014/Dec/25/bjp-to-send-arun-jaitley-to-jammu-and-kashmir-to-keep-all-options-open-698003.html.

(LoC) without passports and visas, with India and Pakistan making some significant concessions on Kashmir.

Jaitley's phone call took the contact to the next level. After his "long chat" with Mufti, PDP president Mehbooba Mufti met Governor N.N. Vohra, indicating an alliance with the BJP.[68] After nearly two months of talks on formulating a common minimum programme of governance, the BJP and the PDP announced their alliance for forming a "popular" government in Jammu and Kashmir. This was the first time that the BJP would participate in governance in the border state. Mehbooba Mufti said that the two parties—known to hold extreme positions—had found a "middle path" and the government that would be formed would not be just about "power sharing" but about "winning hearts and minds of the people of Jammu and Kashmir and the entire country". She claimed that the coming together of the BJP and the PDP would be different from previous alliances since 1947 between the state and central leadership in that for the first time the interest of the people of Jammu and Kashmir and national interest had been kept centre stage. She also said, "The agenda for alliance has kept in mind the priorities, aspirations, development, prosperity and peace of the people of Jammu and Kashmir and is committed to providing a clean, non-corrupt government in the State." This is an opportunity, she said, to bridge the gap with the people of Jammu and Kashmir.[69]

Gujarat

Gujarat was homeland to Jaitley. This is the state that sent Jaitley to the Rajya Sabha in 2000. It was as much Jaitley's battleground as Modi's when Modi decided to take a fresh mandate after the Godhra incident. In 2007, Jaitley

68. Muzamil Jaleel, "Arun Jaitley dials Mufti Sayeed as BJP, PDP 'look' at Jammu-Kashmir options", *The Indian Express*, accessed 25 May 2025, https://indianexpress.com/article/political-pulse/arun-jaitley-dials-mufti-mohammad-sayeed-as-bjp-pdp-look-at-jk-options/.

69. Gargi Parsai, "BJP-PDP Seal Deal on Forming Govt. in J&K", *The Hindu*, accessed 25 May 2025, https://www.thehindu.com/news/national/BJP-PDP-alliance-to-form-govt.-in-JandK/article60514676.ece.

again campaigned for Modi's second electoral campaign during the assembly election in Gujarat. A senior journalist covering the election in Ahmedabad asked Jaitley why he alienated Vajpayee by helping the then chief minister in several legal and political wrangles. Jaitley was on record to state: "I've known Modi for years. We've worked together in Delhi much before he came to Gujarat and I see him as an exceptional talent."[70] This response came at a time when no one could have anticipated Modi becoming the prime minister one day. In 2012, Narendra Modi led the BJP to yet another victory and became the chief Minister for the fourth time. Again, Jaitley strategised Modi's election together with others in Gujarat. In August 2017, then BJP chief Amit Shah appointed Arun Jaitley as the BJP's election in-charge for Gujarat.[71] Four Union ministers—Narendra Singh Tomar, Nirmala Sitharaman, Jitendra Singh, and P.P. Choudhary—were made co-in-charges.[72]

Haryana

The journey of the BJP's rise in Haryana politics is a tale of resilience, strategic alliances, and transformative leadership that has reshaped the state's political narrative. For a long time, Haryana was a bastion of traditional political powerhouses. Initially, the party faced formidable challenges, grappling with rooted regional parties and a deeply entrenched caste-based polity dominated by the likes of the Indian National Lok Dal (INLD) and the Congress. The BJP forged strategic alliances with regional players and leveraged caste dynamics to

70. Saba Naqvi, "Arun Jaitley's relationships ranged far and wide, but the defining equation in his life would be with Narendra Modi", *The Times of India*, accessed 25 May 2025, https://timesofindia.indiatimes.com/blogs/toi-edit-page/arun-jaitleys-relationships-ranged-far-and-wide-but-the-defining-equation-in-his-life-would-be-with-narendra-modi/.

71. "Arun Jaitley Made BJP Poll In-charge for Gujarat, Prakash Javadekar for Karnataka", *The Indian Express*, accessed 25 May 2025, https://indianexpress.com/article/india/arun-jaitley-made-bjp-poll-in-charge-for-gujarat-prakash-javadekar-for-karnataka-4812468/.

72. "Arun Jaitley, Prakash Javadekar BJP's Poll In-charge for Gujarat, Karnataka", *Deccan Chronicle*, accessed 25 May 2025, https://www.deccanchronicle.com/nation/current-affairs/2408.

its advantage. The party's alliance with the SAD in the state proved instrumental in consolidating its support base among the Sikh community, particularly in the politically influential regions of Kurukshetra and Ambala.

The genesis of BJP's rise in Haryana can be traced back to the early 1990s when the party, buoyed by the wave of the Hindutva ideology sweeping across the nation, began to make inroads into the state's political landscape. However, the BJP's fortunes took a dramatic turn with the onset of the twenty-first century. The watershed moment came in 2014 when the BJP secured a historic mandate in the Lok Sabha elections, winning all ten parliamentary seats in Haryana. This resounding victory laid the foundation for the BJP's dominance in the state's political arena. The BJP's meteoric rise in Haryana also coincided with a gradual erosion of the traditional vote banks of regional parties like the INLD and the Congress. The disillusionment among voters with the lacklustre performance and corruption scandals plaguing these parties created a fertile ground for the BJP to capitalise on. Moreover, the BJP's organisational prowess and robust grassroots machinery played a pivotal role in consolidating its electoral gains across the state. The party's relentless focus on booth-level management, cadre mobilisation, and outreach programmes ensured that its message reached every nook and corner of Haryana, thereby broadening its support base.

The culmination of the BJP's rise in Haryana was evident in the 2019 assembly elections when the party emerged as the single largest party winning 40 out of 90 seats and forming the government in alliance with the Jannayak Janta Party (JJP). This electoral triumph underscored the BJP's status as the preeminent political force in the state, relegating traditional rivals to the fringes of Haryana's political spectrum. The BJP's ascendancy in Haryana politics represents a paradigm shift in the state's political dynamics. From being a peripheral player to assuming the mantle of leadership, the party's journey epitomises the power of perseverance, pragmatism, and people-centric governance.[73]

73. "The Remarkable Ascendancy of BJP in Haryana Politics: A Journey of Resilience and Transformation", The Haryana Story, accessed 25 May 2025, https://en.theharyanastory.com/article/515/the-remarkable-ascendancy-of-bjp-in-haryana-politics-a-journey-of-resilience-and-transformation.

Jaitley had a significant association with Haryana politics. His connection with the state's politics began when he was detained in Ambala jail in 1977, where he interacted with several Haryana-based political leaders and activists. In 2013, Jaitley decided that the BJP would go with Haryana Janhit Congress (HJC) rather than the INLD in the assembly and parliamentary elections. In a massive political rally organised by Haryana Janhit Congress president Kuldeep Bishnoi in Hisar on 1 December 2013, Jaitley announced, in the face of stiff opposition from some factions in the BJP, that "Bishnoi will be the Chief Minister if the BJP–HJC alliance comes to power. The alliance is a firm reality and the massive gathering here confirms the alliance's acceptability at the grassroots level".

The function was organised to mark the culmination of a fifty-seven-day-long Haryana Vijay Yatra undertaken by Bishnoi. Jaitley urged the gathering to vote for the alliance to help in electing Narendra Modi as the prime minister and Bishnoi as the chief minister.[74] Modi, addressing a rally in Jammu and Kashmir at the same time on 1 December 2013, referred to the successful Haryana rally to the audience. He said, "I have just been informed by Arun Jaitley Ji that there a sea of people has come to attend the BJP-HJC rally in Haryana in support of alliance."[75] Although in the elections to the Haryana assembly held on 15 October 2014, Bishnoi's party could win only a few seats, the BJP created political history by winning 47 seats in the 90-member assembly. The party got 33.3 per cent vote share in the state.[76] Manohar Lal Khattar became the first Punjabi Khatri chief minister of the state.

All this time, Jaitley continued to practise law, not only to earn his bread and butter, but also to fight many legal political battles for the BJP and its leaders. Despite his deep engagement with his party's work, Jaitley was one of the most sought-after lawyers of the country.

---

74. Vishal Joshi, "Jaitley Confirms BJP-HJC Alliance in Haryana", *Hindustan Times*, accessed 25 May 2025, https://www.hindustantimes.com/india/jaitley-confirms-bjp-hjc-alliance-in-haryana/story-2GTU5BtocKn4i0UiMp6IJO_amp.html.

75. "Shri Narendra Modi addressing 'Lalkar Rally' in Jammu: Speech", YouTube, accessed on 24 August 2025, https://www.youtube.com/watch?v=JHO-H4rERhQ.

76. "India Votes", accessed on 24 August 2025, https://www.indiavotes.com/vidhan-sabha/2014/haryana/240/31.

12

The Brilliant Lawyer

Arun Jaitley was one of the sterling legal minds in the country. He thrived in the district court, excelled in the Delhi High Court, and ultimately became a prominent Supreme Court lawyer, earning the distinction of being one of the highest taxpayers among senior advocates. He was by all means a formidable advocate with an unparalleled grasp of nearly all branches of law. His expertise in arbitration and commercial disputes also earned him recognition in international legal circles. His wit, charisma, unparalleled presence, and meticulous preparation made him an outstanding lawyer and a jurist par excellence. His ability to dissect complex legal issues, combined with his persuasive oratory and strategic brilliance, set him apart as one of the finest legal minds. His legal career was defined by his ability to navigate intricate legal challenges with precision and eloquence. Witnessing him advance legal arguments in sensitive political cases with huge implications was truly a treat.

Jaitley played a stellar role as additional solicitor general of India (1989–90). His contributions to the legal field were not just limited to courtroom battles; he also played a key role in shaping legal policies and reforms, making him a towering figure in India's legal landscape. His role in drafting key legislations demonstrated his commitment to strengthening India's legal framework. Over his illustrious legal career of nearly three decades, he handled some of the most high-profile and complex cases. During the latter part of his career, he started to devote more time as a parliamentarian, and became aware that his legal practice would create a conflict of interest if he were to take larger responsibilities and hold sensitive positions.

In 2004, Jaitley returned to the Supreme Court briefly for legal practice. In 2009, after he was appointed as the Leader of the Opposition in the Rajya Sabha he decided to wind down his law practice. While surprising, this decision underscored Jaitley's commitment to public service. Though he chose a life that kept him away from the Supreme Court during the later years, he worked tirelessly for upholding the rule of law and establishing its principles in the scheme of governance of the country. The fact that Jaitley spent nineteen months in prison opposing the Emergency influenced his zeal to protect the independence of the courts.

Having experienced imprisonment and lived through periods of both centrist and coalition governments, Jaitley firmly believed in the need for judicial oversight to protect constitutional values while reviewing administrative decisions, laws, and policies. No matter how high he rose, he never forgot his roots and always exhibited a soft corner for the Bar. In fact, as the minister for law and justice, Jaitley spearheaded the establishment of the Advocates' Welfare Fund, implemented the scheme of setting up fast track courts, attended to the computerisation of courts, brought amendments in the Motor Vehicles Act, 1988, and the Negotiable Instruments Act, 1881, to facilitate the expeditious disposal of cases, and even inaugurated the high courts of Chhattisgarh, Jharkhand, and Uttarakhand. He exempted lawyers from the purview of GST. Being a lawyer himself, he was a friend of the judiciary in the Cabinet.

Arun Jaitley's legacy as a lawyer and jurist remains unparalleled. Few counsels have this kind of articulation, clarity, and humane personality. His legal acumen and sharp intellect have left an enduring impact on India's legal and judicial landscape. The legal world is poorer for his absence.

★

Jaitley was practically born in Tis Hazari, the North Delhi district court where his father, Maharaj Kishen Jaitley, mainly practised. His early introduction to law as a profession stemmed from his father Maharaj Kishen Jaitley, who was also a lawyer. Having graduated in law from Delhi University in 1977, Jaitley started appearing in Tis Hazari, specialising in cases involving the MCD and the DDA.

His major breakthrough came in the 1980s, when he represented *The Indian Express* in a case challenging an order by Jagmohan Malhotra, then the lieutenant governor of Delhi, which revoked the lease of the newspaper's building and ordered the demolition of portions of it for violating the Floor Area Ratio (FAR) norms. Jaitley successfully argued before the Supreme Court that freedom of expression, vital for newspapers, must be shielded from oppressive forces seeking to silence dissent. His victory secured the Indian Express building, preventing its partial demolition. In October 1985, the Supreme Court overturned the lieutenant governor's order. Jaitley's defence of the Indian Express building became a landmark case. It cemented Jaitley's prominence in the legal arena at the young age of thirty-three. It also brought him in close contact with Ramnath Goenka—the owner of *The Indian Express*—an association that was to benefit Jaitley in many ways in his career. In 1987, Jaitley shifted his practice to the Supreme Court, while continuing to appear before the Delhi High Court. Jaitley had many opportunities to engage in legal jousting—especially in a supporting role to senior lawyer and former BJP politician Ram Jethmalani—while also raising his political profile.

As discussed earlier, Jaitley was advising in a series of legal matters related to interactions between the Enforcement Directorate, under former finance minister V.P. Singh, and Fairfax, an American detective agency that had allegedly been hired to investigate the illegal stacking of black money overseas. In March 1987, Jaitley and Jethmalani successfully defended S. Gurumurthy, RSS ideologue and financial advisor to Goenka, against allegations of having passed classified information to Fairfax, soon after Gurumurthy wrote a series of articles in *The Indian Express* against the Congress and Reliance. A commission headed by two Supreme Court judges was appointed to investigate V.P. Singh, the then defence minister, who had fallen out with Prime Minister Rajiv Gandhi for his relentless pursuit of tax evaders, including Congress-friendly companies such as Reliance. V.P. Singh subsequently resigned from his ministerial post, quit the Congress party, and hired Jaitley for his defence. Upon becoming the prime minister, Singh appointed Jaitley as the additional solicitor general, one of the youngest ever to hold the post.

Soon after, Jaitley shifted his office to Prithviraj Road, sharing the premises with senior lawyer Dushyant Dave. There was no looking back. A story published by *India Today* in March 1997, titled "Legal Eagles", carried short descriptions of a bunch of young eminent lawyers of the country. Arun Jaitley topped the list. Jaitley mentioned therein that "he enjoys every moment in Court". Any litigating lawyer would readily agree with this.[1] In his interview to *India Today,* Jaitley could also be seen hinting that he was moving away from politics and returning to his legal career. But circumstances did not permit him that. Jaitley was made a minister in the Vajpayee government and later a Rajya Sabha MP. Seen as a suave face in the government, he was soon elevated with Cabinet rank as the Union law minister.

In August 1997, he shifted his office to Kailash Colony. His rise continued as he went on to argue countless cases which shaped the country's legal jurisprudence. His clients now included prominent business houses of the country—PepsiCo, Bombay Dyeing and Co. Ltd.

He devised legal strategies for political leaders from the BJP and its friendly parties when they faced political cases. He represented L.K. Advani and other BJP leaders in the Jain Diary Hawala and Babri Masjid demolition cases. He defended Modi in investigations initiated against him after the 2002 Gujrat riots.

Another notable case was his defence of Amit Shah, the former home minister of Gujarat, in the high-stakes Sohrabuddin Sheikh encounter case.[2] Sohrabuddin was a noted mafia who operated in Gujarat, Madhya Pradesh, and Rajasthan, and was carrying a prize on his head in Madhya Pradesh. He had also been convicted under the Terrorist and Disruptive Activities (Prevention) Act, 1987 (TADA). The search conducted by Madhya Pradesh police at his premises in Jhirniya village, Ujjain district, had yielded more than forty AK-56 rifles, hundreds of AK-56 cartridges and hand grenades. He was an absconder from the police agencies of various state governments.

After his encounter on 24–25 November 2005, his brother filed a writ petition in the Supreme Court. The Government of India conceded that the investigations were to be handed over to the CBI. Since objections were raised with regard to the fairness of the CBI, the Supreme Court ordered investigations by a team of police officers of the Gujarat state police under its

1. Prashant Padmanabhan, "Arun Jaitley from the Eyes of a Legal Practitioner: A Tribute", *Bar and Bench*, accessed 25 May 2025, https://www.barandbench.com/columns/arun-jaitley-from-the-eyes-of-a-legal-practitioner-a-tribute.

2. Jyoti Malhotra, "What Makes the Finance-Defence-Company Affairs Minister the Go-To Man in the Narendra Modi Government", *India Today*, accessed 25 May 2025, https://www.indiatoday.in/magazine/cover-story/story/20141110-arun-jaitley-narendra-modi-finance-defence-company-affairs-minister-805687-2014-10-30.

supervision. The state police reconstructed the encounter, conducted scientific investigation under the supervision of the Supreme Court, and implicated and arrested several police officers including three IPS officers. The Supreme Court referred the matter to the CBI. The ground on which the Supreme Court transferred the case to the CBI was that the investigation involved interstate ramifications and the Andhra Pradesh angle of the matter had not been probed.

In July 2010, after the chargesheet was filed, Shah resigned as the home minister and presented himself before the CBI. The CBI arrested Shah and he faced imprisonment for ninety days. Soon Shah was out on bail with the Gujarat High Court accepting that "there is no prima facie evidence against Amit Shah". The CBI challenged the said order and upon the request of the CBI, the Supreme Court ordered Amit Shah to remain out of Gujarat and all political activities.[3] Amit Shah remained outside the state of Gujarat for a period of two years. The high court order was upheld by the Supreme Court.[4] Jaitley not only strategised, but advised Shah on fighting the cases.

Jaitley also strategised Amit Shah's defence in the Tulsiram Prajapati case, an extension of the Sohrabuddin case. The CBI alleged that Tulsiram Prajapati was a witness to the arrest and disappearance of Sohrabuddin while in custody of the police officers, and that he was subsequently eliminated by the Gujarat police. The CBI filed a chargesheet against Amit Shah just a few months before the Gujarat Legislative Assembly elections which were scheduled to be held before December 2012. Amit Shah had to approach the Supreme Court. On 8 April 2013, the Supreme Court held that no separate chargesheet could be filed in this case since the CBI itself had alleged that both the cases were similar, and it merged the chargesheet with the Sohrabuddin case chargesheet thereby preventing the CBI arresting Amit Shah once again.

In December 2014, a CBI special court at Mumbai discharged Amit Shah of all charges relating to his involvement in the alleged killing of Sohrabuddin and Tulsiram Prajapati. Jaitley wrote a blog on 30 December 2014 calling the discharge "The Vindication of Amit Shah".[5] "Arun Jaitley," Amit Shah said, "was there whenever I was in trouble in my life ... like an elder brother he held

---

3. Arun Jaitley, *A New India: Selected Writings 2014–19* (Juggernaut, 2020), pp. 307–10.
4. Ibid.
5. Ibid.

my finger and took me out of trouble. I will have to acknowledge it. He did it without fear. In my case he did not bother about his public image."[6]

Jaitley was Jayalalithaa's lawyer in the disproportionate assets case dating back to 1996 when the DMK government, then in power, suo motu filed a case against Jayalalithaa. It was based on the complaints by DMK member K. Anbazhagan and Janata Party president Subramanian Swamy (Swamy had given a petition to the then Tamil Nadu governor). The Tamil Nadu government alleged that Jayalalithaa had amassed Rs 66.6 crore, which was disproportionate to her known sources of income. The assets named in the case include farmhouses and bungalows in Chennai and its suburbs, vast tracts of agricultural land in many parts of the state, farmhouse in Hyderabad, tea estate in the Nilgiris, jewellery, industrial sheds, and cash in bank accounts and investments. Apart from Jayalalithaa, her close aide Sasikala, Sasikala's nephew V. Sudhakaran, and her sister-in-law Ilavarasi were also named in the case.

After the elections in 2001, the AIADMK returned to power. The DMK moved the Supreme Court asking the case to be transferred from Tamil Nadu alleging witnesses were turning hostile as Jayalalithaa's party was in power. In 2003, the case was transferred from Chennai to Bangalore.[7]

Jaitley was a key figure in the 2G spectrum case, where he represented several accused individuals, arguing on the nuances of administrative law and the allocation of natural resources. His deep understanding of constitutional principles allowed him to present compelling arguments that influenced judicial interpretations.

In 1998, he contributed significantly to the Third Judges case,[8] where the President sought clarification on judicial appointments. Jaitley's insights helped solidify the collegium system for appointing judges to the high courts and the Supreme Court. In Special Reference No. 1 of 1998, popularly referred to as the "Third Judges case", Jaitley had assisted the nine-judge Constitutional

6. "Amit Shah On Arun Jaitley's 'Contribution' To Cricket Amid Row On Statue", NDTV, accessed on 24 August 2025, https://www.ndtv.com/india-news/amit-shah-on-arun-jaitleys-contribution-to-cricket-amid-row-on-statue-2344542.

7. Sam Daniel and Radhika Iyer, "Timeline: Disproportionate Assets Case Against Jayalalithaa", NDTV, accessed 25 May 2025, https://www.ndtv.com/india-news/timeline-disproportionate-assets-case-against-jayalalithaa-569806.

8. In Re: Under Article 143(1) Of The ... vs Unknown, AIR 1999 SC 1.

bench of the Supreme Court, which reinterpreted its judgment in the "Second Judges case" by expounding who should be a part of the "collegium" and clarifying the question of "primacy" of the Chief Justice's opinion in case of disagreement with other collegium members.

In 2002, when the ECI expressed concerns about holding timely elections in Gujarat, Jaitley, representing the BJP, successfully argued before the Supreme Court that the commission had a constitutional obligation to ensure elections within the mandated timeframe. This victory paved the way for Modi's electoral success and his subsequent rise to national leadership.

Jaitley assisted the Constitutional bench of the Supreme Court which upheld the validity of the 27 per cent reservation granted to OBCs in education and jobs while ruling that such quota benefits could only be granted after the "creamy layer" was eliminated from the list of OBCs.[9] *Ashoka Kumar Thakur vs Union of India* is a landmark case that has shaped the discourse on reservations in higher educational institutions in India.[10] The case primarily dealt with the constitutional validity of the Constitution (93rd Amendment) Act, 2005, and the Central Educational Institutions (Reservation in Admission) Act, 2006. It raised critical issues about the extension of reservations to OBCs and Socially and Educationally Backward Classes (SEBCs) in central institutes, the exclusion of the so-called "creamy layer", and the balance between social justice and merit in admissions. The case is significant not only for its impact on the reservation policy, but also for its interpretation of fundamental rights and the basic structure doctrine of the Constitution of India.

Jaitley assisted the Supreme Court in examining the legal and constitutional foundations of the reservation policy. The court held that the Constitution (93rd Amendment) Act was valid insofar as it applied to state-maintained and aided educational institutions. The amendment was not seen to violate the basic structure of the Constitution when these institutions were considered. The ruling made it clear that the reservation policy was not applicable to unaided institutions, as imposing such reservations there would infringe on the right under Article 19(1)(g) to carry on an occupation. A key decision was that if the creamy layer was not excluded, the amendment could be

---

9. *Ashoka Kumar Thakur vs Union of India*, *Law Bhoomi*, available at https://lawbhoomi.com/ashoka-kumar-thakur-v-union-of-india/.

10. Ibid.

rendered ultra vires. The court emphasised that the exclusion of the creamy layer was necessary to ensure that the benefits of reservations reached the truly disadvantaged. The court held that the identification of the creamy layer should be left to the discretion of the government. It recognised that there were no strict, immutable guidelines for this purpose and that the government could decide on parameters such as family income and occupational status. While upholding the reservation policy, the court balanced the principle of merit with the need for social justice. It noted that merit should not be understood solely in terms of academic scores, but should also take into account social and economic disadvantages. This observation was crucial in ensuring that the reservation policy did not compromise the overall standards of education while striving to uplift underprivileged sections of society.

The court upheld the constitutional validity of Article 15(5) by clarifying that special provisions for backward classes did not conflict with the principles of equality enshrined in Article 14. The court underscored that minority educational institutions were categorised as a separate class. They enjoyed protection under Article 30 and were thus exempt from the ambit of Article 15(5). This distinction ensured that the reservation policy did not inadvertently affect the autonomy of minority institutions, which have their own constitutional safeguards. *Ashoka Kumar Thakur* (*supra*) stands as a seminal case in the landscape of Indian constitutional law.

In the landmark case of *P.A. Inamdar vs State of Maharashtra*,[11] Jaitley assisted the seven-judge Constitutional bench of the Supreme Court, which inter alia held therein that both minority and non-minority unaided professional educational institutions have an obligation and a duty to maintain requisite standards of professional excellence by giving admissions based on merit and making it equally accessible to eligible students through a fair and transparent admission procedure and a reasonable fee structure.[12]

Two pivotal developments shaped the course of Indian cricket—the decision to sell television rights for matches, and the creation of the Indian Premier League (IPL). Jaitley advised the Board of Control for Cricket in India (BCCI).

---

11. *P.A. Inamdar & Ors vs State of Maharashtra & Ors*, 2005 (6) SCC 537.

12. Anushri Joshi, "Case Study: P.A. Inamdar vs. State of Maharashtra", *Desikaanoon*, accessed 25 May 2025, https://desikaanoon.in/case-study-p-a-inamdar-vs-state-of-maharashtra/.

In the early 1990s, when Jagmohan Dalmiya and Inderjit Singh Bindra, both veteran cricket administrators, decided to take on the Government of India and defend the BCCI's right to telecast its own cricket matches and support the game of cricket with revenues generated by television broadcasting rights, Jaitley was their lawyer. The government contended that "national security" would be threatened if uplinking was allowed to private parties. Jaitley succeeded in getting an interim order from the Supreme Court and finally won the case. Thanks to the battle fought by the Dalmiya–Bindra duo supported by Jaitley, airwaves were freed in India and free speech on television became a reality and more meaningful.

Having economically empowered the BCCI with television money, Dalmiya realised the power of "eyeballs". India alone accounted for more than 75 per cent of television audiences and commensurate sponsorship money. India's influence in the International Cricket Council (ICC) increased. Dalmiya became the president of the ICC and India became a superpower in international cricket.[13]

Saurav Ganguly says, "I remember a phone call (he) made during the 2003 World Cup in South Africa. We had lost the first game and the whole country went berserk but he (Jaitley) said that the association supports you and you play well. These small things matter, he was a great human being."[14]

★

Jaitley's grasp of law and facts was remarkable. He could be getting a haircut, watching the news on television, and fielding political phone calls while being briefed on a matter by a junior.[15] As a junior lawyer, I instructed Jaitley as a senior counsel in many cases in the 1990s–2000s. Each time he would be

---

13. Arun Jaitley, *A New India: Selected Writings 2014–19* (Juggernaut, 2020), pp. 315–16.

14. "Amit Shah unveils Arun Jaitley's statue at DDCA premises", *The Indian Express*, accessed on 24 August 2025, https://indianexpress.com/article/sports/cricket/amit-shah-unveils-arun-jaitleys-statue-at-ddca-premises-7123349/.

15. Abhishek Sharma, "To Sir with Love: A Tribute to Arun Jaitley by a Former Junior", *Bar and Bench*, accessed 25 May 2025, https://www.barandbench.com/columns/to-sir-with-love-a-tribute-to-arun-jaitley-by-a-former-junior.

munching on some or the other savouries during the briefing. Yet, such was his brilliance, Jaitley would be attentively listening. He liked junior lawyers who focused on the core issue rather than give a long description of the case. Often the client would be disappointed by the distraction. But we who briefed him regularly knew Jaitley was not only listening, he was also grasping the core issues of the case.

He would rarely say a word to reassure the client who would carry the impression that Jaitley had been indifferent and unconcerned, but, in court Jaitley was so brilliant, he would know all the facts of the case and ensure that the case was won.[16] He commanded an exceptional memory and could speak in court about any matter related to the case. In a Delhi High Court hearing on cable television when the judge inquired about television penetration in India, Jaitley, without referring to any notes, eloquently discussed the evolution of Indian television, citing statistics he remembered from his time as the information and broadcasting minister.[17] As a senior advocate, his ability to turn a case with startlingly simple and effective legal analysis was unparalleled. Above all, whether as a lawyer or politician, the law was his first love. From stories about his father and his ilk of trial lawyers in Punjab who couldn't pronounce dates in English to the finer nuances of constitutional law, Arun Jaitley loved the law and the courts like few did.

Junior lawyer Dushyant K. Mahant has this to say about Jaitley:

> Watching him argue a case in court was magic. Not only was he facile with his own arguments, but any counters from the other side were quick to be rebutted. In one hearing in the High Court, just as he stood up to argue, I remember the opposing counsel cutting in and putting across his points vehemently. In fact, Her Honour Aruna Suresh remarked, "Mr. Counsel, you are making your arguments on the presumption that I will grant relief to the other side but Mr Jaitley

16. Narendra Modi, "Condolence Message", in *The Discussant: Journal of Centre for Reforms, Development and Justice*, Special Edition, An Obituary to Arun Jaitley, Vol. VII, No. 3 (July–September 2019), pp. 12–13.

17. Abhishek Sharma, "To Sir with Love: A Tribute to Arun Jaitley by a Former Junior", Bar and Bench, accessed 25 May 2025, https://www.barandbench.com/columns/to-sir-with-love-a-tribute-to-arun-jaitley-by-a-former-junior.

has not even started his arguments." Justice Suresh did grant relief to Jaitley-ji after hearing arguments from both sides. After leaving the court, Jaitley-ji politely told that lawyer from the other side, "Don't be so aggressive."

★

There is a saying that a man's worth is determined not by how he treats his equals, but by how he treats his juniors. As a senior advocate, Jaitley left a long list of juniors who learnt the art of advocacy from him. Even his detractors agree he took a personal interest in looking after juniors and ensuring they got established as legal practitioners. He had his share of detractors but never held a grudge against anyone. Beyond his high-profile cases, Jaitley was known for mentoring numerous junior lawyers, fostering their careers, and earning respect even from his detractors. His commitment to nurturing talent left a lasting legacy in the legal community. Jaitley never explicitly lectured his juniors on the importance of hard work and integrity; his actions spoke louder than words.[18]

One could often see Jaitley, when free from a case, standing in the corridors of the Supreme Court, surrounded by lawyers, regaling them with his wisdom and experience. True to the timeless traditions of the Bar, Jaitley had a passion for and became known for actively mentoring young lawyers. He ensured their well-being by assisting them in establishing independent practices or joining reputable law firms. Some of his juniors are known to have been elevated to the bench also.

Finally, he proved that one can be personally successful while firmly standing for others. For all his achievements, as a statesman, finance minister, law minister, senior advocate, party leader, representative of India in various forums abroad, it was his kindness as a human that he will be remembered for. His dear friend Mukul Rohatgi says, "Jaitley lived only for others. For me, he was instrumental in my appointment as Attorney General. He lent a helping

---

18. Abhishek Sharma, "To Sir with Love: A Tribute to Arun Jaitley by a Former Junior", *Bar and Bench*, accessed 25 May 2025, https://www.barandbench.com/columns/to-sir-with-love-a-tribute-to-arun-jaitley-by-a-former-junior.

hand to countless people, in the profession or otherwise. His kindness spread like sunshine and gave warmth to many." Legal scholar Arghya Sengupta said:

> When I had earlier asked Jaitley how he turned out to be so sensitive, unlike several of his battle-hardened colleagues, with a twinkle in his eye, he said that he belonged to the only institution in the country—the Parliament—which was accountable to so many. He was being kind to Parliament too, while never losing an opportunity to demonstrate his ready and ever-visible wit. That is the Arun Jaitley I will remember—twinkly eyes, a half-smile, making razor-sharp arguments that were beautiful in their simplicity.[19]

Gracious and sensitive, Jaitley was the first to host a grand lunch for senior advocate Sidharth Luthra when he was appointed as the additional solicitor general in July 2012. Jaitley got a common friend to do the invitations as Luthra had been appointed by the UPA government, and, Luthra believed, Jaitley did not want to embarrass him.[20] Luthra represented Jaitley in the criminal defamation case against Arvind Kejriwal and others before a magistrate.

Not only did Jaitley go out of the way to support his chamber's juniors and all the members of his staff, but he also extended the same familial affinity and affection to all his colleagues and friends. Eminent lawyer Pooja Mahajan, who was once Jaitley's junior recalls:

> Jaitley Sir was very generous. We were one of the few chambers where a senior counsel paid generously to his juniors. Besides monthly stipend, which was at par with most mid-level law firms, we were paid ten per cent of every opinion we assisted him with. Given the fees he

---

19. Arghya Sengupta, "For Arun Jaitley, Law Was an Intellectual Passion", *The Wire*, accessed 25 May 2025, https://thewire.in/politics/arun-jatiley-tribute-arghya-sengupta.

20. Sidharth Luthra, "Arun Jaitley: A Distinctive Lawyer, a Fine Human Being", *Hindustan Times*, accessed 25 May 2025, https://www.hindustantimes.com/analysis/arun-jaitley-a-distinctive-lawyer-a-fine-human-being/story-ibzYrSb3LL88VuBKqjL4PL.html.

> charged, ten per cent was a substantial amount. A part of my expense to study at Oxford was met from the money I earned while working in his chamber. When I returned from Oxford, I applied for a job at a leading law firm which didn't generally didn't hire lawyers unless they were from one of the national law schools. When Jaitley Sir found out, he just picked up the phone and called the firm's managing partner and requested him to give me a chance. I got the job. It made all the difference to my career.

In times of need, Jaitley was always a friend indeed. He might have skipped a happy occasion or two, but he seldom missed a prayer meeting of a bereaved colleague or a call from a troubled friend. Jaitley's generosity knew no bounds. Rajat Sharma, the head of India TV, said, "He was a friend to all, especially those in need. I have been fortunate to know him since 1974, when he selflessly helped me, a struggling student, with my SRCC fees."[21]

Paras Kuhad, a former additional solicitor general during the UPA era, shared in an interview that he first met Jaitley in the mid-1980s. In 1992, while based in Jaipur, Kuhad suffered a serious eye injury that required multiple surgeries. Jaitley, who was visiting Jaipur, went to see Kuhad. When Kuhad mentioned that he might postpone the second surgery due to its high cost, Jaitley enquired about the exact amount. Upon learning it was around Rs 5–6 lakh, Jaitley advised Kuhad against taking such a risk. Later that evening, he surprised Kuhad by sending him a cheque for Rs 7.5 lakh. Kuhad is on record to state he was deeply moved by Jaitley's extraordinary generosity, especially considering the significant value of that money at the time.[22]

---

21. "Grief of Arun Jaitley's demise will forever be with me: Rajat Sharma remembers his dear friend", India TV, accessed on 8 November 2025, https://www.indiatvnews.com/news/india-video-rajat-sharma-remembers-arun-jaitley-india-tv-special-show-544619.

22. Arvind Panagariya, "View: Arun Jaitley Was a Formidable Lawyer, Great Communicator and a True Human Being", *The Economic Times*, accessed 25 May 2025, https://economictimes.indiatimes.com/news/politics-and-nation/view-arun-jaitley-was-a-formidable-lawyer-great-communicator-and-a-true-human-being/articleshow/70832511.cms?from=mdr.

In 2007, a group of landowners approached Jaitley to represent them in the Supreme Court. Despite their limited financial resources, their lawyer believed Jaitley was their best hope. Jaitley agreed to take the case pro bono, successfully argued it, and secured a favourable verdict. He even declined the modest fee they had collectively raised.[23] In another instance, a prominent industrial family facing legal troubles sought Jaitley's services for numerous cases. While initially hesitant, Jaitley agreed to represent them solely for bail proceedings when he believed the authorities were unfairly targeting them. Despite receiving a substantial but unsolicited payment, Jaitley returned the cheque without hesitation, reaffirming his unwavering integrity.[24] Jaitley readily took on pro bono cases, such as representing medical students whose admissions had been unfairly cancelled. Upon learning that his fee had already been paid, Jaitley promptly returned the payment from the students, deeply moving them.[25]

He was a man of faith. Unlike many top lawyers today, he never asked for an advance amount from clients, relying on their honesty.[26] Jaitley was also known for his presence of mind. He was a thorough gentleman, well known for his unshakeable integrity and for being a stickler for professional ethics. Every penny he earned, he often said, was accounted for and reported to the tax authorities.

Both the bench and the Bar were proud of him. Once, a Constitution bench of the Supreme Court headed by then Chief Justice B.N. Kirpal was hearing a Presidential Reference on the 2002 Gujarat Assembly elections. K.K. Venugopal, representing the ECI, made a reference to the appointment of a person as a minister even before he became a member of the House. He referred to an instance from Kerala where E.K. Nayanar was made the chief

---

23. Dushyant K. Mahant, "Memories of Jaitley the Lawyer: When He Argued a Case for Free", *The New Indian Express*, accessed 25 May 2025, https://www.newindianexpress.com/nation/2019/Aug/24/memories-of-jaitley-the-lawyer-when-he-argued-a-case-for-free-2023702.html.

24. Abhishek Sharma, "To Sir with Love: A Tribute to Arun Jaitley by a Former Junior", *Bar and Bench*, accessed 25 May 2025, https://www.barandbench.com/columns/to-sir-with-love-a-tribute-to-arun-jaitley-by-a-former-junior.

25. Ibid.

26. Shweta Punj and Uday Mahurkar, "Arun Jaitley: A Politician and a Gentleman", *India Today*, accessed 25 May 2025, https://www.indiatoday.in/magazine/obituary/story/20190909-arun-jaitley-a-politician-and-a-gentleman-1592958-2019-08-30.

minister and subsequently won an assembly seat. Kapil Sibal, representing one of the parties, stood up and made a mention: 'Mr. Venugopal need not go to Kerala to find such a minister. We have our own example here. He has become a minister and subsequently an MP. And we are proud of that example!' Every judge looked at Jaitley, who was seated in the front row with a smiling face. He was younger to all of them and was already a former minister.[27]

★

There is a saying—once a lawyer, always a lawyer. Even in Modi's Cabinet, Jaitley's hand was clearly visible on all important legal issues, be it the National Judicial Appointments Commission (NJAC) or appointment of important law officers. As Vajpayee and Modi's minister, Jaitley helped shape views on the contentious Section 377 of the Indian Penal Code, 1860, which the Supreme Court watered down in September 2018 to the extent that it no longer penalised consensual sexual relationship between adults in any form. He prevailed on the government that the Centre should not take a stand on the matter and leave it for the court to decide.

Jaitley masterminded the "Triple Talaq" Bill criminalising the practice of instant divorce among Muslims. This legislation aims to protect Muslim women from the arbitrary and discriminatory practice of being divorced by their husbands through the mere utterance of three words. The new law seeks to criminalise those who, in defiance of the law, still resort to this practice and drive their wives to destitution. The debate surrounding this issue was intense, with strong arguments on both sides. The Supreme Court has already declared instant talaq as unconstitutional, and yet in the absence of a deterrent, it can at best amount to a civil wrong with no penal consequences.

In his blog posted in February 2019, Jaitley said that a recent case from Bareilly relating to the obnoxious practice of Nikah-Halala in Islamic personal law had shocked his conscience. A lady who was married in 2009 was divorced twice by her husband through Triple Talaq, once in 2011 and subsequently

---

27. Prashant Padmanabhan, "Arun Jaitley from the Eyes of a Legal Practitioner: A Tribute", *Bar and Bench*, accessed 25 May 2025, https://www.barandbench.com/columns/arun-jaitley-from-the-eyes-of-a-legal-practitioner-a-tribute.

in 2017. The family prevailed upon the husband to accept her back. On both occasions, she was sedated and asked to undergo Nikah-Halala, on the first occasion with her father-in-law and on the subsequent occasion with her brother-in-law. They both raped her. A similar case was reported by the PTI on 2 September 2018 as having taken place in the Sambhal district of Uttar Pradesh.

That in the twenty-first century there could be such gross violation of the dignity of women in the world's largest democracy should make every head hang in shame. After raping this lady, both the father-in-law and brother-in-law used the weapon of Triple Talaq to divorce the victim so that she could be accepted by her husband. "If Triple Talaq had not been a permitted mode of divorce in India, would this incident emanating from a no-fault-impulsive divorce have taken place?" Jaitley asked in his blog. A number of Muslim men and conservatives were choosing to even ignore the Supreme Court judgment.[28] Some incidents were so unconscionable and repulsive that they shake the conscience of the society and compel it to take remedial measures. Many communities, over the last several decades, have brought incremental but significant changes in their personal laws. The object and direction of these changes have been to ensure that the right to live with dignity and gender equality is ensured, and the rights of women and children are protected. Some practices which survived for centuries (such as Sati and Untouchability) are now considered unconstitutional, he wrote in his blog.

"On basic principles of humanity, justice, and fair play, would it be right, irrespective of religion, to give to the husband a unilateral right to end the marriage?" he asked in his blog posted in July 2019. The fear of the husband uttering three words will always keep the wife subjugated and bear the injustice. Divorce, in India, takes place either by consent of both parties on agreed terms or one of the parties approaches the court for divorce on the grounds that the spouse has committed a "matrimonial misconduct" (the grounds for divorce in Indian law). Most cases end in a settlement with a reconciliation or a divorce where the wife is provided either monthly maintenance or a large lump sum of money which will support her. The basic principle of matrimonial law is

---

28. Arun Jaitley, "Does the Bareilly 'Nikah-Halala' Not Shock Your Conscience?", accessed 25 May 2025, https://www.arunjaitley.com/does-the-bareilly-nikah-halala-not-shock-your-conscience/.

that no person can take advantage of his own wrong. The Sharia law[29] was an exception. The husband may have wronged the wife and still, despite his own matrimonial misconduct, divorce her by uttering three words to dissolve the marriage. This is against all cannons of humanity, justice, and fair play. If this practice is adopted by others, many women would be driven to destitution.[30]

Jaitley wrote in his blog:

> I have consistently held the opinion that there must be a recognised distinction between two aspects which stem out of religious interpretations. The first is the "rituals" of a religion. Rituals cannot be decided by the law. They remain squarely within the right to practice one's religion. However, fundamental rights belong to all. One section of the society cannot be denied these rights. What affects the right of a citizen—in this case the Muslim wife—cannot be determined by a religion. After the Constitution came into force, rights emanating from birth, rights of a minor, rights in relation to marriage, divorce, succession, adoption, rituals etc., belong to every citizen. They should necessarily be compatible with fundamental rights. Granting an arbitrary right to a husband to orally and instantaneously divorce his wife does not deal with any ritual which is in the domain of religion. In a society governed by a Constitution and the rule of law, prima facie, this practice of oral divorce violates both the right to equality and the right of a woman to live with dignity. It is long overdue that the courts re-examine whether the rights being deprived to a citizen on the grounds of personal law violate the constitutional guarantees.[31]

29. Sharia law refers to the disciplines and principles that govern the behaviour of a Muslim individual towards his or herself, family, neighbours, community, city, nation, and the Muslim polity as a whole, the Ummah (global Muslim community) and everyone under Islam's jurisdiction. Similarly, Shariah governs the interactions between communities, groups, and social and economic organisations.

30. Arun Jaitley, "'Talaq' without a Social Security", accessed 25 May 2025, https://www.arunjaitley.com/talaq-without-a-social-security/.

31. Ibid.

It is crucial to acknowledge that India is still a developing nation where social security for women remains inadequate. In divorce proceedings, the premise that "no one should benefit from their wrongdoing" generally applies. However, Triple Talaq allows husbands to unilaterally dissolve the marriage, leaving their wives vulnerable to destitution. This is fundamentally unjust and incompatible with basic human dignity and equality principles. In contrast, developed countries with robust social security systems often have more liberal divorce laws. These systems typically include provisions for spousal support, asset division, and other measures to ensure the financial well-being of women after divorce, Jaitley argued.

Jaitley vehemently defended making a civil contract into a criminal offence. Demanding dowry, indulging in bigamy or polygamy, indulging in cruel behaviour (including mental cruelty) are all criminal offences. A bounced cheque or a defamation may be a civil wrong but both have penal consequences in criminal law. Merely to oppose a progressive legislation, one does not have to invent a new jurisprudence, he wrote in his blog. Those with short-sighted vision have repeatedly argued that since the Supreme Court has declared the practice as unlawful, why punish a husband who is indulging in an unlawful act. If the Triple Talaq right used by him is unlawful and does not exist, why send him to jail? The Supreme Court, by striking down the practice of Triple Talaq, has merely made a declaration of the law. This declaration has to be followed by a legislation which punishes the offending spouse for indulging in this cruel act despite it being declared unlawful.

Many conservatives would still practice this irrespective of what the court has said. There is data available post the judgment which establishes that this is actually happening on the ground. Besides being tried for the offence in a court, obviously the husband will have to pay maintenance to his wife. Both these will have a strong deterrent effect on those who want to use the weapon of Triple Talaq. They will think a hundred times before using it due to the onerous consequences of its illegality. "I have no doubt that once an example is made out of some people, the fear of its consequences will lead to minimising this practice. If this law is not enacted, the judgment of the Supreme Court will turn into a futile academic exercise where the practice is illegal; however, if you still indulge in it no penal consequence visits you," Jaitley wrote in his blog.[32]

Jaitley hailed The Muslim Women (Protection of Rights on Marriage) Act, 2019, as a significant step towards ensuring justice and equality for Muslim women. It addresses a long-standing injustice and upholds the fundamental rights enshrined in the Indian Constitution.

★

Jaitley would firmly but respectfully disagree with the Supreme Court on many occasions. Be it on the manner of appointment to the Supreme Court and high courts, or some other decision. Jaitley expressed disagreements with the historic Supreme Court judgment on Section 377 of the Indian Penal Code that decriminalised consensual gay sex and called sexuality a part of free speech. Jaitley said he felt that the verdict raises questions on restraining any form of homosexual or bisexual activity in a school hostel, prison, or army frontier. He also differed on a segment of the top court's ruling on adultery, and said that it may end up converting the Indian family system into a Western family system. On the Supreme Court allowing women's entry into the Sabarimala shrine, he said such a ruling cannot happen on select practices as it may have many social consequences.

"The judgment decriminalising gay sex was fine but the problem comes when writing these historical judgments, you get carried away and want to be part of history and therefore you go a step further," said Jaitley. He said he agreed with the reasoning given by the court in the judgment that sexual activity is part of Article 21 of the Constitution that guarantees the right of life and that one cannot be discriminated on the basis of sex. However, he said he completely disagreed with the reasoning that sexual activity is part of free speech.

> Because I think that's little excessive and consequences of that may not be on decriminalisation. Free speech is entirely a different gambit. It

32. Ibid.

> can be restrained on the reasons of sovereignty, security, public order and so on and mind you there is tendency of creating new fundamental rights everyday … So when you convert this into a fundamental right and say it's free speech then how do you restrain any form of sexual activity, homosexual or bisexual in a school hostel, prison, army frontier.

Stating that this requires further debate, Jaitley said this reasoning was not necessary for deciding the Section 377 case which decriminalised gay sex. On the Supreme Court ruling on adultery, he said some of the judges said these are matrimonial offences and personal wrongs and not public wrongs. "Therefore, it is outside the purview of criminal law. Would that cover bigamy or polygamy also which are personal wrong? Would that cover cruelty? Would that cover dowry offences? Now this logic covering them, it would be a wholly anti-women judgement," he said. He said he was not in dispute that the "very badly worded section" on adultery needed to be quashed, but "the later view may find a reference in some Western journals very favourably but it may end up converting Indian family system into Western family system where the fragility of marriage as an institution itself will increase. Therefore you probably require to debate the second part of the observation which again was not necessary for deciding this case." On the Sabarimala ruling, Jaitley said, "If you want to take a progressive step, Articles 14 and 21 will apply against all religions."[33]

The judges respected his view. But once, when he had criticised the SC order quashing the NJAC in 2015 in his Facebook post titled "NJAC Judgement: An Alternative View", a well-argued critique of the Constitution bench judgment in the NJAC case, a judicial magistrate ordered that he be tried for sedition and encouraging mutiny. Questioning Jaitley's post, he then proceeded to record that an order of a court could be questioned only by following a procedure prescribed by law. The magistrate even went to the extent of holding that since no person is entitled to create or generate hatred or contempt against

---

33. "Sexuality and Free Speech are Different Issues: Arun Jaitley on Section 377 Verdict", *India Today*, accessed 25 May 2025, https://www.indiatoday.in/india/story/sexuality-and-free-speech-are-different-issues-arun-jaitley-on-section-377-verdict-1357789-2018-10-07.

an elected government established by law, Jaitley had prima facie done the same, as his comments "undoubtedly spread hatred and contempt against a duly elected government".

Jaitley then approached the Allahabad High Court, which quashed the magistrate's order. While doing so, Justice Yashwant Varma observed that Jaitley's piece did not "incite the people to insurrection or rebellion". "Disrespect (of the Supreme Court), even if it were assumed that the article did so, does not render the action liable to prosecution for offenses under section 124A or section 505. The right to air an opinion, to dissent, intellectual discourse are the heart and soul of the freedom of speech and expression which stands conferred upon all citizens by our Constitution," Justice Varma recorded in his judgment. It further observed that the magistrate appeared "to have closed his eyes to the well-settled view that healthy criticism or even intellectual disagreement with a particular view of a judge contained in a judgment of the court is not a crime", adding that this held true even if the view expressed was "unacceptable or even unpalatable to some".

The court also noted that before passing the order against Jaitley, the magistrate would have done well to remember the words written by Justice V.R. Krishna Iyer in his judgment in *Baradakant Mishra vs Registrar of Orissa High Court*:

> Vicious criticism of personal and administrative acts of Judges may indirectly mar their image and weaken the confidence of the public in the judiciary, but the countervailing good, not merely of free speech but also of greater faith generated by exposure to the actinic light of bona fide, even if marginally overzealous, criticism cannot be overlooked. Justice is no cloistered virtue … The magistrate in the opinion of the court clearly failed to apply judicial mind, acted irresponsibly and failed to bear in mind the caution and circumspection which should have preceded his assuming jurisdiction and issuing summons.[34]

34. Maneesh Chhibber, "When a Facebook post almost got Arun Jaitley tried for sedition", *The Print*, accessed on 24 August 2025, https://theprint.in/politics/when-a-facebook-post-almost-got-arun-jaitley-tried-for-sedition/179224/

Jaitley was very patient, tolerant, and forgiving, and could take any amount of criticism as a politician and opposition in court. But he was unsparing if anyone was to question his integrity which he guarded with zeal.

★

Jaitley hung his lawyer jacket in 2009 to focus entirely on his role as the Leader of the Opposition in the Rajya Sabha. In 2009, when he quit, he told Rajat Sharma in an interview that his earnings as a minister were less than 10 per cent of what he earned from his legal practice.[35]

35. Dushyant K. Mahant, "Memories of Jaitley the Lawyer: When He Argued a Case for Free", *The New Indian Express*, accessed 25 May 2025, https://www.newindianexpress.com/nation/2019/Aug/24/memories-of-jaitley-the-lawyer-when-he-argued-a-case-for-free-2023702.html.

13

Leader of the Opposition in the Rajya Sabha (2004–14)

In 2009, the BJP tasted defeat in the general elections for the second consecutive term. The Congress party came back to power with an increased majority. Ensuring the "Right to Work" and a loan waiver to farmers worth Rs 275,000 crores helped it beat back anti-incumbency. It managed to get 206 seats in the Lok Sabha, increasing its 2004 tally by 61 seats. The Indo-US civil nuclear deal was not an issue that resonated with or attracted voters during the elections. Few understood—or cared about it. But urban Indians approved of the way in which it had brought India closer to the United States, which was a destination for many Indians.

Manmohan Singh, who would go on to head the UPA for five more years, was admired for the way in which he had resolutely pursued the deal. His handling of the global financial crisis of 2007–09, and the rapid growth of the economy since 2004, had come in for acclaim from middle-class Indians who had made good. However, the Manmohan Singh government was unlike any other that existed before or after. No full-term, rather two-term, prime minister was as hemmed in as he was. Sonia Gandhi took the political decisions and had a say in major policy initiatives. The prime minister let Pranab Mukherjee, another powerful figure in the government, run much of the administration through key decision-making bodies like scores of groups of ministers. As a result, Manmohan Singh's authority was severely curtailed, and he worked under constraints.[1]

The Opposition is an essential part of any democratic government and the most important part of Parliament.[2] The government governs and the Opposition criticises.[3] The leader of the largest recognised Opposition party is invited as the Leader of the Opposition[4] in both the Houses of Parliament, by the chairman of the Rajya Sabha or the speaker of the Lok Sabha as the case may be. The task of the Leader of the Opposition is unlike that of the Leader of the House, but it is nevertheless of considerable importance.[5]

Although new to India as an office,[6] the Leader of the Opposition arose out of practice in England and has no official function either under legislation or the rules of the House.[7] In England, Her Majesty's Opposition is Her Majesty's alternative government. Her Majesty's Opposition is, therefore, second in importance to Her Majesty's Government and the Leader of the Opposition

---

1. Neerja Chowdhury, *How Prime Ministers Decide* (Aleph, 2023).
2. Ivor Jennings, "Government and Parliament" (Chapter XV), in *Cabinet Government* (Cambridge University Press, 1959), pp. 472–510.
3. "Role of the Leader of the House, Leader of the Opposition and Whips", *Parliament of India, Rajya Sabha* (July 2020), p. 14.
4. The Salary and Allowances of Leaders of Opposition in Parliament Act, 1977 defines the "Leader of the Opposition", in relation to either House of Parliament, as "member of the Council of States or the House of the People, as the case may be, who is, for the time being, the Leader in that House of the party in opposition to the Government having the greatest numerical strength and recognised as such by the Chairman of the Council of States or the Speaker of the House of the People, as the case may be".
5. Ivor Jennings, "Government and Parliament" (Chapter XV), in *Cabinet Government* (Cambridge University Press, 1959), pp. 472–510.
6. It was only in 1969 that for the first time since Independence, the two Houses had recognised the Opposition party [Congress Party (Opposition) formed after the split in the Congress party in November 1969] and a Leader of the Opposition in each House. See, M.N. Kaul and S.L. Shakdher, *Practice and Procedure of Parliament*, edited by Anoop Mishra, 7th Edn (Metropolitan for Lok Sabha Secretariat, 2016), pp. 156–57.
7. Ivor Jennings, *Cabinet Government* (Cambridge University Press, 1959), p. 79.

is almost Her Majesty's alternative prime minister. Technically, however, he is only the leader, for the time being, of the chief opposition party.[8]

There may be several parties in the Opposition, but the Opposition means the second main party temporarily in a minority, with leaders experienced in office who are ready, when the time arises, to form an alternative government. This affords a guarantee that its criticism will be directed by a consistent policy and conducted with responsibility—not in spirit calculated to ruin the game for the sake of the prize.[9] Among other things, the Leader of the Opposition watches for encroachments on the rights of minorities, and demands debates when the government is trying to slip away without parliamentary criticism. He must be in his place more often and be familiar with all the tricks of a skilled parliamentarian and all the opportunities available under the rules of the House.[10] In performing his duties and obligations, the Leader of the Opposition has to take into account not only what he is today, but what he hopes to be tomorrow.[11]

Although the voters denied the BJP a place on the treasury benches in 2009, the party retained the strength to nominate the Leader of the Opposition in both Houses of Parliament. By now, Jaitley had acquired a decade-long experience in Parliament and made his mark as a parliamentarian, both as a minister in Vajpayee's government from 1999 to 2004, and later sitting on the Opposition bench for five years from 2004 to 2009.

In June 2009, he was appointed Leader of the Opposition in the Rajya Sabha, a position he occupied initially from 3 June 2009 to 2 April 2012, and then from 3 April 2012 to 26 May 2014,[12] for nearly five years. When the issue of appointment of the Leader of the Opposition came up in 2009, Venkaiah Naidu proposed that Jaitley be chosen. Jaitley however, insisted that Naidu

---

8. Ivor Jennings, *Cabinet Government* (Cambridge University Press, 1959), p. 79.

9. Campion (Ed.), *Parliament: A Survey* (1952), p. 30.

10. Ivor Jennings, *Cabinet Government* (Cambridge University Press, 1959), p. 84.

11. M.N. Kaul and S.L. Shakdher, *Practice and Procedure of Parliament*, Edited by Anoop Mishra, 7th Edn (Metropolitan for Lok Sabha Secretariat, 2016), p. 156.

12. "Role of the Leader of the House, Leader of the Opposition and Whips", *Parliament of India, Rajya Sabha* (July 2020), p. 19.

deserved it more. Finally, Naidu prevailed and Jaitley relented.[13] Naidu himself went on to become the vice president of India and ex-officio chairman of the Rajya Sabha on 11 August 2017.

Spending many years in the Opposition as well as in the treasury benches had given Jaitley a holistic vision on Parliament. He was mindful of the high traditions of the Office of Leader of the Opposition and the enormous responsibility that came with the appointment. But being the Leader of the Opposition was a different league. What was expected from him as the Leader of the Opposition was effective criticism of the government and cornering it on as many issues as possible. He decided to devote himself fully to the responsibility his party entrusted him with.

He made one of the most difficult decisions of his life—he quit his flourishing practice the same year (2009). Later, in Rajat Sharma's show on *Aap Ki Adalat*, when asked why he chose to sacrifice hundreds of crores he could have earned by continuing his law practice while performing as the Leader of the Opposition, Jaitley answered he was not the first to quit a thriving law practice to serve the nation. His learnings from his political life had been fulfilling and he had no regrets.[14]

★

When the Congress breached the 200-mark in the May 2009 elections, it appeared that freed of Left Front support, UPA-II was assured of a trouble-free five-year term. By the time Manmohan Singh took the oath of office, the number of MPs supporting the government had gone upwards of 300. But, in truth, the numbers were more make-believe than real. All four external supporters—the SP, the BSP, RJD, and JD(S)—were going to drive a hard bargain.

---

13. M. Venkaiah Naidu, "Our Regular Meetings Were for Good, and Food for Thought", in *The Discussant: Journal of Centre for Reforms, Development and Justice*, Special Edition, An Obituary to Arun Jaitley, Vol. VII, No. 3 (July–September 2019), pp. 17–19.

14. *Aap Ki Adalat*, accessed on 4 September 2025, https://www.youtube.com/watch?v=jVAbPUTr1dY

During the term of UPA-I, the Lok Sabha Speaker called for a division of votes on twenty-one occasions. Twenty of these were non-serious divisions, posing no threat whatever to the government. The only time a division portended danger was after the Left Front's withdrawal. The division of numbers on 22 July 2008, the day Prime Minister Manmohan Singh tested his majority in the House, was: 275 for and 256 against.[15] It was a close shave for the government, but fortunately for UPA-I, its first and only serious test came towards the end of its term—with just eight months left for the general elections.

While UPA-I remained largely free of scams and judicial rebukes from the Supreme Court, its second term proved to be a Leader of the Opposition's delight, as the government lurched from one scandal to another, grappling with crisis after crisis over the next five years. The scams—2G corruption scam, Coal Allocation (Coalgate), Commonwealth Games (CWG) scandal, bribery charges relating to posting in railway ministry, Adarsh housing scam, and bribery charges in the steel ministry—hit the regime, offering the Opposition one opportunity after the other to attack UPA-II.

Jaitley was not the one to let the opportunity go. He went after UPA-II vociferously, highlighting the failures of the Congress-led coalition. He emerged as a formidable critic, systematically dismantling the government's credibility. With his sharp legal mind and articulate arguments, Jaitley exposed the irregularities in policy decisions, accusing UPA-II of crony capitalism and policy paralysis. Coming down heavily on the prime minister, Jaitley said the country cannot afford to have "a non-politician" as a prime minister, however "attractive" he might look. Without naming Manmohan Singh, he said politicians are not known by their years in the government but by the "footprints they leave behind". He was quick to praise former Prime Minister P.V. Narasimha Rao, who, he said, brought about "a turning point" in economic policies. He said that recent history had not been very kind to Rao who worked at a time when a clarity was yet to emerge in economic policies.[16]

---

15. Vidya Subrahmaniam, "One Year of UPA-II: Numbers Without Comfort", *The Hindu*, accessed 25 May 2025, https://www.thehindu.com/opinion/op-ed/One-year-of-UPA-II-numbers-without-comfort/article16301602.ece.

16. "Jaitley Hits Out at UPA Leadership", *The Pioneer*, accessed 25 May 2025, https://www.dailypioneer.com/2014/sunday-edition/jaitley-hits-out-at-upa-leadership.html.

Jaitley became the loudest and the most emphatic voice against scams and corruption. And his was no ordinary voice. When he stood up to speak, members would hear in rapt attention. His speeches contained verifiable facts. Although unsparing in his questioning, his demeanour carried immense dignity. His speeches were marked by incisive analysis, wit, and a relentless focus on accountability. Besides attacking the government on corruption, Jaitley raised other pertinent issues.

The second terms of the UPA commenced with the 2007–08 global financial crisis, which began to impact India from 2009 onwards. Jaitley assaulted UPA-II on food inflation. In 2008–09, the fiscal deficit was 6.1 per cent of GDP, which rose quickly to 6.6 per cent in 2009–10. It remained high at 5.9 per cent even in 2011–12 and began to come under a semblance of control only subsequently. The UPA left power with a fiscal deficit of 4.5 per cent.[17]

Jaitley took on the government for its failure to deal with terrorism effectively. The 26/11 Mumbai terrorist attack figured prominently in the 2009 polls. Advani repeatedly hurled the charge of "weak leader" at Manmohan Singh and said he felt "pity" for him rather than anger. In Parliament, Jaitley took over from Advani. "Thanks to the soft approach of the UPA," opined Arun Jaitley, 'India today has emerged as a very soft state … 10 Pak terrorists demonstrated so shockingly how vulnerable and weak India is."[18] Jaitley's speeches echoed in the high ceilings of the Rajya Sabha as he had the government on the mat on a series of corruption scandals and what he termed as "policy paralysis". "We created several institutions which were perceived to be safeguards against corruption. They are either helpless spectators or have been seriously compromised." He was merciless in his attack:

> The manner in which senior ministers of the government have jumped to defend the indefensible commercial transactions of a member of the Congress Party's First family indicates that the current controversy is being utilized to display loyalty rather than to enforce probity. Politically

---

17. T.C.A. Sharad Raghavan, "UPA-2 Faced the Same Economic Issues Modi Govt Does Now. But There's One Difference", *The Print*, accessed 25 May 2025, https://theprint.in/opinion/standard-deviation/upa-2-faced-the-same-economic-issues-modi-govt-does-now-but-theres-one-difference/1272049/.

18. Vinod Mehta, *Lucknow Boy: A Memoir* (Penguin, 2011), pp. 241–42.

connected people cannot be debarred from business. However, the kind of entrepreneurship displayed in this case where windfall gains are monumental and investment is miniscule. Somebody needs to look into these transactions to determine whether they are bona fide business transactions or favours. There obviously is a lot more than what meets the eye. The possibility of windfall gains emanating from a "political equity" investment intended to reap "political dividends" cannot be obviated. Each one of the above instances establishes existence of unfair and unacceptable transactions. There is a legitimate apprehension that institutions intended to be a watch-dog on these practices have been seriously compromised. Citizens Groups are being told that the State will not take any action. Loyalty is more important than probity. The citizens must go to court and establish a case. The citizens are mere whistle blowers; they have to bring these cases into public domain. It is the responsibility of the State to investigate these cases. If the State shirks from its responsibility, unconventional methodologies of exposure will overtake the existing public discourse. The Comptroller and Auditor General (CAG) is an established institution performing its functions. The government prefers to assault it rather than follow its sage audit advice. The experience of the JPCs shows enormous clout of the government to prevent truth from surfacing on the mere strength of numbers. Even the Public Accounts Committee (PAC) is being prevented from doing its job particularly in the case of 2G spectrum allocation scam. The Central Bureau of Investigation (CBI) was statutorily created to investigate and prosecute cases of corruption. Its credibility is today a suspect. The CBI is currently functioning on a premise that the UPA must be helped wherever it can be; the opponents of this government must be framed and those in the middle such as the SP and BSP must be under a perpetual sword hanging on their head. This is the methodology for managing parliamentary numbers.[19]

---

19. Arun Jaitley, "Jaitley's Blog Attacking Gandhi Dynasty: Why Is There 'Negativism'?", *India Today*, accessed 25 May 2025, https://www.indiatoday.in/india/north/story/arun-jaitley-blog-why-is-there-negativism-118408-2012-10-10.

The parliament debates in the monsoon session of 2011 covered a range of issues. Speaking on national security and terrorism, Jaitley cited the Mumbai terrorist attack as another example of the failure of the government in checking terrorism owing to its weak policies and soft approach. In the CAG report on CWG, he said the report had again exposed the nexus of the Congress party, government officials, and contractors in looting public money. He also spoke at length on the impeachment motion of Justice Soumitra Sen and effectively demolished Sen's defence citing instances of his misconduct in misappropriation of funds. He also took the government to task for failing to address the concern of the people on corruption and undemocratically trying to muzzle the voice of the civil society.[20]

UPA-II appeared defenceless against Jaitley's tirade. One entire Parliament session—the winter session of 2011—was washed out (because of demands to set up a JPC on 2G), as well as the second half of the budget session 2013 (due to Coalgate).[21] As a result, drafts of key legislation, such as the Land Acquisition Bill, the Food Security Bill, and the Insurance and Pension Bill were left in a limbo. The 2013 budget session has gone down as one of the least productive in Parliament history. The Opposition's effective diatribe led to resignations by many ministers—scam-tainted or otherwise. From DMK nominated ministers A. Raja and Dayanidhi Maran (both post-2G) to Congress leaders Subodh Kant Sahay (Coalgate), Pawan Kumar Bansal (bribery in railway appointments, though not directly) and Ashwani Kumar (interference in the CBI report on Coalgate), were forced to quit.

Policy paralysis set in as files stopped moving and bureaucrats stopped acting out of fear of the 3Cs—courts, CAG, Central Vigilance Commission (CVC)—which coincided with Pranab Mukherjee's leadership of the finance ministry.[22] The "indecisiveness" and policy paralysis had caused recurring harm to the investment environment in the country, slackening of FDI, and breaking of communication between the government and the main Opposition, Jaitley

20. "Arun Jaitley in Parliament", Bharatiya Janata Party (August 2011), p. 1.

21. Puja Mehra, *The Lost Decade (2008–18): How India's Growth Story Devolved into Growth without a Story* (Penguin, 2019), pp. 49–51.

22. Ibid.

roared.[23] Such was Jaitley's acumen that the UPA government often worried whether its proposed legislation would withstand his scrutiny.

Over the years, Jaitley cleverly brought Modi in debates, citing the Gujarat model of governance and made out a case for a strong and decisive leadership. Contrasting the UPA government with "the strong leadership" in Gujarat, Jaitley said though Modi came under relentless criticism of his political opponents, he chose not to respond and instead went ahead with his "agenda" that helped Gujarat do a developmental leapfrog. He pointed out that Saurashtra had at one time "no drinking water" but agricultural growth had "doubled" during Modi's governance and the rural economy has turned stronger. The Gujarat government developed ports all along the coast which had helped fishermen, cited the case of "milk revolution", and drew attention to the fact that Gujarat was now known for "growth in manufacturing sector".

Referring to the non-traditional thinking in the "Gujarat model", Jaitley said that the Ahmedabad Development Authority had developed good quality urban homes at "half the price in the country". He said reduction in the cost of houses owed it to the policy in Gujarat under Chief Minister Modi that "instead of shrinking land availability expand it". "I think it was decisiveness at the leadership level [that was responsible for] 'the success' in Gujarat," he said. "Bureaucracy also fine-tuned to new political culture and to the eventual model that grew," he added.[24]

★

On 9 March 2010, a historic bill granting 33 per cent reservation for women in the Lok Sabha and state assemblies was passed by the Rajya Sabha after two days of high drama that saw suspension of seven members who disrupted proceedings violently. The Congress–SP–BSP–RJD understanding came unstuck over the Women's Reservation Bill. The bill was pushed by the government despite the threat of withdrawal of support by the SP and the RJD,

---

23. "Jaitley Hits Out at UPA Leadership", *The Pioneer*, accessed 25 May 2025, https://www.dailypioneer.com/2014/sunday-edition/jaitley-hits-out-at-upa-leadership.html.

24. Ibid.

and passed by a two-thirds majority. The Constitution (108th Amendment) Bill, 2008, could get through with "unequivocal" support from the BJP and the Left Front in the Upper House where the ruling UPA coalition was in a minority. Jaitley once again played a pivotal role for his party.

The passing of the bill in the Rajya Sabha witnessed unruly and dramatic scenes on the day it was moved in the House for consideration. It could not be taken up on the day the motion was moved because of unruly scenes. Protesting MPs ran amuck, snatching papers, tossing files, and tearing a copy of the bill. Taking no chances, the parliamentary stenographers who record the House proceedings cleared their table of all movable objects, including heavy reference books, paperweights, pen knives, and files. The bill could not be taken up.

Sonia Gandhi cracked the whip following the first day's fiasco. Congress leaders went into hyperactive mould. The ruling party then took the extreme position that there would be no debate, only voting on the bill. The next day, Jaitley took the precaution of bringing three copies of his speech. He left one for safekeeping with the deputy chairperson. That day some thirty-five marshals formed a protective ring stretching from the chairperson's desk to the note-takers' table in the well of the House.

Jaitley started his speech after the voice vote even as the arrangements for electronic voting were in progress and the television channels flashed the news that the bill had been passed. Finding that Jaitley's speech was audible, as the heckling had largely subsided with the removal of protesting MPs, the ruling party followed Jaitley's cue and went ahead with the debate, abandoning the voting midway.[25] The 245-member House had an effective strength of 233. Prime Minister Manmohan Singh and Leader of the Opposition Arun Jaitley described the measure as "momentous and historic".[26]

Amidst all this chaos, Jaitley did not lose his sense of humour. He sent a chit to civil aviation minister Praful Patel in the Rajya Sabha stating in jest, "You

---

25. Coomi Kapoor, "No Permanent Friends or Enemies", *The Indian Express*, accessed 5 May 2025, https://indianexpress.com/article/opinion/columns/no-permanent-friends-or-enemies/.

26. "Rajya Sabha Clears Women's Quota Bill", *India Today*, accessed 25 May 2025, https://www.indiatoday.in/india/story/rajya-sabha-clears-womens-quota-bill-68983-2010-03-08.

look like a medical sales representative." He was alluding to the fact that Patel had removed his coat but still wore his tie. Patel wrote back, "Considering what happened yesterday, I may well become one." Patel was referring to the passage of the Women's Bill in the Rajya Sabha, which meant he could no longer count on re-election to Parliament from his family seat of Bhandara in Maharashtra.[27]

Chairperson M. Hamid Ansari later sent a thank you letter to Jaitley.

2G Spectrum Scam

Then arrived the moment that marked the beginning of the end of the Manmohan Singh-led government's popularity among the people of the country. It was accused of causing a colossal loss to the public exchequer in 2G spectrum allotment. Jaitley grabbed the opportunity with both hands, tearing into UPA-II in Parliament. On 10 November 2010, the day after the winter session of Parliament began, Vinod Rai, the Comptroller and Auditor General of India (CAG), held a press briefing and told reporters that he had sent an audit report on the 2G spectrum allotments by the telecom ministry to the government. He refused to share the details of the findings, in line with a loosely followed tradition: Parliament, when in session, has the first right to know.[28]

The report sparked a political storm that would not subside until the Lok Sabha polls four years later. The CAG report tabled in Parliament later, mentioned that telecom minister A. Raja had valued 2G spectrum at 2001 prices while allotting it in 2008, inflicting a revenue loss of Rs 176,700 crore on the exchequer. The figure, in large font size, was published on the front pages

---

27. Coomi Kapoor, "No Permanent Friends or Enemies", *The Indian Express*, accessed 5 May 2025, https://indianexpress.com/article/opinion/columns/no-permanent-friends-or-enemies/.

28. Puja Mehra, *The Lost Decade (2008–18): How India's Growth Story Devolved into Growth without a Story* (Penguin, 2019), pp. 49–51.

of newspapers across the country.[29] From here onwards, it was a downward slide all the way for UPA-II.

The opening of the telecom sector is indeed a success story, a showcase for the success of economic reforms. More investment, better technologies, competition, quality, and a complete absence of shortage have been the high points of the success story. When the government opened up the sector in 1994–95 to the private sector, there were many sceptics about the private sector being put in control of communications. Within years every critic was proved wrong. Public sector monopoly had led to a sluggish growth of the sector. Contrary to popular perception, mobile telephones proved to be a boon for the common and weaker sections. It hugely improved India's tele-density. The waiting list became a part of history. Costs were radically slashed down; linemen were no longer required. Most Indians felt better connected. The National Telecom Policy, 1999 formulated by the NDA government made improvements in the policy. It switched to a revenue-sharing model which led to reduction in the cost to the operator and increased the volumes substantially. The increased volumes ensured much larger revenue to the government and cheaper services to the consumers.[30]

The UPA government inherited this success story of telecom in 2004. In 2007, an open licence regime was recommended. Pursuant to this, the government invited applications for telecom licences. Nine licences were awarded which entitled each party to a spectrum. The Department of Telecommunications fixed the price at Rs 1,650 crore, the same rate that had last been allotted in 2003, based on the auction-determined price of 2001.This is what the CAG questioned in its report. The telecom market had expanded since 2001, the economy had grown, and the prospect of the number of consumers had increased. Even otherwise, calculated on the basis of the net present value, there would have to be a fundamental difference between the values in 2001–03 and those in 2007–08. This was compounded by three out of the nine awardees of the licences finding buyers / collaborators from the international

29. Maanvi, "2G 'Scam': How the CAG Report Gave Us a Number for Corruption'", *The Quint*, accessed on 4 September 2025, https://www.thequint.com/videos/news-videos/2g-spectrum-scam-verdict-a-raja-cag-report-vinod-rai-kanimozhi.

30. Arun Jaitley, "2G Spectrum Scam", *Articles & Speeches by Arun Jaitley: A Compilation* (Universal Law Publishing Co. Pvt. Ltd., 2014), p. 23.

market, utilising the permissible 74 per cent FDI policy of the government, thus making a profit through artificial valuation. None of the licensees had started the service, not a single subscriber was added. All that existed was a shell company along with a spectrum at Rs 1650 crore.[31]

Parliament was in session. The BJP led by Jaitley, launched a frontal attack on the government. The telecom ministry tried defending its decision stating it was based on the New Telecom Policy of 1999 and a Cabinet approval of 2003, and was thus in line with the policies formulated by previous governments. Jaitley tore into the defence with his sharp and analytical retorts. He focused on the loss caused to the public exchequer accusing the government of corruption.

> The valuation of the companies allotted spectrum overnight enhanced to 2 billion dollars (approximately). Shares were transferred to foreign collaborators/buyers at that value. The difference in the price at which licence was awarded and at which it was sold was at a minimum Rs 6000–7000 crore. The nine licensees collectively along with spectrum were thus alleged to have been allotted at an under-valuation which exceeds Rs 60,000 crore.[32]

The CAG report, he thundered, 'had shattered the confidence in the credibility of governmental functioning. The biggest success story of economic reforms had now become a monumental scam.'[33]

The CBI was forced to register a regular case. The Supreme Court sent A. Raja and top executives of telecom companies to Tihar jail in February 2011. The court directed the Central government to constitute a special court for hearing cases related to the 2G spectrum allocation. A year later, the Supreme Court took the extraordinary step of cancelling the 122 licences issued by

31. Ibid.

32. Ibid.

33. Arun Jaitley, "Shri Arun Jaitley on 'Telecom Story'", Bharatiya Janata Party, accessed 25 May 2025, https://www.bjp.org/interviews-and-articles/shri-arun-jaitley-telecom-story.

Raja's ministry. The cancellation at one stroke reset the telecom industry.[34] The damage was done—not just to UPA-II, but to the whole economy.

As the campaign gained credence on the strength of CAG Vinod Rai's reports, the public mood turned against the government of the day. Under pressure from the Opposition, UPA-II agreed to appoint a JPC to examine the matter of allocation and pricing of telecom and spectrum. Sensing a victory, Jaitley rose to support the motion for its appointment, but not missing out another opportunity to hit the government. He accused the government of allowing lobbyists to dictate policy. In his speech he said:

> The telecom sector is a grim reminder of how a success story can be hijacked for private gains. The institution of lobbyists has surfaced in India, in a structured manner in the telecom sector. Regrettably, middle men, lobbyists and corporate have tried to influence ministerial appointments and appointments of policy makers .... In the telecom sector, this relationship has become too close for comfort.

"It is these aberrations," he suggested, "the Joint Parliamentary Committee has to seriously look into ... [and] examine any possible collusion between the policy makers and the beneficiaries. If such collusion is influenced by any extraneous consideration, the same must be accounted for." He ended on a high note, "The success of the telecom sector cannot be allowed to be tainted because of the role of certain individuals. India should not pay for the misdeeds of some."[35]

When the report of the JPC, approved by a slender majority, was laid on the table of the Rajya Sabha, Jaitley rose to speak to rapt attention. "The strategy is to first indulge in acts of corruption and then subvert constitutional institutions in order to cover them up," he said to thundering applause from

---

34. Puja Mehra, *The Lost Decade (2008–18): How India's Growth Story Devolved into Growth without a Story* (Penguin, 2019), pp. 59–60.

35. Ram Kripal Sinha, "Brief Talking Points Made by Shri Arun Jaitley, Leader of Opposition, Rajya Sabha on the Resolution Relating to JPC", Bharatiya Janata Party, accessed 25 May 2025, https://www.bjp.org/speeches/brief-talking-points-made-shri-arun-jaitley-resolution-relating-jpc.

the Opposition benches. The principal issues that the JPC had to examine were whether spectrum could be given at 2001 prices; whether the goalposts could be shifted in relation to the procedure; and whether the prime minister and the finance minister were in the know of and privy to the decisions taken by the then telecom minister. He said the majority report bypassed most of these issues. "If we want that the dignity of the Parliamentary institutions be maintained, we must ensure that the truth surfaces and not be covered up," he said. He accused that the note of dissent given by the Opposition MPs had been edited. By doing so, the chairman of the committee had committed a breach of privilege.

Though Jaitley invited a ruling from the Chair on this issue, no ruling came. Later in a social media post he wrote, "The only consolation I have is that the Government stands exposed. The Emperor is without clothes. Even a Parliamentary cover-up through a JPC will not save it of the embarrassment."[36]

Coal Allocation Scam

The next major scam of the UPA-II era surfaced at a time when the 2G spectrum scandal had already created a deep political upheaval. It was again a CAG report which took the lid off the Rs 1.86 lakh crore scam in allotment of coal blocks—what came to be known as Coalgate, and which became one of the biggest cases of corruption reported under UPA-II. A number of coal blocks, which were not in the production plan of Coal India Limited and the Singareni Collieries Company Limited (SCCL), were identified and a list was prepared. A total of 216 blocks were allocated between 1993 and 2010, but some were taken away at different points in time. In the end, the number of allocated blocks stood at 194. The CAG accused the government of "inefficient" allocation of coal blocks between 2004 and 2009. The CAG report, placed in Parliament in August 2012, pegged the loss to the exchequer at Rs 1.86 lakh crore. The UPA government claimed that the CAG's presumptive

---

36. Arun Jaitley, "JPC Cover Up Adds to PM's Embarrassment", accessed 25 May 2025, https://www.arunjaitley.com/jpc-cover-up-adds-to-pms-embarrassment/.

loss theory was flawed. After the coal scam was reported, Manmohan Singh offered to resign from the prime minister's post if found guilty.

The CVC ordered a CBI enquiry into the allegations following complaints by BJP MPs Prakash Javadekar and Hansraj Ahir. In April 2013, Parliament's standing committee on coal and steel in its report tabled in Parliament said that the allocation of coal blocks between 1993 and 2008 was done in an unauthorised manner. It also said that allotment of mines where production had not started should be cancelled. A public interest litigation moved in the Supreme Court sought cancellation of all the 194 coal block allotments. The court, monitoring the CBI probe into the coal scam, asked the agency not to disclose probe details to the government. Then CBI director Ranjit Sinha told the Supreme Court that the investigation report had been shared with the law minister, leading to Ashwani Kumar resigning from the office.

On 11 June 2013, the CBI registered an FIR against minister of state in the coal ministry, Dasari Narayana Rao, and an industrialist. Subsequently, the Supreme Court decided to set up a special CBI court where all coal block allocation cases would be tried. On 24 September 2014, the Supreme Court quashed the allocation of 214 coal blocks. The Lok Sabha passed a bill paving way for fresh auction of the coal blocks deallocated by the court. A special court ordered the CBI to examine former Prime Minister Manmohan Singh. In April 2015, the CBI filed a chargesheet against former Jharkhand Chief Minister Madhu Koda, former minister of state for coal, Dasari Narayana Rao, and thirteen others. The special court held Koda of cheating and criminal conspiracy in December 2017. Koda was later convicted on charges of corruption.[37]

In the meantime, Parliament was stalled. The stalemate continued on one of the greatest corruption scandals in Indian history. Jaitley attacked the dubious coal block allocations by the government.

Allocation of natural resources had been a subject matter of public debate in the previous two decades, particularly with the entry of the private sector in infrastructure development. Minerals are an important natural resource. The private sector has a great role to play in the development of the mineral-based industries. However, the policy of allocation of these natural resources had

---

37. "Explained: What Is the Coal Scam All About", 25 May 2025, https://www.indiatoday.in/india/story/explained-what-is-the-coal-scam-all-about-in-which-madhu-koda-is-held-guilty-1106352-2017-12-13.

been discretionary, leaving ample scope for allocation on account of corrupt and collateral motives.

Jaitley said, "The government took a correct policy decision on June 28, 2004 that competitive bidding be introduced in the coal block allocation policy."[38] He also cited opposition from states to competitive bidding. Jaitley tore into the defence.

> For most of the next five years the Prime Minister was the coal minister. The exploitation of coal blocks allotted between 2004 and 2012 is negligible. For most of these coal blocks, statutory and environmental permissions have not been given. The Prime Minister's argument that pending change of policy to competitive bidding, the allocation was necessary for the growth of GDP is eyewash. None of these coal blocks have contributed to the GDP. They have only contributed to the huge valuation of the private sector allottees and a corresponding opportunity and real cost to the Public Exchequer.

Jaitley took on what he termed "the Prime Minister's alternative defence that his government was handicapped by the Opposition from the coal and lignite states to competitive bidding". He alleged, "The present MoS, Coal Shri Prakash Jaiswal admitted in the Parliament on December 21, 2009 that the majority of the states had agreed to the competitive bidding process. Thus to shift the blame to the states is a very poor alibi. Federalism cannot be blamed for the corruption of the UPA." In any case, "In any federal polity, it is legitimate for the states to be concerned about the development of power production in their own states," he said, defending the states.[39] Jaitley was unstoppable. "The Prime Minister must own full and real responsibility. Let him cancel these 142 discretionary allocations, put them on auction and test whether they had been allocated at a fair price."[40]

---

38. Arun Jaitley, "Dubious Defence of Coal Block Allocations", Bharatiya Janata Party, accessed 25 May 2025, https://www.bjp.org/interviews-and-articles/article-dubious-defence-coal-block-allocations-shri-arun-jaitley.

39. Ibid.

40. Ibid.

★

Other scandals followed: financial irregularities in organisation of the Commonwealth Games (CWG), corruption charges against then minister of steel, Virbhadra Singh. Jaitley continued to attack the government in the Parliament and outside. Jaitley led the party's charge against Justice M.S. Liberhan, former Chief Justice of Andhra Pradesh High Court, appointed by the P.V. Narasimha Rao government in December 1992 to head a commission of inquiry into the demolition of the Babri Masjid. He slammed the Liberhan Commission report as a "tragedy of errors", citing factual mistakes in the voluminous report. Pointing out errors.[41]

★

18 August 2011 was a watershed day in the Rajya Sabha. Soumitra Sen, a Calcutta High Court judge, was on the verge of becoming the first judge in the country to be impeached. Minutes before the proceedings started on the matter, Jaitley entered the Upper House with a large number of books. They looked heavy and new. Later, Jaitley told curious reporters that he had spent more than Rs 35,000 on the books to prepare for the debate that closely resembled a courtroom drama with frequent references to evidence, legal provisions, and spirited arguments from all sides. The motion was passed by the Rajya Sabha but Sen, accused of misappropriation of funds, resigned before it came up before the Lok Sabha.

A day prior to the debate in the Rajya Sabha, he summoned Sidharth Luthra. At about 9:30 p.m., Luthra along with his colleagues, visited his home. In an hour-long discussion, he focused on crucial facts such as the personal use of funds by the judge (which had taken us weeks and months to analyse). The next day, armed with cheques used by the judge, his credit card vouchers, bank

---

41. Bharatiya Janata Party, "Brief of the points of speech by Shri Arun Jaitleyji Leader of the Opposition (Rajya Sabha) while participating in the debate on Justice Liberhan Commission Report", accessed on 5 September 2025, https://www.bjp.org/speeches/brief-points-speech-shri-arun-jaitleyji-leader-opposition-rajya-sabha-while-participating

statements, purchase bills of books, and details of gifts to the judge's friends from funds to be held in trust, he convinced Rajya Sabha members—and the motion for removal of a judge was approved for the first time in Indian history.[42]

The impeachment debate in the Rajya Sabha on 18 August 2011, led by Jaitley, highlighted significant concerns regarding judicial misconduct. He presented a detailed argument against a judge accused of misappropriation of funds and procedural irregularities, emphasising the importance of accountability within the judiciary. Jaitley illustrated the gravity of the accusations by presenting specific instances where the judge allegedly misrepresented facts. He pointed out that the committee responsible for the inquiry had mistakenly attributed a bank account to the judge, which actually belonged to another individual named "Sumitra". This misattribution raised questions about the committee's competence and the validity of the charges against the judge. He detailed how the judge had been accused of misappropriating funds.

Jaitley criticised the inquiry process, stating that the judge was not given a fair opportunity to present his case. He mentioned that the inquiry committee had not utilised all available evidence, including bank statements, which could have proven the judge's innocence. Jaitley argued that the absence of these crucial documents compromised the integrity of the inquiry, leading to a flawed conclusion. He pointed out discrepancies in the financial records presented by the judge. Jaitley asserted that the judge failed to provide satisfactory explanations for substantial withdrawals from his accounts, which were instead found to be self-withdrawals that did not benefit workers or the purported investments.

"The implications of this case extend beyond the individual involved," Jaitley said. Emphasising the necessity for a transparent and accountable judicial appointment process, Jaitley argued for the establishment of a National Judicial Commission. He advocated for a balanced system involving both the judiciary and executive branches to prevent the recurrence of such misconduct. In addition, Jaitley called for an examination of the judicial system that allows judges to be judged solely by their peers. He suggested that this practice could

---

42. Sidharth Luthra, "Arun Jaitley: A distinctive lawyer, a fine human being", *Hindustan Times*, accessed on 5 September 2025, https://www.hindustantimes.com/analysis/arun-jaitley-a-distinctive-lawyer-a-fine-human-being/story-ibzYrSb3LL88VuBKqjL4PL.html.

lead to a lack of accountability and transparency, reinforcing the need for a reformed approach to judicial appointment and oversight.

Through his detailed arguments, Jaitley underscored the essentiality of maintaining judicial integrity and accountability. The impeachment debate raised critical questions about the current judicial system and the processes that govern it, ultimately advocating for reforms to ensure that the judiciary operates with the highest ethical standards.[43]

★

Jaitley's effectiveness lay in his ability to present complex scams in simple terms, putting the government on the defensive. He highlighted how corruption under UPA-II had stalled economic growth and eroded public trust. His attacks were not just rhetorical but backed by evidence, making it difficult for the ruling coalition to counter him effectively. The Opposition, under his leadership, successfully turned Parliament into a battleground over governance failures, forcing the government into repeated explanations and damage control. UPA-II's inability to convincingly address these allegations weakened its position, contributing to its eventual defeat in the 2014 elections. Jaitley's role as a vocal and strategic opposition leader was instrumental in shaping the narrative against the government, making UPA-II a textbook case of how corruption scandals can dominate political discourse.

In the wake of scams and investigations, the government machinery stopped functioning amidst fears of a witch hunt. The Opposition became a clear beneficiary of a wave that was created against the government in office.[44]

Jaitley received flak for stalling Parliament. He was often accused by the Congress of legitimising the use of disruptions to prove a political point. In August 2012, when the coal block allocation scam erupted, Jaitley justified disruptions by saying, "There are occasions when obstruction in Parliament

43. Bharatiya Janata Party, "Speech in Rajya Sabha: Impeachment: Sh. Arun Jaitley: 18.08.2011", accessed 25 May 2025, https://www.youtube.com/watch?v=AKA1XTUdHEw.

44. Puja Mehra, *The Lost Decade (2008–18): How India's Growth Story Devolved into Growth without a Story* (Penguin, 2019), pp. 59–60.

brings greater benefits to the country"—a remark that was often used by the Congress and other opposition parties to justify their stand when the BJP wanted order in the House after winning power in 2014.

He knew the role of the Opposition and the Leader of the Opposition well. The Opposition and the government are carried on alike by agreement. The minority agrees that the majority must govern, and the majority agrees that the minority should criticise. The process of parliamentary government will break down if there was absence of mutual forbearance. A few days later, Jaitley corrected his position, saying, "Parliamentary obstructionism should be avoided. It is a weapon to be used in the rarest of the rare cases."[45]

When Prime Minister Manmohan Singh accused the BJP of cynicism and "a mindless environment of negativism", Jaitley responded that it would have been better if the prime minister had honestly introspected as to why this "environment" has been created in the first place. He said:

> Corruption in governance and public life appears to be overflowing. It has crossed the limits of tolerance. The poison which perpetuates this negativism therefore must be expunged from the system. That alone will create a positive environment. Banish corruption, investigate corruption cases honestly and punish the corrupt—that will create a more positive environment. If you put a lid on cases of corruption, the cynicism in negativism will grow. Popular anger has emerged because of lack of accountability. Probity and accountability alone will eliminate this "negativism".[46]

He left behind a series of memorable interventions as the Leader of the Opposition. This include his speech in 2008 in the immediate aftermath of the 26/11 terror attacks, when he censured the UPA government for reducing

45. Saubhadra Chatterji, "Whether in Oppn or Govt, He Left an Indelible Mark on Parliament", *Hindustan Times*, https://www.pressreader.com/india/hindustan-times-st-noida/20190825/282312501730942?srsltid=AfmBOoqOU9t9pg4OQKqXh67tnXJfo8T2VceGUCyl5FYl15tw3sGFeeWO.

46. Arun Jaitley, "Jaitley's Blog Attacking Gandhi Dynasty: Why Is There 'Negativism'?", *India Today*, accessed 25 May 2025, https://www.indiatoday.in/india/north/story/arun-jaitley-blog-why-is-there-negativism-118408-2012-10-10.

India to a weak state,[47] and his speech in 2011 during the Lokpal debate where he famously said, "If we are creating history, let us not create a bad one."[48]

Jaitley believed that criticizing the government and its ministers was an essential duty of the Opposition. The duty of the Opposition is to oppose. That duty is the major check upon corruption and defective administration. It is also the means by which individual injustices are prevented. This duty is hardly less important than that of the government.[49] He attacked the Congress, but he never made personal attacks on any leader. The acrimony between the BJP and the Opposition escalated over the years, but Jaitley never lost his friends in the opposition camps.

He was a vocal critic of Prime Minister Manmohan Singh during the scam-tainted UPA-II regime, but after the 2014 results came out, he wrote in a blog: "Unquestionably, Dr Manmohan Singh was a very good finance minister." Jaitley's decimation of the UPA's defence of the 2G telecom scam in the Upper House didn't mean that he and former Prime Minister Manmohan Singh didn't subsequently talk in the corridors of Parliament. In fact, Jaitley went to meet Manmohan Singh, later telling journalists that Manmohan Singh's break-free budget in 1991, under P.V. Narasimha Rao, had had a great deal of impact on his thinking.[50]

He had immense respect for former President Pranab Mukherjee. At any function held in Parliament's Central Hall, Jaitley was often seen seated beside Mukherjee, engrossed in a long conversation.[51]

---

47. Nitin Gadkari, "Arun Jaitley Helped BJP Set the Narrative", in *The Discussant: Journal of Centre for Reforms, Development and Justice*, Special Edition, An Obituary to Arun Jaitley, Vol. VII, No. 3 (July –September 2019), pp, 20–22.

48. Ibid.

49. Ivor Jennings, "Government and Parliament" (Chapter XV), in *Cabinet Government* (Cambridge University Press, 1959), pp. 472–510.

50. Jyoti Malhotra, "Budget 2014: Staid and Sturdy with Arun Jaitley", *India Today*, From the India Today archives (2014), accessed 25 May 2025, https://www.indiatoday.in/india-today-insight/story/from-the-india-today-archives-2014-budget-2014-staid-and-sturdy-with-arun-jaitley-2570842-2024-07-23.

51. Saubhadra Chatterji, "Whether in Oppn or Govt, He Left an Indelible Mark on Parliament", *Hindustan Times*, https://www.pressreader.com/india/hindustan-times-st-noida/20190825/282312501730942?srsltid=AfmBOoqOU9t9pg4OQKqXh67tnXJfo8T2VceGUCyl5FYl15tw3sGFeeWO.

As a parliamentarian, Jaitley was superb. Shashi Tharoor said that "it was a pleasure questioning him in the Lok Sabha because his answers were both knowledgeable and precise. When my party gave me the honour of speaking in debates on his budget proposals, I could be sure he would respond effectively to the arguments he could rebut, while cheerfully ignoring those he had no answer to."[52] Abhishek Manu Singhvi once wrote that phrases like "perennial pessimists" and "eternal naysayers" were Jaitley's gift to the political lexicon, used like a scathing but effective scalpel.

"Once, as both Arun and I were coming out of the Rajya Sabha after hearing our good friend Sitaram Yechury make an impassioned plea as to why practitioners like doctors, lawyers, chartered accountants, engineers and also industrialists should not be allowed to be MPs for alleged conflicts of interest, we ran into Sita in the lobby. Before I could speak, Arun said, 'Sita wants a Parliament not only of the unemployed but also the unemployable!' This '*gagar mein sagar*' talent, as the Hindi proverb goes, was Arun's special gift," stated Singhvi. Jaitley's wit and sense of humour did not leave him till the end.[53]

Congress leaders admit that when they were in power, Jaitley reached out to them, his political rivals, exchanging civilities and reaffirming personal equations and, indeed, helping the government pass several bills in the Upper House. "His extraordinary competence and his ability to maintain relations across party lines meant that we passed a record number of bills in the Rajya Sabha," conceded Congress leader Rajeev Shukla. Shukla would often take Congress ministers to meet Jaitley and iron out irritants. An astounding seven bills relating to the HRD ministry headed by Kapil Sibal could be passed only when Shukla brought Jaitley on board.[54]

---

52. "Shashi Tharoor Pens Tribute, Says Arun Jaitley Was Every Non-BJP Person's Favourite BJP Person", *Outlook*, accessed 25 May 2025, https://www.outlookindia.com/national/india-news-obituary-arun-jaitley-every-non-bjp-persons-favourite-bjp-person-news-337083.

53. Abhishek Manu Singhvi, "Arun Jaitley Possessed the Rare Skill to Communicate Simply, Analytically and Calmly", *The Economic Times*, accessed 25 May 2025, https://economictimes.indiatimes.com/news/politics-and-nation/arun-jaitley-possessed-the-rare-skill-to-communicate-simply-analytically-and-calmly-abhishek-manu-singhvi/articleshow/70822329.cms?from=mdr.

54. Jyoti Malhotra, "Budget 2014: Staid and Sturdy with Arun Jaitley", *India Today*, From the India Today archives (2014), accessed 25 May 2025, https://www.indiatoday.in/

Jaitley also did not hesitate to publicly laud Opposition MPs when they fared well. During his interactions with media persons, he often praised RSP Lok Sabha MP N.K. Premachandran and CPI(M)'s former Rajya Sabha member P. Rajeev—both come from Kerala and are strongly opposed to the BJP—for their eagerness to study bills and debate in the House.[55]

A legal mind with astute skills in drafting legislation, Jaitley did not hesitate to extend his drafting skills to the then UPA government when it was struggling to clear the nuclear liability bill, crucial for carrying out the Indo-US civil nuclear deal.[56] Former Maharashtra Chief Minister Prithviraj Chavan, who was handling the bill as the Minister of the State in the PMO, recalled that Jaitley had "kept aside the hard stand advocated by some in his party" to help the government in a "national cause". Chavan said:

> When the government was struggling with the clause on nuclear accident liability (it did not have the numbers, as the Left was against it), I approached the BJP. I went to Arun Jaitley and told him (that) it's important for the country, and we had worked hard to reach this point. He looked at the draft and made some changes to make it acceptable to more (parties). We modified the Bill, and the BJP supported it.

The bill was passed after the government deleted the words "done with the intent to cause nuclear damage and such act" from Clause 17(*b*). Had Jaitley taken a "hard stand", the bill could not have been passed, Chavan said.[57]

Jaitley played a key role in the Upper House. As the Leader of the Opposition, he was a great support for the Rajya Sabha chairman, and a consummate strategist knowing when to take a hard position and when to accommodate the

---

india-today-insight/story/from-the-india-today-archives-2014-budget-2014-staid-and-sturdy-with-arun-jaitley-2570842-2024-07-23.

55. Liz Mathew, "Arun Jaitley: Mentor to the Young, MP Who Helped UPA Govt on Nuclear Bill", *The Indian Express*, accessed 25 May 2025, https://indianexpress.com/article/india/arun-jaitley-dead-mentor-to-the-young-mp-who-helped-upa-govt-on-nuclear-bill-5934494/.

56. Ibid.

57. Ibid.

other side.[58] Even when his health was fast deteriorating, in January 2019, just before he left for the United States for treatment, he decimated the Opposition attack on the Rafale issue by laying out all the facts threadbare.[59] He was conferred with the award for being the best parliamentarian for the year 2010.[60] The award was instituted by the Indian Parliamentary Group in 1994. Then Lok Sabha Speaker Meira Kumar had constituted an Award Committee to select the member for the award for the three years and recommend it to the executive committee of the Indian Parliamentary Group. The Award Committee's recommendation of Jaitley for the award was unanimously accepted by the executive committee. Later, the BJP published a compendium of his speeches in Parliament.[61]

Jaitley's impressive performance as Leader of the Opposition over five years elevated him to a stature where he was frequently seen as a potential contender for the prime minister's office, a job he held no interest in—that was for his friend Modi. His untiring and unceasing attack eventually framed the 2014 general elections as a contest between stability and chaos, and helped generate the momentum that carried the Modi-led BJP to a historic victory.

---

58. M. Venkaiah Naidu, "Our Regular Meetings Were for Food, and Food for Thought", in *The Discussant: Journal of Centre for Reforms, Development and Justice*, Special Edition, An Obituary to Arun Jaitley, Vol. VII, No. 3 (July–September 2019), pp. 17–19.

59. Nitin Gadkari, "Arun Jaitley Helped BJP Set the Narrative", in ibid, pp. 20–22.

60. PTI, "Arun Jaitley, Karan Singh & Sharad Yadav Best Parliamentarians", *The Times of India*, accessed 25 May 2025, https://timesofindia.indiatimes.com/india/arun-jaitley-karan-singh-sharad-yadav-best-parliamentarians/articleshow/18833724.cms.

61. "Arun Jaitley in Parliament", Bharatiya Janata Party (August 2011).

14

Pitching Modi as Prime Minister

In 2011, much before Modi's name surfaced as a potential prime ministerial candidate for the 2014 general elections, Jaitley had told many colleagues that Modi would be the prime minister in 2014. He was the natural choice in 2014, Jaitley told journalist Kumkum Chadha. In fact, Jaitley and Modi had started preparing the foreground for Modi's rise in national politics way back in 2005 at a time when there were many charges against Modi about his involvement in the Gujarat riots. In May 2005, when Jaitley was the Leader of the Opposition in the Rajya Sabha, in a conversation with Robert Blake, deputy chief of mission at the US Mission in New Delhi, Jaitley had predicted the change in leadership and defended Modi. He said, L.K. Advani would lead the party for another two to three years, "after which one of five next generation leaders would take the reins".

He was visibly pained by the revocation of Modi's visa by the United States. Jaitley complained that he could not understand how the United States could take such an action against the party that had initiated the transformation of United States–India relations. When Blake attempted to explain the "rationale and legal basis" for the US decision, Jaitley argued that it would have been better for the United States to let the chief minister visit the United States. Eight years later, Modi's name was announced as the BJP's prime ministerial candidate for the 2014 elections.

The crowning of Modi as the NDA's prime ministerial candidate was a nail-biting political thriller with the BJP planning to wait for the election results before biting the bullet. Jaitley was its chief scriptwriter. In the months preceding the formal announcement of Narendra Modi as the BJP's prime ministerial candidate in 2014, Jaitley worked tirelessly behind the scenes to build consensus around the selection for his friend Narendra Modi.

Although the BJP had lost two elections in a row, the prospects for 2014 elections appeared bright. The Congress-led government had never looked more vulnerable. During its first term, as it sought to liberalise and grow the economy like never before, it had enjoyed widespread popularity. At times it looked as if the unassuming prime minister, Manmohan Singh, could walk on water. Now it appeared rudderless, tired, and battered after being hit by a succession of scandals.

The Anna Hazare Movement against corruption, countrywide protests against the gang-rape of a twenty-three-year-old student in a moving bus in Delhi, beheading of two Indian soldiers on the border by Pakistan troops, aggressive incursion by the Chinese, the torture and subsequent death of Indian prisoner Sarabjit Singh in a Pakistani jail, are but a few incidents which showed the government in a poor light, with a prime minister who was unable to provide strong decisive leadership. He was being ridiculed for his silence than praised for his actions, which had rendered him more of a liability than an asset that he was considered during UPA-I.

Mulayam Singh Yadav and Mayawati—two regional satraps of Uttar Pradesh—were, indeed, extending outside support but they were seen as being part of the alliance more for their own good than the UPA's. This, and with key allies DMK and All Indian Trinamool Congress (TMC) pulling out of the alliance had left the UPA government in an unenviable position.

The worst was still to come. The differences in approach between the two power centres—Prime Minister Manmohan Singh and Congress president Sonia Gandhi—did not help an already battered UPA. The economic situation was nothing to boast of either. The indicators showed an alarming decline during UPA-II compared with UPA-I. The economy had slipped from a high growth rate of 9.3 per cent in 2005–06 to 6.5 per cent in 2011–12. The second tenure of the UPA witnessed inflation (wholesale price index) skyrocketing from 4.47 per cent in 2005–06 to 8.94 per cent in 2011–12, while agriculture growth declined from 3.96 per cent to 2.5 per cent during the same period.

Persistent high food inflation, high current account deficit, trade deficit—not to speak of crony capitalism—too marred the prime minister's second term in office. Some key faces of the Hazare Movement formed the Aam Aadmi Party (AAP) in 2012. The arrival of the AAP and the fall of the Congress proved to be catalysts for cementing the alliance of big business with Hindutva at the national level. To use Narendra Modi's vocabulary, the empire or the "Delhi Sultanate" was on shaky ground. It was time to push forward.

Every opposition party in a democracy everywhere in the world likes to claim that it's time for a change, but political cliché or not, there was ample evidence that—across India—change was exactly what people were looking for. There were battle-hardened party leaders in Delhi quite capable and more than ready to be the BJP standard-bearer. Foremost among them was Advani, Modi's long-time mentor. And yet, Advani never pushed his own candidacy publicly any more than Modi did. But Advani, who had once been a crucial part of Modi's political life-support system, was now the biggest threat to Modi's hopes of becoming prime minister. Advani was also in his mid-eighties and had led the party to defeat in the last general elections, making him even less credible in the eyes of the BJP's cadre.

★

Narendra Modi had rapidly emerged as Chhote Sardar, a strong leader who could offer a challenge to the UPA. Even as the Ram Janmabhoomi movement gained momentum, Modi was chosen as Advani's "sarthi", a term used for Lord Krishna as Arjun's charioteer in the Mahabharata, when Advani decided to take out the rathyatra which changed Indian politics forever. Modi had minutely planned his mentor's rathyatra in Gujarat.

Firmly in the saddle with two-thirds majority after the 2002 win in the Gujarat assembly elections, Modi got into the development mode in 2003, inaugurating the "Resurgent Gujarat" business summit—an earlier avatar of Vibrant Gujarat—and also embarking on Gujarat Siddhi Yatra to celebrate achievements of his one-year rule. He introduced the Karmayogi Abhiyaan, a campaign launched to transform the bureaucracy and deliver better governance to improve efficiency of government officials. The successful Vibrant Gujarat summits, where captains of industry hailed him as the next prime minister, helped build Brand Modi.

The big jolt came in March 2005, when the United States revoked his visa on grounds of suppression of religious freedom. The European Union followed suit. With the West ignoring him, Modi started to look eastwards, especially to Japan, South Korea, Singapore, Australia, Taiwan, Hong Kong, and China. On 12–13 January 2007, Modi organised the Vibrant Gujarat Global Summit, a summit unlike a regular trade fair. Although it too had its share of sundry stalls of various countries, corporations, and quasi-governmental outfits, the big difference was that the big guns of Indian industry were in attendance—Ratan Tata, Mukesh Ambani, Shashi Ruia, and K.V. Kamath—besides non-resident Indians (NRIs). Japan became a partner country for the Vibrant Gujarat summit in 2007. The meet announced it had notched up investments to the tune of Rs 2.5 lakh crore. Pharma giant Wokhardt's Habil F. Khorakiwala, who had just taken over as the president of the Federation of Indian Chambers of Commerce and Industry (FICCI), described Modi as a "dynamic visionary"; Ratan Tata, whose small car project in West Bengal was then mired in a mighty mess, said, "You are a fool if you are not in Gujarat."

The highlight of the 2007 summit was Special Economic Zones (SEZs). The Chief Minister Modi pointed out to the large gathering and said that Gujarat was among the first states to enact a SEZ law titled "Gujarat Special Economic Zone Act" in 2004, even before the Centre did in 2005. In a speech designed as much for the industrialists, as for a mass audience (it was also broadcast), he came up with one of those lines that make for catchy headlines: the whole of Gujarat, Modi said, is a SEZ—S for Spirituality, E for Entrepreneurship, and Z for Zeal. The hall resonated with loud applause.

Modi believed that Vibrant Gujarat would work in his state as Gujarat was different: it had the highest rate of urbanisation at 40 per cent. Additionally, there was a historical context to what was unfolding in Gujarat. In the course of the twentieth century, some of the most popular mass movements in the state were reactionary in nature. The Bharatiya Kisan Sangh, affiliated to the RSS, mobilised the community of Patels and had two million members in Gujarat by 2007. The Swami Narayan sect too had contributed to a heightened Hindu identity. This therefore was the socio-political milieu in which Narendra Modi first made his mark as a mass politician. By 2007, Narendra Modi was also cultivating Gujarati sub-nationalism by cleverly turning the tables on his opponents. For instance, every time there were protests against constructing the Sardar Sarovar Project (SSP) on the Narmada river that had displaced villagers and tribals, Modi would seize the opportunity and announce a protest of his own, against the slow progress of the project in a state prone to water shortage. In speeches, he called those who opposed the dam "five-star activists from Delhi and Bombay".

On 12–13 January 2011, more than 10,000 businessmen from 100 countries descended on Gandhinagar for the fifth instalment of Vibrant Gujarat. On the first day of the summit—held inside the newly-constructed Mahatma Mandir, a monument to Gandhi in the unlikely form of a convention centre—the stage was crowded, in keeping with the usual tradition at Indian public events. Eighty people were seated on the dais in three rows, but all eyes were on the man at the centre, the organiser and unquestioned star of the show—Narendra Modi. Among those sitting next to him were the Japanese ambassador and the Canadian high commissioner, and these men were in turn flanked by the two most prominent ambassadors from India Inc., Ratan Tata and Mukesh Ambani. Another three dozen corporate chairmen and CEOs were also on stage, along with the prime minister of Rwanda and the president of the United States–India Business Council. Modi announced from the stage that he wished to see the United States as a partner country at the next summit. By the time it was all over, the businessmen had promised investments in excess of $450 billion, the largest-ever sum for a single event in an emerging economy. The five summits since 2003 generated investment pledges worth $920 billion for Gujarat.

Modi managed to bury the past and resurrect his prospects for political advancement. He was now the Vikaas Purush, or Development Man. For the first families of Indian business, Modi was "the next leader of India", "a visionary", "the unstoppable horse", and "the CEO who can lead the country", to quote just a sampling of the effusive endorsements.

The United Kingdom too announced the re-establishment of trade ties with Gujarat after a moratorium of ten years. Modi led a business delegation to the United Kingdom, where human rights group welcomed him with black flags. China rolled out a red carpet for Modi in 2011. Big car companies like Tata, Ford, and Maruti Suzuki had by now driven into the state, giving a boost to Modi's development plank.

On his sixty-second birthday, on 17 September 2011, Modi launched his Sadbhavana Mission, a three-day fast, a move clearly aimed at securing a larger national role. Later, he pointed with pride to the constituency of Jamnagar on the west coast, a town that is 90 per cent Muslim where BJP scored a victory in municipal elections. In municipal elections in 2013, all twenty-four of the

BJP's candidates, who were Muslims, won, sweeping aside the Congress, which had dominated the area politically since Independence.

★

From 2002 to 2012, Modi won every single election for his party in the state of Gujarat.

Rajnath Singh was appointed the BJP president in December 2005. His reconstruction of the BJP as an organisation started generating results in the elections. From 2004 to 2007, the NDA allies led by the BJP won in eight states. They made progress in the states of Karnataka, Bihar, and Punjab and obtained support from backward castes.

Rajnath dropped Modi from the BJP's Parliamentary Board, the party's apex decision-making body. The reason given was that there was a conflict of interest in being a state chief minister as well as being on the panel to select election candidates. The move was unexpected. Jaitley was removed as chief party spokesperson. Senior journalist Saba Naqvi wrote at the time that Rajnath Singh admitted to her in an interview that Narendra Modi's exclusion from the Parliamentary Board was "seventy per cent a decision of the RSS and thirty per cent his own choice", while Arun Jaitley's removal as national spokesperson "was an equal, fifty-fifty decision between him and the RSS. The interview created a furore in the party and Sangh circles. Rajnath Singh denied it point-blank.

Meanwhile, the newly appointed spokesperson, Ravi Shankar Prasad, issued an official statement saying that the interview contained certain statements that the president had never made; that his observations had been deliberately distorted and quoted out of context; and that there was a palpable and malicious attempt to convey a negative image of the BJP.

However, during his next tenure as the BJP president (January 2013–July 2014), Rajnath Singh more than compensated by reading the writing on the wall—Narendra Modi was the star on the ascendant and there was no point in going against the tide, as it were. Rajnath Singh would later play a big role in enabling Modi overcome resistance to his national ambitions from the veteran, L.K. Advani.

★

Jaitley's formidable legal skills remained an asset for Modi and his close associate Amit Shah when both came under CBI scrutiny—first in connection with the post-Godhra riot cases and later in encounter killing cases. By then, after four years of investigations, in February 2012, the Special Investigation Team (SIT) appointed by the Supreme Court gave a clean chit to Modi in the Gulberg massacre case, among the nine most crucial ones reinvestigated by the Supreme Court-appointed SIT, in which sixty-nine persons in a Muslim-dominated housing society were massacred. It soon filed a closure report indicating that its inquiry found no prosecutable evidence against Modi and fifty-nine others in the particular case.

On 31 August 2012, Modi appeared on the new digital platform to participate in a live and interactive Google+ Hangouts session, moderated by actor Ajay Devgn. Modi was heading into his third state assembly election and Google was aggressively promoting the Hangouts feature. The broadcast proved to be a happy meeting ground for both the politician and the platform. The video chat had to be delayed, starting an hour later than 8 p.m. as scheduled, because, as an apologetic Devgn told viewers who had logged in, Google+ "system crashed with so much of traffic and it took us an hour to manage that".

"I have been watching 30–40 friends from Google here for the past one hour who have been working hard to figure out how to clear the traffic," began Modi. "Traffic policemen on the road don't get as much trouble as the trouble my friends here were facing," he quipped as he too apologised for the delay, before going on to thank Google and say that the platform was "catching the pulse of the globe". The chat itself had been advertised for four days prior to 31 August on the chief minister's personal website, www.narendramodi.in, and drew in 20,000 advance questions. Modi answered eighteen of them in the 114-minute broadcast, which was ultimately seen by over 788,000 viewers.

Presaging all the touchpoint messages of strong nationalism, developmentalism, techno-governance, and a new modernity rooted in tradition that would eventually define Modi's nationwide messaging, the chat also encapsulated the core communications style that would ultimately define Brand Modi. Even the choice of topic, "Strong and Glorious India Long Cherished by Swamy Vivekananda", served to subliminally connect the Gujarat chief minister to the cultural confidence symbolised by Swami

Vivekananda, who captured the Indian imagination in 1893 at the Parliament of the World's Religions.

Further, with Modi becoming the first politician in India to appear on Hangouts, the chat underscored his image as a leader who embraced digital change and technology, as did his messaging on Google. At a time when most mainstream media houses would not interview Modi without asking questions about the post-Godhra violence in 2002, the choice of moderator was crucial. Devgn had just delivered a hit with the Hindi film *Singham* a year earlier, and starred in the successful *Bol Bachchan* and *Son of Sardar* in 2012. Choosing an actor at the height of his career to anchor the session added to the novelty and spectacle of the event.

It was an early version of the celebrity model that drove the Modi interview with the Bollywood actor Akshay Kumar in 2019, which helped change the political narrative in India ahead of the 2019 general elections. As with the "non-political" interview with Akshay Kumar, the 2012 Hangouts session with Devgn focused far more on the personal side of the man, with topics ranging from the intricacies of the Modi kurta to the rise of the Asian century.

The story goes that Google+ had first approached Rahul Gandhi for a session. As a young first-time MP who was still new to politics, he would have been the perfect fit for a young tech platform looking to engage the youth through celebrities. Rahul Gandhi is said to have refused the offer, and the company then approached Modi, says journalist Brajesh Kumar Singh, who covered the event in Ahmedabad. Modi's response, he recalls, was: "How quickly can we do this?" Among global politicians, only then US President Barack Obama and then Australian Prime Minister Julia Gillard had been on Hangouts thus far. The platform was looking for celebrities to engage with in India. Bollywood stars Shah Rukh Khan and Aamir Khan, as well as cricketer Mahendra Singh Dhoni, were among the celebrities who had featured on Google Hangouts. Modi became the first politician to join this list.

At the time of the Devgn Hangout in 2012, Modi had 8 million followers on Twitter (rising to 61.5 million by September 2020), 6 million on Facebook (growing to 45.8 million by 2020). He was already way ahead of all other Indian politicians (barring Shashi Tharoor at the time) on social media. Rahul Gandhi, for example, did not even join Twitter until May 2015, and started tweeting under his own name only from May 2018. Modi, however, was willing to go the whole hog with a social platform, using it to directly reach his voters, bypassing what he may have seen as the distorting lens of the media. In response to a question on the chat from a self-confessed fan on how he managed to stay calm despite media criticism, Modi said he welcomed criticism as such, but argued that what he faced in the country was not criticism, but allegations by vested interests.

Modi's dominance of the digital world became a national talking point in 2014, when he used social media and his hologram rallies to great effect. Yet, his embrace of technology as a force multiplier in politics predates the 2014 general elections. Modi first deployed 3D holograms of himself not in 2014, but in the 2012 Gujarat assembly elections. Soon after that, in March 2013, while addressing the Google Big Tent summit, again via Google Hangouts, he argued:

> "Technology in Politics" plays a crucial role ... The internet has therefore truly empowered the citizen. It has forced the politician to perform, not just promise. In a way, it has become a challenge for the political class. The time has come for the political class to adapt to this change and reinvent itself! It needs to stop running away. It needs to embrace the internet's many powerful facets. ... In this age of internet democracy, citizens are netizens, who transcend the geographical borders of countries and continents. No wonder it is called the Wired Republic.

All of this was indicative of how Modi viewed digital communication long before he became the BJP's prime ministerial candidate.

From pioneering the use of campaign audio and videocassettes in the 1980s during the Ram Janmabhoomi movement to adapting early to satellite television in the 1990s, and from Modi holograms in 2014 to dominating Facebook and WhatsApp messages in 2019, the BJP has always operated at the confluence of technology and politics. In the late 1980s and up to 1992, the party powered its outreach on the Ram Janmabhoomi movement with roadside Re 1 sales and mass distribution of audiocassettes containing fiery speeches on Ram by Uma Bharti and Sadhvi Ritambhara. The BJP's Ram Janmabhoomi movement also rode the Videocassette Recorder (VCR) boom, in the pre-internet and pre-satellite television days, right into middle-class homes, through videocassettes containing religious. In many ways, these strategies reshaped direct political communications in India.

★

Jaitley played a key role in building Modi's image as a crusader for development through his many interventions on his blog.

> Any riot, be it inspired by religious, caste or any other frenzy, leaves huge wounds behind. It causes death, injury, loss and suffering. It divides the society, it polarizes people on basis of their birthmarks. Every civilized society has to free itself from the menace of such social tensions. Gujarat for a long time had an unfortunate history of such riots, small or big. It was men and events which triggered such conflicts, the last of such major riots being in the year 2002. As a section of the media revisits the Gujarat riots of 2002 it is equally important to look at Gujarat ten years after the riots. Gujarat has finally had a riot-free decade. Hopefully, the unfortunate events of 2002 will never be repeated. Gujarat's agenda today is no longer a social divide. It is economic development, improvement in the life of every citizen and a desire to compete with the most successful societies in the world. The memories of 2002 are not revived by the Gujaratis. They are revived by elements within the society whose relevance exists in reviving the sad memories of past. The burning of compartment No. S-6 in the Sabarmati Express on 27th February, 2002 was a barbaric act. It was planned by mischievous elements with the intention of generating communal trouble in the country. It stunned the society. Many were misled into a retaliatory action. The violence was so widespread that the security apparatus of the State was outnumbered. The army had to be called in to take positions. A very large number of innocents lost their lives due to this violence. Hundreds were killed even in police firing. Contrast this with the anti-Sikh riots in New Delhi in 1984 where not one person died in police firing.

Jaitley commended Modi for coming out shining through a serious test of leadership.

> Should he have allowed the environment of the State to be dominated by the agenda set by Godhra and the post-Godhra riots? There were many who wanted that agenda to continue. The Chief Minister and the Government overcame various odds to change the agenda. The greater good of the largest number of people was the ultimate object. The State embarked upon an unprecedented growth story, undeterred by hostilities. The State GDP grew by double digit. The State used its potential to become India's manufacturing hub. The port infrastructure was strengthened with the advantage of a large hinterland available to Gujarat. Its road network now compares with the developed world. Agriculture which was crippled due to water shortage has multiplied at an impressive double digit growth rate, thanks to the Sardar Sarovar project which the State managed to achieve despite political and judicial obstacles. Electricity being provided 24 hours a day became a great achievement. Red-tapeism was eliminated in economic decision making. This incentivized domestic and international investors to look at Gujarat as the prime investment destination in India. Corruption-free government became the brand image of the State and its Chief Minister. Today, irrespective of religious or caste affiliations, the Gujaratis are looked upon as entrepreneurs who being free from the shackles of indecisiveness are facilitated by a political leadership to be a part of peace and prosperity. The world today knows Gujarat for the growth story and for its immense economic potential. The advantages of this growth have trickled down. Enriched revenues of the State have been used for various social and poverty alleviation schemes.

Jaitley said the divide between Hindus and Muslims of Gujarat was a matter of the past; Hindus and Muslims were both a part of the state's growth story. This had been acknowledged by most studies which have observed that the Muslims minority in Gujarat is economically much better than most other parts of the country. Gujarat had changed its agenda, much to the dislike of the Congress party leadership and some NGOs which work as its front.

Jaitley accused the Congress of propaganda against Modi as they were unable to take him on electorally.

> The changed agenda does not suit their politics. It is therefore necessary for them to keep the riot-torn image of Gujarat alive. Politically they have been on the losing side. Narendra Modi cannot be defeated by the Congress Party in the elections. The strategy therefore is to use other methodologies to fight him. The initial strategy was to use a section of the media which rejoiced in anti-Modi stories. Rumours, falsehood and propaganda were convenient instruments. For years we were narrated a horrific story of a lady victim who was pregnant and her stomach was torn apart. The entire story was manufactured and no fact could be proven. The Gujarat Police found no evidence against Modi in the riots case. The courts were petitioned to appoint an SIT. The SIT of Gujarat Police officers found no evidence against him. It was replaced by an SIT comprising former CBI officials. Media reports indicate that there is no evidence against Modi. They found no prosecutable evidence against Modi. A further arrangement was made which went outside the Code of Criminal Procedure. The investigator's findings would be reviewed by a lawyer—an amicus curiae. Is the process of hounding to continue till facts can be manufactured to suit the politics of some? The Home Minister of the State, against whom no evidence was available in two prior investigations, was charge-sheeted and arrested by CBI in an encounter case. A bare analysis of the charge sheet and the accompanying evidence indicates the falsity of the evidence. Voluminous evidence is available of a disgruntled police officer communicating with the Pradesh Congress leadership on how to implicate Modi. The State Congress leadership even sent to him a blueprint of the legal process required to be followed in order to implicate the Chief Minister. Every encounter is not a fake encounter. India has suffered at the hands of Maoist violence, cross-border terrorism and various other forms of insurgency. Police and security forces have often clashed with these insurgents. In the last one decade the list of State-wise encounters would show that the number of encounters in Gujarat were amongst the least. Every other State can be trusted to presume that the encounter is genuine or it can

appoint its own mechanism to investigate the encounters. However, the judicial yardstick to investigate encounters in Gujarat is different. In an astonishing case where a lady activist of the Laskar was killed along with some others, the Central Government withdrew its affidavit supporting the encounter as genuine and real. The LeT website had owned her up as LeT operative. A court has now appointed an SIT which includes an officer nominated by the NGOs and the Central Government to investigate the case. Motivated investigators will hardly be fair. In all other States the Lokayukta would be appointed on the advice of the Council of Ministers but in the case of Gujarat, the Governor can ignore the recommendation of the Council of Ministers. A Court has found this to be legally acceptable. Several legislations passed by the State Assembly are either waiting assent of the Governor or of the Central government. The NGOs which are actively campaigning against Gujarat in the past ten years have simultaneously pleaded for those who burnt the Sabarmati Express which started the sordid saga of 2002. The UPA Government chose to appoint a carefully chosen retired judge of the Supreme Court to opine in an inquiry that the fire in the Sabarmati Express started from inside. The last one decade has been a challenging one for the State of Gujarat. There was a history of social tensions. Gujarat now has had a riot-free decade. It has tried to move away from the past. It has embarked upon a road to economic growth. The tragedy of Gujarat is that since Modi's opponents can't defeat him politically, they hide behind NGOs and a section of the media. One can only hope the Judiciary keeps out of this political thicket and remains even handed. The guilty must be punished but the attempt at media trials and manufacturing of evidence must end. Harmony and growth will be the best healers. The future road map of Gujarat will be a battle between those who want Gujarat to be caught in the time frame of 2002 and those who believe that this century promises to be the one of Gujarat's. Gujarat has now to overcome the challenge of this negative energy.

★

While there were some in the media who kept pointing fingers at Modi for the 2002 riots, a section of India was by then anxious to see Modi become the prime ministerial candidate. The middle classes were falling under the thrall of the idea of a strong leader in an age of drift; the young saw Modi as dynamic; women were overtly enamoured of this big, strong man; according to statistics reeled out by the BJP, even Muslims in Gujarat and elsewhere had come to accept him as the inevitable leader. Even before his candidature as the prime minister, loyalists fought for him on internet forums and media. An army of human rights lawyers, activists, and riot victims had failed to get him in any legal trouble. No Indian leader had faced the kind of censure he did in the West (when many countries denied him visas), and still build a reputation as a wealth generator of Gujarat. Many dismissed the groundswell as a structured narrative systematically being promoted by an overzealous band of Modi loyalists.

Modi had assiduously built the cult of personality, prevailing over cadre, leaders, region, and ideology. He had succeeded in juxtaposing Gujarat's development with his own image. He had worked both on the notion of Hindu identity and regional pride, at times positing Gujarat against the Centre. In his home state of Gujarat, he had taken complete control over the state apparatus, running the affairs through bureaucracy. Most significantly, he presented himself as the wealth generator in a "vibrant" Gujarat, a leader committed to basics—bijli, sadak, paani. A leader who meant business, in a post-liberalisation, increasingly urbanised, aspirational India.

Sensing the groundswell in his favour, Modi cast his eye on the rest of India with a determined Jaitley by his side. Jaitley realised the possibilities of converting the groundswell of support into a decisive electoral mandate in the 2014 elections. Jaitley, with his fabled access to Delhi power circles, turned himself into Modi's point person in the national capital. Besides negating the challenge of Advani's bid for another shot at prime ministership, Jaitley made sure that organisational support for Modi was expressed unequivocally at the Goa session of the party in 2013. The perception that he had developed close associations with a section of the Delhi media gave rise to accusations of perception management benefiting his party and government—an allegation not uncommon among the behind-the-scenes operators of major political parties.

Advani, Modi's mentor, however, questioned the projection of Narendra Modi as the prime minister. Advani believed that after Atal Bihari Vajpayee, he was the senior party leader with a stellar record of service. But by then, the RSS had made many categorical statements about the need for the old guard to retire and younger faces to take leadership positions. Nitish Kumar's unhappiness with Modi's candidature helped Advani make an argument, but it was not adequate in the face of the support within the BJP for the chief minister of Gujarat.

However, many in the BJP were convinced that "if the BJP was the party best placed to benefit from this mood, why put the likelihood of victory at risk by selecting a controversial and potentially divisive candidate like Narendra Modi?" Better, perhaps, to play safe and go for a more consensual, if less exciting, candidate. Modi, after all, had no experience at the national level and had never been elected to Parliament. Advani, once the party's nationalist hard-man, could now be seen as the unifying alternative to Modi—an extraordinary turn in itself. The BJP had begun a journey from "untouchability" to acceptability in the era of Atal Bihari Vajpayee when the wishes of allies were given primacy, and figures like Nitish were ministers at the Centre. "Project Modi" involved turning the Vajpayee model on its head. It placed a commanding figure at the fulcrum during a period when the BJP had evolved into a credible political force and the primary axis around which regional parties coalesced in opposition to the Congress. There were therefore strong arguments within the party against Narendra Modi being the prime ministerial candidate.

At the same time, there were also strong arguments being made within the BJP to turn inwards, and rebuild its core under a leader whom the cadres saw as charismatic. This was amply clear at every BJP gathering where Modi seemed to be the only chief minister to inspire the rank and file. Huge chants would go up every time he entered a meeting. Modi, quite simply, had prevailed in the mind of the cadre. One argument was that in the age of a squabbling leadership, Modi was the only leader who could manage the backroom moves of the RSS. The Gujarat chief minister was also pushed to the forefront like a subaltern hero, the OBC who had little time or patience for the machinations of the Brahmins who dominated the RSS. Again, insiders argued that Modi was the right man to disrupt the carefully ordered world of the traditional elites in the brotherhood of the Sangh.

★

The BJP's rank and file began clamouring for a bigger role for Modi. On 22 January 2013, Rajnath Singh, the party veteran and the former party chief, once again took over as the BJP president, following Nitin Gadkari's resignation. Rajnath Singh's new team had twelve vice presidents, ten general secretaries, fifteen secretaries, and seven spokespersons, besides a twelve-member Central Parliamentary Board, a nineteen-member Central Election Committee, and a five-member Central Disciplinary Committee. With more than seventy names in various capacities, Rajnath Singh's team included veterans such as the Bihar strongman C.P. Thakur, Balbir Punj, Mukhtar Abbas Naqvi, Kiran Maheshwari, and Smriti Zubin Irani as vice presidents, and Amit Shah, Dharmendra Pradhan, Varun Gandhi, P. Muralidhar Rao, and Rajiv Pratap Rudy as general secretaries. He made Poonam Pramod Mahajan, daughter of late party leader Pramod Mahajan, the secretary. Saroj Pandey succeeded Smriti Irani as the Mahila Morcha chief and Anurag Thakur was given another term as the head of the Bharatiya Janata Yuva Morcha (BJYM). The team also included numerous prabharis, "handlers", who were in charge of various states.

The one appointment that made the headlines was Narendra Modi's in the BJP Central Parliamentary Board, the highest decision-making organ of the party. During Rajnath Singh's first tenure (2005–09), Modi was excluded from the same body as he would have been the only chief minister on the Central Parliamentary Board, which seemed unfair to the other serving chief ministers. It was the death of veteran leader Balasaheb Apte that led to one vacant seat on the Central Parliamentary Board. In the midst of calls for Narendra Modi's name to be announced as the party's prime ministerial candidate, the appointment was seen as a sign of things to come. Unlike the old guard, Rajnath Singh was not unaware of ground realities.

In fact, this time around, Rajnath Singh really had no choice but to induct Modi into the party's Parliamentary Board. Ever since Modi was re-elected as the chief minister of Gujarat for a third term in 2012, the BJP's rank and file had been clamouring for Modi to be projected as the party's prime ministerial candidate in the next general elections scheduled for 2014. It seems, however, the decision to bring back Modi to the BJP's Parliamentary Board was not entirely unanimous. There is evidence to suggest that there were some within the BJP who were wary of the appointment of Modi, as they were afraid of being upstaged. But the mood among the party cadre was such that Modi's induction could no longer be avoided. This was not only because of his remarkable electoral success in Gujarat, but also due to the recognition that Modi was the party's most popular and saleable face.

At the two-yearly Vibrant Gujarat summit held in January 2013, Modi was the toast of India's corporate captains, including Ratan Tata, Mukesh Ambani, and Anand Mahindra. This, of course, was not something new, as Modi has traditionally been a favourite of corporate India. A striking feature of the summit, however, was the attendance of a number of delegates from the United States, Britain, Canada, and Japan. Many foreign governments, including the United States, which were wary of associating with Modi after the 2002 riots in Gujarat had by now softened their line. For the sceptics, it was the clout of Modi speaking. Rajnath Singh knew that winning the people's mandate necessitated all hands on deck.

Politics is the art of the possible. The sublime skill of managing contradictions came handy here for the BJP's backroom warhorse Jaitley. He was by now oiling the back channels and using his clout in the media to build popular support for Modi. In April 2013, grilled at the Town Hall over Narendra Modi's imminent march to Delhi and the BJP's quintessential dilemma about his acceptability, Jaitley said that a groundswell of support was building up for Modi. As a master strategist, and a cricket honcho, he didn't believe political battles were won or lost till the last ball is bowled. Speaking at the Headlines Today's Right To Be Heard programme, Jaitley said:

> There's a growing interest in Modi as the PM candidate. This is due to a groundswell building up among the people. And it's just not because of a media buzz. When there was a media blitzkrieg against him, he had the strength to survive by addressing audiences over the heads of the media. There are few Indian politicians who have the courage to do that. I think Modi has made a huge mark on Indian polity.

C.P. Thakur, the former BJP state president of Bihar and Union health minister, also campaigned vociferously for Modi's projection as the party's prime ministerial candidate. Thakur argued, "Modi is the BJP's only chance at victory. He is the tallest leader. He motivates the cadre and presents a strong alternative. He should be projected as PM candidate—anything short of that will harm our prospects."

Thakur worked tirelessly to convince the BJP's leaders in Delhi that parting ways with the JD(U)—the inevitable fallout of Modi's elevation—would in fact be in the party's best interests. "The more acrimonious our separation, the better it is for the BJP. Now no one can prevent Modi from coming to campaign in Bihar." At a formal meeting with Rajnath Singh, Arun Jaitley, and Ram Lal on 18 April 2013, long before the Goa conclave, Thakur and a handful of other Bihar BJP leaders strongly argued that Modi's projection would be far more important for the party's prospects in the state than sticking with the JD(U). There were many others who shared this view: failing to name Modi as the prime ministerial candidate would will only dilute the party's message and diminish its appeal.

For all practical purposes, the media and a large chunk of the political dispensation within the country had, by the end of April 2023, assumed Narendra Modi would be the BJP's prime ministerial candidate. Based on the rumours, the BJP's allies within the NDA had also begun to voice their opinion. Some of them, such as the SAD, were on the same page as the BJP. Sukhbir Singh Badal, the president of the SAD, pitched Modi's name in January 2013 and came out in support of Modi's developmental track record, thanks to his excellent rapport with Jaitley. After all, Jaitley had been the in-charge of Punjab for many years and he had stitched a formidable alliance for the BJP with the SAD, and a personal friendship with Badal.

Others like the Shiv Sena in Maharashtra and Nitish Kumar in Bihar were problematic. The possibility of a crucial NDA ally Nitish Kumar walking out of the alliance could be the biggest hurdle in Modi's elevation. But Jaitley said, "Politics is not about everything coming to you easily. Managing contradictions is the art of governance. In 1989, V.P Singh became Prime Minister with support of BJP and Left. Once every week, he would hold dinner diplomacy with both the Left and BJP to stay in power. I am continuously in touch with Nitish Kumar. There's nothing to worry."

BJP's National Executive Meeting, Goa, June 2013

June 2013 was a tumultuous month for the BJP, the principal opposition party. The possibility of Narendra Modi being given a greater responsibility for the 2014 elections, if not being named as the party's prime ministerial candidate, had become apparent before the 2013 national executive meeting. L.K. Advani, Yashwant Sinha, Jaswant Singh, B.C. Khanduri, and a few more, including Uma Bharti, decided to give the meeting a miss. While Ravi Shankar Prasad, who was the Deputy Leader of the Opposition in the Rajya Sabha, was in Sri Lanka with a delegation, newly appointed general secretary Varun Gandhi was in Paris due to some personal reasons. This made it abundantly clear what an uphill task it would be to get the leadership to jointly put their weight behind a single candidate. Jaitley was in the forefront in ensuring that the plan was carried out. While Sushma Swaraj backed Advani, Jaitley led the Modi supporters.

On 9 June 2013, the final day of the executive meeting, Rajnath Singh was the last person to speak. In his twenty-five-minute-long address, Rajnath Singh sounded the clarion call. As his address drew to an end, Rajnath Singh proposed the creation of a central campaign committee and then, without further ado, announced Narendra Modi as its chairman, to a thunderous applause that took a while to die. Rajnath Singh asked Modi to join the others on the podium. The announcement was so unexpected that there was no bouquet to felicitate Modi with. So Rajnath Singh picked up one lying next to the lectern, which had been given to someone else before, and handed it to him. Rajnath Singh's unexpected and terse announcement was clear enough of what lay ahead. The appointment brought Narendra Modi one step closer to being made the party's prime ministerial candidate.

After the national executive meeting, Arun Jaitley, Rajnath Singh, and Narendra Modi addressed the Karyakarta meeting at Taleigao Community Centre in Panaji on the same day. Addressing the workers, Rajnath Singh said his decision to make Modi the campaign committee chief was not for the party, but for the country. He said he had no hesitation in taking this significant decision as this was well deserved. Arun Jaitley said that the time had come to give the country a strong leadership. Addressing the party's cadre, Arun Jaitley said that by naming Modi as the head of the poll panel, BJP president Rajnath Singh had given a new direction to the politics of this country. Talking about a strong leader, senior party leader Jaitley said, "Taking decisions is the hallmark of a strong leader." Comparing the BJP and the Congress, Jaitley said, "Our party is not a dynastic party. In a party where views are taken from thousands of workers, taking decisions are not easy." Jaitley added, "By taking a decision on Modi, Rajnath has given a face to not only the emotions of the cadre of BJP but that of crores of people of this country." However, he emphasised that the responsibility bestowed on the Gujarat chief minister was not easy.

Lambasting the Congress for policy paralysis and corruption, Jaitley said, "Congress has made this country leaderless. It is not being able take decisions ... The economic situation of the country is in a bad shape. Investment is down. Poverty is rising. Corruption is on a high ... This is the most corrupt government in India's history." The BJP leader also did not spare Prime Minister Manmohan Singh and criticised him for being seen as a weak prime minister. "Never in the history of India has the office of PM been seen in this manner. The office of the PM has become a target of humour, jokes and sarcasm," he said.

Jaitley also praised all the states where the BJP was in power and extolled the party's chief ministers for their ability to take decisions. He categorically stated that for the BJP, the poll campaign for the 2014 general elections had started. Jaitley said, "When the appropriate time comes, the best within the system takes over. Even when we had the tallest leader in our party, Atal Bihari Vajpayee, it was only on the eve of the 1996 elections, that Advani announced Atal-ji's name as leader of the party."

While the Advani camp had been busy theorising about a "compromise formula" with the RSS, its chief, Mohan Bhagwat, was quick to clarify that Modi was his final choice. At an RSS function in Meerut on 18 June 2013, one day after the JD(U) parted ways with the BJP, Bhagwat made a veiled reference to the "secularist" objections Advani and Nitish Kumar had put forth against Modi—the only national leader in the BJP who could be considered an icon of hard Hindutva in the same way Advani once was. "Whether somebody likes it or not," Bhagwat said, "Hindutva is the only way to bring about change in the country. It is where the country's respect lies."

The writing was on the wall: Modi would lead the BJP into the next elections with the staunch backing of the RSS. Given that the "last hurdle" to declaring Modi the prime ministerial candidate—Nitish Kumar—had now been removed, it was only "a matter of time" before the party made an official announcement, which was likely to come after the assembly elections scheduled in five states: Delhi, Chhattisgarh, Madhya Pradesh, Rajasthan and Mizoram in December 2013.

As expected, Nitish Kumar decided to part ways with the BJP. His decision was political rather than ideological, in spite of his recent speeches about secularism. The BJP had never won more than 182 seats in a Lok Sabha election, and if it couldn't top that figure in 2014, its putative allies might be in a position to demand an alternative to Modi—or, Kumar presumably hoped, to put forth one of their own for the position. Other regional parties who might consider an alliance with a Modi-less BJP—like the TMC in West Bengal, the BJD in Odisha, or the TDP in Andhra Pradesh—were also eyeing the electoral arithmetic. Jaitley was confident that Modi's was a wave and that he could lead the saffron party to a sweeping victory. In the event Nitish Kumar's help was needed at that stage, he was hopeful of bringing Kumar back into the fold. If the BJP had enough seats to form the government, but not enough to install Modi as the prime minister, Jaitley's ties with Kumar would help him immensely. But if Modi managed to lead the BJP to more than the historic high of 182 seats, and become the prime minister, he would still need friends in Delhi, where Jaitley was a powerful ally with clout in the media and the corporate world.

★

Modi did not have to wait till December. The BJP decided much earlier to bet on him. Ending weeks of backroom manoeuvrings at the behest of the RSS, on 12 September 2013, Narendra Modi was named the NDA's prime ministerial candidate after the party's Central Parliamentary Board unanimously elected the Gujarat chief minister as the one to lead them in the Lok Sabha elections. Immediately after the board meeting, Modi, accompanied by other members, barring Advani and ailing former Prime Minister Atal Bihari Vajpayee, walked into the media conference room. Amid sound of conch shells, BJP president Rajnath Singh made the announcement, followed by his brief media statement. The twelve-member board meeting was attended by Rajnath Singh, Murli Manohar Joshi, M. Venkaiah Naidu, Nitin Gadkari, Sushma Swaraj, Arun Jaitley, Narendra Modi, Ananth Kumar, Thawar Chand Gehlot (the most noticeable face of the BJP for the SCs from Madhya Pradesh), and Ramlal (a senior RSS leader). The Shiv Sena also announced its support to Modi's candidature.

"We will leave no stone unturned to ensure BJP's victory," said Modi. Later, he also coined a slogan "nayi soch, nayi ummeed" (new thinking, new hope) before party cadres and vowed that the BJP would contest the 2014 polls on good governance and development plank, while continuing to raise issues like corruption and price rise. Jaitley later acknowledged that despite many hurdles, on 13 September 2013, the BJP managed to decide on the candidature of Narendra Modi as the prime minister.

After Modi was declared the BJP's prime ministerial candidate, BJP president Rajnath Singh, senior leader Jaitley, and former president Gadkari visited Gujarat to meet Modi, discuss prospective changes in the Gujarat government, and plan a course of action in Delhi. The meeting symbolised change in the party—Modi as the new power centre and Jaitley as his confidante. Major decisions had been traditionally taken by the party's Parliamentary Board, its highest decision-making forum, which included party veterans L.K. Advani and Murli Manohar Joshi, besides Sushma Swaraj, M. Venkaiah Naidu, Ananth Kumar, Thawar Chand Gehlot and Ramlal as its members. This time it was Modi and Jaitley taking key decisions on matters in Delhi and Gujarat. Amit Shah had yet to emerge as a power centre. Revenue minister Anandiben Patel emerged as the consensus candidate to take over as chief minister of Gujarat.

The 2004 general elections demonstrated that national outcomes were essentially an aggregate of state-level results, with no discernible all-India pattern. Even neighbouring states often voted in opposite directions. The 2009 general election results, however, presented a different analysis. In most parts of the country there was a visible pro-incumbency trend. The Congress did better than its otherwise natural strength in the states. The urban constituencies voted overwhelmingly in favour of the Congress. The performance of the Congress in states like Haryana, Delhi, Uttar Pradesh, Madhya Pradesh, Rajasthan, and Gujarat was much better than its strength in the legislative assemblies of those states.

Jaitley was confident that the results of the 2014 general elections were going to be different. The very acceptable persona of Manmohan Singh in 2009 had been adversely affected. Corruption, indecisiveness, weak leadership, price rise, and the terrible state of the economy have created a huge anti-incumbency environment. The Congress had withered away in Andhra Pradesh on account of a political split. It had lost partners in West Bengal and Tamil Nadu on whom it had piggy-backed to success in 2009. The political issues evolving in the run-up to the general elections were loaded against the Congress. The Congress now looked upon its new leader, Rahul Gandhi, as a possible saviour.

With Modi as the BJP's candidate, it was clear that the nature of the contest would be more presidential. In the 2009 general elections, the Congress and the BJP shared 323 Lok Sabha seats among themselves. This figure was not likely to reduce in the forthcoming elections. With anti-incumbency working against the Congress, the party's alliance being in shambles in several states and the near sweep situation of 2009 in urban India likely to be reversed, the odds were loaded against the Congress. The possibility of the BJP forging way ahead appeared real.

15

Abki Baar Modi Sarkar

Though named prime ministerial candidate in September 2013 for the 2014 general elections, Narendra Modi was still the chief minister of Gujarat. He chose to operate out of Gandhinagar in Gujarat, leaving Delhi in the trusted hands of his friend Jaitley. Amit Shah was chosen to focus on Uttar Pradesh. At the same time, Modi sent some of his trusted advisers on an undercover mission around the country to get a first-hand idea of the situation on the ground. They did not declare that they represented Modi, so as to avoid any biases while they collected the information. These intelligence inputs were crucial to the design of his messages to the people. The way he thought about it was that his campaign had to be national but his appeal had to be local to the people.[1] In his own mind, Modi had divided the campaign into three phases. The first, "the preparatory period", which was over by then. The second, from September to early December, would focus on the upcoming legislative assembly elections in four key states, including Delhi, while planning the details of the third phase, the national campaign, to come soon after.[2]

At the heart of the planning was, obviously, Modi himself, while Jaitley, and the BJP's national treasurer and the head of the party's information communication campaign committee, Piyush Goyal, played the role of facilitators and enablers of the campaign. The BJP set up twenty committees

---

1. Lance Price, *The Modi Effect: Inside Narendra Modi's Campaign to Transform India* (Hodder & Stoughton, 2015), p. 101.

2. Ibid.

to focus on various aspects of electioneering as early as July 2013 with the intent of campaigning in states including Madhya Pradesh, Chhattisgarh, Rajasthan, and so on, where local elections were due ahead of the national polls. The campaign committee was led by the likes of senior bigwigs Jaitley, Amit Shah, and Sushma Swaraj. Another team led by Amit Shah, former cricketer Navjot Singh Sidhu, and Poonam Mahajan set out to woo new voters. There was even a panel led by Rajiv Pratap Rudy, Prakash Javadekar, and so on to mobilise intellectuals, and another committee to campaign in the informal sector. A group had also specially been set up to highlight the misrule of the UPA. There was also a committee to handle social media, and another core committee for media, besides an election commission cell.[3]

The BJP also roped in Piyush Pandey, who in turn brought in Ogilvy and Mather (O&M) agency Soho Square for the BJP's poll extravaganza. Pandey was initially reluctant to associate with political campaigning. David Ogilvy, O&M's founder who is often hailed as the father of advertising, was against the idea of working with politicians. One of the many hazards of working with them, David Ogilvy had argued, was not being paid on time besides having to mislead consumers about cantankerous politicos. This was why Pandey had held back in the past. But after Modi spoke to him,[4] Pandey yielded.

Pandey had worked with Modi for more than three years, making commercials for Gujarat Tourism. Pandey's apprehension, however, was whether his creative freedom would be appreciated by politicians. "There was scepticism on our part," he admitted. "We wondered what it would be like working for a political party without a marketing manager—which is what we were used to in our day-to-day work. These were political heavyweights with strong points of view. How much space would we get to express ourselves? Who would be the decision-maker? All these questions came to mind." However, after meeting BJP leaders such as Arun Jaitley, Amit Shah, Nirmala Sitharaman, Prakash Javadekar, and Piyush Goyal, his fears were allayed a bit. These appeared to be a sorted-out group of people who were very clear about what they wanted, he thought.[5] Pandey then roped in Shoojit Sircar—the National Award-winning

---

3. N.P. Ullekh, *War Room: The People, Tactics and Technology Behind Narendra Modi's 2014 Win* (Roli, 2015, 2019), pp. 36–51.

4. Ibid.

5. Ibid.

director of Bollywood films such as *Vicky Donor* and *Madras Cafe*—in making close to ten short films every night. Manish Sherawat, an animation expert, made television spots featuring Modi for broadcast during the Indian Premier League (IPL) cricket matches. Sherawat is a product of the National Institute of Design (NID), a premier design school based out of Ahmedabad.

★

Piyush's team operated out of a virtual fortress in Taj Vivanta near Khan Market soon after they were brought on board in late 2013. Designing advertisements that were both appealing and meaningful to a wider audience was crucial for the BJP, especially given its past missteps in this area. Exactly ten years earlier, in the 2004 general elections, the BJP-led coalition—which was awash in corporate cash—lost despite a high-voltage campaign titled "India Shining". Voters decisively rejected the ruling Hindu nationalist party, confirming fears that India's so-called economic boom during the NDA rule did very little to lift the fortunes of the majority. The NDA, having made the strategic blunder of advancing the elections by six months, suffered a heavy defeat in the country's first fully electronic polls.

Amit Shah and Jaitley insisted on a presidential-style campaign with the entire focus on Modi because his popularity was, according to an internal survey, much higher than his party's. Jaitley had publicly stated a year ago that a Rahul Gandhi versus Narendra Modi battle would be quasi-presidential, and Modi would score over Rahul in the electoral contest. Anti-incumbency against the UPA was strong, and the elections were thus fought both on that sentiment and on the positive appeal of hope embodied by Narendra Modi.[6]

Shah respected Jaitley as an election strategist and as a politician who understood the media like no other leader in the party. Their camaraderie strengthened in July 2010 when Shah was put behind bars after being charged by the CBI in the Sohrabuddin fake encounter case. Jaitley visited Shah in Ahmedabad's Sabarmati jail to show solidarity—a gesture Shah never forgot. Jaitley was vocal about his admiration for his younger colleague's unflagging energy, and commitment to the party ideology.

---

6. Arun Jaitley, *A New India: Selected Writings 2014–19* (Juggernaut, 2020), pp. 344–45.

On 30 October 2010, the Supreme Court gave Shah twenty-four hours to leave Gujarat. Shah came straight to Jaitley's house. Jaitley was livid. He immediately had his house in New Delhi's Bengali Market cleaned, stocked it with provisions, and offered that Shah move in. Shah didn't have to take up the offer finally, but he was touched by the generous gesture.[7] Jaitley became Shah's closest ally in his political and legal travails.[8] He defended Shah, accusing the then political government at the Centre for implicating Shah; he then said that there was legally no admissible evidence against Shah. Jaitley was amongst the few voices that consistently maintained over the years that the prosecution of Amit Shah was politically motivated.[9] As already mentioned earlier, as the Leader of the Opposition, he wrote a letter to Prime Minister Manmohan Singh on 27 September 2013 to the effect.

Jaitley and Shah believed that the campaign should provide a political expression for a failing economy; just as material progress relieves political anxieties, economic anxieties convert quickly into political upheavals. That is also when radical politicians who challenge the prevailing order trounce the ruling establishment. This was exactly how they wanted to pitch Modi to voters. His campaign for the 2014 elections was to be premised on projecting him as an anti-establishment challenger subverting the prevailing order for a better future. Some senior BJP leaders did at one point suggest making the campaign more about the party than a personality, but no other voice endorsed it.[10] Pandey later said in an interview that he found BJP leaders like Jaitley and Sitharaman very helpful.[11]

---

7. "Shah Broke Down When Jaitley Lost His Only Election", *The Times of India*, accessed 25 May 2025, https://timesofindia.indiatimes.com/india/shah-broke-down-when-jaitley-lost-his-only-election/amp_articleshow/70824179.cms.

8. P.R. Ramesh and N.P. Ullekh, "Axis of Power 2014", *Open*, accessed 25 May 2025, https://openthemagazine.com/features/india/axis-of-power-2014/.

9. "Sohrabuddin Case: Jaitley Praises Ruling on Amit Shah, Say He Was Targeted to Get to Modi", *Firstpost*, accessed 25 May 2025, https://www.firstpost.com/politics/sohrabuddin-case-jaitley-praises-ruling-on-amit-shah-say-he-was-targeted-to-get-to-modi-2023937.html.

10. N.P. Ullekh, *War Room: The People, Tactics and Technology Behind Narendra Modi's 2014 Win* (Roli, 2015, 2019), pp. 36–51.

11. Ibid.

When Pandey first presented his campaign concept to the BJP team, there was discomfort. This was something out of the ordinary, something unheard of for a political campaign. Instead of being narrated a tale, the viewer was being asked to stretch his or her imagination and visualise what may have happened in the past. Instead of overt suggestion, this was a covert emotional appeal disguised as a rational argument. It was precisely what one would expect from one of the largest and most acclaimed advertising experts in the world. Pandey observed that a few key people in the BJP core team were true leaders and decision-makers who made his job easier. Once, for instance, Nirmala Sitharaman—whom he called a "great confidence-giver"—took him aside at a meeting and told him, "You are absolutely right. Stick to your point. Otherwise, this meeting can go haywire. I love what you're doing."

In another instance, when Pandey presented short animated films to be shown on television during the IPL matches, she encouraged him in a similar way, saying, "This is brilliant stuff." In yet another instance, there was a debate over the use of the word "*pragati*" versus "*vikas*", both of which mean "progress". Pandey wanted to use the term "*pragati*" in one of the advertisements, as it is more easily understood by the common man, but some of the party workers wanted to use the word "*vikas*", often flouted by politicos. Modi's main man Amit Shah put an end to the discussion, saying curtly, "Cut the crap. The ad-agency people are saying pragati, use that. Move on."

"All it takes is two or three key people to say they love it, and then everyone else falls in line. Decisions are made by leaders, not committees," said Pandey.[12]

Pandey's team made close to ten short films every night. The last line of each commercial "*Abki baar Modi sarkar*" (This time Modi's government) was inspired largely from the motto "*Abki bari Atal Bihari*" (This time, Atal Bihari) used successfully in the 1990s by the BJP for Vajpayee. This was to be lapped up by the public and went on to become the key refrain of the entire election campaign. While Pandey wrote the hugely popular "*Abki baar Modi Sarkar*" and "*Janta maaf nahi karegi*" (Public will not forgive) slogans for numerous commercials, Praveen Khandelwal wrote the equally powerful "*Achche din aane waale hain*" (Good days are coming) that continues to be a hit among Modi admirers.

---

12. Ibid.

At the peak of the poll campaign, *"Abki baar Modi Sarkar"* was the most potent slogan and one of the most popular election catchphrases ever in the history of Indian elections. The highly striking Hindi phrase was an instant hit with the man on the street. It went viral on the internet and the remarkable coherence of the ad campaign perhaps foretold Modi's decisive win.

Lyricist Prasoon Joshi created a full-length song in the initial stages of the election campaign, *"Saugandh mujhe iss mitti ki, mein desh nahi mitne doonga"* which featured Modi's voice punctuating a high-decibel passionate appeal for political change. It was launched at a press conference by Arun Jaitley, who had played a major role in the creation of the song.

Manish Sherawat made television spots featuring Modi for broadcast during the IPL cricket matches. "I needed someone who could keep things confidential and who was also highly creative. Manish and I worked as a two-man team—I would write the script and Manish would make the storyboard," Pandey said. It was an out-of-the-box campaign, and it had to be, Pandey posited. "The audience is very different out there—they were young and they would be high on cricket when these ads were to be broadcast. I couldn't very well do something with a lot of *rona dhona* (crying). I told the BJP guys I wanted to make an animation film. We would use satire; we would be inspired by the cartoonists of the world," Pandey added.

Initially, Team BJP were taken aback, but eventually they decided to let the expert do his job and got on with theirs. "I did seventeen of those, they were twenty seconds each. They became a rage overnight," Pandey remembered.[13] The first of the animation series launched with the line: *"Bina captain ke team karegi haar, Isliye abki baar Modi Sarkar"* (Without a captain, the team will lose / That is why, this time, Modi government).

With a bespectacled cricket umpire as protagonist, the cartoons were simply sketched black lines on a saffron background with a cheeky sense of humour that relied on the audience's knowledge of politics to make their point. The first one was a dig at the Congress party's lack of leadership; another showed a cricketer offering the umpire wads of cash, which the umpire refused, hinting at the "corruption-free" promise of "Modi Sarkar".

A rewarding commercial made by Pandey that had a huge impact on the ground was one that guided people to press on the lotus symbol on the

13. Ibid.

electronic voting machine. Titled *"kamal par button dabao"* (press the button next to the lotus flower), it was launched in the light of complaints that rivals were using Modi's name to misinform illiterate people that his symbol was the cycle, elephant, and so on. One of the videos in the campaign showed a person sitting and pressing a button on and off. Another person says to him, "Why are you pressing the button? There is no electricity." The first person says, "I know that; I am just practising. When I press the lotus button, there will be electricity."

Pandey later said that selling Modi was easy.

> He is an ad man's delight. He is a doer as evident from his own rallies in the first part of the campaign. He is a person with tremendous energy—would anyone doubt that? He travelled like a maniac; it was insane to see his schedule. Everywhere he went, he changed scripts to match the audience and circumstances, and then he went and delivered them with the same energy as he'd done in the morning somewhere else. So it was a concentrated effort on a daily basis: there was advertising, there were *karyakartas* on the ground, there were 3D rallies and then there were people on social media doing their bit. It was a mega-strategic affair. I don't think any party has thought of their strategy this well, in India at least.

No ad assault or reach-out programme using hi-tech would have made an impact if the party machinery hadn't worked with clockwork precision—the kind they themselves admit had never been attempted before.

The BJP had in place a "highly reasonable team of party workers" to vet commercials to make sure that they fit in perfectly with its political vision. A BJP team at its Ashoka Road office in Delhi, led by the likes of UK-based Modi supporter Manoj Ladwa, had the task of endorsing all television and print commercials along with other slogans to ensure their compatibility with the overall campaign. For example, a lot of attention had to be paid to ensure that each video and poster had the BJP symbol, lotus, on it. Also, each radio ad or brief film had to be region-specific. It wouldn't release propaganda material that denounced law and order problems in BJP-ruled states. There were many other benchmarks too.

"We had to take extreme caution, be alert all the time and give utmost attention to detail. The planning we did at the BJP headquarters—which was monitored by party leaders such as J.P. Nadda and Jaitley—was quite extraordinary," said Vijay Chauthaiwale who was part of a team of pros based out of the BJP headquarters whose task was to coordinate between war rooms. This team was spearheaded by Ladwa, who, interestingly, was at the forefront of a years-long campaign demanding a visa for Modi in the United Kingdom—which Modi got even before he was elected as the prime minister.

Pandey attributed the success of the campaign to leaders like Amit Shah, Arun Jaitley, Nirmala Sitharaman, Piyush Goyal, and a few others who took important decisions at crucial moments. "Otherwise, these discussions in committees would not end till the cows came home," he laughed heartily.

Despite his reluctance to accept credit for the BJP's win, there is no doubt that Pandey's advertisements contributed no less to the creation of the Modi juggernaut than rallies and the hi-tech campaign managed by the likes of social media supporters, grassroots volunteers, various party panels, and the RSS, concede BJP leaders.

All this did not come without a cost, however, and Pandey always insisted on working with world-class production teams. He didn't want to create "Doordarshan-style" (DD) films, he said, referring to India's government-owned national television, looked down upon by media professionals for its shoddy production quality. In the first instance, he had put his foot down and said a short film would cost upwards of Rs 15 lakh, and, to his pleasant surprise, party leaders agreed.

> Though they had expected the budget to be around Rs 5 lakh per film, they understood my point. I asked them, do you want a DD kind of film? I can make it for Rs 5 lakh. But I won't put my name to it, because it's not me. Secondly, it wouldn't do them any good either. Did they want to make a film for the sake of making a film or were they making a film that would have an impact and get talked about? Modi would brush aside conformists who wanted to stick to tried-and-tested slogans and themes for the Gujarat Tourism campaign. Modi's attitude was: "I have hired an expert. The expert has given me a good

> reason of how we could be different from others. Who said we have to follow a format?" That is the beauty of the man.[14]

There was complete clarity about the core messaging of the campaign. On his part, Narendra Modi was promising *achche din* (good days), that became synonymous with a strong leader fixing the rot and corruption. The campaign was all about Modi Shining, Modi Smiling, Modi Descending, Modi Coming, Modi Waving, Modi Speaking, and so on. Brand Modi was all around us, on television, in billboards, on radio, in print ads, and so on. The phrase "presidential style" would be somewhat inadequate to describe the contours of the campaign to those who did not see it for themselves.[15] Inside a building in Lodhi Estate in New Delhi, professionals brainstormed about getting the pitch right for each stage of the electoral battle. They looked into details about getting traction on social media platforms, jingles, and slogans. Then came the formal release of advertisements that were created by Soho Square. But as mentioned before, at each stage, various loyalists were consulted.

Javadekar ran a tight press office operation with the help of party's head of media, Shrikant Sharma. Everybody was at their desks by 6.30 in the morning to read the newspapers and monitor the main national radio and television broadcasts between 7.00 a.m. and 11.00 a.m. At 9 o'clock there would be a teleconference with the main political leaders, like Arun Jaitley and Rajnath Singh. They would discuss the main issues that were running in the media and decide how the party should respond. At 11.00 somebody, usually one of the politicians, would make a statement in front of the cameras on behalf of the party and perhaps take one or two questions.

The main news conference would be at 3.00 p.m., when journalists could ask whatever they liked. The team would then meet again to assess how their stories were running in the media and to answer any last-minute questions from the BJP spokespeople who would represent the party on the evening discussion shows. These programmes took up a lot of time and effort and

14. N.P. Ullekh, "Abki Baar Modi Sarkar: Whose Line Was It Anyway?", *Scroll.in*, accessed 25 May 2025, https://scroll.in/article/721624/abki-baar-modi-sarkar-whose-line-was-it-anyway.

15. Saba Naqvi, *The Saffron Storm: From Vajpayee to Modi* (Penguin, 2018), p. 238.

it was part of Javadekar's job to make sure all the spokespeople around the country knew what to say—"the line to take". He would hold a teleconference call, using audio bridge technology, every afternoon. "There are nearly two hundred state-level spokesmen and panellists who go on the various TV shows. In every Indian language now, in each state, there are at least ten news channels, out of which at least five do live debates in the evening. So, it's a big thing."[16]

★

Towards the fag end of Modi's chief ministership, Gujarat's economy had continued to grow well above 10 per cent for over a decade, and a new slogan was coined by Modi to indicate the state's inclusive growth: "*Sauno saath, sauno vikas*" (Cooperation of all, development of all). When Modi became the prime ministerial candidate, the Hindi translation of the Gujarati slogan became a national catchphrase: "*Sabka saath, sabka vikas*." A month later, Modi was at the Shri Ram College of Commerce in Delhi talking to a packed audience of students about his vision for India.

In October 2013, Jaitley travelled to New Jersey to address the Overseas Friends of BJP (OFBJP)-USA community, a brain child of Mahesh Mehta and Mukund Mody. Between 1960 and 2000, the Indian population in the United States had grown rapidly, more than doubling every decade; simultaneously, the community's political concerns and social needs grew as well. Indian political organisations at the time began paying more attention to the political potential of the diaspora.[17] The foundation of the OFBJP is an interesting story. Mehta, the OFBJP's national coordinator, met M.S. Golwalkar in Ahmedabad, in 1947. Mehta was ten years old at the time; his father was involved with the RSS, and the encounter with the group's second chief left a strong impression. "His eyes looked through me, as if penetrating me," Mehta recalled. "I was instantly glued to him." Meeting Golwalkar set Mehta on a lifelong path of service to

16. Lance Price, *The Modi Effect: Inside Narendra Modi's Campaign to Transform India* (Hodder & Stoughton, 2015), pp. 153–54.

17. Vanya Mehta, "Foreign Returns", *Caravan Magazine*, accessed 25 May 2025, https://caravanmagazine.in/reportage/foreign-returns.

the Sangh Parivar—first in India, and then abroad as the founder of the VHP of America (VHPA).

At the age of twenty-two, Mehta left home to spend a year as an RSS worker in "villages and tribal areas" in Gujarat. In 1969, after earning a master's degree in chemical engineering from the University of Baroda, he moved to the United States, where he eventually came to work in the field of membrane technology. Mehta had intended to return to India, but soon became heavily involved with the overseas activities of the VHP. Noting Mehta's success in organising Hindu youth camps in Massachusetts, the VHP's co-founder and general secretary S.S. Apte insisted that Mehta stay in the United States, telling him, "Don't go back to India, you will be required here."

In the mid-1970s, Mehta was also involved with another group, the Friends of India Society International (FISI), which emerged from a 1975 protest against the Emergency, held outside the Indian Consulate in New York. The society's secretary-general was Mukund Mody, the man who eventually founded the OFBJP. By 1970, Mehta had founded the first international chapter of the VHP. In 1990, Mody met top BJP officials in India. In *India at the Crossroads*, a collection of conversations with prominent Indian Americans by the writer Prem N. Chopra, Mody talked about joining forces with like-minded NRIs to oppose Indira Gandhi from abroad, and then later to advocate for shifts in Indian foreign policy, such as allowing dual citizenship. He said that leaders including L.K. Advani "decided to open cells of BJP in foreign countries to remove misconceptions and educate people about the policies of the BJP before the national elections". Some members of the FISI, and other BJP supporters, rallied to form the OFBJP.[18]

On 10 October 2013, hundreds of enthusiastic supporters of Modi thronged the TV Asia USA auditorium at Edison, New Jersey, to hear Jaitley. TV Asia, headquartered in Edison, is a pro-BJP network that targets the South Asian community. The attendees were members of the United States chapter of the OFBJP. The mood was jubilant. OFBJP-USA leaders gave an enthusiastic welcome to Jaitley. Jaitley thanked the Indian diaspora who had gathered at a short notice to accord him a warm welcome.[19] He said, "India is undergoing a transition period for the last two decades; confidence emerged after the

18. Ibid.
19. Ibid.

economy was opened that unleashed an enormous energy effectively showcasing India to the rest of the world." He went on to recount how the country was losing direction because of the UPA government's misgovernance and massive corruption leading to the Nehru era's growth rate of slightly above 3 per cent and equalling Somalia's growth rate. He said that during the NDA government's tenure, India achieved a growth rate in the range of 7–10 per cent.

Jaitley thundered from that dais that in a democracy a prime minister should lead from the front and should be decisive and strong, but in the case of the UPA government, the prime minister watched haplessly as his own party vice president derided Cabinet decisions, that too on foreign shores. "Foreign policy is directionless with neither established policy nor strategy and today India's neighbourhood became dangerous with Pakistan and China making incursions at will. We share a porous border with Bangladesh which also adds to our woes with illegal immigration," he said. He pointed out that a systematic misuse of government agencies such as CBI against political opponents and allies alike had become a norm. There was unease everywhere and people were frustrated. The conditions were favourable to the BJP and people were looking for a strong and decisive leader, Narendra Modi, who had provided good governance in his state of Gujarat. Jaitley assured the supporters that once the BJP and the NDA came to power, they would work hard to turn up the economy, and improve the internal and external security situation. He urged the Indian diaspora to contribute in every form to help the BJP bring the change. Jaitley received a standing ovation.[20]

★

The 2014 Lok Sabha elections, as predicted and as planned by Modi and Jaitley, turned out to be one-sided. The BJP secured a majority of its own. The NDA won with a very comfortable majority. India was blessed with a single-party majority government after three decades. Hopes soared, aspirations rose sky-high, and every section of the population looked forward to a new dawn.

---

20. Arun Jaitley, "Arun Jaitley Speech in New Jersey", in *Articles & Speeches by Arun Jaitley: A Compilation* (Universal Law Publishing Co. Pvt. Ltd., 2014), pp. 231–32.

Indians wanted to vote for an economy in which more and more people would get quality jobs, health, and education.[21]

Modi's reliance on Jaitley did not end with the election. The friendship was further bolstered after Modi became the prime minister. New to the maze of Lutyens' Delhi in 2014, Modi needed Jaitley to make forays into and familiarise himself with the corridors of power. While Amit Shah worked on strengthening the BJP, Modi banked on Jaitley to deal with any problem that his government might face.

It was not just what Modi said, but how and where he said it that seemed to have special resonance in Uttar Pradesh. At a rally in Gorakhpur on 23 January 2014, Modi asked the crowd, "How many hours do you get electricity?" They responded with, "We don't get power." Modi reminded them that in Gujarat there was twenty-four-hour electricity, and taunted the leader of the SP state government, Akhilesh Yadav, saying he would never be able to turn Uttar Pradesh into Gujarat. "You need a fifty-six-inch chest to do that," announced Modi. Because of its significance, the state got more than its fair share of mega-rallies, with people travelling huge distances only to hear him speak.

★

Jaitley kept a diary during the last leg of campaigning in May 2014. In it he recorded his thoughts on a range of topics.[22] He later shared that the high point of this election was the energy displayed by Modi. During the campaign Modi had not missed a single meeting. He visited every nook and corner of India, and even in areas where the BJP was not strong enough, he managed to create a momentum in favour of the BJP.[23] Another high point of the election was the huge rallies and a very large turnout. The campaign strategies also expanded. Besides conventional public contact programmes, the use of media,

---

21. Puja Mehra, *Lost Decade (2008–18): How India's Growth Story Devolved into Growth Without a Story* (Penguin Random House, 2019), pp. 128–29.

22. Arun Jaitley, *A New India: Selected Writings 2014–19* (Juggernaut, 2020), p. 331.

23. Ibid., 344–45.

advertisements, and social media was quite extensive. Jaitley believed that in future elections, multiple modes of campaigning are bound to expand.[24]

Modi created the wave, with media and advertising acting as force multipliers, and then he deftly rode to a stupendous victory. Running in nine phases from 7 April to 14 May, the 2014 general elections was the longest-ever in the history of independent India. Modi finally appeared on screen in a national television studio on Saturday, 12 April, by which time the first two rounds of voting had already happened. He chose to grant the exclusive to the popular Hindi-language show *Aap ki Adalat*. The studio was set up as usual in a courtroom format, with the interviewee "in the dock" in the centre and the audience surrounding him at a distance. The programme received the highest TV ratings in India's history. Official monitoring figures showed that 74 per cent of news viewers in the country tuned in to watch.

Despite a hectic day on the campaign trail, Modi was in sparkling form, buoyed up by the enthusiastic reaction of the studio audience, who started chanting his name and applauding as soon as he appeared. It went on for over an hour, and while it wasn't exactly a grilling, and Modi was clearly in control of what he wanted to say, nobody could claim that the difficult issues hadn't been raised. He was asked about the Gujarat riots, the ban on him entering the United States, his attitude towards Muslims, the charge that his image was all spin and didn't always fit the facts, and much else besides.[25]

As the campaign drew to a close, Jaitley said, "I have no doubt that large turnouts necessarily mean a decisive vote. A decisive vote in this election can only be a pro-Modi, pro-BJP or pro-NDA vote. As polling will draw to a close today, exit polls will be telecast. Pollsters normally have a tendency to err on the side of caution." He also made a prescient prediction that the Congress party would respond to defeat by setting up a committee to come out with a report on reasons for loss.[26]

Towards the end of the campaign, the national BJP team booked an entire floor in Varanasi's Surya Hotel in the cantonment area. The hotel became the venue for press conferences which were held each day by BJP spokespersons.

---

24. Ibid.

25. Lance Price, *The Modi Effect: Inside Narendra Modi's Campaign to Transform India* (Hodder & Stoughton, 2015), pp. 158–59.

26. Arun Jaitley, *A New India: Selected Writings 2014–19* (Juggernaut, 2020), p. 331.

Next to the Surya Hotel is the Radisson Hotel, where the big guns of the party moved in. Amit Shah stationed himself there, as did journalists Swapan Dasgupta and Ashok Malik who were expected to explain the Modi phenomena to foreign journalists. After his election campaign in Punjab, Arun Jaitley also came over for a few days. He played host to the media.[27]

★

20 May 2014 turned out to be a historic moment for the BJP. The BJP won 282 seats on its own, safely past the halfway point of 272 seats. The biggest recovery for the party happened in Uttar Pradesh. The BJP won 71 of the 80 seats in the elections.

India had shifted on its axis and elected an individual who projected himself as the Supreme Leader. All the opposition towards Modi just a few months ago was a thing of the past. Jaitley's tireless efforts over the last two years had come to fruition. The election results brought a break from the long period of coalition governments, where no party had crossed the majority mark of 272 seats on its own. The NDA tallied 336 seats, thus accounting for the largest majority government since the 1984 general elections. With over 814 million people voting, this was the largest election in the world. The Congress, the second largest party, had garnered only 44 seats or 8.1 per cent of the votes.[28] Modi won from Varanasi. He polled 581,022 votes, securing 56.37 per cent of the votes polled in the constituency. The runner-up Arvind Kejriwal of AAP got 209,238 votes. Congress's Ajay Rai got 75,614. Modi's margin of victory was 3.71 lakh votes.

The NDA's historic win under Modi, which brought the BJP to power with a full majority after three decades, marked not just a political triumph but also a personal vindication for Jaitley, who had stood firmly behind Modi's leadership despite internal and external challenges. For Jaitley, the victory was a moment of validation. He had been one of the earliest voices within

---

27. Saba Naqvi, *The Saffron Storm: From Vajpayee to Modi* (Penguin, 2018), p. 245.

28. "Election Results 2014: India Places Its Faith in Moditva", *Times of India*, accessed 25 May 2025, https://timesofindia.indiatimes.com/news/election-results-2014-india-places-its-faith-in-moditva/articleshow/35224486.cms.

the BJP to advocate for Modi as the party's prime ministerial candidate, even when sections of the party and allies were sceptical. The resounding mandate proved that Modi's leadership, combined with Jaitley's strategic acumen, had struck a chord with the Indian electorate.

The 2014 victory also brought a sense of relief for Jaitley. The BJP had suffered two consecutive defeats in 2004 and 2009, and there was growing pressure to reinvent itself. Modi's elevation as the face of the campaign was a bold gamble, and Jaitley had been instrumental in ensuring party unity behind this decision. The landslide win silenced critics and reinforced Jaitley's belief in Modi's mass appeal. As someone who had worked tirelessly behind the scenes—drafting policies, negotiating alliances, and countering opposition narratives—Jaitley felt a deep sense of fulfilment seeing their collective efforts bear fruit.

The BJP's campaign slogan may have been "*Abki baar Modi Sarkar*", but, as Congress leader Abhishek Manu Singhvi jocularly told Arun Jaitley in Parliament's Central Hall, the reality is "*Abki baar Jaitley Sarkar*".[29] However, while the Modi wave swept several parts of India including the north, Jaitley, one of the chief architects of this victory, lost his own election from Amritsar against former Punjab Chief Minister Captain Amarinder Singh of the Congress, despite Modi campaigning for him.

---

29. "Why Arun Jaitley is Modi's 'Chanakya'", Rediff, accessed 25 May 2025, https://m.rediff.com/money/slide-show/slide-show-1-union-budget-why-arun-jaitley-is-called-as-modis-chanakya/20140705.htm.

16

The Defeat in Amritsar

On 17 May 2014, *The Telegraph* headline screamed—"How the mighty fell—Jaitley jolt lone blot in 'ocean' of joy." The newspaper reported that the only bad news for the BJP in its dream-come-true election performance in May 2014 came from Amritsar, where the party's key strategist Arun Jaitley failed to surmount the heaviest of odds in his debut Lok Sabha contest.[1] Jaitley lost to the Congress party's Amarinder Singh by about 1.02 lakh votes from the hotly contested seat. Jaitley's defeat brought a deep sense of disappointment amid euphoria in the BJP camp. To Jaitley, the key strategist behind the BJP's 2014 victory, his own trouncing was a big setback. Amritsar was his first foray into a popular election after forty years. He had last contested the DUSU presidency in 1974.

Jaitley had been a member of the Rajya Sabha all these years—first elected in 2000 and re-elected in 2006, 2012, and 2018. Jaitley was thrice elected to the Rajya Sabha from Gujarat and two of these terms came when Modi was the chief minister of the state. The fourth was from Uttar Pradesh. It is ironical that the best performing MP failed the people's test in 2014. The defeat was a rare personal setback for him as even the Modi wave could not help his fortune.

But Jaitley put up a brave face. Playing down his disappointment, he said his loss was "a drop" in the "ocean" of his party's massive triumph. Modi and

---

1. Sanjay K. Jha and Radhika Ramaseshan, "How the Mighty Fell—Jaitley Jolt Lone Blot in 'Ocean' of Joy", *The Telegraph*, accessed 25 May 2025, https://www.telegraphindia.com/india/how-the-mighty-fell-jaitley-jolt-lone-blot-in-ocean-of-joy/cid/182957.

Amit Shah were equally disappointed. Modi gave Jaitley a reassuring call.[2] Some in the BJP were already discussing Jaitley's fate in the wake of Amritsar rout. Many recalled that when Jaswant Singh lost in 1998, Prime Minister Atal Bihari Vajpayee, who had been keen to make him finance minister, was forced to nominate him as the deputy chairman of the Planning Commission instead. Jaswant was later brought into the Rajya Sabha and subsequently appointed finance minister.

In 1998, Vajpayee's political confidant Pramod Mahajan too lost the Lok Sabha polls. Vajpayee however, inducted him as his political secretary in the PMO and later got him a Rajya Sabha berth before absorbing him into his Cabinet. Amritsar became a sort of 'Hanamkonda' for the BJP, the constituency in the undivided Andhra Pradesh from where P.V. Narasimha Rao had contested in 1984 and lost despite the major upsurge in favour of the Congress almost all over the country. Rao was defeated by little known C. Janga Reddy of the BJP at a time when the Congress won as many as 414 Lok Sabha seats in the wake of assassination of Indira Gandhi. Rao was later elected from Ramtek in Maharashtra. In the 1984 elections, Hanamkonda was one of the two seats the BJP had won all over the country. The other seat was in Gujarat from where A.K. Patel had won.

The electoral debacle, however, did not alter Jaitley's standing in the BJP. Like Rao, who had become an important Cabinet minister in the Rajiv Gandhi government, Jaitley was also tipped to find a place in the Modi government. As the most trusted confidante of Narendra Modi, Jaitley was not only inducted in the Cabinet but given two key portfolios—finance and defence—the first time these portfolios were held by one minister. In fact, he was at the forefront of planning with the prime minister his new Cabinet and other key appointments.

★

On 15 March 2014, the BJP announced its decision to field Jaitley as its candidate for the Lok Sabha elections from Amritsar, the second-largest city in the western state of Punjab. It was decided that out of the total thirteen Lok Sabha seats in Punjab, the BJP would field its candidates in three—Amritsar, Gurdaspur, and

2. As told by Dr Narinder Dhruv Batra, Jaitley's close friend.

Hoshiarpur—while the rest would be contested by its coalition partner, the SAD. A few days later, the BJP announced Hindi cinema's star Vinod Khanna's candidature from Gurdaspur parliamentary seat. He had won the seat thrice before, but lost in 2009 polls to Congress's Partap Singh Bajwa. Vijay Sampla was picked to contest from Hoshiarpur.

Traditionally a Congress stronghold, Amritsar had backed BJP's Navjot Singh Sidhu since 2004. Sidhu was elected from Amritsar thrice—two general elections in 2004 and 2009, and one by-election in 2007. When he first won the election from Amritsar in 2004, Sidhu trounced six-time Congress MP Raghunandan Lal Bhatia by a convincing margin of over 110,000 votes.[3] Sidhu was forced to resign in 2016 after he was convicted by the Punjab and Haryana High Court in a road rage case. After his conviction was stayed by the Supreme Court, Sidhu bounced back to win the 2007 by-election by defeating then Punjab finance minister Surinder Singla of the Congress by 77,626 votes.[4]

The BJP believed that Amritsar was a safe choice for Jaitley to make his electoral debut. However, many people, even within the party, were surprised at the choice. There was not just anti-incumbency against the SAD, the BJP's ally ruling Punjab since 2007, there was a marked a wave of discontent. Punjab was perhaps the only state where the Modi wave was largely missing as it showed in the results.[5] The state was struggling with poor infrastructure, rotting cities, and agricultural decline.

In the run-up to the 2014 elections, Sidhu had become a matter of embarrassment for the party. He had lost considerable influence in the constituency. He managed to win the seat in the 2009 Lok Sabha polls by a small margin of 7500 votes. Since then, he had concentrated more on his television appearances, rather than spending time in Amritsar. Furthermore, Sidhu started criticising Chief Minister Parkash Singh Badal and SAD president Sukhbir Singh

---

3. Bhatia, who had won from Amritsar in 1972, and again in the 1980, 1985, 1992, 1996, and 1999 elections, is a member of the Congress.

4. Kamaldeep Singh Brar, "The Rise and Fall of Navjot Singh Sidhu, the Politician", *The Indian Express*, accessed 25 May 2025, https://indianexpress.com/article/cities/amritsar/the-rise-and-fall-of-sidhu-the-politician-7926824/.

5. Vaibhav Vats, "The Urbane Face of the B.J.P. Nervous in Electoral Debut in Amritsar", *The New York Times*, accessed 25 May 2025, https://archive.nytimes.com/india.blogs.nytimes.com/2014/04/30/b-j-p-s-urbane-face-nervous-in-electoral-debut-in-amritsar/.

Badal. He openly pitched himself against the Punjab government, of which the BJP was a part. He took on BJP ministers and leaders and left no scope for the party to accommodate him. His opponents had put up "missing" posters with a reward in Amritsar constituency after Sidhu did the vanishing act from his seat for a few months in 2011.[6] Frequent public outbursts of his MLA wife Dr Navjot Kaur Sidhu, and her rebellious attitude against her own government despite being its chief parliamentary secretary, was not going down well with the party leadership. There were also concerns around the unpopularity of Bikram Singh Majithia, a local legislator from Amritsar and revenue minister in the Punjab state government, who has been accused of running a drug racket in the state.[7] What could also go against Jaitley was the eviction of Sikh farmers from BJP-ruled Gujarat's Kutch region.[8]

The Badals were insistent that Jaitley fight from Amritsar. The BJP's local leadership, including Anil Joshi and senior leaders demanded that Jaitley be given the Amritsar ticket. In a way, the move was targeted at easing out Sidhu from the scene. The BJP thought Jaitley's entry would ensure that the BJP and SAD leadership will stand unitedly behind him. But, a star campaigner for the BJP in other states, the BJP could not afford to let the three-time MP from Amritsar sulk. Sidhu was called by the BJP national leadership to Delhi and offered a seat in Delhi. However, he refused to contest from anywhere but Amritsar. Sidhu gave a small window to the party leader—he would only contest from Amritsar, but he was willing to make way for Jaitley if he was to contest from Amritsar. Sidhu was assured he could soon salvage some pride if he got back to Parliament via the Rajya Sabha route in 2014 itself.[9]

---

6. PTI, "'Missing' Posters of Navjot Singh Sidhu on Amritsar Roads Again After 10 Years", NDTV, accessed 25 May 2025, https://www.ndtv.com/india-news/missing-posters-of-navjot-singh-sidhu-on-amritsar-roads-after-10-years-2454926.

7. Vaibhav Vats, "The Urbane Face of the B.J.P. Nervous in Electoral Debut in Amritsar", *The New York Times*, accessed 25 May 2025, https://archive.nytimes.com/india.blogs.nytimes.com/2014/04/30/b-j-p-s-urbane-face-nervous-in-electoral-debut-in-amritsar/.

8. Manjeet Sehgal, "Clash of Titans in Amritsar: Jaitley vs Amarinder Singh", *India Today*, accessed 25 May 2025, https://www.indiatoday.in/mail-today/story/its-a-leap-of-faith-for-jaitley-in-amritsar-185874-2014-03-23.

9. As told by a BJP leader who did not wish to be named.

It was clear that Amritsar was not going to be a cakewalk despite the rapidly building Modi wave. "You could have contested from Delhi or Gujarat. I am not sure if Amritsar is the right choice," a friend had then opined to him. Another source said, "Some of his well-wishers tried to persuade Jaitley to contest from New Delhi or Jaipur but he perhaps thought the AAP would be a thorn in his side in the capital." Another party man suggested Jaipur.[10]

★

Jaitley had a long political association with Punjab and was familiar with the state's political landscape. He had remained involved in Punjab politics much before his candidature from Amritsar was announced. He had been in charge of Punjab for his party for many years and had championed a formidable and successful alliance with the SAD. He had a good understanding of the state's politics. The BJP's rise to national prominence in the 1990s had been accompanied by its spectacular growth in the northern regions. It had ruled state governments in Uttar Pradesh, Delhi, Himachal Pradesh, Rajasthan, Gujarat, Haryana, Madhya Pradesh. Punjab, however, stayed elusive with the BJP playing a second fiddle.

Jaitley was mindful that the ground situation in Amritsar was not very favourable. The Akalis, however, insisted he give Amritsar a shot, saying he wouldn't even need to be present—they would take care of the campaign. The Punjab BJP too was adamant that Jaitley contest from Punjab. Jaitley was hesitant about contesting an election. Not that he was afraid of losing, he just thought it would take too much of his time which he could utilise strategising for winning many other seats by his party. But when picked for Amritsar, Jaitley decided to honour the party's choice. Amritsar had a special place in his heart. His mother Ratan Prabha was born and brought up in Amritsar. His parents had arrived in Amritsar from Lahore during the Partition in 1947 after they were forced to leave Lahore at the time of the Partition. Jaitley's parents stayed

10. Vaibhav Vats, "The Urbane Face of the B.J.P. Nervous in Electoral Debut in Amritsar", *The New York Times*, accessed 25 May 2025, https://archive.nytimes.com/india.blogs.nytimes.com/2014/04/30/b-j-p-s-urbane-face-nervous-in-electoral-debut-in-amritsar/.

with his mother's relatives in Amritsar before relocating to Delhi after a few years. Jaitley's grandmother was also from a prominent family of Amritsar. Besides, being a Punjabi, he was confident that people would see him as an insider. He had worked hard for Punjab with the party. From one room to a big party office, the BJP expanded the Amritsar office due to Jaitley's efforts.

On 7 April 2014, Jaitley filed his nomination papers for the Amritsar Lok Sabha seat. He was accompanied by his family and former Himachal Pradesh Chief Minister Shanta Kumar and SAD MP Naresh Gujral. A sprawling banquet hall mostly reserved for weddings had been transformed into Jaitley's campaign headquarters; it swelled with party workers, journalists, and dozens of Jaitley's relatives. After filing nomination, Jaitley disappeared into a back room, where he held long discussions with party leaders to prepare for what could be the most critical moment of his political career.

On Sunday evening, crowds assembled at Novelty Chowk, in the heart of Amritsar, where Jaitley was due to make an appearance. A newspaper reported that when Jaitley made his public appearance, he lacked the swagger of natural politicians, appeared ill at ease in the raucous delirium as his motor cavalcade navigated the streets of Amritsar. His body language remained stiff, and he could barely bring himself to smile. Waving is almost second nature to politicians, but Jaitley often seemed lost, staring impassively into the crowd.

Later that evening, Jaitley drove to address a rally in New Amritsar, a modern enclave on the outskirts of the city. A small stage had been erected on a wide avenue, and several leaders of the SAD, including Bikram Singh Majithia, joined Jaitley. Jaitley, speaking to a small crowd, reiterated the pitch that could be the key to victory in Amritsar: Jaitley's stature and importance in a future government in New Delhi, likely to be headed by the BJP. "I want to plead with Amritsar: Join yourself with the Modi wave," he said. "To make Amritsar a successful city, we need to add Delhi's power to it."[11]

Jaitley's reputation as a reformist and a clean politician preceded him to Amritsar. A voter, Surinder Sharma, a forty-nine-year-old doctor, told the media, "This man has vision. He will do good work and be our voice in Parliament." BJP workers from Amritsar, who were campaigning for Jaitley, were enthused. A BJP worker said, "He is a good man. We are desperate for him to win. But if anyone defeats him, it will be the Akalis." An accurate

11. Ibid.

prediction based on ground reality that Jaitley's own party leaders failed to sense. There was a strong anti-incumbency wave against the Akalis that the BJP had underestimated and later admitted—the defeat in Amritsar was the result of a "grave error of judgement".

A week later, the Congress chose Amarinder Singh, a political heavyweight and a former chief minister of Punjab, to run against Jaitley. Although Amarinder only reluctantly agreed to contest the polls at the behest of AICC president Sonia Gandhi, the Patiala royal scion enjoyed a huge following among Congress supporters in Punjab. The entry of Amarinder rattled the BJP's Amritsar plan. What had initially seemed a straightforward and smooth ride for Jaitley was transformed into one of the most competitive and high-profile contests of this election. Jaitley found himself thrust into a contest far tougher than he expected. The odds were stacked against Jaitley who was contesting his first election in late-mid-career.[12] Jaitley realised, probably a trifle too late, the disruption it caused to their planning, but he decided to put up a spirited fight against Amarinder.

Jaitley contested the Amritsar election with lots of energy. He fought to win. "It was an example for us how a politician should face challenges," recalled former Amritsar Mayor Bakshi Ram Arora. Jaitley released his vision paper for Amritsar—he wanted to turn the holy city into a business hub.[13] He was pleased with the response to his rallies. On 25 April 2014, Narendra Modi addressed five rallies in Punjab. Accompanying him were Chief Minister Parkash Singh Badal and state BJP president Kamal Sharma. Each of these rallies was extremely well attended. Modi described Jaitley as a "precious diamond" at an election rally in Amritsar.[14]

---

12. Sankarshan Thakur, a commentator on India's right wing and a roving editor at *The Telegraph* newspaper.

13. Kamaldeep Singh Brar, "Jaitley remained involved in Punjab politics at ground level much before contesting from Amritsar", *The Indian Express*, accessed on 4 September 2025, https://indianexpress.com/article/india/arun-jaitley-death-demise-punjab-politics-contesting-amritsar-punjab-5933649/.

14. "Arun Jaitley: Modi's 'Precious Diamond', Original Chanakya Was a Master at Working Levers of Power", *The Times of India*, accessed 25 May 2025, https://timesofindia.indiatimes.com/india/arun-jaitley-modis-precious-diamond-original-chanakya-was-a-master-at-working-levers-of-power/articleshow/69562898.cms.

Former Chief of the Army Staff General V.K. Singh addressed a large gathering of ex-servicemen who were aggrieved by the fact that, notwithstanding the promise of implementing "One Rank One Pension", the notification giving effect to the announcement had not been issued. Additionally, the UPA's weak policy on national security had adversely impacted the mindset of those who see national security as priority. "The geopolitical realities compel us to analyse that any future aggression may see the buildup of Pakistan and China axis. Our defence purchases and preparedness have seriously suffered. Under A.K. Antony, the Raksha Mantralya has been virtually rudderless and without direction," Jaitley said.[15] Writing in his campaign diary posted in his blog, he said, "Each of these rallies was extremely well attended. The enthusiasm at the rallies, coupled with large attendance, was a giveaway." Jaitley added:

> The most significant section where the Modi appeal is clearly visible is the youth. His ability to charge up and motivate the younger generation has been most evident. In an environment of disillusionment with governance, he appears to have become a nucleus of hope. Even those who did not attend the rally were seen analysing the political impact of his visit to each of the constituencies. The mind space of Amritsar was entirely consumed by Modi's visit … Modi seemed to be inspiring a certain degree of confidence in the people that he is capable of delivering what he promises. Practitioners of aspirational politics have, therefore, put their weight behind him.[16]

He believed that Modi's visit to Punjab was going to be a game changer.[17] When Captain Amarinder Singh was asked about how he was coping with a "strong opponent" like Jaitley, he put up a bold front, "If he was Leader

---

15. Arun Jaitley, "The Campaign Diary—26/04/2014", Bharatiya Janata Party, accessed 25 May 2025, https://www.bjp.org/interviews-and-articles/article-shri-arun-jaitley-campaign-diary-26042014.

16. "Modi's Visit to Punjab a Game-changer: Jaitley", *The Pioneer*, accessed 25 May 2025, https://www.dailypioneer.com/2014/sunday-edition/modis-visit-to-punjab-a-game-changer-jaitley.html.

17. Ibid.

of the Opposition in the Rajya Sabha, I was the Chief Minister of this State, so what?"[18]

For Jaitley, the foray into a direct electoral contest became a tough one as the Congress hurled the "outsider" tag at him in a constituency dominated by Sikh voters. Being a Sikh, Sidhu had an additional appeal in the prestigious constituency. But Jaitley was hopeful as Hindu leaders have also done decently well in the Amritsar constituency. Congress stalwart Bhatia had won Amritsar a record six times. The equations changed after 2004 when the BJP introduced Sidhu in this constituency.

Initially, Jaitley rented a house on Lawrence Road for two months which was also his election office. Sangeeta Jaitley and Sonali camped in Amritsar. Sangeeta's family too carried influence in Amritsar. Although her father Girdhari Lal Dogra hailed from Jammu and Kashmir, Girdhari Lal's brothers Kishan Chand and Darbari Lal were settled in the holy city. However, both of them had passed away over a decade and a half ago.[19] During the 2014 Lok Sabha elections, Sangeeta actively supported Jaitley's political campaign, holding street-corner meetings and managing his other political affairs discreetly from behind the scenes. She ensured full day catering of food, tea, and beverages like lassi.[20] Such was the goodwill he enjoyed in the legal fraternity that when he campaigned for the Amritsar seat in 2014, scores of Delhi's top lawyers took time off from their high-paying billable hours to stomp the streets of the city for him.[21]

When Captain Singh created a din calling him an "outsider", Jaitley had to take a big decision to quieten them. He purchased a 340-square-yard,

---

18. Chander Suta Dogra, "An Uphill Task for Jaitley in Amritsar", *The Hindu*, accessed 25 May 2025, https://www.thehindu.com/elections/loksabha2014/an-uphill-task-for-jaitley-in-amritsar/article5953943.ece.

19. Neeraj Bagga, "With Jaitley's Passing Away, Amritsar Loses Connection to One of BJP's Tallest Leaders", *The Tribune*, accessed 25 May 2025, https://www.tribuneindia.com/news/archive/punjab/with-jaitley-s-passing-away-amritsar-loses-connection-to-one-of-bjp-s-tallest-leaders-822217/.

20. As told by Jaitley's confidante Narinder Dhruv Batra.

21. Coomi Kapoor, "A Man of Open Heart and Mind, Arun Jaitley Had Friends Across Divide", in *The Discussant: Journal of Centre for Reforms, Development and Justice*, Special Edition, An Obituary to Arun Jaitley, Vol. VII, No. 3 (July–September 2019), pp. 52–55.

five-bedroom house in the Green Avenue locality of Amritsar.[22] But that, too, was greeted with much heckling. He was accused of buying a house in a plush residential area of the city to offset the "outsider" tag.[23] Captain Amarinder demanded that the ECI disqualify Jaitley, pointing at the timing of the purchase of the house. Jaitley went on to contest irrespective of these allegations. He dismissed the "outsider" tag, saying he was a frequent visitor to Amritsar and had relatives there.[24]

Captain Amarinder carefully avoided any talk about the UPA's ten-year rule at the Centre. The Patiala royal scion, who had an elite personal style, had shed some of his royal ways and was reaching out to the ordinary people. While Sidhu had accused the Badals of ignoring Amritsar, Amarinder executed a lot of development work during his tenure as the chief minister. As the seat was on the radar of the Congress high command, Amarinder's detractors were not able to raise their heads.[25]

Captain Amarinder fired a daily volley of strategically aimed ammo at the SAD–BJP combine on a range of issues from misrule and high-handedness of the state government, to unemployment, drugs, and personal attacks on Jaitley, as well as the ruling Badals. Jaitley, fighting his first Lok Sabha election, was taken aback by the stridency of the attacks. "I am disappointed by the level of political discourse that Capt. Singh is indulging in," he said in the first week of his campaigning. Captain Amarinder, however, was clear on his strategy. He said that battles cannot be fought being on the defensive. But typical of Jaitley, he maintained his dignity, choosing his words carefully, never making any personal attack.

But it became clear to Jaitley he was facing two unexpected hurdles in this high-stakes election. He encountered strong anti-incumbency sentiment

---

22. Yudhvir Rana, "When Arun Jaitley Bought a House in Amritsar", *The Times of India*, accessed 25 May 2025, https://timesofindia.indiatimes.com/city/amritsar/when-jaitley-bought-a-house-in-amritsar/articleshow/70823720.cms.

23. Chander Suta Dogra, "An Uphill Task for Jaitley in Amritsar", *The Hindu*, accessed 25 May 2025, https://www.thehindu.com/elections/loksabha2014/an-uphill-task-for-jaitley-in-amritsar/article5953943.ece.

24. Manjeet Sehgal, "Clash of Titans in Amritsar: Jaitley vs Amarinder Singh", *India Today*, accessed 25 May 2025, https://www.indiatoday.in/mail-today/story/its-a-leap-of-faith-for-jaitley-in-amritsar-185874-2014-03-23.

25. Ibid.

against the SAD–BJP in virtually every assembly segment of the constituency. Narendra Modi attempted to wash over this anger and replace it with the prospect of Punjab getting goodies from the Centre if the NDA came to power.[26] The glaring absence of sitting MP Navjot Singh Sidhu, Jaitley's one-time protégé, did not help.

"When Mr. Jaitley came to our locality, people asked him why the BJP chose to ignore Mr. Sidhu and field him instead. The latter spent Rs 2 crore from his pocket for Amritsar," said Hitesh Uberoy, a businessman. "It would have been nice had he come, but I understand his sentiments," Jaitley said.[27]

The RSS put its might behind Jaitley. An army of RSS workers made this border town of Punjab their temporary home in the days before the polling date. Morning walkers encountered them as they fanned out into the city's mohallas and lanes at daybreak to campaign for Arun Jaitley.[28] Not only the RSS, but big businessmen from Gujarat flew in and out discreetly to work on the business lobbies. Droves of Jaitley supporters and friends campaigned furiously for him; and not without reason. When the ruling SAD–BJP in Punjab persuaded the BJP brass to field Jaitley from Amritsar, it was done with the assurance that the seat would be easy pickings.[29] The battle for Amritsar, which went to the polls on 30 April 2014, was anything but.[30]

In a desperate move, Badal caused ripples in the political circles after he introduced Jaitley as a future deputy prime minister at a rally in Attari. On his part, Jaitley said he was not looking for any position, but would work for the people of Amritsar. "I am not looking for any position. What he (Badal) had in his mind is quite legitimate, that Amritsar needs a good voice at the Centre. I am reasonably qualified to be that effective voice," Jaitley said.

Jaitley believed in the power of vote; even one vote could make a difference—"Those who missed the vote failed in their primary duty as a citizen."[31] He

---

26. Chander Suta Dogra, "An Uphill Task for Jaitley in Amritsar", *The Hindu*, accessed 25 May 2025, https://www.thehindu.com/elections/loksabha2014/an-uphill-task-for-jaitley-in-amritsar/article5953943.ece.

27. Ibid.

28. Ibid.

29. Ibid.

30. Ibid.

31. Arun Jaitley, *A New India: Selected Writings 2014—19* (Juggernaut, 2020), p. 332.

was enrolled in the Gandhinagar parliamentary constituency, having been a member of the Rajya Sabha from Gujarat, three times in a row. He was faced with a dilemma: "Do I leave my own constituency in Amritsar to cast my vote or do I skip my vote?" On the day of polling, Jaitley decided to travel to Gujarat to cast his vote even if that meant a hectic and tiring day-long journey. After a visit to the Golden Temple and the Durgiana Mandir in the morning, Jaitley travelled to each of the nine assembly segments. By the time almost 50 per cent of the votes had been cast, Jaitley along with Sangeeta flew into Gandhinagar to vote. He returned to Amritsar by the evening. "It was tiresome but satisfying," he later noted in his daily diary.[32]

★

When the results were announced for the longest-ever elections in the history of independent India, the big shock came from Amritsar. Jaitley had failed to ride the "tsunamo".[33] Modi is said to have been devastated. Jaitley was already in Delhi. He had sensed his defeat after the polling was over. Reports from the ground were not positive. Defeat looked imminent. Modi called Jaitley and assured loss and win are part of electoral life.[34]

Amit Shah too was shocked. On the morning of 16 May, he was glued to the television screen in his rented accommodation in New Delhi's Jangpura. Soon, it was clear the BJP was sweeping Uttar Pradesh—a feat that was attributed to Shah's micromanagement as the party general secretary and state in-charge. It should have been time for celebration, but there was one thing that wasn't quite right. He saw Jaitley trailing in Amritsar. Shah was hopeful till he called some grassroots workers in Punjab. It was all over, they said: Jaitley was losing. Shah broke down, and so did his wife Sonal.[35]

---

32. Ibid.

33. The Modi wave leading to the BJP's massive victory in 2014 general elections was compared to a tsunami and referred to as tsunamo.

34. As informed by Narinder Dhruv Batra, who claimed he was with Jaitley when Modi called.

35. "Shah Broke Down When Jaitley Lost His Only Election", *The Times of India*, accessed 25 May 2025, https://timesofindia.indiatimes.com/india/shah-broke-

As counting progressed, it was becoming clear that the Modi wave that had swept most of the country had not made much impact in Amritsar. As per the seat-sharing arrangement between the two allies in Punjab, the BJP contested 23 assembly seats out of the total 117 in Punjab. The BJP trailed on 15 of the 23 assembly segments it contested as per the arrangement. In most other Punjab constituencies, the SAD was able to neutralise the Congress as the AAP ate into anti-incumbency votes, polling 2 to 3 lakh votes. Amritsar had voted against the ruling combine's decision of imposing a series of taxes, especially on traders, the prevailing lawlessness and drug menace, absence of basic facilities to residents, among others.[36] Jaitley was collateral damage.

Solace for the state BJP lay in the fact that its vote share increased by just about 1 per cent since 2012. It was a wake-up call for the state BJP. This defeat came as a major embarrassment more for the SAD, than its ally. It was the SAD's senior leadership, including party patron and Chief Minister Parkash Singh Badal, who persuaded Jaitley to contest polls from Amritsar, little knowing what the Congress had in store for them.

Despite an entire BJP team, led by state president Kamal Sharma camping in Amritsar, the party could not avert a defeat in the holy city. Out of the 11 assembly segments that the party won in the last assembly elections in 2012, the BJP trailed in 6. Jaitley trailed from Amritsar (North), the constituency of Punjab local bodies minister Anil Joshi, by a big margin of 16,726 votes. Jaitley lost with a margin of 32,198 votes in the constituency of Dr Navjot Kaur Sidhu, the BJP MLA from Amritsar (East). In Amritsar (West) assembly constituency, where Kamal Sharma was made in charge of the campaign, Jaitley trailed by 36,957 votes.[37] Surprisingly, the only segment where Jaitley got more votes than Amarinder Singh was from the constituency of revenue minister Bikram Singh Majithia.

---

down-when-jaitley-lost-his-only-election/amp_articleshow/70824179.cms.

36. Monika Malik, "Jaitley Fails to Ride Tsunamo, Loses Amritsar Constituency", *The Pioneer*, accessed 25 May 2025, https://www.dailypioneer.com/2014/india/jaitley-fails-to-ride-tsunamo-loses-amritsar-constituency.html.

37. Gurpreet Singh Nibber, "BJP's State Unit in the Line of Fire After Jaitley's Defeat", *Hindustan Times*, accessed 25 May 2025, https://www.hindustantimes.com/chandigarh/bjp-s-state-unit-in-the-line-of-fire-after-jaitley-s-defeat/story-WcG8zMHXczp3ZTSB2OuuYI_amp.html.

The fact could not be ignored that Jaitley's own men scripted his defeat. Joshi and Sharma, both regarded as Jaitley's protégés, persuaded him to contest from Amritsar.[38] BJP's Sidhu was the party's lone Sikh face at the national level, and many believed that the party's move to do away with the cricketer-turned-politician and replace him with a Hindu face was a wrong move. Captain Amarinder said that a "disconnected" SAD leadership had "misled" the BJP leader into contesting from Amritsar.[39]

Jaitley's loss had come as a dark cloud in the BJP's largely blue sky at a time when he was projected as the next finance minister and "Punjab's voice in the Parliament".[40] Anil Joshi sent his resignation to state BJP president Kamal Sharma on the counting day, when Jaitley's defeat was more than sure, accepting moral responsibility.[41] "It was not a defeat of Arun Jaitley, since he is man of high character, and neat and clean image. In fact, this is defeat of local leadership which couldn't turn up as per the desired expectations. It is my failure as well as of the local leadership," said Anil Joshi. "I don't deserve Ministry in the Punjab Government after what happened here."[42] The state unit would remember the polls for a long time, for all the wrong reasons.[43] BJP leaders in Punjab entrusted with the task of ensuring Jaitley's victory lost face. They failed to give a clear picture to Jaitley about the poll scenario building up against him. The Punjab BJP called a meeting of its core group on

---

38. Ibid.

39. Monika Malik, "Jaitley Fails to Ride Tsunamo, Loses Amritsar Constituency", *The Pioneer*, accessed 25 May 2025, https://www.dailypioneer.com/2014/india/jaitley-fails-to-ride-tsunamo-loses-amritsar-constituency.html.

40. Ibid.

41. Gurpreet Singh Nibber, "BJP's State Unit in the Line of Fire After Jaitley's Defeat", *Hindustan Times*, accessed 25 May 2025, https://www.hindustantimes.com/chandigarh/bjp-s-state-unit-in-the-line-of-fire-after-jaitley-s-defeat/story-WcG8zMHXczp3ZTSB2OuuYI_amp.html.

42. Monika Malik, "Jaitley Fails to Ride Tsunamo, Loses Amritsar Constituency", *The Pioneer*, accessed 25 May 2025, https://www.dailypioneer.com/2014/india/jaitley-fails-to-ride-tsunamo-loses-amritsar-constituency.html.

43. Gurpreet Singh Nibber, "BJP's State Unit in the Line of Fire After Jaitley's Defeat", *Hindustan Times*, accessed 25 May 2025, https://www.hindustantimes.com/chandigarh/bjp-s-state-unit-in-the-line-of-fire-after-jaitley-s-defeat/story-WcG8zMHXczp3ZTSB2OuuYI_amp.html.

27 May 2014 in New Delhi to discuss the election results. Outgoing MP Sidhu was conspicuous by his absence and that had also affected Jaitley's prospects.

The SAD formed a committee to introspect and find out the reasons for the poor performance of the party, but in the last few weeks of the campaign it had become increasingly clear that the SAD cadre did not work hard enough.[44]

While his defeat fuelled bitterness among BJP leaders and workers against the SAD, Jaitley did not change his approach on handling the SAD–BJP alliance in Punjab. He remained the strongest advocate of continuing the alliance in Punjab. BJP leaders often wondered why, despite tensions with the alliance partner and phases of bitterness, he gave a long rope to the SAD in Punjab. Till his death, he continued to serve as a bridge between the two parties. Despite his defeat from Amritsar, the city continued to reverberate in his heart. "Amritsar always had a special place in the heart of Jaitley. He not only laid the foundation of IIM, Amritsar, but also began Amritsar Smart City project," said Punjab BJP chief Shwait Malik.[45]

In 2017, he was back in Amritsar, campaigning for his party. He urged the city's residents to vote for BJP candidate Rajinder Mohan Singh Chhina in the bypoll in the Amritsar Lok Sabha constituency. Chhina, the former vice president of the party's state unit, had lost the assembly elections from the Amritsar West seat in 2007.[46]

---

44. As told by Jaitley's close friend who was in Amritsar and handling finance. He wished to remain anonymous.

45. "Jaitley's 'Safe' Run Ends with Amarinder's entry", *Deccan Herald*, accessed 25 May 2025, https://www.deccanherald.com/amp/story/archives/jaitleys-safe-run-ends-amarinders-2183635.

46. Rohan Venkataramakrishnan, "Things Missing from BJP's Amritsar Campaign: Clarity, Allies and a Defence of Demonetisation", *Scroll.in*, accessed 25 May 2025, https://amp.scroll.in/article/827405/things-missing-from-bjps-amritsar-campaign-clarity-allies-and-a-defence-of-demonetisation.

17

Modi's Minister and Confidante

At 2.30 p.m. on 20 May 2014, a delegation of fifteen members of the NDA led by Rajnath Singh, the president of the BJP met the President. The other members of the delegation were Lal Krishna Advani, Murli Manohar Joshi, Arun Jaitley, Sushma Swaraj, Venkaiah Naidu, Nitin Gadkari, Ananth Kumar, Thawar Chand Gehlot, Parkash Singh Badal, Chandrababu Naidu, Uddhav Thackeray, Ram Vilas Paswan, Neiphiu Rio, and Sukhbir Singh Badal. A letter stating that Narendra Modi had been elected as the leader of the BJP parliamentary party was handed over to the President. Later, at 3.15 p.m., Narendra Modi called on the President as the elected leader of the BJP parliamentary party. The President appointed Narendra Modi as the prime minister of India and requested him to advise the names of others to be appointed members of the council of ministers.[1]

Narendra Modi was sworn in as India's fifteenth prime minister on 26 May 2014, the first to be born after Independence. Forty-five ministers, twenty-four with Cabinet rank, were sworn in after him. Rather than holding it in the Durbar Hall, Rashtrapati Bhavan, which can barely accommodate 500 guests, Modi chose the grand forecourt of the Rashtrapati Bhavan for the occasion. Rajpath was lit up—it was a public spectacle played out on live television. More than 3000 invites were sent out. Only days earlier, an emotional Modi

1. "President Appoints Narendra Modi as Prime Minister, Oath Taking Ceremony on May 26", Press Information Bureau, Government of India, President's Secretariat, available at https://www.pib.gov.in/newsite/PrintRelease.aspx?relid=105107.

had wept in Parliament's central hall while formally accepting his party's leadership; Advani had cried as well. For a fleeting moment, it seemed like a tearful reunion of the old and new orders within the BJP parivar.

His swearing-in ended a ten-year-long tenure of the Indian National Congress and signalled a major shift in the nation's politics. Interestingly, *Firstpost* drew a parallel between this significant day for Indian politics and the world of music when back in 1967, the legendary British band, The Beatles, released *Sgt. Pepper's Lonely Hearts Club Band*, a ground-breaking album that would go on to revolutionise rock 'n' roll music forever. The album cover featured The Beatles in colourful styled outfits surrounded by cardboard cut-outs of famous personalities. Designed by Peter Blake and Jann Haworth, it is widely regarded as one of the most influential album covers in history. Critically acclaimed, *Sgt. Pepper's* won four Grammy Awards, including Album of the Year and the first rock long-play record to receive the honour. It stayed at the top of the UK Albums Chart for twenty-seven weeks and topped the Billboard 200 in the United States for fifteen weeks. Beyond commercial success, the album cemented the band's place as cultural trailblazers of the 1960s.[2]

Modi's Cabinet was a lean, mean machine. UPA-II had twenty-nine Cabinet ministers. Team Modi had only twenty-three ministers.[3] With a total of forty-five ministers, it was the exact size of Atal Bihari Vajpayee's 1998 Cabinet. Under the UPA, sixty-eight ministers looked after fifty-one ministries; in the Modi government, forty-five ministers handled fifty-two departments. The Ministry of Overseas Indian Affairs was put back under the Ministry of External Affairs. Corporate affairs, a ministry held by a different minister from finance in UPA-II, was back under the finance ministry. In the infrastructure sector, one of Modi's key thrust areas, road transport and highways and shipping and ports were combined under a single ministry. Similarly, power, coal, and new and renewable energy were brought under a single ministry though petroleum

2. "History Today: When Narendra Modi Took Oath as India's 15th Prime Minister in 2014", *Firstpost*, accessed 25 May 2025, https://www.firstpost.com/explainers/history-today-when-narendra-modi-took-oath-as-indias-15th-prime-minister-in-2014-13890814.html.

3. Sandeep Unnithan and Jayant Sriram, "How Modi's First Union Cabinet Took Shape", *India Today*, from the India Today archives (2014), accessed 25 May 2025, https://www.indiatoday.in/india-today-insight/story/from-the-india-today-archives-2014-how-modis-first-union-cabinet-took-shape-2551069-2024-06-09.

remained a standalone ministry. The related ministries of urban development, housing and poverty alleviation were placed under a single charge while rural development, Panchayati Raj and drinking water and sanitation were grouped together. If a single minister was in charge of multiple subjects, decision making could be definitely quickened.[4]

Late on Sunday evening, ahead of Cabinet formation, the information department of the Gujarat government issued a detailed statement—"Shri Narendra Modi has made a Dent in Formation of Ministries"—that appeared to anticipate the shape of the incoming administration which assumed office on Monday evening (26 May 2014). "For the first time, he adopted the guiding principle of 'Minimum Government and Maximum Governance' and also rationalisation with a commitment to bring a change in the work culture and style of governance. It is a good beginning in transforming entities of assembled ministries to organic ministries. It will bring more coordination between different departments, will be more effective and bring a speed in process," the statement said. Elaborating further, the statement confirmed one Cabinet minister will head a cluster of related ministries. "The focus is on convergence in the activities of various ministries where one Cabinet minister will be heading a cluster of ministries who are working in complementary sectors," it said. The guiding philosophy was to cut the top layers while expanding the government at levels where it interacted with people. Seventeen related ministries were combined into seven different groups. "Mr Modi is eventually aiming at smart governance where the top layers of government will be downsized and there would be expansion at the grassroots level," the Gujarat government statement said. Things were going to be different this time around, starting with ministry formation, the statement appeared to suggest. "Shri Narendra Modi is aware of the high expectations of the people….' it stated.[5]

---

4. Ibid.

5. "Narendra Modi's Cabinet: Rajnath Singh, Sushma Swaraj & Arun Jaitley Make It to Top 7?", *The Economic Times*, accessed 25 May 2025, https://economictimes.indiatimes.com/news/politics-and-nation/narendra-modis-cabinet-rajnath-singh-sushma-swaraj-arun-jaitley-make-it-to-top-7/articleshow/35616141.cms?from=mdr.

One of Modi's most pressing tasks was to pick his team of ministers to deliver on the promises articulated in his campaign speeches and the BJP's election manifesto. The 2014 "Cabinet for change" was crafted after days of hectic consultations in Delhi's new power triangle—Keshav Kunj, the RSS office in Jhandewalan; the BJP headquarters on Ashoka Road; and Gujarat Bhawan in Delhi (Modi moved into 7 Race Course Road after minor renovation by May-end). Modi, Jaitley, and Amit Shah decided who should be inducted in the council of ministers and their portfolios. For four days, he was busy with the formation of the ministry and discussing various alternatives to ensure effective governance, convergence, and coordination between various ministries. Earlier, due to political instability and the prevalence of multi-party governments, the process of forming ministries was almost always carried out in a fragmented manner.[6] The original list had been prepared by Modi's confidantes, Arun Jaitley and Amit Shah, then vetted by the RSS. The final touches, including portfolio distribution, were done by Modi himself. The choices reflected the pool of talent available to him, but also Modi's style of functioning.[7]

Most senior leaders were accommodated in the Cabinet. Rajnath Singh got the home affairs department.[8] Nitin Gadkari was given the surface transport ministry; his old job as the BJP president was given to Amit Shah. Sushma Swaraj was made external affairs minister. Jaitley, whom Modi implicitly trusted, was given the heavyweight finance, defence, and corporate affairs portfolios. Two new ministries were created—the Ministry of Skill Development and Entrepreneurship headed by Assam's Sarbananda Sonowal and the Department of Water Resources, River Development and Ganga Rejuvenation headed by Uma Bharti. Smriti Irani, who had failed to unseat Rahul Gandhi, went to the sensitive human resources department that included education policy. Jaitley's stamp on the Modi Cabinet was discernible.[9] On his advice, Modi gave

---

6. Ibid.

7. Rajdeep Sardesai, *2014: The Election That Changed India* (Penguin, 2015).

8. Veterans like L.K. Advani and Murli Manohar Joshi were not inducted as they fell afoul of Modi's age ceiling of seventy-five for ministerial berths.

9. Sandeep Unnithan and Jayant Sriram, "How Modi's First Union Cabinet Took Shape", *India Today*, From the India Today archives (2014), accessed 25 May 2025, https://www.indiatoday.in/india-today-insight/story/from-the-india-today-archives-2014-how-modis-first-union-cabinet-took-shape-2551069-2024-06-09.

key portfolios to three young leaders—Nirmala Sitharaman, Minister of the State for Commerce and Industry who handled key departments like World Trade Organisation; Piyush Goyal, Minister of the State for Power, Coal, New and Renewable Energy; and Dharmendra Pradhan, Minister of the State for Petroleum and Natural Gas.[10]

Three BJP spokespersons were rewarded with ministerial berths—Ravi Shankar Prasad, Nirmala Sitharaman, and Prakash Javadekar. Sanjeev Balyan served as Minister of State in two ministries—agriculture, under first-time Cabinet minister Radha Mohan Singh, and food processing industries, under another first-time Cabinet minister, Harsimrat Kaur Badal. The BJP's closest allies were rewarded with some of the best portfolios.[11] The new Cabinet sent a clear message—the Modi government had a trusted core. Arun Shourie, who had been left out of the team, went so far as to suggest that only three men really mattered in the Government of India, calling the concentration of power frightening. Others welcomed the prospect of decisive leadership and clear lines of authority.[12]

★

Jaitley took the oath dressed in sparkling white kurta-pyjama and an elegant ivory-coloured half jacket. As already mentioned, he was the first person in independent India's history to hold the finance and defence portfolios at the same time. Many finance ministers, such as Morarji Desai, Indira Gandhi, and Manmohan Singh, have gone on to be prime ministers. Pranab Mukherjee went on to become the President, while some prime ministers, Rajiv Gandhi and

---

10. Jyoti Malhotra, "What Makes the Finance-Defence-Company Affairs Minister the Go-To Man in the Narendra Modi Government", *India Today*, accessed 25 May 2025, https://www.indiatoday.in/magazine/cover-story/story/20141110-arun-jaitley-narendra-modi-finance-defence-company-affairs-minister-805687-2014-10-30.

11. Sandeep Unnithan and Jayant Sriram, "How Modi's First Union Cabinet Took Shape", *India Today*, From the India Today archives (2014), accessed 25 May 2025, https://www.indiatoday.in/india-today-insight/story/from-the-india-today-archives-2014-how-modis-first-union-cabinet-took-shape-2551069-2024-06-09.

12. Lance Price, *The Modi Effect: Inside Narendra Modi's Campaign to Transform India* (Hodder & Stoughton, 2015), p. 248.

V.P. Singh, have held the defence portfolio at the same time. Arun Jaitley had failed to win his own seat in the election, yet he was at the centre of ministry formation. Not only was he inducted as a Cabinet minister but given the most significant role. By giving Jaitley key ministries (and two out of four portfolios that comprise the Cabinet Committee on Security), Modi's signal was clear—he held Jaitley in high esteem.[13] It was also indicative of the faith Modi reposed in Jaitley's capabilities to deliver the economic reforms Modi envisioned. It was not just a payback—as perceived by many—for Jaitley's loyal friendship and strategic planning in Modi's election as the prime minister. Modi considered Jaitley's legal expertise, economic understanding, and political experience crucial in shaping the new government's policies.

The economy needed to be revived, investor confidence needed to be restored, and bold reforms were expected. Modi was aware of the challenges ahead; he knew that the real work was just beginning. Jaitley was the most experienced of all in carrying out important economic reforms in the Vajpayee government. Jaitley held many important portfolios under Vajpayee—law and justice, commerce, information and broadcasting, shipping, disinvestment, corporate affairs, and even civil aviation for some time. He was the man Modi could ask for advice, or from he could receive blunt counsel, even occasional disagreement, knowing he had no conspiratorial motive, no hidden agenda.[14]

To Jaitley, the trust Modi reposed in him was deeply moving. The BJP's spectacular win under Modi was not just a political milestone but a deeply personal moment for Jaitley—one that reaffirmed his legacy as a key architect of India's new political era and his own contributions to the BJP's resurgence. The idea of a "Modi wave" was no longer theoretical; it had materialised into an unprecedented mandate. The victory was a testament to his faith in Modi's leadership. Yet, he realised that the victory also brought immense responsibility; the expectations were sky-high.

---

13. Jyoti Malhotra, "What Makes the Finance-Defence-Company Affairs Minister the Go-To Man in the Narendra Modi Government", *India Today*, accessed 25 May 2025, https://www.indiatoday.in/magazine/cover-story/story/20141110-arun-jaitley-narendra-modi-finance-defence-company-affairs-minister-805687-2014-10-30.

14. Ashok Malik, "Arun Jaitley's Demise, An Irreplaceable Loss to the Nation", in *The Discussant: Journal of Centre for Reforms, Development and Justice*, Special Edition, An Obituary to Arun Jaitley, Vol. VII, No. 3 (July–September 2019), pp. 56–59.

The Indian economy in 2014 was not in an enviable position by any standards. The country's once-compelling growth story, scripted by the 1991 team of Prime Minister P.V. Narasimha Rao, Finance Minister Manmohan Singh, and secretary of ministry of finance, Montek Singh Ahluwalia, had lost its lustre. India's economy was grappling with sluggish growth and declining investor confidence due to a series of high-profile corruption cases, among other reasons. Growth was low, inflation was on the rise, deficits were widening, corruption was rampant, and policymaking was in paralysis. In the third quarter of 2013, India's overall growth had faltered, reaching a nadir of just 4.8 per cent. At the end of 2013, India was the recipient of less than 1 per cent of the global stock of FDI; in terms of outward FDI, the country's share of the global FDI stock was even smaller. Consumer inflation was at an all-time high, with prices rising by an average of 11.2 per cent in November. India was experiencing a serious problem of "stagflation", stagnating growth combined with inflation.[15] Export markets were experiencing economic sluggishness.[16] India's impact on commodity markets on the demand side had also been comparatively small, considering its large population. The rupee had taken a beating. The share of manufacturing in GDP had stagnated at 15 per cent. A chronically energy-starved nation, India couldn't seem to find enough supply to satisfy its growing middle class or to run the businesses that would fuel growth further.

The Modi government was elected when India was already a part of the "Fragile Five", a term coined by a little-known research analyst at Morgan Stanley in the summer of 2013 identifying Turkey, Brazil, India, South Africa, and Indonesia as economies which had become overly dependent on skittish foreign investment to finance their growth ambitions. The government had no options. It was committed to reforms. "Reform or Perish"—that was the challenge before the Indian economy. Therefore, the government systematically and consistently introduced several reforms spread over a five-year period.[17]

---

15. "India's Economy in the 2014 Election", Albright Stonebridge Group, available at https://dgagroup.com/insight/indias-economy-2014-election/.

16. "India in 2014: Elections and Economy", Center for Strategic and International Studies, available at https://www.csis.org/analysis/india-2014-elections-and-economy.

17. Arun Jaitley, *A New India: Selected Writings 2014–19* (Juggernaut, 2020), pp. 45–52.

Many multinational corporations were facing disputes over transfer pricing—the value of which had sharply climbed from $1.8 billion in 2009 to $11.3 billion in 2012, according to the *Financial Times*. Private investments were already held up and bad debts were piling up. The fiscal space had been stretched beyond manageable deficit limits. Such a state of affairs was completely out-of-sync with the aspirations of a young nation, 65 per cent of whose population was below thirty-five years of age and restless for opportunities to move ahead. The global economy had still not recovered from the shock of the 2008 financial crisis and most developed economies remained vulnerable. Trade stayed stagnant, marked by a shift towards protectionism. Geopolitical equations, particularly in the Middle East, continued to be volatile, pushing crude prices to historic highs. Both domestic and global developments created huge turbulence for the Indian economy.[18]

Expectations were high, though the government's finances were in a mess. Having been elected on the strength of dizzying expectation and a promise of ushering *achche din* for India, the foremost priority was ensuring rapid and somewhat equitable growth—to build India's capacity.[19] Jaitley was determined to turn crisis into an opportunity, and make Modi's term a transformational moment in the history of India.

As soon as Jaitley occupied the western part of North Block, the red sandstone building that houses the ministry of finance, he started preparing to present the first budget of the Modi government in late July. By not occupying the South Block office where the defence minister sits, Jaitley indicated that he was only a temporary occupant in the defence ministry till any "alternative arrangements" were made. This time Jaitley shifted to the government bungalow at 4 Krishna Menon Marg, the first government accommodation he occupied.

Modi and Jaitley formed a mutual admiration society. The two had, long ago, in 1999, expressed their admiration for each other on two episodes of Rajeev Shukla's television show *Rubaru*. Modi dated their relationship to the JP Movement, and described Jaitley as "a rare combination in politics", an "activist, an intellectual, articulate, very clean, and also a very friendly man". Though some had doubted Jaitley's abilities at first, Modi said, "The best

---

18. Bibek Debroy, Anirban Ganguly and Kishore Desai (Eds.), "Editorial Note" in *Making of New India: Transformation Under Modi Government* (Wisdom Tree, 2019).

19. Ibid.

thing about Arun-ji is his total dedication to whatever work he is given. A person who has such dedication in life rarely fails." When Shukla subsequently interviewed Jaitley about Modi, Jaitley returned the compliments, calling Modi a "tough taskmaster", a "disciplinarian", and a "creative" politician.[20] As columnist Ashok Malik eloquently put, "This kind of mutual affection between two ambitious leaders is difficult to grasp, especially in the otherwise brutal universe of politics."[21]

★

Prime Minister Modi and his team hit the ground running immediately after assuming office. The very first Cabinet decision was to set up a special investigation team headed by retired Supreme Court judge M.B. Shah to bring back Indian black money stashed abroad. A 2010 study by the US-based non-profit Global Financial Integrity estimated that Indians had spirited away $500 billion overseas. The message was clear: the government was willing to take the ecosystem of corruption and black money head-on. Jaitley's ministry would be responsible for the clean-up. Jaitley realised that although five years is not a long period in the life of a nation, it could be a turning point in its direction towards progress. Jaitley recalled how in 1991 Prime Minister P.V. Narasimha Rao was confronted with an economic crisis. The economic situation compelled reforms and became an important watershed in Indian history. He recalled how the first NDA government under Vajpayee took key decisions with regard to infrastructure creation and prudent fiscal management. Bold policies on telecom and national highways made significant impacts on the economy.[22]

Jaitley devoted the next five years championing some of the most complex economic reforms to deliver Modi's vision. With this he combined his own zeal and philosophy of a nationalist welfare state. He hit all the right notes in

20. Praveen Donthi, "Talk of the Town", *Caravan Magazine*, accessed 25 May 2025, https://caravanmagazine.in/reportage/talk-town.

21. Ashok Malik, "Arun Jaitley's Demise, An Irreplaceable Loss to the Nation", in *The Discussant: Journal of Centre for Reforms, Development and Justice*, Special Edition, An Obituary to Arun Jaitley, Vol. VII, No. 3 (July–September 2019), pp. 56–59.

22. Arun Jaitley, *A New India: Selected Writings 2014–19* (Juggernaut, 2020), pp. 45–52.

his tenure as the minister of finance. He took over from where he had left in 2004 and championed many key reforms needed in the rapidly changing global geopolitical landscape, restoring economic health and accelerating growth. Jaitley's tenure saw the implementation of critical reforms—GST, Insolvency and Bankruptcy Code (IBC), demonetisation, rejuvenation of banking sector, monetary policy, digital economy, financial inclusions through Aadhaar and Pradhan Mantri Jan Dhan Yojna, amendments to regulatory systems—all of which contributed to the modernisation and formalisation of the Indian economy.

He is also credited with the clean-up of non-performing assets in the banking system. Jaitley was a strong advocate for economic liberalisation and drove reforms that granted businesses both the ability to operate freely and the means to exit the market effectively through the IBC. Jaitley's efforts completed a crucial phase in Indian economic reform, which had previously addressed freedom of entry and operation, but lacked a robust mechanism for business closure. He was determined to destroy the system which favoured those who defaulted on loans. Indians, for long, have been used to hearing announcements of new schemes and initiatives whenever the government changes. However, what was remarkably different this time was that clear and ambitious timelines were set for each initiative. These timelines were declared upfront to the nation by the prime minister himself. In doing so, he told the nation that he was going to make himself accountable for ensuring that development targets were achieved in a time-bound manner.[23]

Jaitley seamlessly juggled many other roles leaving an indelible mark in whichever room he was asked to sit, in the North or South Block or Shastri Bhawan.[24] He was even given additional charge of defence when Manohar Parrikar's health deteriorated. His tenure as the defence minister saw a number of big-ticket reform measures. Jaitley's guiding hand and legal mind were responsible for major legislative accomplishments in Modi's first term outside of his own portfolios. He was the man who explained the government's

---

23. Bibek Debroy, Anirban Ganguly and Kishore Desai (Eds.), *Making of New India: Transformation Under Modi Government* (Wisdom Tree, 2019), pp. ix–xiv.

24. M. Venkaiah Naidu, "Our Regular Meetings Were for Good, and Food for Thought", in *The Discussant: Journal of Centre for Reforms, Development and Justice*, Special Edition, An Obituary to Arun Jaitley, Vol. VII, No. 3, (July –September 2019), pp. 17–19.

position when a bill to ban "triple talaq" was brought. The historic legislation for abrogation of Article 370 of the Constitution was drafted by him. Informally called "scholar minister" in political circles, he could be the Man Friday of anyone at the helm. Prime Minister Modi even deputed Arun Jaitley to represent the Government of India at the unveiling of Gandhi's statue in Parliament Square, London, on 14 March 2015.

The I&B ministry was another ministry close to Jaitley's heart. In his first budget, he set up a new plan scheme and allocated Rs 100 crore to encourage growth in the community radio sector. This scheme increased 400 permissions for setting up of community radio stations to. He announced that the Film & Television Institute, Pune, and Satyajit Ray Film & Television Institute, Kolkata, would be accorded status of institutes of national importance. He also announced that a National Centre for Excellence in Animation, Gaming and Special Effects would be set up.[25]

He continued on disinvestment where he left in Vajpayee's term. Given the sensitive nature of disinvestment work, critical files were carried to the finance minister by hand.[26] "I would usually approach his affable Additional Private Secretary Bhatia to sneak me in, given the FM is always occupied. Jaitley Saheb would ask a few questions and put his signatures on the file out of implicit faith in his officers," wrote Ashok Pal Singh who worked in Jaitley's ministry as joint secretary.[27]

A group of ministers rechristened "alternate mechanism" had been set up under the Modi government. The finance minister chaired it, and Nitin Gadkari, the transport minister, was a permanent member. The minister, under whose administrative control the Central Public Sector Enterprise (CPSE) came, was the third member of the group. Ashok Pal Singh was involved with the power ministry where there were a maximum number of single-ministry transactions.

---

25. Arun Jaitley, "Budget 2014–2015", available at https://www.indiabudget.gov.in/doc/bspeech/bs201415.pdf.

26. Ashok Pal Singh, "Arun Jaitley: An Ex-Official Recounts Friendly Meetings & a Salvaged Deal", *The Quint*, accessed 25 May 2025, https://www.thequint.com/voices/blogs/arun-jaitley-an-ex-official-recounts-friendly-meetings-a-salvaged-deal.

27. Ibid.

There was a familiar pattern to the afternoon meetings; they always started on time with the relaxed finance minister at the head of the table. While getting briefed on the transaction, he would regale the group of ministers along with Ashok Pal Singh with anecdotes. Often, an assistant would bring cut fruits and vegetables. Waiting for his ministerial colleagues to arrive, Jaitley would tell the other four members, tongue in cheek, "One never turns up but unfailingly signs up to the decision taken by him. The other always comes fifteen minutes late starting from his nearby office only when told the meeting has commenced!" While waiting for the delinquent minister, concerns were aired to Jaitley about disinvestment deals getting probed and concerned officers facing the music of investigative agencies post-retirement.

Showing great empathy, he prompted amendments to the Prevention of Corruption Act, 1988 to shield honest officers. He suggested vetting disinvestment transactions by an ombudsman after persuading a former Chief Justice of India to take the position.[28] His understanding was that no agency would frivolously probe a deal vetted by a former Chief Justice. The concern was touching as well as reassuring. Not surprisingly, record disinvestments took place under his charge. A tentative book was built before unleashing a disinvestment transaction. It was a mega offer for sale. The issue was undersubscribed at 2 p.m. with the closing bell at the stock exchange to go at 3.30 p.m. There was panic in the ministry. Ashok Pal Singh wrote, "The Secretary was in a panic when I entered her room. She told me, 'I am running to the residence of the FM, and you don't leave the monitor in my place till you see the issue fully subscribed.'" A die-hard public sector investor was playing truant. On reaching the residence of the minister, the secretary learnt that Jaitley was resting. Jaitley came into the drawing room, rubbing his eyes. The secretary dialled the chairman and managing director (CMD) of the company and put the phone in his hand. Soon after that, Ashok Pal Singh reported to the secretary, sipping tea with the finance minister, that the issue stood fully subscribed.[29] Two weeks later, the CMD was provided with an excel sheet showing the killings his company was making out of investments in the government offerings.[30]

28. Ibid.

29. Ibid.

30. Ibid.

Jaitley fought hard to eliminate corruption in all forms. The spate of scandals that had singed the collective conscience in the recent past has steeled the government's resolve to fight this menace together. He sincerely believed that transparency and people's awareness were the best antidote against corruption, and that the government needed to set up effective mechanisms such as a strong Lok Pal to deal with corruption with an iron hand. He worked relentlessly towards this goal as that was the way to go for India of the twenty-first century.[31]

Even when he was not a law minister in Modi's Cabinet, Jaitley's hand was clearly visible on all important legal issues. It was on his advice that Mukul Rohatgi was appointed as Attorney General of India.[32] Rohatgi is also on record that generally when he met Prime Minister Modi as Attorney General to discuss any legal issues, he would defer him to Jaitley. *"Jaitley-ji se vimarsh kar lein"* (please consult Jaitley-ji).[33]

Jaitley was a friend of India, never discriminating against any state on political basis, although politically he was unsparing of Opposition-ruled states. It was Jaitley who allocated funds for Lord Jagannath's "Nabakalebar" and approved the commemorative coin to mark the occasion. He also sanctioned funds for the commemoration of 200 years of Paika rebellion. In his untimely death, the people of Odisha lost a friend and a well-wisher, Dharmendra Pradhan said.[34]

Jaitley was the brain behind the coal ordinance promulgated in the backdrop of Supreme Court order quashing 214 coal blocks to companies since 1993. The Coal Mines (Special Provisions) Ordinance, 2014 was promulgated on 21 October 2014. Later, the Coal Mines (Special Provisions) Bill, 2014, was introduced in the Lok Sabha on 10 December 2014, during the winter session, by the Minister of Coal, Piyush Goyal, to amend the Coal Mines (Nationalisation) Act, 1973 and the Mines and Minerals (Development and

31. Arun Jaitley, My Vision, accessed 25 May 2025, https://www.arunjaitley.com/my-vision/.

32. "On the record with Sunetra Choudhury", *Hindustan Times*, accessed on 5 September 2025, https://www.htsmartcast.com/news-podcasts/on-the-record.

33. Ibid.

34. "Rich Tributes Pour in for Former Minister Arun Jaitley Across Party Lines", *The New Indian Express*, accessed 25 May 2025, https://www.newindianexpress.com/states/odisha/2019/Sep/05/rich-tributes-pour-in-for-former-minister-arun-jaitley-across-party-lines-2029652.html.

Regulation) Act, 1957. The bill sought to replace the Coal Mines (Special Provisions) Ordinance, 2014. The bill could not be passed. Less than twenty-four hours after Parliament adjourned sine die for the winter session with key legislations left pending due to disruptions, the Modi government pushed through the coal sector reforms by approving promulgation of the ordinance. The coal allocation ordinance was passed by the Lok Sabha, but it was not allowed to be taken up for discussion in the Rajya Sabha. The revival of mining was necessary for the financial empowerment of the eastern states and to provide employment to lakhs of people. That ordinance was re-promulgated. Arun Jaitley told reporters that it would facilitate e-auction of coal blocks to private companies for captive use and allot mines directly to PSUs. The process for auctioning the first set of twenty-four coal mines began the following day.

Jaitley was also the brain behind the deregulation of diesel prices as well as the increase in price of natural gas from domestic fields from the existing $4.2 per million British thermal unit (mbtu) to $5.6 per mbtu. Gas pricing had been a particularly hot-button issue, with Arvind Kejriwal of the AAP and CPI's Gurudas Dasgupta accusing the previous UPA government's C. Rangarajan Committee of favouring Mukesh Ambani's Reliance Industries Limited (RIL) by recommending that the price be increased to $8.4 per mbtu.[35]

Far removed in tastes and habits, Modi and Jaitley intuitively shared the same sense of righteousness, and were guided by the same moral compass. It showed in the Modi–Jaitley team's unwillingness to provide evergreen bank loans, to finance giveaways and loan write-offs, or to compromise on fiscal deficit targets just to win short-term political popularity. When he believed in something, Arun Jaitley could be very obstinate—as obstinate and as steadfast as Narendra Modi. No wonder Jaitley was an obvious, able, and steady first mate as Modi took command of the government in 2014.[36] At the same time, even though Modi and Jaitley were friends, Jaitley observed decorum and protocols. After Modi became the prime minister, he wrote, "Political relationships are more

35. Jyoti Malhotra, "What Makes the Finance-Defence-Company Affairs Minister the Go-To Man in the Narendra Modi Government", *India Today*, accessed 25 May 2025, https://www.indiatoday.in/magazine/cover-story/story/20141110-arun-jaitley-narendra-modi-finance-defence-company-affairs-minister-805687-2014-10-30.

36. Ashok Malik, "Arun Jaitley's Demise, An Irreplaceable Loss to the Nation", in *The Discussant: Journal of Centre for Reforms, Development and Justice*, Special Edition, An Obituary to Arun Jaitley, Vol. VII, No. 3, (July–September 2019), pp. 56–59.

complex than simple friendships. Mr Modi is now prime minister and I respect him for who he is."[37]

★

Jaitley's talents also lay in his ability to be the firefighter for any public relations disaster that hit the BJP. Jaitley also emerged as the undoubted key strategist for the NDA in its first term from 2014 to 2019. When West Bengal's Chief Minister Mamata Banerjee was on a warpath with the BJP, it was Jaitley who could make her see reason. So also with the late J. Jayalalithaa of AIADMK, once the chief minister of Tamil Nadu.[38] His ability to spin a situation to the advantage of the BJP on television and in Parliament earned him many admirers, even among his political adversaries. Whether he was speaking from the Opposition bench or from the treasury side, Jaitley was heard by everyone in rapt attention. People knew that he would always bring in a unique point of view to the issue being debated. When his precision and intellectual depth found an outlet on the internet through blogs, his brilliant analyses reached a wider audience and further enriched public discourse.[39] When he began to blog in September 2013,[40] even while the medium was a new one, Jaitley's enormous powers of persuasion made the transition seamlessly from soaring speeches to searing blogs.

Jaitley defended the government vigorously describing the Congress's allegations as a case of "concocted falsehood". Jaitley argued that Prime Minister Modi should be commended for securing the Rafale fighter jet deal, which he claimed saved the country thousands of crores of rupees. Jaitley asserted that false figures regarding the aircraft's purchase price were circulated publicly and that efforts were made to obscure the distinction between a basic aircraft and a weaponised version. He emphasised that all facts related to the

---

37. Kumkum Chadha, *The Marigold Story: Indira Gandhi & Others* (Westland, 2019), p. 338.

38. Ibid., p. 334.

39. Arun Jaitley, *A New India: Selected Writings 2014–19* (Juggernaut, 2020), pp. vii–ix.

40. Arun Jaitley, https://www.arunjaitley.com/

purchase were presented before the Supreme Court, which comprehensively rejected the challenges to the deal. He stated that the court examined and upheld the necessity of the purchase, the quality of the aircraft, the pricing, the process, and the offset issues.[41]

In his blog "The Rafale Falsehood Repeated" posted on 8 August 2018, Jaitley addressed what he perceived as another attempt to discredit the Indian government by disseminating false information regarding the 2016 Inter-Governmental Agreement for the acquisition of Rafale fighter jets. It is particularly awful that this effort came shortly after the failure of a similar attempt in Parliament, he wrote.[42] In his blog post "15 Questions that Expose Congress Party's Falsehood on Rafale", Jaitley addressed the criticism and allegations made by the Congress regarding the Rafale deal between the Indian and French governments. Jaitley posed a series of questions to the Congress party, challenging them to provide factual responses and accusing them of making allegations without understanding the details of the Rafale deal.[43]

Jaitley was often considered the third most powerful man in the party, behind Prime Minister Narendra Modi and BJP president Amit Shah. All party spokespersons flocked to him for advice. He was the BJP's and Prime Minister Modi's chief trouble-shooter. Be it path-breaking reforms in any sphere and showcasing the government's achievements, or fiercely defending controversial policies, or launching a frontal attack on the Congress, or stitching and salvaging alliances, few could have been more effective. He was the most effective interlocutor of the government in and outside Parliament, articulating its position and perspectives on all major socioeconomic and political issues.

He had the innate and unique ability of offering solutions without compromising on the basic position and view of the government and his party. While he acquitted himself as an outstanding parliamentarian and an eloquent orator, what made Jaitley different was his knowledge and grasp of national and

---

41. Arun Jaitley, "The Compulsive Contrarian and His Manufactured Logic", accessed 25 May 2025, https://www.arunjaitley.com/the-compulsive-contrarian-and-his-manufactured-logic/.

42. Arun Jaitley, "The Rafale Falsehood Repeated", accessed 25 May 2025, https://www.arunjaitley.com/the-rafale-falsehood-repeated/.

43. Arun Jaitley, "15 Questions that Expose Congress Party's Falsehood on Rafale", accessed 25 May 2025, https://www.arunjaitley.com/15-questions-that-expose-congress-partys-falsehood-on-rafale/.

international issues. He worked hard to keep abreast of contemporary issues with a 360-degree view of socioeconomic and geopolitical implications.[44] Jaitley liked reading and held his own views in the discussion on subjects as diverse as modern history, law, judiciary, economy, politics, or cricket. He thrashed out issues with ease. His approach was one of gentle persuasion rather than diktat, which is why measures like the GST and IBC, among others, will remain his enduring legacy. Then environment minister Prakash Javadekar once called him a "super strategist".[45] Jaitley always thought of persuasion and ideology as more powerful than noise and catchy remarks to make a point. He held on to nuance with élan, made subtlety a powerful instrument, and believed that a turn-of-phrase would endear the person to the listener. For him, etiquette and grace were never to be compromised. And neither were the principles of integrity in public life—it was a quality he deeply valued.[46]

He believed that parliamentary debate should focus on issues and not on individuals as it would help in understanding an alternative view point. "If you concentrate merely on policies, attack the policies, attack the views and put forward your own views, most people will try to understand this alternative viewpoint. But if you waste your entire time on attacking a person, he would be also coining the best of phrases on how to get even with you and the result will be a decline in the quality of public discourse. That is precisely what we are suffering in this country," Jaitley once said.[47]

---

44. M. Venkaiah Naidu, "Our Regular Meetings Were for Good, and Food for Thought", in *The Discussant: Journal of Centre for Reforms, Development and Justice*, Special Edition, An Obituary to Arun Jaitley, Vol. VII, No. 3 (July–September 2019), pp. 17–19.

45. "Arun Jaitley, Modi's 'Precious Diamond', original Chanakya was master at working levers of power", https://timesofindia.indiatimes.com/india/arun-jaitley-modis-precious-diamond-original-chanakya-was-a-master-at-working-levers-of-power/articleshow/69562898.cms.

46. Jyoti Pande Lavakare, "A Common Name, a Father's Light", *The Indian Express*, accessed 25 May 2025, https://indianexpress.com/article/opinion/columns/a-common-name-a-fathers-light-10080578/.

47. "Parliamentary Debate Should Focus on Issues, Not on Individuals: Jaitley", *Business Today*, accessed 25 May 2025, https://www.businesstoday.in/pti-feed/story/parliamentary-debate-should-focus-on-issues-not-on-individuals-jaitley-153178-2018-10-03.

Jaitley's budget speeches from 2014 to 2017 were marked by eloquent use of poetry to inspire hope and optimism. In 2015, Jaitley sought to rally the public with a couplet that acknowledged past challenges but expressed determination to overcome them: "We have grown some flowers, some more still need to be grown. The difficulty though is that till now there are many old thorns in the garden."[48] The following year, he drew on poetic imagery to highlight the government's resolve in the face of adversity:[49]

Kashti chalane walo ne jab haar kar di patvaar hamein
Lehar lehar toofan mile aur mauj mauj majhdhaar hamein
Phir bhi dikhaya hai hamne aur phir ye dikha denge sabko
In haalaaton mei aata hai dariya karna paar hamein

Jaitley's most memorable poetic turn came in 2017, as he sought to inspire the public to embrace the government's economic reforms, including demonetisation:[50]

Is mod par ghabra kar na tham jaiye aap
Jo baat nayi usse apnaiye aap
Darte hai nayi raah par kyun chalne se
Ham aage aage chalte hai aaiye aap
Nayi duniya hai, naya daur hai, nayi hai umang
Kuch the pehle ke tarike, to kuch hai aaj ke rang dhang

48. Mannu Arora, "Jaitley's Poetic Turns in Four Budgets. What Will His Fifth Budget Speech Highlight", *Economic Times*, accessed 25 May 2025, https://cfo.economictimes.indiatimes.com/news/jaitleys-poetic-turns-in-four-budgets-what-will-his-fifth-budget-speech-highlight/62688693.

49. Ibid.

50. Ibid.

Through these evocative verses, Jaitley aimed to instil a sense of optimism and determination in the face of economic challenges, rallying the public behind the government's transformative agenda.[51]

Jaitley's wit was hard to match. During the course of his nearly forty-minute speech—interrupted by an adjournment—soon after Rahul Gandhi finished his speech, Jaitley quoted a line from the 1964 James Bond film *Goldfinger*. "If it is once, it's happenstance, it can happen. If it is twice, it is a coincidence. And if it is thrice, it's a conspiracy," Jaitley said, to describe the Congress as an alleged conspirator in multiple defence scams.[52]

Be it as a minister or as a parliamentarian, Jaitley carried obvious influences of both his mentors—Vajpayee and Advani. As a minister, Jaitley was never harsh on the bureaucrats, a quality he picked up from Vajpayee. As prime minister, Vajpayee could convey more to his subordinates than what he desired by staying polite, but firm. Jaitley listened patiently to his colleagues and officers, another quality he picked from his mentor Vajpayee. Like Vajpayee, he allowed a discussion on almost every subject and eventually reconciled the conflicting viewpoints depending on their merits.[53]

There were many other similarities in both Vajpayee and Jaitley. Both loved food. Ministers in the Vajpayee government still occasionally speak about the quality of snacks served in his Cabinet meetings. Jaitley even loved to experiment with food when he travelled internationally. In India, he had his own favourite places in various cities, and occasionally, when he got off the train in the morning, he would have breakfast at one of them before reaching home.[54] Jaitley was a refined food connoisseur. The poet in him also nurtured a dreamer, one who dreamed in the light of his own vision. Many of those were born out of his idealism. In fact, several lines of different poems that he wrote reflected his own mood. Jaitley was a fan of songs in the cinema of the 1960s—the golden era of Indian cinema.

---

51. Ibid.

52. "James Bond Meets Rafale: Jaitley Quotes Goldfinger to Tear into Rahul Gandhi's Family", *India Today*, accessed 25 May 2025, https://www.indiatoday.in/india/story/arun-jaitley-james-bond-goldfinger-rafale-debate-rahul-gandhi-family-1421938-2019-01-02.

53. Arun Jaitley, *A New India: Selected Writings 2014–19* (Juggernaut, 2020), p. 320.

54. Arun Jaitley, *A New India: Selected Writings 2014–19* (Juggernaut, 2020), p. 320.

Both Vajpayee and Jaitley are also remembered for their oration both in Parliament and outside. In Parliament, both were heard in pin-drop silence. At public meetings, audiences would wait for hours for Vajpayee's arrival. His speeches were always infused with humour, and his quick wit made his instant responses unmatched. Vajpayee's choice of words, his turn of phrase, and the poetic touch he brought to his expression gave him the rare ability to explain even the most complex issues in simple language. Jaitley, himself a gifted orator, often acknowledged that he was deeply influenced by Vajpayee's speaking style—the first time he heard him speak, in 1967, when he was still a school student.

> There was a political rally near my house in Delhi for the 1967 general elections. He came to address that rally. He already enjoyed a formidable reputation as a great orator. He was on the way to becoming an iconic political leader. Many youngsters used to repeat the sentences that they heard in his speech. They imitated his style. I became a student activist of ABVP in 1970. Atalji was a familiar face in both Parliament and political rallies. We had invited him for several speeches in the Delhi University. Whenever we wanted some issues to be raised in Parliament, we rushed to brief him. My acquaintance with him started in 1973 when I was a student leader in Delhi University. Thereafter, I started interacting with him frequently. He has been a great listener. He used to occasionally react to some enthusiastic ideas, which we gave, with humour.[55]

★

Outside Parliament, Jaitley contributed to political discourse through his articles in which he often targeted the Congress. "*Tukde-tukde* gang" and "*chunavi* Hindus" were among the coinages he used to target the Congress and its leaders.

---

55. Ibid., p. 305.

Jaitley was also front-ending the party's strategies. When it came to party *karyakartas*, he was fiercely protective of them, and would do anything to safeguard their legitimate interests.[56] As a true leader, he mentored many young leaders and ministers even before the BJP formed the government in 2014. As Nirmala Sitharaman recalled:[57]

> In person, though, he was never proficient with praise. When I did something well enough by his standards—initially a press conference, later a parliamentary answer—his pat-on-the-back, as it were, would be limited to a "hmm" and a nod. That was enough, especially because it reinforced to me the biggest lesson there is to remember: At work, in politics or otherwise, you can't rest on your past successes. There were always ten other things that needed our attention. Sometime between 2011–2012, as I was on the way back after a particularly tough day in the TV studios, I got a call from him. He asked if I was alright, and told me to meet him the next day. I did so promptly. What he said then will stay with me a long time: "Don't try to win the evening with an argument," he said. "Gently put the facts across, and you'll win the day."

Jaitley's governance style was "balanced", with his reactions to most situations being well-considered and appropriate. Jaitley avoided extremism, instead opting for a measured, middle-of-the-road approach that allowed him to carry people along. It was this skill that helped him navigate complex political waters, including the successful passing of GST.[58]

---

56. Jyoti Pande Lavakare, "A Common Name, a Father's Light", *The Indian Express*, accessed 25 May 2025, https://indianexpress.com/article/opinion/columns/a-common-name-a-fathers-light-10080578/.

57. Nirmala Sitharaman, "A Shishya's Tribute to Arun Jaitley", *The Indian Express*, accessed 25 May 2025, https://indianexpress.com/article/opinion/columns/arun-jaitley-dead-bjp-finance-mentor-nirmala-sitharaman-5936231/.

58. S.N. Thyagarajan, "Raian Karanjawala on His Friends Ratan Tata, Arun Jaitley, and Rupert Murdoch", *Money Control*, accessed 25 May 2025, https://www.moneycontrol.com/news/trends/legal/raian-karanjawala-on-his-friends-ratan-tata-arun-jaitley-and-rupert-murdoch-11266571.html.

As a professional, Jaitley's skills sharpened his acumen, helped him dissect issues and situations in a split second. He could get to the heart of the matter straightaway, which, of course, is a great advantage in India's highly competitive politics. What also distinguished him from other politicians was the capacity to be prompt and witty. Congress politician Jairam Ramesh, who locked horns with Jaitley in the Rajya Sabha often enough, once called him "Bedi+Pras+Chandra+Venkat" for his "extraordinary spinning skills". He recalls that Jaitley enjoyed the description hugely. Bishan Singh Bedi, Erapalli Prasanna, B.S. Chandrasekhar, and S. Venkataraghavan made up Indian cricket's famous "spin quartet" of the late 1960s and the 1970s.[59]

Having sat on the Opposition bench for long, he held the Opposition in great respect. He also applauded performing MPs. On the occasion of the retirement of CPI(M) Rajya Sabha MP from Kerala, P. Rajeev, Jaitley remarked, "Mr Rajeev was industrious in digging out procedure and rules of debates in the House and kept the ruling benches on their toes." He then urged his friend from the CPI(M), Sitaram Yechury, to bring back Rajeev to the Rajya Sabha. Such mutual respect and consideration for political opponents are rare qualities in politics.[60]

★

Arun Jaitley was dogged by ill health soon after he took oath as a minister in 2014. The alarm bells rang when Jaitley was reading out his first budget speech. His family members were in the Visitors' Gallery at the historic moment to hear him speak. Jaitley began his speech well but as he proceeded, he looked uncomfortable and sought permission from the Chair to sit down and complete his speech. According to the rules of the Lok Sabha, a member is expected to speak from his allotted seat and must rise while speaking. However,

---

59. Anita Joshua, "Arun Jaitley: Mr Fixit, with Friends Everywhere", *The Telegraph*, accessed 25 May 2025, https://www.telegraphindia.com/india/arun-jaitley-mr-fixit-with-friends-everywhere/cid/1700063#goog_rewarded.

60. Gargi Parsai, "In RS, Clamour for P. Rajeev's Return", *The Hindu*, accessed 25 May 2025, https://www.thehindu.com/news/national/in-a-rare-gesture-mps-ask-cpim-to-bring-back-rajeeve-to-rajya-sabha/article7133930.ece.

an exception was granted to Jaitley because he was not looking well.[61] His obvious ill health could not have escaped the notice of the prime minister, as well as the rest of the country. It was Modi who advised Jaitley to heed the doctors' recommendation to undergo gastric bypass surgery. Initially, Jaitley was adamant and refused the procedure. The prime minister took a personal interest in his health, speaking directly to Jaitley's family to persuade him to proceed with the surgery without delay. He called Jaitley's son and daughter, Rohan and Sonali, for breakfast at 7 Race Course Road[62] (renamed as 7 Lok Kalyan Marg), telling them that they urgently needed to persuade their father to go in for bariatric surgery "as he had several years of productive work ahead of him" and needed to be healthier than he was, a family source confirmed.[63]

Rohan had just returned to India in 2014 and started practising as a lawyer.[64] He was set to get married the same year but Jaitley had to take a short sabbatical—a three-month break to undergo a kidney transplant and later he was forced to travel to the United States for treatment. In September 2014, Jaitley underwent bariatric surgery to treat weight gain that he suffered because of a long-standing diabetic condition. On 14 May 2018, Jaitley underwent renal transplant surgery at AIIMS. His friends, Modi and Amit Shah, were there to help.

Jaitley was diabetic from a young age. He grew up eating the rich, tasty food of Old Delhi: jalebis, kachoris, and rabri faludas. His father would often bring large packets of food from Chandni Chowk and Jaitley would be the first to devour them. "I have lived a life of 'imprisonment' for thirty-three years: walking, exercise, yoga, medical tests, a one-chappati meal, and a 99 per cent

---

61. Kumkum Chadha, *The Marigold Story: Indira Gandhi & Others* (Westland, 2019), pp. 331–32.

62. The official residence of the Indian prime minister.

63. Jyoti Malhotra, "What makes the finance-defence-company affairs minister the go-to man in the Narendra Modi Government", *India Today*, accessed on 4 September 2025, https://www.indiatoday.in/magazine/cover-story/story/20141110-arun-jaitley-narendra-modi-finance-defence-company-affairs-minister-805687-2014-10-30.

64. Rohan Jaitley completed his schooling from the Delhi Public School, R.K. Puram. From there he went on to study law at the Amity Law School, Noida. He obtained a master's degree from Cornell University in the United States.

vegetarian diet," said Jaitley.[65] In July 2005, while walking near his home in South Delhi's Kailash Colony with his friend Ranjit Kumar,[66] a senior lawyer, he started coughing and complained of breathlessness. Jaitley was rushed to Escorts Hospital. Noted heart surgeon Naresh Trehan who lived near enough reached fast, and fortunately "everything worked out". A few days later, Jaitley, then fifty-two years old, had triple bypass surgery.[67] Jaitley never let the world know of the many medical setbacks he faced.

Modi would keep tabs on Jaitley's progress in hospital, even visiting him at Max Hospital, where Jaitley was admitted, on the eve of his departure to the United States. In January 2019, Jaitley had a soft tissue cancer surgery in the United States. The prime minister was in constant touch with Jaitley's family. He would call him two–three times a day from New York and Washington, between speaking at the United Nations General Assembly and meeting US President Barack Obama.

Despite frequent visits to the hospital and subsequent long recuperating spells from 2014 to 2019, Jaitley continued to be the most important minister until his condition deteriorated further because of multiple ailments. He fought his health issues with fortitude and courage. Despite his medical condition, he would come to the rescue of the Modi government through his periodic commentaries on social media which became a repository of political judgment. But his failing health deprived him of the opportunity to present the final budget of the Modi government's first term.

On 12 March 2018, Jaitley was fielded for the Rajya Sabha from Uttar Pradesh, after having represented Gujarat in the Upper House for three terms. Jaitley filed his nomination papers at the Tandon Hall of the Uttar Pradesh assembly complex in the presence of Uttar Pradesh BJP chief Mahendra Nath Pandey, deputy chief ministers Keshav Prasad Maurya and Dinesh Sharma,

---

65. Kumkum Chadha, *The Marigold Story: Indira Gandhi & Others* (Westland, 2019), pp. 331–32.

66. Ranjit Kumar went on to become solicitor general in the Modi government.

67. Praveen Donthi, "Talk of the Town", *Caravan Magazine*, accessed 25 May 2025, https://caravanmagazine.in/reportage/talk-town.

Uttar Pradesh Cabinet ministers Shrikanth Sharma and Anupama Jaiswal, and party leader Hero Bajpai.[68] He was elected on 3 April 2018.

Jaitley's life changed after frequent surgeries. He had to make adjustments in his food habits. Arvind Subramanian wrote that when he first arrived in Delhi, tales of Jaitley's love for food were already legendary. It was sad therefore to see him, more recently, fulfilling his daily protein requirements by forcing down a few slices of paneer or a simple boiled egg. Often, Gopal—his Man Friday and a figure worthy of a Bollywood biopic—would attempt to refill his plate as though serving the old Arun Jaitley, only to be waved off with an irritable reminder that things had changed. The irritation, it seemed, was directed less at Gopal and more at the reality of his own altered circumstances.

However, that Jaitley could not slake his own appetite did not stop him from holding forth on Indian cuisines or from enthusiastically ordering for me the best chhole bhature or butter chicken in town whenever he could.[69] Almost till the end, he never gave up hope and continued to fight.

It was widely predicted that Modi would be back as the prime minister in 2019. His political opponents were in disarray; his own party was solidly behind him and he had clearly defined goals that were closely aligned with the hopes and expectations of an electorate impatient for change. Meeting those expectations would require more than one term in office. Sustaining the hopes, on the other hand, would demand evidence of real progress sooner rather than later.[70] Jaitley refused to contest the election to the Lok Sabha this time. Due to ill health, Jaitley remained physically absent from the election campaign in 2019 but kept the pot of his attacks on the Congress boiling on social media and continued his tirade till the very last days.

On 23 May 2019, the results of the national elections were announced and the BJP won 303 seats in Parliament, its highest tally ever, giving it a simple

---

68. "Arun Jaitley Files Nomination for Rajya Sabha Polls from Uttar Pradesh", *Mint*, accessed 25 May 2025, https://www.livemint.com/Politics/sSQ007TiJktR3WiXwh1u3H/Arun-Jaitley-files-nomination-for-Rajya-Sabha-polls-from-Utt.html.

69. Arvind Subramanian, "Arun Jaitley Hit All the Right Notes in His Tenure As the Minister of Finance", *Livemint*, accessed 25 May 2025, https://www.livemint.com/news/india/arun-jaitley-hit-all-the-right-notes-in-his-tenure-as-the-minister-of-finance-1559153248243.html.

70. Lance Price, *The Modi Effect: Inside Narendra Modi's Campaign to Transform India* (Hodder & Stoughton, 2015), p. 246.

majority in a Parliament that has 545 seats. The Modi-led BJP had by now expanded its popular vote share to 37.4 per cent in 2019, way above the 23.75 per cent vote share and 182 Lok Sabha seats won by the BJP under its first prime minister, Atal Bihari Vajpayee, in 1999.

Jaitley's superb four-decade-long political career was sadly cut short by failing health. He wrote to Prime Minister Narendra Modi ahead of the swearing-in in May and opted out of the new government.[71] In a special gesture, Modi visited him at his residence a day ahead of taking the oath.

71. "Arun Jaitley writes letter to PM Modi, opts out of new cabinet citing health reasons", *The Times of India*, accessed on 4 September 2025, https://timesofindia.indiatimes.com/india/arun-jaitley-opts-out-of-new-cabinet/articleshow/69555700.cms.

18

A Die-hard Nationalist

It is tempting to view the BJP as a party—and the Modi government in particular—through the prism of ideology, given the BJP's own projection of itself as an ideological organization. One of the anticipated outcomes of Prime Minister Narendra Modi's tenure was the elevation of nationalism to the centre of political discourse. There is, undeniably, a strong Hindu nationalist strand within the BJP, rooted in the belief that Indian nationhood is defined by an enduring cultural bond—one that must be preserved and nurtured, and which predates the idea of 'constitutional patriotism' that emerged after 1950.[1]

Despite his deep political engagement, the perception of Arun Jaitley as a technocrat rather than a full-blooded politician persisted. In truth, he was far more layered. He could laugh easily, share jokes, and hold forth on law, cricket, or Hindi cinema with his friends—some of whom belonged to the BJP. He could also play the charming socialite, though he neither drank nor stayed up late, usually beginning to yawn by 11 p.m. But when it came to politics, Jaitley's convictions were firmly ideological. He backed every 'Hindu' turn of the BJP, most notably the decision to make Ayodhya a political rallying point. A staunch nationalist, he worked quietly on the abrogation of Articles 370 and 35-A months before the bill was introduced; he was deeply disturbed when L.K. Advani lauded Mohammad Ali Jinnah in Pakistan; and from as early as 1999,

1. Bibek Debroy, Anirban Ganguly and Kishore Desai (Eds.), *Making of New India: Transformation Under Modi Government* (Wisdom Tree, 2019), pp. 3–9.

he was one of Narendra Modi's most ardent supporters. On matters central to the party's ideology, Jaitley never hesitated, never wavered, and never doubted.[2]

Jaitley subscribed to Hindutva politics but was never confined by it. His political temperament was more in the Vajpayee mould—liberal, pragmatic, and inclusive. Though he shared the saffron worldview, he opposed the demonisation or marginalisation of minorities. He criticised what he saw as "Muslim appeasement," but never the Muslim community itself. His life, like that of many political realists, was not without its contradictions,[3] but he was a nationalist to the core. In fact, he deserves credit for articulating common-sense nationalist ideas in a manner that was persuasive, balanced, and remarkably smooth. At a time when the English-language media had little positive to say about the BJP, and the RSS was often portrayed as a group of regressive elements hostile to modernity and freedom, Jaitley played a pivotal role in making nationalism appear intelligent, modern, and even aspirational to an entire generation of educated youth.[4]

For Jaitley, Indian nationalism lay at the core of both policy and public discourse—imbued with its own distinct character and uniquely Indian expression. The resurgence of nationalism, therefore, took many observers by surprise. For decades, nationalism had been dismissed as outdated, even burdened with a somewhat disreputable connotation. Jaitley said, "Nationalism is a good word but it is considered bad only in India."[5] As Makarand R. Paranjape eloquently put it, "Indian nationalism, however, is not quite as negative or defensive. It is a positive, even assertive, upsurge. Its central theme, tone, and tenor is the expectation that India can be great again…."

---

2. Swapan Dasgupta, "An Asset to BJP in the Coalition Game", in *The Discussant: Journal of Centre for Reforms, Development and Justice*, Special Edition, An Obituary to Arun Jaitley, Vol. VII, No. 3 (July–September 2019), pp. 48–49.

3. "Arun Jaitley: The Half Liberal Among Saffron Supremacists", *National Herald*, accessed 25 May, 2025, https://www.nationalheraldindia.com/obituary/arun-jaitley-the-last-liberal-of-the-ruling-right-wing-camp.

4. "A Tribute to the Man Who Brought 'Nationalism' to Our Drawing Rooms", *OpIndia*, accessed 25 May 2025, https://www.opindia.com/2019/08/a-tribute-to-the-man-who-brought-nationalism-to-our-drawing-rooms/.

5. PTI, "Nationalism a Bad Word in India: Jaitley", *The Pioneer*, accessed 25 May 2025, https://www.dailypioneer.com/2017/india/nationalism-a-bad-word-in-india-jaitley.html.

A renewed confidence in India has also revived the country's civilisational mission—something that had remained dormant, if not entirely forgotten, since Independence. A century ago, it was the idea of *swaraj* that endowed Indians with a sense of both moral and spiritual superiority over their colonial rulers. Over time, however, this awareness of India's higher purpose was suppressed and obscured. But what, indeed, is India's civilisational mission? Few take the time to reflect on it. As Sri Aurobindo observed, India rises for *dharma*, not for narrow self-interest. If one were to define the essence of such *dharmic* nationalism, India's distinctive contributions would include non-dualism in metaphysics, *swaraj*—or non-aggressive autonomy—in politics, and inclusiveness in culture.[6]

As a patriotic Indian, Jaitley was concerned about the mass infiltration of Bangladeshis which had changed the demographic character of Assam, West Bengal, and some districts of Bihar; he was particularly concerned by the consequences of the domination of the ethnic Assamese in Assam. Infiltration not only creates pressure on national resources, it is also a matter of national security. Every district in Assam adjacent to the Siliguri Corridor or Chicken's Neck[7] has witnessed a significant demographic change due to infiltration. Even the Supreme Court described it as a silent invasion of India. An infiltrator should not be confused with a refugee. A refugee is a person who is persecuted on account of his religious beliefs or political views, while an infiltrator gatecrashes only for economic opportunities. To place them at par would be naïve, Jaitley wrote in one of his blogs.[8]

He defended the National Register of Citizens (NRC), arguing that the territory and citizens are the two most important aspects of a sovereign state. He stated that the principal duty of any government is to defend the borders of the country, prevent any trespass, and ensure the safety and security of its citizens. He asserted that sovereignty and citizenship are the core of India's identity and that the country's interests must be prioritised over political

6. Bibek Debroy, Anirban Ganguly and Kishore Desai (Eds.), *Making of New India: Transformation Under Modi Government* (Wisdom Tree, 2019), pp. 21–28.

7. Siliguri Corridor, commonly known as the 'Chicken's Neck' is a narrow 22-km-wide strategic corridor in West Bengal that connects north-eastern states to the rest of the country. This narrow stretch is bordered by Nepal, Bangladesh, Bhutan, and China.

8. Arun Jaitley, *A New India: Selected Writings 2014–19* (Juggernaut, 2020), pp. 335–36.

considerations. Independent India has faced a major challenge in protecting its sovereignty in Jammu and Kashmir, a bone of contention between India and Pakistan from the time of India's partition in 1947. Even Assam was a sore point at the time of Partition, with Pakistan resenting its inclusion in India. Jaitley cited historical accounts by Pakistani and Bangladeshi leaders suggesting their claims over Assam, and highlighting the strategic importance of the region. He emphasised that the NRC was essential to protect India's sovereignty, as it helps distinguish between refugees, illegal migrants, and citizens. Jaitley warned that the consequences of large-scale illegal migration from Bangladesh have been dire for Assam, leading to a demographic change that could potentially result in the loss of the strategically vital lower Assam region to Bangladesh. He argued that no "misconceived and mistaken notions of secularism" should come in the way of addressing this issue. Jaitley stressed that India's sovereignty is not a "play thing" and should not be compromised for the sake of "imported vote banks".[9]

Jaitley never tired of underlining how India has succeeded as the world's largest democracy, where many other nations have failed. He wrote:

> The resilience of our democracy is truly remarkable. Except for a brief aberration when the dark clouds of Emergency hovered on the horizon, our journey on the path of democracy has taken us from strength to strength. We have surmounted many challenges on the way in a spirit of unity and amity. This great country is unique for the diversity in language, culture and religion which in a subtle way binds all of us into an essential oneness of being an Indian first and foremost.[10]

He believed that the challenges before India are even bigger and more complicated. Democracy confers on every citizen the right to equality and guarantees liberty of thought and freedom of speech and expression. It

---

9. Arun Jaitley, "National Register of Citizens—Sovereignty vs Vote Bank", accessed 25 May 2025, https://www.arunjaitley.com/national-register-of-citizens-sovereignty-vs-vote-bank/.

10. Arun Jaitley, "My Vision", accessed 25 May 2025, https://www.arunjaitley.com/my-vision/.

mandates the state to take steps to enable every citizen to access opportunities in education, employment, and health care. While India has succeeded in some measure to achieve the goals enshrined in the Constitution, much remains to be done. People's aspirations today are more visible than ever before. Because of the slow pace at which things have improved for the common man in the past few decades, there is also a growing impatience and a sense of restlessness. People want the present situation to change and change fast. They want the constitutional guarantees given to them years ago to be redeemed in real life. They want the economy to have a sustained high growth so that jobs are created for the many unemployed youth. They want the political class to shed its hypocrisy and work for the upliftment of the people in a sincere and transparent manner. They want corruption to be eliminated in all forms. Education and health care should be made affordable and accessible. Infrastructure, be it roads, rails, bridges, ports, or airports, should be developed. They want all forms of social inequality, discrimination, abuse, and exploitation to end soon.[11]

On 12 May 2014, as the polling ended for what was the world's largest democratic election, Jaitley proudly wrote, "The strength and resilience of Indian democracy has been most visible during this campaign. Despite momentary tensions and criticisms the elections have ended in a manner which could be a proud moment for Indian democracy."[12]

"I invite you to join hands with me in this crusade. Jai Hind"—the note on the home page of his website continues to remind us of his passionate vision.[13] "The crusade must continue. We should join hands to make India the nation of his vision," it appeals to the Indians.[14]

★

---

11. Arun Jaitley, "My Vision", accessed 25 May 2025, https://www.arunjaitley.com/my-vision/.
12. Arun Jaitley, *A New India: Selected Writings 2014–19* (Juggernaut, 2020), pp. 344–45.
13. Arun Jaitley, "My Vision", 25 May 2025, https://www.arunjaitley.com/my-vision/.
14. Arun Jaitley website, accessed on 4 September 2025, https://www.arunjaitley.com/my-vision/

The BJP has long been guided by three unwavering articles of faith: the construction of a Ram Mandir in Ayodhya, the enactment of a Uniform Civil Code, and the abrogation of Article 370. Jaitley was deeply invested in all three, though he was most vocal about Article 370. His final tweet—posted on 5 August 2019, just days before his death—was a jubilant one, celebrating the historic abrogation of Article 370, which had accorded special status to Jammu and Kashmir. The tone of that message reflected his profound sense of fulfilment. For years, Jaitley had argued that Article 370 was an anachronism—a temporary provision that had outlived its purpose and only fostered separatism in the region. He hailed the government's move as a monumental step toward true national integration.[15] The "temporary and transient provision cannot be treated as permanent, it had to go," he wrote on X, the micro blogging handle.[16] The decision of the government would help the people of Jammu and Kashmir the most as it would bring more investment, more industry, more private educational institutions, more jobs, and more revenue, he tweeted.[17] His last blog, written on 6 August 2019, shortly before his death on 24 August 2019, reflected his profound elation at this transformative decision. It was the fulfilment of a lifelong dream. He praised Prime Minister Narendra Modi and home minister Amit Shah for the "monumental decision" to revoke the special status of Jammu and Kashmir, calling it a "historical wrong" that has been "undone".[18] The prime minister had described it as an emotional moment for the party, and Jaitley's final blog, too, was on the same issue. "The popular belief that the promise BJP made on Article 370 is an unachievable slogan has been proved wrong," Jaitley.[19]

Jaitley understood the legal complexities involved in the abrogation and played a crucial behind-the-scenes role in strategising the move, ensuring that the government's decision was constitutionally sound. His blog, the

---

15. Arun Jaitley on X, https://x.com/arunjaitley/status/1158269065309200385.

16. Arun Jaitley on X, https://x.com/arunjaitley/status/1158269074553442304.

17. Deepshikha Ghosh (Ed.), "'Historical Blunder Corrected': Arun Jaitley As Article 370 Scrapped", NDTV, accessed 25 May 2025, https://www.ndtv.com/india-news/historical-blunder-corrected-says-arun-jaitley-as-article-370-for-jammu-and-kashmir-scrapped-2080453.

18. Jaitley's blog

19. Arun Jaitley, *A New India: Selected Writings 2014–19* (Juggernaut, 2020), pp. vii–ix.

text of which was carried by many national newspapers,[20] highlighted how the government had "legally and democratically" undone what previous administrations had considered too politically risky to touch. He took pride in the fact that the decision was passed with an overwhelming majority in Parliament, reflecting a national consensus. For Jaitley, this was not just a BJP victory but a triumph for India's unity and sovereignty. Yet, in his blog, Jaitley stayed humble, not taking credit for his role.

It was only a year later that Sangeeta Jaitley revealed that the bill for the abrogation of Articles 370 and 35-A was drafted by her husband, a task assigned to him by Prime Minister Narendra Modi. "Prime Minister had told Arun (Jaitley) to draft such a bill for abrogation of Article 370 and Article 35A that could withstand any legal scrutiny even if it is challenged in the Supreme Court," she disclosed in a video message commemorating the first anniversary of the historic decision. It was implemented effectively by Home Minister Amit Shah and it "all happened under the leadership of Prime Minister Narendra Modi", she added.

Narrating the sequence of events, Sangeeta Jaitley said that in the days before the bill was to be moved in Parliament, she found her husband "engrossed in reading the J&K Constitution" (J&K had its own constitution by virtue of Article 370) and asked him why. He replied, "Article 370 has to be abrogated." She disclosed that there was a meeting between the prime minister, home minister, and Arun Jaitley, where it was decided to abrogate Article 370 with a legally sound draft of the bill, which Arun Jaitley then prepared.[21] There was a flurry of activity in Jaitley's house before the bill for abrogation was tabled in the House. Officials from the PMO and the Ministry of Home Affairs were in and out to discuss the draft with him.[22] Shah called Jaitley to seek his

---

20. "Arun Jaitley Death: Full Text of Former Finance Minister's Last Blog", *Business Today*, accessed 25 May 2025, https://www.businesstoday.in/latest/economy-politics/story/arun-jaitley-death-full-text-of-former-finance-minister-last-blog-224724-2019-08-24.

21. "Abrogation Bill Was Drafted by Arun Jaitley, Reveals His Wife", *Tribune*, accessed 25 May 2025, https://www.tribuneindia.com/news/j-k/abrogation-bill-was-drafted-by-jaitley-reveals-his-wife-122624/.

22. Interaction with Sangeeta Jaitley.

"ashirvaad" soon after the Rajya Sabha cleared the way for the voiding of Article 370 and reorganisation of Jammu and Kashmir.[23]

★

Abrogation of Article 370—a permanent fixture on BJP poll manifestos—fulfilled a foundational demand of the BJP and its predecessor. The party's hard position on Kashmir is older even than the Ram Janmabhoomi struggle, which the party formally embraced as a political goal only with the 1989 Palampur Resolution. The integration of Kashmir, by contrast, was a fundamental party goal for the Jana Sangh right from 1951.[24] From the very start of the first day of the establishment of the BJS, it announced that India should withdraw the Kashmir issue from the United Nations (UN) as the state was an integral part of India and that the part of Kashmir under Pakistan administration should be liberated.[25]

From 1846 to 1858, Jammu and Kashmir was a princely state in a subsidiary alliance with the British East India Company and subsequently, under the British Crown. The princely state was created after the First Anglo-Sikh War (1845–46) when the East India Company, which had annexed the Kashmir Valley from the Sikhs as war indemnity, sold it to the Maharaja of Jammu, Gulab Singh, for Rs 75 lakh. During the British Raj, Jammu and Kashmir retained a degree of sovereignty, except in matters relating to defence, foreign affairs, and communications. The state also barred outsiders from owning property within its borders. In 1947, when India gained Independence, Maharaja Hari Singh—the ruler of Jammu and Kashmir—initially chose to remain neutral, refusing to join either India or Pakistan. However, his stance changed dramatically in October 1947, when tribal militias from the newly created Pakistan, supported

---

23. "Shah Broke Down When Jaitley Lost His Only Election", *The Times of India*, accessed 25 May 2025, https://timesofindia.indiatimes.com/india/shah-broke-down-when-jaitley-lost-his-only-election/amp_articleshow/70824179.cms.

24. Nalin Mehta, *The New BJP: Modi and the Making of the World's Largest Political Party* (Westland, 2022).

25. "History and Development of Bharatiya Janata Party", Bharatiya Janata Party, accessed 25 May 2025, https://www.bjp.org/historyanddevelopment.

by its establishment, invaded the state. Faced with this crisis, the Maharaja urgently sought military assistance from New Delhi. The Indian government agreed to intervene—on the condition that Hari Singh sign the Instrument of Accession.[26]

Hari Singh agreed and the Instrument of Accession was signed on 26 October 1947, which was accepted by Lord Mountbatten, the then Governor-General of India, under the provisions of the Indian Independence Act. Clause 7 of the Instrument of Accession emphasised that Jammu and Kashmir's accession to India was conditional upon the state retaining the right to have a significant degree of autonomy.[27] This clause was a foundational element that eventually led to the creation of Article 370. In July 1949, negotiations started on giving effect to Clause 7 in the Constitution of India being drafted by the Constituent Assembly. The discussions continued for months. On 17 October 1949, Article 370 was adopted by the Constituent Assembly. On 26 January 1950, the Constitution of India was enacted. Its Article 370 set the framework for Jammu and Kashmir's relationship with the rest of India giving it a special status.

Article 370 set three broad frameworks. Firstly, Article 370 stipulated India would not make laws in Jammu and Kashmir outside the scope set out by the Instrument of Accession, without the "concurrence" of its government. Secondly, it stated that except Article 1, which declared India as a "Union of States", and Article 370 itself, no part of the Constitution would apply to Jammu and Kashmir. The President of India could make any provisions of the Constitution to apply to the state with "modifications" or 'exceptions', but required only "consultation with the Government of the State". Thirdly, Article 370 itself could not be amended or repealed—unless the Constituent Assembly of Jammu and Kashmir consented to it.[28]

---

26. Instrument of Accession of Jammu and Kashmir, available at https://cjp.org.in/wp-content/uploads/2019/08/instrument_of_accession_of_jammu_and_kashmir_state.pdf.

27. Clause 7 of the Instrument of Accession: Nothing in this Instrument shall be deemed to be a commitment in any way as to acceptance of any future Constitution of India or to fetter my discretion to enter into arrangement with the Governments of India under any such future Constitution.

28. Advay Vora, "Article 370 of the Constitution: A Timeline", *Supreme Court Observer*, accessed 25 May 2025, https://www.scobserver.in/journal/article-370-of-the-

The decision came under strong attack from the Hindu community of Jammu led by the Praja Parishad and Buddhist groups from Ladakh. The Praja Parishad had been set up by RSS pracharak Balraj Madhok (later a founding member of the Jana Sangh) in November 1947, with the aim of forcing full integration of the state with India. The Praja Parishad's agitation, organised around the slogan "*Ek Vidhan, Ek Nishan, Ek Pradhan*" (One Constitution, One Symbol, One Premier), gained momentum when the Jana Sangh, the Hindu Mahasabha, and the Ram Rajya Parishad decided to back it.

Although having accessed Kashmir to India, Sheikh Mohammad Abdullah resented the frequent orders from New Delhi and wrote to Nehru on 10 July 1950:

> I have several times stated that we acceded to India ... despite our having so many affinities with Pakistan ... because we thought our programme will not fit with their policy. If, however, we are driven to the conclusion that we cannot build our state on our own lines, suited to our genius, what answer can I give to my people and how am I to face them?[29]

On 31 October 1951, seventy-five members of the Jammu and Kashmir Constituent Assembly gathered for the first time on an autumn day in Srinagar. They belonged to the National Conference Party led by then prime minister of Jammu and Kashmir, Sheikh Abdullah. Their goal was to draft a Constitution for Jammu and Kashmir.

The Kashmir agitation became a key Jana Sangh priority after the 1952 general elections. On 10 February 1952, the BJS met in Delhi and passed a resolution asking the government to withdraw the issue from the UN.[30] The resolution stated that the accession of Kashmir to India was full and it was

---

constitution-a-timeline/.

29. Arun Kumar Banerji, "Kashmir Muddle~I", *The Statesman*, accessed 25 May 2025, https://www.thestatesman.com/opinion/kashmir-muddlei-1503103866.html.

30. "52.05 Withdraw Kashmir Issue from UNO", in *Bharatiya Jana Sangh Party Documents: 1951–72*, Vol. 4: Resolutions on Internal Affairs (Bharatiya Jana Sangh, 1973), p. 19.

wrong to offer a plebiscite and take the matter to the UN where it was not justice that governed votes, but power politics and Cold War tactics.[31]

On 29 May 1952, the Jammu and Kashmir Legislative Assembly accepted the proposal of joining the Indian federation. To bridge the gap between divergent perceptions of Article 370 between the Centre and the state, a deal, known as the Delhi Agreement, was struck on 24 July 1952 between the National Conference (read Sheikh Abdullah) and Nehru.[32] There was an agitation against the pact led by the Praja Parishad.[33] The Jana Sangh declared that the State Constituent Assembly's decision to have a separate flag for Kashmir and its recommendation that the state be an autonomous republic within the Indian republic were a clear violation of India's sovereignty and the spirit of the Indian Constitution.[34] The Praja Parishad strongly agitated against this and the BJS supported it. In Parliament, Syama Prasad Mookerjee delivered a strong speech against it. The agitation in Jammu and Kashmir intensified. Prem Nath Dogra, the leader of the Praja Parishad, met Mookerjee in Jullundur (now Jalandhar), during the Punjab Jana Sangh session on 8 November 1952, and the two leaders discussed the Kashmir Satyagraha plan.[35]

In 1953, when Jana Sangh leaders sat in a conference to finalise a new constitution for the party, they simultaneously passed a resolution demanding the "full accession of Kashmir to India".[36] In March 1953, a satyagraha began in

---

31. Bhupender Yadav and Ila Patnaik, *The Rise of the BJP: The Making of the World's Largest Political Party* (Penguin, 2022).

32. Arun Kumar Banerji, "Kashmir Muddle~I", *The Statesman*, accessed 25 May 2025, https: / / www.thestatesman.com / opinion / kashmir-muddlei-1503103866.html.

33. Bhupender Yadav and Ila Patnaik, *The Rise of the BJP: The Making of the World's Largest Political Party* (Penguin, 2022).

34. "52.24 Integrate Kashmir Movement", in *Bharatiya Jana Sangh Party Documents: 1951–72*, Vol. 4: Resolutions on Internal Affairs (Bharatiya Jana Sangh, 1973) 22–24.

35. Devesh Khandelwal, *Pledge for an Integrated India* (1st edn., Prabhat Prakashan, 2016), p.180.

36. Bharatiya Jana Sangh Party Documents, 1951-72, accessed on 4 September 2025, https: / / www.google.com search?q=1953+Jan+Sangh+resolution+Full+Accession+of+Kashmir&rlz=1C5CHFA_enIN1103IN1103&oq=1953+Jan+Sangh+resolution+Full+Accession+of+Kashmir&gs_lcrp=EgZjaHJvbWUyBggAEEUYOTIHCAEQIRigATIHCAIQIRiPAjIHCAMQIRiPAtIBCTE3NjUzajBqN6gCCLACAfEFQMStcI8_lO8&sourceid=chrome&ie=UTF-8

Delhi with the demand for the complete integration of Jammu and Kashmir. On 11 May, Mookerjee entered Jammu and Kashmir without a permit. He was arrested and taken to Srinagar. To enter Jammu and Kashmir, over 10,750 satyagrahis participated in the agitation from all over the country.[37] Syama Prasad Mookerjee's arrest in Kashmir and his mysterious death on 23 June 1953 while in police custody ended the agitation;[38] the satyagraha was put on hold.[39] On 9 August, Sheikh Abdullah had to be arrested after being removed from the post of prime minister. Between 1952 and 1972, the Jana Sangh passed as many as twenty-four political resolutions on Kashmir—almost one-third of all its resolutions on the wider issue of national unity.

After a five-year process, on 26 January 1957, the Constitution of Jammu and Kashmir came into force with a declaration—"The State of Jammu and Kashmir is and shall be an integral part of the Union of India." The day before that, on 25 January 1957 the Constituent Assembly of Jammu and Kashmir was dissolved at 12.00 noon. The president of the Constituent Assembly, Ghulam Mohammed Sadiq, announced: "Today this historic session ends and with this the Constituent Assembly is dissolved." The Constituent Assembly made no express recommendation to dilute Article 370.[40]

Jaitley understood the complexities of the state, having been an active member of his party's core team on Kashmir for decades. As Vajpayee's minister, Jaitley was appointed as the interlocutor to hold talks with representatives belonging to the widest socio-political spectrum in the state.[41] On 26 June 2000, the Jammu and Kashmir Assembly adopted a report of the State Autonomy

---

37. "History and Development of Bharatiya Janata Party", Bharatiya Janata Party, accessed 25 May 2025, https://www.bjp.org/historyanddevelopment.

38. "Syama Prasad Mookerjee and the Communalist Alternative", in D.A. Low (Ed.), *Soundings in Modern South Asian History* (University of California Press, 1968), pp. 358–66.

39. "History and Development of Bharatiya Janata Party", Bharatiya Janata Party, accessed 25 May 2025, https://www.bjp.org/historyanddevelopment.

40. Advay Vora, "Article 370 of the Constitution: A Timeline", *Supreme Court Observer*, accessed 25 May 2025, https://www.scobserver.in/journal/article-370-of-the-constitution-a-timeline/.

41. L.K. Advani, *My Country, My Life* (Rupa, 2008), pp. 687–93.

Committee (SAC)[42] and asked the Centre to immediately implement it. The SAC recommended return of the constitutional situation in Jammu and Kashmir to its pre-1953 status, by restoring to the state all subjects for governance except defence, foreign affairs, currency, and communication. MLAs belonging to the BJP, JD(U), Congress, and a few other regional parties voted against the motion. The resolution shocked the nation. The Union Cabinet, at its meeting on 4 July, rejected the autonomy resolution.[43]

In December 2001, Pakistan-based terrorists carried out an attack at the Indian Parliament, killing seven security personnel and endangering the lives of Indian parliamentarians. This led to a mass mobilisation of Indian troops along the border, codenamed Operation Parakram.[44] The military build-up did not lead to a war, but the operation brought close to a million battle-ready soldiers eyeball-to-eyeball on the Indo-Pak border. Bilateral tension persisted through 2002 because of another terror strike against an Indian military facility in Jammu and Kashmir even as ceasefire violations continued to rise on the Line of Control.

The NDA government decided to hold talks with the Jammu and Kashmir government. Jaitley, BJP general secretary at the time, was appointed as the representative of the Indian government to hold talks with the state government and political parties there on the issue of devolution of greater powers to the state. Deputy Prime Minister Advani announced the appointment of Jaitley on the floor of the Lok Sabha.[45] Jaitley was to be assisted by Union home ministry officials, the government announced on 17 July 2002. The Jammu and Kashmir government was to be represented by senior minister Ghulam Mohiuddin

---

42. The state government set up a committee to examine the question of restoration of autonomy to the state of Jammu and Kashmir vide Government Order No. 1164-GAD of 1996 dated 29 November 1996, available at https://vifdatabase.com/wp-content/uploads/2018/05/autonomy.pdf.

43. L.K. Advani, *My Country, My Life* (Rupa, 2008), pp. 674–79.

44. Operation Parakram was launched by the Indian military after the terrorist attack on its Parliament at New Delhi on 31 December 2001. The might of the Indian military was mobilised for an impending war with Pakistan.

45. Rajeev Deshpande, "J&K Autonomy Issue: Arun Jaitley Named Centre's Interlocutor", *India Today*, accessed 25 May 2025, https://www.indiatoday.in/magazine/nation/story/20020729-j-k-autonomy-issue-arun-jaitley-named-centres-interlocutor-794742-2002-07-28.

Shah and some others.[46] The Opposition criticised Jaitley's appointment stating that it was wrong to appoint a party-man as an interlocutor to represent the government. The government strongly defended the appointment of Jaitley; he is the best man for the job, it said. Jaitley was accorded Cabinet minister rank.[47]

On 25 July 2002, as the Centre's official mediator on the state's future, the latest in a long line of envoys, Jaitley met the senior minister of the National Conference, Ghulam Mohiuddin Shah, in New Delhi. The BJP informed the RSS that Jaitley's appointment as a negotiator was to discuss devolution of powers and not autonomy; the government may even consider creating a regional council for Jammu.[48]

In July 2003, there was another audacious terrorist attack on the Indian Army's leadership in Jammu. The situation became dire in Jammu and Kashmir. The previous years had been volatile. The year 2001 saw the killing of the highest number of militants and security forces. In terms of civilian casualties, 2002 was the worst.[49]

Amidst all this, in 2004, the Jammu and Kashmir Legislative Assembly passed the Jammu and Kashmir Permanent Residents Disqualification Bill (the Disqualification Bill), which proposed that women who married non-state subjects could no longer claim state subject status and would thereby lose both preferential treatment in government hiring and the ability to acquire new property in the state. Various political actors decried the Disqualification Bill's violation of Kashmiri women's fundamental rights under the Indian

---

46. "Onkar Singh, "Swami Defends Jaitley's Appointment as J&K Interlocutor", *Rediff*, accessed 25 May 2025, https://m.rediff.com/news/2002/jul/18onkar.htm.

47. Arun Jaitley, "Letter by Shri Arun Jaitley Leader of the Opposition (Rajya Sabha) to the Prime Minister on the Report of the Working Group Constituted by the Government of Jammu & Kashmir on 'Strengthening Relations between State and the Centre'", Bharatiya Janata Party, accessed 25 May 2025, https://www.bjp.org/hi/pressreleases/letter-shri-arun-jaitley-leader-opposition-rajya-sabha-prime-minister-report-working.

48. "No Autonomy for J&K: BJP to RSS", *The Times of India*, https://timesofindia.indiatimes.com/india/no-autonomy-for-jk-bjp-to-rss/articleshow/16354864.cms.

49. Jayanth Jacob and Aurangzeb Naqshbandi, "41,000 Deaths in 27 Years: The Anatomy of Kashmir Militancy in Numbers", *Hindustan Times*, accessed 25 May 2025, https://www.hindustantimes.com/india-news/the-anatomy-of-kashmir-militancy-in-numbers/story-UncrzPTGhN22Uf1HHe64JJ.html.

Constitution, while proponents of the Disqualification Bill issued apocalyptic pronouncements about the end of constitutionally guaranteed autonomy for Jammu and Kashmir if the Disqualification Bill failed to pass. Arguments for and against the Disqualification Bill fell largely along the lines of a false and dangerous dichotomy, casting feminism and Kashmiri autonomy as inherent opposites.[50]

In the wake of all this violence and tension, the BJP government in Delhi decided to start a peace process and appointed interlocutors to find a solution to Kashmir. Home Minister Advani started dialogue with leaders of the moderate faction of the All Parties Hurriyat Conference (APHC), an umbrella group of religious and political parties and Kashmir's most prominent separatist organisation. Two rounds of talks were held in New Delhi on 22 January and 27 March 2004. The Centre's interlocutors were, first, K.C. Pant, deputy chairman of the Planning Commission, then Arun Jaitley, and later N.N. Vohra, a high-ranking former bureaucrat. They held discussions with various groups.

The NDA lost the election in 2004. UPA-I continued the dialogue with the APHC.

But, beyond the political dimensions, the abrogation held a deep personal significance for Jaitley. A committed progressive nationalist, he had been part of the broader ideological movement that viewed Kashmir's full integration as essential to India's civilisational identity. His last writings radiated a sense of completion, as if he had lived to see one of India's most contentious issues resolved. Knowing that his time was limited, Jaitley's final message was one of hope—a belief that Kashmir would now progress without the shackles of separatism. His words were not just those of a statesman but of a man who had seen his life's work bear fruit. For Jaitley, a lifelong advocate of national integration, this was not just a political victory but the culmination of a decades-long ideological struggle, of his party, and his own. In his last blog, he recalled that when the Instrument of Accession was signed, the Congress did not allow the refugees who migrated to India from West Pakistan at the time of Partition to settle in Jammu and Kashmir. It trusted Sheikh Abdullah

50. Sehla Ashai, "The Jammu and Kashmir State Subjects Controversy of 2004", *Drexel Law Review*, Vol. 2, No. 2 (2010), p. 537, available at https://drexel.edu/law/lawreview/issues/Archives/v2-2/ashai/.

to head the state who converted the state into a personal kingdom; Pakistan was more than enthusiastic in trying to exploit the situation.[51]

A nationalist politician who believed in policies that advanced the welfare of the people, Jaitley termed Article 35-A as an arbitrary provision that gave the right to the state government to discriminate between citizens living in the state and outside; some were declared as permanent residents while leaving out the others, children of some could get government jobs and own property while others could not, the heirs of women marrying outside the state were disinherited from owning or inheriting property. Article 35-A was introduced on 14 May 1954 by President Rajendra Prasad to implement the terms agreed to in the Delhi Agreement of 1952 of the Indian Constitution through the Constitution (Application to Jammu and Kashmir) Order, 1954, issued under Article 370. The Presidential Order guaranteed territorial integrity to Jammu and Kashmir and introduced Article 35-A which conferred special rights to permanent citizens of Jammu and Kashmir. This order was passed with the concurrence of the Constituent Assembly of Jammu and Kashmir. It demarcated permanent residents with exclusive right to purchase land, seek state government employment, and other benefits in education and health care. The others, called "non-permanent residents", were not privy to these privileges.

He considered Article 35-A a barrier to prosperity in the state as no investor was willing to set up any industry, hotel, private educational institutions, or private hospitals since no investor could buy land or property, and their wards could not get government jobs or admission to colleges. This also prevented reputed institutions from setting up educational institutions in Jammu and Kashmir, leaving its youth to travel all over for higher education. Engineering colleges and hospitals, including super-speciality facilities set up by the central government stayed underutilised or unutilised because professors and doctors from outside were unwilling to work in the state due to restrictions on access to state's resources. Article 35-A dismantled the state's economy, hurt the common people of the state the most, and denied them a booming economy, economic

51. Arun Jaitley, "PM Narendra Modi and HM Amit Shah Achieve the Impossible", accessed 25 May 2025, https://www.arunjaitley.com/pm-narendra-modi-and-hm-amit-shah-achieve-the-impossible/.

activity, and jobs, Jaitley argued.[52] He emphatically advocated for abolition of Article 35-A, claiming it as an unconstitutional provision surreptitiously included by a Presidential Notification in the Constitution in 1954; it was neither a part of the original Constitution framed by the Constituent Assembly, nor did it come as a Constitutional Amendment under Article 368 of the Constitution which requires an approval by two-thirds majority of both the Houses of Parliament.

In the 2015–16 Union Budget, Arun Jaitley announced the establishment of an All India Institute of Medical Sciences (AIIMS) and an Indian Institute of Management (IIM) for Jammu and Kashmir. He noted that the earlier NDA government under Atal Bihari Vajpayee had proposed an AIIMS for Jammu, but the subsequent UPA government had downgraded the project to an upgradation of the Government Medical College there.

Jaitley further informed Parliament that the Ministry of Home Affairs (MHA) had approved an increase in the monthly cash relief for Kashmiri migrants—from Rs 1,650 to Rs 2,500 per person. The MHA would release the funds, as it bears the entire cost of this relief. Recalling that a special allocation of Rs 500 crore had already been announced for migrant rehabilitation, Jaitley mentioned that the Jammu and Kashmir government had submitted a proposal of Rs 5,820 crore seeking a revision of the 2008 Prime Minister's Package, with an upward revision of most of its components.

In the previous year's budget, Jaitley had announced an Indian Institute of Technology (IIT) for Jammu. Continuing that momentum, he allocated Rs.90 crore in 2015–16 for construction of godowns by the Food Corporation of India and state governments in Jammu and Kashmir, the Northeast, and other emerging procurement regions. He also unveiled a new scheme—Skill Empowerment and Employment in Jammu and Kashmir (SEE J&K), Himayat—aimed at training one lakh youth from rural and urban areas of the state over five years.

Additionally, the National Centre for Design and Product Development was designated as the nodal agency for conducting a baseline survey and preparing a Detailed Project Report (DPR) for a Jammu and Kashmir crafts project,

52. Arun Jaitley, "The Rule of Law and the State of Jammu & Kashmir", accessed 25 May 2025, https://www.arunjaitley.com/the-rule-of-law-and-the-state-of-jammu-kashmir/.

including the formation of a Special Purpose Vehicle (SPV). An initial sum of Rs 25.5 lakh had been released for this purpose, Jaitley added.

On a previous budgetary proposal for setting up of Solar Parks and Ultra Mega Solar Power Projects, Jaitley said the scheme was approved by the Cabinet on 12 December 2014. Of Rs 200 crores kept in the last budget for upgrading the indoor and outdoor sports stadiums to international standards in Jammu and Kashmir, Jaitley said the proposal had been prepared.[53]

★

Jaitley was in favour of democratising the state's politics, but desired the state's mainstream parties to do more to isolate separatists. He was in favour of giving more space to mainstream parties in the Kashmir valley despite political differences so that the separatist space shrunk. But he expressed disappointment with the political families who had dominated that mainstream space since 1947—two based out of Srinagar and one in New Delhi; even when they condemned terrorism, it was always with "ifs" and "buts". Only when they distance from separatism completely, that violence and terrorism can end, he believed.[54]

At the same time, Jaitley made it clear that India would never accept the demand for separation. It had already given a loud and clear message both to the separatists/terrorists and Pakistan that azadi was not a possibility. He was angry when the two parties issued statements that the constitutional link between the state and the country was based on the solemn assurance of Article 35-A; if there was no Article 35-A, it would break the link, they resolved. Jaitley argued that Article 35-A was not there in 1947 when the Instrument of Accession was signed in the month of October. It was not there even in 1950,

---

53. Sanjeev Pargal, "Jaitley Announces AIIMS, IIM for J&K; Upgradation of Leh Palace", *Daily Excelsior*, accessed 25 May 2025, https://www.dailyexcelsior.com/jaitley-announces-aiims-iim-for-j-upgradation-of-leh-palace/.

54. Arun Jaitley, "The Rule of Law and the State of Jammu & Kashmir", accessed 25 May 2025, https://www.arunjaitley.com/the-rule-of-law-and-the-state-of-jammu-kashmir/.

when the Constitution came into force. It was only surreptitiously inserted in 1954. How could then it be the essential constitutional link, he asserted.[55]

Jaitley favoured strong steps to end terrorism. He argued that while conventional election issues like poverty, employment, and infrastructure were important, national security and terrorism were even more critical for India's long-term future. Jaitley highlighted the high cost of terrorism, including loss of lives, disruption of daily life, social tensions, and hindered development in Jammu and Kashmir. He argued that a strong government was necessary to combat terrorism effectively and integrate the region fully. He criticised the "soft measures" and "appeasement" policies of the past and emphasised the need for a firm approach. He expressed disappointment over the role the two parties were playing and that they were advocating for secession.[56]

A.M. Singhvi, a fellow parliamentarian of Jaitley, himself an eloquent speaker, recalled a strong speech by an Opposition member barely a year ago in the Rajya Sabha on the opportunism and failures of the BJP–PDP coalition in Jammu and Kashmir. Though he was not slated to speak, Jaitley was straining at the leash to intervene, since Jammu and Kashmir was close to his heart, apart from being his "sasural". Exercising his right to do so as the leader of the House, he made an impromptu, extempore, and masterful intervention for over twenty minutes, reeling off historical sequences, dates, and events since the 1950s, coupled with penetrating analysis, displaying his legendary memory, and also his ability to collate complex historical data into a simple, lucid, and prima-facie convincing narrative, even for the Opposition.[57]

★

---

55. Arun Jaitley, "Ek Desh Mein Do Vidhan, Do Pradhan", accessed 25 May 2025, https://www.arunjaitley.com/ek-desh-mein-do-vidhan-do-pradhan/.

56. Arun Jaitley, "The Rule of Law and the State of Jammu & Kashmir", accessed 25 May 2025, https://www.arunjaitley.com/the-rule-of-law-and-the-state-of-jammu-kashmir/.

57. Abhishek Manu. Singhvi, "Arun Jaitley Possessed the Rare Skill to Communicate Simply, Analytically and Calmly", in *The Discussant: Journal of Centre for Reforms, Development and Justice*, Special Edition, An Obituary to Arun Jaitley, Vol. VII, No. 3 (July–September 2019), pp. 35–37.

Not many may be aware that Jaitley played a key role in assembling the evidence submitted to the Supreme Court in the Ram Janmabhoomi case, supporting the argument that Ayodhya was the revered site of Lord Rama's birth. Ashok Singhal and Jaitley spent long hours in his Kailash Colony office poring over historical literature that could strengthen the case for the temple. It was during this research that they found, in sacred texts attributed to Guru Nanak, an account of the Sikh guru's visit to Ayodhya, where he refers to it as the place of Rama's birth. This reference, along with other material, became an important part of the documentation bolstering the claim.

★

In his last blog on 6 August 2019, Jaitley wrote that Prime Minister Modi had rewritten history. Parliament had given "a verdict that Dr. Syama Prasad Mookerjee's vision on Kashmir was the correct one and Panditji's dream solution has proved to be a failure". He expressed deep satisfaction, writing that the move would bring "peace, development, and democracy" to the region. He believed that the special status had only fuelled alienation, corruption, and terrorism, and its removal would allow Kashmir to truly become part of India's constitutional and economic mainstream.

Jaitley's passing just weeks after Article 370's abrogation marked the end of an era. His last blog stands as a testament to his unwavering belief in "one India, one Constitution"—a principle he championed till his last breath. For Jaitley, the abrogation was not just a policy shift; it was the fulfilment of a national destiny, and he departed with the quiet satisfaction of a mission accomplished. He was a man who loved his country more than anything else and his country benefitted greatly from his hard work and commitment. He lived an extraordinary life and will be remembered fondly for his many achievements, being a nationalist-progressive leader, and for many, his greatest achievement lies in swinging the entire generation of educated youth to the political right.

19

A Reformist Finance Minister

When Narendra Modi took over as prime minister in 2014, his government inherited a stumbling economy. Growing at a robust pace around 2008, the Indian economy had fumbled due to both domestic and global developments. Enticed by the growth in 2008, the private sector committed huge investments in core sectors such as infrastructure, power, and steel. However, a significant portion of those investments was made without due diligence.[1] Risks related to project implementation (land acquisition, forest clearances, environment clearances, other statutory approvals, etc.) and cash flows (revenue realisation vis-à-vis committed expenditures) started emerging. Businesses could not handle the resultant stress and projects started getting abandoned midway.[2] Investments turned unproductive, leading to considerable piles of bad debt. This choked the flow of funds into the system—a situation that fathered the non-performing asset (NPA) crisis, a challenge that the country was struggling with in 2014.

Outside India, the global economy had still not recovered from the shock of the 2008 financial crisis and most developed economies remained vulnerable. Trade stayed stagnant, marked by a shift towards protectionism. Crude prices were at historical highs owing to the geopolitical equations, particularly in

1. Bibek Debroy, Anirban Ganguly and Kishore Desai (Eds.), *Making of New India: Transformation Under Modi Government* (Wisdom Tree, 2018), pp. ix–xiv.

2. Ibid.

the Middle East, continuing to be volatile.[3] As mentioned earlier, less than a year ago then, India had also been relegated to an unflattering pack of the "Fragile Five" economies—along with Brazil, South Africa, Indonesia, and Turkey—after the rupee had plummeted due to the so-called "taper tantrum".[4] Crises often act as catalysts for transformation—economic upheavals tend to enable, or even compel, reforms. The need for reform arises only when existing policies are seen to have failed, and a crisis represents the most acute form of such policy failure.[5] When an economy becomes trapped in a Pareto-inferior equilibrium—where resources are misallocated and all participants remain confined to suboptimal outcomes—only bold interventions can break the impasse and steer it towards a more efficient and welfare-enhancing state. Such interventions, which may entail exposing domestic markets to competition, raising taxes, or reducing public spending, are typically unpopular and face strong resistance. Yet, the hardship endured during a crisis often makes these otherwise painful choices more acceptable. The severe welfare losses experienced in times of turmoil tend to overshadow the discomfort caused by an uneven sharing of reform burdens. In this way, economic instability can paradoxically open the path to a more prosperous equilibrium.[6]

While liberation of the economy in the 1980s facilitated faster GDP growth and some poverty reduction, it depended on massive, unsustainable fiscal deficits. Foreign debt piled up, and India went bust in 1991. The balance of payment crisis of 1991 became a pivotal moment in India's economic trajectory, leading to the opening of the Indian economy to a second wave of reforms. The GDP had dropped to 3 per cent at the time the balance of payment crisis

---

3. Ibid.

4. The 2013 taper tantrum resulted after the US Federal Reserve indicated that it was planning to wind down its programme of quantitative easing, resulting in global investors withdrawing money from emerging economies in anticipation of rising yields in the US bond markets.

5. Allan Drazen and William Easterly, "Do Crises Induce Reform? Simple Empirical Tests of Conventional Wisdom", *Economics and Politics*, Vol. 13, No. 2 (2001), pp. 129–57, available at http://econweb.umd.edu/~drazen/DrazenEasterly.EP72001.pdf.

6. William Easterly and Ross Levine, "Africa's Growth Tragedy: Policies and Ethnic Divisions", *The Quarterly Journal of Economics*, Vol. 112, No. 4 (1997), pp. 1203–50, available at https://www.jstor.org/stable/2951270.

occurred in 1991. Decades of overspending had driven the country to the verge of default on its foreign debt. The country, for the first time, had to pledge 20 tonnes of gold to investment bank UBS on 30 May that year to secure a $240-million loan. It pledged gold three more times after that sale, shipping 46.8 million tonnes of the yellow metal to secure $400 million in loans from the Bank of England and Bank of Japan. All this gold was repurchased by December of that year.[7] Clearly, a new policy was needed.

The collapse of the Union of Soviet Socialist Republic (USSR) showed that more socialism was not the answer, and so the government turned from autarky to globalisation, and from public sector domination to an economy driven by the private sector. Though under immensely adverse circumstances and extreme pressure, India grabbed the opportunity offered by the crisis with both hands and introduced systemic changes.[8] The Narasimha Rao-led government with Manmohan Singh as the finance minister took over on 21 June 1991 and launched a raft of economic reforms, including the dismantling of the Licence Raj.[9] As India stepped out of the shadows of socialism and into the new world of capitalism, a number of reforms were initiated aimed at supporting a free market economy. In a single stroke, the new industrial policy—Statement on Industrial Policy of 24 July 1991—did away with investment licencing and myriad entry restrictions. It also ended the public sector monopoly in many sectors and initiated a policy of automatic approval for FDI up to 51 per cent.

Public sector monopoly was limited to eight sectors selected on security and strategic grounds. All other sectors were opened to the private sector. The pre-entry scrutiny of investment decisions was done away with; emphasis shifted to controlling and regulating monopolistic, restrictive and unfair trade practices rather than making it necessary for the monopoly house to obtain prior approval of government for expansion, establishment of new undertakings,

---

7. "A Short History of Indian Economy 1947–2019: Tryst with Destiny & Other Stories", *Livemint*, accessed 25 May 2025, https://www.livemint.com/news/india/a-short-history-of-indian-economy-1947-2019-tryst-with-destiny-other-stories-1565801528109.html.

8. Manmohan Singh, the then finance minister of India, charged with the reforms, said, quoting Victor Hugo, "No power on Earth can stop an idea whose time has come", at the conclusion of his speech after introducing the economic reforms in Parliament in 1991.

9. Sumant Batra, *Corporate Insolvency: Law and Practice* (Eastern Book Company, 2017).

merger, amalgamation and takeover, and appointment of certain directors. The 1990s reforms were also accompanied by the lifting of exchange controls that had served as an extra layer of restrictions on imports. The government devalued the rupee by 22 per cent against the dollar from Rs 21.2 to Rs 25.8 per dollar. Importers were authorised to purchase foreign exchange in the open market at a higher price, effectively ending the exchange control.

India also carried out a substantial liberalisation of trade in services. Doors were opened wider to private sector participation, including participation by foreign investors in many key sectors.[10] The cumulative impact of years of reform and globalisation helped the Indian GDP to average more than 7 per cent in the early 2000s. But the four years from 2009 to 2013 were a new low for India. In 2014, India was on the verge of another economic crisis.

★

When Jaitley assumed the office of finance minister in May 2014, he had an onerous responsibility on his shoulders—of reinstating the fading growth story of the country. The mandate of the elections was also quite telling. It was the first time in three decades that one single party was able to draw an absolute majority. Clearly, high expectations and aspirations were pinned on the new government in office. His first task was to rejuvenate the economy and the mood of the nation. During its first two years in office, the government's foremost goal was to revive the Indian economy to its long-term growth potential of 8 per cent (6.5 per cent per capita) and to convey to citizens how crucial this was for generating employment and improving public welfare. Arun Jaitley envisioned India as a welfare state dedicated to uplifting the poorest, the differently abled, and the marginalised. For such a state to function effectively, it must possess substantial financial resources, which can only be secured through strong and sustainable revenue systems.

10. Arvind Panagariya, "India in the 1980s and 1990s: A Triumph of Reforms", IMF Working Paper WP/04/43 (2004), available at https://www.imf.org/external/pubs/ft/wp/2004/wp0443.pdf.

> In order to garner revenues, we need long-term sustained economic growth. The state must fulfil its role as a facilitator for economic growth by creating the right environment for stimulating entrepreneurship and investment. The long-term India story is intact even today. Our manufacturing sector has to spring forward and transcend years of neglect. Our youth have to be imparted the skills required to become employable and get absorbed in the expanding manufacturing sector. We need to step up investment flows to the agricultural sector and improve productivity and streamline marketing systems so that the farmer gets his due even as food prices remain affordable for our growing population. India has to be made ready for taking the lead in a world that is increasingly becoming globalised. We have some of the richest resource bases in the world. Our human resources are ranked the best in the world. What is needed today is the right leadership, which can rise over narrow partisan interests and do what is best in the nation's interest. We have to be big on ideas and go all out to implement them.[11]

Modi and Jaitley decided to turn the impending crisis into an opportunity. The two finalised and launched an ambitious programme of reforms to revitalise the economy. The next ten years became a transformative decade marking a significant chapter in India's economic history. The role of a finance minister is uniquely important and critical in governance and policymaking in any nation. Understanding the manner in which a nation's finance minister deals with policy matters is also another way of revisiting its economic history.

A finance minister's job is not just to present the annual statement of government finances or the budget. It is also meant to provide leadership to all the key economic policies pertaining to the finances of the government and its policies on trade and industry. Politically also, the finance minister is a key member of a government's top policymaking team or the Cabinet. The finance minister's relationship with the prime minister is a key element when it comes to the manner in which the economic policies of a government are framed and implemented. Indeed, the quality of the relationship between the

---

11. Arun Jaitley, "My Vision", accessed 25 May 2025, https://www.arunjaitley.com/my-vision/.

prime minister and the finance minister often determines the quality of policy and economic governance in a country. India is no exception.

A central premise here is that finance ministers do not operate outside the realm of politics. Even though they are influenced by inputs from technocrats and economic counsel from experts, they often have to tailor their decisions in light of the prevailing political reality. The decisions these finance ministers take provide material for a comprehensive study of the country's political economy. In some cases, they follow the technical advice they receive, but in many cases they go by their own political gut, even if they have to sacrifice their job as a consequence. The finance minister plays a critical role in every major economic policy decision taken by the government. Naturally, over the years, the importance of the finance minister too increased within the government.[12]

Perhaps these were the reasons Modi picked Jaitley as the finance minister; he checked all the boxes. Modi and Jaitley decided that the country needed a resolute reform package. It was essential to return to the broader goal of modernising the tax system by consolidating the numerous state and central levies into a few (three or four) and simplifying them through the streamlining of exemptions and deductions, along with a lowering of marginal rates.[13] Large investments were needed. Measures were required to regain investor confidence and make India attractive to foreign investors. This could not be done without improving India's ranking on World Bank's Ease of Doing Business.[14]

---

12. A.K. Bhattacharya, *India's Finance Minister, From Independence to Emergency (1947-1977)* (Penguin, 2023), p. xvii.

13. Bibek Debroy, Anirban Ganguly and Kishore Desai (Eds.), *Making of New India: Transformation Under Modi Government* (Wisdom Tree, 2019), pp. 89–102.

14. After data irregularities on Doing Business 2018 and 2020 were reported internally in June 2020, the World Bank management paused the next Doing Business report and initiated a series of reviews and audits of the report and its methodology. The Business Ready (B-READY) report, which replaced the Ease of Doing Business report, is the World Bank's new flagship report benchmarking the business environment and investment climate in most economies worldwide. The report assesses the regulatory framework and public services directed at firms, and the efficiency with which regulatory framework and public services are combined in practice. With data that are comparable across economies and over time, B-READY provides actionable evidence to promote reforms for a stronger private sector. The first B-READY report was launched on 3 October 2024, available at https://www.

Jaitley's budgets were marked by important reforms. If newspapers are any barometer of popular sentiment, a glance at *The Times of India*'s front-page headlines on post-budget days between 2014 and 2019 provide a sense of how perceptions of the Modi government's economics changed over time. If 2014 ("FM makes money for you") and 2015 were high on euphoria and hope ("Make it, India"), by 2016, the winds were clearly changing ("Glowing in the wind", "But it's bad news for the 'rich' as govt shifts focus"). By 2017, the Modi government had clearly started veering leftwards ("Wooing have-nots, hitting have-nots") and by 2018–19, it was in full election mode ("It all adds up to 2019"; "2019 … Modi goes full steam"). In Modi's second term, the front-page newspaper headlines on the budget remained lukewarm ("FM stumps rich, bats for investment" in 2019 and "New tax deal for the common man" in 2020, or "Long, wobbly flight to recovery").[15]

In his first budget speech, Jaitley said:

> The people of India have decisively voted for a change. The verdict represents the exasperation of the people with the status-quo. India unhesitatingly desires to grow. Those living below the poverty line are anxious to free themselves from the curse of poverty. Those who have got an opportunity to emerge from the difficult challenges have become aspirational. They now want to be a part of the neo middle class. Their next generation has the hunger to use the opportunity that society provides for them. Slow decision making has resulted in a loss of opportunity. Two years of sub five per cent growth in the Indian economy has resulted in a challenging situation. We look forward to lower levels of inflation as compared to the days of double digit rates of food inflation in the last two years. The country is in no mood to suffer unemployment, inadequate basic amenities, lack of infrastructure and apathetic governance. … As Finance Minister

---

worldbank.org/en/businessready. For Ease of Business, see "Ease of doing business score and ease of doing business ranking" (Chapter 6) in *Doing Business 2020* (World Bank Group, 2020), pp. 77–86, available at https://openknowledge.worldbank.org/bitstream/handle/10986/32436/9781464814402_Ch06.pdf.

15. Nalin Mehta, *The New BJP: Modi and the Making of the World's Largest Political Party* (Westland, 2022).

> I am duty bound to usher in a policy regime that will result in the desired macro-economic outcome of higher growth, lower inflation, sustained level of external sector balance and a prudent policy stance. The Budget is the most comprehensive action plan in this regard. In the first Budget of this NDA government that I am presenting before the august House, my aim is to lay down a broad policy indicator of the direction in which we wish to take this country. The steps that I will announce in this Budget are only the beginning of a journey towards a sustained growth of 7–8 per cent or above within the next 3–4 years along with macro-economic stabilisation that includes lower levels of inflation, lesser fiscal deficit and a manageable current account deficit. Therefore, it would not be wise to expect everything that can be done or must be done to be in the first Budget presented within forty five days of the formation of this Government.[16]

Jaitley's first budget (2014–15) reflected his early focus on strengthening the foundation. It acknowledged the critical link between a healthy banking sector and a robust economy. He recognised the need for substantial capital infusion to meet Basel-III norms and hinted at potential bank consolidation. He also laid the groundwork for financial inclusion through initiatives like the Pradhan Mantri Jan Dhan Yojana (PMJDY) and the creation of differentiated banking models, paving the way for small and payment banks.

His second budget (2015–16) was aimed at building on the foundation he laid in the first. The second budget emphasised leveraging the postal network for more significant financial access and proposed the Banks Board Bureau to improve governance in state-run banks. He introduced the Mudra Yojana, facilitating accessible loans up to Rs 20 lakh for small business owners. The Micro Units Development & Refinance Agency Ltd. (MUDRA) Bank was introduced to boost small business lending, aiming to "fund the unfunded". In his budget speech for 2015–16 on 28 February 2015, he stated:

---

16. Arun Jaitley, "Budget 2014–2015", available at https://www.indiabudget.gov.in/doc/bspeech/bs201415.pdf.

> Bankruptcy law reform that brings about legal certainty and speed, has been identified as a key priority for improving the ease of doing business. SICA (Sick Industrial Companies Act) and BIFR (Bureau of Industrial and Financial Reconstruction) have failed in achieving these objectives. We will bring a comprehensive Bankruptcy Code in fiscal 2015–16, that will meet global standards and provide necessary judicial capacity.[17]

In his third budget (2016–17), Jaitley addressed systemic issues. As the Insolvency and Bankruptcy Code (IBC) gained momentum, Jaitley proposed a similar framework for financial institutions, recognising the need for a specialised resolution mechanism. He also formalised the Monetary Policy Committee and supported state-run banks through recapitalisation. Bank consolidation efforts were also announced.

Jaitley also revived the Varishtha Pension Bima Yojana. In his first budget speech, he said:

> The NDA Government during its last term in office had introduced the Varishtha Pension Bima Yojana (VPBY) as a pension scheme for senior citizens. Under the scheme a total no. of 3.16 lakh annuitants are being benefitted and the corpus amounts to Rs 6,095 crore. I propose to revive the scheme for a limited period from 15 August, 2014 to 14 August, 2015 for the benefit of citizens aged 60 years and above. A large amount of money is estimated to be lying as unclaimed amounts with PPF, Post Office, saving schemes, etc. These are mostly out of investments belonging to the senior citizens and on their demise, remain unclaimed for want of relevant payment instructions. I propose to set up a committee to examine and recommend how this amount can be used to protect and further the financial interests of the senior citizens. The committee will give its report not later than December this year. The government is fully committed to the social security and welfare of employees serving in the organised sector. The Government

---

17. "General Budget 2015–16", available at https://www.irtsa.net/pdfdocs/Budget-2015-16_Highlights_and_Summary.pdf.

> is notifying a minimum pension of Rs 1,000 per month to all subscriber members of EP Scheme and has made an initial provision of Rs 250 crore in the current financial year to meet the expenditure. Further, increase in mandatory wage ceiling of subscription to EPS from Rs 6,500 to Rs 15,000 has been made and a provision of Rs 250 crore has been provided in the current budget. For the convenience of the subscribers, EPFO will launch the "Uniform Account Number" Service for contributing members to facilitate portability of Provident Fund accounts.[18]

Demonetisation in late 2016 created another kind of opportunity for his ministry to introduce a new wave of reforms. In his next budget (2017–18), Jaitley focused on navigating the post-demonetisation landscape. Presented on 1 February 2017, just months after the demonetisation move, the budget redefined India's economic landscape and paved the way for the rollout of GST in July 2017. It focused at revitalising the economy in the wake of the disruptions caused by demonetisation while steering India toward a digital, cashless future.

The budget promoted Bharat Interface for Money (BHIM) Payments app and BHIM Aadhaar Pay for digital transactions and offered incentives for cashless payments by small businesses. Other key announcements included allocation of further funds for bank recapitalisation, emphasising and strengthening the stressed asset resolution framework with the IBC and Securitisation and Reconstruction of Financial Assets and Enforcement of Security Interest (SARFAESI) amendments, and doubling the lending target for the Mudra Yojana. Tax relief for banks through increased NPA provisions was also introduced. The concept of electoral bonds was unveiled. The corpus of the Long Term Irrigation Fund was increased; Mission Antyodaya was launched to lift one crore households out of poverty, building one crore houses under the Pradhan Mantri Awas Yojana; and disinvestment of select public sector enterprises initiated.

---

18. Arun Jaitley, "Budget 2014–2015", available at https://www.indiabudget.gov.in/doc/bspeech/bs201415.pdf.

Jaitley also announced the abolishing of the Foreign Investment Promotion Board (FIPB) to boost FDI, which was in line with the government's "Maximum Governance, Minimum Government" principle. Overall, the 2017 budget represented a departure from tradition and focused on implementing significant reforms while emphasising development initiatives across various sectors. Jaitley called it a budget to "Transform, Energise, and Clean India", focusing on transparency, efficiency, and inclusivity.

In a historic move, Modi and Jaitley decided to discontinue the institutional arrangement of a separate Railway budget, ending a ninety-two-year-old tradition.[19] The 2017–18 budget was a single integrated budget of the Centre's finances. The merger of the Railway budget with the Union budget ended a colonial-era practice that had continued for nearly a century.[20] The merger decision stemmed from a National Institution for Transforming India (NITI) Aayog white paper, "Dispensing with the Railway Budget", by Bibek Debroy and Kishore Desai.[21] Jaitley informed Parliament that the rationale behind the merger was to provide a more comprehensive overview of the government's financial position. Jaitley argued that this would bring the Railways to the "centre stage of the government's fiscal policy" and enable better multimodal transport planning.[22] He oversaw the merger of the Railway budget with the Union budget. This change, implemented in 2017, integrated railway financial provisions into the broader national budget, streamlining the budgetary process.

---

19. Press Information Bureau, "Merger of Rail Budget With Union Budget", Government of India, Ministry of Railways, available at https://www.pib.gov.in/newsite/PrintRelease.aspx?relid=153672.

20. Saptaparno Ghosh, "2017: Breaking Conventions; Reflecting on GST, Demonetisation", *The Hindu*, accessed 25 May 2025, https://www.thehindu com/business/budget/2017-budget-breaking-conventions-reflecting-on-gst demonetisation/article69162659.ece.

21. Merger of Rail Budget With Union Budget, Press Information Bureau, Government of India, Ministry of Railways dated 16 November 2016, accessed on 4 September 2025, https://www.pib.gov.in/newsite/PrintRelease.aspx?relid=153672.

22. Saptaparno Ghosh, "2017: Breaking Conventions; Reflecting on GST, Demonetisation", *The Hindu*, accessed 25 May 2025, https://www.thehindu.com/business/budget/2017-budget-breaking-conventions-reflecting-on-gst-demonetisation/article69162659.ece.

The separate Railway budget originated in 1924, following recommendations from the 1920–21 Acworth Committee. In 1901, the recommendations of the Thomas Robertson Committee led to the formation of the Railway Board, later formalised in 1905 and reconstituted again in 1908 after the Railway Finance Committee submitted its recommendations. The 1905 Indian Railway Board Act conferred the powers or functions of the central government under the Indian Railways Act of 1890 on the Railway Board. Subsequently, following the recommendations of the Acworth Committee (1920–21), there was the Separation Convention of 1924, leading to the separation of Railway finances from general finances. When the proposal for resolution was presented to the legislative assembly in 1924, the government stated the following:

> In the first place, as far as State Railways are concerned, we want to abolish altogether this system of programme revenue voted for a year. We want to establish a proper depreciation fund, a depreciation fund arranged in a scientific and intelligible manner. Secondly, we want to build up Railway reserves. We want to build them up in order that our finances may be more elastic, in order that we may have provision to equalize dividends. And generally, we want to introduce a system of finance which while maintaining unimpaired the centrality of this House and while ensuring to general revenues a fair return from their Railway property, will be more suited to the needs of a vast commercial undertaking. Finally, and most important of all, we want to establish the principle, it is right and proper that the tax-payer, the State, should get a fair and stable return from the money it has spent on its Railways; but if you go further, if you take from the Railways more than that fair return, you are indulging in a concealed way in one of the most vicious forms of taxation, namely a tax on transportation. One of the objects we have most at heart in putting these proposals before this House is to establish that principle.[23]

---

23. "Interim Report of the Committee for Mobilization of Resources for Major Railway Projects and Restructuring of Railway Ministry and Railway Board", Ministry of Railways, available at https://indianrailways.gov.in/railwayboard/uploads/directorate/HLSRC/Interim_Report.pdf.

It was traditionally presented a few days before the Union budget. Post-independence, John Mathai presented the first independent Railway budget. This practice ended when the government merged the two, with Jaitley presenting the inaugural combined budget for the 2017–18 fiscal year. Since then, a unified budget presentation has become standard. This integration streamlined resource allocation and fiscal planning for the Railways. Despite the merger, the Ministry of Railways continues as a departmental commercial entity, with separate budget estimates and demand for grants. The Ministry of Finance now handles all legislative aspects, including a unified Appropriation Bill that incorporates railway estimates. The merger has facilitated integrated, multimodal transport planning and provides the Ministry of Finance with greater flexibility in resource allocation.

Another significant change was advancing the budget presentation to 1 February from the usual 28 February for effective and efficient implementation. India has seen annual budgets being presented on 28 February since Independence, though the time of presentation was changed from 5 p.m. to 11 a.m. in 1999. However, the presentation of the budget on 28 February delayed its approval by Parliament to April/May of the financial year for which it has been presented. In India, the first quarter of the financial year, from April to June, is the most productive period to carry out development work and undertake capital expenditure. The late approval of the budget affected the extent and flow of the government's development expenditure. The change was done to avoid a Vote on Account and pass a single Appropriation Bill for the upcoming fiscal year before the current one ended, allowing government departments to fully utilise the available working season.

Internationally, a good majority of countries treat the calendar year as the financial year. Bibek Debroy, then member of NITI Aayog, was a vocal proponent of changing the financial year (1 April to 31 March) to calendar year (1 January to 31 December). He produced a paper bringing out the history of the financial year and the deliberations that had taken place several times in the past to change the financial year. The prime minister noted this and expressed that he was in favour of considering a change in India's financial year at the full meeting of the NITI Aayog in early 2016. The government appointed a committee under noted economist and former Chief Economic Advisor Shankar Acharya to delve further into this question. The Shankar Acharya

Committee included several heavyweights, including former Cabinet secretary K.M. Chandrasekhar and former NITI Aayog vice-chairman Rajiv Kumar.

The committee conducted a dispassionate examination of the subject. It catalogued both the pros and cons of switching over to 1 November or 1 January as the beginning of the financial year. Both dates, 1 November and 1 January, suffered from a difficulty in India's context. With Diwali falling between 16 October and 15 November, it was expected to cause considerable administrative difficulty to compile budget documents and numbers on account of large staff unavailability owing to the festive season. December also suffered from this problem. The compilation of global practices also suggested that the calendar year was not a universal practice; a large number of countries still followed 1 April or other dates—such as 1 July and 1 October—as the commencement of the new financial year.

Jaitley was convinced that moving the date to November or January offered many challenges. He advised the prime minister to advance the budget from 28 February to 1 February. An unstarred question[24] was asked in the Lok Sabha on 15 July 2019 on the subject: Whether the government had decided to change the commencement of the financial year from January instead of April and, if so, the details thereof and whether it had taken the views of the states before implementing the change. The government replied that no such decision had been made.

The 2017–18 budget was presented on 1 February 2017, the first since 1924. All parliamentary approvals were obtained, with the demands for grants, appropriation bills, and Finance Act passed before the beginning of the financial year 2017–18. This enabled all fiscal expenditures to be taken up from the very commencement of the financial year. These reforms transformed the budget implementation system much more drastically than any budgetary reforms undertaken in the past. With a focus on transparency, inclusivity, and modernisation, the 2017 budget was a bold vision to transform India into a cleaner, more efficient, and globally competitive economy.

Jaitley's budget of 2017–18 was also unprecedented in terms of fiscal architecture, reforms, and management of the central government's finances. The distinction between Five-Year Plan and Non-Plan expenditure, which had

---

24. Unstarred questions are not taken up for oral answer in the question hour; a written reply is sufficient.

defined India's expenditures since the 1950s, had been done away with. The focus was now solely on revenue and capital expenditure. This was a move towards simplifying the budget structure.

With much of the economic reforms rolled out, Jaitley's next budget (2018–19) aimed at continuing reforms. He reiterated the benefits of demonetisation, including reduced cash circulation and a broader tax base. He emphasised the transformative impact of the IBC and the role of recapitalised banks in supporting growth. He detailed the bank recapitalisation plan, which involved raising substantial capital through various means, including recapitalisation bonds. Finally, he addressed the growing interest in cryptocurrencies, ruling out their legal tender status but acknowledging the potential of blockchain technology. The 2018 pre-election budget of the Modi government focused heavily on rural India, addressing concerns raised by the BJP's reduced majority in the Gujarat elections. The budget included increased minimum support prices for farmers, substantial increases in farm credit, "Operation Greens" for vegetable price control, and a large-scale health insurance scheme.

While previous budgets emphasised initiatives like smart cities, Jaitley's last budget prioritised rural infrastructure, housing, and roads, aiming to boost rural consumption and job creation. However, implementation details for many schemes, like Ayushman Bharat and calculation methods for Minimum Support Price (MSP), were lacking, raising concerns. Despite deviating slightly from the fiscal consolidation path, market borrowings remained lower than expected, maintaining fiscal prudence. Corporate tax relief was limited to smaller companies, and the new long-term capital gains tax initially caused market jitters, though it recovered. The real estate sector saw continued support for affordable housing. Overall, the budget, while populist in its rural focus, raised concerns about implementation and lacked significant measures to boost investment and job creation, despite maintaining fiscal stability. While the budget addressed agriculture, it fell short in job creation, investment, and exports.

★

Under Arun Jaitley's stewardship, the economy witnessed a wave of structural reforms and a series of difficult yet decisive policy actions. His tenure was marked by a transformative vision that harnessed technology to reshape the nation's economic landscape. Jaitley revamped the insolvency framework, culminating in the enactment of the IBC in 2016—an achievement that removed a major bottleneck to sustained growth. Equally historic was the introduction of the Goods and Services Tax (GST) in 2017, a reform that redefined India's indirect taxation by unifying multiple levies, enhancing compliance, and simplifying business operations. The success of GST owed much to Jaitley's tenacity and persuasive leadership. He was also instrumental in building India's digital payments ecosystem, with the Unified Payments Interface (UPI) emerging as a central pillar—driving unprecedented transaction volumes and revolutionising the way Indians engage with the economy.

Goods and Services Tax

Jaitley heralded GST, a blue-chip reform that will go down in history as one of the most ground-breaking economic reforms in Indian taxation. India has been substantially a tax non-compliant society. Taxation departments of the government have been a source of harassment which dissuaded people from coming into the tax net.[25] Tax rates were abnormally high. Jaitley decided to cut down the interface between the assessing officers, businessmen, and inspectors. As Modi's first term was nearing completion, Jaitley wrote in his blog:[26]

> The last five years will be considered momentous in this journey. No taxes have been increased. In fact, after sixty-seven years of increase, tax rates have moved downwards. In a bold step spread over a five-year period, income up to rupees five lakh has been exempted from income-tax. Even deductions available to the taxpayers have been increased to encourage and incentivise savings. The Goods and Services Tax has

---

25. Arun Jaitley, *A New India: Selected Writings 2014–19* (Juggernaut, 2020), pp. 45–52.

26. "Agenda 2019—Part-8 The Fourteen Iconic Reforms of Prime Minister Narendra Modi's Government", Bharatiya Janata Party, accessed 25 May 2025, https://www.bjp.org/interviews-and-articles/article-agenda-2019-part-8-fourteen-iconic-reforms-prime-minister-narendra.

> enforced one tax across the country, eliminated barriers and made inspectors disappear. Both income-tax and GST returns are filed on the net and assessments are done on the net. No interface, no corruption. Queries are raised on the net and responses are given on the net. The number of assessees filing returns with reduced tax rates in income-tax has risen close to double in the five-year period. The GST will increase the assessee base in the first twenty-one months of its implementation by almost eighty per cent. The ideal tax policy of simplification, no interface, lower rates and higher collections, has been implemented.[27]

Implementing GST would not have been possible without Jaitley's persistence and persuasive skills. The biggest tax reform in Indian history has simplified the tax structure of the country by replacing the erstwhile multi-layered complicated tax system. It brought all indirect taxes under one uniform tax system. Apart from easing the taxation framework of the country, the move truly integrated India into a single market, allowing for easy movement of goods across state borders. This has enhanced the ease of doing business for the economy, facilitating a high-growth trajectory.

Insolvency and Bankruptcy Code, 2016

Another blue-chip reform Jaitley piloted is the IBC. Indiscriminate lending by public sector banks (PSBs) had created large NPAs. The banking system was under stress. It was unable to support growth. Existing schemes and systems were not working.[28] Intended to be a transformative piece of legislation, the IBC sought revolutionary and cultural transformation in the insolvency and bankruptcy landscape by creating a comprehensive code for insolvency and bankruptcy for corporates and individuals. It established a new architecture for insolvency resolution and liquidation. Besides prescribing a new legislative

---

27. Arun Jaitley, *A New India: Selected Writings 2014–19* (Juggernaut, 2020), pp. 45–52.

28. Arun Jaitley, *A New India: Selected Writings 2014–19* (Juggernaut, 2020), pp. 45–52.

framework, it established many new institutions and led to operationalisation of NCLT, an institution conceived in 2002.[29]

The IBC changed the debtor–creditor relationship. Defaulting managements were removed and debtor companies were going in for resolutions with either new promoters taking over or by sale of assets. Banks finally started recovering their bad debts. No one can now cheat the banks and get away, Jaitley asserted.[30]

Banking Reforms

The global financial crisis of 2008 left the Indian economy largely unscathed. Encouraged by this resilience and a period of strong growth, Indian companies embarked on an aggressive wave of investments, often based on overly optimistic projections. Consequently, the financial health of both banks and corporates deteriorated, giving rise to what came to be known as the "twin balance sheet problem".

By the end of March 2017, bad loans accounted for almost 10 per cent of the country's banking assets. Due to these factors, credit to the private sector had virtually stagnated, bringing investments across the country to a standstill. When Jaitley entered the North Block, the banking sector was on the brink of crisis. In his first budget, Jaitley said:

> Financial stability is the foundation of a rapid recovery. Our banking system needs to be further strengthened. To be in line with Basel-III norms there is a requirement to infuse Rs 240,000 crore as equity by 2018 in our banks. To meet this huge capital requirement we need to raise additional resources to fulfil this obligation. While preserving the public ownership, the capital of these banks will be raised by increasing the shareholding of the people in a phased manner through the sale of

---

29. Mani Gupta, Aman Choudhary, and Saumya Upadhyay, "Overview of India's Insolvency and Bankruptcy Code", *Global Restructuring Review*, accessed 25 May 2025,https://globalrestructuringreview.com/review/asia-pacific-restructuring-review/2023/article/overview-of-indias-insolvency-and-bankruptcy-code.

30. Arun Jaitley, *A New India: Selected Writings 2014–19* (Juggernaut, 2020), pp. 45–52.

> shares largely through retail to common citizens of this country. Thus, while the government will continue to have majority shareholding, the citizens of India will also get direct shareholding in these banks, which currently they hold indirectly. We will also examine the proposal to give greater autonomy to the banks while making them accountable.[31]

He also noted that the rising NPAs of PSBs were a matter of concern for the government. He announced that six new DRTs would be set up at Chandigarh, Bengaluru, Ernakulum, Dehradun, Siliguri, and Hyderabad. He also said that the government would work out effective means for revival of other stressed assets.[32] Together with RBI, he took many bold decisions to restore the health of the ailing PSBs In 2017, Jaitley announced a huge recapitalisation plan for PSBs amounting to a whopping Rs 2.11 lakh crore over a span of two years. Ensuring capital adequacy brought financial stability and kick-started the lending process, which was crucial for the sustenance of the investment activity within the country.

Fiscal Deficit

The average inflation during UPA-II was about 10.4 per cent. For five years Jaitley struggled to bring down the fiscal deficit—the amount that the government borrows for its working. He succeeded in bringing down the fiscal deficit and largely avoided any big slippage in his term as the finance minister. If low crude oil prices helped the government contain the deficit, many policy decisions made the job difficult. Yet, by containing the fiscal deficit, Jaitley won for India a rare rating upgrade from Moody's Investors Service—a global organisation which provides data, intelligence, and analytical tools to business and financial leaders to help make decisions.[33]

---

31. Arun Jaitley, "Budget 2014–2015", available at https://www.indiabudget.gov.in/doc/bspeech/bs201415.pdf.

32. Ibid.

33. "Arun Jaitley's Five-Year Struggle to Bring Down Fiscal Deficit", *The Economic Times*, accessed 25 May 2025, https://economictimes.indiatimes.com/news/

The central fiscal deficit was badly disrupted in 2008–09 because of the global financial crises (GFC), peaking at 6.5 per cent of GDP in 2010–11, despite a sharp recovery and windfall of non-tax revenues from telecom auctions. It had been on a slow but steady downtrend since then after spiking to 5.9 per cent in 2011–12. The revenue deficit had followed a similar track (from 5.2 per cent and 4.5 per cent of GDP in the same two years). The average gross fiscal deficit was projected to be -3.6 per cent from 2014–15 to 2018–19 under the Modi government, compared to -5.3 per cent from 2009–10 to 2013–14 under UPA-2. In his first budget speech in July 2014, Arun Jaitley said that the government would retain the fiscal deficit target for 2014–15 at 4.1 per cent of GDP and reduce it further to 3 per cent by 2016–17. The fiscal deficit which had touched a high of 5.7 per cent in 2011–12, was brought down to 4.8 per cent in 2012–13 and further to 4.5 per cent in 2013–14. ⊠Jaitley added:

> My predecessor (P. Chidambaram) had set up a very difficult task of reducing the fiscal deficit to 4.1 per cent of GDP in [the] current year. Considering that we had two years of low GDP growth, an almost static industrial growth, a moderate increase in indirect taxes, a large subsidy burden and not so encouraging tax buoyancy, the target of 4.1 per cent fiscal deficit is indeed daunting. Difficult, as it may appear, I have decided to accept this target as a challenge. One fails only when one stops trying. My road map for fiscal consolidation is a fiscal deficit of 3.6 per cent for 2015–16 and 3 per cent for 2016–17. I am conscious of the fact that the Iraq crisis is leaving an impact on oil prices and the situation in the middle-east continues to be volatile. Monsoon this year appears more unpredictable. While inflation has remained at elevated levels relative to what is perceived as acceptable, there has been a gradual moderation in WPI recently, from a high of 7.35 per cent in 2012–13 and 5.98 per cent in 2013–14. But we are still not out of the woods. We also must fully address the problem of black money which is the curse of our economy. Faced with these adversities we have no option but to undertake some bold steps in order to enhance economic activity and spur growth in the economy. These steps are

---

economy/indicators/arun-jaitleys-five-year-struggle-to-bring-down-fiscal-deficit/articleshow/67568015.cms?from=mdr.

only the beginning of our effort to revive the growth spirit of the Indian Economy. They are directional.[34]

Jaitley was able to meet the target set by Chidambaram.[35] The decline in global oil prices following the GFC obviously helped Jaitley. However, the government followed a prudent policy by offsetting part of the decline by raising excise taxes, which had earlier been raised when oil prices rose.

Jaitley unveiled a road map for fiscal consolidation, with the 3 per cent fiscal deficit target to be achieved in three years instead of two. The government was able to meet its revised targets, bringing the deficit down to 3.9 per cent in 2015–16, 3.5 per cent in 2016–17, and 3 per cent by 2017–18. However, the government could not strictly adhere to the 2003 Fiscal Responsibility and Budget Management (FRBM) Act's glide path, citing structural disruptions in the economy, particularly the implementation of GST.

In 2016–17, Jaitley maintained the 3.5 per cent fiscal deficit target, but set up a committee to review the FRBM Act, as the government believed the targets were too rigid. The committee recommended a fiscal deficit target of 3 per cent until 2020, 2.8 per cent in 2020–21, and 2.5 per cent by 2023. Jaitley pegged the fiscal deficit at 3.2 per cent in 2017–18 and committed to achieving 3 per cent the following year. However, he later revised the 2017–18 target to 3.5 per cent, which the government could meet.

In his 2018–19 budget speech, Jaitley praised the government's record in containing the fiscal deficit. However, concerns arose when the government's deficit touched 114.8 per cent of the full-year estimates by November 2018.[36] The average inflation during the NDA's first term was less than 4.5 per cent. As

---

34. Arun Jaitley, "Budget 2014–2015", available at https://www.indiabudget.gov.in/doc/bspeech/bs201415.pdf.

35. "Arun Jaitley's Five-Year Struggle to Bring Down Fiscal Deficit", *The Economic Times*, accessed 25 May 2025, https://economictimes.indiatimes.com/news/economy/indicators/arun-jaitleys-five-year-struggle-to-bring-down-fiscal-deficit/articleshow/67568015.cms?from=mdr.

36. "Arun Jaitley's Five-Year Struggle to Bring Down Fiscal Deficit", *The Economic Times*, accessed 25 May 2025, https://economictimes.indiatimes.com/news/economy/indicators/arun-jaitleys-five-year-struggle-to-bring-down-fiscal-deficit/articleshow/67568015.cms?from=mdr.

Modi's first term was nearing completion in 2018, Jaitley wrote with satisfaction in his blog on 18 March 2019: "Today the CPI inflation is below 2.5 per cent."[37]

International Financial Services Centre

In April 2015, Prime Minister Modi approved the establishment of an International Financial Services Centre (IFSC) within Gujarat International Finance Tec-City (GIFT City) in Gandhinagar.[38] It was further resolved that a unified regulatory body would oversee all financial activities conducted there, given that services such as banking, equity trading, bond issuance, and insurance are typically governed by strong individual regulators like the Reserve Bank of India (RBI), the Securities and Exchange Board of India (SEBI), and the Insurance Regulatory and Development Authority of India (IRDAI).

India had long aspired to establish an international financial hub. The Mistry Committee, constituted in 2005, had proposed creating such a centre in Mumbai, accompanied by an ambitious financial reform agenda. However, Prime Minister Modi chose to locate it in GIFT City instead.

Again, the responsibility fell on Jaitley. Jaitley directed the Department of Economic Affairs to prepare the bill; it drafted the International Financial Services Centres Authority (IFSCA) Bill under his guidance. The consultation process with the law ministry and other concerned ministries was quickly completed and the Cabinet approved the bill without any changes. The IFSCA Bill was introduced in the Rajya Sabha by the acting finance minister Piyush Goyal on 12 February 2019. It was referred to the Standing Committee on 22 February. The bill was taken up for consideration in Parliament in November 2019, and passed in December 2019. The International Financial Services Centres Authority Act, 2019, was published in the Gazette of India on 19 December 2019. India had its unified regulator for IFSC, one of the first in the world.

37. Arun Jaitley, *A New India: Selected Writings 2014–19* (Juggernaut, 2020), pp. 45–52.

38. GIFT City was established in 2008, when Narendra Modi was the chief minister of Gujarat. Soon after, the process of transferring financial functions to IFSC started with GIFT City authorities playing the role of facilitators.

Injeti Srinivas, who was secretary in the Ministry of Corporate Affairs, was appointed as its first chairperson. The IFSC GIFT City has grown into a good international financial centre, thanks to numerous tax concessions granted by the government over the years and functions/services transferred to it. Bonds are being issued and listed in IFSC; a few equity stock exchanges have been set up; many banks have established their branches and offices there; and other financial services providers are also trooping in.

Foreign Direct Investment

The stressed banking system had its impact on the investment cycle. In his very first budget in 2014, Jaitley proposed to raise the FDI limit in insurance and defence manufacturing from 26 per cent to 49 per cent. Jaitley said:

> The policy of the NDA government is to promote FDI selectively in sectors where it helps the larger interest of the Indian economy. FDI in several sectors is an additionality of resources which helps in promoting domestic manufacture and job creation. India today needs a boost for job creation. Our manufacturing sector in particular needs a push for job creation. India today is the largest buyer of Defence equipment in the world. Our domestic manufacturing capacities are still at a nascent stage. We are buying substantial parts of our Defence requirements directly from foreign players. Companies controlled by foreign governments and foreign private sectors are supplying our Defence requirements to us at a considerable outflow of foreign exchange. Currently we permit 26 per cent FDI in Defence manufacturing. The composite cap of foreign exchange is being raised to 49 per cent with full Indian management and control through the FIPB route. The Insurance sector is investment starved. Several segments of the Insurance sector need an expansion. The composite cap in the Insurance sector is proposed to be increased up to 49 per cent from the current level of 26 per cent, with full Indian management and control, through the FIPB route. To encourage development of Smart Cities, which will also provide habitation for the neo-middle

> class, requirement of the built up area and capital conditions for FDI is being reduced from 50,000 square metres to 20,000 square metres and from USD 10 million to USD 5 million respectively with a three year post completion lock in. To further encourage this, projects which commit at least 30 per cent of the total project cost for low cost affordable housing will be exempted from minimum built up area and capitalisation requirements, with the condition of three-year lock-in. FDI in the manufacturing sector is today on the automatic route. The manufacturing units will be allowed to sell its products through retail including E-commerce platforms without any additional approval.[39]

Jaitley also promised a phased reduction of the corporate tax rate from 30 per cent to 25 per cent over four years, though this did not happen for all private businesses. His 2015–16 budget introduced the concept of a "place of effective management" (PoEM) to rationalise tax residency of companies and announced a comprehensive bankruptcy code. It also formed the MUDRA Bank to provide credit facilities to Micro, Small and Medium Enterprises (MSMEs), especially those promoted by SC/ST entrepreneurs. A composite FDI + FPI (Foreign Portfolio Investment) cap was introduced to simplify foreign investment limits.

In 2016–17, Jaitley cut corporate tax to 29 per cent for companies with turnover under Rs 5 crore and further eased FDI norms in sectors like insurance, pensions, and asset reconstruction. To address tax avoidance by multinational corporations, he introduced new Base Erosion and Profit Shifting (BEPS) documentation norms and an "equalisation levy" on their digital ad revenues.

Jaitley continued reducing corporate tax rates in subsequent budgets, extending the 25 per cent rate to companies with turnover up to Rs 250 crore by 2018–19. He also abolished FIPB, paving the way for more FDI reforms. FDI in insurance and defence were raised to 49 per cent. Several other conditions on FDI in construction, single, and multi-brand retail and Railways have also been eased, though progress on FDI in retail trade has been halted. The determined effort to expand the participation of Indian private industry in defence, and

39. Arun Jaitley, "Budget 2014–2015", available at https://www.indiabudget.gov.in/doc/bspeech/bs201415.pdf.

to reform public sector defence research and development and production, is expected to produce huge benefits in the years to come. From a worrisome situation on the investment front, fixed capital formation, which is an indication of investment, moved up to about 14 per cent.[40]

Factor Markets/Capital Market/Financial Market

Several actions were taken or initiated to improve the capital markets and technology transfers under Jaitley's watch. The 2015–16 budget announced a slew of measures to improve the functioning of capital markets, several of which required legislative changes. The Forward Markets Commission was proposed to be merged with SEBI, a long-delayed step in creating modern futures and forwards markets for commodities. Other institutional reforms included the establishment of a Financial Redressal Agency, a sector neutral agency for redressal of grievances against all financial service providers;[41] a Financial Data Management Centre;[42] a Financial Sector Appellate Tribunal; and a Resolution Corporation. The pass-through provisions available to mutual funds were also given to Real Estate Investment Trusts (REITs).

Financial Inclusion

The Indian example in financial inclusion is globally quoted as a role model. About 35 crore bank accounts under the Pradhan Mantri Jan Dhan Yojana were opened and every poor household has been connected to banks. As against 58 per cent of households in 2014, every willing household was connected to the banking system. Crores of poor people have received accident and life

---

40. Arun Jaitley, *A New India: Selected Writings 2014–19* (Juggernaut, 2020), pp. 45–52.

41. Press Information Bureau, "Task Force on Financial Redressal Agency", Government of India, Ministry of Finance, available at https://www.pib.gov.in/newsite/PrintRelease.aspx?relid=123713.

42. "Financial Data Management Centre (FDMC)", available at https://dea.gov.in/sites/default/files/Financial%20Data%20Management%20Centre_0.pdf.

insurance at a normal and negligible cost under the subsidised government schemes. More than sixteen crore MUDRA loans have been given to small entrepreneurs for creating avenues of self-employment.[43]

Eliminating Corruption

The NDA government's anti-corruption agenda leaned heavily on the finance ministry under Jaitley. Behind many reforms by Jaitley was the goal to eliminate corruption and tax evasion.[44] The war against black money was driven by him. From enacting stringent black money legislation to passing laws enabling the confiscation of fugitive offenders' properties and curbing their civil rights, the government undertook several major tax and policy initiatives to tackle illicit wealth. Double taxation avoidance treaties with Mauritius, Cyprus, and Singapore were renegotiated, and international agreements were concluded to enable real-time exchange of financial information on assets held by Indians abroad. Jaitley also institutionalised the monetary policy framework, enhancing transparency in the Reserve Bank of India's process of setting interest rates. Additionally, he persuaded Prime Minister Modi to adopt the Electoral Bond scheme, aimed at bringing greater transparency to political funding.

Jaitley said:

> Demonetisation has proved to be a significant step towards formalisation of the Indian economy. It compelled people to deposit their high currency cash into the banking system, account for the deposits by paying taxes or otherwise. It brought a behavioural change in how India spends its money. The real test of demonetisation is "has it led to higher tax collections and higher digital transactions?" The unequivocal answer is "yes".[45]

43. Arun Jaitley, *A New India: Selected Writings 2014–19* (Juggernaut, 2020), pp. 45–52.

44. Ibid., p. 63.

45. Ibid., pp. 35–37.

He led the transformation to the digital economy from the front. Jaitley noted that the government eliminated all discretions which governments, bureaucrats, and politicians had. There is no power in any individual or group of individuals to grant favours, largesse, or contracts to individuals. Systems have been established and all contracts can only be awarded through a market mechanism.[46]

Aadhaar

The rollout of Aadhaar—the Unique Identity Number (UID) assigned to every Indian citizen—was another milestone reform overseen by Jaitley. It marked a transformative move towards technology-driven and digitised governance. By enabling direct transfers to beneficiaries' bank accounts, Aadhaar eliminated leakages and the role of intermediaries, ensuring that individuals receive their entitlements from central, state, and local government programmes seamlessly and transparently.

While Nandan Nilekani—the co-founder and chairman of Infosys Technologies Limited, and the founding chairman of the Unique Identification Authority of India (UIDAI) in the rank of a Cabinet minister from 2009 to 2014—was rightfully credited for conceiving, initiating, and implementing the idea of having a UID for every citizen of India during the UPA government, it was under Jaitley that Aadhaar was given statutory form. When Jaitley took charge of the finance ministry, there was no law governing it. This triggered a serious legal challenge. While Nandan Nilekani pushed hard to get Aadhaar statutory recognition, a senior minister in the UPA blocked it. The BJP, while in Opposition, had some reservations particularly with regard to non-citizens being enrolled.

Immediately after the formation of the NDA government, a presentation was made to Prime Minister Modi by Nandan Nilekani where Jaitley was also present. At the conclusion of the presentation, the prime minister, in consultation with Jaitley and the others present, immediately decided to go ahead with the idea of Aadhaar. A new law—the Aadhaar (Targeted Delivery

---

46. Ibid., pp. 45–52.

of Financial and Other Subsidies, Benefits and Services) Act, 2016—was passed. The law aimed to eliminate duplicate and fake beneficiaries and ensured that subsidies and benefits reach the intended recipients.[47]

The essence of the new law lay in addressing inefficiencies in the government's vast subsidy expenditure for the poor. These subsidies had long been disbursed in indeterminate amounts to vaguely defined groups, with numerous ineligible or duplicate claimants—and even beneficiaries who did not exist. By introducing a biometric-based unique identity, the law aimed to eliminate such distortions and ensure that benefits reached only the rightful recipients.

After its passage in Parliament, the legislation faced a constitutional challenge before the Supreme Court. The Court upheld the fundamental idea of a unique identity system, dismissing claims that it infringed upon the right to privacy. It ruled that Aadhaar aligns with the principles of constitutional trust, limited government, and good governance, while empowering the marginalised. At the same time, the Court instituted multiple safeguards to prevent misuse and protect individual rights. The judgment of the Supreme Court, authored by Justice A.K. Sikri, added balance to the concept of Aadhaar.[48]

The Aadhaar (Targeted Delivery of Financial and Other Subsidies, Benefits and Services) Bill, 2016, was passed by Parliament on 16 March 2016. It was notified on 26 March 2016. Several other sections of the Act which had initially not been notified were notified on 12 September 2016. Ninety-nine per cent of the population of India above the age of eighteen has Aadhaar. Many state support schemes, including some by the Direct Benefit Transfer (DBT) mechanism, have been linked to Aadhaar. Pratyaksh Hanstantrit Labh / Direct Benefit Transfer for LPG (PAHAL) and Ujjwala beneficiaries are given cooking gas subsidies through DBT in their Aadhaar-linked bank accounts; crores of ration card holders stand linked; crores of Mahatma Gandhi National Rural Employment Guarantee Act (MGNREGA) scheme card holders get wage payment through DBT in their bank accounts. So do the 1.93 crore beneficiaries and other beneficiaries of the National Social Assistance Programme (NSAP).

---

47. Arun Jaitley, "Benefits of the Aadhaar—Where It Stands Today", accessed 25 May 2025, https://www.arunjaitley.com/benefits-of-the-aadhaar-where-it stands-today/.

48. Arun Jaitley, *A New India: Selected Writings 2014–19* (Juggernaut, 2020), pp. 45–52.

The income tax department has already linked crores of PAN card holders with their Aadhaar numbers. The government estimated that Rs 90,000 crore has been saved in the last few years till March 2018 through the use of Aadhaar. Several duplicate beneficiaries, non-existent beneficiaries, and fake beneficiaries have been eliminated. The Digital Dividend Report prepared by the World Bank estimates that India can save Rs 77,000 crore every year through the use of Aadhaar. The savings through Aadhaar could fund three schemes of the size of Ayushman Bharat. The total number of subsidy transactions through Aadhaar are almost about 425 crores. The total amount of subsidy transferred through Aadhaar now equals Rs 169,868 crore. With the elimination of middlemen, the benefits go directly to the bank accounts.

In all fairness, Jaitley credited Nandan Nilekani, who started it, and the bureaucrat Dr Ajay Bhushan Pandey, who as chief executive officer of UIDAI subsequently provided it with direction and expansion. Jaitley masterminded the government strategy to repel the legal challenge.[49]

Ayushman Bharat

The Ayushman Bharat scheme was launched on 23 September 2018 to provide 40 per cent of the poorest Indians free hospitalisation up to an expenditure of Rs 5 lakh a year.

India's healthcare system has long suffered from deep structural deficiencies. Beyond the shortage of medical institutions relative to its vast population, several other issues persist. While many public and private hospitals meet global standards and offer services at costs far below international levels, these remain unaffordable for a large section of Indians. Government employees and those in public institutions are generally covered by state-sponsored healthcare schemes, and members of the armed forces receive care within their own medical infrastructure. Some private companies also provide limited health benefits to their staff. Yet, nearly 63 per cent of Indians still bear the burden of healthcare expenses out of pocket, with many unable to afford essential

49. Ibid., pp. 35–37.

treatment. Low insurance coverage, inadequate financial protection, and high personal medical costs remain critical challenges.

Introduced as one of the most significant health initiatives since Independence, the Ayushman Bharat scheme seeks to address these gaps by providing greater access to affordable care for the poor. It also aims to strengthen hospitals as institutions—particularly in Tier-II and Tier-III cities—by ensuring a steady flow of patients and promoting the expansion of healthcare infrastructure across the country.[50] Another benefit expected is an increase in health sector jobs. Jaitley expected that overall, it will help create an accountable health system because beneficiary feedback is an integral part of its implementation.

In the first 100 days, 6.85 lakh patients were provided hospital treatment; 5.1 lakh claims availed of the scheme, for which payment was released. This averaged 5000 claims per day for the first 100 days. No patient has had to pay a single rupee. As awareness of the scheme increases, it is anticipated that in the next few years, over one crore families will benefit each year. Jaitley's target was 100 per cent coverage. Besides important state-supported institutions, private institutions have now been established mainly around large metropolitan towns or Tier-I or Tier-II cities. The total number of hospitals—both government and private—covered by this scheme at the end of 100 days numbered 16,000 and they are increasing steadily, Jaitley announced in his blog.[51]

Over half of the hospitals implementing the scheme are from the private sector. This allows patients to register at any empanelled facility and receive treatment worth up to Rs 5 lakh entirely through a cashless and paperless process. Jaitley termed the scheme "a game changer" in health care. Many people from weaker sections of society, who had previously avoided hospital treatment in order to avoid the burden of an unbearable payment, have benefited from this scheme.[52]

---

50. Cities in India have been classified into Tier-I, Tier-II, and Tier-III categories. The most developed ones are called Tier-I, and the underdeveloped ones are called Tier-II and Tier-III cities. The classification is based on factors like population, infrastructure, and economic activity.

51. Arun Jaitley, *A New India: Selected Writings 2014–19* (Juggernaut, 2020), pp. 32–34.

52. Ibid.

Judicial Reforms

Jaitley consistently called for a holistic reform of the judiciary, emphasising the need for transparent criteria in judicial appointments and for addressing the issue of judges' post-retirement roles. A steadfast advocate of judicial independence, he frequently spoke out to uphold the autonomy and integrity of the institution. At the same time, he was critical of the collegium system for appointing judges to the Supreme Court and High Courts. He strongly supported the 99th Constitutional Amendment that sought to create a National Judicial Appointments Commission (NJAC), reflecting the BJP's long-standing stance on the matter. Jaitley, however, expressed deep disappointment when the Supreme Court invalidated the amendment. He wrote that Indian democracy cannot be "a tyranny of the unelected".

Social Sector Reforms

Jaitley was particularly proud of the Swachh Bharat Mission—a vision of Prime Minister Modi. It was launched on 2 October 2014 throughout the length and breadth of the country as a national movement aiming to achieve the vision of a "Clean India" by 2 October 2019. While leading the mass movement for cleanliness, the prime minister exhorted people to fulfil Mahatma Gandhi's dream of a clean and hygienic India. Towards the end of five years in government, Jaitley recounted with satisfaction that the Swachh Bharat Mission had connected 99 per cent rural homes to sanitation and had become a flagship success story.

Jaitley also worked on improving the education of the girl child, reducing the number of dropouts from schools, and increasing remuneration for those employed in the formal sector such as Accredited Social Health Activist (ASHA) in Anganwadi. The minimum wages have been increased by about 45 per cent. The gratuity limit has been increased from Rs 10 lakh to Rs 20 lakh. Income eligibility for bonuses has been increased from Rs 7000 to Rs 21,000. The implementation of the One Rank One Pension (OROP) scheme, and the increase in the government share from 10 per cent to 14 per cent in the New Pension Scheme have helped the salaried class. The contributory pension scheme was extended to 10 crore informal-sector workers. These measures, Jaitley noted, also had a tremendous economic impact.[53]

Electoral Reforms

Jaitley had a long-standing commitment to ensuring transparency in political funding. During his tenure as law minister in the Vajpayee government, he introduced measures to promote cheque-based, tax-deductible donations and required their disclosure to both the tax authorities and the Election Commission of India (ECI). Companies were granted tax exemptions for openly declaring such contributions in their financial statements, while political parties were mandated to report all cash donations exceeding Rs 720,000 to the ECI. Later, as finance minister and one of the government's key policymakers, Jaitley remained deeply determined to curb the flow of black money in elections.[54]

In his 2017 budget speech, Jaitley said that the situation had "only marginally improved" after these measures, as "political parties continue to receive most of their funds through anonymous donations, which are shown in cash". In paragraph 164 of his budget speech (2017–18), Jaitley announced that electoral bonds would be introduced to bring "transparency in electoral funding". "Even 70 years after Independence, the country has not been able to evolve a transparent method of funding political parties, which is vital to the system of free and fair elections," he said.

The Finance Bill presented along with the budget proposed specific changes in the RBI Act of 1934 and Income-tax Act of 1961 for institutionalising electoral bonds. The RBI Act, 1934, was amended to empower the central government to authorise any scheduled bank to issue an electoral bond. An electoral bond was defined to mean "a bond issued by any scheduled bank under the scheme" notified by the central government. The amendment to the Income-tax Act made contributions through electoral bonds eligible for

---

53. Ibid., pp. 45–52.

54. Subhash Chandra Garg, *We Also Make Policy: An Insider's Account of How the Finance Ministry Functions* (HarperCollins, 2023), pp. 28–30.

deduction under Section 80GGB, similar to other corporate donations, but without requiring companies to specify the recipient political party in their accounts. It was observed that many donors hesitated to contribute via cheques or other transparent channels, fearing that disclosure of their identities could lead to adverse repercussions. This concern was identified as a key reason why companies avoided making direct political donations from their own accounts.

Arun Jaitley proposed "electoral bonds" to be issued "in accordance with a scheme that the Government of India would frame". These electoral bonds could be purchased by donors from "authorised banks against cheque and digital payments only". He argued that electoral bonds ensured white money donations through banking channels. Donors purchase bonds (declared in their accounts), parties deposit them in declared accounts, and the SBI maintains donor records. While the donor–party link remains masked, the system ensures transparency in transaction trails.

The budget announcement generated considerable controversy. Fearing that the scheme would divert all corporate political funding to the ruling party, the Opposition in general opposed the Electoral Bond scheme.

Model Code of Conduct

Another area that Jaitley wanted to reform was the Model Code of Conduct (MCC) in ensuring free and fair elections. He recalled when the MCC lacked statutory backing, existing only as a directive. The first NDA government, under Atal Bihari Vajpayee, and the then ECI, sought to rectify the inadequacy. Jaitley, who was overseeing the law ministry then, along with Chief Election Commissioner Dr M.S. Gill, formulated consent terms concerning the MCC. These terms were submitted to the Supreme Court in a pending dispute and were subsequently accepted and approved, giving the MCC statutory support under Article 324[55] of the Constitution. This strengthened the MCC considerably.

55. Article 324. *Superintendence, direction and control of elections to be vested in an Election Commission*—(1) The superintendence, direction and control of the preparation of the electoral rolls for, and the conduct of, all elections to Parliament and to the Legislature of every State and of elections to the offices of President and Vice-

Jaitley explained that Article 324 empowers the ECI to take necessary steps for conducting fair elections. While existing statutes cover many aspects of election conduct, Article 324 fills any legislative gaps. The Supreme Court, he stated, had consistently interpreted Article 324 as not applying to areas already covered by legislation. This principle, he argued, also applied to the MCC, which derived its authority from Article 324.

Jaitley then addressed the interplay between the MCC and the right to free speech. He acknowledged that specific electoral offences were covered by law, and in those areas, the law prevailed. The MCC, he argued, operated in the remaining areas. He observed a growing trend among political parties, particularly the Congress, to allege MCC violations by their opponents. He

---

President held under this Constitution shall be vested in a Commission (referred to in this Constitution as the Election Commission).

(2) The Election Commission shall consist of the Chief Election Commissioner and such number of other Election Commissioners, if any, as the President may from time to time fix and the appointment of the Chief Election Commissioner and other Election Commissioners shall, subject to the provisions of any law made in that behalf by Parliament, be made by the President.

(3) When any other Election Commissioner is so appointed the Chief Election Commissioner shall act as the Chairman of the Election Commission.

(4) Before each general election to the House of the People and to the Legislative Assembly of each State, and before the first general election and thereafter before each biennial election to the Legislative Council of each State having such Council, the President may also appoint after consultation with the Election Commission such Regional Commissioners as he may consider necessary to assist the Election Commission in the performance of the functions conferred on the Commission by clause (1).

(5) Subject to the provisions of any law made by Parliament, the conditions of service and tenure of office of the Election Commissioners and the Regional Commissioners shall be such as the President may by rule determine:

Provided that the Chief Election Commissioner shall not be removed from his office except in like manner and on the like grounds as a Judge of the Supreme Court and the conditions of service of the Chief Election Commissioner shall not be varied to his disadvantage after his appointment:

Provided further that any other Election Commissioner or a Regional Commissioner shall not be removed from office except on the recommendation of the Chief Election Commissioner.

(6) The President, or the Governor of a State, shall, when so requested by the Election Commission, make available to the Election Commission or to a Regional Commissioner such staff as may be necessary for the discharge of the functions conferred on the Election Commission by clause (1).

emphasised the fundamental nature of Article 19(1)(a), guaranteeing free speech, which, he asserted, could not be diluted, even during elections. He stressed that the MCC should be interpreted in a way that respects, rather than restricts, free speech, which is only subject to the restrictions outlined in Article 19(2). He believed the ECI had a responsibility to protect free speech, enforcing provisions only where election law was violated or where speeches fell within the permissible restrictions of Article 19(2). The MCC and the right to free speech, he argued, must coexist harmoniously.

Jaitley provided examples to illustrate his point. He cited a prime minister's appeal to first-time voters to remember the sacrifice of martyrs when voting, without mentioning any party or candidate. He also mentioned a comment about the demographic composition of the Congress president's constituency in Wayanad. He suggested that deeming such speeches as MCC violations could jeopardise the MCC's constitutionality concerning free speech. He cautioned against such interpretations, reiterating that the MCC did not diminish free speech.[56]

★

Jaitley's impact on India's economic evolution and his pioneering reforms across multiple domains remain unparalleled. His vision of nationalism sought to make India stronger, self-reliant, and economically dynamic—expressed with calm conviction rather than rhetoric or hyperbole. He embodied a rare blend of intellect, integrity, and empathy, standing out as both a visionary statesman and a humane leader.

A firm believer in cooperative federalism, Jaitley championed greater fiscal empowerment for the states. Acting on the Fourteenth Finance Commission's recommendation to raise the states' share in central tax revenues to 42 per cent—a notable 10 per cent increase from the Thirteenth Commission's proposal—the central government promptly accepted the change. As a result, states became financially more robust and autonomous. The structure of the

---

56. Arun Jaitley, "Model Code of Conduct Does Not Take Away the Right to Free Speech", accessed 25 May 2025, https://www.arunjaitley.com/model-code-of-conduct-does-not-take-away-the-right-to-free-speech/.

GST Council further reflected this spirit of partnership, granting states two-thirds of the voting power while the Centre retained one-third, ensuring a balanced and collaborative approach to fiscal governance.[57]

Arvind Subramanian, who worked as the Chief Economic Advisor in Jaitley's ministry termed him as a "dream boss": non-interfering, trusting, encouraging, and protecting.[58] When he learnt that Jaitley would not be joining the government in Modi's second term due to ill health, he wrote:

> Mr Jaitley's manner is so easy because he is totally comfortable in his skin. I never glimpsed vanity or edginess or the other manifestations of a prickly ego, which are almost occupational prerequisites for a politician. As a result, staff of the ministry of finance actually looked forward to meeting him, knowing that they could explain their positions forthrightly, without the risk of put-downs, beratings or humiliations.[59]

With his legal background, Jaitley possessed an exceptional ability to read swiftly and grasp complex material with ease. Bureaucrats enjoyed working under him—his gentle demeanour and attentive listening allowed him to understand both people and their work deeply. He was thoughtful and placed great trust in his officers, inspiring loyalty in return. Known for his sharp wit and engaging storytelling, he had a warmth that endeared him to colleagues. His stature and grace as a leader made serving with him both an honour and a delight. He cared for his officers.

On one occasion, Subramanian approached Jaitley for assistance in securing proper housing for junior officers of the Indian Economic Service (IES), many of whom spent the first fifteen years of their careers in substandard transit quarters in New Delhi. Jaitley was visibly affected after seeing photographs

---

57. Arun Jaitley, *A New India: Selected Writings 2014–19* (Juggernaut, 2020), pp. 45–52.

58. Arvind Subramanian, "Arun Jaitley Hit All the Right Notes in His Tenure As the Minister of Finance", *Livemint*, accessed 25 May 2025, https://www.livemint.com/news/india/arun-jaitley-hit-all-the-right-notes-in-his-tenure-as-the-minister-of-finance-1559153248243.html.

59. Ibid.

of the dilapidated apartments where these officers lived and hearing their accounts of the embarrassment they felt when family members visited. Deeply moved, he took personal initiative—persistently engaging with the then urban affairs minister—to ensure that land was allotted for the IES, paving the way for the construction of new and dignified housing.[60]

Throughout his term, he conducted himself with utmost statesmanship. The Fourteenth Finance Commission chaired by Dr Y.V. Reddy envisaged a radical decentralisation of fiscal resources inviting concerns from many leaders that the recommendations would constrain the Centre, and thereby backfire. But Jaitley responded that the Finance Commission's views should be respected, because the institution had served India so well for so many decades. And his persuasive skills carried the day.[61]

He rarely kept files pending for clearance. Ashok Pal Singh, who worked in Jaitley's ministry as the joint secretary, wrote:

> On one occasion, a file had to be cleared urgently, but the FM was in Kolkata. The flight kept getting delayed. Realising my discomfort, [Additional Private Secretary] Bhatia told me, "Sir, I will get the file signed whenever the FM returns and send it to your house but be ready to come to his residence should he want to discuss it even if it is midnight." Around 12.30 that night, my phone rang, and the screen bore the dreaded name of Bhatia! Bleary-eyed, I took the call only to be told the FM had just cleared the file.[62]

Even though Jaitley could have well taken credit for championing or shepherding many reforms, he preferred to credit his leader Prime Minister Modi, party, and officers in the ministry. When Subramanian decided to return to the United States on account of pressing family commitments, Jaitley posted a heartfelt thanks to Subramanian on his social media on 20 June 2018:

---

60. Ibid.

61. Ibid.

62. Ashok Pal Singh, "Arun Jaitley: An Ex-Official Recounts Friendly Meetings & a Salvaged Deal", *The Quint*, accessed 25 May 2025, https://www.thequint.com/voices/blogs/arun-jaitley-an-ex-official-recounts-friendly-meetings-a-salvaged-deal.

> His early diagnosis of the twin balance-sheet had led us to adopt the macro-economic strategy of higher public investment in the budget of 2015–16. He conceptualised JAM (Jan Dhan, Aadhaar, Mobile) as a database for availing public benefits. He contributed to the debate of federalism by conceptualising that Indian federalism has not merely to be cooperative but also competitive. He came out with new ideas and policy reforms in the sectors of clothing, fertilisers, kerosene, power and pulses. His report on the Revenue Neutral Rate was of great use in forging a consensus which led to the constitution amendment enabling the GST. He participated in every meeting of GST, gave his independent views and was heard in rapt attention by almost every finance minister.

Jaitley added that Subramanian would walk into his room, at times several times a day, addressing Jaitley as "minister" to give either the good news or otherwise. Jaitley said that Subramanian was not a spokesman of the government but an advisor who analysed and thought several steps ahead. He credited Subramanian with futuristic ideas on rationalisation of removal of "subsidies for the rich", universal basic income, climate change, from "socialism without entry and capitalism without exit". "He elevated the quality of the analysis and the presentation of ideas for public deliberation in his four economic surveys. His documents for four years were treated by several independent critics as one of the best ever produced," Jaitley wrote.[63] The cover of Subramanian's book *Of Counsel: The Challenges of the Modi–Jaitley Economy* aptly captures their relationship.[64]

Similarly, when Hasmukh Adhia, the finance secretary, was due to retire at the end of November 2018, Jaitley posted a note acknowledging his valuable contributions. Adhia had been in the finance ministry for four years and had been holding the responsibility of the revenue secretary for the past three years. Jaitley wrote:

---

63. Arun Jaitley, *A New India: Selected Writings 2014–19* (Juggernaut, 2020), pp. 317–18.

64. Arvind Subramanian, *Of Counsel: The Challenges of the Modi–Jaitley Economy* (Penguin, 2018).

> As secretary, financial services, Dr Adhia showed his leadership in the implementation of various social security programmes of the government through banking services. His contributions in successfully accomplishing the Mudra Yojana has been laudable. His tenure as the revenue secretary will be remembered for various initiatives where he provided the bureaucratic leadership in shaping and implementation of the policy. The campaign against black money both within and outside the country was the initial highlight of the revenue department. The income tax department now functions online with no physical interface between the assessee and the assessment official.

Jaitley acknowledged Adhia's role in GST reform. "It was his efforts supported by his team of officers of centre and state governments, which made it possible to hit the deadline of 1st July 2017. Rate reductions and smoothening of the rough edges were also achieved in a record time by Adhia's team," Jaitley wrote. He also credited Adhia's tenure for an exponential increase in the tax base and the tax realisations, supported by the Central Board of Direct Taxes (CBDT) and Central Board of Indirect Taxes and Customs (CBIC). Jaitley said:

> He was unquestionably a highly competent, disciplined, no-nonsense civil servant and of course, with impeccable integrity. His only diversion from his duties was his passion for spirituality and yoga. The government wanted to use his capability and experience in some alternative capacity. He had informed me earlier this year that he would not work for a single day after 30 November 2018. His time thereafter belongs to his favourite passion and of course his son. I wish him all the best for his post retirement life. Thank You, Dr Adhia.[65]

At the same time, Jaitley was less than impressed with a senior bureaucrat in the finance ministry who habitually sought to claim credit for every reform, eager to win favour with the Prime Minister's Office and advance his own aspiration of becoming the RBI governor. Despite his disapproval, Jaitley

---

65. Arun Jaitley, *A New India: Selected Writings 2014–19* (Juggernaut, 2020), pp. 324–25.

remained courteous in his dealings with the officer. After Nirmala Sitharaman succeeded him as finance minister in 2019, the officer was eventually relieved of his position. He later authored a book in which he took credit for many of the key reforms implemented during Prime Minister Modi's first term.

The media often drew comparisons between Arun Jaitley and Manmohan Singh. Both shared the distinction of being influential political figures without a significant personal electoral base—a factor commonly seen as limiting their authority within their respective parties and governments. Yet, each commanded substantial respect and influence in his own way. Singh's stature rested on his reputation for integrity and his role as the architect of the 1991 economic reforms, while Jaitley's influence derived from his legal acumen, administrative competence, parliamentary mastery, and talent for building consensus. What remains an intriguing question for history is how empowered they each truly felt—and whether they sometimes conducted themselves as though their influence were less than it actually was.[66]

The series of reform measures introduced by Jaitley have been crucial in easing the business environment of the country. After the implementation of the insolvency law and the tax reform measures, the Ease of Doing Business report for 2018 released by the World Bank saw India make the highest-ever jump of 30 points in the history of the index (from 130 in the 2017 report to 100 in 2018). In a strong validation of the GST reform, India recorded its most significant improvement in the "paying taxes" category, rising by fifty-three positions. The World Bank noted that since 2003, India has carried out thirty-seven reforms—nearly half of them within the past four years. While the *Doing Business* rankings are not the only metric influencing investment decisions, this progress bolsters global investor confidence by demonstrating the government's steadfast commitment to economic reform.

National highways, rural roads, port connectivity, number of airports, surplus power, modernisation of the Indian Railways, more resources for urban infrastructure, and significant resources for rural infrastructure were the hallmarks of infrastructure improvement during the first term of the Modi

---

66. Arvind Subramanian, "Arun Jaitley Hit All the Right Notes in His Tenure As the Minister of Finance", *Livemint*, accessed 25 May 2025, https://www.livemint.com/news/india/arun-jaitley-hit-all-the-right-notes-in-his-tenure-as-the-minister-of-finance-1559153248243.html.

government.[67] Rural roads, housing, sanitation, electrification, and cooking gas have all been added to infrastructure. Farmers were assured a minimum support price (MSP) providing returns of at least 50 per cent above their production costs. In addition, a subsidised crop insurance programme was introduced alongside an income support scheme worth Rs 75,000 crore, under which small and marginal farmers received Rs 6,000 annually. Further, Rs 60,000 crore was allocated through MGNREGA to strengthen rural livelihoods.[68]

Despite the spate of reforms undertaken, the economy grew at an average of 7.3 per cent between 2014–15 and 2017–18. And this growth performance was the highest among all the major economies of the world. In fact, as per International Monetary Fund (IMF) estimates, India's average rate of growth between 2014 and 2017 was about 4 percentage points higher than the rest of the world and nearly 3 percentage points higher than that achieved by emerging markets and developing economies.

Over the decade after 2014, India's GDP per capita has seen a remarkable increase. In 2014, the GDP per capita was approximately US$ 5000; by 2022, it had risen to over US$ 7000, marking a 40 per cent increase.[69] This growth trajectory is based on purchasing power parity. This means that the purchasing capacity of the Indian populace has grown. Today, India is the fastest-growing major economy in the world. India's economy outperforms most major markets, expanding at an annual average rate of 6 per cent. In 2013, India's economy was the tenth largest in the world; by 2023, at close to US $ 3.7 trillion, it had risen to fifth, above France and the United Kingdom. India is expected to become the third-largest economy by 2027 and expected to achieve a market capitalisation of US $ 10 trillion by 2030.[70]

---

67. Arun Jaitley, *A New India: Selected Writings 2014–19* (Juggernaut, 2020), pp. 45–52.

68. Ibid.

69. "10 Years of Modi Govt: How Has the Indian Economy Fared?", *Firstpost*, accessed 25 May 2025, https://www.firstpost.com/explainers/10-years-of-narendra-modi-government-how-indian-economy-fared-13773879.html.

70. PTI, "Reforms in Last 10 Yrs Are Foundation of Growth over Next Decade: Jefferies", *Business Standard*, accessed 25 May 2025, https://www.business-standard.com/economy/news/reforms-in-last-10-yrs-are-foundation-of-growth-over-next-decade-jefferies-124022200578_1.html.

In 2022–23, India's GDP total was US $ 3.7 trillion and per capita was US$ 2612, marking an 11.67 per cent rise from the previous year's US$ 2238. In 2021, there was a 16.98 per cent increase from US$ 1913 in 2020, which saw a 6.68 per cent decrease from 2019. India reached the fifth position globally on the nominal GDP rank in 2023 and on a per capita income basis, India has ranked 139. Nearly 70 per cent of India's GDP is driven by domestic and private consumption. Its GDP is fuelled by government spending, investments, and exports. India's equity markets have witnessed significant growth, with the Bombay Stock Exchange market capitalisation now above US $ 4 trillion, making it the fifth largest in the world. This growth reflects increased investor confidence and overall economic dynamism. India's foreign exchange reserves have seen a substantial increase, rising from US$ 304 billion in 2014 to US$ 642 billion in February 2024.

This increase has been driven by robust FDI inflows, strong exports, and prudent forex management by RBI.[71] The diversified reserve base provides stability and confidence to investors and policymakers. According to the IMF, India's economy is projected to grow at a rate of 6.6 per cent in 2025 and 2026, surpassing China's projected growth of 4.6 per cent and far exceeding the United Kingdom's expected growth of 0.6 per cent. This underscores India's robust economic policies and growth strategies. In the ten years since 2014, the world has taken more notice of India than ever before. The elephant, that veteran investor David Roche once described as slow and trundling but reliable, is moving ahead, steadily, gathering pace. Roche admitted India is now a viable alternative to China.[72]

Jaitley will be remembered for laying the foundation of this growth. No wonder, Arun Jaitley has settled into national memory as a reformer of the economy. As the successful finance minister of a $2-trillion economy growing at clip faster than China, Jaitley was the toast of his global colleagues and of

---

71. "10 Years of Modi Govt: How Has the Indian Economy Fared?", Firstpost, accessed May 25, 2025, https://www.firstpost.com/explainers/10-years-of-narendra-modi-government-how-indian-economy-fared-13773879.html.

72. Charmaine Jacob, "India Is a 'Slow Trundling Elephant' but a Viable Alternative to China, Says Veteran Investor David Roche", CNBC, accessed May 25, 2025, https://www.cnbc.com/2023/10/23/india-is-a-slow-trundling-elephant-but-a-viable-alternative-to-china-david-roche.html.

the world media at the annual Davos meet of the World Economic Forum held between 20 and 23 January 2016.

20

An Impactful Defence Minister

Jaitley's two terms as defence minister were brief, yet impactful. In the first term of the Modi government, Jaitley was in-charge of the defence ministry from 26 May to 9 November of 2014, before Manohar Parrikar was brought in from Goa to helm it. Jaitley was once again given charge of the defence ministry on 14 March 2017 after Parrikar quit the Union Cabinet to become the chief minister of Goa until Prime Minister Modi finalised a successor for Parrikar. Jaitley held charge till he was succeeded by Nirmala Sitharaman on 3 September 2017. He is the only finance minister ever to also hold the defence portfolio and, thereby, in charge of the country's economic as well as external security.

His tenure saw the clearance of a number of big-ticket reform measures and the simplification of the military acquisition process. When he took additional charge of the defence ministry from Parrikar, his priority was ensuring continuity in the country's overall defence policy. Parrikar had initiated some reforms during his tenure, but many were yet to be taken to their logical conclusions, such as the creation of a Chief of Defence Staff and new unified commands. Some key challenges that faced the new defence minister included strengthening the defence production sector, plugging operational gaps in military capabilities, ushering in reforms in higher defence management, and fixing the civil–military divide. The Indian military was facing critical equipment shortages, with aging platforms like the Mikoyan-Gurevich-21 (MiG-21) fighters and Cheetah helicopters in urgent need of replacement. The procurement process under the previous government had stalled.

Over the years, the Modi government has laid emphasis on making India 'Aatmanirbhar' or self-reliant in defence. Jaitley introduced several reforms in the defence sector to take his prime minister's vision forward. In his two brief stints as defence minister, Jaitley cleared the path for ushering in a raft of long-pending reforms in the armed forces and came out with key policy initiatives to make India self-reliant in defence production and simplify the military acquisition process. He also approved a number of key decisions to bring in reforms in the Navy and the Air Force.[1] As the defence minister, Jaitley's focus was to strengthen combat capabilities of the Army, the Navy, and the Air Force, considering the changing regional security matrix and geopolitical dynamics.

Just hours before Arun Jaitley was to take over as the defence minister in South Block, a MiG-21 fighter jet of the Indian Air Force (IAF) crashed in Jammu and Kashmir's Anantnag district, killing the young pilot who parachuted onto high-tension wires. The incident rang yet another alarm bell on one of IAF's cruellest dilemmas: It has no choice but to continue operating over 200 vintage MiG-21s designed in the 1950s. The UPA government sat on a proposal to buy 126 Rafale aircrafts for two years after the French beat competitors from the United States, Russia, and Sweden to win the world's largest military deal valued at Rs 42,000 crore in 2011. Then defence minister A.K. Antony pointed to the Tejas Light Combat Aircraft as an alternative for Rafale. The indigenous plane, however, was yet to enter combat service, even three decades after the project began.[2] Now, the task had fallen on Jaitley.

When Jaitley entered his South Block office, he found his table piled up with pending files on critical but costly replacements for India's antiquated war machines, including MiG-21s, dubbed 'flying coffins' as an alarming number had crashed; twelve in the past five years alone. That much of this hardware was desperately needed was beyond doubt, for it was critical to India's defence preparedness. The Army aviation corps pilots, for instance,

---

1. PTI, "In Two Stints as Defence Minister, Arun Jaitley Ushered in Major Military Reforms", *Hindustan Times*, accessed 25 May 2025, https://www.hindustantimes.com/india-news/in-two-stints-as-defence-minister-arun-jaitley-ushered-in-major-military-reforms/story-d8Yrut3ul4m1HkUvqM6CSP.html.

2. "Jaitley Faces Tough Task to Balance Two Portfolios with Ease", *India Today*, accessed 25 May 2025, https://www.indiatoday.in/magazine/nation/story/20140616-arun-jaitley-defence-minister-narendra-modi-government-mig-21-crash-804027-1999-11-29.

still flew 120 Cheetah light utility helicopters, literally to the edge of their endurance and service lives, to take supplies to soldiers at the high-altitude posts in Siachen. Like the MiG-21, the Cheetah was designed in the 1950s. A replacement had been delayed by over a decade. There was a need for M777 howitzers for the Army's artillery corps, but the defence ministry had not imported a gun since the Bofors scandal over a quarter century ago. At least 10 of the pending proposals worth over Rs 66,894 crore were "low-hanging fruits"; having completed technical evaluations, they were in the penultimate stage before the military and the bureaucracy could sit down with foreign contractors to negotiate prices.

Representatives of French jet-maker Dassault had held some 500 meetings with Hindustan Aeronautics Limited (HAL) in the past two years, and believed they could sign the contract for the Rafale fighter before the end of the financial year 2014–15.[3]

On 24 June, just a month into office, Jaitley was at Sena Bhavan in Delhi to inaugurate his first Naval Commanders' Conference, which proved to be an eye-opener for him. He was bombarded with opinions and feedback from the Navy brass and most of it concerned the slow pace of military acquisition. In his interaction with the Army and the Air Force brass too, who had also made detailed presentations for Jaitley's benefit earlier in the same month, the forces expressed fears of losing their fighting edge over rivals in India's neighbourhood due to delays caused by the long-winded procedure of clearing purchase proposals. Jaitley's encounter with the five Navy Commanders led by Navy chief Admiral Robin K. Dhowan and the noise made by these top officers brought to the defence minister's notice the need to change South Block's culture of defence procurement.[4]

Holding the defence ministry as a temporary charge, Jaitley was faced with a dilemma. On the one hand, he would have to send proposals to the finance ministry and, on the other, he had to find resources to pay for them in the Union budget due in the first week of July. The previous defence budget

---

3. Ibid.

4. N.C. Bipindra, "Winds of Change to Speed Up Defence Deals", *The New Indian Express*, accessed 25 May 2025, https://www.newindianexpress.com/thesundaystandard/2014/Jun/29/winds-of-change-to-speed-up-defence-deals-630027.html.

was heavily skewed towards personnel costs, leaving limited funds for new equipment. It was by no means an easy task. India's growth rate of 4.7 per cent was the lowest in twenty-five years. Inflation was at 8.6 per cent and fiscal deficit was over 4.5 per cent of GDP. He had to balance the need for fiscal prudence with the urgent requirements of military modernisation. The UPA government's delays in procurement had exacerbated the problem. Large-scale imports would strain the budget further.

The Modi government was determined to boost indigenous defence production. However, there was pressure to make quick, off-the-shelf purchases to address immediate needs. Jaitley's challenge, therefore, was to balance a Rs 230,000-crore budget that is traditionally skewed towards manpower costs rather than acquiring new hardware. India spent nearly 66 per cent of its defence budget on salaries of personnel, and only 33 per cent on acquiring equipment. And of the acquisition cost, nearly 90 per cent went in paying annual instalments for deals already signed. This left little cash for fresh acquisitions. So, Jaitley would have to significantly increase the budget.

He faced another related issue: The defence ministry had ignored a series of proposals for radical restructuring or downsizing to increase its fighting power. Each of the three services (Army, Navy, and Air Force) still projected its hardware requirements separately. This led to a huge backlog of acquisitions which the slow-moving ministry was unable to clear. The minister would also have to find money for the Army's gigantic manpower accretion plan: A new mountain strike corps of 90,000 soldiers, nearly the size of the British Army, that was going to cost Rs 64,700 crore.[5] Though devoting all his attention to preparing the Union budget, Jaitley set big plans in motion for India's defence apparatus as well.

In 2014, in his first budget, Jaitley emphasised on attracting foreign investment by raising the FDI cap in defence to 49 per cent from 26 per cent. The capital outlay for defence was also increased by Rs 5000 crore, including Rs 1000 crore for railway development in border areas. In 2015, he raised defence by spending 7.7 per cent, with an outlay of Rs 246,727 crore for 2015–16

5. "Jaitley Faces Tough Task to Balance Two Portfolios with Ease", *India Today*, accessed 25 May 2025, https://www.indiatoday.in/magazine/nation/story/20140616-arun-jaitley-defence-minister-narendra-modi-government-mig-21-crash-804027-1999-11-29.

over the previous year's budgetary estimates and 10.95 per cent over revised estimates. The capital expenditure for buying new weapons and equipment was increased to Rs 94,588 crore. In line with Prime Minister Modi's thrust on expanding the defence industrial base in the country and enhancing self-reliance in the defence sector, apart from venturing into exporting military items, Jaitley allocated resources for the modernisation of the military and announced a defence budget of Rs 2.58 lakh crore for 2016–17, a hike of 9.7 per cent over the previous year's revised estimates. The allocation for military modernisation was Rs 87,209.63 crore.

The 2017 budget yet again saw a hike of 6 per cent, as a result of which the Army accounted for 57 per cent, or Rs 1.49 trillion, of the country's defence budget.[6] However, the actual expenses reached Rs 417,242 crore, constituting 19.48 per cent of the central government's expenditure. In 2018, India allocated Rs 2.95 lakh crore for military spending during 2018–19, a modest hike of 7.8 per cent over the previous year's budget. The allocation of Rs 295,511.41 crore represents a growth of 7.81 per cent over budget estimates (Rs 274,114.12 crore) and 5.91 per cent over revised estimates (Rs 279,003.85 crore), respectively for the financial year 2017–18. Out of Rs 295,511.41 crore allocated for the financial year 2018–19, Rs 195,947.55 crore was allocated for revenue (net) expenditure and Rs 99,563.86 crore for capital expenditure for the defence services and the organisations/ departments under the Ministry of Defence. The amount of Rs 99,563.86 crore, allocated for capital expenditure, included modernisation-related expenditure. The capital allocation for the Ministry of Defence under BE 2018–19 was 33.1 per cent of the total central government expenditure on Capital Account, which was Rs 300,441 crore.[7] The budget included a capital outlay of Rs 99,563 crore for buying new weapons and systems. As the finance minister, Jaitley emphasised the government's focus

---

6. Gireesh Chandra Prasad and Tarun Shukla, "Indian Army Set for Overhaul as Govt Clears Reforms", *Mint*, accessed 25 May 2025, https://www.livemint.com/Politics/6Fhf3niqk5XpcCcOJ21PvO/Indian-Army-set-for-major-reforms-Defence-minister-Arun-Jai.html.

7. "Defence Budget 2018–19", Press Information Bureau, Government of India, Ministry of Defence, available at https://www.pib.gov.in/Pressreleaseshare.aspx?PRID=1518784.

on modernising and enhancing the military's operational capabilities.[8] In his budget for 2018–19, Jaitley as the finance minister proposed setting up of two defence industrial corridors to promote domestic production.[9]

Documenting War History

War histories shape national identity, influencing how countries perceive their past and future. For example, documenting colonial wars or independence struggles helps nations reconcile with their history and build a unified narrative. Documenting war history is crucial for preserving collective memory, learning from past mistakes, and honouring those who lived through conflict. Wars shape nations, alter borders, and transform societies, making their accurate recording essential for future generations. Historical records of wars provide factual accounts that counter misinformation and propaganda. Without documentation, events can be distorted, leading to historical revisionism. Accurate war histories ensure that sacrifices, atrocities, and geopolitical realities are remembered truthfully. Studying past conflicts helps societies understand the causes of war—whether political, economic, or ideological—and develop strategies to prevent future violence. The post-World War II establishment of the United Nations, for instance, was a direct response to documented wartime failures. War documentation preserves the stories of soldiers, civilians, and victims, ensuring their experiences are not forgotten. Memorials, archives, and oral histories give voice to those who suffered or died, fostering respect and empathy across generations.

One of the major initiatives by Jaitley was to bring the focus on documenting India's war history, a hugely neglected area. Lamenting the lack of war

---

8. "Budget 2024: Modi Govt's Big Announcements in Defence in Past 10 Years", *Hindustan Times*, accessed 25 May 2025, https://www.hindustantimes.com/business/budget-2024-modi-govts-big-announcements-in-defence-in-past-10-years-101706705165329.html.

9. PTI, "In Two Stints as Defence Minister, Arun Jaitley Ushered in Major Military Reforms", *Hindustan Times*, accessed 25 May 2025, https://www.hindustantimes.com/india-news/in-two-stints-as-defence-minister-arun-jaitley-ushered-in-major-military-reforms/story-d8Yrut3ul4m1HkUvqM6CSP.html.

documentation in India, Jaitley, as information and broadcasting minister in 1999–2000, said the country's war history needed to be popularised using the digital media. He instructed officials to begin compiling a comprehensive war history of the Indian armed forces. This project, he said, would educate future generations about the significant role Indian soldiers have played in various conflicts, including World War I. Twelve lakh Indians had fought in the war. The history, he instructed, should be presented in multiple formats.

Sela Pass

Jaitley approved construction of the Sela Pass, a significant step towards enhancing defence preparedness.[10] The Sela Pass tunnel was to be constructed by the Border Roads Organisation (BRO) at an altitude of 13,000 feet on the road connecting Tezpur, Assam, to Tawang in the West Kameng district of Arunachal Pradesh. The cost of Rs 687 crore, including a pre-construction cost of Rs 10 crore and four-year maintenance cost of Rs 15.63 crore was sanctioned for the project.[11] The tunnel was to provide all-weather connectivity to Tawang across Sela Pass on the Balipara–Chariduar–Tawang Road, boosting the preparedness of the armed forces and augmenting the socioeconomic development of the border region.

Comprising two tunnels and a 9.075-kilometre approach road, the Sela Pass was designed for a traffic density of 3000 petrol cars and 2000 diesel trucks per day, with a maximum speed of 80 kilometre per hour.[12] The foundation stone of the tunnel was laid by the prime minister on 9 February 2019, and the construction commenced on 1 April 2019. The tunnel was completed in just five years, overcoming challenges of difficult terrain and adverse weather conditions, using the drill and blast technique as part of the New Austrian

---

10. "Defence Budget 2018–19", Press Information Bureau, Government of India, Ministry of Defence, available at https://www.pib.gov.in/Pressreleaseshare.aspx?PRID=1518784.

11. "PM to Open World's Longest Bi-Lane Road Tunnel in Sela Pass Next Month", *Defence Watch*, accessed 25 May 2025, https://www.defencewatch.in/defence-news/pm-to-open-worlds-longest-bi-lane-road-tunnel-in-sela-pass-next-month.

12. Ibid.

Tunnelling Method, and incorporating safety features of the highest standards. The BRO described the project as one of the most difficult projects executed in the country.[13]

On 9 March 2024, Prime Minister Modi dedicated to the nation the Sela Tunnel project during the Viksit Bharat Viksit North East programme in Itanagar, Arunachal Pradesh. The project will not only provide a faster and more efficient transport route in the region, but is of strategic importance to the country.[14]

Foreign Direct Investment

In May 2001, the defence industry sector, which was hitherto reserved for the public sector, was opened up to 100 per cent for Indian private sector participation with FDI permissible up to 26 per cent, both subject to licensing. The Defence Production Policy, 2011 then aimed at achieving substantive self-reliance in the design, development, and production of equipment/weapon systems/platforms required for defence in as early a time frame as possible; creating conditions conducive for the private industry to take an active role in this endeavour; and enhancing the potential of small and medium-sized enterprises (SMEs) in indigenisation and broadening the defence research and development (R&D) base of the country.

The policy also highlighted the need to build up a robust indigenous defence industrial base by proactively encouraging larger involvement of the Indian private sector in design, development, and manufacture of defence equipment. India met 60 per cent of its defence requirements through imports. The invitation to foreign investors was also an attempt to shrink the country's trade deficit while equipping India with up-to-date manufacturing abilities. Previous efforts to liberalise the defence sector in 2001 were met with a lacklustre response. One of the key reasons for this was that private defence firms lacked

13. Ibid.

14. "Prime Minister Shri Narendra Modi Virtually Dedicates to the Nation Sela Tunnel from Itanagar, Arunachal Pradesh", Ministry of Defence, available at https://www.pib.gov.in/PressReleaseIframePage.aspx?PRID=2012962.

control in the companies they were expected to invest in. Ultimately, the sector saw negligible interest from foreign investors who spent only US $ 5 million since the sector was liberalised. This was in stark contrast to the billions being poured into other sectors, and in 2010, the defence industry was ranked the least attractive for FDI, coming behind soap and timber.[15]

In 2010, India's Ministry of Commerce and Industry circulated a discussion paper arguing for FDI limits to be raised to 74 per cent. Plans to increase FDI in defence were key to the BJP's election manifesto.[16] However, there were disagreements on the limits of foreign investment in defence among India's two largest industry bodies, the FICCI and the CII. While the CII argued for greater foreign investment in the sector for its ability to boost jobs in manufacturing, the FICCI warned that raising the FDI cap to 74 per cent would hinder the development of Indian intellectual property (a FICCI insider argued, "If permitting 100 per cent FDI for building products for the world's largest cellular phone market has not spawned a single world-class Indian company that manufactures cellular handsets or infrastructure, how will it happen in defence?").[17]

An announcement to further liberalise the sector came in Arun Jaitley's first budget speech in June 2014, which promised an increase in FDI from 26 to 49 per cent, albeit with significant qualifications. In August 2014, India's Department of Industrial Policy and Promotion (DIPP) formally put in place the increased Foreign Direct Investment (FDI) caps. The FDI limit of 49 per cent was composite and included all point of foreign investments, that is, FDI, Foreign Institutional Investors (FII), Foreign Portfolio Investment (FPI), Non Resident Investments (NRIs), Foreign Venture Capital Investor (FVCI), and Qualified Foreign Investors (QFI), a press note said.[18] The FDI

---

15. "Foreign Direct Investment in India's Defense Sector", DGA, available at https://dgagroup.com/insight/foreign-direct-investment-indias-defense-sector/.

16. Ibid.

17. Ajai Shukla, "CII & FICCI Disagree on Raising FDI in Defence", *Business Standard*, accessed 25 May 2025, https://www.business-standard.com/article/economy-policy/cii-ficci-disagree-on-raising-fdi-in-defence-114061200145_1.html.

18. "FDI in Defence Sector", Press Information Bureau, Government of India, Ministry of Defence, available at https://www.pib.gov.in/newsite/PrintRelease.aspx?relid=112371.

policy in the defence sector was applicable to defence industries, subject to industrial licensing under the Industries (Development and Regulation) Act, 1951. The list of defence products requiring industrial licence was notified vide DIPP Press Note No. 3 (2014 Series) dated 26 June 2014.[19] Frank Kendall, the Pentagon's chief defence buyer and key official for the United States on the Defence Technology and Trade Initiative (DTTI), said that the DTTI, when implemented, "would have a transformative impact on bilateral defence relations and enhance India's defence industry and military capabilities".[20]

In 2016, the government relaxed FDI norms in several sectors including defence. Under the newly notified rules, licences would be awarded by the DIPP in consultation with the Ministry of Defence and would not require additional oversight from the Department of Defence Production, as had previously been the case. However, the major qualifying condition for FDI continued to be that the firm must be owned and controlled by Indian residents, largely for security concerns. Other new stipulations include the opening up of investment to portfolio investors, who had previously been prevented from making investments. In another development, there would be no lock-in period for transfer of equity and thus equity could be transferred from one non-resident to another pending government approval. All sales could only be made to central and state governments (except in the case of non-lethal products). Further, production capacity would be decided at the time of granting a licence.

Certain riders on investment prevented the move from generating much enthusiasm. As Phil Shaw, head of Lockheed Martin's India operations, put it: "Over 50 percent is the key where you are able to control the business a little bit more than at 26 or 49 percent. Where we have a lot of intellectual property and investment in a particular product, we are not necessarily going to want to send it to India and then not have control over that particular technology."[21]

---

19. "List of Defence Items Requiring Industrial License", Press Information Bureau, Government of India, Ministry of Commerce & Industry, available at https://www.pib.gov.in/newsite/PrintRelease.aspx?relid=105881.

20. "Foreign Direct Investment in India's Defence Sector", DGA, available at https://dgagroup.com/insight/foreign-direct-investment-indias-defense-sector/.

21. "Foreign Direct Investment in India's Defense Sector", DGA, available at https://dgagroup.com/insight/foreign-direct-investment-indias-defense-sector/.

Strategic Partnership

Jaitley's most significant initiative as defence minister was his push to make India a hub for defence manufacturing through the unveiling of the long-awaited Strategic Partnership Model in May 2017. It was under his tenure that this key reform finally received approval. Earlier, when Defence Minister Manohar Parrikar released the Defence Procurement Policy (DPP) 2016 at Defexpo 2016, several appendices were missing, most crucially, the chapter on Strategic Partnerships, a vital component for the success of the "Make in India" initiative in defence production. The government had then announced that this chapter would be finalised after further deliberations. At that stage, private firms were eager to secure major manufacturing contracts, including large-scale projects for aircraft, submarines, and land systems, traditionally dominated by the public sector. However, internal disagreements within the government over the structure of the Strategic Partnership Model delayed the policy's completion. Consequently, India remained heavily dependent on imports for around 65 per cent of its defence requirements, continuing to be the world's largest arms importer, a reflection of the limited success of its defence research and production ecosystem.[22]

The Comptroller and Auditor General (CAG) report highlighted that the Indian Army was facing a critical shortage of ammunition, with stocks sufficient for only around ten days of war, against the required forty days. Jaitley informed the Rajya Sabha that while the CAG report referenced a point in time, "significant progress has since been made"; "procedures have been simplified, powers decentralised, and the armed forces are now reasonably and sufficiently equipped".[23]

When Jaitley took over as the defence minister, he pushed for the private sector to play a major role in the production of weapon systems for the armed

22. Rajat Pandit, "Arun Jaitley Promises Continuity of Policy in Defence Ministry", *The Times of India*, accessed 25 May 2025, https://timesofindia.indiatimes.com/india/arun-jaitley-promises-continuity-of-policy-in-defence-ministry/articleshow/57636081.cms.

23. PTI, "Armed Forces Sufficiently Equipped: Jaitley", Rediff, accessed 25 May 2025, https://www.rediff.com/news/report/armed-forces-sufficiently-equipped-jaitley/20170725.htm.

forces. In the United States, Britain, Germany, Japan, South Korea, etc., it is the private sector that is behind state-of-the-art defence products; China being the exception where anything and everything belongs to the state. "In contrast, India has been nurturing the white elephant in the Defence Research and Development Organisation (DRDO) which has been the bane behind continuing imports of bulk of our defence needs," said the former Director General of Information Systems, Lieutenant General P.C. Katoch.[24] India imports 70 per cent of its military hardware from different countries.[25]

Under the new policy, select private Indian firms were allowed to collaborate with foreign entities to build military platforms like submarines, fighter jets, helicopters, and armoured vehicles/main battle tanks in India. The policy envisaged establishment of long-term strategic partnerships with Indian defence majors through a transparent and competitive process wherein Indian companies would tie up with foreign military firms to set up domestic manufacturing infrastructure. Jaitley said that the strategic partnership policy in defence would help attract FDI as global investors would be assured of orders. He said unless the opening of the FDI rules was accompanied by some reasonable possibility of getting orders, an investor was not going to set up an establishment in the country. Entry of foreign investors "is linked to the kind of orders they will get and the only entity which can place the orders is the Government of India. There are no two procurers, there is only one and that is why the strategic partner policy now has been brought in as it will supplement the FDI policy," he said, explaining the reasons for the poor response of investors in the sector. He added that whether a strategic partner entered through the FDI route or via a technology collaboration, they would have the freedom to choose their mode of participation. Regarded as a landmark reform, the Strategic Partnership Model sought to build a robust

---

24. Lt. General P.C. Katoch (Retd), "Strategic Partnership Policy—Needs Speedy Conclusion", SP's MAI, accessed 25 May 2025, https://www.spsmai.com/experts-speak/?id=353&q=Strategic-partnership-policy-Needs-speedy-conclusion.

25. PTI, "Strategic Partnership to Help Attract FDI in Defence: Arun Jaitley", *The Indian Express*, accessed 25 May 2025, https://indianexpress.com/article/india/strategic-partnership-to-help-attract-fdi-in-defence-arun-jaitley-4684286/.

defence manufacturing ecosystem in India by engaging both large domestic corporations and the Micro, Small, and Medium Enterprises (MSME) sector.[26]

Jaitley invited leading private sector representatives from major industry bodies to review the progress of the Strategic Partnership policy and to explore the launch of four key projects in its first phase—the development of new submarines, naval utility helicopters, a single-engine fighter aircraft for the Indian Air Force, and the Future Infantry Combat Vehicle (FICV) for the Army.[27] The first project under the policy was soon finalised, under which the Indian Navy would procure 111 utility helicopters at a cost of over Rs 21,000 crore.[28]

Modernisation of the Army

The Indian Army has a total strength of around 12 lakh personnel and is one of leading ground forces globally. A manpower-intensive army with ageing systems and platforms must undertake periodic scrubbing of its overall structure in order to make it battle-worthy in a digital age. In consultation with the prime minister and Army top brass, Jaitley decided to reform the Indian Army in a planned manner. Jaitley allocated Rs 2.74 lakh crore for defence spending in 2017–18, including Rs 86,488 crore for modernisation. In the 2018–19 budget, the amount of Rs 99,563.86 crore, allocated for capital expenditure, included modernisation-related expenditure.[29]

---

26. Ibid.

27. Lt. General P.C. Katoch (Retd), "Strategic Partnership Policy—Needs Speedy Conclusion", SP's MAI, accessed 25 May 2025, https://www.spsmai.com/experts-speak/?id=353&q=Strategic-partnership-policy-Needs-speedy-conclusion.

28. PTI, "In Two Stints as Defence Minister, Arun Jaitley Ushered in Major Military Reforms", *Hindustan Times*, accessed 25 May 2025, https://www.hindustantimes.com/india-news/in-two-stints-as-defence-minister-arun-jaitley-ushered-in-major-military-reforms/story-d8Yrut3ul4m1HkUvqM6CSP.html.

29. "Defence Budget 2018–19", Press Information Bureau, Government of India, Ministry of Defence, available at https://www.pib.gov.in/Pressreleaseshare.aspx?PRID=1518784.

One of the major reforms included redeployment and restructuring of approximately 57,000 posts of officers, junior commissioned officers, and other ranks and civilians, for improving operational preparedness. Civilian posts would also be restructured and redeployed in different wings of the armed forces for improving efficiency. A Committee of Experts under the chairmanship of Lieutenant General (Retd.) D.B. Shekatkar was constituted to recommend measures for enhancing combat capability and rebalancing defence expenditure of the armed forces with an aim to increase "teeth to tail ratio"—the amount of supply and support personnel (tail) for each combat soldier (tooth). The committee had suggested ninety-nine recommendations for structural changes in the Army and out of which the defence ministry accepted sixty-five after consultations with all the stakeholders.[30] It was agreed that all these reforms would be completed in a planned manner before the end of 2019.

It was decided to close down thirty-nine military farms in a time-bound manner. Other important reforms involved optimisation of signals establishments to include radio monitoring companies, corps air support signal regiments, air formation signal regiments, composite signal regiments, and merger of corps operating and engineering signal regiments.[31] This was the first time that any government had undertaken such a move, one that had been resisted by the armed forces for the long time. But the government was resolute. The net effect of these measures is that various functions in the Army have been reorganised in the changed environment of economy and technology.[32]

---

30. "Big and Far-Reaching Reform Process Is Being Initiated in the Army: Arun Jaitley", *Desh Gujarat*, accessed 25 May 2025, https://deshgujarat.com/2017/08/30/big-and-far-reaching-reform-process-is-being-initiated-in-the-army-arun-jaitley/#google_vignette.

31. "Modi Government Approves First Phase of Reforms in Army, 57,000 More Officers to Get Combat Roles", *Swarajya*, accessed 25 May 2025, https://swarajyamag.com/insta/modi-government-approves-first-phase-of-reforms-in-army-57000-more-officers-to-get-combat-roles.

32. Gireesh Chandra Prasad and Tarun Shukla, "Indian Army Set for Overhaul as Govt Clears Reforms", *Mint*, accessed 25 May 2025, https://www.livemint.com/Politics/6Fhf3niqk5XpcCcOJ21PvO/Indian-Army-set-for-major-reforms-Defence-minister-Arun-Jai.html.

Jaitley acknowledged the need to expedite the modernisation and induction of new military hardware, with many proposals stuck in the pipeline.[33] He simplified the procurement procedure. "One aspect of the procurement culture that the Jaitley-led ministry intends to change is the number of tables that a file with the purchase proposal has to go through," a bureaucrat said. A procurement proposal for any military equipment is typically initiated by the concerned branch of the Armed Forces. After passing through multiple layers of scrutiny—usually involving at least half-a-dozen officers—the file reaches the Ministry of Defence. Once forwarded from Army Headquarters, it undergoes another round of review by several officials, including the Joint Secretary overseeing that branch, the Director General (Acquisition), the Defence Secretary, and finally the defence minister. The proposal is then examined by the Defence Procurement Board and the Defence Acquisition Council, which grants the final approval.

If the estimated cost of acquisition exceeds Rs 1,000 crore, the matter is referred to the Cabinet Committee on Security (CCS) for clearance. Proposals below that threshold are decided within the Ministry of Defence, often in consultation with the Ministry of Finance, which may seek further clarifications before concurrence. Once approved, the file returns to the service headquarters, which then issues the tender and initiates the acquisition process.

"Every file need not move up and down an indefinite number of times," Jaitley said after his interaction with the men in white. "Our defence forces want their requirements to be fulfilled and the procedure to be speeded up. The government will try to proceed further on this issue." Jaitley acknowledged the pace of modernisation and induction of hardware for the Army and Air Force. He said, "There were many proposals for acquisitions for the armed forces in the pipeline and there is a good case for these processes to be expedited."

33. N.C. Bipindra, "Winds of Change to Speed Up Defence Deals", *The New Indian Express*, accessed 25 May 2025, https://www.newindianexpress.com/thesundaystandard/2014/Jun/29/winds-of-change-to-speed-up-defence-deals-630027.html.

One Rank One Pension

In a historic move to address long-standing disparities in pension benefits, India launched the One Rank One Pension (OROP) scheme, a decision that would change the lives of its military veterans. For years, veterans had fought not just on the battlefield, but also for equal recognition in their post-service lives, particularly when it came to pension benefits. With the introduction of OROP, the government took a bold step to ensure that soldiers who had served the nation with unwavering dedication would be treated fairly. This initiative marked a momentous commitment to honour the sacrifices and service of those who had protected the country, promising them the respect and financial security they deserved.[34]

On 23 October 2014, during his Diwali visit to the Siachen Glacier, Prime Minister Narendra Modi reaffirmed his commitment to implementing OROP, a pledge earlier echoed by Arun Jaitley in his budget speech on 10 July 2014. However, on 7 November 2015, the government issued a new order that effectively diluted the promise, turning OROP into what critics termed a "One Rank, Five Pension" scheme. Under this revision, soldiers who had opted for premature retirement were excluded from its benefits, a significant move, given that nearly 46 per cent of servicemen retire prematurely. As highlighted by the Koshyari Committee, only about 1,000 of the Army's 13 lakh soldiers serve until the retirement age of sixty. The vast majority—jawans and junior commissioned officers—retire much earlier, most between the ages of thirty-eight and forty, and about 10 per cent by forty-six. Consequently, a large section of the force stands deprived of the full benefits originally envisioned under the OROP scheme. The 7 November 2015 order covered all personnel who had retired until 30 June 2014.[35]

The introduction of OROP has proven to be a game-changer for lakhs of ex-servicemen and their families, ensuring that military personnel are treated with the respect they deserve throughout their post-retirement lives. At its core,

---

34. "One Rank One Pension (OROP) in India", Ministry of Defence, available at https://www.pib.gov.in/PressReleaseIframePage.aspx?PRID=2071572.

35. "One Rank One Pension (OROP) to the Defence Forces Personnel", Government of India, Ministry of Defence, available at https://www.desw.gov.in/sites/default/files/OROP-DESW-MOD_0.pdf.

OROP is a simple yet profound idea: that military personnel retiring in the same rank and with the same length of service should receive the same pension, regardless of their date of retirement. The principle addresses the disparity in pension benefits faced by former soldiers due to inflation, changes in pay scales, and the evolving nature of service conditions over time. The scheme directly benefits ex-servicemen and their families by ensuring that the pension gap between current and retired personnel is bridged periodically. The successful implementation of OROP in 2014 was not only a policy shift but a significant gesture of the government's gratitude and respect towards those who served the nation. The OROP order issued by the government on 7 November 2015, brought into effect a uniform pension system for all retired defence personnel, ensuring that the same rank with the same length of service would get equal pension benefits. The policy's primary elements include:

1. *Re-fixation of pensions*: The pension of all past pensioners was re-fixed based on the pensions of personnel who retired in 2013, starting from 1 July 2014. This created a new benchmark for pensions, with all retirees getting equal benefits for their service.
2. *Periodic revision*: The pension is to be re-fixed every five years, ensuring that it continues to reflect changes in the pay and pension structure.
3. *Arrears payments*: Arrears of pension were to be paid in equal half-yearly instalments, although the arrears for family pensioners and gallantry awardees were paid in a single instalment.
4. *Safeguarding above-average pension*: Personnel drawing pensions higher than the average are protected, ensuring that they do not lose out on the benefits of OROP.
5. *Inclusive of all ex-servicemen*: The order covered all personnel who retired up to 30 June 2014, and provided a robust framework for revising pensions for all ranks, including family pensioners.

The demand for OROP had been a long-standing issue, lingering for over forty years. Several government committees and commissions had examined the matter, but each time, the proposal was dismissed, mainly due to financial constraints and administrative complexities. The third Central Pay Commission was the first to address the issue in a comprehensive way, recommending weightages in qualifying service for pensions. Over the years, committees like the K.P. Singh Dev Committee (1984) and the Sharad Pawar Committee (1991) also studied the matter, but failed to offer a definitive solution. Despite these setbacks, the demand persisted, with the Standing Committee on Defence and other forums continuing to advocate for its implementation.[36]

The Indian Ex-Service Movement filed a petition in the Supreme Court demanding the original OROP. The Modi government strongly opposed this in the Supreme Court. Instead of describing OROP as the right of the soldiers, it was called a policy decision of the government's will. Not only this, the Modi government argued that the court cannot give directions on a policy decision leading to economic burden. On 16 March 2022, the Supreme Court dismissed this petition for OROP.

The OROP scheme has benefitted over 25 lakh veterans and their families, bringing much-needed financial security to the ex-servicemen community. The scheme has not only improved the standard of living for retired military personnel but has also ensured greater dignity for their service to the nation. For many veterans, this was a long-awaited recognition of their contributions, bridging the gap between their sacrifices and the rewards they received post-retirement. OROP has also had significant social and emotional value. It has contributed to a stronger bond between the Indian government and its military veterans, signalling the nation's commitment to those who serve and protect its sovereignty. For the families of soldiers, many of whom live with the sacrifices of their loved ones, this policy brought a sense of fulfilment and acknowledgement.[37] Although the central government approved the OROP scheme, Jaitley emphasised the need to ensure its smooth implementation within the government framework. However, several stakeholders felt the scheme did not go far enough; they insisted that specific provisions be added before it was fully rolled out.

Besides the estimated one-time outgo of Rs 10,000–12,000 crore on pension arrears, the recurring annual additional cost was expected to be Rs 8000–10,000 crore. As mentioned earlier, the government's 7 November notification announcing the implementation of OROP for over 25 lakh ex-servicemen and war widows failed to satisfy many veterans. Their objections sparked controversy, with several groups threatening to resume their agitation. The

36. "One Rank One Pension (OROP) in India", Ministry of Defence, available at https://www.pib.gov.in/PressReleaseIframePage.aspx?PRID=2071572.

37. Ibid.

protesting veterans declared, "We reject this notification, as it reflects one of the seven anomalies we had repeatedly highlighted to the government following its announcement on OROP." They further expressed disappointment that their demand for a multi-member independent commission to address these issues had been ignored.[38]

Jaitley was once again given additional charge of defence after Parrikar was sent back to Goa in March 2019. Jaitley told the prime minister that he wished to focus entirely on the finance portfolio. He was succeeded as the defence minister by Nirmala Sitharaman. Jaitley hailed the appointment of a woman colleague as the country's first, full-fledged defence minister and said that it sends a global message. "It is great for the country, not just for the women. It also sends a message globally," Jaitley said. Till then, eighteen of fifty-one European nations have had women defence ministers, starting with the appointment of Elisabeth Rehn in Finland in 1990. Norway has had five women defence ministers, Sweden three.[39] Sitharaman became India's first woman defence minister after Indira Gandhi, who held the post when she was the prime minister. Her appointment came in the backdrop of the aggravated tension with Pakistan and China, which had triggered concerns about the lack of a full-time defence minister. She was also the second woman minister in the CCS—the first was external affairs minister Sushma Swaraj.

"Both ladies in the CCS have established their competence, both are recognised as ladies with substance, who have earned a front-line position for themselves," Jaitley said. Asked if with a woman as defence minister, women in combat may become a reality, Jaitley said, "That was one area in which I wasn't able to do much." Combat roles involve a gender barrier that few nations have done away with. But Army chief Bipin Rawat assured that a plan was in place to allow women in combat roles and the process would begin with induction of women as military police.[40]

---

38. "One Rank One Pension—Why Veterans are Protesting?—Top 10 things to Know", *GConnect*, accessed 25 May 2025, https://www.gconnect.in/defence-services/one-rank-one-pension-why-veterans-are-protesting.html.

39. Anindita Sanyal (Ed.), "Arun Jaitley Says 'Global Message' in Appointing Woman Defence Minister", NDTV, accessed 25 May 2025, https://www.ndtv.com/india-news/arun-jaitley-says-global-message-in-appointing-nirmala-sitharaman-as-defence-minister-1745500.

40. Ibid.

21

Jaitley: A Man for All Seasons

What William Shakespeare said could well have applied to Arun Jaitley. "The elements / So mix'd in him that Nature might stand up / And say to all the world 'This was a man!'"[1] He truly was. Arun Jaitley was an extraordinary human being. He was not just a towering figure in Indian politics and law; he was, above all, a man of extraordinary warmth, compassion, and generosity. He was widely recognised as a remarkable orator, a distinguished lawyer, and a senior politician who served as the Union finance and defence minister. However, his humanitarian side is less known to the public. To those who knew him beyond the public eye, he was a loyal friend, a connoisseur of good food, and a humanitarian at heart. He was an out-and-out family man and, despite his busy schedule, made time for his children when they were growing up. In more ways than one, Arun and Sangeeta Jaitley complemented each other, both being true-blue Punjabis: hospitable and warm.[2]

Jaitley revered his mother. In her book, Kumkum Chadha wrote, "I vividly recall one of the first paintings that was carted to Arun Jaitley's make-shift office in the government bungalow as finance minister, was his mother's. I happened to ask him about it. He was quiet for a while as if trying to gather images that had perhaps blurred. Ratan Prabha, Arun Jaitley's mother, didn't

---

1. William Shakespeare, *Julius Caesar*, Act 5, Scene 5.
2. Kumkum Chadha, *The Marigold Story: Indira Gandhi & Others* (Westland, 2019), p. 326.

live to witness her son's fame as India's finance minister. She died of cancer in 1991."[3]

Jaitley's sharp legal mind and political acumen were matched only by his ability to make people feel valued—whether through thoughtful gestures, wise counsel, or his legendary hospitality. Beneath his composed exterior lay a deeply empathetic soul—one who quietly helped countless individuals in need, never seeking recognition. Whether mentoring young politicians and lawyers, supporting his own staff or that in the courts or of the ministries he headed, or standing by friends in times of crisis, Jaitley's kindness knew no bounds. His life was a testament to the belief that true greatness lies not just in professional achievements but in the ability to touch lives with sincerity and grace. He could disarm even the most formidable of opponents with swift repartee.

He possessed an unbeatable capacity to make one feel he had said much more than what he should have, and yet said precious little. His felicity of expression could be so overpowering that one would forget to trick him with a counter-question. He was likeable because he could be trusted that he would never cross the Lakshman Rekha.[4] These multiple skills and talents make for a rare combination. To find them in one individual is special—and Arun Jaitley was special. Yet, beyond this—much, much beyond this—he had one attribute that made him an absolutely compelling friend, colleague, interlocutor, and mentor: trust. He radiated trust. He was a person who both a tycoon and an ordinary party worker in the BJP office could go to with a problem and be assured of a fair hearing. He was an extraordinary man whose reputation cut across party lines.[5]

Among the best things about Jaitley was his versatility. One could talk to him about fashion—he knew all the brands; one could talk to him about Kashmiri and embroidery work—he would know all its history. As the anchor said in his introduction of Jaitley at the time of announcing the ET Lifetime of

---

3. Ibid.

4. "Arun Jaitley: Batting for the BJP", Rediff, accessed 25 May 2025, https://m.rediff.com/election/2009/apr/27slde1-interview-with-arun-jaitley.htm.

5. Ashok Malik, "Arun Jaitley's Demise, An Irreplaceable Loss to the Nation", in *The Discussant: Journal of Centre for Reforms, Development and Justice*, Special Edition, An Obituary to Arun Jaitley, Vol. VII, No. 3 (July–September 2019), pp. 56–59.

Public Service Awards in December 2019 to Jaitley, "He was a man who could explain the fine print of GST rules and the fine art of swing bowling."[6] He couldn't have put it better. One could talk to Jaitley about his favourite dhabas for kulcha in Amritsar, or where to get the best dosas in Chennai. He was like a living encyclopaedia who knew everything from politics to economics to sport to fashion and food. Suhel Seth said, "No one I know spoke with as much authority about *Devdas* and Derivatives or about *Lamhe* and Law or for that matter about Tendulkar and TADA."[7]

A few anecdotes cannot do justice to his personality, his influence, or his legacy. Jaitley was such a powerhouse that the limited words in this chapter cannot do justice to the person he was; an entire book could be written on his personal life. In fact, more than one biography would be needed to capture the goodness his personal and professional lives carried.

People's Person

It is lonely at the top. Whether they want it or not, the highest office distances the leader from people. Jaitley was an exception—he was people's people. Jaitley's ground-floor office in Parliament was a nerve centre with politicians of all hues dropping by. In his office, as well as in the more exclusive Central Hall, he was the consummate political artist, reaching across the political aisle to call in old friendships that delivered political results and helping new politicians find their feet. People flocked to meet him because it was great being around him. He had intimate knowledge of men and matters, partly because of his prodigious memory.

Jaitley had an earthy sense of humour and a friendly demeanour. 'Half of Delhi claims to know you," a television journalist once remarked to Jaitley,

6. *The Economic Times*, "ET Lifetime of Public Service Award for Former FM (Late) Arun Jaitley: Sangeeta Jaitley Full Speech", accessed 25 May 2025, https://www.youtube.com/watch?v=hQ3FKeuDtA0.

7. "Suhel Seth: Jaitley Was the Most Principled Man I Knew", *Open*, accessed 25 May 2025, https://openthemagazine.com/cover-stories/suhel-seth-jaitley-was-the-most-principled-man-i-knew/#google_vignette.

who reportedly replied, 'Half the Delhi won't be lying.'"[8] He was a brilliant raconteur who was the centre of attraction in many gatherings, whether in Lodhi Gardens after a walk, at a dinner party, or when it came to the media. He could regale one with great stories and nuggets of information, which could make one feel part of the club—a validation that one was part of something important. He loved a durbar. His birthdays used to be celebrated in the park. He could set up an adda—an "off-the-record durbar" in media parlance—anywhere: in his drawing room, the debriefing room at the party headquarters, a park, or the Central Hall of Parliament.

There was the mobile version, a veritable feast for hangers-on, lobbyists, and friends, at his morning or evening walk in Delhi's Lodhi Gardens, an idyll littered with fifteenth-century tombs, or the garden near his house. Anyone could join in. Jaitley initially started walking in a park opposite Sama Nursing Home after moving to the Kailash Colony house. In 2009, when Jaitley became the Leader of the Opposition, security officials asked him to move to a more secure location due to security concerns. Jaitley moved the walks to Lodhi Gardens.

He would be driven by his close lawyer friend and neighbour Ranjit Kumar, from his Kailash Colony residence to Lodhi Gardens in a white Mercedes SUV.[9] Jaitley did not know how to drive a car and never possessed a driving licence. Former Attorney General Mukul Rohatgi joined Jaitley and Ranjit Kumar. A walking group was formed. Members of the opposition parties, senior police officers, doctors, bureaucrats, lawyers, businessmen, and journalists would also accompany them at times. The walk itself was more in the nature of a stroll and Jaitley would hold forth on a range of issues.[10] After the walk, the group would sit at the benches in a particular spot and engage in thoughtful

8. Praveen Donthi, "Talk of the Town", *Caravan Magazine*, accessed 25 May 2025, https://caravanmagazine.in/reportage/talk-town.

9. "Morning Walk, Birthday Ritual at Lodhi Gardens: Delhi Will Remember Arun Jaitley", *Hindustan Times*, accessed 25 May 2025, https://www.hindustantimes.com/india-news/morning-walk-birthday-ritual-at-lodhi-gardens-delhi-will-remember-arun-jaitley/story-NSxJ39otZuABf2B4RA7YHK.html.

10. Ibid.

conversations, crack jokes, and laugh together. Jaitley seldom talked about politics during the walks.[11]

Laloo Prasad, the tea vendor at Lodhi Gardens who had been serving this group tea and lemonade for around fifteen years, said, "I never had a conversation with him, just greeted him and he was very gentle." From Lodhi Gardens, some in the group would go to India International Centre for breakfast.[12] Prem Grover, a real estate businessman close to Arun Jaitley, would organise Jaitley's birthday every year after the walk. At 6 a.m. every 28 December, a motley group of politicians, lawyers, journalists, and businessmen used to assemble at the green-coloured benches across the Bada Gumbad in Lodhi Gardens to celebrate Jaitley's birthday. Usually dressed in a branded woollen jacket with a golf cap, the BJP leader would begin his birthday with his Lodhi Gardens morning-walk friends and with sweetened milk tea, lemonade, cake, bread pakoras, and an assortment of sweets.[13]

In 2014, after he took over as the defence and finance minister, and around the time his health issues cropped up again, Jaitley decided to walk in his 2 Krishna Menon residence, although he would still make the occasional appearance in Lodhi Gardens, like on his birthday. His morning-walk group missed the days spent with a man who was their "friend first and a big politician later". The spot in Lodhi Gardens where they gathered is now known as the "Jaitley Corner".[14]

Jaitley also held a durbar in Parliament. Sitting in Central Hall, whenever one would see a huge gathering of reporters anywhere, one would find Jaitley at the centre engaged in endless *gup-shup* with journalists, sharing his wisdom

---

11. Ibid.

12. Mudita Girotra, "A Friend First and a Politician Later, Say Jaitley's Lodi Gardens Friends, *The New Indian Express*, accessed 25 May 2025, https://www.newindianexpress.com/nation/2019/Aug/24/a-friend-first-and-a-politician-later-say-jaitleys-lodi-gardens-friends-2023697.html.

13. "Morning Walk, Birthday Ritual at Lodhi Gardens: Delhi Will Remember Arun Jaitley", *Hindustan Times*, accessed 25 May 2025, https://www.hindustantimes.com/india-news/morning-walk-birthday-ritual-at-lodhi-gardens-delhi-will-remember-arun-jaitley/story-NSxJ39otZuABf2B4RA7YHK.html.

14. Atul Mathur, "Delhi University Launched Arun Jaitley in Politics", *The Times of India*, accessed 25 May 2025, https://timesofindia.indiatimes.com/city/delhi/du-launched-jaitley-in-politics/articleshow/70823570.cms.

and getting insights into trends shaping the world. The joke in Parliament's corridors was that no other finance minister spent so much time chatting with journalists as Jaitley did.[15] His detractors would often wonder how a finance minister found the time to hold his durbars, keep himself so well informed about the goings-on in every political party, and do the fire-fighting for his party.[16]

He was a perennial favourite of the media. He was an interesting conversationalist with seemingly endless anecdotes, and he had wide connections with the media. Conversations with him were always freewheeling—they would start with politics, transition to cricket but often end with food.[17] Traditionally, the Central Hall of Parliament is a kind of rendezvous point for politicians and journalists. In a known tight-lipped Modi regime, Jaitley was the prime minister's trusted point person with the Opposition and the media.[18] With a prime minister who is said to be work-obsessed and with little time for anything else, it was Jaitley who was left to deal with the media.

Jaitley was, above all, a storyteller. His door was more often open than those of most of his colleagues. Parliament correspondents looked forward to his daily appearance in the Central Hall, certain that he would come armed with an engaging anecdote or a sharp, witty remark. He seldom let them down—there was always a morsel of insider gossip or a humorous story that had caught his keen eye. Jaitley also shared an easy chemistry with the camera. A born headline-maker, he instinctively knew what soundbite the television journalist was after, and his memorable one-liners frequently made it to the news tickers.[19]

---

15. Anita Joshua, "Arun Jaitley: Mr Fixit, with Friends Everywhere", *The Telegraph*, accessed 25 May 2025, https://www.telegraphindia.com/india/arun-jaitley-mr-fixit-with-friends-everywhere/cid/1700063#goog_rewarded.

16. Ibid.

17. Shweta Rajpal Kohli, "Arun Jaitley and the Art of Communication", LinkedIn, accessed 25 May 2025, https://www.linkedin.com/pulse/arun-jaitley-art-communication-shweta-rajpal-kohli/.

18. Coomi Kapoor, "A Man of Open Heart and Mind, Arun Jaitley Had Friends Across Divide", in *The Discussant: Journal of Centre for Reforms, Development and Justice*, Special Edition, An Obituary to Arun Jaitley, Vol. VII, No. 3 (July–September 2019), pp. 51–55.

19. Narendra Modi, "Condolence Message", in ibid., pp. 12–13.

The term "Khan Market gang" was coined by him, as were many other such witticisms. He was India's Communicator-in-Chief.[20] Shweta Rajpal recalled the time spent in Davos, her seventh year of covering the World Economic Forum Annual Meeting 2019, but the first one since the BJP government came to power.

> I was standing outside his hotel in sub-zero temperatures, doing a live link and waiting to film the footage of his arrival. As Mr Jaitley was walking in, I requested him for an interview, and he obliged immediately. No preparation, no agenda, no travel fatigue, no egos. And the magic began. It was the kind of magic you'd witness each time a mike was put in front of him. As expected, in 3 minutes flat, I got the big headline I was looking for—his plans to discuss the hot-button black money issue with his Swiss counterpart. Ask any TV journalist and they'll tell you, it didn't matter if you interviewed Mr Jaitley for two minutes or twenty, he would decide your headline even before you'd asked the first question.

Jaitley was often accused of being indiscreet and too candid for his own good. In his memoir *Editor Unplugged: Magnates, Netas and Me*, editor Vinod Mehta wrote that "although hung up on upward political mobility and, possibly, the biggest gossip in Delhi", Jaitley "likes the company of literate journalists and keeps himself well informed". When Mehta's *Outlook* magazine did a cover story on "India's Best Gossips", in 2009, Jaitley took top spot. "For the lawyer-politician, gossip is not just social currency or amusement, it is a genuine passion," the piece said. "Journalists lucky enough to be invited into his inner circle say ... he entertains them with his rich fund of stories about the private lives of everyone, including journalists and editors."

---

20. Shweta Rajpal Kohli, "Arun Jaitley and the Art of Communication", LinkedIn, accessed May 25, 2025, https://www.linkedin.com/pulse/arun-jaitley-art-communication-shweta-rajpal-kohli/.

Many people insisted that journalists sympathetic to Jaitley acted as mouthpieces for the opinions he wouldn't publicly voice.[21] But his well-known penchant for banter and *gup-shup* was never to hurt or malign anybody.[22]

Arun Jaitley had few rivals, if any, in Indian politics thanks to his capacity to charm the media. "If you do a Google search there is one politician against whom you will not find anything negative. His own track record is totally sanitised in media despite over four decades in public life," said Madhu Kishwar, an academic and the author of *Modi, Muslims and Media: Voices from Narendra Modi's Gujarat*.[23] Arun Jaitley had a soft spot for young journalists. At one point, the government had reason to believe that sensitive information was reaching the media prematurely. As a result, entry for journalists was tightened amid protests. However, Jaitley recognised the value that young reporters could bring. He believed they could provide fresh insights through their reporting.[24]

And then there was the "adda" at home.[25]

Very few know, while Jaitley could speak for hours on stage, in Parliament, and in social gatherings, he would become reserved once he stepped off it. In contrast to his confident and articulate persona as a parliamentarian, Jaitley was known to be a shy individual often seen blushing when complimented.

---

21. Praveen Donthi, "Talk of the Town", *Caravan Magazine*, accessed 25 May 2025, https://caravanmagazine.in/reportage/talk-town.

22. Nirmala Sitharaman, "A Shishya's Tribute to Arun Jaitley", in *The Discussant: Journal of Centre for Reforms, Development and Justice*, Special Edition, An Obituary to Arun Jaitley, Vol. VII, No. 3 (July –September 2019), pp. 23–25.

23. Praveen Donthi, "Talk of the Town", *Caravan Magazine*, accessed 25 May 2025, https://caravanmagazine.in/reportage/talk-town.

24. Ashok Pal Singh, "Arun Jaitley: An Ex-Official Recounts Friendly Meetings & a Salvaged Deal", *The Quint*, accessed 25 May 2025, https://www.thequint.com/voices/blogs/arun-jaitley-an-ex-official-recounts-friendly-meetings-a-salvaged-deal#read-more.

25. Jyoti Malhotra, "Budget 2014: Staid and Sturdy with Arun Jaitley", *India Today*, From the India Today Archives (2014), accessed 25 May 2025, https://www.indiatoday.in/india-today-insight/story/from-the-india-today-archives-2014-budget-2014-staid-and-sturdy-with-arun-jaitley-2570842-2024-07-23.

Man of Principles

Arun Jaitley was a man of principles, ethics meant the world to him. There was a premium on ethics which he insisted must precede friendships. Short-change Jaitley, and he was unlikely to either forget or forgive. He had a clear assessment of what was morally right, and what was not. "Arun can be very touchy, but you won't ever get to know. If you are upfront, half the battle is won. Otherwise, you just don't make the cut. Play fair, chances are that he may help you. Play foul and you are in for trouble," is how Raian Karanjawala analysed Jaitley.[26]

Jaitley was always mindful of avoiding misuse of public funds. He practised what he preached. He stayed in party accommodations instead of five-star hotels during travel for party meetings. He was punctilious about financial matters and extremely careful about not squandering or receiving state largesse. Senior Congress leader and MP A.M. Singhvi narrated a poignant example which occurred during the inauguration of the Uttarakhand High Court in Nainital in the early noughties. As law minister, Jaitley arrived at his official accommodation and enquired about the stay charges. Assuming it was a routine enquiry, the caretaker informed him that the rate was Rs 200 per night for guests and Rs 100 rupees for government officials. Without hesitation, Jaitley produced Rs 300 to cover his stay and that of a friend accompanying him. He insisted on paying, leaving a lasting impression on the caretaker. The caretaker later remarked to the friend that this minister was destined for greatness, as he had never before witnessed such a conscientious approach to public funds.[27]

Top businessmen in London queued up to oblige Jaitley. "They would send their cars, but Jaitley would always take a tube. His morality is impeccable. It is these small, albeit important things which are the measure of an honest

---

26. Kumkum Chadha, *The Marigold Story: Indira Gandhi & Others* (Westland, 2019), p. 333.

27. Dr Abhishek Manu Singhvi, "Arun Jaitley: In Memoriam", *The Times of India*, accessed 25 May 2025, https://timesofindia.indiatimes.com/blogs/straight-candid/arun-jaitley-in-memoriam/.

man. Many politicians would do it because they are being watched, but Arun would do it even when no one is looking," said Abhishek Manu Singhvi.[28]

Jaitley is believed to have recused himself from matters pertaining to the Rs 20,000-crore Vodafone tax dispute and delegated decision-making in this regard to his junior minister Nirmala Sitharaman. Jaitley recorded on file that all issues relating to the Vodafone tax case be referred to Minister of State for Finance Sitharaman or Revenue Secretary Shaktikanta Das. In case of an unresolved issue or a conflict, Jaitley desired that the matter be referred to Prime Minister Narendra Modi. No reason for Jaitley's decision was given, but it may be linked to the fact he could have been associated with either parties in the case in his capacity as a senior lawyer.

Vodafone was locked in twin tax disputes with the government—one pertaining to its 2007 acquisition and the other the transfer pricing case involving Vodafone India Services. While the basic tax demand was Rs 7990 crore, the total outstanding, including interest and penalty, was estimated to have risen to Rs 20,000 crore. The Supreme Court had ruled in Vodafone's favour in 2012 and said the company was not liable to pay any tax over the acquisition of assets in India from Hong Kong-based Hutchison. The government, however, amended the tax laws with retrospective effect to undo the Supreme Court judgment and claim taxes from Vodafone.[29] Vodafone, in its arbitration notice, expressed interest to move ahead with the arbitration without waiting for the Income Tax Appellate Tribunal (ITAT) decision on the Rs 3700-crore transfer pricing case. The appointment of former Supreme Court judge R.C. Lahoti as arbitrator in the tax case was approved by Sitharaman; Jaitley stayed away from the decision-making.

When Jaitley was the finance minister, customs officials at Delhi airport seized his luggage suspecting that some medical devices were contraband. The officials faced no repercussions for their actions—surprising in a country like India, where in an imperfect rule-of-law system, power often shields those

---

28. Kumkum Chadha, *The Marigold Story: Indira Gandhi & Others* (Westland, 2019), p. 328.

29. PTI, "Vodafone Case: Jaitley Recuses Himself from Decisions", *The Hindu*, accessed 25 May 2025, https://www.thehindu.com/business/Industry/vodafone-case-jaitley-recuses-himself-from-decisions/article6126758.ece.

aligned with it. Instead, he complied with the directions issued and ultimately commended the officials for doing their job.[30]

Yet Jaitley did not bother what people would say on how he spent his own money. He was known for his fondness for exclusive pens, watches, and shawls. At home, Jaitley was known to display these, particularly the beautifully embroidered *jamavar* which was said to be a personal favourite of his. He often said with a fierce, childish delight, "It's my money, and I will spend it the way I want." Jaitley possessed a strong sartorial sense, including his elegant use of the *jamawar* shawl on cold winter days and his preference for *bandgala* suits when travelling abroad on official work.

In Punjabi weddings, a gift of cash called *sagan*, a distorted version of shagun, literally meaning, auspicious, was at one time the norm. Till the late 1960s, people would give Rs 10, or the affluent even Rs 1000, and if they were family, the custom was to give a piece of jewellery. The women of a household would maintain a diary listing the amount of money against the names of guests and relatives. Jaitley's daughter Sonali's wedding invitation came with a request to not bring any gifts.[31] Someone pushed an envelope into Sonali's hands on the day of the wedding reception, but the guest withdrew after he had got a "look" from Jaitley.[32]

There was, however, one politician Jaitley could not stop from transgressing the "no gifts" rule, because she was a woman and, more importantly, the head of a party which for years had shared a love–hate relationship with the BJP, and was also known to be mercurial. A few days after the wedding, Jaitley had apparently driven down to her official bungalow in Lutyens' Delhi, and explained to her the sentiment of not accepting gifts.[33] Neither Jaitley nor her interviewer provided the name of the leader, leaving the reader guessing.

---

30. Arghya Sengupta, "For Arun Jaitley, Law Was an Intellectual Passion", *The Wire*, accessed 25 May 2025, https://thewire.in/politics/arun-jatiley-tribute-arghya-sengupta.

31. Virendra Kapoor, "Blessings Only", *The Wire*, accessed 25 May 2025, https://openthemagazine.com/special/blessings-only/#google_vignette.

32. Kumkum Chadha, *The Marigold Story: Indira Gandhi & Others* (Westland, 2019), pp. 331–32.

33. Ibid.

Amrit Mathur who was the chief operating officer of Delhi Daredevils when Jaitley was the Delhi and District Cricket Association (DDCA) president said:

> Jaitley was a man of many parts but in all his roles, one quality stood out. He always, always played straight, hitting across the line was never an option. His was a bat that had a big middle and no edges. Cricket is about scoring runs but equally important is the manner of making those runs. If the same yardstick is used to judge people, the verdict can only be unanimous: Jaitley ji was pure class![34]

Union minister Dharmendra Pradhan described Jaitley's way of life aptly: "Because his personal life was a bedrock for the principles he held dear, Jaitley ji was never disinclined to speak inconvenient truths—but in inoffensive and effective ways that only a gifted raconteur and a person with deep convictions could achieve."[35]

Humble, Kind-Hearted, and Mentor to Many

Jaitley's humility and generosity knew no bounds. His support to his staff—financial, economic, moral, medical, and educational—was legendary. Jaitley was deeply committed to the well-being of his staff, treating them as part of his extended family. He had a personal staff of around ten individuals, including his driver Jagan and the assistant Padma, who had been associated with him for two to three decades. Gopal Bhandari is not someone most people would know. Nor would anyone, except lawyers who briefed Jaitley, have heard of Surender or Padam. These people didn't just work for Jaitley; they were his family, treated with the greatest respect and care.

---

34. Amrit Mathur, "Jaitley Ji Played with a Straight Bat, Was Pure Class", in *The Discussant: Journal of Centre for Reforms, Development and Justice*, Special Edition, An Obituary to Arun Jaitley, Vol. VII, No. 3 (July–September 2019), pp. 69–71.

35. Dharmendra Pradhan, "Arun Jaitley Gave Me Mantra to Deal with Doubt & Dilemma", in ibid., pp. 26–28.

The clerkage collected for senior counsel by his office was used to build houses for almost all his staff and also to educate their children, even abroad. One of them is a partner in India's top law firm. Jaitley made a qualitative difference in their lives. He was deeply committed to the well-being of his staff, treating them as part of his extended family. He ensured that their medical needs were taken care of and that their children's education were provided for.[36] As an unsaid rule, the children of his personal staff studied at Carmel Convent School in Chanakyapuri, the same institution where Jaitley's own children studied. If someone wished to study in a foreign country, Jaitley would make efforts to facilitate their admission to the same educational institutions. Three of his assistants' children were studying in foreign institutions. One of the two daughters of Jaitley's kitchen manager was studying in London. One son of his assistant Gopal is a doctor and another is an engineer.

Suhel Seth recalled, "Many years ago, Arun Jaitley was very, very excited. Not because he had won yet another case in his path-breaking career as a lawyer; not even because of some political goal he had scored. But only because his stenographer's daughter had topped her college and found herself a job with a multinational in the US. It was an education that Jaitley had funded."[37]

Back in 2005, Jaitley had gifted his car to his assistant O.P. Sharma's son Chetan when he was studying law. Jaitley was very particular about extending financial help. He would give pocket money to his children by cheque. He would pay salaries and any other remuneration by cheque. He had set up a welfare fund during his legal practice. He used to manage this fund through a trust.[38] It would be an understatement to say that his death orphaned at least twenty-five families.[39]

---

36. Dr Abhishek Manu Singhvi, "Arun Jaitley: In Memoriam", *The Times of India*, accessed 25 May 2025, https://timesofindia.indiatimes.com/blogs/straight-candid/arun-jaitley-in-memoriam/.

37. "Suhel Seth: Jaitley Was the Most Principled Man I Knew", *Open*, accessed 25 May 2025, https://openthemagazine.com/cover-stories/suhel-seth-jaitley-was-the-most-principled-man-i-knew/#google_vignette.

38. "Arun Jaitley's Extended Family and His Impeccable Gesture...", *The Asian Age*, accessed 25 May 2025, https://www.asianage.com/india/all-india/240819/arun-jaitleys-extended-family-and-his-impeccable-gesture.html.

39. Dr Abhishek Manu Singhvi, "Arun Jaitley: In Memoriam", *The Times of India*, accessed 25 May 2025, https://timesofindia.indiatimes.com/blogs/straight-candid/

Legal interns were paid with expensive legal books which they could not afford. He followed and mentored scores of young lawyers, advising them carefully on how to chart their careers. He kept track of their personal lives.[40]

Despite his high position, Jaitley maintained his humble nature. Recalling the initial years of the Indian Premier League (IPL), Amrit Mathur said that his phone would invariably ring early in the morning, with Jaitley, then president of the DDCA, making routine calls to check if everything was fine. Mathur also said, "That gesture, him calling instead of me, was so typical of the generous and large-hearted person that was Mr Jaitley. Everything—protocol / position / seniority—demanded I (the chief operating officer of Delhi Daredevils) report to him but he was not bound by these things. He never let anybody know he was Arun Jaitley—a man of immense stature and enormous power."[41]

Jaitley consistently made time for his friends and persons dear to him. When with his friends, he was just a friend with no airs of a powerful man. Jaitley had a special fondness and joy in children. Madhu Trehan remembered that Jaitley once visited a home for the arrival of a baby, bringing a thoughtful gift handpicked by his wife, Dolly. She also remembered watching in amusement as a two-year-old presented him with a basket, instructing him to find Easter eggs, and Jaitley, without hesitation, joined in the playful search. She further recalled, "Arriving at my daughter's eclectic wedding in Goa, he sportingly followed the dress code of lungi and kurta."

Despite his prominent position, he remained the same warm-hearted Punjabi friend at his core.[42] Thomas Kunnunkal, the former principal of St. Xavier's Senior Secondary School, Delhi, fondly recalled a memorable incident involving Arun Jaitley, a prominent alumnus from the 1969 batch. During an annual alumni dinner of the school held when Jaitley was the finance minister, he attended as a guest of honour. As usual, he parked his car on Raj Niwas

---

arun-jaitley-in-memoriam/.

40. Madhu Trehan, "The Measure of a Man", *Newslaundry*, accessed 25 May 2025, https://www.newslaundry.com/2019/08/24/the-measure-of-a-man.

41. Amrit Mathur, "Jaitley Ji Played with a Straight Bat, Was Pure Class", in *The Discussant: Journal of Centre for Reforms, Development and Justice*, Special Edition, An Obituary to Arun Jaitley, Vol. VII, No. 3 (July–September 2019), pp. 69–71.

42. Madhu Trehan, "The Measure of a Man", *Newslaundry*, accessed 25 May 2025, https://www.newslaundry.com/2019/08/24/the-measure-of-a-man.

Marg and walked to the school. A humorous twist unfolded when young students, unaware of his identity, charged him the standard entry fee. Jaitley, recognising the confusion, paid the cost with a chuckle.[43]

Jaitley's generosity knew no bounds. He picked up medical bills for countless people, especially children. Jaitley was diagnosed with diabetes at the young age. Perhaps it was his illness that drew him to help those around him who were suffering from any sickness. He would often call eminent doctors he knew and ask them to take care of a person in need, including RSS leaders, journalists, and junior lawyers.

Every year, on his birthday, Jaitley and Sangeeta and the two children visited an orphanage close to his home, a ritual that happened on every special occasion in the Jaitley household. Instead of the ubiquitous party, Jaitley spent time with kids at the orphanage—not just feeding them but supporting them in multiple ways as he had always done. Jaitley loved children and was an avowed believer that education is the first pillar of a more opportunity-laced and equal society, which explained the emphasis on education and employability in his first budget.[44]

His province of influence straddled the world of politics, judiciary and cricket and whose helpful nature had earned him IOUs aplenty. Not all those he helped were people with connections. Some of them were ordinary folk, like those he befriended first during his morning walks.[45] B.S. Sethi was not in Jaitley's circle of friends but remembered that he was always available to meet people.[46] Prem Grover recalled, "I remember when my daughter-in-law

---

43. Abhishek Dey, "'He Always Stayed in Touch': Former School Principal Remembers Ex-FM Arun Jaitley", *Hindustan Times*, accessed 25 May 2025, https://www.hindustantimes.com/delhi-news/he-always-stayed-in-touch-former-school-principal-remembers-ex-fm-arun-jaitley/story-FIqAXpPienIkoIhMRBdwnM.html.

44. "Suhel Seth: Jaitley Was the Most Principled Man I Knew", *Open*, accessed 25 May 2025, https://openthemagazine.com/cover-stories/suhel-seth-jaitley-was-the-most-principled-man-i-knew/#google_vignette.

45. Anita Joshua, "Arun Jaitley: Mr Fixit, with Friends Everywhere", *The Telegraph*, accessed 25 May 2025, https://www.telegraphindia.com/india/arun-jaitley-mr-fixit-with-friends-everywhere/cid/1700063#goog_rewarded.

46. Mudita Girotra, "A Friend First and a Politician Later, Say Jaitley's Lodi Gardens Friends", *The New Indian Express*, accessed 25 May 2025, https://www.

died in 2009, Mr Jaitley cancelled his birthday celebrations to be with us. That was the man that he was."[47]

Many of the people he mentored are today in key positions in government. Several ministers in Modi's Cabinet are his protégés. His former juniors in the law practice have risen high in the profession. He was proud that the children of his office staff had performed extremely well in their respective professions, thanks to his generosity and encouragement.[48] Jaitley countlessly mentored younger colleagues in his party. "Yet, if mentorship is the hallmark of a political career, I've had the best. Did I have a role in the selection of the mentor? None at all, and that is where the role of Providence is," wrote Nirmala Sitharaman in an emotional tribute to Jaitley.[49] Dharmendra Pradhan wrote:

> He hand-held junior colleagues like me in the BJP, galvanised our strengths and worked on our weaknesses… . Jaitley ji has been a brother, a fatherly-figure, a mentor and friend to me—from guiding me on my children's education to advising me on how to live and how to spend. In my years of close interaction with him, I have never seen him in a dilemma. Whether it be a difficult or a joyful moment, he has been calm and inspiring. The ameliorative effect of good company, I believe, is irreplaceable given all the ordinariness and weaknesses that a human being carries. With Jaitley ji's departure, the world seems a little greyer to me today. As I grapple with an interplay between memory and loss, one message comes with immense certitude: my life has been touched with nobility and a great man's company.[50]

---

newindianexpress.com/nation/2019/Aug/24/a-friend-first-and-a-politician-later-say-jaitleys-lodi-gardens-friends-2023697.html.

47. Ibid.

48. Coomi Kapoor, "Arun Jaitley: The Politician Who Won Hearts Across All Divides", *Financial Express*, accessed 25 May 2025, https://www.financialexpress.com/opinion/arun-jaitley-the-politician-who-won-hearts-across-all-divides/1685857/.

49. Nirmala Sitharaman, "A Shishya's Tribute to Arun Jaitley", in *The Discussant: Journal of Centre for Reforms, Development and Justice*, Special Edition, An Obituary to Arun Jaitley, Vol. VII, No. 3 (July –September 2019), pp. 23–25.

50. Dharmendra Pradhan, "Arun Jaitley Gave Me Mantra to Deal with Doubt & Dilemma", in *The Discussant: Journal of Centre for Reforms, Development and Justice*,

Senior Advocate Maninder Singh was among the many mentees of Jaitley, and personally very dear to Jaitley and Sangeeta, who acted as hosts at Maninder's wedding reception. The family of young Maninder, who married lawyer Pratibha (now a judge of Delhi High Court), did not recognise members of the Bar invited to the wedding. Jaitley and Sangeeta decided to receive the guests. When Jaitley decided to hang his lawyer boots, he passed on his major clients to Singh, who made Jaitley proud, going on to become the additional solicitor general of India.

Minister in PMO Jitendra Singh confessed it was Jaitley who brought him into politics. Singh was closely associated with the activities and programmes of the Sangh Parivar and was also a core committee member of Shri Amarnath Yatra Sangharsh Samiti, which spearheaded the Amarnath land agitation. He said, "One February afternoon, while sitting in his 9 Ashoka Road chamber, Arun Jaitley suggested whether I was ready to formally take over the responsibility as a party office-bearer of the BJP. ... I did not straightway respond in too many words but while leaving the room, I stood at the door, looked back at him and said, 'Hope, that would not make a laughing stock of me.' He looked up, smiled and, a man of few words as he was, he said: 'You will carve a niche for yourself.'" Singh added, "I am not sure whether I had faith in myself, but I had huge faith in Arun Jaitley. In the topsy-turvy and need-based politics of today, Arun Jaitley had the commitment and capacity to stand up for a junior or a colleague if he was convinced about what he was doing. He could also take up cudgels for a colleague or a friend 'in absentia' without the person concerned even being aware of it."[51]

Vijay Jolly writes, "I was a rocking BJP MLA from 2003 to 2008 in Delhi Assembly. It was Arun Jaitley who convinced me to contest from the New Delhi seat against then Congress chief minister Sheila Dikshit in 2008 Delhi assembly polls. Jaitley motivated me to publicly challenge the then powerful chief minister. I dutifully followed his dictates. I lost the New Delhi polls

---

Special Edition, An Obituary to Arun Jaitley, Vol. VII, No. 3 (July–September 2019), pp. 26–28.

51. Dr Jitendra Singh, "The Best Brain in the Country, Arun Jaitley Leaves Behind a Void in Many Lives", in ibid. pp. 31–34.

narrowly, but won the hearts of millions with my style and never-die spirit. All thanks to Jaitley's motivations!"[52]

The list of Jaitley being there for friends in times of crisis is too long to enumerate. "When I was charged with contempt of court by the Supreme Court, public and private crises, he was there. There was no question of him asking for anything in return, not even gratitude. He just moved on. The magic and natural grace of Arun was he never allowed us the anxiety of asking for help. We never had to. Arun Jaitley was there for us and for countless others," said Madhu Trehan.[53] Coomi Kapoor, his long-time friend, wrote, "In my last interaction with Arun Jaitley ... he made a stray comment which could well serve as his epitaph. He said he made it a point to help whenever he was in a position to do so and he had been amply rewarded by the goodwill he enjoyed—he was speaking in the context of an opposition leader who found himself friendless in his recent legal difficulties."[54]

Lawyer Neeha Nagpal says:

> My most vivid childhood memory of Arun Uncle is of visiting his home every Diwali for lunch. To me, he will always be my father's old college friend, someone deeply rooted in our family history. He once received a collage of pictures from a DU student rally. He instantly sent it to my brother and me as the collage had lots of pictures of our father too. Papa (Late Mr Inderjit Nagpal) and Arun Uncle shared a bond that began in their youth and has lived on through their children.
>
> After my father's untimely passing in May 2009, Arun Uncle became a steady pillar of strength and guidance for us. In many ways, he filled the void of a father figure for my brother and me. In our weakest moments, he ensured we did not falter or lose direction.

---

52. Vijay Jolly, "Jaitley was my DU senior whom I always referred to as the Big Boss", *The Week*, accessed on 4 September 2025, https://www.theweek.in/news/india/2019/08/28/arun-jaitley-the-go-getter.html.

53. Madhu Trehan, "The Measure of a Man", *Newslaundry*, accessed 25 May 2025, https://www.newslaundry.com/2019/08/24/the-measure-of-a-man.

54. Coomi Kapoor, "Arun Jaitley: The Politician Who Won Hearts Across All Divides", *Financial Express*, accessed 25 May 2025, https://www.financialexpress.com/opinion/arun-jaitley-the-politician-who-won-hearts-across-all-divides/1685857/.

Professionally, he encouraged me to embrace hard work with horse-blinker focus. He often said, nothing can substitute sincerity. I once had an intense discussion on Section 29A of the IBC with him. He explained its relevance in the Indian context with such clarity and conviction that it stays with me till date. He constantly pushed my brother to quit smoking, and once, half-serious and half-playful, told him that he had raised taxes on cigarettes specifically to deter young smokers like him.

Arun Uncle was larger than life. His kindness had no limits. His intellect and emotional depth were remarkable. His elephantine memory will remain his most defining trait. He will remain irreplaceable in our lives.

Doston ka Dost

Arun Jaitley's circle (or circles) of friends was enormous.[55] The BJP and the political world gave him cherished comrades and colleagues, revered seniors, and admiring juniors. Some friends were from his student politics days and others belonged to the legal fraternity. Others were befriended in the post-Emergency civil liberties watchdog institutions. Some co-activists of that era moved to the left and became hostile to the BJP, but Jaitley always maintained an equation and a polite working relationship with them; at times this was politically useful for his party, but that's another story. His various interests—from cricket to cinema, Hindi film songs to travel, and of course food—expanded his circle still further.[56]

A warm-hearted Punjabi at his core, Jaitley was *yaaron ka yaar.* Amongst his closest friends from the legal profession were Raian Karanjawala, Mukul Rohatgi, and senior advocate Rajeev Nayyar. Jaitley first met Karanjawala in 1972 when they were students at SRCC. Karanjawala fondly recalled getting

55. Ashok Malik, "Arun Jaitley's Demise, An Irreplaceable Loss to the Nation", in *The Discussant: Journal of Centre for Reforms, Development and Justice*, Special Edition, An Obituary to Arun Jaitley, Vol. VII, No. 3 (July–September 2019), pp. 56–59.

56. Ibid.

involved in student politics and English debating due to Jaitley's influence. They were family friends who would holiday together and have weekly Saturday lunches together, a tradition that continued for years.[57]

Mukul Rohatgi recalled the period between 1978 and 1998 when his chamber was adjacent to Jaitley at the high court. "Our chambers in the High Court used to be next to each other. We still have those chambers. In court, we used to oppose each other very often. In the heat of the moment, we used harsh words as well but later we would sit as friends," Rohatgi said.[58]

His friends outside the profession included Rajat Sharma and Inderjit Nagpal. His SRCC gang—Supreme Court judge Rohinton Fali Nariman, Karanjawala, and Rajat Sharma—has remained close. Journalist Swapan Dasgupta was Jaitley's another dear friend.[59] When Jaitley was arrested during the Emergency, Karanjawala and Nagpal were one of the few who maintained regular contact with him. They would visit Jaitley in court when he was brought from jail for a particular case.

Another close friend was Narendra Modi. Congress leader Madhavrao Scindia and former hotelier and part-politician Lalit Suri were his dear friends.[60] In 2001, after the tragic death of Madhavrao Scindia in a plane crash, Jaitley, who was the law minister at the time, accompanied Scindia's son Jyotiraditya in an Air Force aircraft to retrieve the body.

Shobhana Bhartia, chairperson of *Hindustan Times*, former Rajya Sabha member, and close friend of Jaitley, remembered that he represented Scindia in the Jain hawala case in 1996. "It didn't matter to us that we belonged to

---

57. S.N. Thyagarajan, "Raian Karanjawala on His Friends Ratan Tata, Arun Jaitley, and Rupert Murdoch", *Money Control*, accessed 25 May 2025, https://www.moneycontrol.com/news/trends/legal/raian-karanjawala-on-his-friends-ratan-tata-arun-jaitley-and-rupert-murdoch-11266571.html.

58. Mudita Girotra, "A Friend First and a Politician Later, Say Jaitley's Lodi Gardens Friends", *The New Indian Express*, accessed 25 May 2025, https://www.newindianexpress.com/nation/2019/Aug/24/a-friend-first-and-a-politician-later-say-jaitleys-lodi-gardens-friends-2023697.html.

59. Jyoti Malhotra, "Budget 2014: Staid and Sturdy with Arun Jaitley", *India Today*, From the India Today Archives (2014), accessed 25 May 2025, https://www.indiatoday.in/india-today-insight/story/from-the-india-today-archives-2014-budget-2014-staid-and-sturdy-with-arun-jaitley-2570842-2024-07-23.

60. Ibid.

different ideological persuasions. Madhavrao, Lalit, Arun and I as well as several others were friends in our private lives. What remains remarkable, though, is the 61-year-old Jaitley's ability to cut across party lines and separate the political from the personal that is increasingly rare in India today," Bhartia said.[61]

Pranab Mukherjee, as the UPA's finance minister, confessed at an Idea Exchange programme of *The Indian Express* that the man he most admired from the Opposition ranks was Jaitley, the then Leader of the Opposition in the Rajya Sabha. Indeed, Jaitley had several good friends across the political spectrum—from the NCP's Sharad Pawar to BSP's Mayawati to SAD's Parkash Singh Badal to TDP's Chandrababu Naidu to Congress's P. Chidambaram, Anand Sharma, and Rajeev Shukla to SP's Ram Gopal Yadav—and equally important, each of them return the compliment.[62] It is widely speculated that Chidambaram would have never got arrested had Jaitley been alive.

Jaitley and Pawar go back a long way, their friendship cemented by their mutual love for cricket. In fact, when Pawar wanted to become the BCCI president in 2005, naturally he counted on Jaitley to bring in the requisite support.[63] He had a long association with the Badals of the Akali Dal. His numerous contacts benefited his party in stitching up alliances, reaching political agreements, and fire-fighting.[64] Senior CPI(M) leader Sitaram Yechury had known Jaitley since the mid-1970s when he led the Students' Federation of India and Jaitley led the AVBP, and both student parties shared the spoils of the 1977–78 DU elections.

In the words of Singhvi, Arun Jaitley's friendships were defined by their profound depth, unwavering loyalty, and unconditional nature. Singhvi recounted one particularly poignant example involving a close college friend of Jaitley's, who was also a colleague at the Bar. When this friend faced a

61. Ibid.

62. Jyoti Malhotra, "What Makes the Finance-Defence-Company Affairs Minister the Go-to Man in the Narendra Modi Government", *India Today*, accessed 25 May 2025, https://www.indiatoday.in/magazine/cover-story/story/20141110-arun-jaitley-narendra-modi-finance-defence-company-affairs-minister-805687-2014-10-30.

63. Ibid.

64. Coomi Kapoor, "A Man of Open Heart and Mind, Arun Jaitley Had Friends Across Divide", in *The Discussant: Journal of Centre for Reforms, Development and Justice*, Special Edition, An Obituary to Arun Jaitley, Vol. VII, No. 3 July–September 2019), pp. 51–55.

seemingly serious medical condition many years ago, Jaitley, who was serving as a minister at the time, immediately set aside all other obligations to be by his friend's side. Jaitley travelled to Mumbai and remained at the hospital, tending to his friend day and night. Despite his significant official responsibilities, Jaitley personally answered all calls made to his friend's mobile phone, ensuring uninterrupted support and care. Singhvi recalled that when the colleague recounted this incident to him, his eyes welled up with tears as he remembered Jaitley's steadfast devotion and compassion during a time of great personal difficulty.[65]

Singhvi also recalled an interesting anecdote. A mutual friend recounted a heart-warming incident that occurred in London. When a staff member complimented Jaitley on his stylish blazer, Jaitley, with his characteristic generosity, took the staff member to Marks and Spencer and purchased a blazer and a tie for him. As the staff member donned his new attire, Jaitley playfully remarked, "*Raju ab ban gaya gentleman*" (Raju has now become a gentleman).[66]

Several of Jaitley's associations were more than four decades old, as with former Samata Party spokesman Shambhu Srivastava, who first met Jaitley during their student days back in the 1970s. Srivastava, who came into regular contact with Jaitley in the 1990s when they would lock horns at television studios, said, "He was a great host. All of us who knew him well have lost count of the number of meals we had at his Kailash Colony house."[67]

Many of Jaitley's contacts across parties go back to those heady days of student politics. His cellmate in jail during the Emergency, socialist Vijay Pratap, had an interesting aside: "Jaitley's first introduction to politics, ironically enough, began at a Left-oriented study circle in Delhi University." Out of jail, Jaitley and Vijay Pratap remained in touch. "Like alumni associations, we had an informal association of jail ward mates and we used to meet occasionally,"

---

65. Dr Abhishek Manu Singhvi, "Arun Jaitley: In Memoriam", *The Times of India*, accessed 25 May 2025, https://timesofindia.indiatimes.com/blogs/straight-candid/arun-jaitley-in-memoriam/.

66. Ibid.

67. Anita Joshua, "Arun Jaitley: Mr Fixit, with Friends Everywhere", *The Telegraph*, accessed 25 May 2025, https://www.telegraphindia.com/india/arun-jaitley-mr-fixit-with-friends-everywhere/cid/1700063#goog_rewarded.

Vijay Pratap quipped, remembering with nostalgia a political era when friendships could bridge ideological divides.[68]

Cricket

Jaitley was not merely a cricket enthusiast; he was actively involved in the game's administration—one of the many roles he embraced in public life. Before he was appointed Cabinet minister in 2014, he was the president of the DDCA. Elected unopposed in 1999, he remained in the position as the president of the DDCA until 2013, for close to thirteen years—one of its longest-serving presidents. He also served as the vice president of BCCI, and as a member of the Governing Council of IPL. He quit the DDCA and BCCI positions in 2013 much before Modi became the prime minister in 2014.

His deep commitment to cricket was evident in the many improvements made in the game's administration during his stint at the DDCA, BCCI, and IPL. Jaitley gifted Delhi a world-class cricket stadium in Feroz Shah Kotla. He increased the stadium's capacity to accommodate more fans besides constructing world-class dressing rooms. His stature as a respected political leader played a crucial role in bringing in resources like installation of floodlights at the Feroz Shah Kotla and a complete renovation of the stadium.

Cricket was dear to Jaitley, he could recall dates, players, and their performances from the past that would astonish even a statistician. No less was his interest in the progress of Delhi's young cricketers.[69] He would remember the names of players who would do well in the Under-19 circuit, for instance, and monitor their performances. He would also do his bit to help the cricketing fraternity even after his stint as the DDCA president was over. It wasn't unusual for Jaitley to call Delhi selectors and coaches to check on the progress of Under-16 and Under-19 players they had not heard of. Mathur recalled, "In the 30 odd years I knew and worked with him in cricket, Mr Jaitley's love for

---

68. Ibid.

69. Amrit Mathur, "Jaitley Ji Played with a Straight Bat, Was Pure Class", in *The Discussant: Journal of Centre for Reforms*, Development and Justice, Special Edition, An Obituary to Arun Jaitley, Vol. VII, No. 3 (July–September 2019), pp. 69–71.

the game always came through. Our conversations invariably and inevitably centered on cricket. He could access facts quicker than Google, precise to the smallest detail, extracting stats from his formidable memory with the effortless ease of a top lawyer. His recall was extraordinary, sometimes scary, as he could refer to a chance remark made years ago as if uttered just the day before."[70]

As he helmed the DDCA, talented players from in and around the national capital emerged and flourished on the biggest stage. Virender Sehwag, Virat Kohli, Shikhar Dhawan, and Ishant Sharma, besides Gautam Gambhir, are some of the names that shone in international cricket with him at the top. Under his leadership at the DDCA, many players got a chance to represent India.

If Jagmohan Dalmiya laid the foundation for the BCCI's current form, it was Jaitley who took it forward. At the BCCI, he was the ultimate go-to person, such was his personal charm and universal appeal. Whatever the issue, regardless of the persons involved, Jaitley would be objective. In the fragmented unruly dynamics of the BCCI, he was an adviser, a problem solver, and a consensus builder. There can be no better example of a brilliant individual selflessly playing for the team.[71]

When the IPL was being formed, Jaitley crafted legal documents to allow for the coexistence of Test cricket, one-day internationals, and the IPL. He deftly navigated it in the initial period, getting permissions and approvals.[72] The IPL provided opportunities to a multitude of players, offering the young players in particular a dream platform. When the entire IPL plan was being formulated, there were many hurdles, but Jaitley, with his tremendous patience and legal expertise, worked tirelessly day and night, ensuring the IPL's successful launch. Whenever there was a legal issue, regardless of which party was in power, everyone's gaze turned towards Jaitley.

Jaitley was a friend, an ally, a protector, and an unfailing insurance cover for the Delhi franchise—Delhi Capitals (earlier Delhi Daredevils). Each time there was a hiccup, a minor disagreement or dispute, all one had to do was to ask for help. To Delhi Capitals, he was the Supreme Court that resolved issues on merit, with complete fairness. Jaitley took keen interest in the

70. Ibid.

71. Ibid.

72. Ibid.

commercial results and the team's on-field performance. When Delhi recruited a young Andre Russell (unknown at that time even to some in the franchise support staff), he surprised everyone by commending the selection of the impactful all-rounder.[73]

When Virender Sehwag could not find a venue for his wedding at any hotel in Delhi as all were sold out, Jaitley graciously offered his official bungalow at 9 Ashoka Road for the wedding in 2004.[74] Parmod Jain, a veteran cricket official, narrated an anecdote when the Delhi team, under Bishan Singh Bedi as the coach, complained about "poor" hotel accommodations during a Ranji Trophy match in Jaipur. Jaitley ordered the team to be shifted to a five-star hotel. From then onwards, he ensured that Delhi players always stayed in decent hotels. Jaitley also "ensured the club cricketers got good facilities in the local league", demonstrating his commitment to improving the sport at all levels.[75]

Jaitley faced one of his toughest tests when, with Kirti Azad's support, Delhi Chief Minister Arvind Kejriwal of the Aam Aadmi Party accused him of financial irregularities in the DDCA during his tenure as its president, calling for his resignation. The allegations rattled the usually composed and articulate statesman Jaitley. He was furious. For a man who had built his reputation on integrity and professionalism, these accusations would have been deeply personal. Jaitley had always prided himself on his clean image in public life, and the allegations struck at the core of his credibility. He would have felt not just politically targeted but also personally wronged, given that he had never before faced such direct and public accusations of impropriety.

Renowned for his legal acumen and composed demeanour, Jaitley responded with uncharacteristic sharpness. His background in law and long experience in political combat may have given him confidence in his defence, yet the emotional strain of such allegations was undeniable. Though he projected calm in public, the charges likely stirred deep frustration and indignation in private.

---

73. Ibid.

74. "When Arun Jaitley Hosted Virender Sehwag's Wedding at His Bungalow", *Catch News*, accessed 25 May 2025, https://www.catchnews.com/cricket-news/when-arun-jaitley-hosted-virender-sehwag-s-wedding-at-his-bungalow-170532.html.

75. Vijay Lokapally, "Arun Jaitley—Delhi Cricket's Visionary Administrator", *Sportstar*, accessed 25 May 2025, https://sportstar.thehindu.com/cricket/arun-jaitley-passes-away-delhi-cricket-ddca-sehwag-aakash-chopra/article29252174.ece.

Moreover, the timing of the allegations was significant. They came at a time when the BJP was already engaged in fierce political battles with the AAP in Delhi. Jaitley, as a key strategist for the BJP, would have seen Kejriwal's move as a calculated political attack rather than a genuine expose. This would have added to Jaitley's resentment, as he believed the allegations were baseless and politically motivated. Despite his composed public demeanour, Jaitley's strong-worded statements and legal actions suggested a man determined to clear his name at all costs. He dismissed the allegations as "false and defamatory" and expressed confidence that the truth would prevail.

Amid charges and counter-charges, Prime Minister Narendra Modi had expressed his faith in his finance minister: "*Advani ji jitney pavitra hain, Jaitley ji utne hee hain*" (Jaitley is as pure as Advani).[76] Virender Sehwag, Ishant Sharma, and Gautam Gambhir came out in support of Arun Jaitley on Twitter stating that he was an exemplary DDCA president.

He filed a defamation suit against Kejriwal and other AAP leaders, indicating how seriously he took the matter. His decision to take the matter to court rather than engage in a media war reflected his belief in due process and his disdain for what he saw as mudslinging. It ended with an unconditional apology to him by Kejriwal. Jaitley was deeply hurt by the false allegations that had been made. Yet, in his characteristic large-hearted manner, he accepted the apology.[77]

While this vindication would have been satisfying, the episode undoubtedly left a mark. For a leader who valued his reputation above all, the public tarnishing of his image—even if later disproven—would have been a painful chapter in his political career.

In 2024, Jaitley's son, Rohan, defeated Kirti Azad to be elected as the president of the DDCA for the third successive term.

After his death, Feroz Shah Kotla ground was named in the honour of Arun Jaitley. Apart from cricket, he guided and assisted numerous sports

---

76. Kumkum Chadha, *The Marigold Story: Indira Gandhi & Others* (Westland, 2019), p. 329.

77. Sidharth Luthra, "Arun Jaitley: A Distinctive Lawyer, a Fine Human Being", *Hindustan Times*, accessed 25 May 2025, https://www.hindustantimes.com/analysis/arun-jaitley-a-distinctive-lawyer-a-fine-human-being/story-ibzYrSb3LL88VuBKqjL4PL.html.

organisations.[78] Whether it was a government undertaking or a private company, he would ensure that sports received the necessary funding. Home Minister Amit Shah has admitted having personally benefitted from Jaitley's advice many times.[79] As with his other spheres of influence, so with cricket: Jaitley kept an open house for cricketers and was ever keen to meet new blood, players or cricket journalists. All of this added to his aura—the self-assured presence of a man who could summon his legal prowess at a moment's notice to win any argument.[80] He never sought any recognition for his contributions to sports.

Favourite Pastime

Arun Jaitley's favourite pastime, besides indulging in fine cuisine and gossiping, was watching classic films, with the Hindi movie *Waqt* being a particular favourite. Singhvi recounted that during a cruise that docked at Dubrovnik, while Jaitley's family members went out to explore the picturesque city, Jaitley opted to stay behind and immerse himself in watching *Waqt* as well as other beloved Punjabi comedies. Jaitley's deep appreciation for good food and nostalgic cinema was integral to his persona.[81] "Jaitley had an elephantine memory. He could recollect a movie of the 1960s, word by word and scene by scene," Ranjit Kumar recollected.[82] Jaitley enjoyed Hindi film songs; legendary

78. "Amit Shah Shares Stories of Arun Jaitley's Love for Cricket", *The Quint*, accessed 25 May 2025, https://www.youtube.com/watch?v=Q5tHuIxuDg4.

79. Ibid.

80. Anita Joshua, "Arun Jaitley: Mr Fixit, with Friends Everywhere", *The Telegraph*, accessed 25 May 2025, https://www.telegraphindia.com/india/arun-jaitley-mr-fixit-with-friends-everywhere/cid/1700063#goog_rewarded.

81. Dr Abhishek Manu Singhvi, "Arun Jaitley: In Memoriam", *The Times of India*, accessed 25 May 2025, https://timesofindia.indiatimes.com/blogs/straight-candid/arun-jaitley-in-memoriam/.

82. "Morning Walk, Birthday Ritual at Lodhi Gardens: Delhi Will Remember Arun Jaitley", *Hindustan Times*, accessed 25 May, 2025, https://www.hindustantimes.com/india-news/morning-walk-birthday-ritual-at-lodhi-gardens-delhi-will-remember-arun-jaitley/story-NSxJ39otZuABf2B4RA7YHK.html.

poet Neeraj's *"Kaarwan Guzar Gaya Gubaar Dekhte Rahe"* was one of his all-time favourites.[83]

Karanjawala told journalist Kumkum Chadha how Jaitley loved Hindi movies, and how Jaitley was particularly fond of the 1969–70 comedy *Padosan* which he had not only watched several times, but always carried with him while travelling.[84] He admired Sahir Ludhianvi and Dev Anand.[85] Karanjawala claimed he had heard Jaitley reel off the colour of Dev Anand's shirts in *Johnny Mera Naam*, or recall dialogues from other films.[86]

Great Host, Renowned Foodie

Food was his greatest love besides friends. His deep, almost legendary, passion for food was an integral part of his persona. A connoisseur of fine cuisine, Jaitley often indulged in gourmet experiences, making his culinary preferences a topic of interest among friends, colleagues, and food enthusiasts. He was the "go-to man" for the best Punjabi food in town. He would wax eloquent about the food in Roshanara Club, one of the oldest in Delhi, established in 1922, or speak endlessly about the channa bathura that Kwality, Connaught Place, New Delhi continues to serve till date. It is said that it was he who had not only introduced the Amritsari kulcha to Delhi, but also Harisons Caterers, who make the best seekh kababs.[87]

---

83. Ravi Shankar Prasad, "In Remembrance: Arun Jaitley Was an Affectionate Elder Brother to Me and Leaves Fond Memories", *The Times of India*, accessed 25 May 2025, https://timesofindia.indiatimes.com/blogs/toi-edit-page/in-remembrance-arun-jaitley-was-an-affectionate-elder-brother-to-me-and-leaves-fond-memories/.

84. Kumkum Chadha, *The Marigold Story: Indira Gandhi & Others* (Westland, 2019), p. 322.

85. Amrit Mathur, "Jaitley Ji Played with a Straight Bat, Was Pure Class", in *The Discussant: Journal of Centre for Reforms, Development and Justice*, Special Edition, An Obituary to Arun Jaitley, Vol. VII, No. 3 (July–September 2019), pp. 69–71.

86. Kumkum Chadha, *The Marigold Story: Indira Gandhi & Others* (Westland, 2019), p. 322.

87. Ibid., p. 330.

A renowned foodie and quintessential Delhiite, he was known to meticulously plan the next day's lunch menu even during breakfast the previous day. He had a refined palate and enjoyed both traditional Indian dishes and international delicacies. His favourite cuisines ranged from rich Punjabi fare—reflecting his North Indian roots—to Mughlai, Continental, and even Chinese.

While Jaitley appreciated a wide variety of dishes, he had a special weakness for sweets. Traditional Indian mithais like gulab jamun, rasmalai, and jalebi were among his favourites. Colleagues often joked about his inability to resist a well-made dessert, even during strict health regimens. His sweet tooth was so well-known that friends and supporters would often gift him premium sweets from renowned shops across India.

He was particularly fond of Delhi's culinary scene, frequently dining at iconic establishments like Karim's for its legendary kebabs, Bukhara for its dal and tandoori delicacies, and Moti Mahal for butter chicken. He cherished Sunday lunches at Moti Mahal in Greater Kailash. Jaitley had been a Moti Mahal fan since childhood, frequenting the Greater Kailash outlet along with his friends to engage in long chats as he gulped his favourite burra and chicken pakoda. Restaurant chain owner Monish Gujral recollected that Jaitley, a quintessential Delhiite, would also visit the Daryaganj outlet where his love affair with these two dishes began.[88] Jaitley's fondness for the restaurant was also evident when he came as the chief guest to launch the first book by Gujral titled *Moti Mahal's Tandoori Trail* in 2004. Recalling a fond memory, Gujral said that when KFC first entered India and failed to make a mark, Jaitley quipped that it was because of Moti Mahal's unbeatable chicken pakodas.[89]

Arun Jaitley was a great host. His residence in Delhi often became a hub for discussions over plates of delicious food, blending politics with gastronomy. Unassuming and approachable, he personally ensured each guest's plate was filled with his recommended dishes, creating an intimate and warm atmosphere that belied his high-profile role as India's finance minister.

---

88. "Arun Jaitley Was a Food Lover Who Relished Chicken Pakoda, Burra and Amritsari Kulcha", *The New Indian Express*, accessed 25 May 2025, https://www.newindianexpress.com/thesundaystandard/2019/Aug/25/arun-jaitley-was-a-food-lover-who-relished-chicken-pakoda-burra-and-amritsari-kulcha-2023860.html.

89. Ibid.

When it comes to Arun Jaitley and his relationship with food, "foodnotes" would be a more fitting term than simply "anecdotes".[90] Ashish Sood, his party colleague and former general secretary of Delhi BJP, recollected that his gatherings were never complete without chicken, chhole-bhature, or parathas. Sometimes parathas would be ordered from Murthal, other times chhole-bhature from Kwality restaurant in Connaught Place.[91]

His love for street food was also notable; he occasionally enjoyed chaat, especially at Delhi's famous outlets like Prince Paan and Nathu's Sweets. These weren't just meals but occasions for long chats with friends, fuelled by his favourite burra and chicken pakoda. A true Delhiite, his face lit up as he reminisced about his regular visits to Shahjahan Road for its famous street-side chaat, his unwavering love for the legendary rasgullas of Gopala Sweets, and his preference for samosas over any other Indian snack.

In the words of Prime Minister Modi, Jaitley was an "encyclopaedia on the subject of food ... whenever we used to go outside, we definitely used to have one meal with him". In a podcast with Zerodha co-founder Nikhil Kamath, Prime Minister Modi reminisced how Jaitley used to advise him on matters of food and restaurants. Modi said, "Earlier, when I used to work for the party organisation, our Arun Jaitley Ji was very fond of food. He knew exactly which restaurant in which city of India served the best food."[92] Perhaps if he was a politician of this era, his Instagram handle would have been the go-to place for images of delectable gustatory treats.[93] Former vice president of India

---

90. Dr Abhishek Manu Singhvi, "Arun Jaitley: In Memoriam", *The Times of India*, accessed 25 May 2025, https://timesofindia.indiatimes.com/blogs/straight-candid/arun-jaitley-in-memoriam/.

91. "Arun Jaitley Was a Food Lover Who Relished Chicken Pakoda, Burra and Amritsari Kulcha", *The New Indian Express*, accessed 25 May 2025, https://www.newindianexpress.com/thesundaystandard/2019/Aug/25/arun-jaitley-was-a-food-lover-who-relished-chicken-pakoda-burra-and-amritsari-kulcha-2023860.html.

92. "'Arun Jaitley Was a Foodie': PM Modi Recalls Visiting Restaurants with Veteran BJP Leader", Republic, accessed 25 May 2025, https://www.republicworld.com/india/arun-jaitley-was-a-foodie-pm-modi-recalls-visiting-restaurants-with-veteran-bjp-leader.

93. "Arun Jaitley—The Foodie Who Ensured His Guests Were Fed Even When He Couldn't Indulge", *DNA*, accessed 25 May 2025, https://www.dnaindia.com/india/photo-gallery-arun-jaitley-the-foodie-who-ensured-his-guests-were-fed-even-when-he-couldn-t-indulge-2784481/india/photo-gallery-arun-jaitley-the-foodie-who-

Venkaiah Naidu recounted, "Both of us were foodies. In the early days, we used to go to all the popular restaurants and try different kinds of cuisine. He was a regular at my residence. His house was the only place I used to visit on sociocultural occasions. While dining we used to talk and exchange notes on various emerging issues. Our regular meetings were both for food and food for thought."[94]

For Jaitley, food was more than just sustenance—it was a medium for bonding. Journalist Gaurav Sawant recalled on Twitter how Jaitley would always ensure his guests were well-fed with "chaat, kachori, mithai, hot milk with saffron, and a thick layer of malai". He remembered how Jaitley would ensure others ate "till they could eat no more".[95]

During his tenure as the finance minister, even Jaitley's South Block office was known for its hospitality, with snacks and tea served generously to visitors. His staff often ensured that meetings included good food, reflecting his belief that shared meals fostered better conversations. Jaitley always ensured visiting journalists were treated to lavish food. Harsimrat Kaur Badal wrote:

> I used to always tell him, you are more like a Sardar, because of your large-hearted persona. He was a like a typical Punjabi foodie. There was a lunch in his chamber at the end of every Parliament session with food from all parts of the country, and leaders across parties would be present. I once told him that I was going to bring lunch from Punjab after the House was adjourned after the President's address. I brought sarson ka saag and makki ki roti because I knew how much he liked

---

ensured-his-guests-were-fed-even-when-he-couldn-t-indulge-2784481/loved-cricket-and-food-2784482.

94. M. Venkaiah Naidu, "Our Regular Meetings Were for Food, and Food for Thought", in *The Discussant: Journal of Centre for Reforms, Development and Justice*, Special Edition, An Obituary to Arun Jaitley, Vol. VII, No. 3 (July–September 2019), pp. 17–19.

95. "Arun Jaitley—The Foodie Who Ensured His Guests Were Fed Even When He Couldn't Indulge", *DNA*, accessed 25 May 2025, https://www.dnaindia.com/india/photo-gallery-arun-jaitley-the-foodie-who-ensured-his-guests-were-fed-even-when-he-couldn-t-indulge-2784481/india/photo-gallery-arun-jaitley-the-foodie-who-ensured-his-guests-were-fed-even-when-he-couldn-t-indulge-2784481/loved-cricket-and-food-2784482.

> it. He told me that I must make it an annual routine, which became a tradition since then.[96]

Jaitley once spent a remarkable three hours searching for Saravana Bhavan, a renowned South Indian restaurant, during a trip to Vancouver. One friend of Jaitley recalled an instance where Jaitley left a famous, Michelin-rated Indian restaurant in New York because he was unable to find his preferred accompaniments of "*nimbu achar*" (lemon pickle) and "*hari mirch*" (green chillies). However, the restaurant owner and Jaitley later became good friends and even exchanged several cherished recipes. The same friend also recounted Jaitley's dedication to procuring authentic Indian cuisine, even if it meant travelling for over five hours round-trip from Zurich to Lausanne to pick up home-cooked delicacies from a highly regarded Sikh gentleman in Lausanne.[97]

Despite his love for eating, Jaitley managed to keep himself fit for long. In 1999, a journalist who took Jaitley out for a "Lunch with *Business Standard*" interview wrote:

> As we sat down for the meal, it was a spritely Jaitley who surprised me with an unlikely question. "Can you guess my age?" he asked, obviously proud of the way he looked after his health and fitness. "You must be around 40," I stammered more because of the suddenness of the question than its complexity. "No, I am close to the 50s," he said with a glint in his eye. At 47, he hardly looked like the person who would be picked by providence to be subjected to multiple morbidities in later years.[98]

---

96. Harsimrat Kaur Badal, "A Go-To Person for Many, Arun Jaitley Mastered Facts Across Genres", *Hindustan Times*, accessed 25 May 2025, https://www.hindustantimes.com/india-news/a-go-to-person-for-many-he-mastered-facts-across-genres/story-TLiRJLvQJooMxP2iOYrXAK.html.

97. Dr Abhishek Manu Singhvi, "Arun Jaitley: In Memoriam", *The Times of India*, accessed 25 May 2025, https://timesofindia.indiatimes.com/blogs/straight-candid/arun-jaitley-in-memoriam/.

98. Ajay Singh, "When Jaitley Asked Me to Guess His Age…", *Governance Now*, accessed 25 May 2025, https://www.governancenow.com/news/regular-story/when-jaitley-asked-me-to-guess-his-age.

For Jaitley, Amritsar held a special place, its culinary reputation as "the Food Capital of India" being a significant draw for his repeated visits. His love for the city's food was reflected in his Facebook post—The Campaign Diary—30 April 2014—where he recollected his link with Amritsar. "I have always regarded Amritsar as the Food Capital of India," he posted. Amritsari kulcha with chanas, of course, topped his list of favourite dishes. Be it paratha, lassi, Amritsari fish, mutton chaaps, and Makhan fish, Jaitley mentioned them all fondly. Such was his knowledge about food that he could rattle the names of eateries, restaurants, and hotels. "When Jaitley was young, he used to come to our grandfather's shop ... In 2014, he came twice and relished kulchas and lassi as he recalled the love and affection he got from this city," recollected Pawandeep Singh, the owner of Kulcha Land.[99]

When Arun Jaitley's Amritsar election campaign was drawing to a close, after six weeks in the vibrant city, it was time to move on to other states. But before leaving, he wanted to experience Amritsar's incredible food scene—a culinary journey that had been a highlight of his time there. He had always considered Amritsar the Food Capital of India, and his recent stay only reinforced that belief.

A traditional Amritsar breakfast featured stuffed parathas or chhole puri. Many families outsourced this dish to renowned halwais rather than making it at home. Each neighbourhood boasted its specialists, but Kanahya on Lawrence Road was particularly famous for its potato-enhanced chana masala. Accompanying it was the ubiquitous Amritsari lassi. Ahuja and Gian were especially well-regarded for their lassi, even rumoured to offer a cure for insomnia! For vegetarian dishes, Kesar reigned supreme, holding the title of Amritsar's most famous dhaba. Bharawan, with its various branches, provided another excellent vegetarian alternative for both locals and tourists. Surjit was the undisputed champion for non-vegetarian fare. Its tandoori chicken, Amritsari fish, and mutton chops (prepared like old English cutlets) were exceptional. The Makhan fish was a particular gourmet delight. Another establishment he hadn't yet tried but which came highly recommended was

---

99. "Arun Jaitley Was a Food Lover Who Relished Chicken Pakoda, Burra and Amritsari Kulcha", *The New Indian Express*, accessed 25 May 2025, https://www.newindianexpress.com/thesundaystandard/2019/Aug/25/arun-jaitley-was-a-food-lover-who-relished-chicken-pakoda-burra-and-amritsari-kulcha-2023860.html.

Beera, also known for its high-quality chicken. Finally, a morning tea at Giani Tea Stall was a must. This wasn't just a cup of tea; it was where the city's gossip started—Jaitley's personal replacement for Delhi's Lodhi Gardens tea gatherings.

In his later years, Jaitley's love for rich food clashed with his declining health. After undergoing bariatric surgery in 2014, he had to adopt a strict diet, avoiding sugar and heavy dishes. However, those close to him revealed that he sometimes indulged in moderation, unable to completely resist his favourite flavours. Despite his health challenges, Jaitley's enthusiasm for food remained undiminished. He continued to appreciate well-cooked meals, even if he could no longer enjoy them as freely as before.

★

Jaitley weathered many storms, but on the outside, he always appeared calm. He believed in getting on with life; he neither prayed for benefits, nor sought out astrologers to pre-empt what was in store for the future. His mother was very religious, and his home has a temple with many gods. Jaitley kept up his equation with what perhaps his mother had initiated—he did share a private moment with the gods every day, by lighting a diya before he set out to seek out many more challenges.[100]

Jaitley's "rational" approach and ability to appeal to various sections of society, as well as his great sense of humour and infectious smile made him a lovable person. Madhu Trehan recalled:

> While many will laud Arun Jaitley's political career and address his public persona, the true measure of a man is how he gave of himself to others. It is an intangible, unquantifiable quality. Especially, he himself never boasted about what he did for others. When my father's soul left his body, dozens of strangers came out of the woodwork to tell us amazing stories of how he had helped them. We did not know.

---

100. Kumkum Chadha, *The Marigold Story: Indira Gandhi & Others* (Westland, 2019), p. 338.

> Quietly, he had been paying for someone's college in the US, another said he came to him during the Partition wearing only a vest, a woman who said he had intervened to stop a forced marriage, too many to list. Similarly, it will be impossible to find a friend of Arun Jaitley's who does not have a story. Although he loved to talk about anything and everything, full of fascinating stories, one never heard him tell a story about how he helped someone. ... The measure of the man was his innate altruistic character. Though nothing can bring back the splendour of the friendship, we will grieve not. We will find strength in what he gave us: himself. (Apologies to William Wordsworth). Many will now say, he is no more. Yes, he is irreplaceable. He was always there for us. He will be within us as we learn to be for our friends as he was. He will always remain here with us. Forever.[101]

We have lost a decent man, a good human being, a large heart, a magnanimous disposition, a piercing intellect, a great orator, an even better communicator, an able lawyer, and a pillar for his party.[102]

---

101. Madhu Trehan, "The Measure of a Man", *Newslaundry*, accessed 25 May 2025, https://www.newslaundry.com/2019/08/24/the-measure-of-a-man.

102. Dr Abhishek Manu Singhvi, "Arun Jaitley: In Memoriam", *The Times of India*, accessed 25 May 2025, https://timesofindia.indiatimes.com/blogs/straight-candid/arun-jaitley-in-memoriam/.

22

The End of an Era

With the demise of Arun Jaitley Ji, I have lost a valued friend, whom I have had the honour of knowing for decades. His insight on issues and nuanced understanding of matters had very few parallels. He lived well, leaving us all with innumerable happy memories.[1] Arun was a very close friend who was a stalwart blessed with a lot of talent with a multifaceted personality. I miss his presence.[2]—Prime Minister Narendra Modi

★

Towards the end of NDA's term in 2019, Jaitley was confined to his house, rarely moving out, but the flood of ministers, politicians, and journalists to his house continued. He would meet some from a distance. Only a few close friends were allowed in his room. He slept on a long rest chair as sleeping on

---

1. "PM Modi Gets Emotional, Condoles His 'Dear Friend' Arun Jaitley's Demise", *The Times of India*, accessed 25 May 2025, https://timesofindia.indiatimes.com/india/pm-modi-gets-emotional-condoles-his-dear-friend-arun-jaitleys-demise/articleshow/70822369.cms.

2. Narendra Modi, "Condolence Message", in *The Discussant: Journal of Centre for Reforms, Development and Justice*, Special Edition, An Obituary to Arun Jaitley, Vol. VII, No. 3 (July –September 2019), pp. 12–13.

the bed was painful.[3] Even as his health faltered, his days were marked by an undying commitment to public service. He would frantically write his blogs. His last blog was on Article 370. Jitendra Singh recalled that when Jaitley was writing a piece on Article 370 and wanted to check on one or two facts, he called him.[4]

On 9 August 2019, Jaitley was admitted to the hospital after he complained of breathlessness. In a late-night statement on 9 August, AIIMS said Jaitley was undergoing treatment under the supervision of a multidisciplinary team of doctors. Over the next few days, a galaxy of leaders from several political parties visited the former Union minister at AIIMS to enquire about his health. Soon after Jaitley was admitted in the Intensive Care Unit of AIIMS, Prime Minister Narendra Modi paid a visit to the hospital. Amit Shah visited Jaitley every day. President Ram Nath Kovind and RSS chief Mohan Bhagwat visited AIIMS to enquire about his health. Union ministers Rajnath Singh and Uttar Pradesh Chief Minister Yogi Adityanath visited the hospital to check on the condition of the BJP leader.

A man who had navigated the corridors of power with unmatched wit and wisdom, Jaitley faced his declining health with the same dignity that had defined his political career. Confined to hospital rooms and away from the limelight he once commanded, he remained a guiding force for his party, offering counsel until his last breath. On 11 August, when Vice President M. Venkaiah Naidu visited Jaitley in hospital, Jaitley, his hand in Naidu's, looked at his friend and gesticulated that all will be well. Naidu had hardly expected it would be his last handshake with him.[5]

When preparing to get ready to be taken to AIIMS, Jaitley confided in a friend, "I have got everything that I sought from life. I wanted to become a student leader, I reached the top, I wanted to make my mark in legal practice, I reached the top, I entered politics, became the Leader of Opposition and

---

3. As told by a close family friend of the Jaitleys.

4. Dr Jitendra Singh, "The Best Brain in the Country, Arun Jaitley Leaves Behind a Void in Many Lives", in *The Discussant: Journal of Centre for Reforms, Development and Justice*, Special Edition, An Obituary to Arun Jaitley, Vol. VII, No. 3 (July–September 2019), pp. 31–34.

5. M. Venkaiah Naidu, "Our Regular Meetings Were for Food, and Food for Thought", in *The Discussant: Journal of Centre for Reforms, Development and Justice*, Special Edition, An Obituary to Arun Jaitley, Vol. VII, No. 3 (July–September 2019), pp. 17–19.

Union Minister, my children are now well settled … I do not have any more wish to fulfil. If I come through (this phase of treatment), I would like to quit politics, and only read books and write books."[6]

Saba Naqvi, a senior journalist, who met Jaitley in hospital in his last days wrote that she had suggested to him that when he got better, he should write his autobiography. Jaitley smiled but said he was struggling to read now.[7]

Sadly he was not to return. Arun Jaitley breathed his last at 12.07 p.m. on Saturday, 24 August 2019, after having been on life support for two weeks. He was only sixty-six years old.

Amit Shah, who was by Jaitley's side overseeing his treatment, broke down. "His death is a personal loss for me. I have not just lost a senior party colleague but also a member of my family, who guided me for several years," he said.[8] Over the years, Shah and Jaitley had bonded strongly. Their affinity made many, both within the BJP and outside, envious. There were attempts to drive a wedge between them. Political circles buzzed with gossip about Shah chafing at Jaitley's "restraining" presence. But there was hardly any truth in it. While Jaitley acknowledged in public the authority of "adhyaksh ji", in private, the voluble leader didn't keep silent about his fondness for "Amit bhai". There were times, too, when the two disagreed strongly on certain decisions but Jaitley never doubted Shah's prerogative or intent. Shah found Jaitley too soft when it came to judging people, almost "too naïve" for his own good. Shah gave Jaitley the latitude he would not extend to others. Till Jaitley's last breath, Shah trusted him for advice on crucial issues.[9]

---

6. Rajat Sharma, My Opinion, "Arun Jaitley: My Friend, Guardian and Guide", accessed 25 May 2025, https://rajatsharma.in/arun-jaitley-my-friend-guardian-and-guide/.

7. Saba Naqvi, "Arun Jaitley's Relationships Ranged Far and Wide, But the Defining Equation in His Life Would Be with Narendra Modi", in *The Discussant: Journal of Centre for Reforms, Development and Justice*, Special Edition, An Obituary to Arun Jaitley, Vol. VII, No. 3 (July–September 2019), pp. 60–62.

8. Swati Bhasin (Ed.), "'Personal Loss For Me': Home Minister Amit Shah on Arun Jaitley's Death", NDTV, accessed 25 May 2025, https://www.ndtv.com/india-news/arun-jaitley-dies-home-minister-amit-shah-on-arun-jaitleys-death-says-it-is-a-personal-loss-for-me-2089772.

9. "Shah Broke Down When Jaitley Lost His Only Election", *The Times of India*, accessed 25 May 2025, https://timesofindia.indiatimes.com/india/shah-broke-down-when-jaitley-lost-his-only-election/amp_articleshow/70824179.cms.

Shah consulted Jaitley on all important matters, even when Jaitley was in hospital in 2014 or later when he went to New York for treatment. On the intervening night of 25–26 September in 2014, Jaitley was in a hospital in New Delhi for complications following a bariatric surgery. Shah had just been made the BJP president and was wrestling with the thorny issue of whether the party should contest assembly elections in Maharashtra without allies. Shah went to the hospital to check on Jaitley who, defying the doctor's advice, began discussing politics with Shah.[10]

Prime Minister Narendra Modi, was in Bahrain.[11] He offered to come back, but was dissuaded by Jaitley's family in view of his engagements.[12]

At AIIMS, as news of his death spread, people from all walks of life—from ministers and tycoons to party workers, from lawyers to family friends—wept openly as they crowded the corridors of the hospital to pay their last respects. The moist eyes and ashen faces in the spheres in which he once held sway—the courts, Parliament, the cricket fraternity, the media, Lodhi Gardens, the world of commerce, the corridors of power, BJP offices—reflected the universal affection in which he was held.[13] Jaitley touched the lives of most with whom he interacted. Aravind Subramanian said:

> Mr Jaitley is humane and kind, ever willing to help, on matters both big and small. To help—perhaps more important, he wanted to help, wanted to extend the legendary Jaitley generosity as widely as possible, for this is part of his DNA. The Jaitley mystique—of being the best-connected man in town, holder of the *darbaars* of who's who, friend

---

10. Ibid.

11. "PM Modi Gets Emotional, Condoles His 'Dear Friend' Arun Jaitley's Demise", *The Times of India*, accessed 25 May 2025, https://timesofindia.indiatimes.com/india/pm-modi-gets-emotional-condoles-his-dear-friend-arun-jaitleys-demise/articleshow/70822369.cms.

12. Swati Bhasin (Ed.), "Arun Jaitley Cremated with State Honours, Top Leaders Present", NDTV, accessed 25 May 2025, https://www.ndtv.com/india-news/arun-jaitley-to-be-cremated-today-leaders-pay-last-respects-2090025.

13. Coomi Kapoor, "A Man of Open Heart and Mind, Arun Jaitley Had Friends Across Divide", in *The Discussant: Journal of Centre for Reforms, Development and Justice*, Special Edition, An Obituary to Arun Jaitley, Vol. VII, No. 3 (July–September 2019), pp. 51–55.

> to all enemies—is, I suspect, founded on and reinforced by the help that he extended to all those he knew (and the countless he did not), and by the fact that there were few in Delhi who were not beneficiaries of the Jaitley largesse.[14]

Jaitley was cremated at the Nigambodh Ghat with full state honours in the presence of political leaders across party lines and supporters on 25 August. In the morning, Jaitley was moved from his South Delhi residence to the party headquarters on Deendayal Upadhyay Marg amidst chants of *"Jaitley ji amar rahein"* (long live Jaitley), where thousands, including top party leaders and Union ministers, paid tribute to him. BJP workers and mourners queued up outside the BJP headquarters where Arun Jaitley's casket, wrapped in the national flag, was placed. Cutting across party lines, a number of political leaders paid their respects to Arun Jaitley. In the afternoon, the mortal remains draped in the Tricolour were carried in a procession from the BJP office to the cremation ground in a vehicle decorated with flowers.

Vice President M. Venkaiah Naidu, BJP veteran L.K. Advani, Defence Minister Rajnath Singh, Union Home Minister Amit Shah, and BJP working president Jagat Prakash Nadda were among Jaitley's former colleagues in attendance. Union ministers Nirmala Sitharaman, Smriti Irani, and Anurag Thakur; BJP MPs Vijay Goel and Vinay Sahasrabuddhe; and Congress leaders Jyotiraditya Scindia and Kapil Sibal were among those present at the cremation ground. Chief ministers of Maharashtra, Gujarat, Karnataka, Bihar, and Uttarakhand, Devendra Fadnavis, Vijay Rupani, B.S. Yediyurappa, Nitish Kumar, and Trivendra Singh Rawat, respectively, were also there. Senior Congress leader Motilal Vora, NCP leaders Sharad Pawar and Praful Patel, RLD leader Ajit Singh and former Andhra Pradesh chief minister and TDP leader N. Chandrababu Naidu also paid respects to Jaitley. As the last rites were being performed by Rohan Jaitley, it started raining.

Modi could not attend his funeral, "a burden", he said in an emotional breakdown, "that will always be on my heart". "I can't imagine that I am so

---

14. Arvind Subramanian, "Arun Jaitley Hit All the Right Notes in His Tenure As the Minister of Finance", *Livemint*, accessed 25 May 2025, https://www.livemint.com/news/india/arun-jaitley-hit-all-the-right-notes-in-his-tenure-as-the-minister-of-finance-1559153248243.html.

far here while my friend has gone away. Some days ago, we lost our former External Affairs Minister *behen* Sushma ji. Today I have lost my friend Arun," he said.[15] It was "'upsetting and unbelievable" that someone he had known since their youth was no more'".[16]

The Indian cricket team, which stepped out on Day 3 of the first Test match against the West Indies in Antigua, wore black bands when they heard of his death. As tributes poured in from across the political spectrum, it became evident that Arun Jaitley was not just a leader but an institution—one whose void would be hard to fill.

Paying tribute to Jaitley, President Ram Nath Kovind said he was a brilliant lawyer, a seasoned parliamentarian, and a distinguished minister, who contributed immensely to nation-building. Jaitley possessed a unique ability of discharging the most onerous responsibility with poise, passion, and studied understanding. "His passing leaves a huge void in our public life and our intellectual ecosystem. My condolences to his family and associates," the President wrote.[17] The President also visited Jaitley's house to pay his condolences to his family.[18]

Vice President Naidu wrote, "I did not expect Arun would say goodbye forever so soon. I am unable to reconcile to the fact that he will not be back at work and I can't seek him whenever needed as usual. I have relied on his wise counsel and sagacity for over 40 years since our college days."[19]

---

15. Swati Bhasin (Ed.), "Arun Jaitley Cremated with State Honours, Top Leaders Present", NDTV, accessed 25 May 2025, https://www.ndtv.com/india-news/arun-jaitley-to-be-cremated-today-leaders-pay-last-respects-2090025.

16. "Former Finance Minister Arun Jaitley Cremated with State Honours", *The Hindu*, accessed 25 May 2025, https://www.thehindu.com/news/national/former-finance-minister-arun-jaitley-cremated-with-state-honours/article29252540.ece.

17. "President Kovind, PM Modi & other top leaders pay tributes to former union minister Arun Jaitley", *The Print*, accessed on 4 September 2025, Sourcehttps://theprint.in/politics/president-kovind-pm-modi-other-top-leaders-pay-tributes-to-former-union-minister-arun-jaitley/281627/

18. "President Kovind pays tribute to Arun Jaitley", *Business Standard*, accessed on 4 September 2025, https://www.business-standard.com/multimedia/video-gallery/general/president-kovind-pays-tribute-to-arun-jaitley-89770.htm

19. M. Venkaiah Naidu, "Our Regular Meetings Were for Food, and Food for Thought", in *The Discussant: Journal of Centre for Reforms, Development and Justice*, Special Edition,

The RSS posted on its Twitter handle a joint statement of its chief Mohan Bhagwat and general secretary Suresh Bhaiyyaji Joshi paying tributes to the former finance minister and BJP stalwart: "This talented and learned leadership is no more now. Jaitley had begun his social and political life at a very young age. The country is progressing on the path of development in various fields for which his contribution was necessary as well as important. May his soul rest in peace," the statement said.[20] Mohan Bhagwat said, "The country is progressing on the path of development in various fields for which his contribution was necessary as well as important."

An emotional Nitin Gadkari wrote, "Arun ji was an intellectual reservoir for us. His areas of expertise were so vast that often the range of his knowledge would surprise me. Law, finance, and defence were subjects in which he had special expertise. On his day, I would rate him as better than the best that India has ever produced in these fields."[21]

The most moving tribute came from Nirmala Sitharaman. 'Arun Jaitley, my guru, my mentor, and my moral strength, is no more. Ever grateful for the role you played, Arun ji,"[22] she wrote.

"What Arun Jaitley meant to me, is perhaps an enigma even to me. But, what I know for sure is that the void which he has left for me and many others like me, to whom he was a mentor, friend, and guide, would be difficult to fill—at least in our lifetimes,"[23] wrote Jitendra Singh.

Political leaders cutting across parties, condoled the death of Jaitley. Congress president Sonia Gandhi said she was "deeply pained and distressed by the untimely passing away of Shri Arun Jaitley. His contributions to public

---

An Obituary to Arun Jaitley, Vol. VII, No. 3 (July–September 2019), pp. 17–19.

20. PTI, "RSS Mourns Jaitley's Death", *Deccan Herald*, accessed 25 May 2025, https://www.deccanherald.com/india/rss-mourns-jaitleys-death-756659.html.

21. Nitin Gadkari, "Arun Jaitley Helped BJP Set the Narrative", in *The Discussant: Journal of Centre for Reforms, Development and Justice*, Special Edition, An Obituary to Arun Jaitley, Vol. VII, No. 3 (July–September 2019), pp. 20–22.

22. Nirmala Sitharaman, "A Shishya's Tribute to Arun Jaitley", in *The Discussant: Journal of Centre for Reforms, Development and Justice*, Special Edition, An Obituary to Arun Jaitley, Vol. VII, No. 3 (July–September 2019), pp. 23–25.

23. Dr Jitendra Singh, "The Best Brain in the Country, Arun Jaitley Leaves Behind a Void in Many Lives", in ibid., pp. 31–34.

life will be remembered forever. Mr Jaitley had a long innings as a public figure, parliamentarian and minister and his contributions to public life will forever be remembered".[24] Senior Congress leader Abhishek Manu Singhvi said, "It was a cruel hand of destiny, which prevented him from joining what might have been his most glorious innings in Modi 2.0. We just saw the sad demise of a decent man in politics, known for his great lawyering, his skilful management of the Upper House of Parliament as Leader of the House, his magnanimity, his earlier stellar role for his party as the Leader of the Opposition in the Rajya Sabha, his amiable and genial nature and his foodie vices."[25]

Another Congress leader Shashi Tharoor said:

> I developed a personal fondness for him quite distinct from my increasingly vehement disagreement with his political views. This persisted when I finally returned to India at the end of my UN career and joined politics. Though we were now on opposite ends of the political spectrum, we resumed a cordial friendship. I dropped in to see him once in a while, even when I was a union minister and he was Leader of the Opposition, and he returned the compliment. When my wife passed away, he came home and spent an hour with me as I sat bereft, shell-shocked and inconsolable. ... With Arun's passing, the nation has lost a fine public servant, a minister of rare distinction and a man whose interventions—whether in speeches or blogs—made significant contributions to the national discourse. The BJP, too, has lost one of its few public figures who could reach easily across the aisle and appeal to constituencies who were not considered "natural" supporters of the party. His talent for conciliation and comradeship, transcending ideologies and political loyalties, will be sorely missed in our increasingly polarised politics.[26]

24. "Grieving Loss of Arun Jaitley" in ibid., pp. 15–16.

25. Dr Abhishek Manu Singhvi, "Arun Jaitley Possessed the Rare Skill to Communicate Simply, Analytically and Calmly", in ibid., 35–37.

26. Shashi Tharoor, "Was Every Non-BJP Person's Favourite BJP Person", in ibid., pp. 63–65.

Yogi Adityanath said, "He was a senior and seasoned leader. He was an eloquent orator and doyen of parliamentary working and a legal luminary. He always presented his facts in a very logical manner and commanded respect from politicians from every political party. Shri Jaitley will be remembered for his work in the finance, defence and many other ministries of Government of India. His demise is an irreparable loss to the nation, who was representing Uttar Pradesh in the Rajya Sabha."[27]

Tributes poured in from the corporate world, eminent lawyers, and people who worked closely with Jaitley. Vikram Kirloskar, the president of the CII, called Jaitley a "true reformer" and "keen advocate" of economic liberalisation. He said Jaitley's leadership in introducing GST and IBC "represented a historic transformation" and "added immensely to the economic framework". Deepak Parekh, the chairman of Housing Development Finance Corporation Limited, said, "Today the nation has lost one of its tallest leaders. The country will always be beholden to him for leading one of India's most significant reforms of recent times, which was the introduction of GST. His uniqueness lay in his ability to be a consensus builder." Shardul S. Shroff, the executive chairman of the law firm Shardul Amarchand Mangaldas, said Jaitley "believed in the reality of *Vasudhaiva Kutumbakam* (the world is one family) ... He was a friend of friends. The smallest inconvenience of his friends moved him to help. Such souls are rare and immortal. They never die."[28]

According to M.S. Sahoo, the chairman of the Insolvency and Bankruptcy Board of India (IBBI), Jaitley was a strong advocate for economic liberalisation in India. Sahoo credited Jaitley with driving reforms that granted businesses both the ability to operate freely and the means to exit the market effectively through the IBC. He argued that Jaitley's efforts completed a crucial phase in Indian economic reform, which had previously addressed freedom of entry and operation, but lacked a robust mechanism for business closure. Sahoo

---

27. Yogi Adityanath, "Condolence Message", in ibid., p. 14.

28. Rajeev Jayaswal, "Arun Jaitley's Focus on Key Reforms Reshaped Indian Economy", *Hindustan Times*, accessed 25 May 2025, https://www.hindustantimes.com/india-news/arun-jaitley-s-focus-on-key-reforms-reshaped-indian-economy/story-16RC8SdKeBlUj7MSwFBs8J.html.

also stated that Jaitley will be remembered for destroying the previous system which heavily favoured those who defaulted on loans.[29]

A "Shradhanjali Sabha" was organised by the BJP at the Jawaharlal Nehru Stadium.[30] Modi, who was on an official tour when Jaitley passed away, paid an emotional tribute at the Sabha.[31]

> I never thought a day will come when I'll have to pay tribute to my friend. We were friends for so long but I couldn't pay my last respects to him … I miss his presence. Whatever work Jaitley got, he added tremendous value to that. We will all remember Arun ji. His life inspires us to work harder for the nation … BJP and Arun Jaitley Ji had an unbreakable bond. We will miss him.[32]

In a Full Court Reference, the Supreme Court paid rich tributes to Arun Jaitley.[33]

Arun Jaitley lived his life with purpose, leaving behind a legacy of intellect, pragmatism, and enduring influence. There was an inescapable feeling that his passing away brought to an abrupt end a political career that had entered its most powerful period. 'In the Bharatiya Janata Party, a party he faithfully served to the last; in the government—of which he was no longer minister but

---

29. K.R. Srivats, "Jaitley Was Champion of Economic Freedom in India: IBBI Chief Sahoo", *The Hindu Business Line*, accessed 25 May 2025, https://www.thehindubusinessline.com/news/jaitley-was-champion-of-economic-freedom-in-india-ibbi-chief-sahoo/article29245779.ece/amp/.

30. Jimmy Jacob (Ed.), "'Able Leader, Encyclopaedia, Close Friend': PM's Tribute to Arun Jaitley", NDTV, accessed 25 May 2025, https://www.ndtv.com/india-news/pm-modis-tribute-to-arun-jaitley-able-leader-encyclopaedia-close-friend-2098798.

31. "PM Modi's Tribute to Arun Jaitley: Close Friend, Blessed with So Much Talent", *The Indian Express*, accessed 25 May 2025, https://indianexpress.com/article/india/pm-modis-tribute-to-arun-jaitley-close-friend-blessed-with-so-much-talent-5984438/.

32. Narendra Modi, "Condolence Message", in *The Discussant: Journal of Centre for Reforms, Development and Justice*, Special Edition, An Obituary to Arun Jaitley, Vol. VII, No. 3 (July–September 2019), pp. 12–13.

33. "Full Court Reference in the memory of Late Shri Arun Jaitley", on 15 October 2019, available at https://cdnbbsr.s3waas.gov.in/s3ec0490f1f4972d133619a60c30f3559e/documents/fcr/arun_jaitley_booklet_07012020.pdf.

still a guidance counsellor—and in Indian public life more generally, Jaitley has and will be succeeded by many. He will never be replaced," said Ashok Malik.[34]

Jaitley's imprint on the political and legal landscape of India and as tutor to some of the most successful politicians of this generation including his friend Modi will remain indelible. He has left behind a rich legacy. His was a life of great personal success and of enormous contribution to national life and character. History will render its own verdict on Jaitley's performance as the finance minister between 2014 and 2019.

But historians should be warned: many of his achievements were not easily visible, nor has he received enough credit for the many reforms that took place under his watch. But it may strike us even more today that he did not really care: what mattered to him was the achievement, not who got the credit; he was only doing his job—delivering the vision his party and Prime Minister Modi had promised 1.4 billion Indians.

---

34. Ashok Malik, "Arun Jaitley's Demise, an Irreplaceable Loss to the Nation", in *The Discussant: Journal of Centre for Reforms, Development and Justice*, Special Edition, An Obituary to Arun Jaitley, Vol. VII, No. 3 (July–September 2019), pp. 56–59.

Part II

Jaitley's Flagship Reforms

23

Shepherding the GST: A Historic Reform

On the first day of July 2017, the biggest tax reform of Independent India was rolled out from the precincts of the Central Hall of Parliament, marking a transformative shift from the fragmented pre-GST tax regime. Hailing the reform, Prime Minister Modi said:

> In the process of nation building, we often arrive at a moment which leads us to a path-breaking juncture and opens up a plethora of opportunities imploring us to aspire for new dreams. At the stroke of the midnight hour today, together we shall ensure a pioneering future of the nation. Within a few moments from now, our nation will embark upon a new economic regime. The entire 1.25 billion citizens of the country are a witness to this historical event. I do not believe that this process of GST is restricted to the scope of the economy only. This momentous occasion stands today as a testimony to the concept of co-operative federalism in Indian democracy. This hallmark day was possible due to the relentless efforts put in over decades by several stalwarts under whose guidance various teams developed this GST framework.[1]

---

1. Bhanu Priya, "Full Text of PM Narendra Modi's Speech at GST Launch from Parliament", NDTV, accessed 25 May 2025, https://www.ndtv.com/india-news/full-text-of-pm-narendra-modis-speech-at-goods-and-services-tax-launch-from-parliament-1719236.

Foremost among those who India will remember for this historical reform is Arun Jaitley. As the finance minister, and the government's key strategist, Jaitley shepherded the visionary reform, forging consensus among diverse states for the complex indirect tax reform, standing as a testament to his political acumen. GST was an astonishingly successful feat of political deal-making, inconceivable without the deft skills of Jaitley.[2] It was an achievement of political consensus-building in a difficult, fractious democracy. Thirty or more regional governments coming together, giving up their sovereignty for the larger common good of creating one market in India, improving tax compliance, creating a robust revenue base for the country, and creating the fiscal environment for higher investment and growth was no mean task.

This would be unimaginable in any other federal system, including the European Union and the United States. In the latter, states would rather secede than enter into any such collective tax arrangements, and the rabid upholders of states' rights would probably pick up pitchforks in revolt.[3]

It was also an achievement of administration, in which Centre and state tax departments worked together to create one tax; and an achievement of technology, in which new systems were created, integrating many diverse ones, making the taxpayer–tax authority interface more seamless. None of this could have happened without the dedication and goodwill of many people, from state governments to central civil servants, most notably, Revenue Secretary Hasmukh Adhia, Secretary of Department of Economic Affairs Shaktikanta Das, the Tamil Nadu-cadre Indian Administrative Service officer, and Chief Economic Advisor Arvind Subramanian, then Jaitley's key officials in the finance ministry. But it was Jaitley who managed to bring together all the different political factions, economic interests, and idiosyncratic personalities, and get the Constitutional Amendment and GST Bill passed. Jaitley will go down in history for successfully championing this landmark reform.

Intellectually, GST was decades in the making, involving many of India's greatest economists, from Raja Chelliah, who first mooted the idea of a value-added tax for India decades ago, to Vijay Kelkar, who boldly recommended a

---

2. Arvind Subramanian, *Of Counsel: The Challenges of the Modi–Jaitley Economy* (Penguin, 2018), pp. xxxiv–xli.

3. Ibid.

single-rate structure for GST.[4] The tax reforms had been in discussion under different regimes, but the idea of GST as a concrete thought was first mooted in 1999 during a meeting between then Prime Minister Atal Bihari Vajpayee and his economic advisory panel which included three former RBI governors: I.G. Patel, Bimal Jalan, and C. Rangarajan. Vajpayee set up a committee headed by then finance minister of West Bengal Asim Kumar Dasgupta, a CPI(M) leader, to design a GST model. The Dasgupta committee was also tasked with putting in place the backend technology and logistics for rolling out a uniform taxation regime in the country.[5]

In 2003, Vajpayee tasked Vijay Kelkar, the then advisor to the finance ministry, to take the idea forward. A taskforce under Kelkar was established which proposed a comprehensive GST to deal with the myriad problems and complications of India's taxation system. Before the recommendations could be implemented, the Vajpayee government was replaced with Manmohan Singh's UPA-I government in 2004. A year later, the Thirteenth Finance Commission headed by Kelkar projected that GDP would grow further by 1.7 per cent if GST were to be implemented.[6]

Then finance minister P. Chidambaram mooted the proposal in his budget speech for the year 2006–07, setting 1 April 2010 as the deadline for introducing GST. In 2009, Pranab Mukherjee took over as the finance minister from Chidambaram. He announced the basic structure of GST, as designed by the Dasgupta committee, which had continued to work even under Chidambaram on the GST design framework. Mukherjee retained the April 2010 deadline set by his predecessor. Public announcement for the rollout of GST from 2010 was made in the year 2006. However, no further progress could be made for a long period after this initial announcement as consensus on knotty issues remained elusive. Then in Opposition, the BJP opposed the basic structure of

---

4. Ibid.

5. "Thirteenth Finance Commission: 2010-2015", Volume I: Report, December 2009, available at https://fincomindia.nic.in/asset/pdf/commission-reports/13fcreng.pdf.

6. Ibid.

GST on many counts. Modi, who was then Gujarat chief minister, was also averse to GST.[7]

After detailed deliberations and negotiations in the Empowered Committee of State Finance Ministers, the Constitution (115th Amendment) Bill, 2011, was introduced by Mukherjee. It was referred to the Parliamentary Standing Committee which submitted its report in August 2013. Given the political dynamics in UPA-II's term, passing of the GST Bill proved impossible. The bill lapsed with the dissolution of the fifteenth Lok Sabha. The GST rollout was postponed.

★

Before July 2017, the Indian indirect tax regime was highly fragmented.[8] The Centre and states were separately taxing goods and services. There were many taxes like excise duty, service tax, value-added tax (VAT), central sales tax (CST), purchase tax, entertainment tax, and octroi. In addition, there was a multiplicity of rates, laws, and procedures. An entrepreneur faced as many as seventeen inspectors, seventeen returns, and seventeen assessments. The rate of taxation prevalent at that time was exorbitantly high. The standard rate of VAT and excise duty was 14.5 per cent and 12.5 per cent respectively. To this could be added CST and the cascading effect of tax on tax. The standard rate thus became 31 per cent on a large number of commodities. The assessees had only two options—either to pay a high rate of tax or to evade it. Tax evasion was prevalent to a large extent.

India comprised multiple markets. Each state was a separate market because the rate of tax could be different. This caused a heavy compliance burden. Imposition of tax on tax was another serious problem. For example, VAT

---

7. "PM Modi explains why he opposed GST for years as Gujarat CM", *The Hindustan Times*, accessed 6 October 2025, https://www.hindustantimes.com/india-news/issuesi-raised-with-gst-as-cm-were-solved-after-i-became-pm-says-modi/story-x2hO49LBPiQMl4XqadIWzJ.html

8. "One Nation–One Tax: Good and Services Tax", Government of India, Ministry of Information and Broadcasting, available at https://static.pib.gov.in/WriteReadData/specificdocs/documents/2023/may/doc202351190701.pdf.

was levied on a value that included excise duty. The input tax credit chain broke as goods moved from one state to another, resulting in hidden costs for the business. Further, pre-GST, there were tax nakas (checkpoints) at every interstate border, creating bottlenecks in interstate transport of goods. Interstate sales became inherently inefficient because trucks had to wait for hours and days at the state borders. As a result, the logistics sector remained inefficient and that adversely impacted businesses. Every state was effectively a distinct market for the industry as well as consumer. An industry's choice of locating factories or warehouses was heavily influenced by the prevailing tax regime rather than pure business consideration. This made an industry uncompetitive.[9]

Jaitley was convinced that GST was a key component needed for improving the framework for doing business and it could be an answer to many perennial problems faced by entrepreneurs. In his first budget speech, Jaitley made his intention clear.

> The debate whether to introduce a GST must now come to an end. We have discussed the issue for the past many years. Some states have been apprehensive about surrendering their taxation jurisdiction; others want to be adequately compensated. I have discussed the matter with the states both individually and collectively. I do hope we are able to find a solution in the course of this year and approve the legislative scheme which enables the introduction of GST. This will streamline the tax administration, avoid harassment of the business and result in higher revenue collection both for the Centre and the states. I assure all states that the government will be more than fair in dealing with them.
>
> The sovereign right of the government to undertake retrospective legislation is unquestionable. However, this power has to be exercised with extreme caution and judiciousness keeping in mind the impact of each such measure on the economy and the overall investment climate. This government will not ordinarily bring about any change retrospectively which creates a fresh liability. Hon'ble members are aware that consequent upon certain retrospective amendments to the

---

9. Ibid.

> Income Tax Act, 1961 undertaken through the Finance Act, 2012, a few cases have come up in various courts and other legal fora. These cases are at different stages of pendency and will naturally reach their logical conclusion. At this juncture I would like to convey to this August House and also the investors community at large that we are committed to provide a stable and predictable taxation regime that would be investor friendly and spur growth. Keeping this in mind, we have decided that henceforth, all fresh cases arising out of the retrospective amendments of 2012 in respect of indirect transfers and coming to the notice of the assessing officers will be scrutinised by a High Level Committee to be constituted by the Central Board of Direct Taxes (CBDT) before any action is initiated in such cases. I hope the investor community both within India and abroad would repose confidence in our stated position and participate in the Indian growth story with renewed vigour.[10]

Keen to craft a flawless GST, Jaitley turned to Kelkar for advice who apparently advised the finance minister to go for a "pure GST" that would exempt no goods or services at all, not even real estate, liquor, and petroleum products, and would have a single rate—between 10 per cent and 12 per cent. This view eventually acquired the epithet: "one nation, one tax".[11] Jaitley got on to the task of preparing the bill. Simultaneously, he had commenced negotiations with the Empowered Committee (EC). The EC was originally set up on 17 July 2000 by the Government of India with the state finance ministers of West Bengal, Karnataka, Madhya Pradesh, Maharashtra, Punjab, Uttar Pradesh, Gujarat, Delhi and Meghalaya as members. The objective was to monitor the implementation of uniform floor rates of sales tax by states and union territories, to supervise the phasing out of the sales-tax-based incentive schemes, to decide milestones and methods of states to switch over to VAT and to scrutinise reforms in the Central Sales Tax system existing in the country.

---

10. Arun Jaitley, "Budget 2014–2015", available at https://www.indiabudget.gov.in/doc/bspeech/bs201415.pdf.

11. Puja Mehra, *The Lost Decade (2008–18): How India's Growth Story Devolved into Growth without a Story* (Penguin, 2019).

Subsequently, state finance ministers of Assam, Tamil Nadu, Jammu & Kashmir, Jharkhand and Rajasthan were also notified as the members of the EC. On 12 August, 2004, the Government of India decided to reconstitute the EC with state finance/taxation ministers of all states as its members. The body was later registered as a society under the Societies Registration Act, 1860. To strengthen the EC, the Thirteenth Finance Commission recommended that a grant of Rs 30.00 crore be made to EC, so that they could pursue GST-related research work and enhance capacities.[12]

A master at the art of building consensus, Jaitley succeeded in securing near-unanimous recommendations of the EC, also supported by the Congress-ruled states. In early December 2014, when the Constitution amendments were discussed in the EC meeting, several state finance ministers were highly critical of the Centre, and suggested that at this rate, GST could not be introduced. In the afternoon, when the state finance ministers met Jaitley, he suggested that a small group of state finance ministers could meet him and discuss all issues in detail.

"In the evening, the way Jaitley handled the meeting was an experience. He heard them out and suggested that he could sit with them through the night to discuss their concerns. But he insisted that the matter needed to be resolved. He showed that kind of determination. The state finance ministers came back around 8–8.30 that evening and the meeting went on till late in the night. We met the next day and again a few days later. He negotiated with great skill—being very firm, where it was required, and yet being accommodating. For instance, he did not yield on petroleum being kept out of GST but agreed that the rate of levy could be decided later," said Shaktikanta Das.[13] A confident Jaitley introduced the Constitution (122nd Amendment) Bill, 2014, in Parliament on 19 December 2014.

Front-ending the efforts to build consensus in favour of the bill, he emphasised on the need to replace the highly inefficient tax regime, characterised by a

---

12. Department of Revenue, Ministry of Finance, Government of India, accessed on 25 September 2025, https://dor.gov.in/introduction-empowered-committee-state-government

13. Shaktikanta Das, "A Unique Combination of Knowledge, Intelligence and Wisdom", in *The Discussant: Journal of Centre for Reforms, Development and Justice*, Special Edition, An Obituary to Arun Jaitley, Vol. VII, No. 3 (July–September 2019), pp. 66–68.

complex indirect tax system, with the Centre and states levying multiple taxes on goods and services under the seventeen overlapping Central and state taxes. The bill became a political football between the Congress and the BJP. The Congress opposed the GST reform as proposed, politically. Jaitley reminded the Congress that it was the UPA government that had proposed the GST, and that even the Constitution amendment was piloted by the UPA.

The three members of the Congress party circulated a note of dissent on the bill.[14] They proposed that a rate of GST be fixed in the Constitution not exceeding 18 per cent. They further proposed that the expression "supply" should not apply to goods and services supplied by one unit of a firm to another unit of the same unit of the firm. They also recommended that the share of local bodies in revenue buoyancy be included in the draft constitutional amendment. The Congress suggested increasing the voting representation of states in the GST Council from two-thirds to three-fourths. Additionally, the party urged that Goa be granted special category status under the GST framework.

Since Parliament was not functioning when the dissent note was circulated, Jaitley rebutted the Congress's note on his website,[15] stating that the rates of taxation have to be left to the GST Council to decide depending on factors such as economic conditions, revenue buoyancies, etc. On exclusion of "supply" to goods and services supplied by one unit of a firm to another unit of the same unit of the firm, he said GST charged on supply of goods and services would be VATable and not have any cascading effect. As regards the share of local bodies in the revenue buoyancy, Jaitley argued such allocation would be contrary to the 73rd Amendment to the Constitution which gives State Finance Commissions the responsibility of making such recommendations. Increasing the state's voting power, thereby reducing the Centre's voting power from one-third to one-fourth, would be contrary to the decision taken by UPA-II on 30 April 2013. The majority required in the GST Council for taking a decision is three-fourths. In fact, the Congress proposal would mean that if all the

---

14. Manoj C.G, "Congress' 8-point dissent note throws spanners in the GST works", *The Indian Express*, accessed on 26 September 2025, https://indianexpress.com/article/india/india-others/congress-dissent-note-throws8-spanners-inthe-gst-works/

15. Arun Jaitley, My Thoughts, "Dissent or Disruption—The Congress Party's Position on GST", accessed 25 May 2025, https://www.arunjaitley.com/dissent-or-disruption-the-congress-partys-position-on-gst/.

states get together and decide that the Centre should have a lower GST rate, they could deplete revenues of the Centre almost completely. On Goa, Jaitley argued that Goa has the highest per capita income in the country and special status was not justified.

In the dissent note, the Congress proposed that any dispute with regard to GST should be adjudicated by a GST Tribunal chaired by a person who has been a judge of the Supreme Court or chief justice of a high court. Disagreeing with the proposal, Jaitley wrote that political issues have to be settled politically and not by judges; the power of deciding the modalities of adjudication and settlement of disputes in the bill would rest with the GST Council.

Jaitley implored the Congress to support the great reform.

★

The bill was passed by the Lok Sabha in May 2015 where the NDA had absolute majority. It, however, got stuck in the Rajya Sabha, where the ruling alliance did not have a majority. To clear the two-thirds of the votes in the Rajya Sabha, support from the Congress's seventy members was required. But the government and the Congress were at loggerheads over the passage of crucial legislations including GST. The BJP doubled the efforts to ensure the passage of the bill.

Late in July 2015, Jaitley and Arvind Subramanian held deliberations with leaders of the Congress, the Left Front, the Trinamool Congress, the SP, and the JD(U) to garner support for the passage of the bill. CPI(M) general secretary Sitaram Yechury, P. Chidambaram, who had just been elected to the Rajya Sabha, and Congress leader Anand Sharma were among those who participated in the separate rounds of discussions. The government was also in touch with the AIADMK leader and Tamil Nadu Chief Minister J. Jayalalithaa.

Jaitley met Congress president Sonia Gandhi and former Prime Minister Manmohan Singh to extend an invitation for his daughter Sonali's wedding. It is widely believed that he used the opportunity to discuss the GST Bill, although both sides denied there was any discussion.[16] Jaitley then met Rahul Gandhi to

16. Mehboob Jeelani, "BJP Warms Up to Congress for GST Bill", *The Hindu*, accessed 25 May 2025, https://www.thehindu.com/news/national/BJP-warms-up-to-

extend an invitation to his daughter's wedding. They had an hour-long chat and Rahul Gandhi is stated to have assured his party's support on condition that some of the provisions the Congress had objected to be taken care of.[17]

Jaitley advised Modi to make the first move to break the ice. In a major reach-out to the main Opposition, Modi invited Sonia Gandhi and Manmohan Singh over tea at his residence on 17 November 2015. Jaitley and Parliamentary Affairs Minister M. Venkaiah Naidu were also present at the meeting that lasted forty-five minutes.[18] On Manmohan Singh's advice, the Congress set aside its political differences with the ruling party to discuss the GST.[19] Sonia Gandhi nominated Anand Sharma for the interlocution with the government on GST. Jaitley nominated revenue secretary Hasmukh Adhia and Arvind Subramanian to negotiate. Chidambaram and Jaitley handled the back-channel talks with Sharma, Adhia, and Subramanian.

The Congress raised three main demands in exchange for supporting the bill. Jaitley placed these before the states, a large number of which were ruled by BJP governments, but they vetoed two of three: the demand for a constitutional cap of 18 per cent and an independent dispute resolution mechanism headed by a judge. Following this the Congress had no option but to change its stand on the two issues.[20] The central government, on the other hand, approved the third demand—of dropping a proposal for a provision regarding the imposition

---

Congress-for-GST-Bill/article60297273.ece#.

17. Mehboob Jeelani, "Jaitley Meets Rahul, 'Broaches GST Issue'", *The Hindu*, accessed 25 May 2025, https://www.thehindu.com/news/national/arun-jaitley-meets-rahul-gandhi/article7892383.ece.

18. "Sonia, Manmohan Meet Modi over Tea", *The Hindu*, accessed 25 May 2025, https://www.thehindu.com/news/national/Sonia-Gandhi-Manmohan-Singh-meet-Narendra-Modi/article60230142.ece.

19. Abhay Vaidya, "GST Architect Vijay Kelkar Says It's a Win for India's Federalism", *Hindustan Times*, accessed 25 May 2025, https://www.hindustantimes.com/pune-news/gst-architect-vijay-kelkar-says-it-s-a-win-for-india-s-federalism/story-c9lZZ3BxxMX36jVR9r4qmM.html.

20. Puja Mehra, *The Lost Decade (2008–18): How India's Growth Story Devolved into Growth without a Story* (Penguin, 2019).

of a 1 per cent interstate tax over and above the GST rate—that the states had approved.[21]

The bill finally hit the goalpost in 2016 in the monsoon session of Parliament; it was finally passed in the Rajya Sabha on 3 August 2016 with certain amendments, and thereafter by the Lok Sabha again on 8 August 2016. Only the AIADMK staged walkouts in both the Houses ahead of voting on the bill. History was made but not before the country got to witness one of the finest debates in the history of Indian Parliament.

The erosion of parliamentary debate and decorum has become a defining feature of contemporary politics. Yet, the parliamentary discussion on the Constitutional Amendment Bill in August 2016 stood out as a remarkable exception. In its content, tone, and exchange of ideas, the debate rose well above the prevailing standards, offering a rare display of substance and civility. It brought together two formidable constitutional lawyers, Arun Jaitley and P. Chidambaram, whose incisive and substantive exchanges left the millions watching—and, in spirit, India's founding fathers—immensely proud of the country's parliamentary democratic tradition. This was Indian democracy at its finest.[22]

On the floor of the House, the government reached across the aisle, and the Opposition and regional parties walked half the distance to see the constitutional amendment through. The political system set aside grudges and differences in the interest of the most significant tax reform in Independent India, thanks to Jaitley's persistent efforts and all political parties and government rising about their differences in the larger interest of the country. On 3 August 2016, when the bill was cleared by the Rajya Sabha, Arvind Subramanian could be seen hugging Hasmukh Adhia. Subramanian ranked the moment as one of the high points of his tenure.[23]

Speaking in the Lok Sabha, Modi, noting that all parties had risen above their ideological differences in support of the amendment, said, '... the GST

---

21. "New Cabinet-Approved GST Bill drops 1% Inter-State Sales Tax, *The Wire*, accessed on 26 September 2025, https://thewire.in/politics/new-cabinet-approved-gst-bill-drops-1-inter-state-sales-tax.

22. Arvind Subramanian, *Of Counsel: The Challenges of the Modi–Jaitley Economy* (Penguin, 2018), pp. xxxiv–xli.

23. Ibid.

could not be seen as the victory of a party or government ... It is the victory for the democratic ethos of India and a victory for everyone". The bill would have been in trouble in the Rajya Sabha due to the BJP's lack of numbers and the reluctance of some states, but in the end all parties backed it, he said.[24]

The bill was later passed by more than fifteen states and received the assent of the President of India on 8 September 2016, and enacted as the Constitution (101st Amendment) Act, 2016, conferring simultaneous power upon Parliament and the state legislatures to make laws governing goods and services. A Presidential Ordinance was issued to extend the GST provisions to Jammu and Kashmir. Later, Arun Jaitley introduced The Central Goods and Services Tax (Extension to Jammu and Kashmir) Bill, 2017—to replace the ordinance. Kelkar stated that the clearance of GST by Parliament was a win for India's federalism and a great beginning for making a unified market.[25]

The GST regime paved the way for laying the foundation for a seamless national market, reshaping India's tax landscape and driving economic growth. It consolidated taxes into a single system, unifying India into a single market; it replaced seventeen complex taxes and cesses. Interstate barriers and entry taxes were abolished. It streamlined taxation by eliminating cascading taxes, bureaucratic hurdles, and interstate barriers, fostering a unified national market. The entertainment tax levied by the states ranged from 35 per cent to 110 per cent. The assessees had to file multiple returns, entertain multiple inspectors, and additionally face the inefficiency—trucks being stranded at the state boundaries for days altogether. GST changed this scenario completely. Today, there is only one tax, only online returns, no entry tax, no truck queues, and no interstate barriers.

★

24. "Amended GST Bill Gets Parliament Green Signal", *The Hindu*, accessed 25 May 2025, https://www.thehindu.com/news/national/Amended-GST-Bill-gets-Parliament-green-signal/article60484521.ece.

25. Abhay Vaidya, "GST Architect Vijay Kelkar Says It's a Win for India's Federalism", *Hindustan Times*, accessed 25 May 2025, https://www.hindustantimes.com/pune-news/gst-architect-vijay-kelkar-says-it-s-a-win-for-india-s-federalism/story-c9lZZ3BxxMX36jVR9r4qmM.html.

The GST framework provided for the constitution of the GST Council to make recommendations to the Union and the states on issues related to GST such as the goods and services that may be subjected to or exempted from GST, model GST laws, principles of levy, principles that govern place of supply, threshold limits, GST rates including the floor rates with bands, special rates for raising additional resources during natural calamities/disasters, special provisions for certain states, etc. The GST Council was constituted on 12 September 2016, setting firmly into motion the rolling out of GST. The establishment of the Goods and Services Tax Network (GSTN), a special purpose vehicle designed to automate business processes with equal participation from the Centre and the states, was another significant milestone in advancing the implementation of GST.[26]

After the legislative procedure was over, Jaitley's next task was to spearhead the smooth functioning of the GST Council and rollout GST's smooth implementation, an undertaking not free of challenges. The GST Council is India's first statutory federal institution where both the Centre and the states have pooled their fiscal rights in a collective forum to create one common market. Both had agreed to jointly sit and decide key matters concerning GST. The all-powerful council was chaired by the Union finance minister, with the Centre's voting share fixed at one-third of the total votes cast, while the collective voting strength of the states was assigned a weightage of two-thirds. A proposal could be adopted only if the total weighted votes of members present and voting in its favour amounted to at least three-fourths of the total.

As the council's chair, typical of his approach, Jaitley preferred to work through consensus, avoiding the need to vote. He forged consensus among states, securing bipartisan support for the GST and fostering a cooperative federalist spirit within the GST Council from the very first meeting held on 22–23 September 2016. The GST Council held periodical meetings to continuously review and rationalise GST tariffs under Jaitley's chairmanship, taking thousands of decisions often without voting, and despite external political noise, setting an incredible precedent which recognised the delicate balance of India's federalism.

---

26. "One Nation–One Tax: Good and Services Tax", Government of India, Ministry of Information and Broadcasting, available at https://static.pib.gov.in/WriteReadData/specificdocs/documents/2023/may/doc202351190701.pdf.

Jaitley's skilful navigation of the sensitivities of India's federal structure through the GST Council stands as a testament to his political acumen. True to his character, Jaitley credited the members of the GST Council with the council's success. Notwithstanding the political position their parties took, the state finance ministers displayed a high level of statesmanship and acted with maturity despite the "political noise outside".[27] The council worked on the principle of consensus, adding to the credibility of the decision-making process. Jaitley said, "I am sure this trend will continue in future. The meetings have witnessed an intense debate on several issues, which has been an excellent example of 'deliberative democracy'. Opposing viewpoints have ended up in convergence and so far all issues have been decided by a consensus."[28]

Arvind Subramanian shared:

> Sometimes, I used to wonder whether Mr Jaitley is being excessively democratic, because allowing everyone in the GST Council to express their views made for painfully long and tedious meetings. I often wanted him to intervene more forcefully to end the discussion. After all, hadn't Clement Atlee famously said that "democracy as discussion only works, if at some point people stop talking"? But he was more patient and wiser than me. Now, it is clear that Mr Jaitley's efforts will have a lasting, durable impact because he created a strong, democratic institution that will outlive the individuals who created it.[29]

As Jaitley's health started failing, and he had to travel abroad for treatment, the GST Council, in its twenty-eighth meeting, thirteen months after the new tax's imposition, abandoned the principle of consensus to press ahead with impromptu rate cuts. State finance ministers called the proceedings in the

---

27. Arun Jaitley, "The Role of the GST Council", accessed 6 September 2025, https://bfsi.eletsonline.com/gst-proved-to-be-both-consumer-assessee-friendly-jaitley/

28. Arun Jaitley, "Two Important Issues before the GST Council", accessed 25 May 2025, https://www.arunjaitley.com/two-important-issues-before-the-gst-council/.

29. Arvind Subramanian, "Arun Jaitley Hit All the Right Notes in His Tenure As the Minister of Finance", *Livemint*, accessed 25 May 2025, https://www.livemint.com/news/india/arun-jaitley-hit-all-the-right-notes-in-his-tenure-as-the-minister-of-finance-1559153248243.html.

council meeting "undemocratic, unpleasant, unfortunate, and non-egalitarian. Council member and Punjab finance minister Manpreet Singh Badal left the meeting midway, saying that the rate cuts had not been listed on the agenda, rendering the process 'unfair and undemocratic." The GST Council's non-BJP members were especially vocal.[30]

Jaitley faced severe criticism for not levying a single-slab tax. He vociferously defended GST, and the multi-tier tax system, arguing a single slab was unsuitable for India's income diversity. Essential items remained exempt or low-taxed, while luxury/sin goods attracted higher rates. He anticipated future rate rationalisation as revenues stabilised. Urging critics to acknowledge GST's success in simplifying taxation, boosting compliance, and unifying India's market, he emphasised that responsible policymaking, not populism, would sustain India's economic progress. With the critics he argued that:

> … a single slab is possible only in extremely affluent countries where there are no poor people. It would be inequitable to apply a single rate in countries where there are a large number of people below the poverty line. The direct tax is a progressive tax. The more you earn, the more you pay. An indirect tax is a regressive tax. In the pre-GST regime, the rich and the poor, on various commodities, paid the same tax. The multiple slab system not only checked inflation, it also ensured that the Aam Aadmi products are not exorbitantly taxed. Illustratively, a Hawai chappal and a Mercedes car cannot be taxed at the same rate. This is not to suggest that the rationalisation of slabs is not needed. That process is already on. Except on luxury and sin goods, the 28% slab has almost been phased out. Zero and 5% slabs will always remain. As revenue increases further, it will give an opportunity to policy makers to possibly merge the 12% and 18% slab into one rate, thus effectively making the GST a two-rate tax.[31]

---

30. "GST Council's rush job angers some FMs of Opposition-ruled states", *Business Standard*, accessed 6 September 2025, https://www.business-standard.com/article/economy-policy/gst-council-s-rush-job-angers-some-fms-of-opposition-ruled-states-118072300031_1.html.

31. Arun Jaitley, My Thoughts, "Two Years After GST", accessed 25 May 2025, https://www.arunjaitley.com/two-years-after-gst/.

★

In Mann ki Baat, an Indian radio programme hosted by Prime Minister Narendra Modi in which he addresses the people of the nation, Modi said, "I call GST, Good and Simple Tax."[32]

The GST encountered fierce opposition from traders and small enterprises. The Congress termed GST Gabbar Singh Tax.[33] "GST is still not a simple tax. It is Gabbar Singh Tax and when Congress will be back in power it will change it into a simple tax and turn it into one tax rather than five different taxes," said Rahul Gandhi.[34] The story of India often demands a touch of hyperbole to make sense of its many contested narratives. The GST was one such idea—long awaited, ambitious, and transformative. It was widely acknowledged that India's tax system was as intricate as the nation itself, and successive governments had only added to its complexity. Simplifying and streamlining it required immense political courage—and a willingness to take risks. That is precisely what GST achieved, driven by a noble principle: meaningful innovation challenges the comfort of the status quo and inevitably disrupts.

GST's rollout was far from smooth; in its early days, it posed real challenges for small entrepreneurs. Yet, no major reform takes root without turbulence, and resistance to change is only human. True leadership lies in holding firm to conviction—and that is exactly what Arun Jaitley did. While the initial implementation saw teething troubles and temporary disruptions as businesses adapted to the new tax regime, external shocks such as demonetisation and

---

32. Bibek Debroy, Anirban Ganguly, Kishore Desai, *Making of New India, Transformation Under Modi Government* (Wisdom Tree, 2019), pp. 143–45

33. Gabbar Singh is a villainous character from the 1975 Hindi film *Sholay.* The character of a khaki-attired dacoit twirling a pistol, spitting tobacco, squishing flies and humans with equal nonchalance, flashing a sinister grin, played by late actor Amjad Khan became the ultimate personification of cinematic evil. His dialogues like *"Soja, nahi toh Gabbar Singh aa jayega"* carried a chilling authority that sent shivers down the spine.

34. "Rahul Gandhi says Congress will change Gabbar Singh Tax into simple tax", Gujarat Pradesh Congress Committee website, accessed 6 October 2025, https://www.incgujarat.com/rahul-gandhi-says-congress-will-change-gabbar-singh-tax-into-simple-tax/.

the COVID-19 pandemic further compounded the challenges. Nonetheless, GST remains a defining reform in India's economic journey.[35]

Jaitley acknowledged the economic hardships the GST implementation may have imposed, particularly on smaller firms. Explaining it as "creative destruction", crucial for long-term growth and a more transparent economy, he urged the parties to bear with the transitional difficulties in national interest. With Jaitley's tireless efforts, the new system settled down within the first few weeks of the implementation. Despite problems, India's transition to the new tax regime has been one of the smoothest globally, and rewarding for the economy and citizens. Online compliance replaced bureaucratic interfaces.

GST remains the biggest tax reform since Independence, arguably, one of the greatest fiscal policy reforms in Indian economic history.[36] It is a fully technology-driven system. It ended long queues of trucks and goods carriers at highway toll plazas freeing goods movement across states. Credible studies point to an improvement of over 33 per cent in transport time after GST implementation. Millions of litres in petrol and diesel have also been saved apart from decongesting arterial roads.[37]

Critics of GST, however, claim that it hurts savings and harms every section of society. GST has also been criticised for placing many goods in higher tax slabs leading to stress on the middle class. In September 2025, in a major decision, GST rates went through a significant rehash. Rehabilitating the GST reform on an ongoing basis would be a fitting tribute to Jaitley and crucial for economic recovery.

---

35. Bibek Debroy, Anirban Ganguly, Kishore Desai, *Making of New India, Transformation Under Modi Government* (Wisdom Tree, 2019), pp. xv–xvi

36. Arvind Subramanian, *Of Counsel: The Challenges of the Modi–Jaitley Economy* (Penguin, 2018), pp. xxxiv–xli.

37. "One Nation–One Tax: Good and Services Tax", Government of India, Ministry of Information and Broadcasting, available at https://static.pib.gov.in/WriteReadData/specificdocs/documents/2023/may/doc202351190701.pdf.

24

The IBC: A Blue-chip Reform

The Insolvency and Bankruptcy Code (IBC) stands as one of Arun Jaitley's enduring gifts, not only to India but to the entire Global South. As India charts its course in a rapidly evolving world order, aspiring to emerge as a leading power, it continues to anchor its rise in the well-being of the Global South and in the pursuit of the global good. More prominent than ever in international calculations, India is prepared to shoulder new responsibilities and seize fresh opportunities. It envisions an era of inclusive growth and development, grounded in its civilisational values and rich heritage. At the heart of this vision lies the steady and disciplined advance of an economy guided by sound laws and forward-looking policies, an approach that embodies the principle: think local, look global. The IBC exemplifies this philosophy, a model law that seamlessly blends global best practices with India's unique institutional and economic realities.[1]

Jaitley's contribution to insolvency reforms goes way back before the IBC was enacted in 2016. The National Company Law Tribunal (NCLT), the specialised bankruptcy tribunal, which was notified as the Adjudicating Authority under the IBC on 1 June 2016, was itself conceived in 2002 under Jaitley's watch as the law minister.

The Sick Industrial Companies Act of 1985 (SICA), the then law for the revival and rehabilitation of distressed companies, had proved to be ineffective.

---

1. Sumant Batra, *Corporate Insolvency: The Road to Viksit Bharat* (Eastern Book Company, 2025), pp. 1072–87.

The winding up of companies took even longer in India. An application for winding up on any ground, including pursuant to recommendation made under the SICA, was required to be filed under the Companies Act, 1956 (now 2013 Act). Noting the failure of the SICA and the delay in winding up of companies, the government set up a committee under Justice V. Balakrishna Eradi, to suggest suitable reforms for changes in law relating to insolvency of companies. On the basis of the recommendations of the Eradi Committee, the 1956 Act was amended through the 2002 Act. The SICA was repealed in 2003, but the repealing law could not be notified as the NCLT proposed by the 2002 Amendment got entangled in litigation.[2]

However, much before the 2002 Act was passed, on 27 September 1997, Jaitley entrusted me with the responsibility of setting up an advocacy body for insolvency reforms which came to be known as INSOL India. Justice D.P. Wadhwa, then a judge of the Supreme Court of India, had just returned from Adelaide after attending the conference of INSOL International, a global federation of insolvency fraternity. Impressed by the advanced insolvency laws in developed countries, he requested Jaitley to take steps for setting up a member association of INSOL International in India which could serve as a platform for learning from other jurisdictions and advocate insolvency reforms in the country.

Jaitley convened a meeting of judges and lawyers on 27 September 1997 at the India Habitat Centre, Delhi, to explore the setting up of the India chapter of INSOL International. A day before the meeting, Jaitley asked me if I was willing to take the responsibility of setting up the association. I got pulled into restructuring practice at the age of twenty-six. I was only thirty-one years old when Jaitley made the offer to me. I was overwhelmed.

At the meeting, it was resolved to set up an association of judges, lawyers, and accountants which would advocate insolvency reforms. Justice Manmohan Sarin, then a judge of the High Court of Delhi, was appointed as the first president, and I as its founder secretary. A two-member committee, consisting of Jaitley and me, drafted the charter of the association. We proposed INSOL India as the name of the association. The formation of INSOL India fulfilled the long-cherished desire of members of the legal fraternity, chartered accountants, company secretaries, and other individuals, bodies, and institutions in India

2. Ibid., pp. 18–39, 154–78.

to establish an association to promote closer cooperation, exchange ideas, disseminate information, and foster a deeper understanding of insolvency and related laws.

My exposure to insolvency systems outside of India began in 1997 with Jaitley entrusting me with this responsibility. Soon Jaitley became the law minister, and we could make good use of the work we had done in two years. One thing led to another, and soon, I was selected by INSOL International to serve as a nominee director on its board. Jaitley gifted me a set of Montblanc pens in the presence of a large gathering of judges and lawyers. I had the distinction of serving on the INSOL International Board for ten years, including as its vice president and president (as the youngest and the first Asian to head the organisation). He told me on many occasions that I had made him proud.

In the early noughties, green shoots of free economy were beginning to be seen. The market started changing in India after the opening of the economy in the 1990s and the introduction of large-scale reforms. But the journey of insolvency reforms remained painfully slow. The legal framework for insolvency remained ineffective for decades, even as reforms in the other areas of economic laws moved rapidly after the liberalisation of the Indian economy in 1991. To attract foreign investment, policymakers focused heavily on reforming entry laws but neglected improvements in exit laws, underestimating the role the insolvency system plays in winning investor confidence. Only some incremental measures were taken which led to a fragmented and fractured insolvency regime. The RBI issued a number of one-time schemes for settlement of dues between lenders and borrowers from time to time. Some of these failed to produce the desired results, as lenders were scared that writing off loans might cause investigating bodies to come after them and question the merits of each waiver.[3]

NPAs continued to rise in banks and financial institutions in the absence of an effective insolvency law. This prompted the enactment of the Securitization and Reconstruction of Financial Assets and Enforcement of Security Interest Act, 2002 (SARFAESI Act). Drawing inspiration from several Asian nations in the aftermath of the Asian financial crisis, the government introduced the

3. Sumant Batra, *Corporate Insolvency: Law and Practice* (Eastern Book Company, 2017), pp. 3–20.

SARFAESI Act to create a framework for establishing private sector asset reconstruction and securitisation companies.

In 2004, Prime Minister Manmohan Singh directed the setting up of the J.J. Irani Committee to overhaul the company law. I saw an opportunity to address flaws in the half-baked insolvency framework in the 2002 Act. I met then minister of corporate affairs, Prem Chand Gupta, and requested that the terms of the Irani Committee be expanded to include a review of the insolvency law. The Department of Corporate Affairs in the Ministry of Finance had just been carved out and the new ministry (Ministry of Corporate Affairs) was headed by a Cabinet minister. With some effort, I was able to persuade Prem Chand Gupta to take up the matter with Prime Minister Manmohan Singh to review the 2002 Act. He had to consult the prime minister, as the ink on the 2002 Act had yet to dry, and it was not going to be an easy policy decision to take back to Parliament. We met the prime minister. After hearing us patiently, the prime minister, a man of few words, gave us the unhesitating go-ahead. As an economist and having worked in the IMF, Prime Minister Manmohan Singh understood the importance of the insolvency law. The terms of reference of the Irani Committee were modified and insolvency reform was included. I was inducted into the Irani Committee.[4]

The Irani Committee proposed significant legislative changes to make the restructuring and liquidation process speedy, efficient, and effective. The government introduced the Companies Bill, 2012, in Parliament to implement reforms recommended by the Irani Committee. The bill proposed the introduction of a new discipline of insolvency professionals. While the proposed law allowed the debtor to continue in possession, an independent oversight of the insolvency practitioner over the debtor was provided. However, the debtor was to be dispossessed if it failed to submit a resolution plan satisfactory to the creditors' committee within the prescribed time. The provision for setting up of a creditors' committee was introduced. Moratorium could be granted only on determination of bankruptcy of companies which was moved to default test from balance sheet test provided under the SICA. The NCLT was to function as a special bankruptcy court. Timelines were prescribed for each stage of proceedings.

---

4. Sumant Batra, *Corporate Insolvency: The Road to Viksit Bharat* (Eastern Book Company, 2025), pp. 18–39, 154–78.

UPA-I failed to pass the law during its parliamentary term. The bill was reintroduced by UPA-II but was not taken up with the urgency it deserved. By then the advocates of insolvency reforms, banking sector investors, and even development institutions supporting reforms were completely frustrated by the delay. There was a policy paralysis in the last two years of UPA-II. The bill could only be passed on 8 August 2013, a few months before UPA-II's parliamentary term was to end. There was no time left to implement the law. Moreover, the clouds over the setting up of the NCLT had also not fully cleared. It was still entangled in litigation before the Supreme Court. The legal framework in vogue for bankruptcy resolution (winding up of a company on inability to pay debts) continued to be in the Companies Act, 1956, pending notification of the amended provisions in the Companies Act, 2013.[5]

Many chapters of the Companies Act, 2013, were notified; the chapters relating to the insolvency law were not.

★

Fast forward to 2014, when Narendra Modi took over as the prime minister, India's overall growth had faltered, reaching a nadir of just 4.8 per cent in the third quarter of 2013. The rupee had taken a beating, slumping to Rs 68 per dollar in the summer of that year. The country's once-compelling growth story had lost its lustre, as foreign and domestic investments were hit by policy paralysis, and clearances for big-ticket infrastructure projects were held back on environmental grounds.[6] Measures were required to improve India's ranking on World Bank's Ease of Doing Business.[7] An improvement in insolvency law was a prerequisite to this.

---

5. Ibid.

6. Sumant Batra, "Introduction" in *Corporate Insolvency: Law and Practice* (Eastern Book Company, 2017), pp. 32–39.

7. After data irregularities on Doing Business 2018 and 2020 were reported internally in June 2020, the World Bank management paused the next Doing Business report and initiated a series of reviews and audits of the report and its methodology. The Business Ready (B-READY) report is the World Bank's new flagship report benchmarking the business environment and investment climate in most economies worldwide. The

There were other reasons for urgency, including the frightening levels of stress that had built in the Indian banking sector over the course of a few years. The alarming proportion of NPAs was severely impacting the availability of much-needed credit to inject investment into the economy. It wouldn't be an exaggeration to say that PSBs in particular were on the verge of a crisis in 2014 due to their high NPAs.[8] The twin balance sheet (TBS) problem also emerged. The TBS problem is an economic issue that refers to the simultaneous existence of two interconnected balance sheet problems—one within the corporate sector and the other within the banking sector. Firms typically over-expand during a boom time, generally with support of liberal credit.[9] In these cases, their revenues often do not match debt service obligations and their balance sheets get stretched. As they default on their debts, balance sheets of banks also get stretched. This leads to a situation where the firms with stretched balance sheets are unwilling to invest any further, while other firms cannot invest as banks with stretched balance sheets are not able to lend any more. Many other factors contributed to the incidence of NPAs in the banks,

Over time, the government introduced a series of incremental measures aimed at cleansing the banking system of the NPA menace and revitalising the

---

report assesses the regulatory framework and public services directed at firms, and the efficiency with which regulatory framework and public services are combined in practice. With data that are comparable across economies and over time, B-READY provides actionable evidence to promote reforms for a stronger private sector. The first B-READY report was launched on 3 October 2024, available at https://www.worldbank.org/en/businessready. For Ease of Business, *see* "Ease of doing business score and ease of doing business ranking" (Chapter 6) in *Doing Business 2020* (World Bank Group, 2020), pp. 77–86, available at https://openknowledge.worldbank.org/bitstream/handle/10986/32436/9781464814402_Ch06.pdf.

8. The banking system in India consists of commercial banks and cooperative banks, of which commercial banks account for more than 90 per cent of the banking system's assets. Based on the ownership pattern, commercial banks can be grouped into three types: (1) state-owned banks or PSBs, i.e., SBI and its subsidiaries and the nationalised banks; (2) private banks under Indian ownership; and (3) foreign banks operating in India.

9. The Indian economy was booming in the mid-noughties with growth rates surging to 9–10 per cent per annum. After a brief interruption in sympathy with the global financial crisis, the growth rate improved to about 8.5 per cent from 2009 to 2011. Firms made huge investments with a projected double-digit growth rate, funded mostly by the credit boom.

financial and banking sector. This resulted in a highly fragmented framework of insolvency law and rights of creditors/debtors; none worked. As of 31 October 2015, only about 955 (out of 4636) and 163 (out of 545) cases of court and voluntary winding up were resolved within five years. A significant number of such cases had been pending for more than twenty years. The lengthy process kept substantial corporate assets unrealised and undistributed. The inordinate delay in liquidation proceedings marred the possibilities of rapid use of productive assets lying dormant in these proceedings throughout the country.[10]

Confronted with this crisis, Jaitley decided to accelerate the enactment of a new insolvency law. On 22 August 2014, Jaitley's ministry set up the Bankruptcy Law Reforms Committee (BLRC) under its Department of Economic Affairs to study the "corporate bankruptcy legal framework in India", and submit a report to the government for reforming the system. Dr T.K. Viswanathan[11] was appointed as its chairman. The BLRC was mandated to produce its recommendations without any delay.

During the course of its deliberations, the BLRC decided to divide its work into two parts: (1) examine the present legal framework for corporate insolvency and suggest immediate reforms; and (2) develop an insolvency code for India, covering all aspects of personal and business insolvency. The BLRC submitted an interim report on 11 February 2015.

In his budget speech for 2015–16 on 28 February 2015, Jaitley stated: "Bankruptcy law reform, that brings about legal certainty and speed, has been identified as a key priority for improving the ease of doing business. SICA and BIFR have failed in achieving these objectives. We will bring a comprehensive Bankruptcy Code in fiscal 2015–16, that will meet global standards and provide necessary judicial capacity."[12]

The BLRC submitted its final report on 4 November 2015, in two parts: Volume 1 detailing the rationale and design for legislation, and Volume 2

---

10. Sumant Batra, *Corporate Insolvency: Law and Practice* (Eastern Book Company, 2017), pp. 3–20.

11. Dr T.K. Viswanathan is the former secretary general of the Lok Sabha and a former Union law and legislative affairs secretary.

12. Arun Jaitley, "Budget 2015–2016", available at https://www.indiabudget.gov.in/doc/bspeech/bs201516.pdf.

suggesting a draft Insolvency and Bankruptcy Bill. In its report, the BLRC observed that the existing bankruptcy framework for firms was highly fragmented. The powers of the creditors and the debtors under insolvency law were provided for under different legislations. It proposed a new insolvency and bankruptcy resolution framework which (1) facilitated the assessment of viability of the enterprise at a very early stage; (2) enabled symmetry of information between creditors and debtors; (3) ensured a time-bound process to better preserve economic value; (4) used a collective process; (5) respected the rights of all creditors equally; (6) ensured that, when negotiations failed to establish viability, the outcome of bankruptcy was binding; and (7) provided clarity of priority, and that the rights of all stakeholders are upheld in resolving bankruptcy. The eight chapters of Volume I provide a comprehensive analysis of its suggestions including the economic thinking behind the IBC.[13]

The IBC, together with the underlying reform, in many ways, was a journey into uncharted territory, a leap into the unknown and a leap of faith. Many institutions required for the implementation of a modern insolvency regime did not exist. The law had to be laid down; infrastructure had to be created; capacity had to be built; professions had to be formed; markets and practices had to be developed; and stakeholders had to be made aware of the IBC, accept the change, and learn how to use it.

In its report, the BLRC noted that the legislative track of the implementation would comprise taking the draft law through the consultative process, and public debate, prior to its being tabled in Parliament. Recognising that the setting up of the institutions contemplated in the report might require some time, the BLRC recommended that until such time as the regulator was established, its powers and functions could be exercised by the government, with appropriate transitional provisions provided for in the IBC.[14]

However, Jaitley had a better plan. On the basis of the recommendations of the BLRC, in December 2015, he introduced a bill relating to the IBC in Parliament, with its objectives stated as follows:

---

13. Bankruptcy Law Reforms Committee, "The Report of the Bankruptcy Law Reforms Committee—Volume I: Rationale and Design", Insolvency and Bankruptcy Board of India (November 2015) p. 18, para 3.4.2, available at https://ibbi.gov.in/BLRCReportVol1_04112015.pdf.

14. Ibid.

> An Act to consolidate and amend the laws relating to reorganisation and insolvency resolution of corporate persons, partnership firms and individuals in a time-bound manner for maximisation of value of assets of such persons, to promote entrepreneurship, availability of credit and balance the interests of all the stakeholders including alteration in the order of priority of payment of Government dues and to establish an Insolvency and Bankruptcy Board of India, and for matters connected therewith or incidental thereto.

Jaitley stated that the Code aimed to consolidate and amend laws relating to the insolvency and bankruptcy resolution of corporate persons, partnership firms, and individuals in a time-bound manner. He explained that the current position regarding insolvency and bankruptcy in India involved multiple legislations, which the new bill would address. Regarding the legislative process, Jaitley stated his preference that the bill not be passed as a money bill and instead expressed his willingness to form a Joint Committee with representatives from both Houses of Parliament to discuss the bill. He emphasised the importance of eventually reaching a consensus through amendments and alterations, which is the strength of a parliamentary democracy.

The bill was passed by the Lok Sabha on 28 April 2016 and the Rajya Sabha on 11 May 2016. The Ministry of Finance issued a press release on 11 May 2016, which observed:

> Today is a historic day for economic reforms in India when the Rajya Sabha passed the major economic reform Bill moved by the Government, i.e., "Insolvency and Bankruptcy Code, 2016". This is considered as the biggest economic reform next only to GST. … The Insolvency and Bankruptcy Code is thus a comprehensive and systemic reform, which will give a quantum leap to the functioning of the credit market. It would take India from among relatively weak insolvency regimes to becoming one of the world's best insolvency regimes. It lays the foundations for the development of the corporate bond market, which would finance the infrastructure projects of the future. The

> passing of this Code and implementation of the same will give a big boost to ease of doing business in India.[15]

Thus, the IBC came to be enacted as a critical building block in India's progression towards a mature market economy.

The IBC was notified by the President of India on 28 May 2016. It made amendments to eleven laws, including the Companies Act, 2013, the Recovery of Debts and Bankruptcy Act, 1993, and the SARFAESI Act, 2002, to give effect to the newly codified legislation. The IBC provided for an overhaul of the legal regime for corporate and individual insolvency and bankruptcy, replacing the existing legal regime with a predictable, market-led, and incentive-compliant mechanism. The IBC also plugged a glaring gap by providing the missing third limb of corporate freedom—the freedom to exit or discontinue the business. With the enactment of the IBC, the framework to resolve insolvency resolution of distressed enterprises in an orderly and time-bound manner would take concrete shape in the years to follow. The IMF termed it as a "big bang reform".[16]

★

Under Arun Jaitley's stewardship, India broke from its past record and exceeded all expectations in implementing the IBC. Leading from the front, his ministry demonstrated the highest commitment to insolvency reform and implemented the IBC with full vigour. The unprecedented pace at which it moved to operationalise the IBC probably has no parallel anywhere else in

---

15. "Parliament Passes the Insolvency and Bankruptcy Code", Press Information Bureau, Government of India, Ministry of Finance, available at https://www.pib.gov.in/newsite/printrelease.aspx?relid=145286.

16. International Monetary Fund, "India: 2017 Article IV Consultation— Press Release; Staff Report; and Statement by the Executive Director for India", IMF Country Report No. 2017/054 (February 2017), available at https://www.imf.org/en/Publications/CR/Issues/ 2017/02/22/India-2017-Article-IV-Consultation-Press-Release-Staff-Report-and-Statement-by-the-Executive-44670#:~text=This%202017%20Article%201V%20Consultation%20highlights.

the world. The Government of India (Allocation of Business) Rules, 1961, was amended on 29 July 2016 to entrust the responsibility of administration of the IBC to the Ministry of Corporate Affairs. In less than six months after the enactment of the IBC, subordinate legislation was finalised, most of the institutions were put in place, and the major part of corporate insolvency law was made operational. The entire ecosystem for corporate insolvency was put in place to enable commencement of corporate insolvency proceedings by 1 December 2016.[17] From the setting up of the BLRC to the passing of the IBC and from the establishment of many new institutions under the IBC to the finalisation of rules and regulations took less than two years. The government shifted gears to focus on educating market players and building the capacity of the newly set-up institutions for effective implementation of the IBC. A mammoth exercise was necessary, as the nuances of the insolvency law were not widely understood in India.[18]

★

Although the IBC had become operational for the insolvency resolution process for companies and limited liability partnerships from 1 December 2016, financial institutions had not shown much enthusiasm around the new law. A total of 157 applications (sixty-four before the Mumbai bench, thirty-six before the Delhi bench, fourteen before the Kolkata bench, and forty-three before other benches) were filed by 31 March 2017. Of these, thirty—five filed by operational creditors, seven by financial creditors, and eighteen by corporate debtors—were admitted. Another nineteen applications were either rejected or withdrawn. The remaining were still under process.[19]

---

17. M.S. Sahoo, "Insolvency Reforms: A Road Under Construction", in *Insolvency and Bankruptcy Regime in India: A Narrative* (Insolvency and Bankruptcy Board of India, 2020), pp. 1–18.

18. Sumant Batra, *Corporate Insolvency: The Road to Viksit Bharat* (Eastern Book Company, 2025), pp. 40–79.

19. "The Essence of Time", Vol. 2, *Insolvency and Bankruptcy News*, Quarterly Newsletter of the Insolvency and Bankruptcy Board of India (January–March 2017).

Many of them were sceptical of the IBC because their experience with previous insolvency reforms had not been encouraging. They were still reeling from the erstwhile insolvency regime. Some were of the opinion that the IBC should be first tried out with smaller cases to prepare it and test its ability to handle large stressed assets in the course of time. But the government was determined to roll out the IBC with full vigour.[20]

On 4 May 2017, in an unprecedented move, Jaitley's ministry recommended amendment in the Banking Regulation Act, 1949, by promulgating an ordinance,[21] which authorised RBI to issue directions to banks to initiate proceedings under the IBC for timely resolution of distress in defaulter companies. The Banking Regulation (Amendment) Act, 2017, notified on 25 August 2017, replaced this ordinance. In a sense, it was a leap of faith when the government chose to channel large NPAs into resolution through the still nascent insolvency framework.

An independent advisory committee of RBI shortlisted companies whose fund- and non-fund-based outstanding amount was greater than Rs 5000 crore (US$ 600 million) as on 31 March 2016. The committee identified twelve companies, whose defaulted loans constituted about 25 per cent of the gross NPAs of the banking system at the time, to be referred to the NCLT. These twelve companies were Bhushan Steel Limited; Bhushan Power and Steel Limited; Essar Steel Limited; Electrosteel Limited; Monnet Ispat and Energy Limited (from the steel sector); Alok Industries Limited (from the textiles sector); Jaypee Infratech Limited (from the real estate sector); Amtek Auto Limited (from the automotive sector); Lanco Infratech Limited; Jyoti Structures Limited; Era Infra Limited (from the construction and infrastructure sector); and ABG Shipyard Limited (from the shipbuilding sector). These companies' accounts roughly translated to Rs 2.5 lakh crore (US$ 30 billion) of banks' NPAs. RBI requested the NCLT to accord priority to these cases.[22]

This also nudged the financial creditors to use the IBC for insolvency resolution. Following the RBI's directions, insolvency petitions were filed

---

20. Sumant Batra, *The Jaypee Infra Insolvency Saga* (Om Books International, 2024).

21. The Banking Regulation (Amendment) Ordinance, 2017.

22. "RBI Identifies Accounts for Reference by Banks under the Insolvency and Bankruptcy Code (IBC)", RBI (13 June 2017), available at: https://rbi.org.in/scripts/BS_PressReleaseDisplay.aspx?prid=40743.

with NCLT by the lenders of these twelve defaulting companies. These twelve defaulters have since then become infamous as the "Dirty Dozen", named so by Sanjeev Sanyal, drawing from the title of the 1967 American war film.[23]

The enactment of the IBC and the RBI's crackdown on the bad loans situation[24] were amongst many steps taken to address the NPA issue with urgency. Later, the RBI released another list of twenty-eight companies which owed roughly Rs 2 lakh crore (US$ 24 billion) to banks. The dues of these forty companies[25] together accounted for 40–45 per cent of bad loans in the banking system. The RBI's action to initiate insolvency process in respect of the large defaulters prompted many fence sitters to start using the IBC for resolution of their stressed assets. The action also reaffirmed the government's faith in the new law and its commitment to resolve the NPA crisis.

★

The implementation of the IBC was not without its challenges. From the very outset, its journey was marked by a series of unprecedented twists and turns, demanding swift adaptability and a proactive response to overcome emerging hurdles. The government, the Insolvency and Bankruptcy Board of India (IBBI), and other regulators played a proactive role in swiftly addressing ambiguities in the IBC and related laws as they emerged during case proceedings. Through timely amendments and corresponding regulatory updates, they ensured that the framework evolved along a consistent and progressive trajectory.

Initial revisions in the IBC and its regulations were, however, prompted by the snags experienced in the insolvency process of the twelve largest defaulter accounts, particularly the high-stake case of Jaypee Infratech Limited (JIL). The IBC witnessed six legislative interventions in the first four years since its

---

23. Sumant Batra, *The Jaypee Infra Insolvency Saga* (Om Books International, 2024).
24. Sumant Batra, *Corporate Insolvency: Law and Practice* (Eastern Book Company, 2017), pp. 3–20.
25. Nishank, "Insolvency and Bankruptcy Code (IBC): Whose Loss, Whose Gain?—A Critical Analysis of Performance of Two Years of IBC", Centre for Financial Accountability (May 2019), available at https://www.cenfa.org/wp-content/uploads/2019/07/IBC-Report-Final.pdf.

enactment to strengthen its processes and further its objectives, in sync with emerging market realities. Out of these six, the complexities of JIL influenced three amendments. The others were on account of Essar Steel Limited and Bhushan Power and Steel Limited. Each of the amendments is a milestone on the road of insolvency reforms, reinforcing the primary objective of the IBC, namely, rescuing lives of companies.

The IBBI has also made 102 amendments to its eighteen regulations made under the IBC, out of which twenty-two amendments have been made from April 2022 to March 2023 alone. The amendments continue till date. Many were in the pipeline at the time this book went to press. The IBC has undoubtedly emerged as one of the most dynamic economic legislations of recent times.

The outcomes under the new insolvency regime have been striking. This is evident from the fact that as of December 2024, a total of 8175 cases have been admitted, with 6192 reaching closure. Of these closed cases, 3485 companies—accounting for 56 per cent of the closures—were successfully rescued, while 2707 resulted in liquidation. Among the rescued companies, 1236 cases were closed due to appeal, review, or settlement; 1130 were withdrawn; and 1119 concluded with the approval of resolution plans. The IBC's more broader and significant impact comes from the behavioural change it has induced, particularly the shift in the relationship between creditors and borrowers. It has created an optimal incentive–disincentive mix to facilitate above-board and transparent dealings in creditor–debtor relations. This shift has fundamentally changed the narrative around NPAs or defaults; it is no longer solely a burden on banks but has become a critical concern for borrowers as well.

In a relatively short span, the IBC has emerged as a powerful tool for addressing banking sector stress, contributing significantly to the sharp decline in gross NPAs, which fell to a multi-year low of 2.8 per cent for SCBs in March 2024. It has proven to be an effective remedy to the Twin Balance Sheet (TBS) problem, in which banks were burdened with mounting NPAs while corporations grappled with excessive leverage and debt repayment challenges. The World Bank's "Doing Business 2020" report moved India's ranking to 52 in terms of resolving insolvency, a significant jump from 122 in 2013. I have written in great detail about the outcomes of the new insolvency regime in my four books[26] on the IBC since 2017.

India has benefitted immensely from the IBC. Its impact on the economy has been phenomenal. Jaitley demonstrated how to address the crisis, and turn it into an opportunity. The rest, as the saying goes, is history. The IBC saga is still unfolding; the law has just entered its tenth anniversary. There have been many significant hits and some key misses. While most teething problems have been overcome, some continue to make use of the IBC difficult. Many milestones have been crossed, and many more lie ahead.

26. Sumant Batra, *Corporate Insolvency: Law and Practice* (Eastern Book Company, 2017), Justice A.K. Sikri and Sumant Batra (Eastern Book Company, 2024), Sumant Batra, *The Jaypee Infra Insolvency Saga* (Om Books International, 2024), and Sumant Batra, *Corporate Insolvency: The Road to Viksit Bharat* (Eastern Book Company, 2025).

25

Reforms in the Banking Sector

In the economic organism of a nation, banking serves as the blood coursing through its veins. If there was one sector that was in crying need of help when Jaitley took over as the finance minister in 2014, it was banking. Reeling under the stress of burgeoning bad loans, the banking sector was plagued by a shortage of capital and a crisis of confidence. This was a time when Basel-III[1] capitalisation norms, requiring banks to shore up capital and build contingency capital buffers, were set to kick in. Jaitley recognised that a robust banking sector was critical to power growth.

Over the next five years, he introduced many landmark measures to restore the health of the ailing banking sector. The hints of reforms he would unleash came in his first budget speech made on 10 July 2014. He said:

> As Finance Minister I am duty bound to usher in a policy regime that will result in the desired macroeconomic outcome of higher growth, lower inflation, sustained level of external sector balance and a prudent policy stance. The budget is the most comprehensive action plan in this regard. In the first budget of this NDA government that I am

---

1. As mentioned earlier, Basel III is an internationally agreed set of measures developed by the Basel Committee on Banking Supervision in response to the financial crisis of 2007–09. The measures aim to strengthen the regulation, supervision and risk management of banks.

> presenting before the august House, my aim is to lay down a broad policy indicator of the direction in which we wish to take this country. The steps that I will announce in this budget are only the beginning of a journey towards a sustained growth of 7–8 per cent or above within the next 3–4 years along with macroeconomic stabilisation that includes lower levels of inflation, lesser fiscal deficit and a manageable current account deficit. Therefore, it would not be wise to expect everything that can be done or must be done to be in the first Budget presented within forty five days of the formation of this government ... Financial stability is the foundation of a rapid recovery. Our banking system needs to be further strengthened.[2]

In the same speech, Jaitley acknowledged that Indian banks needed Rs 240,000 crore as equity by 2018 in order to meet the stricter Basel-III capital adequacy norms. He added that the government intended to offload stake in banks to the general public without giving up controlling stake. He also hinted at the Modi government's inclination towards consolidation in the banking sector. He said, "There have been some suggestions for consolidation of public sector banks. The government, in principle, agrees to consider these suggestions." Jaitley also talked about the need for a financial inclusion mission that would meet the needs of the unbanked sections of the society. That eventually led to the Pradhan Mantri Jan Dhan Yojana (PMJDY) which went on to become the world's largest financial inclusion programme. The same budget called for the RBI to create a differentiated banking framework to serve the economy's niche segments more effectively. That laid the foundation of small banks and payment banks.

In the second budget of the Modi government, Jaitley hoped that the country's vast postal network, and its proposed payment bank, will be used by the department to increase the access of the people to the formal financial system. It broached the idea of a Bank Board Bureau to increase the governance of state-run banks. He said:

---

2. Arun Jaitley, "Budget 2014–2015", available at https://www.indiabudget.gov.in/doc/bspeech/bs201415.pdf.

> In order to improve the governance of Public Sector banks, the government intends to set up an autonomous Bank Board Bureau. The bureau will search and select heads of public sector banks and help them in developing differentiated strategies and capital raising plans through innovative financial methods and instruments. This would be an interim step towards establishing a holding and investment company for banks.

To increase the access of small businesses to formal credit, the government proposed the creation of MUDRA Bank with a corpus of Rs 20,000 crore and a credit guarantee corpus of Rs 3000 crore.

The BLRC had, in the meantime, submitted its report. A bill to enact the IBC was tabled in Parliament and referred to the JPC. In his third budget (2016–17), even as the discussions around the IBC gained momentum, a similar framework for financial institutions was envisaged by Jaitley. While presenting the budget, he said that a vacuum existed with regards to the bankruptcy situation in financial firms. To fill the vacuum, he proposed a comprehensive law on resolution of financial firms which will provide, "a specialised resolution mechanism to deal with bankruptcy situations in banks, insurance companies, and financial sector entities. This law, together with the IBC, when enacted, will provide a comprehensive resolution mechanism for our economy."[3]

Another major decision taken in the third budget presented by Jaitley for reforming the banking sector was to provide a statutory basis for the Monetary Policy Committee, which came into effect after an agreement between RBI and the government in this regard in 2015. In the same budget, Jaitley announced Rs 25,000 crore as a recapitalisation measure for the banks and the initiation of the process of consolidation of banks through the Bank Board Bureau.

The 2017–18 budget came in the backdrop of the government's demonetisation measure taken in late 2016. While presenting the budget, Jaitley said that the impact of demonetisation was already visible in terms of lower interest rates and increased digitisation. "There is early evidence of an increased capacity of Banks to lend at reduced interest rates and a huge shift towards digitisation among all sections of society. ... The surplus liquidity in

3. Arun Jaitley, "Budget 2016–2017", available at https://www.indiabudget.gov.in/doc/bspeech/bs201617.pdf.

the banking system, created by demonetisation, will lower borrowing costs and increase the access to credit. This will boost economic activity, with multiplier effects," he added.[4]

Jaitley allocated Rs 10,000 crore for bank recapitalisation in line with the "Indradhanush" roadmap. He also said that the legal framework for resolution of stressed assets had been strengthened with the enactment of the IBC, 2016, and amendments to the SARFAESI and Recovery of Debts and Bankruptcy Act. The finance minister also doubled the lending target to Rs 2.44 lakh crore for FY 2017–18 over the previous year for the Pradhan Mantri Mudra Yojana, the flagship scheme to encourage small businesses. He increased the allowable provision for NPA from 7.5 per cent to 8.5 per cent which would reduce the tax liability of banks. The idea of an Electoral Bond scheme was also announced during this budget for which the finance minister proposed amending the RBI Act, 1934.

Jaitley started off his speech for the 2018–19 budget by stating that the IBC had changed the lender–debtor relationship and that recapitalised banks would support growth. Jaitley talked about the bank recapitalisation plan announced in 2017 which entailed mobilisation of Rs 2.1 lakh crore of capital including issuance of recapitalisation of bonds worth Rs 1.35 lakh crore. Ruling out the status of legal tender for cryptocurrencies, he said that the government would consider using blockchain technology for ushering in the digital economy.

Capitalisation

When Arun Jaitley took charge of the finance ministry in 2014, the government was faced with another challenge with respect to the PSBs. While the Basel norms that required banks' capital to be shored up, including building contingency capital buffers, were kicking in, the resolution of NPLs was virtually grounded. Privatising banks was still not on the agenda. The only option left was to infuse capital in the banks. The Department of Financial Services (DFS), based on the advice of the RBI, demanded Rs 2 lakh crore of

4. Arun Jaitley, "Budget 2017–2018", available at https://www.indiabudget.gov.in/doc/bspeech/bs201718.pdf.

capital infusion. Of the total package of Rs 2.11 lakh crore, the government was to infuse Rs 1.35 lakh crore and the rest was to be raised by issuing equity in the market and selling "non-core" assets. In July 2017, the government was worried about the state of affairs in the PSBs. The government's "Indradhanush" package, which had provided for infusion of Rs 10,000 crore of equity in the PSBs during 2017–18, seemed to be peanuts.

On 24 October 2017, accompanied by Finance Secretary Subhash Chandra Garg, Jaitley walked into the Press Information Bureau's Media Conference Hall to deliver a major announcement: PSBs would receive a capital injection of Rs 2.11 lakh crore, with Rs 1.35 lakh crore coming directly from the government and the balance to be mobilised through market equity issuance and the sale of "non-core" assets. The government shelled out, but very little was raised by the PSBs in the market. Only Punjab National Bank (PNB) raised money. No non-core assets could be sold. The government had to make up the balance capital infusion later.

Jaitley was instrumental in freeing as many as eleven PSBs placed under a prompt corrective action (PCA) framework by the RBI. In December 2018–19, the RBI had placed half the PSBs (eleven out of twenty-one) under the PCA framework. A bank under the PCA framework is a "narrow" bank. It can accept deposits but is barred from extending loans by and large. It can invest its resources in buying government securities. The RBI's PCA framework essentially revolved around two tasks. First, risk-adjusted capital (capital to risk [weighted] assets ratio [CRAR]) should be 9 per cent and the net non-performing loans (NPLs) should be less than 6 per cent of the total risk-weighted loans.

Sometime in January 2019, a few weeks before the presentation of the budget, the government decided that the PSBs would have to be brought out of the PCA framework and an amount of over Rs 1.5 lakh crore would be needed for that. Newly appointed finance secretary, Rajiv Kumar, sent a note to then finance secretary, Subhash Chandra Garg, asking for over Rs 1 lakh crore to bring six banks out of the PCA framework and also to prevent four others from getting covered under PCA (in addition to the eleven already in). His requirement included capital both for meeting the minimum capital adequacy and "growth capital" (needed to expand the loan book). In fact, to meet both, the DFS was relying only on capital infusion. The minimum capital requirement and other conditions literally meant that the banks needed capital of 9 per cent plus the amount by which the net NPAs were greater than

6 per cent. In addition, the DFS asked for growth capital of about Rs 50,000 crore (over and above the minimum regulatory capital for allowing banks to expand lending).[5]

Garg was not in favour of the PSBs' capitalisation by the government. He went to Jaitley and suggested they wait for the results of 31 March to determine the actual amount required. Jaitley was not impressed by Garg's suggestion. He directed Garg to act positively on Kumar's note. Garg recorded a comprehensive note on the file arguing that whatever amount was required by the PSBs to boost capital should be raised by the banks by issuing public equity. Jaitley overruled Garg, writing the longest note Garg had seen in the twenty months he had worked with him. Jaitley rebutted every point Garg wrote, and approved the proposal of the DFS for capital infusion in PSBs. Garg later acknowledged that Nripendra Misra, the principal secretary to the prime minister, later told him (Garg) that he was not in tune with the thinking of the government.[6]

The RBI issued a press release on 31 January 2019, a day before the presentation of the 2019–20 interim budget, removing restrictions under the PCA framework for three PSBs: Bank of India, Bank of Maharashtra, and Oriental Bank of Commerce. Over the years, all PSBs have been brought out of the PCA framework. Central Bank of India was the last one to get its honour back in September 2022.

The Industrial Development Bank of India (IDBI) Bank was the weakest performer among PSBs. By 2018, its NPLs had crossed 27 per cent of its loan book, and it had been reporting substantial losses year after year. The government held over 94 per cent of its equity. Unlike other PSBs, the IDBI Bank did not come into being through nationalisation; it was originally set up by IDBI—a development finance institution established by an Act of Parliament—when banking licences were opened to both public and private players in 1993. IDBI later merged with IDBI Bank, bringing with it a significant burden of NPLs.

The IDBI Act allowed the government to lower its stake to 49 per cent. Unlike other PSBs, there was no legislative restriction of retaining a minimum 51 per

5. Subhash Chandra Garg, *We Also Make Policy: An Insider's Account of How the Finance Ministry Functions* (HarperCollins, 2023), pp. 306–13.

6. Ibid.

cent stake with the government. In other state-run banks, the government has pledged to keep a majority 52 per cent stake. The government was free to sell IDBI Bank like Air India or any other PSU. The government explored the possibility of the International Finance Corporation (IFC) taking over a majority stake in IDBI Bank, on its own or with other associates.[7] The IFC was keen to acquire the stake and was willing to offer about Rs 100 a share to acquire a controlling interest along with other associates (the IFC on its own was allowed to take a maximum 20 per cent stake). However, the deal fell through.[8]

In April–May 2018, Jaitley decided that the government would offer IDBI to Life Insurance Corporation of India (LIC). He brought the PMO on board. But there were three problems. First, the RBI did not allow any single stakeholder to have more than 10 per cent voting rights in a bank. Second, the IDBI Bank was sitting over a big pile of NPLs. It had very little on the retail book and was feared to be making losses. LIC did not know how to run a bank and could not be expected to turn it around. Third, LIC's regulator, the IRDAI, would not permit LIC to have more than a 15 per cent stake in IDBI Bank as a higher stake was not permissible under the investment rules framed under the Insurance Act, 1938, and IRDA Act, 1999.

The IRDAI gave its approval to LIC's purchase of the 51 per cent government stake in IDBI Bank on 30 June 2018. Some more time was taken to get RBI and Cabinet approval. Under SEBI's takeover regulations at the time, if a company acquired more than 25 per cent in another listed company, it had to make an open offer to minority shareholders to buy at least 26 per cent more in the target firm. A request was made to SEBI to exempt LIC from making a public offer. SEBI refused. LIC held about 8 per cent stake in IDBI Bank, which was classified as a public holding. Excluding that, only about 6 per cent of shares were really with the public. LIC decided to acquire up to 26 per cent of shares at a price of Rs 261.73 per share.

---

7. Dheeraj Tiwari, "Government talks with IFC for a strategic sale in IDBI bank", *The Economic Times*, accessed September 2025, https://economictimes.indiatimes.com/industry/banking/finance/banking/government-talks-with-ifc-for-a-strategic-sale-in-idbi-bank/articleshow/49975188.cms?from=mdr.

8. Subhash Chandra Garg, *We Also Make Policy: An Insider's Account of How the Finance Ministry Functions* (HarperCollins, 2023), pp. 306–13.

Shares of the debt-ridden IDBI Bank shot up over 16 per cent in two days, reacting to news that LIC would be making an open offer to minority shareholders of the bank in which it proposed to buy a controlling stake.[9] LIC got another about 3 per cent of shares in the public offer. The government was thus required to sell about 40 per cent of IDBI-issued capital to LIC to enable it to hold 51 per cent equity stake. LIC completed the acquisition of the 51 per cent stake in IDBI Bank in January 2019.

Non-Performing Assets

Of the many reforms in the banking sector Jaitley initiated in the very first year after taking over as finance minister, he will be remembered for bringing down NPAs to manageable levels by adopting many measures including the blue-chip IBC.

When Jaitley entered his North Block office, fortunately, there were green shoots of recovery being seen in the global economy. As per IMF, the world economy was projected to grow at 3.6 per cent in 2014 vis-à-vis 3.0 per cent in 2013, with the Euro area expected to register a positive growth after the contraction witnessed in 2012 and 2013. However, the performance of the US economy with attendant implications for the unconventional monetary policy stance and global financial conditions was pivotal to the fate of global recovery in the coming years. These were the head winds against which the Indian economy would have to manoeuvre its way to attain a high growth trajectory.

Ahead of the first budget, Jaitley was apprised of the annual Article IV (of the IMF's Articles of Agreement) consultations that took place between the IMF and finance ministry officials in Delhi and with RBI Governor Raghuram Rajan in Mumbai early in the year, ahead of the 2014 Lok Sabha elections. The IMF had advised that measures were needed to fully recognise the true asset quality of banks' portfolios irrespective of sectors of the economy (including

---

9. "LIC to make open offer to IDBI Bank minority shareholders; bank's stock spikes 16% in 2 days", *Business Today*, accessed September 2025, https://www.businesstoday.in/latest/corporate/story/lic-to-make-open-offer-to-idbi-bank-minority-shareholders-108559-2018-07-11.

infrastructure and real estate). The IMF noted that the banks were going to require significant new capital injections over the next few years, based on the challenging operating environment, combined with the new Basel-III capital requirements.

The restructured advances were fast increasing. As of March 2013, they comprised 5.7 per cent of the banking system's gross advances, and 7.1 per cent of the PSBs' advances. This would require improvements in the legal and institutional insolvency framework, the regime for insolvency professionals, the functioning of the distressed asset market, and out-of-court settlement procedures. "Restructured assets are usually not considered 'non-performing' in India, and their rapid rise has led some observers to doubt the publicly displayed financial strength of many Indian banks," the IMF had noted. "Restructured loans should be counted towards NPAs immediately after a restructuring, and then moved to the performing bucket only after a period of satisfactory performance."

This was of particular importance for the PSBs. The IMF stress-tested the banks' capital position for the possibility of sudden deterioration in loan quality and evaluated the impact of Basel-III requirements. It found the PSBs in particular to be vulnerable to a change in classification of a significant share of restructured loans to NPAs. Each bank's balance sheet was stressed individually, based on 45 per cent of restructured advances moving to NPAs, and it was assumed that both the PSBs' NPAs and their restructured loans would double. After this, three alternative provisioning ratio scenarios were assessed. In the most severe case, the government's share of the recapitalisation cost was estimated at 5 per cent of the 2012–13 GDP.[10]

As already highlighted, frightening levels of stress had built in the Indian banking sector over the course of a few years. The PSBs' outstanding loans had risen from approximately Rs 18 lakh crore in March 2008 to around Rs 52 lakh crore by March 2014. In the initial years, private banks topped the list of banks with highest NPAs (the private sector Industrial Credit and Investment Corporation of India [ICICI] Bank was at the top). Small and medium-sized private sector banks such as Karnataka Bank, Lakshmi Vilas Bank, Kotak Mahindra Bank, and IndusInd Bank followed ICICI Bank on the list. Among the

10. "India: 2014 Article IV Consultation", IMF Country Report No. 14/57, IMF, available at https://www.imf.org/external/pubs/ft/scr/2014/cr1457.pdf.

few PSBs that figured in the list were Central Bank of India, United Commercial (UCO) Bank, and Syndicate Bank.

By March 2009, the scene began changing gradually. More state-run banks began appearing in the picture. The country's largest lender by assets, State Bank of India and Indian Overseas Bank found a place in the list of top NPA scorers. Still, private sector lenders figured prominently in the list with ICICI Bank and Development Credit Bank (DCB) leading the pack.[11] The gross advances of SCBs had increased from Rs 2,503,431 crore as of 31 March 2008 to Rs 6,875,748 crore as of 31 March 2014. As the firms were making more investments and taking more credit, things started to go wrong. NPAs assumed an alarming proportion, impacting availability of credit needed to inject investment into the economy. NPAs soared the most between the years 2009 and 2012, as gross NPAs increased from Rs 449.57 billion in 2009 to Rs 1124.89 billion in 2011–12 and further to Rs 1644.62 billion in 2012–13. The gross NPAs of the PSBs increased almost four times from March 2010 (Rs 599.26 billion) to March 2014 (Rs 2272.64 billion).[12]

In its Financial Stability Report Issue No. 8[13] (December 2013), the RBI identified five sectors—infrastructure, iron and steel, textiles, aviation, and mining—as stressed sectors. The number had grown from Rs 53,917 crore (in 2008 just after the Lehman Brothers Chapter 11 filing[14]) to Rs 3,41,641 crore in September 2015, i.e., from 2.11 per cent to 5.08 per cent as a percentage of the total loans.[15] Insolvency laws as then existing were of no help in resolving NPAs.

---

11. Dinesh Unnikrishnan and Kishor Kadam, "Explained in 5 Charts: How Indian Banks' Big NPA Problem Evolved Over Years", *Firstpost*, accessed 25 May 2025, https://www.firstpost.com/business/explained-in-5-charts-how-indian-banks-big-npa-problem-evolved-over-years-2620164.html.

12. Sumant Batra, *Corporate Insolvency: The Road to Viksit Bharat* (EBC, 2025).

13. "Financial Stability Report Issue No. 8", RBI, December 2013, available at https://rbidocs.rbi.org.in/rdocs/PublicationReport/Pdfs/FSRDEC301213_FL.pdf.

14. On 15 September 2008, Lehman Brothers Holdings, Inc., the fourth-largest US investment bank, sought Chapter 11 protection, initiating the largest bankruptcy proceeding in US history. The demise of the 164-year-old firm was a seminal event in the global financial crisis.

15. Dinesh Unnikrishnan and Kishor Kadam, "Explained in 5 Charts: How Indian Banks' Big NPA Problem Evolved Over Years", *Firstpost*, accessed 25 May 2025,

NPAs have a vicious effect on the sustainability and growth of the banking system. If not managed properly, they can lead to bank failure. An important business implication of NPAs is that they lead to credit risk management assuming priority over other aspects of the bank's functioning. The bank's whole machinery would be thus preoccupied with recovery procedures rather than concentrating on expanding business if NPAs take priority. A bank with a high level of NPAs would be forced to incur carrying costs on non-income-yielding assets.[16] High NPAs depressed profitability of banks and constrained new lending, specifically in the PSBs. Many borrowing firms reported interest coverage ratio (ICR) of less than 1, meaning that they had little or no capacity to service their debt obligations. This further threatened the banks' balance sheets on account of the over-leveraging of their balance sheets.

The stress was severely impacting the availability of much-needed credit to inject investment into the economy. Because profits were eroded, the PSBs, where the bulk of the bad loans sat, could not raise enough capital to fund credit growth. This caused a significant decline in credit growth from 17 per cent in 2011–12 to 9 per cent in 2014–16. Debts of the top ten stressed corporate groups tripled from 2010–11 to 2015–16. The TBS problem also emerged.

Without credit growth, the economy's return to a high-growth trajectory was difficult. It was clear that the bad-loan problem required urgent and effective resolution. Raghuram Rajan proposed to Jaitley a plan for an asset quality review (AQR) of banks. He warned it could throw up a lot of muck as banks had been sweeping a lot of assets under the carpet. Jaitley decided to deal with the challenge head-on. "Fine, go ahead," Jaitley gave Rajan the green light to "clean up" the system.[17] Years later, Prime Minister Modi complimented Jaitley for bringing out the truth before the nation. The prime minister termed this step by his government as "biting the bullet".

---

https://www.firstpost.com/business/explained-in-5-charts-how-indian-banks-big-npa-problem-evolved-over-years-2620164.html.

16. Sumant Batra, *The Jaypee Infra Insolvency Saga* (Om Books International, 2024), pp. 3-7.

17. "'Go Ahead': What Arun Jaitley Told Raghuram Rajan About Tackling Bad Loans", NDTV, accessed September 2025, https://www.ndtv.com/india-news/raghuram-rajan-interview-bad-loans-go-ahead-what-arun-jaitley-told-raghuram-rajan-about-tackling-bad-loans-7294350

When the RBI ordered an AQR in 2015, the skeletons in the cupboard started tumbling out. It unveiled the true extent of NPAs, which had escalated from Rs 2.26 lakh crore in March 2014 to Rs 8.96 lakh crore in March 2018. The crackdown brought to light the seriousness of the problem. The AQR revealed a sharp increase in NPAs of commercial banks in both public and private sectors, increasing from 3.2 per cent of gross advances in March 2013 to 4.3 per cent in March 2015, and further to 9 per cent by September 2016. It was higher at 12 per cent for PSBs. The NPA problem had turned into a full-blown crisis. The problem continued to fester,[18] NPAs kept growing, while credit and investment kept falling—a festering TBS syndrome.

As stated, things worsened to a great extent by March 2014. The bad loan troubles of government banks began to hit hard despite the best efforts by banks to cover up possible NPA stock to restructured loan categories. PSBs, with eight out of ten banks being government-owned, now dominated the list. In order to help the PSBs struggling with high NPAs, the RBI proposed relaxed norms.[19] Banks were spared from classifying certain assets as NPAs for two more years to reduce the amount of loans that needed to be classified as bad loans; they could thus go easy on provisioning against these bad loans. Less provisioning not only helps banks report higher net profit but, more importantly, the banks effectively would have more capital to deploy. This is because once an asset has been classified as NPA, it reduces the advanceable deposit available with the bank.

The RBI gave a deadline of March 2017 for all banks to clean up their balance sheets. A perverse effect of the slow legal process was that banks began shying away from risks by investing a greater than required proportion of their assets in the form of sovereign debt paper. The state of the insolvency process continued to be highly ineffective and failed to deal with the problem of NPLs.

---

18. "Economic Survey 2016–17", Government of India, Ministry of Finance, available at https://www.indiabudget.gov.in/budget2017-2018/es2016-17/echapter.pdf.

19. "Prudential Norms on Income Recognition, Asset Classification and Provisioning Pertaining to Advances—Projects Under Implementation—Change in Ownership", RBI/2014-15/538, DBR.No.BP.BC.84/21.04.048/2014-15, 6 April 2015; "Prudential Norms on Income Recognition, Asset Classification and Provisioning Pertaining to Advances—Refinancing of Exposures to Borrowers", RBI/2014-15/539, DBR.No.BP.BC.85/21.04.048/2014-15, 6 April 2015; https://www.scribd.com/document/283472773/RBI-Circular-on-EPBG-April-6-2015.

The IBC, 2016, was notified by the President of India on 28 May 2016 to consolidate and amend the laws relating to reorganisation and insolvency resolution of corporate persons, partnership firms and individuals in a time-bound manner for maximization of value of assets of such persons, to promote entrepreneurship, availability of credit and balance the interests of all the stakeholders, including alteration in the order of priority of payment of government dues and to establish an Insolvency and Bankruptcy Board of India, and for matters connected therewith or incidental thereto.

Jaitley assured bankers that the government would protect them when making "commercially prudent" settlements of NPAs. Recognising the reluctance of bankers to settle loans at significant discounts due to fear of later scrutiny, the government aimed to create a safe environment for these decisions.[20] During a quarterly performance review with the PSB heads, Jaitley emphasised the need for banks to be "empowered and protected" to facilitate effective NPA resolution. He urged state-owned banks to expedite the clean-up of their balance sheets, emphasising their full authority to tackle wilful defaulters. He instructed PSBs to act against these defaulters and encouraged them to eliminate their legacy NPAs.

As a result of many measures taken under Jaitley's leadership, there was a significant enhancement in the asset quality of banks. These measures nursed the credit sector back to sound health, and the GNPA ratio shrank to 2.8 per cent in March 2024. The GNPA ratio of Scheduled Commercial Banks (SCBs) took a downward trend, reaching a twelve-year low of 2.8 per cent at the end of March 2024 from its peak of 11.2 per cent in FY18. Lower slippages and a reduction in outstanding GNPAs through recoveries, upgrades and write-offs led to this decrease. The improvement in SCB's asset quality has been broad-based.

GNPA ratio of the agriculture sector remained high at 6.5 per cent at the end of March 2024, but it recorded persistent improvement during the second half of FY24. The GNPA ratio in the personal loans segment improved across all categories. Asset quality improved across all significant sub-sectors within

20. "Will Protect Bankers Who Clean Up NPAs: Arun Jaitley at Review Meeting", *The Indian Express*, accessed 25 May 2025, https://indianexpress.com/article/business/banking-and-finance/arun-jaitley-public-sector-banks-bad-loans-npa-bad-loan-recovery-2838526/.

the industrial sector, barring vehicles and transport equipment. Lower GNPAs and high provisions accumulated in recent years contributed to a decline in net NPAs. As SCBs bolstered their capital base by capitalising reserves from higher profits and raising fresh capital, their CRAR increased to 16.8 per cent at the end of March 2024.

As of the end of March 2024, all banks met this as well as the CET-1 ratios requirement of 13.9 per cent, well above the regulatory minimum. The NIM of SCBs remained robust at 3.6 per cent in March 2024. With growing net interest income and other operating income, and as the need for additional provisions fell, their profit after tax rose by 32.5 per cent in March 2024, in spite of a large increase in operating expenses. Profitability indicators remained strong, with RoE and RoA ratios touching decadal highs in March 2024. Lagged effects of transmission of monetary policy rate increases, and shifts in liquidity conditions led to a 100 basis points increase in the cost of funds as against the 75 basis points rise in the yield on assets in FY24. The yield on assets further improved due to the rise in interest rates.[21]

Piyush Goyal, who was holding charge of the finance ministry when Jaitley was in New York for treatment, stated that the banking system was poised for "very good times ahead" and would be able to support the credit needs of the economy.

Bank Consolidation

Indian PSBs have a long history with respect to mergers and acquisitions. Since Independence, the Indian banking sector has undergone sweeping changes. As people gradually shifted away from the unorganised financial system, reliance on formal banking grew steadily. This period also saw the enactment of the Banking Regulation Act, 1949. To build confidence in an organised banking framework and shield the public from the practices of traditional moneylenders, the government undertook major reforms. Fourteen banks were nationalised in 1969, followed by another six in 1980.

---

21. Sumant Batra, *Corporate Insolvency: The Road to Viksit Bharat* (EBC, 2025), pp. 127–29.

With the 1991 liberalisation, privatisation and globalisation reforms, nationalised banks suddenly found themselves competing with private and foreign banks. This intense competition reshaped the industry, compelling institutions to strengthen their operations and enhance customer services. The global recession of 2008 further disrupted economies worldwide. To navigate this crisis, many industries turned to mergers and acquisitions—and the banking sector was no exception.[22]

Jaitley recognised bank mergers as a viable strategy for strengthening the public sector banking landscape. He had already hinted in his first budget speech that a roadmap for consolidation would be spelt out. Consolidation among the PSBs was also on the agenda of P. Chidambaram, finance minister of the previous UPA government, but the government wanted the proposal to come from the banks which never came. A merger between two banks would have cost the job of one of the chief executives, so no one uttered the 'M' word. After 2014, under Jaitley, this strategy was accelerated in a rigorous way.

Jaitley wanted to act only after weaker banks were first made robust; immediate mergers were not feasible if they resulted in "mega weak banks", he believed.[23] Instead, he focused on strengthening individual banks before considering amalgamations. In March 2016, Jaitley announced the formation of an expert group to address the consolidation of PSBs to create stronger, more robust banks. The bankers also supported the proposal of consolidation of banks in order to have strong banks rather than having a numerically large number of banks.[24] PSB chiefs were asked to submit Memorandums of Understanding (MOUs) detailing their strengths, weaknesses, and potential

---

22. Kruti Paritosh Shah and Navjyot Raval, "Recent Merger and Acquisition in Indian Banking Sector: A Study of Merger of Andhra Bank and Corporation Bank with Union Bank of India", International Conference on Multidisciplinary Research and Innovative Practices (November 2021).

23. Nikhat Hetavkar, Abhijit Lele, "Prefer merger among stronger banks: Arun Jaitley", *Business Standard*, accessed September 2025, https://www.business-standard.com/article/economy-policy/prefer-merger-among-stronger-banks-arun-jaitley-117092300062_1.html.

24. "Finance Minister Shri Arun Jaitley: Experts' Group Would Be Set-Up Immediately to Look into All Issues Related to Consolidation of Public Sector Banks to Have Strong Banks; Second Edition of Two Day Bankers' Retreat 'Gyan Sangam 2.0' Concludes", Press Information Bureau, Government of India, 5 March 2026, available at https://dea.gov.in/sites/default/files/FM_GyanSangam2_Bankerretreat.pdf.

merger options, though concrete merger plans were still in development. The government allocated capital based on these analyses.

Arvind Subramanian was of the view that a more radical solution would be necessary to solve the TBS problem. In this case, the government would have to take bold actions such as changing the Banking Companies (Acquisition and Transfer of Undertakings) Act, 1970 (Bank Nationalisation Act)—one of the holy cows of India's socialist past—to allow privatisation of PSBs. So too must the RBI.[25]

In February 2017, the government approved the merger of the SBI's five associate banks—State Bank of Bikaner and Jaipur (SBBJ), State Bank of Hyderabad (SBH), State Bank of Mysore (SBM), State Bank of Patiala (SBP), and State Bank of Travancore (SBT), with the SBI. Later in March, the Cabinet approved the merger of Bharatiya Mahila Bank (BMB) also with the SBI. The SBI first merged State Bank of Saurashtra (SBS) with itself in 2008. Two years later, State Bank of Indore (SBN) was merged with it. The SBI had approved separate schemes of acquisition for SBP and SBH. There were no share swaps or cash outgoes as they were wholly owned by SBI. The merger took effect from 1 April. This six-way mega merger catapulted the country's largest lender to among the top fifty banks globally in terms of assets. It reduced the number of PSBs to twenty-one. Jaitley reiterated that India doesn't need thirty such banks.

In June 2017, a meeting of top bankers with Jaitley, finance ministry officials, and RBI deputy governor was called to take stock of lenders' financial position and speedy resolution of bad assets. Jaitley informed the group that the central government was "actively working" towards consolidation of banks. He did not disclose too much detail because the issue was price sensitive.[26]

In October 2017, a panel headed by Arun Jaitley was set up to evaluate proposals for mergers among state-run banks, taking the long-awaited move a step forward. Piyush Goyal, the minister for coal and railways, and Defence

---

25. Arvind Subramanian, *Of Counsel: The Challenges of the Modi-Jaitley Economy* (Penguin, 2018), pp. 60–65.

26. "Government Actively Working Towards Bank Consolidation: Arun Jaitley", *The Indian Express*, accessed 25 May 2025, https://indianexpress.com/article/business/banking-and-finance/government-actively-working-towards-bank-consolidation-arun-jaitley-4700328/.

Minister Nirmala Sitharaman were the other two members of the panel that would send final proposals to the government and Parliament for approval.

This was the time when India had twenty-one PSBs, which account for more than two-thirds of the country's banking assets. But a surge in bad loans and lower profitability compared with their private sector rivals triggered calls for consolidation among the state lenders.[27] Sanjeev Sanyal, the principal economic advisor at the finance ministry, suggested that the planned consolidation could potentially reduce the number of state-run banks to between ten and fifteen.[28] The consolidation of the PSBs, which then held approximately 70 per cent of the market share and accounted for over 80 per cent of the banking system's NPAs, was intended to enhance their scale and risk-taking capacity. Jaitley aimed to achieve economies of scale, operational efficiency, and improved risk management through these mergers. He said that consolidation was also expected to improve the banks' ability to manage their credit portfolios, including stressed assets. He believed that consolidation would prevent resource duplication and strengthen banks to withstand economic shocks.[29]

Over the years that followed, Indian PSBs were reduced to twelve in number in August 2019. Dena Bank and Vijaya Bank were combined with Bank of Baroda (BOB) on 1 April 2019. BOB became the third-largest bank after the merger. In the same year, ten banks merged into four. United Bank of India as well as Oriental Bank of Commerce were combined with PNB. As a result of this merger, PNB became the second-largest PSB of India in terms of branch network, after the SBI. Syndicate Bank merged with Canara Bank, making Canara Bank the fourth-largest PSB. Andhra Bank and Corporation Bank combined with Union Bank of India, which became the fifth-largest PSB in the country. Allahabad Bank was merged with Indian Bank. It has now become

---

27. "Arun Jaitley to Head Panel to Oversee State Bank Consolidation", Reuters, accessed 25 May 2025, https://www.reuters.com/article/world/arun-jaitley-to-head-panel-to-oversee-state-bank-consolidation-idUSKBN1D15DX/.

28. Ibid.

29. Komal Gupta, "Govt Sets Up Arun Jaitley-panel to Oversee PSU Bank Mergers", *Livemint*, accessed 25 May 2025, https://www.livemint.com/Industry/MdGonwoHu8KgFriWG8HVuI/Govt-sets-up-Arun-Jaitleyled-panel-on-PSU-bank-mergers.html.

the sixth-largest PSB post-merger. Presently, Union Bank of India is the fourth-largest PSB and Canara Bank, the fifth largest.[30]

In this way, Jaitley ensured that the consolidation combined with capital infusions, contributed to the revival of the PSB sector.

Bank Insolvency

One of Jaitley's few disappointments was his inability to shepherd the Financial Resolution and Deposit Insurance (FRDI) Bill, 2017, to its logical conclusion; the bill had to be withdrawn even as it was under review by the JPC. In 2015, after the BLRC submitted its report, discussions around the enactment of the IBC gained momentum. In his third budget (2016–17), Jaitley proposed a similar framework for financial institutions. He said that a systemic vacuum existed with regard to bankruptcy situations in financial firms and that a comprehensive Code on Resolution of Financial Firms would be introduced in Parliament during 2016–17.

The financial sector in India consists of a range of functionaries. These include banks (commercial banks, RRBs, and cooperative banks); non-banking financial institutions; primary dealers; development financial institutions; insurance companies (including life insurance companies, general insurance companies, and reinsurer companies); securities market functionaries (including merchant bankers, venture capital funds, stock exchanges, depositories, depository participants, qualified depository participants, stock brokers, sub-brokers, debenture trustees, and credit rating agencies); provident and pension funds; housing finance companies; and financial market infrastructures.[31]

The resolution of these entities is governed by different mechanisms in different statutes; no unified legislative framework or regulator exists in relation

30. "The public banks in India", *India Forbes*, accessed September 2025, https://www.forbesindia.com/article/explainers/public-sector-banks-in-india/89933/1.

31. Debanshu Mukherjee and Aditya Ayachit, "Resolution of Distressed Financial Institutions: An Overview of Recent Reforms in India", *National Law School Business Law Review*, Vol. 3, No. 1, Article 9 (2017), pp. 129–38, https://repository.nls.ac.in/cgi/viewcontent.cgi?article=1064&context=nlsblr.

to the management of financial sector distress in the Indian context. The RBI enjoys powers to wind up or amalgamate an SCB (other than the PSBs whose statutes empower the central government) under provisions of the Banking Regulation Act, 1949. This Act provides for the resolution of a banking company by compulsory merger, winding-up, or voluntary merger. The compulsory merger route is the most often used method.[32] In such mergers, the RBI applies to the central government for a moratorium on the banking company, then prepares a scheme for merger with another healthy bank, and finally gets the scheme sanctioned by the central government. Alternatively, the central government could also order the acquisition of the undertaking of a banking company under certain circumstances, upon receipt of a report from RBI. The winding-up route provides that the RBI may apply to the high court to wind up a banking company in specific circumstances. Under the voluntary merger route, a scheme for amalgamation approved by a two-thirds majority of shareholders and sanctioned by the RBI could be used to merge two banking companies. The RBI also enjoys similar powers over cooperative banks.[33] Power to supersede the board of directors in the interests of the public or to secure proper management, apply for moratorium, and prepare scheme of amalgamation, liquidation, and appointment of liquidators is provided under the Banking Regulation Act, 1949, and the Bank Nationalisation Acts, 1970/1980 for SCBs.

The resolution mechanism for several Indian PSBs is provided in the statute that has created them. For example, as per the SBI Act, 1955, the SBI can be placed in liquidation only by the order of the central government, and the liquidation would happen in a manner dictated by the government. Similarly, the RRBs Act, 1976, exempts the RRBs from any laws relating to winding up of companies. Instead, the RRBs can be placed in liquidation only by the order of the central government, and the liquidation would happen in a manner dictated by the government. The resolution of insurance companies is governed by the Insurance Act, 1938. The IRDAI has powers to formulate and sanction

---

32. Prashant Saran and Tulasi Gopinath, "Resolution of Weak Banks: The Indian Experience", *Economic & Political Weekly*, Vol. 45, No. 2(2010), p. 54; Prashant Saran and Tulasi Gopinath, "Weak Bank Resolution Framework in India: Thumbs Up or Down?", *Economic & Political Weekly*, Vol. 46, No. 50 (2011), p. 104.

33. S. 2(gg), Deposit Insurance and Credit Guarantee Corporation Act, 1961.

a scheme of amalgamation and transfer, appoint an administrator for the management of the insurance business, and to cancel, reduce, or vary contracts and agreements if it finds that a life insurer is acting in a manner prejudicial to the interests of the policyholders. It may also decide to wind up the company, in accordance with provisions of the Companies Act, 2013 (2013 Act). The other possibility is that the amalgamation is initiated by the parties, or at the behest of the IRDAI itself.[34]

If a Central Recordkeeping Agency (CRA) or a Pension Fund Manager (PFM) is acting in a manner that is prejudicial to the interest of the subscribers, the central government may, on a report from the Pension Fund Regulatory and Development Authority (PFRDA), if it deems fit, appoint an administrator to manage the affairs of the PFM or the CRA under the direction and control of the PFRDA. The PFRDA has powers to make orders for attachment, retention, preservation, interim custody, and sale of any asset or property, which is regulated by the PFRDA Act, 2013; to supersede the governing board or board of directors or management of the intermediary and appoint an administrator to manage the affairs of the intermediary; and to direct the pension funds to transfer the assets, records, documents, and information to another pension fund at its own cost.[35] The RBI Act, 1934, empowers the RBI to supersede the board of a non-banking finance company (NBFC) and appoint an administrator and advisory committee. The RBI can also file an application for winding up of an NBFC under the 2013 Act if the RBI determines that an NBFC is unable to pay its debt, has become disqualified to carry on the business of an NBFC, has been prohibited by the RBI from receiving deposit, or the continuance of an NBFC is detrimental to public interest or depositors.

On 24 March 2011, the Ministry of Finance established the Financial Sector Legislative Reforms Commission (FSLRC) to overhaul and harmonise the laws, rules, and regulations governing the financial sector. The need for such an exercise was evident, as the institutional framework had evolved piecemeal over more than a century. The FSLRC observed that the regulatory landscape

---

34. Pratik Datta, Varun Marwah and Ulka Bhattacharyya, "Resolving Financial Firms in India: The Way Forward", *NUJS Law Review*, Vol. 13, No. 1 (2020), https://www.amsshardul.com/wp-content/uploads/2020/09/13.1-Datta-Marwah-Bhattacharyya.pdf.

35. Ibid.

had become fragmented, marked by gaps, overlaps, inconsistencies, and opportunities for arbitrage.

On 22 March 2013, the FSLRC made detailed recommendations suggesting a complete overhaul of this fragmented resolution regime, with a modern comprehensive law on resolution. The first version of the draft Indian Financial Code provided detailed provisions for setting up a resolution corporation. Another version of the Code updated the provisions. The FSLRC noted that the failure of financial firms was a part of the regenerative process of market economies. However, on account of the disruptive effect of such failures on the economy, adequate mechanisms have to be instituted to allow smooth exit of failing firms. The commission recommended the institution of a resolution corporation which would allow speedy resolution of financial firms like banks, insurance companies, defined benefit pension funds, and payment systems. The FSLRC envisioned that the resolution corporation would have representation from across the financial regulatory architecture and would carry out the resolution process in the interests of protecting the stability and resilience of the financial system and enhancing financial market efficiency through efficient pricing and allocation of risk.[36]

In parallel, an RBI Working Group (WG), instituted in January 2013, recommended the setting up of a single Financial Resolution Authority (FRA) for resolving all financial institutions and financial market infrastructures in coordination with the respective financial regulators in its report in January 2014.[37] The WG highlighted several gaps between the existing resolution powers and options available to the regulators and the Financial Stability Board Key Attributes. The WG acknowledged the importance of a special or separate resolution framework for financial institutions, distinct from the corporate insolvency regime, for such institutions. The WG specified

---

36. Debanshu Mukherjee and Aditya Ayachit, "Resolution of Distressed Financial Institutions: An Overview of Recent Reforms in India", *National Law School Business Law Review*, Vol. 3, No. 1, Article 9 (2017), pp. 129–38, https://repository.nls.ac.in/cgi/viewcontent.cgi?article=1064&context=nlsblr.

37. "Report of the Working Group on Resolution Regime for Financial Institutions", RBI, Chaired by Dr Arvind Mayaram and Anand Sinha (January 2014), available at https://dea.gov.in/sites/default/files/Report%20of%20the%20Working%20Group%20on%20Resolution%20Regime%20for%20Financial%20Institutions%20.pdf.

that the special regime should extend to all financial institutions—banks as well as non-banking financial institutions—and be robust enough to address failures of small and medium financial institutions as well as failures of large, complex financial institutions. It recommended creating a dedicated "Financial Resolution Authority" to manage the resolution of all financial institutions. This body would need a robust toolkit—such as liquidation, purchase-and-assumption transactions, bridge institutions, good-bank/bad-bank mechanisms, bail-ins, and temporary public ownership—along with the powers to act swiftly and intervene early when an institution showed signs of distress. Government takeover was advised only as a last resort. To enable timely regulatory action, the Commission also proposed a PCA framework with graded, pre-defined triggers.[38]

After the NDA came to power in the Centre, Jaitley set up a committee under the chairmanship of Ajay Tyagi, the then additional secretary of the DEA, to draft and submit the bill. This was in March 2016. The Tyagi committee submitted its report in September 2016; the draft FRDI Bill was drawn up based on the recommendations of this committee. Public comments were invited until 31 October 2016. After considering the suggestions, the Cabinet approved the introduction of the FRDI Bill. Jaitley introduced the FRDI Bill in the Parliament on 10 August 2017. The bill was referred to the JPC. However, it received pushback from a few stakeholders for some of its provisions, including a "bail-in" clause that allowed appropriation of deposits over and above the insured amount. The Opposition termed some of the bill's provisions "anti-people" and "anti-poor", and pointed out that people's money would be used to bail out banks that make bad lending decisions through a corresponding reduction in the claims of depositors.

Jaitley was convinced that the bill sought to protect customers of financial service providers in times of financial distress; it would also help to encourage discipline among the financial service providers by putting a limit on the use of public money to bail out distressed entities.

38. Sikha Bansal and Timothy Lopes, "Resolution Regime for Systemic Financial Firms: The IBC Way or the Other Way?", in *IBC: Idea, Impressions and Implementation* (IBBI, 2022), pp. 137–52, available at https://ibbi.gov.in/uploads/publication/b5fba368fbd5c5817333f95fbb0d48bb.pdf.

I was invited by the JPC to give evidence before it as an expert witness. Deliberations before the JPC being confidential, I cannot reveal the details of my expert testimony given under oath; however, it would be safe to say I supported the bill while offering suggestions for its improvement. To us, criticism stemmed from a lack of complete understanding of the bill's provisions. The FRDI Bill was based on global best practices.

Everyone has long been used to the word "bailout", where governments step in to protect the interests of savers or depositors—like in the United Kingdom when there was a run on the deposits of banks such as Northern Rock, Lloyds Bank, or Royal Bank of Scotland (RBS). There were cases in the United States and other parts of Europe, too. The fact that huge public funds were used for such support, and the criticism that bailouts incentivised bank managements to take risky bets—called "moral hazard" by economists—led governments to seek other solutions. Regulators put in place laws and rules to discourage or prevent such bailouts with new resolution regimes. Losses of these financial firms had to be borne by shareholders and creditors rather than taxpayers.

One of the tools for such a resolution is "bail-in". It allows resolution agencies to override the rights of the shareholders of the firm—this could mean writing down of a company's equity and debt to absorb losses, or converting debt into equity. This could also mean overriding requirements such as approvals by shareholders and disposing of the firm's assets. The Group of Twenty (G20) at its Cannes Summit in 2011 endorsed some of the key attributes of such a form of resolution by "bail-in". In other words, deposit holders do not have any superior claims. The principal aim, of course, is to minimise the cost of any such failures of financial firms to taxpayers. The other objective, as the EU's Bank Recovery and Resolution Directive, 2014, indicates, is that the shareholders of banks and creditors must also pay their share of costs, rather than governments or taxpayers absorbing all losses. The Bank of England (the central bank of the United Kingdom) has been pushing banks in the United Kingdom to set aside more funds to cover for potential failures. The aim, the UK central bank said, is to ensure banks no longer remain "too big to fail", and to make sure that the risks that banks take are properly priced by investors who know they will suffer if things go wrong.[39]

---

39. Shaji Vikraman, "FRDI Bill: Understanding the Basis of Bail-In, and Depositors' Fear", *The Indian Express*, accessed 25 May 2025, https://indianexpress.com/article/

The government vociferously defended the provisions of the bill for months, pointing out that the "bail-in" clause will not adversely impact depositors. The government maintained that the implicit sovereign guarantee for state-run banks would remain unaffected. Prime Minister Narendra Modi had also sought to assure people that the bill was consumer-friendly and would protect the public's deposits.[40]

Jaitley had to travel to the United States for his treatment. Piyush Goyal was asked to hold the fort for Jaitley; he was given charge of the finance ministry. Before Jaitley returned in the third week of August, the bill was withdrawn. Piyush Goyal informed the JPC that the resolution of these issues would require a comprehensive examination and reconsideration. Jaitley was disappointed that a critical component of the financial sector reform—a robust insolvency resolution system for financial institutions—had to be dropped. So was I. Had he been around, he would have persuaded the prime minister to make tweaks in the bill to address any concern rather than withdraw it.

The failure of FIs can cause disruption and major negative externalities, such as a liquidity crunch, the fire sale of assets, and spillovers via the interbank market.[41] The need for a specialised resolution framework for systemic financial entities has been emphasised unequivocally by experts, global institutions and authorities.

In its 98th session, the Governing Council of the International Institute for the Unification of Private Laws (UNIDROIT) agreed to recommend to the General Assembly to include the project on Bank Insolvency in the Work Programme with medium priority. The assigned level of priority was merely formal. The Council asked the Secretariat to conduct further research and provide a more defined scope for the project, as well as further justification of its adequacy as work to be conducted by a global institution.

Pursuant to the Governing Council's mandate, the UNIDROIT Secretariat canvassed international support, conducted legal research and organised an Exploratory Workshop on Bank Insolvency together with the BIS Financial

---

explained/frdi-bill-understanding-the-basis-of-bail-in-and-depositors-fear-4977004/.

40. Ibid.

41. Martin Cihak and Erlend Nier, "The Need for Special Resolution Regimes for Financial Institutions—The Case of the European Union", available at <https://www.elibrary.imf.org/ view/journals/001/2009/200/001.2009.issue-200-en.xml>.

Institute in June 2021. Drawing from the conclusions of the Exploratory Workshop and thorough additional research, at the Governing Council's 100th session in September 2021, the Secretariat presented a detailed account of the feasibility analysis and exploratory work conducted for the project. On that occasion, the Council approved the proposed scope of the project, subject to existing regulatory standards and underlining its focus on smaller banks, agreed to recommend upgrading the project's priority, and authorised the Secretariat to establish a Working Group.

The UNIDROIT project on Bank Insolvency aims at addressing the current gap in the international legal architecture by developing an international soft law instrument covering the key features of bank liquidation proceedings. The UNIDROIT Guidance Document on Bank Insolvency was adopted by the UNIDROIT Governing Council at its 105th session held in May 2025 The RBI was a member of the UNIDROIT working group. I attended UNIDROIT sessions as an observer.[42]

With the UNIDROIT Guidance Document on Bank Insolvency having been framed, the enactment of a law to deal with resolution of financial corporations in India will be a befitting tribute to Jaitley.

---

42. Sumant Batra, *Corporate Insolvency: The Road to Viksit Bharat* (EBC, 2025), pp. 959–67.

26

Managing Demonetisation

At 8 p.m. on 8 November 2016, Prime Minister Narendra Modi delivered an unanticipated address to the nation. The last time the government had made a surprise announcement, the world woke up to the news that Army troops had crossed the Line of Control and carried out high-risk "surgical strikes" behind enemy lines. But that declaration took place in the morning, unlike Prime Minister Modi's 8 November address. Modi said that he wanted to "make a special request" to Indian citizens. "There comes a time in the history of a country's development when a need is felt for a strong and decisive step," he said.

He went on to announce the demonetisation of Rs 1000 and Rs 500 notes with effect from midnight, making these notes invalid. Instead, Indians would get fifty days (until 31 December) to deposit the demonetised currency into their accounts. Automated Teller Machines (ATMs) would be recalibrated to dispense the new, smaller and more plastic-looking Rs 500 and Rs 2000 currency notes. In his speech Modi said that the primary motives for the demonetisation were threefold: to eradicate black money, to remove counterfeit currency, and to stop terror financing.

An article on the BBC portal later termed it as the "great Indian demonetisation" of 2016, and said it would rank among the most impactful economic policy decisions of any country in recent history.[1] Having made

---

1. Parveen Chakravarty, "Viewpoint: Modi's Currency Gamble Damaged Indian Economy", BBC, accessed 25 May 2025, https://www.bbc.com/news/world-asia-

the historic announcement, Modi embarked on a three-day state visit to Japan the next morning.

The press release, issued on 8 November 2016 soon after the address, stated that the decision was made to "... curb financing of terrorism through the proceeds of Fake Indian Currency Notes and use of such funds for subversive activities such as espionage, smuggling of arms, drugs and other contrabands into India, and for eliminating Black Money which casts a long shadow of parallel economy on our real economy...".[2]

Notably, even during the two previous episodes of the demonetisation of high-value notes over Rs 100 in India, on 12 January 1946 and on 16 January 1978, the express objective of the exercise was to contain black marketing or black money. The official announcement in 1946 stated, "The working capital of black market operations is believed to be held in large measure in the form of high denomination notes and the government is aware of the persistent public demand for effective action against these enemies of public welfare." In 1978, the High Denomination Bank Notes (Demonetisation) Act, 1978, which followed the ordinance of the same name on 16 January 1978 demonetising Rs 1000, Rs 5000, and Rs 10,000 notes, also stated that the action was needed because such high-denomination banknotes facilitate "... the illicit transfer of money for financing transactions which are harmful to the national economy or which are for illegal purposes".[3]

It is widely believed that Narendra Modi got the idea of demonetisation, which led to the withdrawal of 86 per cent of the Indian currency in circulation on 8 November 2016, from Anil Bokil, a member of Pune-based think tank,

---

india-41896865.

2. Ministry of Finance, 8 November, 2016, "With a view to curb financing of terrorism through the proceeds of Fake Indian Currency Notes (FICN) and use of such funds for subversive activities, and for eliminating Black Money, Government decides to cancel the legal tender character of the High Denomination bank notes of Rs 500 and Rs 1000 from the expiry of the 8th November, 2016", accessed on 5 September 2025, https://www.pib.gov.in/newsite/erelcontent.aspx?relid=153406.

3. Ashok K. Lahiri, "Demonetization, the Cash Shortage and the Black Money", NIPFP Working Paper Series, Working Paper No. 184 (December 2016), available at https://www.nipfp.org.in/media/medialibrary/2016/12/WP_2016_184.pdf.

Arthakranti Pratishthan (Institution for Economic Revolution).[4] This idea of "lightning strike on black money", a phrase coined by then Chief Economic Advisor Arvind Subramanian, was presented to Modi in July 2013, when he was the chief minister of Gujarat. His decision to go through with it as the prime minister has been termed one of the unlikeliest economic experiments in modern Indian history.

The idea of demonetisation was not new in the BJP's economic thinking. The Jana Sangh, BJP's predecessor, on two occasions, on 18 November 1972 and 16 July 1973, had passed economic resolutions specifically demanding that the Congress government take recourse to demonetisation. Atal Bihari Vajpayee, Jana Sangh president at the time, had contemplated it as far back as 1971. He announced that his party would demonetise currency to eliminate black money if it was voted to power. From the mid-1960s to the mid-1970s, three future prime ministers of India—Vajpayee, I.K. Gujral, and Chandra Shekhar—had demanded demonetisation during parliamentary debates on the economy. For almost a decade (1967–74), the idea enjoyed such cross-party support that it regularly featured in the parliamentary questioning of finance ministers after the presentation of the annual budget.[5] The state government of Uttar Pradesh, led by Charan Singh and consisting of an anti-Congress coalition that included the Jana Sangh, even passed a Cabinet resolution on 3 July 1967 demanding that Prime Minister Indira Gandhi demonetise all currency notes above Rs 10 to arrest the deterioration in the economy.

These debates formed the political backdrop for the Union government's appointment of a committee, led by a distinguished bureaucrat, K.N. Wanchoo, to study the problem of black money. The Wanchoo Committee Report (1971), kept secret for a few months but later presented to Parliament, unanimously recommended demonetisation. Through the 1970s, this idea took such a hold of the country's political imagination that even several prominent Congress leaders—a group of 100 AICC members, the West Bengal Pradesh Congress

---

4. Rohit David, Interview with Anil Bokil in "Demonetisation Being Addressed Partially ... Replace Flawed Taxation System with Banking Transaction Tax", *The Times of India*, accessed 25 May 2025, https://timesofindia.indiatimes.com/blogs/the-interviews-blog/demonetisation-being-addressed-partially-replace-flawed-taxation-system-with-banking-transaction-tax/.

5. Nalin Mehta, *The New BJP: Modi and the Making of the World's Largest Political Party* (Westland, 2022), pp. 268–276.

Committee, and a number of ruling-party MPs—demanded it, foreshadowing the debate around Modi's 2016 decision.

This shows how powerful the idea of demonetisation was for the early Jana Sangh and other Opposition parties in the 1970s, the decade in which Narendra Modi came of age as an RSS pracharak. It is not unreasonable that he would have been familiar with this history when, as a state government head four decades later, he was presented with a demonetisation proposal.[6] This could well have played a role in influencing his decision as the prime minister to attempt uncovering billions of dollars in undeclared wealth.

★

A flurry of rumours began circulating almost immediately after the announcement. Foremost among them was the claim that Jaitley had been kept out of the loop on demonetisation. His friends in the media—long accustomed to receiving discreet tip-offs from their favourite source—struggled to believe he had concealed something of this scale from them. Though Jaitley engaged openly with journalists, he guarded official secrets with equal intensity; he understood precisely where private camaraderie ended and public responsibility began. This time, however, the media misread his silence on demonetisation as proof that Modi had not taken him into confidence.

Jaitley's critics within the party fuelled the narrative that the finance minister had been left out of the loop. He made no attempt to counter these claims, viewing a public clarification as beneath his dignity. Meanwhile, the PMO, the finance ministry, and the RBI all rejected requests filed under the Right to Information Act, 2005, seeking to determine whether Jaitley had been consulted prior to the demonetisation announcement. Privately, Jaitley rubbished the rumours.[7] The air was cleared by power minister Piyush Goyal. While speaking at the annual Hindustan Times Leadership Summit conference in New Delhi

---

6. Ibid.

7. Jayanta Roy Chowdhury, "Figures Who Became Public Faces of the Demonetisation Implementation", *The Telegraph Online*, accessed 25 May 2025, https://www.telegraphindia.com/india/figures-who-became-public-faces-of-the-demonetisation-implementation/cid/1514810.

on 3 December 2016, Piyush Goyal said that Jaitley knew it and kept it a secret despite being "very friendly and open. ... This is the kind of commitment a tall leader has ... when the time comes, they keep [an important information] secret from everybody."[8]

Not only was he aware of the decision before the announcement was made, Jaitley was part of the core group which worked on demonetisation, and also made responsible for piloting it.[9] When asked by a close friend, he quipped, "Do you think such a thing is possible? Can the country's finance minister be kept out of such an exercise?" The friend, an influential journalist, cross-checked this with her sources in the PMO who confirmed that Arun Jaitley was very much part of the plan.[10]

When the idea was first mooted in early 2016, RBI Governor Raghuram Rajan wasn't enthused by the idea. In his book *I Do What I Do*, he wrote that he was asked for his opinion in February 2016 at one of the customary meetings held just days before the budget was to be presented in Parliament by Jaitley. "I was then asked to prepare a note, which the RBI put together and handed to the government. It outlined the potential costs and benefits of demonetisation." There were preliminary discussions before that eventful meeting, but it was after the budget that the process began in earnest.[11] There was some discussion about announcing demonetisation in the budget speech. But it soon became clear that the process required extensive preparation to ensure that both demonetisation and subsequent remonetisation unfolded as smoothly as possible.[12]

---

8. PTI, "Finance Minister Knew about Demonetisation", *The Hindu*, accessed 25 May 2025, https://www.thehindu.com/news/national/%E2%80%98Finance-Minister-knew-about-demonetisation%E2%80%99/article16757097.ece.

9. Jayanta Roy Chowdhury, "Figures Who Became Public Faces of the Demonetisation Implementation", *The Telegraph Online*, accessed 25 May 2025, https://www.telegraphindia.com/india/figures-who-became-public-faces-of-the-demonetisation-implementation/cid/1514810.

10. Kumkum Chadha, *The Marigold Story: Indira Gandhi & Others* (Westland, 2019), p. 335.

11. Raghuram G. Rajan, *I Do What I Do* (Harper Business, 2017).

12. Anand Mishra, "First Discussed Note Ban with RBI in Feb 2016: Shaktikanta Das", *The Indian Express*, accessed 25 May 2025, https://indianexpress.com/article/india/first-discussed-note-ban-with-rbi-in-feb-2016-shaktikanta-das-4535425/.

Jaitley also wanted to examine carefully the legal consequences of demonetisation and its impact on the economy before any decision was taken.[13] As a keen student of constitutional history, Jaitley knew that in 1978, the Janata government had brought a law to scrap high-denomination notes. He was mindful that if he brought in an ordinance on 8 November demonetising Rs 500 and Rs 1000 notes, he would have to bring a law backing the ordinance when Parliament met later that month, giving the Opposition a chance to debate the move and possibly pick holes in it. Being a lawyer, he studied the matter to ensure it would stand scrutiny in courts of law. He decided to use a little-used provision in the RBI Act to issue a simple notification.[14]

Having planned the legal path, Jaitley brought on board Urjit Patel who had replaced Rajan at the RBI. That was quintessential Jaitley, a clever lawyer and strategist at his best plotting India's biggest-ever monetary gambit. In the meantime, from March to April 2016 onward, the government and RBI had very active internal discussions.[15]

Shaktikanta Das, who was the secretary of the DEA in the finance ministry, was entrusted with making the demonetisation drive a success, including conducting studies on its possible impact.[16] Hasmukh Adhia, an enthusiastic supporter of the demonetisation measure, worked closely with Modi and Jaitley. Secretary of financial services, Anjuly Chib Duggal, was also part of the team. The RBI attended the meetings with the core group through the summer.[17] All this time, the core group kept the matter a closely guarded secret. Secrecy was the key to its success.

---

13. Discussions with Jaitley's friend who did not wish his name to be revealed.

14. Jayanta Roy Chowdhury, "Figures Who Became Public Faces of the Demonetisation Implementation", *The Telegraph Online*, accessed 25 May 2025, https://www.telegraphindia.com/india/figures-who-became-public-faces-of-the-demonetisation-implementation/cid/1514810.

15. Anand Mishra, "First Discussed Note Ban with RBI in Feb 2016: Shaktikanta Das", *The Indian Express*, accessed 25 May 2025, https://indianexpress.com/article/india/first-discussed-note-ban-with-rbi-in-feb-2016-shaktikanta-das-4535425/.

16. Das was appointed as the twenty-fifth governor of RBI in December 2018. On finishing his term, Das was appointed principal secretary to the prime minister in February 2025.

17. Raghuram G. Rajan, *I Do What I Do* (Harper Business, 2017).

Even within the core group, members were not always aware of each detail—Rajan's note was not mentioned in the meetings.[18] The core group also worked on the detailed road map of the plan. A major pre-demonetisation question was whether RBI could stockpile extra Rs 100 and Rs 50 notes to ease the cash crunch after withdrawing high-value currency. However, logistical hurdles ruled this out—any sudden spike in printing would have been obvious to staff, whether at modern facilities like Mysuru and Salboni or older presses in Nashik and Dewas.

The timing of the announcement was another critical decision. Officials considered a post-Diwali window, as the festive rush would have subsided, but the final date—8 November—was chosen just weeks prior. There was also a proposal to delay it to a Friday, giving banks the weekend to prepare. Despite tight secrecy, speculation was growing. For instance, during the monsoon Parliament session, nearly 8 per cent of the Rajya Sabha questions to the finance ministry were about black money—more than those on the PSBs—hinting at impending action.[19] Once the political storm had seemingly passed, Jaitley approached the Cabinet to clear an ordinance.[20]

Roughly twenty-four hours before 8 November, the prime minister's core group briefed the heads of the security agencies, including the Intelligence Bureau. Officers lower down the chain were informed only a few hours before the announcement. It was a calculated risk, debated within the core group and ultimately approved. There was no turning back now; India had entered uncharted territory. Before the prime minister went live on Doordarshan, the decision needed the approval of at least one Cabinet body. The natural choice

---

18. Subhomoy Bhattacharjee, "Backroom Story of Demonetisation: From PMO to RBI, How It All Played Out", *Business Standard*, accessed 25 May 2025, https://www.business-standard.com/amp/article/economy-policy/backroom-story-of-demonetisation-from-pmo-to-rbi-how-it-all-played-out-117110700044_1.html.

19. Subhomoy Bhattacharjee, "Backroom Story of Demonetisation: From PMO to RBI, How It All Played Out", *Business Standard*, accessed 25 May 2025, https://www.business-standard.com/amp/article/economy-policy/backroom-story-of-demonetisation-from-pmo-to-rbi-how-it-all-played-out-117110700044_1.html.

20. Jayanta Roy Chowdhury, "Figures Who Became Public Faces of the Demonetisation Implementation", *The Telegraph Online*, accessed 25 May 2025, https://www.telegraphindia.com/india/figures-who-became-public-faces-of-the-demonetisation-implementation/cid/1514810.

was the Cabinet Committee on Security, where the finance minister and the home minister had been steering the exercise over the past year.[21] The defence and foreign ministers, too, needed to be briefed, especially as there would be questions from around the world about demonetisation.

The government made a reference to RBI on 7 November, requesting it to place the matter before the RBI Central Board for consideration. The RBI considered the matter at a meeting of its Central Board on 8 November and gave its nod, hours before the prime minister's announcement.[22] Rumour mills were working full time by then. The list of possible experts who arrived around 7.30 p.m. surprised everyone. There were no security or military experts. Instead, plenty of economists, within and outside the government, filled up the list. Ten joint secretaries had assembled in Shaktikanta Das's room for a review meeting on the evening of 8 November but did not know the purpose.[23] Half an hour later, the prime minister announced demonetisation.[24]

As the cameras began rolling at the prime minister's residence, both Revenue Secretary Hasmukh Adhia and former Economic Affairs Secretary Shaktikanta Das, who were part of the core group, were back at their offices. The core group formed a committee of these joint secretaries and tasks were assigned to them to coordinate with various state governments to look after ATM supplies and other aspects of the remonetisation process.[25] With the prime minister's voice filling up the room, the officers were handed out their assigned duties.

---

21. Subhomoy Bhattacharjee, "Backroom Story of Demonetisation: From PMO to RBI, How It All Played Out", *Business Standard*, accessed 25 May 2025, https://www.business-standard.com/amp/article/economy-policy/backroom-story-of-demonetisation-from-pmo-to-rbi-how-it-all-played-out-117110700044_1.html.

22. Anand Mishra, "First Discussed Note Ban with RBI in Feb 2016: Shaktikanta Das", *The Indian Express*, accessed 25 May 2025, https://indianexpress.com/article/india/first-discussed-note-ban-with-rbi-in-feb-2016-shaktikanta-das-4535425/.

23. Ibid.

24. Subhomoy Bhattacharjee, "Backroom Story of Demonetisation: From PMO to RBI, How It All Played Out", *Business Standard*, accessed 25 May 2025, https://www.business-standard.com/amp/article/economy-policy/backroom-story-of-demonetisation-from-pmo-to-rbi-how-it-all-played-out-117110700044_1.html.

25. Anand Mishra, "First Discussed Note Ban with RBI in Feb 2016: Shaktikanta Das", *The Indian Express*, accessed 25 May 2025, https://indianexpress.com/article/india/first-discussed-note-ban-with-rbi-in-feb-2016-shaktikanta-das-4535425/.

Calls to the police chiefs and chief secretaries in state governments began to go out. It was going to be a long night.[26]

After Prime Minister Narendra Modi announced on 8 November that the old high-denomination notes would cease to be legal tender, Jaitley promptly updated his Facebook status to: "India cannot afford to live with black money any longer. Honesty, integrity and ethical conduct are requirements of India's development."[27] Das and Adhia enthusiastically greeted the measure on social media. Adhia tweeted from his handle: "This is the biggest and the boldest step by the government for containing black money. It is like a surgical strike on black money."[28]

★

After 9 November 2016, which was declared a bank holiday, the withdrawn Rs 500 and Rs 1,000 notes could be deposited—with valid identification—into bank or post office accounts without any limit until 30 December 2016. They could also be exchanged for the new Rs 500 or Rs 2,000 notes, or for the existing Rs 5, Rs 10, Rs 20, Rs 50, and Rs 100 denominations, though initially only up to Rs 4000.[29] This limit was increased to Rs 4500 on 14 November, before such

---

26. Subhomoy Bhattacharjee, "Backroom Story of Demonetisation: From PMO to RBI, How It All Played Out", *Business Standard*, accessed 25 May 2025, https://www.business-standard.com/amp/article/economy-policy/backroom-story-of-demonetisation-from-pmo-to-rbi-how-it-all-played-out-117110700044_1.html.

27. "India can no longer live with black money: Arun Jaitley", Deccan Chronicle, accessed September 2025, https://www.deccanchronicle.com/nation/current-affairs/161116/india-can-no-longer-live-with-black-money-arun-jaitley.html.

28. "Withdrawal of Rs 500, Rs 1000 notes surgical strike on black money: Revenue Secretary", *Mint*, accessed September 2025, https://www.livemint.com/Politics/Oh6wVyxADAGSQxqQ9gOcRK/Withdrawal-of-Rs500-Rs1000-notes-surgical-strike-on-black-m.html.

29. The Government Press Release of 8 November 2016 stated: "(i) Old High Denomination Bank Notes may be deposited by individuals/persons into their bank accounts and/or exchanged in bank branches or Issue Offices of RBI till the close of business hours on 30th December, 2016. (ii) Old High Denomination Bank Notes of aggregate value of Rs 4000 only or below held by a person can be exchanged by him/her at any bank branch or Issue Office of Reserve Bank of India for any

direct exchange was stopped from 25 November 2016.[30] Furthermore, there was a warning that all the cash deposited in an account during the period of 10 November 2016 to 30 December 2016 above a threshold of Rs 2.5 lakh would be matched with the income tax returns filed.[31]

On 28 November 2016, the government introduced the Taxation Laws (Second Amendment) Bill, 2016, in the Lok Sabha.[32] When cash deposited in a bank or post office account could not be reconciled with the assessee's tax returns, the proposed tax burden was raised substantially—from a flat 30 per cent plus surcharge and cess to 60 per cent tax plus a 25 per cent surcharge on that tax, amounting to a total of 75 per cent, along with an additional penalty of 10 per cent of the tax and surcharge, adding another 7.5 per cent.

The proposal also introduced the Taxation and Investment Regime under the Pradhan Mantri Garib Kalyan Yojana, 2016 (PMGKY), offering individuals a chance to declare unaccounted income, pay a steep penalty, and regularise their holdings. Under this scheme, the effective tax rate on the declared amount would be 50 per cent, and 25 per cent of the disclosed income would be locked in for four years in an interest-free government deposit.[33]

---

denomination of bank notes having legal tender character, provided a Requisition Slip as per format to be specified by RBI is presented with proof of identity and along with the Old High Denomination Bank Notes. Similar facilities will also be made available in Post Offices." Available at https://www.pib.gov.in/newsite/erelcontent.aspx?relid=153406.

30. The government press release of 8 November 2016 stated that the limit of Rs 4000 on the exchange of old high-denomination banknotes for other valid ones would be "reviewed after 15 days and appropriate notification issued, as may be necessary". The government press release of 24 November 2016 stated that there will be no over-the-counter exchange of old Rs 500 and Rs 1000 notes after midnight of 24 November 2016. Available at https://docs.google.com/document/d/1i2PicQQQJH-f8iJvstOSz2p8aSXy7ISED6uzJeFCy8Y/edit?tab=t.0.

31. PTI, "Deposits Above Rs 2.5 Lakh to Face Tax, Penalty on Mismatch", *The Economic Times*, accessed 25 May 2025, http://economictimes.indiatimes.com/wealth/personal-finance-news/deposits-above-rs-2-5-lakh-to-facetax-penalty-on-mismatch/articleshow/55337775.cms.

32. Press Release, Government of India, Ministry of Finance, 28 November 2016, accessed September 2025, https://www.pib.gov.in/newsite/erelcontent.aspx?relid=154450

33. Ashok K. Lahiri, "Demonetization, the Cash Shortage and the Black Money", NIPFP Working Paper Series, Working Paper No. 184 (December 2016), available at

Alongside demonetisation, limits were placed on over-the-counter cash withdrawals from bank and post office accounts—Rs 10,000 per day, subject to a weekly cap of Rs 20,000 during the first fortnight. On 25 November 2016, this was revised to a single limit of Rs 24,000 per week with no daily sub-limit. ATM withdrawals were initially capped at Rs 2000 per account per day until 13 November, after which the limit was raised to Rs 2500. For a period, a shortage of small-denomination coins was also reported.

With the demonetisation making landfall, Jaitley set up a war room in his ministry. There were legal, economic, and political consequences which would need to be dealt with. Jaitley was at the forefront of managing on all fronts. About 90 per cent of transactions in India were made in cash in those times. Rs 500 and Rs 1000 notes made up 86 per cent of all cash in circulation at the time. Even as Prime Minister Modi continued his speech, listing out the salient points of how his government and RBI would carry out the demonetisation exercise, people scurried to ATMs, and made frantic calls to understand what was essentially a new world order for India. Huge queues were forming at banks when they reopened after a short holiday. Filling ATMs with eight trillion rupees ($117 billion) in new banknotes to restore liquidity to the economy was even trickier. New Rs 2000 notes were hard to come by and barely any new Rs 500 notes had been printed. India's 200,000 cash dispensers could not handle the new smaller notes and it would take weeks to reconfigure them. Demonetisation forced millions to stand in queues in front of banks as they tried to exchange the banned currency. Even for the withdrawal of the limited sums, there were long queues and endless waits outside banks. The withdrawal of such large cash from the system meant a mammoth operation, affecting nearly everyone in India and beyond. Tempers frayed as hundreds of thousands of people queued for hours outside banks for a third day. Newspapers, Indian and foreign, flashed pictures of serpentine queues outside banks and ATMs seen across the country.[34] Nobel Laureate Amartya Sen criticised the decision.

---

https://www.nipfp.org.in/media/medialibrary/2016/12/WP_2016_184.pdf.

34. "Anger Intensifies Over India's Demonetisation Move", Aljazeera, accessed 25 May 2025, https://www.aljazeera.com/economy/2016/11/17/anger-intensifies-over-indias-demonetisation-move.

As the hue and cry about the failure of demonetisation grew, rumour mills went into overdrive about Arun Jaitley being shown the door.[35]

Unfazed by newspaper criticism, on 11 November 2016, a determined Jaitley appeared before the media and announced it would take time for banks to make changes to ATMs to dispense the new banknotes. He defended ATMs not having enough cash; the machines had not been calibrated before the demonetisation announcement to maintain secrecy. He continued, "It is a massive operation, it will take time."

The banking system was fully equipped to deal with the currency shake-up. The SBI had received Rs 47,868 crore in deposits since the withdrawal of Rs 500 and Rs 1000 notes was announced on 8 November. Total deposits in all the banks were around Rs 2–2.25 lakh crore.

He appealed to the public and stated, "Don't rush to banks right now for exchanging or withdrawing old Rs 500 or Rs 1000 notes as there are massive crowds. Wait for a few days as the scheme is open till December 30. It will take 2–3 weeks to update the hardware and software of ATMs to dispense the new currency because it is a 'long-drawn' process. Customers shouldn't demand a choice of currency at the banks because there may be a shortage. They should accept whatever currency they are getting."[36] He also warned gold traders transacting in old currency; "...the government will monitor any Jan Dhan accounts with suspicious activity," he said. "People should move more and more to cashless transactions as they make life simple," he advised. He also dispelled rumours around new Rs 2000 notes. "GPS chip in Rs 2000 note, reports of digital lockers are rumours," he said.

On 13 November 2016, Rajat Sharma hosted Arun Jaitley as a guest on his widely watched show Aap Ki Adalat. This marked Jaitley's first interview since the demonetisation move. Following the show's format, Sharma invited the finance minister to take the witness stand and respond to "charges", while introducing journalist Vijay Sanghvi as the guest "judge". The segment began

---

35. Kumkum Chadha, *The Marigold Story: Indira Gandhi & Others* (Westland, 2019), p. 336.

36. Dhrubo Jyoti, "No Need to Rush: 10 Things Finance Minister Jaitley Said About Demonetisation", *Hindustan Times*, accessed 25 May 2025, https://www.hindustantimes.com/india-news/don-t-rush-to-deposit-scrapped-notes-10-things-jaitley-said-about-demonetisation/story-0MSTsVfbfwjLcRvAhFCBVM.html.

with a narrated overview of Jaitley's political journey, highlighting his close ties with Narendra Modi and his support during the "dark days of the 2002 riots". Seated in a wooden witness box designed to resemble a courtroom, Jaitley defended the government's demonetisation policy against criticism that it had caused "public harassment", had hurt small traders, and was politically motivated ahead of state elections.

Amid occasional applause from the audience, he reiterated the official stance—that the move would benefit the public in the long run by curbing black money. Sharma did not press him on how this domestic measure would address illicit wealth stored overseas. After an hour of discussion, the "judge" delivered his verdict, stating that Jaitley's explanations were "worth thinking about" and required no further debate. The "judge" also echoed Jaitley's push for digital payments, suggesting the government lower credit-card interest rates.[37]

The episode aired in prime time on India TV, reaching a vast audience. That week, according to the Broadcast Audience Research Council, India TV's viewership was 169 times higher than that of the leading English news channel, Times Now. Among Hindi news channels, India TV ranked second only to Aaj Tak in popularity.[38]

Daily new rules emanated from Jaitley's office over the next few months to deal with the fallout of demonetisation. Shaktikanta Das became the mascot for the drive, fielding questions and holding hurriedly called media conferences to announce rule changes. Hasmukh Adhia managed the backroom planning.

Demonetisation of Rs 500 and Rs 1000 notes in India was different from many other countries' scrapping of high-value notes in two respects—the withdrawal of their legal tender status and continuation with Rs 1000 and Rs 2000 notes.[39] This resulted in a cash shortage. India was a cash-dominated economy. With supplies only from the domestic currency presses, the shortage

---

37. India TV, "Finance Minister Arun Jaitley in *Aap Ki Adalat*—2016", accessed 25 May 2025, https://www.youtube.com/watch?v=1Ob8Ox3ojlk.

38. Atul Dev and Praveen Donthi, "Our Man in the Studio", *Caravan Magazine*, accessed 2 May 2025, https://caravanmagazine.in/reportage/man-studio-rajat-sharma-india-tv.

39. Ashok K. Lahiri, "Demonetization, the Cash Shortage and the Black Money", NIPFP Working Paper Series, Working Paper No. 184 (December 2016), available at https://www.nipfp.org.in/media/medialibrary/2016/12/WP_2016_184.pdf.

was unlikely to disappear by the end of 2016. The impact of the shortage, if it continued, would be fully felt in the last quarter of 2016–17. Das worked closely with the RBI to streamline the printing of new currency notes, and coordinated with other government departments to ensure adequate supply of notes across India, becoming the face of the government during the demonetisation drive.

All this time, Das was also playing a key role under Jaitley's guidance on GST reform which was set to rollout on 1 July 2017; Das was instrumental in coordinating with the states to ensure the successful implementation of the GST. The mild-mannered bureaucrat had the knack of getting things done without being confrontational, a trait he shared with his boss Jaitley. Both made a formidable team together with Adhia, another confidante of Modi. Modi's office monitored the progress hands-on.

★

Jaitley clarified to the people that the aim of demonetisation was not to confiscate the currency; it was a frontal attack on black money and an opportunity for digitisation of the economy, and brought into the fold a mass of assessees in the tax net, who evaded tax by transacting in cash economy. Getting it into the formal economy and making the holders pay tax was the broader objective, he wrote in his blog.[40] The system required to be shaken in order to make India move from cash to digital transactions.[41]

Jaitley admitted that demonetisation was painful but it was necessary to create the psychological milieu for the war against black money to start. It was necessary to squeeze cash to prevent generation of more black money. "You have to squeeze cash because black money generates more black money. Not whatever is in assets is a matter of assessment by the income tax authorities. But whatever is lying in hard cash so that it does not generate anything for the future, has to be squeezed out," he added.[42]

---

40. Arun Jaitley, *A New India: Selected Writings 2014–19* (Juggernaut, 2020).

41. Ibid.

42. "No Question of Roll Back of Demonetisation, Says Jaitley", *The New Indian Express*, accessed 25 May 2025, https://www.newindianexpress.com/nation/2016/Nov/17/no-question-of-roll-back-of-demonetisation-says-jaitley-1539684.html.

In a short time, demonetisation weeded out enormous unaccounted cash from the economy. RBI reported that Specified Bank Notes (SBNs) of an estimated value of Rs 15.28 lakh crore were deposited back as on 30 June 2017. The outstanding SBNs as on 8 November 2016 were of Rs 15.44 lakh crore value. The total currency in circulation of all denominations as on 8 November 2016 was Rs 17.77 lakh crore. Cash became part of the formal economy. The published figure of currency in circulation for the half year ending September 2017 was Rs 15.89 lakh crore. This showed year-on-year variation of (-) Rs 1.39 lakh crore; whereas year-on-year variation for the same period during the previous year was (+) Rs 2.50 lakh crore. This meant that the reduction in currency in circulation was of the order of Rs 3.89 lakh crore.[43] At the same time, it compelled holders of genuine cash to deposit the same in the banks. Cash involves anonymity in transactions. It bypasses the banking system and enables its possessors to evade tax. With the return of Rs 15.28 lakh crore in the formal banking system, almost the entire cash holding of the economy now had an address. It was no longer anonymous. From this inflow, the amount involving suspicious transactions based on various estimates ranged from Rs 1.6 lakh crore to Rs 1.7 lakh crore. By October 2018, the sheer volume of cash deposits that could be linked to specific individuals had led to the identification of 17.42 lakh suspected account holders, from whom responses were obtained online through a non-intrusive process.

In his blog, Jaitley dismissed what he described as an uninformed critique of demonetisation—that nearly all the withdrawn cash eventually made its way back into the banking system. Higher deposits, he argued, strengthened banks' lending capacity. Much of this money also flowed into mutual funds and other investments, becoming fully integrated into the formal financial system.[44]

In the first few days of the demonetisation announcement, the criticism around it had mainly centred on the hardship that it caused the general public. There was anger about the long queues as well as about the near-daily rule changes governing the exchange and withdrawal of cash. The government, however, soon found itself battling criticism on the economic aspect of the decision. There was an attack from all quarters on the government on the

43. Arun Jaitley, *A New India: Selected Writings 2014–19* (Juggernaut, 2020).

44. Ibid.

impact of the demonetisation on the economy, attacks that continue even after nearly a decade.

Although Jaitley's ministry battled the economic impact on a daily basis, coming out of the demonetisation mess unhurt was not going to be an easy task, despite what the decision promised to achieve in the future. No matter how good the stated objectives were (including a shift to a cashless economy), the move to scrap 86 per cent of currency in circulation all of a sudden threw the economy into a crisis situation. Corporate profitability took a hit, lakhs of jobs were reportedly lost in the informal sector, consumer ability to spend were curtailed, farmers were affected as prices crashed, services and manufacturing sectors were impacted, and there was scepticism globally on the rationale behind Modi's currency ban.

Three months after demonetisation was kicked off, the Organisation for Economic Co-operation and Development (OECD) Economic Survey reduced its growth prediction for India from 7.4 per cent to 7 per cent.[45] Speaking at the launch of the OECD Economic Survey for India, Das observed that the OECD survey predicted that India's growth rate would rise to 7.3 per cent in 2017–18 and increase to 7.7 per cent in 2018–19. He said the benefits of the note ban would be felt from April 2017 onwards, and the completion of the remonetisation process would fuel consumption. "From the next quarter, long-term and medium-term benefits and outcomes are going to be very positive," Das said.[46]

Jaitley turned the demonetisation into an opportunity for digitisation of the economy, a key reform under Jaitley's ministry. There was an acceleration of digital transactions. For die-hard nationalist Jaitley, demonetisation was also an effective weapon against terror funding.[47] According to the RBI annual

---

45. "OECD cuts India growth to 7%, says India a star performer", *Mint*, accessed 25 September 2025, https://www.moneycontrol.com/news/business/economy/oecd-cuts-india-growth-to-7-says-indiastar-performer-1033906.html.

46. "Demonetisation Benefits Will Be Clear from April, Says Shaktikanta Das", *Scroll.in*, accessed 25 May 2025, https://scroll.in/latest/830506/demonetisation-benefits-will-be-clear-from-april-says-shaktikanta-das.

47. PTI, "Demonetisation Helped Reduce Terror Activities in Kashmir: Arun Jaitley", *Business Standard*, accessed 25 May 2025, https://www.business-standard.com/article/current-affairs/demonetisation-helped-reduce-terror-activities-in-kashmir-arun-jaitley-117100800272_1.html.

report of 2014–15, almost 600,000 counterfeit notes were detected in 2015 by Indian authorities. RBI data also suggested that the most counterfeited Indian notes were Rs 500 and Rs 1000 printed mainly by state actors in Pakistan. The largest number of counterfeit Indian currency notes was seized from Nepal. Bangladesh was the second most favourite transit route for counterfeit Indian currency notes being smuggled from Pakistan. Reports from law enforcement agencies, confessions of convicted terrorists, and examination by the Financial Action Task Force (FATF) implicated state actors in Pakistan beyond reasonable doubt as being involved in the practice of producing counterfeit Indian currency notes to fund terrorist acts and wage economic warfare against India.

Demonetisation left many terrorist groups unable to operate. Because terrorist organisations largely held their finances in the demonetised notes, activities such as recruitment, weapons procurement, logistical support, payments to over-ground workers, and even bribery became extremely difficult. According to Jammu and Kashmir Police officials, funding for militancy and the separatist movement in the region originates in Pakistan and is sustained through hawala networks operating out of Pakistan, Bangladesh, Nepal, and Dubai. After demonetisation, these networks were forced to find ways to recover their stockpiled Indian currency—a process that could take months or even years. Meanwhile, incidents of stone-pelting and other violent protests began to decline, dropping by 15–20 per cent month after month following the killing of Hizbul Mujahideen commander Burhan Wani on 8 July.[48] The majority of the population had voiced discontent because of the continuous shutdowns, loss of tourist revenue, and the blockade of educational establishments by the separatists. After demonetisation, pelting incidents and violent attacks by protestors declined steadily.[49]

Jaitley also viewed demonetisation as a catalyst for boosting personal income tax collections. By 31 October 2018, receipts for the 2018–19 financial year were

---

48. PTI, "Demonetisation Helped Reduce Terror Activities in Kashmir: Arun Jaitley", *Business Standard*, accessed 25 May 2025, https://www.business-standard.com/article/current-affairs/demonetisation-helped-reduce-terror-activities-in-kashmir-arun-jaitley-117100800272_1.html.

49. "Demonetization—India's Attack on Terrorism", Publications—Study Papers, European Foundation for South Asian Studies (EFSAS), available at https://www.efsas.org/publications/study-papers/demonetization-%E2%80%93-india%E2%80%99s-attack-on-terrorism/.

20.2 per cent higher than in the previous year. Corporate tax collections rose by 19.5 per cent over the same period. In the two years preceding demonetisation, direct tax collections had grown by 6.6 per cent and 9 per cent respectively. In the two years that followed, they increased by 14.6 per cent (including part of the year before demonetisation took effect in 2016–17) and by 18 per cent in 2017–18.

"Similarly, in the year 2017–18, the tax returns filed reached 6.86 crore, an increase of 25% over the previous year. This year, as on 31-10-2018, already 5.99 crore returns have been filed which is an increase of 54.33% compared to the previous year till this date. The new filers added this year are 86.35 lakh," he wrote in his blog.[50] He credited demonetisation for the increase in assessee base. "In May 2014, when the present government was elected, the total number of filers of income tax returns was 3.8 crore. In the first four years of this government, it has increased to 6.86 crore. By the time the first five years of this government are over, we will be close to doubling the assessee base," his blog said.

★

Demonetisation generated a political storm. The Congress accused Modi of causing a massive disruption to the existing social, political, and economic functions of the world's second-largest emerging market.[51] On 18 November 2016, then chief minister of Delhi, Arvind Kejriwal, along with West Bengal Chief Minister Mamata Banerjee organised a protest in front of the RBI office in the national capital to oppose the decision of the government to withdraw Rs 500 and Rs 1000 currency notes. They demanded withdrawal of demonetisation as it was causing hardship to the common man. Jaitley's management of the fallout was not limited to ensuring smooth implementation of demonetisation but also included dealing with the criticism by the Opposition. The issue of

50. Arun Jaitley, "Impact of Demonetisation", accessed 25 May 2025, https://www.arunjaitley.com/impact-of-demonitisation/.

51. Indian National Congress, Key Issues, "Demonetisation: A Modi-Made Disaster", accessed 25 May 2025, https://inc.in/key-issues/demonetisation-a-modi-made-disaster.

demonetisation also rocked Parliament leading to repeated adjournments of the Rajya Sabha as well as the Lok Sabha.

Unfazed by the combined Opposition attack on Prime Minister Narendra Modi in Parliament, Jaitley said the government was firm on cleansing politics and the economy of the country. On the Opposition's demand for a reply by the prime minister on the demonetisation issue in Parliament, Jaitley said:

> Government has a collective responsibility. And therefore it is the prerogative of the government on who should reply to a debate. Bulk of the debate has already taken place. I have attended the debate. And the government will decide who will reply to the debate. If the government thinks it is necessary at an appropriate time for the prime minister to intervene, we will consider it at that stage. But it is not necessary that there is an intervention (by prime minister) in every debate.

The demonetisation decision was challenged in many courts, eventually landing on the doorstep of the Supreme Court. On 2 January 2023, the Supreme Court Constitution bench delivered its landmark judgment upholding demonetisation by 4:1 majority.[52] Justice B.V. Nagarathna dissented. The answer afforded by the Supreme Court that demonetisation was legal was, however, at best, academic. But the judgment provided the public a glimpse into the exercise and also an occasion to reflect on demonetisation itself. The core of the legal challenge to the demonetisation move centred around the interpretation of the phrase "any series" in subsection (2) of Section 26 of the RBI Act which was invoked by the Union government to demonetise bank notes in 2016.

The legal argument was that the Union government could not use this section to demonetise "all series" of bank notes of any denomination as it did with the notification dated 8 November 2016. Justice B.R. Gavai, who authored the judgment on behalf of the majority—Justices S. Abdul Nazeer, A.S. Bopanna, V. Ramasubramanian, and himself—rejected this argument, pointing out that applying the canons of interpretation, "any" can mean "all" unless the interpretation would go contrary to the intent of the law.

---

52. *Vivek Narayan Sharma vs Union of India (2023).*

Justice Nagarathna, on the other hand, argued that such an interpretation would not be sustainable. In her view, any should mean "specified" or "particular", else the section would result in the powers of the Union government being unguided and arbitrary. Justice Nagarathna argued instead that demonetisation of all notes was possible only through the plenary legislation made by Parliament.

Nevertheless, the majority judgment held that the Centre's notification dated 8 November 2016 was valid and satisfied the test of proportionality. The court held:

> Practices such as hoarding "black" money, counterfeiting, etc., when coupled with corruption, are eating into the vitals of our society and economy. Any measure intended to strike at such practices, and thereby eliminate off shoots thereof, such as, terror funding, drug trafficking, emergence of a parallel economy, money laundering including Havala transactions, must be commended. Such measures are necessary to sanitize the economy and society, and enable it to recover from the plague caused by the evils listed hereinabove.[53]

Therefore, it could not be denied that demonetisation in the instant case was a well-intentioned proposal. The court held that the notification dated 8 November 2016, which announced the decision to scrap the high-value currency notes, could not be said to be unreasonable. The Supreme Court accepted the government's views that there was consultation between the Centre and RBI before demonetisation. The court dismissed a batch of petitions challenging the 2016 decision to demonetise Rs 500 and Rs 1000 currency notes and said the decision, being the executive's economic policy, could not be reversed. The power of the central government assigned under Section 26(2) of the RBI Act could not be solely ignored on the ground that demonetisation took place only for a particular series of notes. The Court further emphasised that the fact that the earlier demonetisations of 1947 and 1978 involved the withdrawal of all series of notes did not, in any way, restrict

53. *Vivek Narayan Sharma vs Union of India* on 2 January 2023, *Indian Kanoon*, available at https://indiankanoon.org/doc/164842744/.

the central government's authority in the present case. The court rejected the plea related to extension of the window to exchange older currency. Compared with the demonetisation of the year 1978 where only eight days were assigned to exchange older currencies, the court held that the window of fifty-two days, starting from 8 November 2016, was a reasonable time period.

Sadly, Jaitley was no longer alive to feel the satisfaction or pride of seeing his advice upheld. The Supreme Court's decision once again affirmed his brilliance as a legal mind. Prime Minister Modi would no doubt have offered silent thanks for his friend's counsel.

The political verdict on demonetisation happened, thankfully, while Jaitley was still alive and for which Jaitley did not have to wait very long. In 2017, the state of Uttar Pradesh went to polls. The BJP swept the elections in Uttar Pradesh and also in Uttarakhand in less than six months of demonetisation. The assembly elections were widely regarded as a mini-referendum on Modi's demonetisation decision.

On 11 March, when the results in Uttar Pradesh were declared, it was a surprise for everyone. The BJP won 312 seats, while the SP had 47. The BSP won 19, while the Congress, with 7, could not reach the double digit. The BJP secured a sweeping victory, driven largely by rural voters—ironically, those whose economic interests were believed to have suffered the most. The party's vote share surged by 24.7 percentage points compared to the previous election. Commentators who had written off the BJP after demonetisation admitted they had misread the ground sentiment. It became evident that the poor were prepared to endure their own difficulties, taking a grim satisfaction in seeing the affluent face even greater discomfort. As long as the rich were standing in queues, the poor were willing to bear the strain.

Beaming with pride, Jaitley said, "*Zameen badal rahi hai*", the ground was shifting. It was clear that politics had scored over economics. "*Ameer ko maarne ki khushi kam paise ki peeda se kahin zyada thi,*" said Nitish Kumar, summing up how hitting out at the rich had paid the BJP government rich dividends.[54] The poor understood that black money could not be wiped out in a single stroke but the shock effect of the demonetisation clearly conveyed the government's determination to tackle the problem head-on.

---

54. Kumkum Chadha, *The Marigold Story: Indira Gandhi & Others* (Westland, 2019), p. 336.

27

Digital Economy

★

In the 1996 American film *Star Trek: First Contact*, Captain Jean-Luc Picard remarks in a conversation about twenty-fourth-century societies that "the economics of the future are somewhat different". We may still be far from that imagined future, but even a brief look back at recent decades shows how dramatically our own economic landscape has shifted. Compared with twenty-five, twenty, or even ten years ago, today's modes of producing, acquiring, and consuming goods and services are radically altered—sometimes to the point of being unrecognisable. Much of this transformation stems from the rise of the digital economy.

Put simply, a digital economy encompasses interconnected economic activity enabled by living and working in a digital environment. It is often mistaken for the online transactions that take place across the globe, which are better described as the internet economy. A digital economy extends well beyond the act of purchasing: it includes the infrastructure, platforms, and devices through which people engage with this vast network. In many ways, it represents a contemporary industrial revolution.[1]

---

1. Anna Kucirkova, "A Digital Economy for an Increasingly Connected World", CIAT—Inter-American Center of Tax Administrations, accessed 24 August 2025, https://www.ciat.org/a-digital-economy-for-an-increasingly-connected-world/?lang=en.

India's digital transformation has been nothing short of revolutionary. In 2015, the government launched the Digital India programme—a nationwide effort involving multiple departments—to prepare the country for a digital future. Its core aim is to strengthen the connection between citizens and the state through accessible e-services, and to deliver public services in a transparent and cost-effective manner. Digitalisation carries particular significance for India, where more than 60 per cent of the population resides in rural areas. Creating a digitally connected nation expands access to the benefits and opportunities of a modern economy, helping bridge long-standing economic divides. India's rapid digitalisation has been propelled by a convergence of factors: rising broadband penetration, rapid technological innovation, some of the lowest data costs in the world, and a strong governmental push to build robust digital infrastructure. This environment, in turn, has fuelled a vibrant start-up ecosystem and encouraged entrepreneurship among a young, tech-savvy population that has embraced digital tools with remarkable speed.[2] Digitalisation is aimed at increasing economic efficiency and competitiveness, creating new businesses and products, and addressing challenges relating to increasing financial inclusion, improving governance, and reducing disparities.

The Digital India programme seeks to digitally empower society and the knowledge economy—faceless, paperless, and cashless. India has followed a different strategy in digitisation of its economy vis-à-vis other developed countries. India has an open internet and there is no firewall between it and the rest of the world. However, the difference is that India has leveraged the internet to create a plethora of digital public goods and government services. This has allowed India to connect numerous citizens and provide a more democratic and inclusive digital network and infrastructure.

Underpinning this infrastructure is the "India Stack", a set of open Application Programming Interfaces (APIs), which is unlocking economic building blocks like identity, digital payments, and data, thereby creating a platform for facilitating transactions and providing goods and services. The Aadhaar layer provides online biometric-based digital identities to 1.35 billion individuals. Another layer of the Digital India Stack is UPI. There are over 350

2. "Digitalizing India: A Force to Reckon With", EY India, accessed 25 May 2025, https://www.ey.com/en_in/insights/india-at-100/digitalizing-india-a-force-to-reckon-with.

banks on the network with over 260 million unique users, and the network has grown to become India's largest digital payment network and the world's fifth-largest digital payment network by volume.

The economic impact of digitalisation can be seen across the Indian economy. India's core digital economy share in gross value added (GVA) increased from 5.4 per cent in 2014 to 8.5 per cent in 2019, with a digitally dependent economy estimated to be around 22 per cent of GDP in 2019. In absolute US dollar terms, India's digital economy exhibited a growth rate of 15.6 per cent over the period 2014–19, which was 2.4 times faster than the growth of the overall Indian economy. Digital output multiplier has increased over time from 1.35 in 2014 to 1.52 in 2019, highlighting the role of investments to drive growth. Approximately 62.4 million workers were employed in the digitally dependent economy in 2019.[3] The country's digital economy is expected to grow twice as fast as the rest of the economy, and constitute 13.42 per cent of national income by the end of 2024–25, as against 11.74 per cent in 2022–23. By 2030, India's digital economy will account for nearly a fifth of overall GDP. This is the first such attempt by the government to quantify the size of India's digital economy.[4]

India has long relied heavily on cash transactions, a dependence shaped by limited digitisation, inadequate last-mile financial access, and the prevalence of unaccounted income. Demonetisation placed the country on an accelerated path towards the government's Digital India vision, pushing citizens and businesses alike to engage with the emerging digital economy. The move, however, initially plunged the economy into turmoil. With 86 per cent of the currency in circulation suddenly invalidated, replacement notes were scarce, ATMs had yet to be recalibrated, and people queued for hours—sometimes days—to deposit or exchange old notes at bank branches. For Arun Jaitley, demonetisation represented a pivotal step in formalising India's economy. He made use of Digital India to promote cashless transactions while also bringing more people into the formal banking system and, in the process, expanding

---

3. Ibid.

4. Aroon Deep, "Digital Economy to Constitute Fifth of Indian GDP by 2030: ICRIER Report", *The Hindu*, accessed 25 May 2025, https://www.thehindu.com/business/digital-economy-to-constitute-fifth-of-indian-gdp-by-2030-icrier-report/article69131201.ece.

the tax base. The digital system would result in more deposits with banks, increasing their ability to lend at affordable rates. A healthy banking system would help support growth of the economy, Jaitley believed.[5]

★

Among India's many notable digital public infrastructure achievements, the Unified Payments Interface (UPI) stands out as truly transformative. UPI is a real-time digital payments system that has reshaped the way individuals transfer money, enabling seamless transactions between any two mobile users. It consolidates multiple bank accounts into a single mobile application—regardless of the participating bank—and brings together a range of banking functions, from effortless fund transfers to merchant payments, under one unified platform. It also supports peer-to-peer payment requests, which users can schedule and settle with ease and convenience.

When demonetisation was announced, UPI was on the cusp of being rolled out. Developed and operated by the National Payments Corporation of India (NPCI)—a not-for-profit umbrella organisation that manages retail payment and settlement systems under the guidance of the RBI—UPI was conceived as part of a broader RBI and Indian Banks' Association initiative under the Payment and Settlement Systems Act, 2007, to build a robust national payments infrastructure. Under Arun Jaitley's leadership, NPCI conducted a pilot launch with twenty-one member banks on 11 April 2016. By 25 August 2016, banks had begun uploading their UPI-enabled applications to the Google Play Store, paving the way for its public adoption.

On 30 December 2016, Prime Minister Modi launched BHIM app, another innovation under Jaitley. BHIM allows simple, easy, and quick payment transactions using UPI. Instant bank-to-bank payments can be made and collected using just a mobile number or a Virtual Payment Address (VPA), which serves as a unique identifier for UPI transactions. BHIM is available in

---

5. "Cash Comes at a Cost, Nation Moving Towards Digital Economy: Jaitley", *The Hindu*, accessed 25 May 2025, https://www.thehindu.com/business/Economy/cash-comes-at-a-cost-nation-moving-towards-digital-economy-jaitley/article19992964.ece.

twenty languages, namely, Hindi, English, Tamil, Telugu, Malayalam, Bengali, Odia, Kannada, Gujarati, Marathi, Assamese, Bengali, Bhojpuri, Haryanvi, Marwari, Konkani, Manipuri, Khasi, Mizo, and Urdu. Within ten days of its launch, the BHIM app had one crore downloads from Android Play Store and over two million transactions across the UPI and USSD (Unstructured Supplementary Service Data) platforms. BHIM is interoperable with other UPI applications and bank accounts.

Development of the UPI interface fundamentally changed the behaviour of Indians, with a long-term positive impact on the formalisation of the digital economy in India—through cashless and paperless transactions. It has deepened financial inclusion by bringing in several small businesses and unbanked individuals into the formal economy, creating a financial record and credit history, and allowing these businesses and individuals to access credit. UPI has made provision of an alternate retail payment system and lowered the dependence on existing card-based payment systems. It has enabled an architecture for private players to innovate and develop new business models, for example, fintech (financial technology) and e-commerce solutions. As a result of the development of this stack, the impact of the pandemic, and the growing e-commerce market, digital payments have been exploding, with UPI leading the surge in India and confirming its bright future in the country.

Globally, UPI is among the most successful retail fast payment systems (FPS). Like other widely adopted FPS, it provides simplicity, safety, and security to person-to-person (P2P) and person-to-merchant (P2M) transactions. It has five key attributes: 1) an open architecture infrastructure, 2) multi-party transactability, 3) ease of doing transactions, 4) strict data regulations, and 5) a carefully calibrated regulatory environment.

An open infrastructure simply means that UPI allows third-party developers to build on top of its open platform and create their own app that can be integrated with UPI. Tech companies (big tech and fintech) and banks have free entry to use UPI and/or build their own apps with UPI as the third-party application. UPI allows users to make payments from one bank account to another. They can initiate these payments from their bank account through third-party application providers (TPAPs) such as Amazon Pay, Google Pay, and PhonePe. Big techs can be defined as large companies whose primary activity is digital services. Examples include Google, Apple, or Amazon in the United States, and Alibaba or Tencent in China.

To build a UPI-enabled platform, third-party developers must obtain authorisation from the NPCI and comply with technical specifications, security and privacy standards, testing and certification processes, and other relevant regulations set by the NPCI. UPI also enables multi-application transactions. This means that users registered on any UPI platform can make safe and quick transactions to any other account registered with UPI. These could be accounts linked to third-party payment service providers (PSPs) or bank accounts. Users are not restricted to using a particular bank's mobile app or payment platform but can use the UPI app or any UPI-enabled app to make transactions. This makes UPI a convenient single platform for transactions, eliminating the need for users to maintain multiple accounts or download multiple apps to make payments. Payment over UPI does not depend on full bank account numbers or other information of the recipients. Instead, they can use a mobile number or scan a quick response (QR) code by phone to initiate a transaction.

The use of UPI data is strictly regulated. For this reason, big techs have not been allowed to extract rents from users' transaction data. Users can access their own transaction data from their bank and there are separate data-sharing initiatives, but payment initiators (TPAPs) cannot collect individual transaction data. Finally, regulators in India have carefully calibrated the rules governing the system, supporting competition while being mindful of financial stability. While it is worth underscoring that the associated credit risk remains on the balance sheet of banks and other regulated lenders, the sheer volume of transactions by dominant players raised competition and financial stability concerns.

In 2021, the NPCI announced a restriction on the total volume of transactions processed by any single TPAP in the UPI system, capping it at 30 per cent. TPAPs that surpass the three-month transaction volume limit have been advised to decrease their market share to avoid market disruption and encourage future use.

In the 2017 budget, Jaitley announced concerted steps to strengthen the structural underpinnings of the digital economy, in order to incentivise a bigger uptake of digital payments. The focus of the budget included the establishment of a computer emergency response team for India's financial sector; a computer response team for the financial sector is the most immediate need, given the woefully inadequate cybersecurity infrastructure in India, explicitly brought to light by the mass data breaches of the previous year.

Recognising that the UPI system rolled out in 2016 was a potentially revolutionary step to make banking less cumbersome, the budget provided for promotion of the system via the NPCI-backed BHIM app. The budget also focused on the establishment of a Payments Regulatory Board for digital payments within the RBI. An increase in the uptake of digital payments, especially since demonetisation, and the consequent rise of related issues, highlighted the need for a regulator with specific jurisdiction over such payments.

Finally, the enabling of a merchant version of Aadhaar-enabled payments, primarily targeted towards those who do not have debit or credit cards, was part of the 2017 budget. Prioritising Aadhaar-enabled payment systems has provided a massive push towards a less-cash economy. The lack of access to smartphones, reliable internet, debit cards, and credit cards puts a very significant portion of India's population outside the entire cashless drive. Enabling cashless payments on the back of a biometric-enabled Aadhaar system overcomes this hurdle to a great degree.

These propositions taken together were to go a long way in shoring up the basic structure of a digital economy. Put together, they signified a concerted effort to strengthen the structural underpinnings of the digital economy.[6]

★

Jaitley deserves credit for providing impetus to RuPay, an Indian domestic cards scheme considered and propelled by the NPCI in 2012 to establish a self-reliant and inclusive financial ecosystem. The name "RuPay"—a blend of "Rupee" and "Payment"—immediately signals its Indian identity and lends the brand an unmistakably indigenous character. RuPay represents a breakthrough in the world of card payment systems, becoming India's first home-grown card scheme.[7] Its launch fulfilled the RBI's long-standing aspiration to create a

6. R. Shashank Reddy, "A Credible Digital Push by Arun Jaitley", Carnegie Endowment for International Peace, accessed 24 August 2024, https://carnegieendowment.org/posts/2017/02/a-credible-digital-push-by-arun-jaitley?lang=en.

7. "RuPay—Making India Prominent on the World Map", NPCI, accessed 24 August 2025, https://www.npci.org.in/blog/rupay-making-india-prominent-on-the-world-

widely accepted, open, and multilateral domestic payment arrangement. In 2009, the RBI asked the Indian Banks' Association to establish a not-for-profit entity and develop a domestic alternative—then provisionally called the "India Card"—that would meet the needs of Indian banks. At the time, nearly 90 per cent of Visa transactions and all Mastercard transactions within India were domestic, yet the cost of processing them was high, largely due to the dominance of these foreign networks. RuPay was introduced to lower these transaction costs and encourage greater adoption of digital payments by making online and card-based transactions more affordable and accessible.[8]

Jaitley extended RuPay's purpose beyond just being a payment network to promoting financial inclusion by facilitating transactions for unbanked and underbanked segments of the society. By providing a domestic payment system, RuPay has made banking services accessible to millions of Indians who were previously excluded from the formal financial sector. Thanks to Prime Minister Modi's policy of digital economy and financial inclusion, and Jaitley's efforts as the finance minister, RuPay has made quick inroads into the hinterland. Under Jaitley, RuPay's use was extended to support government initiatives such as Direct Benefit Transfer (DBT) programmes, enabling seamless and secure disbursement of welfare payments to beneficiaries nationwide digitally.

A big boost for RuPay came when Jaitley's ministry prescribed the issuance of RuPay cards to every account holder who opened the account under the Pradhan Mantri Jan Dhan Yojana (PMJDY) launched in 2014. As RuPay gained traction, it expanded its offerings beyond traditional debit and credit cards. It introduced prepaid cards, contactless payments, and e-commerce solutions, catering to the evolving needs of consumers and businesses.[9]

At the Delhi Economics Conclave in 2015, Modi spoke about the emergence of RuPay cards as an alternative to the otherwise duopolistic industry

---

map.

8. Dr R. Gokilavani and Dr R. Durgarani, "Evolution of Digital Economy in India", *International Journal of Marketing and Human Resource Management*, Vol. 9, No. 1 (January–April 2018), pp. 31–39, https://iaeme.com/MasterAdmin/Journal_uploads/IJMHRM/VOLUME_9_ISSUE_1/IJMHRM_09_01_003.pdf.

9. "What Is RuPay And How Does It Work?", RemitFinder, available at https://www.remitfinder.com/blog/what-is-rupay-and-how-does-it-work.

dominated by Visa and Mastercard.[10] Jaitley decided to launch a campaign to create an awareness among people for using more and more RuPay cards which could be a game changer as far as India is concerned.[11] In the 2015 budget, Jaitley had proposed to introduce several measures soon that will incentivise usage of RuPay debit cards. "The benefits of RuPay debit cards are flexibility of the product platform and high levels of acceptance," he stated.[12] He pitched RuPay as healthy competition in the debit and credit card space traditionally dominated by a few international players.

RuPay soon became a domestic alternative to international payment systems like Visa and Mastercard. In 2015, India's total debit-card volume was 925 million. RuPay claimed to power over 500 million cards issued by nearly 1100 banks—giving it more than 50 per cent share in the country's debit-card market by volume, beating the much older duo of Visa and Mastercard. In 2013, RuPay's market share was just 0.6 per cent.[13] RuPay card usage at point-of-sale (PoS) devices jumped 135 per cent to 459 million transactions in the financial year 2017–18 as against 195 million in the previous year. The number of RuPay cards in circulation also grew, having reached 494 million in the financial year 2018 up 35 per cent against 365 million in the previous year. RuPay card usage at e-commerce websites jumped 137 per cent to reach 208 million transactions in the financial year 2018 against just 87.5 million in 2017.

---

10. "RuPay: How a Six-year-old Card Gave the Scare to Global Biggies Such as Visa and Mastercard", The Economic Times, accessed 24 August 2025, https://m.economictimes.com/news/economy/finance/rupay-how-a-six-year-old-card-gave-the-scare-to-global-biggies-such-as-visa-and-mastercard/amp_articleshow/66591913.cms.

11. PTI, "RuPay and Cheques Roadmap for a Robust Economy: FM Arun Jaitley", *The Economic Times*, accessed 24 August 2025, https://economictimes.indiatimes.com/industry/banking/finance/banking/rupay-and-cheques-roadmap-for-a-robust-economy-fm-arun-jaitley/articleshow/46719473.cms?from=mdr.

12. "Budget 2015: Want a Cashless India, Says Arun Jaitley", *India Today*, accessed 25 August 2025, https://www.indiatoday.in/india/story/budget-2015-arun-jaitley-wants-cashless-india-rupay-242436-2015-02-28.

13. "RuPay: How a Six-year-old Card Gave the Scare to Global Biggies Such as Visa and Mastercard", *The Economic Times*, accessed 24 August 2025, https://m.economictimes.com/news/economy/finance/rupay-how-a-six-year-old-card-gave-the-scare-to-global-biggies-such-as-visa-and-mastercard/amp_articleshow/66591913.cms.

In terms of value of payments, in 2018, the transactions stood at Rs 16,600 crore against Rs 5934 crore the year before, a jump of 180 per cent. Jaitley's drive for a less-cash economy in the wake of the demonetisation promoted RuPay card in the interiors of the country where paying with a card was a big novelty just a few years ago. RuPay's total transactions increased to Rs 8430 crore ($1.16 billion) as of September 2018 from Rs 1100 crore before the demonetisation.[14]

The biggest weapon that helped RuPay conquer a big chunk of the market was Jaitley's decision to levy its flat fee. For every RuPay-based transaction, the NPCI charges a flat 60 paise for acquiring and 30 paise for issuing. For instance, if a customer with a RuPay card issued by Bank A pays through Bank B's PoS terminal, as the acquirer, Bank B will pay 60 paise to the NPCI and, as the issuer, Bank A will pay 30 paise. This is a tiny fraction of Visa and Mastercard's merchant-discount rate, which is calculated as a percentage of the actual transaction amount.[15] With the finance ministry's perseverance, the number of RuPay cards in use increased from 282.78 million in the financial year 2016–17 to 964.25 million in the financial year 2023–24. These numbers include both POS and e-commerce RuPay cards and together represent a 240 per cent increase. The value of RuPay cards issued increased from Rs 349.29 billion in the financial year 2016–17 to Rs 2447.30 billion in the financial year2023–24.[16]

In 2018, Mastercard complained to the Office of the United States Trade Representative that the Indian government associated the use of RuPay cards with nationalism, claiming it serves as a kind of national service. Mastercard complained that the Indian government had adopted a series of protectionist measures to the detriment of global companies.[17]

---

14. Ibid.

15. Ibid.

16. "What Is RuPay And How Does It Work?", RemitFinder, available at https://www.remitfinder.com/blog/what-is-rupay-and-how-does-it-work.

17. "RuPay: How a Six-year-old Card Gave the Scare to Global Biggies Such as Visa and Mastercard", *The Economic Times*, accessed 24 August 2025, https://m.economictimes.com/news/economy/finance/rupay-how-a-six-year-old-card-gave-the-scare-to-global-biggies-such-as-visa-and-mastercard/amp_articleshow/66591913.cms.

★

In his blog[18] published on 8 November 2018, marking two years of demonetisation, Jaitley wrote that UPI transactions had grown from Rs 0.5 billion in October 2016 to Rs 598 billion in September 2018. The BHIM app was being used by 1.25 crore people. The value of BHIM transactions had gone up from Rs 0.02 billion in September 2016 to Rs 70.6 billion in September 2018. The share of BHIM transactions in overall UPI transactions was at about 48 per cent in June 2017. Its transactions increased from Rs 8 billion before the demonetisation to Rs 57.3 billion in September 2018 for PoS and from Rs 3 billion to Rs 27 billion in e-commerce. Visa and Mastercard are losing market share in India to indigenously developed payment systems of UPI and RuPay, whose share has reached 65 per cent of the payments done through debit and credit cards.

UPI has extended its capabilities across borders. In July 2021, BHIM UPI partnered with the Royal Monetary Authority (RMA) of Bhutan to implement QR-based payments in Bhutan, adding a new milestone of cross-border financial integration. In August 2022, the UPI and RuPay card schemes signed a memorandum of understanding (MoU) confirming a partnership with the payment solutions provider PayXpert to internationalise the acceptance of its payment solutions in the United Kingdom, starting with UPI-based QR-code payments. In the same year, UPI AutoPay also debuted in the mutual fund segment (and all recurring payments) to digitise its payment landscape by allowing people to pay loan in equated monthly instalments (EMIs) through UPI. The growing scale of operations has improved outreach and transaction costs in domestic as well as cross-border initiatives. On 21 February 2023, a cross-border linkage between India and Singapore went live. The linkage operates through the countries' respective fast payment systems, namely UPI and Singapore's PayNow (PayNowSG), with the aim of enabling cross-border fund transfers using their respective UPI ID, mobile number, or VPA. The collaboration between UPI and PayNow SG has brought significant advancements to cross-border remittances between India and Singapore.

---

18. Arun Jaitley, "Impact of Demonetisation", accessed 24 August 2025, https://www.arunjaitley.com/impact-of-demonitisation/.

Leveraging PayNow SG's peer-to-peer funds transfer service, users can now seamlessly transfer funds using mobile numbers or VPAs in real-time, without the need for bank account details.[19]

Jaitley played a key role in promoting digital payments and UPI. In five years as the finance minister, he ensured UPI set a global benchmark for digital payments by transforming India's financial ecosystem. It created a near-frictionless environment for money transfers. Numerous digital and financial service providers stepped forward to create innovative ways to attract new consumers and build awareness on how to operate digitally. While the United States remains a leader in various fintech innovations, its banking system still lags behind India in payment efficiency. Unless the United States undergoes significant reforms to modernise its payment infrastructure, which will require government and regulatory support, it will continue to fall short of the seamless and instant nature of systems like UPI.[20]

★

The digital economy encompasses the vast range of activity generated by billions of everyday online interactions among individuals, organisations, devices, data, and processes. At its core lies hyperconnectivity, the rapidly expanding interconnectedness of people, institutions, and machines made possible by the internet, mobile technologies, and the Internet of Things (IoT).[21] The digital economy is taking shape and undermining conventional notions

---

19. Giulio Cornelli et al., "The Organisation of Digital Payments in India—Lessons from the Unified Payments Interface (UPI)", SUERF Policy Note No. 355 (August 2024), available at https://www.suerf.org/wp-content/uploads/2024/08/SUERF-Policy-Note-355_-Frost-et-al-1.pdf.

20. Divyam Raj, "India's Unified Payments Interface Has Revolutionized Its Digital Payments Market", Cornell SC Johnson College of Business, accessed 24 August 2025, https://business.cornell.edu/hub/2024/12/20/indias-unified-payments-interface-has-revolutionized-its-digital-payments-market/.

21. Dr R. Gokilavani and Dr R. Durgarani, "Evolution of Digital Economy in India", *International Journal of Marketing and Human Resource Management*, Vol. 9, No. 1 (January–April 2018), pp. 31–39, https://iaeme.com/MasterAdmin/Journal_uploads/IJMHRM/VOLUME_9_ISSUE_1/IJMHRM_09_01_003.pdf.

about how businesses are structured; how firms interact; and how consumers obtain services, information, and goods. The digital economy permeates all aspects of society, including the way people interact, the economic landscape, the skills needed to get a good job, and even political decision-making. India's emerging digital economy has the potential for generating new scientific research and breakthroughs, fuelling job opportunities, increasing economic growth, and improving the lives of people. These changes are happening worldwide. In Kenya, mobile data is being used to identify malaria infection patterns and identify hotspots that guide government eradication efforts. Data from vehicle sensors on delivery trucks, combined with mapping and analytics tools, has helped companies save millions of gallons of fuel and cut emissions—equivalent to removing thousands of cars from the road for an entire year. Likewise, farmers from Iowa to India are drawing on data from seeds, satellites, and sensors to make more informed decisions about what to plant and how best to respond to shifting climate conditions.[22]

In a short period of time, India has built a digital highway across the country which is not merely about communication—it provides access to healthcare, education, governance, and economic opportunity. Broadband usage in India has been growing at an unprecedented pace. Mobile broadband (MBB) subscribers have increased from 345 million to 765 million while traffic per user has seen a jump of 31 per cent over five years reaching 17 GB as of December 2021. As a result, India's data traffic usage from 2017 to 2021 was among the highest in the world, with a compound annual growth rate (CAGR) of 53 per cent. India's Generation Z[23] spends an average of eight hours per day online.

The next wave of smartphone adoption is happening in rural India. It is expected that India would have the second-largest universe of online shoppers

---

22. Victoria A. Espinel, "The Digital Economy: What Is It and How Will It Transform Our Lives?", World Economic Forum, accessed 24 August 2025, https://www.weforum.org/stories/2016/11/the-digital-economy-what-is-it-and-how-will-it-transform-our-lives/.

23. Generation Z is a term used to describe people born roughly between the late 1990s and early 2010s, such as those born from 1997 to 2012. The "Z" follows the pattern of previous generations like Generation X and Generation Y (Millennials). Generation Z is known as the first "digital natives" as they were raised with the internet, smartphones, and social media, shaping them as a tech-savvy, socially conscious, and diverse group.

by 2030, estimated at 500 million to 600 million. Online marketplaces have been exploding across all sectors of the economy. The size of the e-commerce market is expected to grow to US$ 350 billion by 2030.[24]

★

Amongst the first few initiatives of Jaitley's ministry was the launch of the first phase of PMJDY in August 2014. PMJDY is a national mission for financial inclusion aimed at ensuring affordable access to a full range of financial services—banking, savings and deposit accounts, remittances, credit, insurance, and pensions. By enabling every citizen to open a bank account under this scheme, the country's financial resources can be brought into the formal savings system, accessible through net banking as well. A basic savings bank account can be opened at any bank branch or through a business correspondent (Bank Mitra) outlet. PMJDY accounts are being opened with zero balance. Nonetheless, if the account holder wishes to get a cheque book, one should satisfy the minimum balance criteria.[25]

The flagship financial inclusion scheme, PMJDY, was launched for a period of four years. In view of the "runaway success" of the scheme, in 2018, Jaitley decided to make it open-ended with more incentives. He doubled the overdraft limit for account holders to Rs 10,000. The first phase of the PMJDY scheme focused on opening basic bank accounts and issuing RuPay debit cards with inbuilt accident insurance cover of Rs 1 lakh. Besides, it provided basic banking accounts with an overdraft facility of Rs 5000 after six months. The second phase, which began on 15 August 2015, planned to provide microinsurance

---

24. "Digitalizing India: A Force to Reckon With", EY India, accessed 25 May 2025, https://www.ey.com/en_in/insights/india-at-100/digitalizing-india-a-force-to-reckon-with."By providing every citizen with a bank account under this scheme, India's total money can be brought within a savings framework, and it can also be accessed through online banking."

25. Dr R. Gokilavani and Dr R. Durgarani, "Evolution of Digital Economy in India", *International Journal of Marketing and Human Resource Management*, Vol. 9, No. 1 (January–April 2018), pp. 31–39, https://iaeme.com/MasterAdmin/Journal_uploads/IJMHRM/VOLUME_9_ISSUE_1/IJMHRM_09_01_003.pdf.

to the people and pension schemes to unorganised sector workers through business correspondents.

The free accident insurance cover for those opening PMJDY accounts after 28 August 2015 was doubled to Rs 2 lakh with no conditions attached for overdraft of up to Rs 2000. Also, the upper age limit for availing the facility was hiked to sixty-five from the earlier sixty years. As of August 2018, there were approximately 32.41 crore PMJDY accounts having a total deposit balance of Rs 81,200 crore. About 30 lakh people availed the overdraft facility. Fifty-three per cent of the PMJDY account holders are women, while 83 per cent of the total accounts are seeded with Aadhaar.[26] When the number of accounts reached 27.31 crores, a Guinness World Record was set.[27]

26. PTI, "Govt Makes Flagship Financial Inclusion Scheme 'Jan Dhan' Open-ended with More Incentives, Says Arun Jaitley", *Firstpost*, accessed 24 August 2025, https://www.firstpost.com/business/govt-makes-flagship-financial-inclusion-scheme-jan-dhan-open-ended-with-more-incentives-says-arun-jaitley-5126741.html.

27. Pradhan Mantri Jan Dhan Yojana, accessed September 2025, https://www.pmindia.gov.in/en/major_initiatives/pradhan-mantri-jan-dhan-yojana/

28

Dodging India's Mini-Lehman Moment

Sometime in mid-September 2018, the PMO is stated to have received an alarming report—India's mini-Lehman moment—exposing the precarious state of finances in IL&FS (earlier, Infrastructure Leasing and Financial Services) Corporation. The report claimed that IL&FS's assets were heavily overvalued and its debts grossly underrepresented; it was on the verge of defaulting. IL&FS had approximately Rs 16,000 crore of payment obligations for the remaining year, but had no cash flow after incurring operational expenditure. The giant enterprise would go down and take with it several non-banking financial companies and other companies.

A default by IL&FS, a massive financial institution and AAA-rated infrastructure powerhouse, would upend the financial market. There were over 300 companies in the IL&FS group. The conglomerate had raised billions of dollars in the corporate bond market and powered the nation's public project building boom. Its failure would have a cascading effect on the market. The banks, already struggling with NPLs, wouldn't be able to cope with another crisis; the financial system would collapse. It was India's "too big to fail" moment, referring to financial firms so large that their collapse could spark economic chaos. The anonymous report received by the PMO was forwarded to the finance ministry.[1]

---

1. Subhash Chandra Garg, *We Also Make Policy: An Insider's Account of How the Finance Ministry Functions* (HarperCollins, 2023), pp. 243–54.

IL&FS was formed in the late 1990s to support infrastructure development in the country. Following the liberalisation of the economy in the early 1990s, the infrastructure sector—roads, power, urban development, and industrial parks—was opened to private investment. The infrastructure sector was also highly controlled and regulated; various concessions were required from the government for its development. The investment in infrastructure required huge investments upfront, whereas returns came over many decades; in many cases, returns were not even adequate to pay back investments. Considering the risks, the private sector did not show much excitement to invest.

The government opted to pursue a public–private partnership framework, offering regulated and assured returns or viability-gap support. The aim was to create an institution capable not only of extending financial assistance but also of delivering technical solutions for infrastructure development. This vision culminated in the establishment of IL&FS. Initially nurtured within the banking division of the finance ministry's Department of Economic Affairs (DEA), IL&FS took shape before this division was later reorganised into a separate Department of Financial Services. Among its prominent equity holders were India's Life Insurance Corporation (LIC), Japan's Orix Corporation, and the Abu Dhabi Investment Authority.

The government provided all kinds of support to IL&FS; it got loans from multilateral institutions such as the World Bank, Asian Development Bank (ADB), and International Finance Corporation (IFC) for IL&FS's infrastructure projects. Money was raised through short- and long-term bonds that could be traded in financial markets. (If a government wants to borrow money, it usually does so by selling bonds to investors. The investor then received a stream of future payments.) IL&FS was nurtured by some intrepid professionals, Ravi Parthasarathy and Hari Sankaran in particular.

In a way, IL&FS was a strange fish: A private infrastructure financier that lent to risky projects it also owned, while throwing around the weight of non-existent state connections to mask a multiyear liquidity squeeze.[2] The group's venture into buying real estate in India's slowing market backfired.

2. Andy Mukherjee, "Averting India's Mini-Lehman Moment Was the Easy Part", *The Print*, accessed 24 August 2025, https://theprint.in/opinion/averting-indias-mini-lehman-moment-was-the-easy-part/128526/.

As the money drained out, IL&FS defaulted on a series of its loan repayment commitments.

IL&FS's difficulties had been mounting since July 2018, when its founder, Ravi Parthasarathy, resigned, citing health concerns. A series of defaults within the group from August onwards further strained corporate bond yields and triggered a slide in the stock market. That same month, the company's credit rating was cut from AAA to AA+ on its loans and debentures, and by late September, it had been downgraded repeatedly to junk status.[3] This shook investor confidence in non-banking financial institutions.

A few days later, concerns about a severe liquidity crunch at another major housing finance company—Dewan Housing Finance Limited (DHFL)—rose sharply. Around this time, Subhash Chandra Garg, then economic affairs secretary, revealed that Hari Sankaran had met him the previous day to describe the acute liquidity stress IL&FS was facing, while insisting the company remained fully solvent. According to Sankaran, IL&FS held assets worth over Rs 1.2 lakh crore against total debt of less than Rs 80,000 crore. He said he had been on the verge of finalising a deal to sell certain assets to raise the required funds, but an unexpected issue had derailed it. He added that an equity infusion through a rights issue was being planned and would be taken up by the IL&FS board in the coming month. Seeking immediate relief, he urged the government to persuade LIC or SBI to extend a temporary loan of Rs 10,000 crore against IL&FS's assets—funds he said were needed within a day or two to avert a default[4].

Even without the uncanny timing of its troubles erupting a decade after the collapse of Lehman Brothers, there were enough signs to invite comparison between the iconic Wall Street bank and IL&FS. IL&FS was a relatively small yet systemically significant institution, heavily reliant on short-term loans and bonds from wholesale investors, holding largely illiquid, long-term assets, maintaining minimal loan-loss buffers, and intertwined with a wide network of financial entities, including a major insurance company. To call the resemblance

3. "How India Avoided Its 'Lehman Brothers Moment'", BBC, accessed 24 August 2025, https://www.bbc.com/news/world-asia-india-45728881.

4. Subhash Chandra Garg, *We Also Make Policy: An Insider's Account of How the Finance Ministry Functions* (HarperCollins, 2023), pp. 243–54.

striking would be an understatement. Thankfully, in this case, the ugliness was merely skin-deep.[5]

IL&FS operated with far less leverage than Lehman, whose 2008 collapse was rooted in an overwhelming dependence on credit derivative structures embedded in bank balance sheets. These instruments magnified exposures well beyond the value of the underlying assets. The problem was intensified by assumed correlations between derivatives, which shaped capital requirements: portfolios deemed uncorrelated required far less capital than those considered tightly linked. But once the underlying assets began to deteriorate, these assumptions broke down, and prices fell almost in unison. The outcome was a chain reaction of credit exposures unsupported by sufficient capital, triggering sudden failures. This dynamic was evident in products like Minibonds, where Lehman's involvement was limited to acting as a swap counterparty, even though the explicit credit exposures in the instruments themselves were sound.

In contrast, the situation in India, particularly with IL&FS, was fundamentally different. Credit derivatives were notably absent, limiting the potential for uncontrolled exposure build-up without capital backing. IL&FS held tangible infrastructure assets, not derivative instruments, and there were credit and equity buffers in place to reduce systemic risks for banks. The issue, however, was that IL&FS was a privately owned and professionally managed entity (with majority stakes held by private institutions and employees). Yet, when the crisis struck, the responsibility for the bailout once again fell on taxpayers.

★

Jaitley was at once briefed about the situation. His concern was the multiple shocks to the financial markets if IL&FS collapsed. The economy was already grappling with surging fuel prices and a plunging currency. The last thing the government needed was more turmoil in the debt market, with plans

5. Somnath Mukherjee, "IL&FS: It's Not India's Lehman Moment, but Deja Vu on Financial Sector Reforms", *The Economic Times*, accessed 24 August 2025, https://economictimes.indiatimes.com/markets/stocks/news/ilfs-its-not-indias-lehman-moment-but-deja-vu-on-financial-sector-reforms/articleshow/65895652.cms?from=mdr.

underway to raise Rs 2.47 trillion ($ 34.7 billion) through March 2019 to bridge India's fiscal gap. It would surely have been India's mini-Lehman moment.[6]

Several other NBFCs were also under severe strain and seemed at risk of collapsing like IL&FS. Yet Jaitley was firmly opposed to offering any budgetary support or government guarantees to rescue IL&FS. He believed such intervention would set a dangerous precedent. There was also no clarity on how much support would be sufficient, and the likelihood of recovery was minimal, given the weak underlying assets. Extending help, he felt, would send the wrong signal, encouraging every troubled or irresponsible player to turn to the government for a bailout.[7] With polls due in 2019, utilising state-run institutions' funds would have given the Opposition a handle to question the BJP.[8]

Jaitley was intent on acting swiftly; any hesitation, he felt, would damage the government's political capital. His goal was clear: remove Sankaran and his associates from IL&FS. The challenge was determining the mechanism. He asked Injeti Srinivas, then secretary in the Ministry of Corporate Affairs, whether IL&FS could be taken to the National Company Law Tribunal (NCLT) under the Insolvency and Bankruptcy Code (IBC). Although the IBC was designed for resolving insolvencies of non-financial entities and did not ordinarily apply to companies like IL&FS, it did grant the government limited flexibility under its Section 227 to bring certain financial service providers within its ambit.

The authority granted under Section 227 had been preserved when the IBC was enacted, given the uncertainty surrounding any future legislation for financial service providers and the potential scope of such a law. After discussions, Jaitley concluded that the IBC—still in its early stages and already burdened with a heavy caseload since becoming operational in December 2016—was not the right forum. IL&FS, he felt, was too large and complex to be channelled through the IBC process. Instead, replacing the IL&FS management

---

6. Interview with Sanjeev Sanyal, then finance ministry's principal financial advisor.

7. Subhash Chandra Garg, *We Also Make Policy: An Insider's Account of How the Finance Ministry Functions* (HarperCollins, 2023), pp. 243–54.

8. Andy Mukherjee, "Averting India's Mini-Lehman Moment Was the Easy Part", *The Print*, accessed 24 August 2025, https://theprint.in/opinion/averting-indias-mini-lehman-moment-was-the-easy-part/128526/.

through NCLT orders under Sections 241 and 242 of the Companies Act, 2013—similar to the intervention in the Satyam case—seemed to him a more effective course of action.[9]

On 25 September, Jaitley met LIC chairman V.K. Sharma, RBI deputy governor Viral Acharya, SBI chairman Rajnish Kumar, and Central Bank of India managing director Pallav Mohapatra. A day later, Jaitley met RBI governor Urjit Patel and other officials at his residence. The following day, on Jaitley's instructions, Garg met shareholders of IL&FS, including LIC and SBI. Separately, the RBI met LIC and Orix representatives in Mumbai. In the meantime, Jaitley's team sent a confidential note to Injeti Srinivas recommending that the NCLT be approached for the "reconstitution" of the IL&FS board.[10] The decision was taken by Jaitley after the government had quietly reached out, at least two days earlier, to former bureaucrats and then current bankers to orchestrate a board coup.[11]

The petition was filed before the Mumbai branch of NCLT on the morning of 1 October 2018. NCLT heard the matter the same day in view of its urgent nature and ordered the immediate suspension of the IL&FS board. Upon the recommendation of the government, NCLT appointed Uday Kotak, Vineet Nayyar, G.N. Bajpai, G.C. Chaturvedi, Malini Shankar, and Nand Kishore as directors. A few days later, the appointment of former Rajasthan chief secretary C.S. Rajan was also confirmed by NCLT. Bajpai left within a month's time as he had some conflict of interest. The board was mandated to restructure the firm and arrange fresh funds so that existing projects don't stop.

A fraud investigation was initiated to look into financial mismanagement. All this happened in less than fifteen days. Jaitley was able to avert a major crisis in the financial sector. A comprehensive press note was issued by DEA highlighting how the supersession of the discredited IL&FS board by the one

---

9. In 2009, a corporate scandal in a leading Indian IT firm, Satyam, forced the ruling Congress party-led government at the time to step in.

10. "The untold tale behind government's shock takeover of IL&FS", *Mint*, accessed September 2025, https://www.livemint.com/Industry/W1yKVh8sqjqrH7mLORXWqO/The-untold-tale-behind-governments-shock-takeover-of-ILFS.html.

11. Ibid.

appointed by NCLT could bring the financial system of the country back from the brink.[12]

Speaking at an Associated Chambers of Commerce and Industry of India (ASSOCHAM) event a few days later, Jaitley said, "A weak leadership, within days of crisis, could not have handled IL&FS the way the present government did, and therefore a crisis in the making was handled with swiftness."[13] Jaitley had indeed averted India's mini-Lehman moment.

The Serious Fraud Investigation Office (SFIO) conducted an investigation into the affairs of IL&FS and presented an interim report to NCLT. The report revealed that the group had been working based on an "unsustainable pyramidal model", in which the holding company and its subsidiaries borrowed short-term funds from the market and lent to various special purpose vehicles (SPVs) implementing projects at much higher rates of interest. The holding company further burdened the SPVs with things like brand fees, consultancy fees, project guarantees, and advisory fees. It meant that while the debt of the SPVs kept mounting, the holding company and its key subsidiaries had strong balance sheets, at least on paper.

According to the SFIO report, in certain projects (or SPVs), the IL&FS group levied a range of charges: the parent entity collected brand and advisory fees; its subsidiary, IL&FS Financial Services Limited (IFIN), billed loan syndication, merchant banking, and success fees; while IL&FS Transportation Networks Limited (ITNL) imposed project management and claim management fees. The report noted that it was easy for IL&FS to load these fees onto the SPVs because the same individuals held decision-making roles across multiple group companies, including board positions. Unsurprisingly, the company's revenue—from brand fees, consultancy fees, and similar charges—rose from Rs

12. Press Information Bureau, Government of India, Ministry of Corporate Affairs, "Government in public interest moved NCLT to supersede Management of IL&FS on grounds of mismanagement", dated 1 October, 2018; "NCLT allows appointment of a new Board & approves induction of Six directors", accessed September 2025, https://www.pib.gov.in/newsite/PrintRelease.aspx?relid=183864.

13. PTI, "A Weak Leadership at the Centre Could Not Have Handled IL&FS Crisis, Says Arun Jaitley", *Business Today*, accessed 24 August 2025, https://www.businesstoday.in/latest/economy-politics/story/weak-leadership-centre-not-handled-ilfs-crisis-arun-jaitley-151556-2018-10-16.

64.6 crore in 2015–16 to Rs 212.3 crore in 2017–18, figures the SFIO described as "fabricated, inflated, or not genuine".[14]

★

Having ensured minimal damage from IL&FS's failure, Jaitley turned his attention to some of the giant NBFCs facing stress. They too needed an urgent resolution, but not in the same way as IL&FS. However, these financial service providers (FSPs) could be resolved under the IBC, decided Jaitley. He instructed Srinivas to operationalise the IBC for FSPs under Section 227 of the IBC. A sub-committee of the Insolvency Law Committee was constituted under M.S. Sahoo, the then chairperson of the Insolvency and Bankruptcy Board of India (IBBI),[15] to submit its recommendations on the following terms of reference: 1) FSPs or categories of FSPs that can be notified under Section 227 of the IBC for the purpose of their insolvency and liquidation proceedings based on inputs received from DEA and other financial regulators; 2) the regulatory framework that may be required for dealing with such FSPs; and 3) in light of the current financial stress in certain NBFCs and Housing Finance Companies (HFCs), the possibility of covering them under specific framework duly factoring the recent amendments made to the RBI Act, 1934, by the Finance Act, 2019.[16]

The Sahoo committee observed that, given the absence of a dedicated framework for resolving FSPs and the recent crises in the sector, an enabling mechanism under Section 227 of the IBC was essential for handling such entities. It noted that Section 227 was broad in scope and allowed the central government, in consultation with the relevant financial regulator(s), to bring specific FSPs under the IBC—either in its existing form or with necessary

14. Ashish Gupta and Jui Mukherjee, "IL&FS: Solving the Puzzle", *Fortune India*, accessed 24 August 2025, https://www.fortuneindia.com/enterprise/ilfs-solving-the-puzzle/102980.

15. Sumant Batra, *Corporate Insolvency: The Road to Viksit Bharat* (EBC, 2025), pp. 968–86.

16. "Report of the Sub-Committee of the Insolvency Law Committee for Notification of Financial Service Providers under Section 227 of the Insolvency and Bankruptcy Code, 2016" (October 2019), available at https://ibbi.gov.in/uploads/resources/ca0c7be35204c196451a5f4918e08292.pdf.

modifications—through rules issued under this provision. The committee recommended amending Section 227 to explicitly permit adjustments to the insolvency resolution and liquidation provisions of the IBC when applied to FSPs, thereby strengthening the legal robustness and long-term viability of the framework. Ultimately, it emphasised, it would be for the appropriate financial regulator to decide whether—and when—to invoke this framework for a given FSP or category of FSPs.[17]

On 15 November 2019, the Ministry of Corporate Affairs notified the Insolvency and Bankruptcy (Insolvency and Liquidation Proceedings of Financial Service Providers and Application to Adjudicating Authority) Rules, 2019 (FSP Rules) for resolving specified NBFCs registered with RBI. The FSP Rules came into effect the same day. Jaitley did not live to see the FSP Rules being notified. He passed away a few months earlier, on 24 August.

The resolution process of some large FSPs—DHFL, SREI Infrastructure Finance Limited and SREI Equipment Finance Limited (SREI), and Reliance Capital Limited—was initiated under the FSP Rules. Jaitley would have been satisfied with the speedy and efficient resolution of these entities.

DHFL, one of the country's largest NBFCs, was the first to be pushed into the IBC under the FSP Rules. DHFL experienced a significant decline starting from December 2019 and began defaulting on loan repayments. It was also accused of financial irregularities, including diversion and siphoning of funds. Its insolvency process revealed that DHFL owed over Rs 1 lakh crore to its creditors, with claims admitted by the administrator amounting to around Rs 87,000 crores. It had more than 77,000 deposit holders. The resolution plan for DHFL, led by Piramal Capital & Housing Finance Limited, was approved for a total financial consideration of Rs 33,250 crores.

The resolution plan for SREI involved claims amounting to Rs 33,050.43 crores. Out of this, Rs 13,784.76 crores was realised, which represented 42.12 per cent of the admitted claims. The realisation as a percentage of the liquidation value was significantly higher at 280.74 per cent. The resolution applicant for this case was the National Asset Reconstruction Company Limited.

For Reliance Capital Limited, the claims admitted amounted to Rs 26,088.97 crores. The amount realised from the resolution plan was Rs 9661 crores, which

17. Ibid.

was 37.03 per cent of the admitted claims. The realisation as a percentage of the liquidation value was 73.42 per cent.

The financial distress among some banks, NBFCs and HFCs drew attention to the fragmented legal framework on resolution of FSPs in India. While the government was quick to extend the IBC to the relatively bigger NBFCs and HFCs, they are not a substitute for a comprehensive framework for resolution of financial firms.

29

Electoral Reforms

A healthy democracy depends on dynamic political parties and genuinely competitive elections. Parties serve a number of essential functions: they articulate and aggregate citizens' interests, shape public policy, recruit and develop political leadership, and organise the functioning of Parliament and government.[1] Robust party competition and energetic election campaigns are vital to any democracy. To operate meaningfully—whether contesting elections, governing, or holding those in power to account—parties and their candidates rely heavily on financial backing. Sustained organisational work and campaigning simply cannot be carried out without substantial funding.

Traditionally, political parties in India financed themselves through private donations and membership dues.[2] Corporate contributions to political parties were legal, subject to certain restrictions, and required disclosures in the company's financial statements. Political funding has been central to the issue of political corruption in India, reducing accountability, distorting representation, and introducing asymmetry in policymaking and governance.

---

1. S. Bartolini and P. Mair, "Challenges to Contemporary Political Parties", in L. Diamond and R. Gunther (eds), *Political Parties and Democracy* (Johns Hopkins University Press, 2001), pp. 327–44.

2. M.V. Rajeev Gowda and E. Sridharan, "Reforming India's Party Financing and Election Expenditure Laws", *Election Law Journal, Vol. 11, No. 2 (2012), pp. 226–40*, https://casi.sas.upenn.edu/sites/default/files/upiasi/Reforming%20India%27s%20Party%20Financing%20and%20Election%20Expenditure%20Laws.pdf.

Arun Jaitley was fascinated with electoral reforms. He led the fight for holding democratic election of office bearers in DU. He believed that the question of the funding of political parties was at the heart of India's democracy and was associated with the journey of political funding reforms as a minister under both Vajpayee and Modi.[3]

In 2003, as Vajpayee's law minister, Jaitley introduced reforms to incentivise cheque donations (tax deductible for donors) to political parties and mandate disclosure to tax authorities and the ECI. In October 2003, he convened a meeting of leaders of all recognised political parties to discuss the rules providing for the system of open ballot for elections to the Council of States (Rajya Sabha) and other proposals on electoral reforms. The Representation of the People (Amendment) Act, 2003, provided for introducing the system of open ballot for elections to the Rajya Sabha. During the consideration of the bill by Parliament, Jaitley assured that the proposed rules would be discussed with political parties before finalisation.

Apart from the system of open ballot for election to the Rajya Sabha, the all-party meeting discussed the amendment of the Constitution to confer upon the other election commissioners the same protection in the matter of removal from office, available to the Chief Election Commissioner under clause (5) of Article 324. The meeting also discussed two additional issues: raising the security deposit required to contest parliamentary and assembly elections, and introducing legislation to ensure that the salaries, allowances, and pensions of the Chief Election Commissioner and other election commissioners—as well as the Election Commission's administrative expenses—are charged to the Consolidated Fund of India.[4]

Jaitley moved the Constitution (91st Amendment) Bill, 2001, which paved the way for changing the anti-defection law in 2003. The 91st Amendment makes it mandatory for leaders switching political parties—whether singly or in groups—to resign as legislative members and seek re-election. It was Jaitley

3. Arun Jaitley, "The Choice of Political Funding—Cheque, Electoral Bonds or Blackmoney from Contractors and Middlemen", accessed 24 August 2025, https://www.arunjaitley.com/the-choice-of-political-funding-cheque-electoral-bonds-or-blackmoney-from-contractors-and-middlemen/.

4. "All Party Meeting on Electoral Reforms", Ministry of Law and Justice (October 2003), available at https://archive.pib.gov.in/release02/lyr2003/roct2003/28102003/r281020034.html.

who formulated the first Model Code of Conduct and strategised with the ECI to provide it statutory strength. On accountability of politicians, Jaitley led the Opposition during the sharply contested battle on the Lokpal Bill in 2011 during UPA-II. "You (government) want to kill the Lokpal while it is still in the womb," he said about the bill. As the Rajya Sabha saw a riveting debate between Jaitley and Abhishek Singhvi over the constitutional validity and implication of the provisions of the proposed law, the Opposition managed to refer the bill to a select committee. Despite being the Leader of the Opposition, Jaitley became a member of the committee and helped the government draft the Jan Lokpal Bill.[5] In 2017, as the finance minister in Modi's first term, Jaitley introduced the instrument of electoral bonds, paving the way for all donations in white. However, in 2025, the Supreme Court ruled that the Electoral Bond Scheme, 2018, was unconstitutional as it did not disclose the funding source to political parties.

★

Over the decades, India has built an intricate framework governing election expenditure, political party financing, and related reporting and disclosure requirements. When the Companies Act, 1956, and the Representation of the People Act, 1951, were first enacted, they contained no provisions regulating political contributions from companies or individuals. Yet within a decade of the inaugural general election of 1951, a troubling nexus between black money and political fund-raising had already begun to surface.[6]

One of the reasons for the emergence of the parallel black money economy was the high taxation regime and highly regulatory and protectionist policy framework that was instituted from the 1950s onward. Some of this black money tended to be pumped back to political parties and candidates to garner

---

5. Liz Mathew, "Arun Jaitley: Mentor to the Young, MP Who Helped UPA Govt on Nuclear Bill", *The Indian Express, accessed 24 August 2025,* https://indianexpress.com/article/india/arun-jaitley-dead-mentor-to-the-young-mp-who-helped-upa-govt-on-nuclear-bill-5934494/.

6. "Black money" is the term applied to funds on which taxes have not been paid or to money raised through illegal activities.

favourable policy decisions. In a remarkable judgment delivered in 1957, a bench headed by Chief Justice M.C. Chagla of the Bombay High Court had issued an early warning to Parliament about the great danger inherent in permitting companies to make contributions to the funds of political parties, which may "ultimately overwhelm and even throttle democracy".[7] In this case, the Tata Iron and Steel Company Limited had originally approached the Bombay High Court for the amendment of its memorandum of association to include the making of contributions to political parties.

In the appellate proceedings, the court noted:

> Democracy in this country (India) is nascent and it is necessary that democracy should be looked after, tended and nurtured so that it should rise to its full and proper stature. Therefore, any proposal or suggestion which is likely to strangle democracy almost in its cradle must be looked at not only with considerable hesitation but with a great deal of suspicion … any attempt on the part of anyone to finance a political party is likely to contaminate the very springs of democracy. Democracy would be vitiated if results were to be arrived at not on their merits but because money played a part in the bringing about of those decisions. The form and trappings of democracy may continue, but the spirit underlying democratic institutions will disappear. History of democracy has proved that in other countries democracy has been smothered by big business and money bags playing an important part in the working of democratic institutions and it is the duty not only of politicians, not only of citizens, but even of a court of law, to the extent that it has got the power, to prevent any influence being exercised upon the voter which is an improper influence or which may be looked at from any point of view as a corrupt influence.[8]

---

7. Suchindran Baskar Narayan and Lalit Panda, "Money and Elections: Necessary Reforms in Electoral Finance", Vidhi: Centre for Legal Policy (January 2018), available at https://vidhilegalpolicy.in/wp-content/uploads/2020/06/Final_Money_and_Elections.pdf.

8. *Jayantilal Ranchchoddas Koticha vs Tata Iron & Steel Co. Ltd.*, (1957) 27 Comp Cas 604.

By the Companies (Amendment) Act, 1960, Section 293-A was included in the 1956 Act to regulate contributions by companies. A few years later, in 1964, the Santhanam Committee on Prevention of Corruption in its report recommended various measures to curb corruption and rising use of black money. It recommended that political parties should maintain and publish the accounts of funds and donations collected from the private sector.[9]

In 1968, Prime Minister Indira Gandhi banned corporate donations to political parties, ostensibly to prevent large business groups from exercising undue influence on politics, though it was speculated that the measure was introduced partly to prevent corporate funding to right-wing Opposition parties like the Swatantra Party which was then rapidly gaining influence in parts of the country.[10] In 1969, by the Companies (Amendment) Act, Section 293-A was again amended to ban contributions to political parties and for political purposes; contravention was punishable with a fine up to Rs 5000, and every officer who defaulted was punishable with imprisonment which could extend to three years, besides being liable to fine.

In 1974, noting that the "objective of limiting expenditure is to eliminate, as far as possible, the influence of big money in the electoral process", the Supreme Court ruled that the party spending on behalf of a candidate should be included in calculating the cap on that candidate's election expenses.[11]

> If there were no limit on expenditure, political parties would go all out for collecting contributions and obviously the largest contributions would be from the rich and affluent who constitute but a fraction of the electorate. The pernicious influence of big money would then play a decisive role in controlling the democratic process in the country. This would inevitably lead to the worst form of political corruption and that in its wake is bound to produce other vices at all levels.

---

9. "Report of the Committee on Prevention of Corruption", Government of India, Ministry of Home Affairs, available at https://archive.org/details/dli.ministry.20223.

10. M.V. Rajeev Gowda and E. Sridharan, "Reforming India's Party Financing and Election Expenditure Laws", *Election Law Journal, Vol. 11, No. 2 (2012), pp. 226–40,* https://casi.sas.upenn.edu/sites/default/files/upiasi/Reforming%20India%27s%20Party%20Financing%20and%20Election%20Expenditure%20Laws.pdf.

11. *Kanwar Lal Gupta vs Amar Nath Chawla, (*1975) 3 SCC 646.

Parliament responded in 1975 by adding Explanations 1 and 2 to Section 77(1) of the RPA, stipulating that unauthorised spending by a political party or by a candidate's supporters would not count towards the candidate's official election expenses. In practice, this allowed candidates to determine what would be included in their expenditure statements, effectively undermining the purpose of the provision. The Supreme Court later upheld this amendment. In 1979, political parties were granted exemptions from income and wealth taxes on the condition that they filed annual returns with audited accounts, reported all donations of Rs 10,000 (about $1,430 at the time) and above, and revealed the identities of such donors.

A major development in the 1980s was the 1985 amendment to the 1956 Act, which introduced Section 293A allowing companies to make contributions to political parties and for "political purposes". The explanation of "political purpose" was broad, covering donations to any person who, to the donor's knowledge, was engaged in activities that could be seen as supporting a political party at the time of the contribution. It also classified as political contributions any direct or indirect corporate spending on advertisements for a political party or on publications benefiting one. In addition to the existing cap on contributions and disclosure requirements, the amendment introduced three further restrictions to regulate such funding.

First, the company (which is not a government company) should have been in existence for more than three years; second, contributions could only be made when a resolution authorising the contributions had been passed at a meeting of the Board of Directors; and third, the penal consequences attached to the violations of the provision were made more stringent. A fine extendable to three times the amount contributed could be imposed, and every officer of the company who was in default of the provision was punishable for a term which could extend to three years and be liable for fine.[12]

In 1989, Parliament inserted Part IV-A into the RPA, providing for the registration of political parties. But the courts held that this power will not extend to deregistration of parties or any enquiry by the ECI into the affairs of the political party.[13] In 1990, the Dinesh Goswami Committee on Electoral

12. *Association for Democratic Reforms vs Union of India on 15 February, 2024, Indian Kanoon, https://indiankanoon.org/doc/121499464/.*

13. *Indian National Congress (I) vs Institute of Social Welfare,* (2002) 5 SCC 685, at page 705.

Reforms set up by the National Front government recommended some state funding in the form of limited support—for vehicle fuel (usually the main campaign expense), rental charges for microphones, the issuance of voter identity slips, and additional copies of the electoral rolls. It did not include spending by independent supporters in the election expenditure limit but made such unauthorised spending a penal offence (as in the United Kingdom).

In 1993, a Confederation of Indian Industry (CII) taskforce proposed making corporate political contributions tax deductible and requiring shareholder approval for board decisions authorising such donations. It also recommended state funding of elections, with resources raised either through a dedicated cess on excise duties or through industry contributions to a state-managed election fund. The distribution of these funds to political parties would be determined by a prescribed formula.[14]

In 1996, the Supreme Court interpreted Explanation 1 to Section 77(1) of the RPA to mean that a political party's election expenses would be added to those of a candidate when assessing compliance with expenditure limits—but only if the party had submitted audited accounts detailing its income and spending.[15] Till then no political party had submitted audited accounts despite notices from income-tax authorities; the court directed political parties to file returns as required by the Income Tax Act, 1961, and Wealth Tax Act, 1957. The RPA was amended to reduce the campaign period from twenty-one to fourteen days.

Another important development in campaign financing occurred in 1998 when the government provided a partial state subsidy in the form of allocation of free time for seven national and thirty-four state parties on the state-owned television and radio networks.[16] In the same year, the Indrajit Gupta Committee on State Funding of Elections made some recommendations for extending

---

14. M.V. Rajeev Gowda and E. Sridharan, "Reforming India's Party Financing and Election Expenditure Laws", *Election Law Journal, Vol. 11, No. 2 (2012), pp. 226–40,* https://casi.sas.upenn.edu/sites/default/files/upiasi/Reforming%20India%27s%20Party%20Financing%20and%20Election%20Expenditure%20Laws.pdf.

15. All India Reporter 1996, Supreme Court 3081.

16. "Scheme for Use of Govt. Owned Electronic Media by Political Parties during Elections", Press Note, Election Commission of India (15 January 1998), available at https://hindi.eci.gov.in/files/file/1569-scheme-for-use-of-govt-owned-electronic-media-by-political-parties-during-elections/.

state support to political parties in kind.[17] The recommendations remained mostly unimplemented.

When Jaitley became the law minister after Ram Jethmalani resigned, he was determined to implement the recommendations of the Indrajit Gupta Committee. In 2003, Jaitley introduced the bill to amend the RPA, the 1956 Act, and the Income Tax Act. The amendments proposed by Jaitley amalgamated most suggestions made by the Indrajit Gupta Committee, as also suggestions made by several parties and experts, so as to cleanse the funding mechanism as far as Indian politics is concerned.[18] Addressing the Lok Sabha on the bill, Jaitley said that the need for the amendments has arisen as:

> … there has been a larger consensus both in the democratic polity of India as also amongst the various political parties that 56 years after Independence, we have still not been able to establish a transparent mechanism by which politics, political activities and political parties in the country are to be funded. … I do recollect that about a year and a half ago the Congress party also had set up an internal committee headed by Dr Manmohan Singh. The committee had made several suggestions in regard to streamlining of this entire process. Therefore, this (Amendment) Bill is really intended to develop this transparent system as an alternative to what many believe has to be no system by which politics is being funded or any invisible system by which it is being funded.
>
> Sir, the ingredients of this Bill are that any person, and "any person" includes not only an individual, a partnership, HUF, also a company, but it excludes Government companies that are entitled to make contributions to a recognised political party. In order to incentivise contributions to be made by cheque, a procedure had been streamlined in this Bill that contributions can be made by cheque as far as individuals are concerned, partnerships are concerned, and HUFs are concerned. This is private money of individuals. There is no

---

17. "Indrajit Gupta Committee Report on State Funding of Elections", Government of India, Ministry of Law and Justice, Legislative Department (1998), pp. 11–45, 55–56.

18. "Discussion on the Election and Other Related Laws (Amendment) Bill, 2003", Lok Sabha Debates, available at https://indiankanoon.org/doc/573436/.

limit imposed on it. But as far as companies other than Government companies are concerned, because it is also shareholders' money, there is an upper cap of five per cent imposed under the Companies Act. More than five per cent of profits cannot be contributed. Whatever is the amount so contributed in order to incentivise donations by cheque, an Amendment is being proposed to the Income Tax Act wherein a suitable deduction as an admissible expenditure for the amount so contributed would be available to the donor under the Income Tax Act. This is intended so as to incentivise persons to give donations to political parties by cheque. There will be an incentive for that in terms of the fiscal regime being amended in that purpose. Political parties in turn will have a responsibility to audit their accounts, to strictly maintain their accounts. They will be required to maintain a list of all donors who donate more than Rs 20,000, in a given financial year. That entire statement of accounts, signed by the authorised person of the political party, would be submitted before the Election Commission each year. So, the object of this Bill is two-fold. One is to switch over from the present system where many believe that contributions are made to political parties through black-money which is generated. As a replacement to this contribution which could be incentivised and be made by cheque, there will be a responsibility on the political parties to maintain their accounts, to audit their accounts, and to regularly file their returns before the Election Commission in addition to the returns being filed before the appropriate income tax authorities. Additionally, the committee, headed by late Shri Inderjit Gupta made certain suggestions with regard to the state funding. We could not implement all the suggestions made by the committee because the states were reluctant to contribute to the funds which were to be created for the state funding. But we decided to make some beginning in this matter, and the beginning which has been suggested in this particular Bill that as far as electronic media is concerned, which include both the public broadcaster and also the private electronic media and the cable channels, the Election Commission would be empowered at the time of elections to draw out a code for them so that there is equitable and fair sharing of time by all political parties as far as the electronic media is concerned. The time would be allocated on the basis of the votes polled by the political parties in the preceding elections. Additionally, voter lists would be made available to political parties and candidates free of cost. There is also an empowering provision in this Bill that depending upon the improvement in the finances both with the central government and the state government, such other facilities at the expenditure of the state, which could be given to candidates at such an election as the financial position improves and also the ability of both the central and the state government improves. Those additional amenities to be given to candidates at elections, could also be provided under this particular Act.

There is also a proposal to add an explanation to Section 77 to obviate any requirement for any ambiguity that may arise in future in relation to the expenditure incurred by a candidate at the time of elections. Candidates incur expenditure on their own behalf, for, at times, when national leaders of political parties visit constituencies or state leaders visit constituencies, the expenditure which is incurred for the visit of these national leaders or state leaders, particularly in relation to their transportation—some may fly in planes or even private planes or helicopters—now if that expenditure is added to the expenditure to be incurred by each individual candidate, then, perhaps, for inviting a state or a national leader of his party, bulk of expenditure of the candidate would be included by that one visit. So, this Bill has clarified—because such ambiguity had arisen in the past—that this expenditure would not be treated as an expenditure attributable to any particular candidate which is in relation to the national and the state leaders of that particular party who incur the expenditure. There are also certain persons in relation to whom there is—because of security requirements—some responsibility of the governments to provide some mechanism in relation to security or such other facilities as in the case of the Prime Minister or other VIPs who are protected VIPs. Now, a lot of government employees, including security personnel, are deployed for such persons to whom security is to be provided or other arrangements are to be made, the expenditure incurred on them also would not be attributable to any particular candidate because such expenditure is not really in furtherance of his election prospects.

> Sir, this is a modest beginning which we are attempting to make to, at least, cleanse the process of politics by which there is a transparent funding mechanism of Indian politics. Parliament, parliamentary democracy and political parties are inherent aspects and components of Indian democracy. What should be the funding mechanism of political parties, candidates, has remained a big question before the public, as a result of which several questions relating to the credibility of politics and political parties are involved.[19]

The Election and Other Related Laws (Amendment) Act, 2003, amending the provisions of the RPA was notified on 11 September 2003. Section 29-C[20] was introduced in the RPA with the purpose of requiring each political party to declare the details of the contributions received. The treasurer of a political party or any other person authorised by the political party must, in each financial year, prepare a report in respect of contributions in excess of Rs 20,000 received by the party from a person or company other than government companies in that financial year. The report prepared must be submitted to the ECI before the due date for furnishing a return of income of that financial year

---

19. Ibid.

20. 29-C. *Declaration of donation received by the political parties.*—(1) The treasurer of a political party or any other person authorised by the political party in this behalf shall, in each financial year, prepare a report in respect of the following, namely:

(a) the contribution in excess of twenty thousand rupees received by such political party from any person in that financial year;

(b) the contribution in excess of twenty thousand rupees received by such political party from companies other than Government companies in that financial year.

(2) The report under sub-section (1) shall be in such form as may be prescribed.

(3) The report for a financial year under sub-section (1) shall be submitted by the treasurer of a political party or any other person authorised by the political party in this behalf before the due date for furnishing a return of its income of that financial year under section 139 of the Income-tax Act, 1961 (43 of 1961) to the Election Commission.

(4) Where the treasurer of any political party or any other person authorised by the political party in this behalf fails to submit a report under sub-section (3), then, notwithstanding anything contained in the Income-tax Act, 1961 (43 of 1961), such political party shall not be entitled to any tax relief under that Act.

under the Income Tax Act. A political party which fails to submit the report shall not be entitled to any tax relief as provided under the Income Tax Act.[21]

★

Despite the progress made through Jaitley's initiative, the problem of political funding remained far from resolved. Election campaigns in India have long relied heavily on unofficial, unaccounted funds. This unchecked flow of black money was not only pushing the country's celebrated democracy towards plutocracy but also deepening public cynicism toward politics and politicians.

In 2013, the UPA-II government introduced electoral trusts through an amendment to the Income Tax Rules, 1962, aiming to preserve donor anonymity, particularly for corporate donors, while still allowing them to claim tax benefits for contributions to political parties. The mechanism, however, fell short of expectations: in 2015–16, nearly 90 per cent of all donations routed through electoral trusts went to the party in power at the Centre. In response, the Election Commission of India issued guidelines on the submission of contribution reports by electoral trusts, exercising its plenary authority under Article 324 of the Constitution.[22]

India's sixteenth general elections held over seven phases in 2014—the longest till then in India's electoral history—was billed as the most expensive elections ever, witnessing an unprecedented flow of black money into the country's electoral process. Analysts claim that a mammoth Rs 400 billion ($6.64 billion), roughly 0.35 per cent of India's GDP, had been pumped into the democratic process.[23] With an estimated spending of more than $5 billion,

---

21. The provision was amended by the Finance Act, 2017 to include a proviso by which the political party was not required to disclose details of contributions received by electoral bonds.

22. Suchindran Baskar Narayan and Lalit Panda, "Money and Elections: Necessary Reforms in Electoral Finance", Vidhi: Centre for Legal Policy (January 2018), available at https://vidhilegalpolicy.in/wp-content/uploads/2020/06/Final_Money_and_Elections.pdf.

23. Niranjan Sahoo, "Black Money Infiltrates Indian Elections", ORF, accessed 24 August 2025, https://www.orfonline.org/research/black-money-infiltrates-indian-elections.

the 2014 elections to the Lok Sabha ranked amongst the costliest in the history of democracy.[24]

Concerned over the corrosive influence of black money, the ECI initiated a series of measures to curb the illicit money flow in 2014 elections and state elections that followed. From laying out elaborate surveillance infrastructure, including flying squads, to setting up parallel accounting teams to track money flow in elections, the ECI showed a measured response to tackling black money. The ECI also came up with the novel idea of setting up a central helpline to aid willing whistle blowers to alert its personnel on any such illicit transactions. Yet the results were not very encouraging. The ECI seized only a fraction of the money involved.[25] Data showed that some 75 per cent of the money going to political parties was from undocumented sources.[26]

When Jaitley took over as the finance minister in 2014, he was determined to bring transparency in election funding. The demonetisation of high-value currency notes in November 2016 had thrust the perennial problem of black money back into focus and the initiatives needed in different sectors to control it. One such sector is politics.

In May 2016, in an unprecedented move, the ECI was forced to rescind the poll notification for two assembly constituencies in Tamil Nadu, where ECI officials reported large-scale distribution of money and gifts to electors by the candidates and political parties.[27] Again, in April 2017, the ECI cancelled

---

24. Suchindran Baskar Narayan and Lalit Panda, "Money and Elections: Necessary Reforms in Electoral Finance", Vidhi: Centre for Legal Policy (January 2018), available at https://vidhilegalpolicy.in/wp-content/uploads/2020/06/Final_Money_and_Elections.pdf.

25. Till 22 April 2014, the ECI and its affiliated agencies have seized an unprecedented Rs 2.6 billion ($43 million) in cash meant to be distributed among voters. *See*, Niranjan Sahoo, "Black Money Infiltrates Indian Elections", ORF, accessed 24 August 2025, https://www.orfonline.org/research/black-money-infiltrates-indian-elections.

26. Milan Vaishnav, "Modi's Crackdown on Black Money Is Bad News for Political Parties, Including the BJP", Carnegie Endowment for International Peace, accessed 24 August 2025, https://carnegieendowment.org/posts/2016/11/modis-crackdown-on-black-money-is-bad-news-for-political-parties-including-the-bjp?lang=en.

27. Dennis S. Jesudasan, "ECI Rescinds Poll Notification for Aravakurichi, Thanjavur Constituencies", *The Hindu*, accessed 24 August 2025, https://www.thehindu.com/news/national/tamil-nadu/ECI-rescinds-poll-notification-for-Aravakurichi-Thanjavur-constituencies/article60509737.ece; "General Election to the Legislative

a bypoll to the R.K. Nagar constituency in Chennai amidst allegations that the state health minister may have distributed as much as Rs 89,00,00,000 to the voters.[28] These are just some isolated instances of the ECI attempting to cope with the problem.

Jaitley decided that it was time to introduce electoral reforms aimed at improving transparency in electoral funding and ensuring that political parties do not misuse the tax benefits provided to them. In paragraph 164 of his budget speech (2017–18), Jaitley announced that electoral bonds would be introduced to bring "transparency in electoral funding". "Even 70 years after Independence, the country has not been able to evolve a transparent method of funding political parties, which is vital to the system of free and fair elections," he said. The Finance Bill presented in February 2017 along with the budget proposed specific changes in the RBI Act, 1934, and Income Tax Act, 1961, for institutionalising electoral bonds.

The RBI Act was amended to empower the central government to authorise any scheduled bank to issue electoral bonds. An electoral bond was defined to mean "a bond issued by any scheduled bank under the scheme" notified by the central government. The Income Tax Act amendment allowed contributions made through electoral bonds as admissible for deduction under Section 88-GGB, like other company donations, without the requirement of mentioning the party in the accounts of the company. These electoral bonds would be "redeemable only in the designated account of a registered political party" and "redeemable within the prescribed time limit from issuance of bond".

Jaitley also limited cash donations to a maximum amount of Rs 72,000 from one person. He argued that electoral bonds ensured white money donations through banking channels. Donors purchase bonds (declared in their accounts), parties deposit them in declared accounts, and SBI maintains donor records. While the donor–party link remains masked, the system ensures transparency in transaction trails.

Assembly of Tamil Nadu, 2016—Holding of Election from 134-Aravakurichi and 174-Thanjavur Assembly Constituencies", Election Commission of India, Order dated 27 May 2016.

28. Gaurav Vivek Bhatnagar, "Breaking Down EC Order on R.K. Nagar By-Poll Cancellation", *The Wire*, accessed 24 August 2025, https://thewire.in/122540/breaking-down-ec-order-on-r-k-nagar-by-poll-cancellation/.

Fearing that the proposed scheme would divert all corporate political funding to the ruling party, the Opposition in general opposed the Electoral Bond scheme. The RBI bureaucracy found the electoral bonds akin to bearer bonds, which could be misused for money laundering. The ECI also felt that the scheme was a non-transparent way of funding. All this weighed on Jaitley's mind. He directed the DEA to frame "the scheme" to be notified by the central government under the powers assumed under the RBI Act. The former DEA secretary, Subhash Chandra Garg claims that he too had doubts about the scheme.[29]

However, Jaitley was convinced that this was the best way forward, that it was necessary to transform the financial management of political parties and promote transparency in political funding by allowing companies to donate from their accounts instead of using cash. He argued that the pre-existing system encouraged money laundering and the formation of shell companies to hide transactions. Jaitley also told Garg that political parties received up to 90 per cent of their funding in cash, which they would break into smaller donations of less than Rs 20,000 each to avoid reporting the actual donors to the ECI. He believed the Electoral Bond scheme would address these issues. The only compromise was that the companies would not disclose which party they donated to, which Jaitley argued would build confidence among the donors.

He explained that both electoral trusts, introduced by then finance minister Pranab Mukherjee in 2010, and electoral bonds ensured the use of white money and increased transparency. However, both mechanisms concealed the identity of the donor linked to the receiving political party. Jaitley explained the state of funding received by political parties to his officials, saying that even a party like the BJP received 90 per cent of its funding in cash. Most of this bulk donation came from companies. The system he had devised was, he recognised, not the best and most transparent, but it was better than any other prevalent system. There would be transparent accounting in companies. He also said other political parties had supported the scheme in private but were not courageous enough to do so in public.

Convinced by Jaitley's arguments, the DEA decided to "push the scheme through" despite his initial apprehensions. A meeting was convened with the

---

29. Subhash Chandra Garg, *We Also Make Money: An Insider's Account of How the Finance Ministry Functions* (HarperCollins, 2023).

RBI and a representative from the ECI in July 2017. RBI's principal concern at that time was to ensure that the electoral bonds were not akin to bearer bonds. The ECI representative did not want to be a party to any decision, as the ECI was in principle against electoral bonds. Nonetheless, there was a discussion between the DEA and the ECI about the features that would make the bonds least unpalatable.[30]

A key challenge was ensuring that all serious political parties had a fair chance to access electoral bonds. While the ECI registered parties and classified them as national or state parties, registration itself was extremely easy—resulting in more than 2500 registered parties. Only a few were nationally recognised, and about fifty to sixty were recognised at the state level. Allowing every registered party to receive electoral bond funding risked misuse and blackmail, and would have made the issuance and oversight of bonds unwieldy.

Since most registered parties had little or no political relevance, extending eligibility to all would effectively create channels to fund individuals or small groups rather than genuine political actors. Conversely, restricting access only to recognised parties would limit the scheme to a very small set of parties.

After considering various alternatives, Garg and the ECI settled on a threshold: any party that had secured at least 1 per cent of the vote in the most recent national or state election would be eligible to receive electoral bonds.

After firming up the key features of the Electoral Bond scheme in the first week of August 2017, Jaitley approved the scheme prepared by his officials and instructed that it be discussed with the PMO. On 14 May 2016, the Finance Act, 2016, had already amended Section 2(1)(j)(vi) of the Foreign Contribution (Regulation) Act, 2010 (FCRA), which defines "foreign source" to allow foreign companies having a majority share in Indian companies to donate to political parties. Previously, foreign companies were prohibited from donating to political parties under the FCRA and the Foreign Exchange Management Act, 1999.

On 31 March 2017, after Prime Minister Modi cleared the scheme, the Finance Act, 2017, amended the RPA; the RBI Act, 1934; the Income Tax Act, 1961; and the Companies Act, 2013. Section 11 of the Finance Act, 2017, amended Section 13-A of the Income Tax Act, exempting political parties from keeping a detailed record of contributions received through electoral bonds.

---

30. Ibid.

Section 135 amended Section 31 of the RBI Act. This permitted the central government to "authorise any scheduled bank to issue electoral bond[s]". Section 137 introduced a proviso to Section 29-C of the RPA, exempting political parties from publishing contributions received through electoral bonds in "Contribution Reports". These reports disclose contributions received by parties "in excess of twenty thousand rupees" from companies and individuals. Section 154 amended Section 182 of the Companies Act, 2013, which removed the upper limit on how much a company could donate to a political party. Previously, companies could only donate up to 7.5 per cent of three years of the company's net profits.[31]

On 2 January 2018, the Ministry of Finance issued a notification that introduced the Electoral Bond Scheme, 2018 (Electoral Bond Scheme).[32] Under the Electoral Bond Scheme, certain branches of SBI were authorised to sell electoral bonds. Bonds could be purchased in denominations of Rs 1000, Rs 10,000, Rs 100,000, Rs 10,00,000, and Rs 10,000,000 from the SBI. They were to be sold for ten days in January, April, July, and October each year. The identity of the purchaser was to remain anonymous to everyone, except the SBI, who had to record the buyer's KYC details. Political parties which secured more than 1 per cent votes "in the last general election to the House of the People or a Legislative Assembly" were eligible to accept donations through electoral bonds. The political parties were required to encash the bond within fifteen days of receiving it. After this period ended, the funds were to be deposited to the Prime Minister's Relief Fund.

Jaitley wrote an article emphasising the need for electoral bonds. On 7 January 2018, the finance ministry released a press note carrying extracts from his article:[33]

---

31. "Constitutionality of the Electoral Bond Scheme", *Association for Democratic Reforms vs Union of India*, *Supreme Court Observer*, available at https://www.scobserver.in/cases/association-for-democratic-reforms-electoral-bonds-case-background/.

32. Electoral Bond Scheme, 2018, available at https://www.scobserver.in/wp-content/uploads/2021/10/Electoral-Bonds-Scheme-2018.pdf.

33. "Why Electoral Bonds Are Necessary", Press Information Bureau, Government of India, Ministry of Finance, available at https://www.pib.gov.in/newsite/PrintRelease.aspx?relid=175452.

India is the largest democracy in the world. However, despite strengthening various institutions for the last seven decades, India has not been able to evolve a transparent political funding system. Elections and political parties are a fundamental feature of parliamentary democracy. Elections cost money. The round the year functioning of the political parties involves a large expenditure. Parties run offices throughout the country. Staff salaries, travelling expenses, establishment costs are regular expenditures of political parties. There has not been a single year where elections either for the Parliament or State Assemblies have not been held. Besides expenditure of individual candidates, political parties have to spend money on election campaigns, publicity, tours, travels and election-related establishments. These expenditures run into hundreds of crores. Yet there has not been a transparent funding mechanism of the political system.

The conventional system of political funding is to rely on donations. These donations, big or small, come from a range of sources from political workers, sympathisers, small business people and even large industrialists. The conventional practice of funding the political system was to take donations in cash and undertake these expenditures in cash. The sources are anonymous or pseudonymous. The quantum of money was never disclosed. The present system ensures unclean money coming from unidentifiable sources. It is a wholly non-transparent system. Most political groups seem fairly satisfied with the present arrangement and would not mind this status-quo to continue. The effort, therefore, is to run down any alternative system which is devised to cleanse up the political funding mechanism.

A major step was taken during the first NDA government led by Shri Atal Bihari Vajpayee. The Income Tax Act was amended to include a provision that donations made to political parties would be treated as expenditure and would thus give a tax advantage to the donor. If the political party disclosed its donations in a prescribed manner, it would also not be liable to pay any tax. A political party was expected to file its returns both with the income-tax authorities and Election Commission. It was hoped that donors would increasingly start donating money by cheque. Some donors did start following this practise but most of them were reluctant to disclose the details of the quantum of donation given to a political party. This was because they feared consequences visiting them from political opponents. The law was further amended during the UPA government to provide for "pass through" electoral trust so that the donors would park their money with the electoral trusts which in turn would distribute the same to various political parties. Both these reforms taken together resulted in only a small fraction of the donations coming in form of cheques.

In order to make a serious effort to carry forward this reform process, I had announced in my budget speech for the year 2017–18 that the existing system would be substantially widened and donations of clean money could be made to political parties in several ways. A donor could enjoy a tax deduction by donating in cheque. Donors were also free to donate moneys online to political parties. A cash donation to a political party could not exceed an amount of Rs 2000. In addition, a scheme of electoral bonds was announced to enable clean money and substantial transparency being brought into the system of political funding.

I do believe that donations made online or through cheques remain an ideal method of donating to political parties. However, these have not become very popular in India since they involve disclosure of donor's identity. However, the Electoral Bond scheme, which I placed before the Parliament a few days ago, envisages total clean money and substantial transparency coming into the system of political funding. A donor can purchase electoral bonds from a specified bank only by a banking instrument. He would have to disclose in his accounts the amount of political bonds that he has purchased. The life of the bond would be only 15 days. A bond can only be encashed in a pre-declared account of a political party. Every political party in its returns will have to disclose the amount of donations it has received through electoral bonds to the Election Commission. The entire transactions would be through banking instruments. As against a total non-transparency in the present system of cash donations where the donor, the donee, the quantum of donations and the nature of expenditure are all undisclosed, some element of transparency would be introduced in as much as all donors declare in their accounts the amount of bonds that they have purchased and all parties declare the quantum of bonds

> that they have received. How much each donor has distributed to a political party would be known only to the donor. This is necessary because once this disclosure is made, past experience has shown, donors would not find the scheme attractive and would go back to the less-desirable option of donating by cash. In fact the choice has now to be consciously made between the existing system of substantial cash donations which involves total unclean money and is non-transparent and the new scheme which gives the option to the donors to donate through entirely a transparent method of cheque, online transaction or through electoral bonds. While all three methods involve clean money, the first two are totally transparent and the Electoral Bond scheme is a substantial improvement in transparency over the present system of no-transparency.
>
> The government is willing to consider all suggestions to further strengthen the cleansing of political funding in India. It has to be borne in mind that impractical suggestions will not improve the cash denominated system. They would only consolidate it.

The Electoral Bond Scheme was challenged before the Supreme Court alleging that it violated the right to information of citizens, and was contrary to the principle of free and fair elections. An affluent person could make financial contributions to political parties with a legitimate possibility of quid pro quo arrangements, the petitions said. On 25 March 2019, the ECI, one of the respondents, filed an affidavit opposing the Electoral Bond Scheme. The affidavit claimed that the scheme is contrary to the goal of transparency in political finance. It also claimed that the ECI had shared a letter to the government on 26 May 2017, warning against the "repercussions/impact on the transparency aspect of political finance/funding". Further, the ECI submitted that exempting political parties from sharing details regarding contributions would keep information on foreign funding in the dark. The affidavit stated, "...unchecked foreign funding of political parties in India, which could lead to Indian policies being influenced by foreign companies".[34]

34. "Counter Affidavit on Behalf of Election Commission of India", *Association for Democratic Reforms vs Union of India,* available at https://www.scobserver.in/wp-

On 1 April 2019, the government submitted a rebuttal to the ECI contention claiming that the Electoral Bond Scheme was "a pioneer step in bringing electoral reforms, to ensure that the spirit of transparency and accountability in political funding is maintained". The government claimed that political parties largely received funds through cash donations, leading to an "unregulated flow of black money".[35] The government assured that these issues would no longer hamper political funding because only one authorised bank, the SBI, could issue such bonds. Further, providing KYC details ensures accountability.[36]

Jaitley defended the Electoral Bond Scheme stating it had been enacted in pursuance of a legitimate state interest—to shift from cash-driven, unregulated, and unaccounted cash-based political donations to a regulated, digital, and legal political donation framework. The provisions of the Electoral Bond Scheme had a specific object and purpose of curbing black money and protecting donor privacy. "Blessed with great wisdom and depth, he [Pranab Mukherjee] realised that merely providing for cheque donations won't bring a change. Donors fear the consequences of their revealed identities being linked to a political party to whom they donated," Jaitley wrote in a blog dated 7 April 2019. He pointed out the hypocrisy of attacks on electoral bonds while electoral trusts were not criticized, given they both operated on the same principle. He concluded by suggesting that NGOs and commentators should consider the larger implications of their criticisms and recognise the improvements in transparency brought about by electoral bonds and trusts. Jaitley criticised NGOs for their reporting on political donations, particularly those claiming the BJP receives disproportionately more funds. He argued that these claims demonstrated a misunderstanding of party funding, emphasising that all parties require similar amounts of money proportionate to the seats they contest. The key difference, he asserted, lies in the method of fund collection, with the BJP favouring legitimate means like cheques and electoral bonds over

---

content/uploads/2021/10/Counter-Affidavit-by-Election-Commission-of-India-against-Electoral-Bonds.pdf.

35. "Rejoinder to the Counter Affidavit", *Association for Democratic Reforms vs Union of India,* available at https://www.scobserver.in/wp-content/uploads/2021/10/Rejoinder-by-the-Ministry-of-Finance-in-Electoral-Bonds-case.pdf.

36. "Constitutionality of the Electoral Bond Scheme", *Association for Democratic Reforms vs Union of India, Supreme Court Observer,* available at https://www.scobserver.in/cases/association-for-democratic-reforms-electoral-bonds-case-background/.

black money. Jaitley urged NGOs and commentators to prioritise systemic progress over ideological opposition.

On 31 October 2023, a five-judge Constitution bench heard arguments over three days. Petitioners argued that the Electoral Bond Scheme increased corporate funding, black money circulation, and corruption. And that voters have a right to information about political parties' source of funding, as it informed the policies and views of that party. The government implored that the scheme was an economic reform and urged the court to refrain from judicial review of an economic policy. On 2 November 2023, the Constitution bench reserved the judgment. On 15 February 2024, the court unanimously struck down the Electoral Bond Scheme. The bench held that the scheme violated the voters' right to information enshrined in Article 19(1)(a) of the Constitution.

Noting that the government had itself classified the scheme as an "electoral reform", the court held that the amendments introduced to make way for the scheme relate to the electoral process and the scheme could not be tested on the parameters applicable to economic policy. It would thus be subject to judicial scrutiny. The court held that the scheme infringed upon the right to information of the voter by anonymising contributions through electoral bonds. Recognising the nexus between the right of citizens and open governance, the judgment held that effective participation in democratic governance was not just a means to an end but an end in itself. Citizens have a duty to hold the government of the day accountable for their actions and inactions, and they can effectively fulfil this duty only if the government was not clothed in secrecy.

Regarding black money, the judgment stated that the scheme was not the only means for curbing black money in electoral finance; there were other alternatives which substantially did so while not impacting the right to information. Stating that at a primary level, political contributions give a "seat at the table" to the contributor, which could translate into influence over policymaking, the judgment noted there was a legitimate possibility that a financial contribution by an affluent person to a political party would lead to quid pro quo arrangements in the form of introducing a policy change or licence granting. The scheme was not fool-proof and gaps would enable political parties to find the particulars of the contributions made to them. Thus, de jure anonymity of the contributors did not translate to de facto anonymity. Notably, the judgment did not cite any instance of such political contributions possibly influencing a policy change or extracting a political favour in the last six years.

Having struck down the scheme, the court directed that the sale of electoral bonds be stopped with immediate effect. The SBI was directed to submit details of the electoral bonds purchased from 12 April 2019 till the date of the decision (15 February 2024) to the ECI. This would include details of the purchaser as well as the political parties that the bonds were given to. Further, the court ordered the ECI to publish the information shared by the SBI on its official website within one week from the receipt of the information. In his separate reasoning, Justice Sanjeev Khanna suggested that the Electoral Trust Scheme introduced in 2013 best realised the objective of the government in a real and substantial manner without significantly impacting the fundamental right of the voter to know.[37]

The Supreme Court decision was a setback to the government. This was perhaps one decision led by Jaitley's ministry that could not stand the scrutiny of law. Jaitley was not alive to respond to the decision. Had he been alive, he would have likely accepted the decision with grace or perhaps persuaded the Supreme Court to allow the government to correct the legal flaws, rather than it being set aside.

★

Another reform Jaitley pursued concerned political defections. For decades, India's political landscape had been marred by frequent party-switching among legislators, leading to chronic instability. The notorious phrase "Aaya Ram, Gaya Ram" emerged in response to this constant churn, as elected representatives repeatedly shifted allegiances and toppled governments in the process. The resulting turmoil deeply worried many responsible political leaders. Over the

---

37. Sumant Batra, "Cleansing Political Funding in India", *Financial Express, accessed 24 August 2025,* https://www.financialexpress.com/opinion/cleansing-political-funding-in-india/3399069/.

years, several attempts were made to craft legislation that could effectively curb such defections.[38]

The legislative path of the anti-defection law has been long and uneven. Its roots can be traced to the 1967 general elections, which produced a mixed outcome for the Congress party. Although it remained in power at the Centre, its Lok Sabha strength fell sharply from 361 to 283 seats. In the same year, Congress lost control of seven state governments as MLAs shifted their loyalties. Amid this turmoil, Congress MP P. Venkatasubbaiah proposed establishing a high-level committee to examine the growing problem of legislators defecting from one party to another. The suggestion triggered intense debate in the Lok Sabha. Opposition members derisively labelled it a "Save Congress" initiative, while Congress leaders accused the Opposition of enticing MLAs to cross over.[39]

Despite the heated exchanges, the Lok Sabha eventually agreed to set up a committee on political defections, chaired by then home minister Y.B. Chavan. The committee defined "defection" as a legislator's voluntary abandonment of allegiance to the party on whose symbol they were elected, except where the shift was the result of a party decision. The Chavan Committee's report underscored that the primary incentive for defections was the prospect of ministerial office. Of the 210 MLAs who defected across seven states, 116 were rewarded with ministerial posts in the governments they helped bring to power. To address this, the committee recommended that defectors be barred from holding ministerial office for one year (or until they were re-elected), that the size of the Council of Ministers be reduced, and that political parties adopt internal codes of conduct to limit such disruptions.

Following the report, two unsuccessful legislative attempts were made to curb defections—the first by Indira Gandhi's home minister, Uma Shankar Dikshit in 1973, and the second by law minister Shanti Bhushan under the Janata Party government in 1978. However, consensus remained elusive,

---

38. P.D.T. Achary, "Explained: What Does the Anti-defection Law Say? What Can Disqualify a Legislator?", *The Indian Express, accessed 24 August 2025, https://indianexpress.com/article/explained/what-can-disqualify-a-legislator-anti-defection-law-goa-congress-crisis-5825943/.*

39. Chakshu Roy, "Explained: The Limits of Anti-defection", PRS Legislative Research, accessed 24 August 2025, https://prsindia.org/articles-by-prs-team/explained-the-limits-of-anti-defection.

primarily due to concerns that a strict anti-defection law might infringe on legislators' freedom of speech, a constitutional right.

The third, a successful attempt, was made in 1985 under the Rajiv Gandhi government. Despite Opposition MPs arguing that the bill would stifle free expression and politicise the Speaker's role, the government swiftly passed the Constitution (52nd Amendment) Act, 1985, in just two days—coinciding with Mahatma Gandhi's death anniversary.[40] According to the 1985 Act, legislators could lose their seats for violating party whips (inside the legislature) or publicly opposing their party (outside the legislature); legislators were protected from disqualification in cases of a split if 1/3rd of party members defected or a merger if 2/3rds joined another party; and the Presiding Officer of the legislature was made the sole authority to adjudicate defection cases.

Almost immediately, political parties began testing the law's limits. Disputes over what constituted a "split" destabilised the V.P. Singh and Chandra Shekhar governments, while Speakers faced accusations of partisanship. In 1992, Lok Sabha Speaker Shivraj Patil remarked, "The Speaker is not expected to dabble in keeping political parties weak or strong, or to discipline Parliamentarians for their party's purposes."[41] The Supreme Court later intervened to clarify what conduct outside the legislature qualified as defection and the extent of the Speaker's powers. While upholding the Speaker's authority, the court also ruled that their decisions were subject to judicial review.

The next significant step in the evolution of the anti-defection framework came in 2003, when Jaitley introduced the Constitution (91st Amendment) Bill to remedy several weaknesses in the existing law. Under the earlier Constitution (52nd Amendment) Act of 1985, a provision allowed that if a split occurred in the original political party—resulting in one-third of its legislators forming a separate group—those legislators would not face disqualification. This provision resulted in large-scale defections and the lawmakers were convinced that the provision of a split in the party was being misused. Therefore, it was proposed to delete this provision.

40. The Congress had over 400 MPs in the Lok Sabha.

41. Chakshu Roy, "Explained: The Limits of Anti-defection", PRS Legislative Research, accessed 24 August 2025, https://prsindia.org/articles-by-prs-team/explained-the-limits-of-anti-defection.

A committee headed by Pranab Mukherjee examined the bill. The committee observed, "The provision of split has been grossly misused to engineer multiple divisions in the party, as a result of which the evil of defection has not been checked in the right earnest. Further it is also observed that the lure of office of profit plays a dominant part in the political horse-trading resulting in spate of defections and counter defections."

The 2003 amendment was passed. The amendment made it mandatory for leaders switching political parties—whether singly or in groups—to resign as legislative members and seek re-election. The 1/3rd split provision which offered protection to defectors was deleted from the law on the committee's recommendation. The 2003 amendment also incorporated the 1967 advice of the Y.B. Chavan committee in limiting the size of the Council of Ministers, and preventing defecting legislators from joining the Council of Ministers until their re-election. With the 2003 amendment deleting the split provision, the only remaining protection against disqualification was the clause relating to mergers under Paragraph 4 of the Tenth Schedule. Though seemingly minor, this change had far-reaching consequences. Its effects were felt in subsequent political events in states like Goa and Karnataka, where defecting MLAs were prevented from immediately joining the government.[42]

Eliminating the split provision encouraged parties to orchestrate large-scale defections—facilitated as "mergers"—rather than smaller, "retail" ones. Legislators began resigning their seats to avoid disqualification and still secure ministerial posts. The cap on the size of the Council of Ministers, in turn, led states to expand the number of parliamentary secretary positions. Speakers also became increasingly entangled in political manoeuvring, actively aiding in the formation or collapse of governments. Since the anti-defection law does not prescribe a time limit for ruling on disqualification petitions, Speakers have issued swift decisions when politically convenient or delayed them for years when circumstances demanded.[43]

---

42. Liz Mathew, "Arun Jaitley: Mentor to the Young, MP Who Helped UPA Govt on Nuclear Bill", *The Indian Express, accessed 24 August 2025*, https://indianexpress.com/article/india/arun-jaitley-dead-mentor-to-the-young-mp-who-helped-upa-govt-on-nuclear-bill-5934494/.

43. Chakshu Roy, "Explained: The Limits of Anti-defection", PRS Legislative Research, accessed 24 August 2025, https://prsindia.org/articles-by-prs-team/explained-the-limits-of-anti-defection.

★

Another electoral reform associated with Jaitley was granting the Model Code of Conduct (MCC) a mandatory character under Article 324 of the Constitution to safeguard free and fair elections. When Vajpayee assumed office in 1999, the MCC had no statutory force and functioned merely as an advisory guideline. The origins of the MCC go back to the 1960 Kerala Assembly elections, when the state administration introduced an initial "Code of Conduct" to regulate the behaviour of political parties. The idea gained wider traction in the 1962 Lok Sabha elections, during which the Election Commission circulated the code to all recognised political parties and state governments.[44]

Jaitley, who was overseeing the law ministry in 1999, believed that Article 324, which empowers the ECI to take necessary steps for fair elections, fills any legislative gaps in existing statutes on aspects of election conduct.

> The MCC is an extremely important and powerful instrument available to the Election Commission for the conduct of free and fair elections. There was a time when the MCC was only directive in nature. There used to be frequent litigation about its legal enforceability ... Vajpayee and the then Election Commission, agreed in principle to give statutory support to the MCC. The Chief Election Commissioner at that time, Dr. M.S. Gill, and the Law Ministry, which I was looking after, entered into consent terms about the MCC.[45]

The consent terms were filed in a pending litigation in the Supreme Court. The Supreme Court had consistently interpreted Article 324 as not applying to areas already covered by legislation. This principle, the government and the ECI argued, also applied to the MCC, which derived its authority from

---

44. B.PAC, A Code for Integrity: Understanding the Model Code of Conduct for Ethical Election, accessed 27 September 2025, https://bpac.in/understanding-code-of-conduct-for-ethical-elections/.

45. Arun Jaitley, "Model Code of Conduct Does Not Take Away the Right to Free Speech", accessed 27 September 2025, https://www.arunjaitley.com/model-code-of-conduct-does-not-take-away-the-right-to-free-speech/.

Article 324. "While law prevails in areas where electoral offences are specifically covered by law, the MCC, operated in the remaining areas," Jaitley wrote in his blog. He emphasised that the MCC cannot dilute the fundamental nature of Article 19(1)(a) of the Constitution, guaranteeing free speech. He stressed that the MCC has to be interpreted in a way that it respects, rather than restricts, free speech, which is only subject to the restrictions outlined in Article 19(2). He believed the ECI had a responsibility to protect free speech, enforcing provisions only where election law was violated or where speeches fell within the permissible restrictions of Article 19(2). The MCC and free speech, he argued, must coexist harmoniously.[46]

The Supreme Court enforced, accepted and approved the consent terms, giving the MCC statutory support under Article 324 of the Constitution. This strengthened the MCC considerably. Since then the MCC acquired more teeth.

The MCC comes into force immediately when the election dates are declared and remains till the results are announced. The MCC applies to all elections from the Lok Sabha and state assemblies to local bodies. It instructs how the ministers of the parties in power must conduct themselves when the MCC is in force. It explains how parties can lodge complaints to the ECI observers in case of a dispute. All organisations, committees, corporations, and commissions funded wholly or partially by the Centre or state are bound by the MCC. While listed political parties and candidates are bound to follow the MCC, even non-political organisations which hold campaigns favouring a political party or candidate are bound to follow specific guidelines mentioned by the ECI.

Political parties and candidates are expected to avoid commenting on the private lives of opponents, restricting their criticism to policies, programmes, past performance, and public conduct. Their social media communications must similarly avoid personal attacks. They must not engage in actions that deepen existing social divisions or incite hostility among caste, religious, or linguistic groups, nor make appeals to such identities to secure votes. All parties and candidates must comply with any restrictive or prohibitory orders in force at venues where meetings are held. Permission from local police is required for the use of public spaces and loudspeakers. For public processions, organisers must provide police with the time, starting and ending points, and the proposed

---

46. Ibid.

route, and receive clearance. Campaign workers must carry identity cards or badges and, if they are not voters, candidates, or authorised election agents for that constituency, must leave the area once campaigning ends. They are also prohibited from disrupting rival meetings, conducting processions past such meetings, or removing or defacing opponents' posters. These are only some of the many obligations set out in the MCC that parties, candidates, and government authorities are required to observe.[47]

The MCC is not a statutory instrument and is not directly enforceable through legislation passed by Parliament; many of its provisions do not carry specific penalties for violation. However, several actions prohibited by the MCC—such as creating tension among caste, religious, or linguistic groups; appealing to communal or caste identities for votes; using places of worship for campaign purposes; bribing, intimidating, or impersonating voters; canvassing within 100 metres of polling stations; transporting voters; disrupting public meetings; distributing liquor on polling day; and holding public meetings within forty-eight hours of the close of polling—are classified as electoral offences or corrupt practices under the Indian Penal Code, 1860 (now the Bharatiya Nyaya Sanhita, 2023) and the Representation of the People Act. These attract penalties under those laws. Complaints related to elections may be made to ECI observers, the returning officer, the local magistrate, the Chief Electoral Officer, or the Election Commission itself, and any directions issued by the ECI, returning officer, or District Election Officer must be strictly followed.

Understanding the significance of the MCC is vital for citizens in ensuring fairness and transparency of elections. Citizens can play a crucial role in promoting responsible and ethical electoral practices by acquainting themselves with the MCC. By doing so, they gain the ability to hold parties and candidates accountable for their conduct throughout the electoral process. When Arun Jaitley contested for the Amritsar parliamentary seat in 2014, he made all efforts to observe the MCC.[48] Its effective enforcement would be a befitting tribute to Arun Jaitley.

---

47. Suchitra Karthikeyan, "What Is Model Code of Conduct, and What Are the Penalties for Violation? | Explained", *The Hindu, accessed 24 August 2025*, https://www.thehindu.com/elections/model-code-of-conduct-explained-when-in-force-guidelines-and-action-on-violations/article67957740.ece.

48. As told by his friend and supporter, Narendra Dhruv Batra.

30

Judicial Independence

Jaitley strongly believed that an independent judiciary is fundamental to a healthy democracy and consistently argued for safeguarding that independence. He rejected the practice of attacking judges simply because their rulings were unfavourable. After all, judges adjudicate matters that affect both the everyday lives of ordinary citizens and the interests of the most powerful commercial and political actors. "Their judgment pleases us at times and leaves us unhappy on many occasions. But that is the reality of the system which we have learned to live with".[1] He advised the media to apply restraint when reporting a court decision. "A judge is not in a popularity race. He owes his commitment only to law, justice, and fairness. A judge is neither to follow the ballot box nor is he to be swayed by the times," Jaitley often reminded the media. Both the media and judiciary have to live with each other. "In order to coexist, both must respect the respective rights of each of these institutions," he wrote in one of his blogs.[2]

> One cannot take upon itself the task of destroying the other. … Mainstream print media conventionally had greater editorial control. The ability to dissect facts and take a balanced view was much higher.

1. Arun Jaitley, "It's Time to Stand up With the Judiciary", accessed 24 August 2025, https://www.arunjaitley.com/its-time-to-stand-up-with-the-judiciary/.
2. Ibid.

> But of late, the rat race for grabbing eyeballs or viewership has begun. A judge is continuously judged every day ... in the course of his personal and judicial conduct. Every time he makes a comment or writes a judgment, every word is scrutinised ... Ordinarily, courts tend to ignore contemptuous criticism. Courts are willing to accept criticism of judgments because that aids the process of legal evolution. The power of contempt is intended to protect the dignity of the court. However, the power of contempt is rarely and sparingly used. A section exploits this judicial refrain of excessively using the power of contempt. However, they themselves have no hesitation in contemptuous behaviour themselves.[3]

Jaitley was sharply critical of those who sought to exert pressure on the Supreme Court, describing them as "institutional destabilisers". He argued that such individuals targeted judges through orchestrated social-media campaigns whenever they failed to secure a favourable order, showing scant regard for truth while posing as champions of the public interest. He condemned their conduct in court as disrespectful—both towards the bench and towards opposing counsel—remarking that they even threatened walkouts when judges disagreed with them. Jaitley cautioned that India had been witnessing repeated assaults by such "institution disruptors" on judges who refused to yield, warning of an ongoing pattern of mass intimidation both within and beyond the courtroom.[4]

He stressed the importance of principled individuals standing by the judiciary when destabilising forces mount their attacks, and argued that those who spread falsehoods to undermine the institution should face exemplary consequences.[5] In his popular blog, he wrote:

> It may not be an exaggeration to say that today both in court and by creating an environment outside, a mass-intimidation of judges is on. Some lawyers have used intimidatory behaviour as a tactic to

3. Ibid.
4. Ibid.
5. Ibid.

> expand their practise. Intimidation and discrediting are important weapons in the hands of these people. Reputation is an integral part of a person's fundamental right to live with dignity. An intimidated judge can fear consequences of a possible view that he is taking. It is, therefore, essential that all well-meaning persons stand with the judicial institution when destabilisers get ready for an assault.[6]

Jaitley feared that the liberal attitude of the courts had emboldened the institution disruptors; they get away because of the magnanimity and the compassion of judges. He also deplored frequent attempts made to get some parliamentarians to sign a motion of impeachment against judges.[7]

Jaitley always defended the Supreme Court as an institution. On 12 January 2018, four senior judges of the Supreme Court—Justices Jasti Chelameswar, Ranjan Gogoi, Madan B. Lokur and Kurian Joseph—called a press conference at the residence of the second senior judge and mounted a virtual revolt against the then Chief Justice of India (CJI) Dipak Misra. Addressing the press, the judges listed, what they termed, a litany of problems afflicting the country's highest court and warned they could destroy Indian democracy. During the conference, they aired their grievances over Justice Dipak Misra's style of functioning.

> The administration of the Supreme Court is not in order, and many things, which are less than desirable, have happened in the last few months. We met CJI this morning. We collectively tried to persuade CJI that certain things aren't in order so take remedial measures but unfortunately our efforts failed. Among the many demands for change put forth by the four senior judges of the court was a "consultation process" among the top five judges of the court (by seniority) in drawing up the roster and work allocation. It is with no pleasure that

6. Ibid.

7. Ibid.

> we have been compelled to do this, administration of the Supreme Court is not in order.[8]

The unprecedented step left both the judiciary and observers taken aback, creating uncertainty about how such open discord within a revered institution would be resolved. The press conference thrust the judges into public view as a divided group.

Jaitley reacted strongly, defending emphatically the office of the CJI: "The Chief Justice of India is the first amongst the equals in the Supreme Court. He is the head of the judicial institutions. He is both the 'Master of the Roster' and the 'Head of the Collegium' which makes binding recommendations for the appointment of judges." He emphasised that the CJI, as the head of the judicial institutions, holds a pivotal position, and his integrity, ethics, scholarship, and fairness reflect the image of India's judiciary. Jaitley warned that if the "Iqbal" or prestige of the judiciary is destroyed, the institution itself would crumble.[9]

Jaitley blamed the development on vested interest at the Bar, the compulsive contrarians, and a set of extra-adventurist lawyers. "A precedent has now been legitimised. His [the CJI's] successors will find it difficult to escape similar treatment. The threat to the independence of the judiciary can also come from the public pressures that these contrarians exert on judges," Jaitley wrote in his blog.[10]

On another occasion, when a former Supreme Court employee made harassment charges against the then CJI,[11] Jaitley criticised the complainant for sensationalising the allegations by distributing copies of her representation

---

8. Krishnadas Rajagopal, *The Hindu*, dated 13 January 2018, "Four SC judges air differences with CJI Misra", accessed 27 September 2025, https://www.thehindu.com/news/national/four-sc-judges-air-differences-with-cji-misra/article22432428.ece

9. Arun Jaitley, "It's Time to Stand up With the Judiciary", accessed 24 August 2025, https://www.arunjaitley.com/its-time-to-stand-up-with-the-judiciary/.

10. Arun Jaitley, "The Compulsive Contrarian and His Manufactured Logic", accessed 24 August 2025, https://www.arunjaitley.com/the-compulsive-contrarian-and-his-manufactured-logic/.

11. Atul Dev, Nikita Saxena, "Supreme Charge", *The Caravan*, 20 April 2019, accessed September 2025, https://caravanmagazine.in/law/former-supreme-court-employee-accuses-cji-ranjan-gogoi-sexual-harassment.

to other Supreme Court judges and the media instead of submitting it to the appropriate committee. Jaitley accused four digital media organisations for lending credence to completely unverified allegations. He expressed his puzzlement at the Opposition party's tendency to lend support to these "fringe campaigns" against judges and the CJI.[12]

At the same time, Jaitley favoured accountability of judges. When The Indian Express carried a detailed account of the alleged incident involving a young intern and a former Supreme Court judge, he advocated that the judge, who was also the chairperson of a state's Human Rights Commission, should step down. Jaitley said this case was different as allegations against the judge had been tested. The CJI had appointed a three-judge inquiry committee to look into the incident. Both the intern and judge had given their versions to the committee. Media reports indicated that the committee has found prima facie substance in the complaint of the intern.

The committee observed that the allegations prima facie disclosed an act of unwelcome behaviour (unwelcome verbal/non-verbal conduct of sexual nature) by the former judge. However, considering the fact that the court on the administrative side did not have a jurisdiction to deal with a retired judge and a former intern, the full court on the administrative side opined that no further follow up action could be taken by the court.[13] It was, therefore, not merely an untested allegation, Jaitley asserted. There was reason to believe on the basis of the report of the three judges that an offence could have been committed. Since the former judge of the Supreme Court held a high position after retirement, Jaitley suggested the judge should step down.

> The judge's insistence on continuing in office raises a few questions. Firstly, if it were a case of a prominent politician rather than a former judge, would the judicial institutions have completely washed their hands off or would they have monitored the investigations? The fact that a former judge of the highest court is involved demands that the standards of judicial scrutiny will have to be higher than the normal.

---

12. Arun Jaitley, "It's Time to Stand up With the Judiciary", accessed 24 August 2025, https://www.arunjaitley.com/its-time-to-stand-up-with-the-judiciary/.

13. Arun Jaitley, "Justice Ganguly Must Demit Office", accessed 24 August 2025, https://www.arunjaitley.com/justice-ganguly-must-demit-office/.

Secondly, in the face of this serious allegation, can he at all discharge his functions as the Chairman of Human Rights Commission? Thirdly, would it not be fair and proper that the former judge contests these allegations as an ordinary citizen rather than a high functionary? If he were to relinquish his office, he would only be protecting the dignity of the office that he occupies. His decision to cling on to his office only establishes that even judges like most in the political positions continue to stick to their office till the intensity of public opinion forces them out.[14]

★

On 18 August 2011, the Rajya Sabha witnessed a historic development. Justice Soumitra Sen of the Calcutta High Court stood on the verge of becoming the first judge in India to be impeached. This was only the second such instance in Parliament's history—and the first time the Upper House voted on an impeachment motion. The earlier case involved Justice V. Ramaswami in 1993, when the Lok Sabha initiated proceedings but the motion fell short of the required two-thirds majority.

As the proceedings were about to commence against Justice Sen, Jaitley, as the Leader of the Opposition, entered the Upper House carrying a substantial stack of weighty, new-looking books. Later, Jaitley explained to inquisitive reporters that he had invested over Rs 35,000 in legal texts to thoroughly prepare for the impending debate. The proceedings closely resembled a courtroom drama, featuring frequent citations of evidence, legal provisions, and fervent arguments from all sides.[15] As the Leader of the Opposition in the Rajya Sabha, Jaitley made a strong pitch for Justice Sen's removal, noting that

---

14. Arun Jaitley, "16th December 2013", accessed 24 August 2025, https://www.arunjaitley.com/16th-december-2013/.

15. Saubhadra Chatterji, "When Arun Jaitley Spent Rs 35,000 to Prep for Rajya Sabha Debate", *Hindustan Times*, accessed 24 August 2025, https://www.hindustantimes.com/india-news/where-you-stand-depends-on-where-you-sit-arun-jaitley-s-immortal-words-on-functioning-of-parliament/story-do48Uz2VJYJnFi8KwP5n4M.html.

right through his tenure as receiver and then a judge of the high court, he never rendered account of the money entrusted to him, and in fact created encumbrances and misappropriated the money, "as an in-house committee appointed by judiciary had found".[16]

"Today is an occasion which is both sad and historic. We have all assembled here in an alternative capacity of Parliament where we perform a function where we decide the fate of a man who has conventionally been deciding the fate of others. Though this is a political House, it performs a judicial function," Jaitley said.[17] He reminded the House:

> We are conscious of the fact that the power of impeachment is intended to be exercised in the rarest of the rare cases. The power of impeachment of a holder of a constitutional office is an authority or jurisdiction given to us to remove a man in order to save the dignity of his office. The office gets precedence over the man who occupies it. And if we find that the man is guilty of any misdemeanour, in the case of a judge, a proven misconduct or incapacity, we impeach him so that we can ensure that the dignity of the office of judge that he occupies can be maintained. This power, Sir, is both punitive and also a deterrent power. We regulate the exercise of this power by Article 124(4) in the case of a judge of a Supreme Court and read with it Article 217 in the case of a judge of a High Court. The two grounds on which a judge, in either case, can be impeached is either proven misbehaviour or incapacity. In this case, Mr Yechury's Motion is confined to the first ground, i.e. proven misbehaviour. Sir, when these articles were being drafted by the Constituent Assembly, Shri Gopalaswamy Iyengar had expressed the hope that, perhaps, these powers would never be used. He espoused the confidence that, at least, in his lifetime it will never be used. His prophecy was partly correct because it was not used in his lifetime.

---

16. "Arun Jaitley in Parliament: Fight Against Terror Is a Battle—India Cannot Afford to Lose", Bharatiya Janata Party, available at https://www.bjp.org/files/books-monographs/arun-jaitley-fight-against-terrorism.pdf.

17. Ibid.

Sir, as times have passed by, there are too many whispers and too many aberrations which we are confronted with. It is only a very rare case which comes to this House for consideration. And, therefore, Sir, we are now living in a changed time where the level of vigilance and the standards of probity will also have to be higher. The judges will also have to realise that Judiciary is no longer an institution which lives on ivory towers. Judges, like most of us here and others holding constitutional offices or high offices, also now live in glass houses. And, therefore, whether it is public or it is the media or it is the litigant or it is the Bar, they eventually become the best judges of judges.

Their conduct is also going to be watched and watched very closely. This is not to say that we can make unfounded allegations against a Judge because a Judge in ordinary circumstances speaks only through his judgments and he is not able to defend himself. Therefore, we have to be very cautious about every word that we say as right to speak, both inside and outside this House that Judges and the Judiciary is an institution which cannot be thrown to the wolfs. It cannot be made an object of unfounded allegations but it will also like other institutions have to stand by the scrutiny of all times. When, Sir, a Judge is sought to be impeached through a procedure, what are really the standards we expect from the Judge? Do we expect from a Judge to resort to every technicality which is available to him? Do we expect a Judge to say that "I will not enter the box so that I cannot be questioned; there are hard facts which I will not be able to answer?" Or, do we expect a Judge to be a role model as a litigant and then candidly states every question that is put to him because system cannot suffer for a Judge who is stigmatised? A Judge who is stigmatised can really never be in a position to represent the face of rule of law in India and be a Judge as far as others in the society are concerned. Therefore, Sir, when a Judge says, "I will not appear myself and answer the questions, or, that first that prove the allegations against me and let me see how much you have in your pocket against me, only then I will let you know what my response is", that is not the case of an ideal Judge facing an inquiry. It has been repeatedly said and we hear rightly so these days that holders of high offices must be like Caesar's wife, they must be above suspicion. Caesar divorced his second wife because he suspected her of an illicit relationship. Even though the charge was not fully proved, he went through divorce because he said, "Caesar's wife, considering the position she is in, must be unsuspectable." So, a Judge cannot really say, "First prove an allegation against me beyond reasonable doubt and only then I will come up and tell you whether I have an answer to give or not." A Judge by his very character must be "unsuspectable". His position must be such that nobody can point a finger to him. We have, Sir, heard the presentation of the learned Judge at length. Sir, I have had an opportunity to read the entire record which the Secretariat has served and distributed to the Members. At times I got an impression whether the facts which I have read are similar to the facts which I was hearing from the learned Judge. Sir, when we were young lawyers we were all trained that if in a given case you are strong on facts, you bang the facts first. If you are weak on facts but strong on law, you bang the law. And, if you are weak on the both, then you bang the desk, at least, you will appear to be confident. I was wondering what the facts are. The facts are in a very narrow compass. One does not have to go into a complicated circle of facts in order to determine that there are many other cases in the Judiciary where people are accountable. Of course, there are other cases in the Judiciary also where the persons should be accountable. In the matter of probity or lack of probity, there is no right of equality. There are other people who have committed offences while being Judge and got away with it ... [that] is no ground available to any Judge to say that "I must also get away from this offence". In the matter of violation of law there is no Article 14. Article 14, the Right to Equality, applies in the matter of application of law not in the matter of violation of law. Therefore, to discredit other Judges and say, "Well, there are others like this and, therefore, I must get away" is never an argument available to any citizen, least of all, to a Judge.[1]

On 18 August 2011, the Rajya Sabha passed the impeachment motion against Justice Soumitra Sen of the Calcutta High Court, clearing the first stage for his

1. Ibid.

removal. This was the first time in the country's history that an impeachment motion against a judge had been passed by either House of Parliament. As many as 189 members voted in favour of the motion to impeach the fifty-three-year-old judge after a two-day debate on the issue. Seventeen members voted against. Members belonging to the BSP opposed the motion. TMC MPs were absent during voting. The impeachment motion was to come up before the Lok Sabha following week. If passed by a 2/3rds majority in the Lok Sabha, the motion was to be referred to the President who would order Justice Sen's removal as a judge. But Justice Sen, who was accused of misappropriating funds, resigned before the matter could be brought before the Lok Sabha.

Notably, while impeachment proceedings against Justice Sen were being debated in the Parliament, Justice P.D. Dinakaran, Chief Justice of the Sikkim High Court, against whom the Rajya Sabha chairman had set up a judicial panel to look into allegations of corruption, resigned in July 2011 before impeachment proceedings could be initiated against him. He was facing charges of corruption, land-grab, and abuse of judicial office.

★

While Jaitley fought fiercely for independence of the institution and dignity of judges, he believed firmly that the judiciary should respect the executive's turf and favoured a greater role for the executive in the appointment of judges. Jaitley was vocally critical of the prevailing collegium system for its lack of transparency, subjectivity, and potential for favouritism. He advocated for a more objective and transparent system based on clear criteria.

India holds the unusual distinction of being a democracy in which judges effectively appoint themselves. The Emergency left a marked imprint on the judiciary, and the process of appointing Supreme Court judges was no exception. It would not be inaccurate to say that the shift from the appointment system envisioned by the Constitution's framers to the one in operation today can, to a significant extent, be traced back to the impact of the Emergency.

The balance of power between the executive and the judiciary in the appointments process gradually but markedly shifted in favour of the judiciary in the decades after the Emergency. This swing was a response to the executive's dominance during the Emergency, particularly in matters concerning the judiciary. The excesses of that period have often been invoked to justify granting the judiciary primacy in appointments.[2] Over time, and through a succession of judicial rulings, the courts steadily curtailed the executive's role in the selection of judges.

By way of background, in 1993, the Supreme Court held that the power of appointment of judges of the Supreme Court and high courts would hereinafter wrest with a collegium of senior-most judges of the court. A judicial collegium to appoint judges of the Supreme Court and high courts was a response to feared executive overreach in appointments.[3] In interpreting the appointments provisions under Articles 124(2) and 217(1), the seven-judge majority (with five judges writing through Justice J.S. Verma) held that when constitutional authorities disagree over judicial appointments, the Chief Justice of India's view must prevail. This view was to reflect the collective opinion of the judiciary, expressed through the CJI. To form it, the CJI—as the judiciary's representative—was required to consult the two senior-most judges, constituting the judicial collegium, along with any other judge possessing relevant knowledge. The court further held that no appointment could be finalised by the President without a clear, affirmative recommendation from the CJI.

Soon after the genesis of the idea of the collegium to appoint judges, there was a stand-off between the executive and the judiciary. The interpretive confusion led to a Presidential Reference where nine questions were asked of the Supreme Court by the President.[4] In a unanimous opinion, the court firmly underlined the significance of the collegium and gave a concrete shape to it.[5] The judgment broadened the collegium to include the CJI and the

---

2. T.R. Andhyarujina, "A Committed Judiciary: Indira Gandhi and Judicial Appointments", in Arghya Sengupta and Ritwika Sharma (eds), *Appointment of Judges to the Supreme Court of India: Transparency, Accountability, and Independence* (Oxford University Press, 2018), pp. 18–30.

3. *Supreme Court Advocates-on-Record Association vs Union of India*, (1993) 3 SCC 441.

4. Arun Jaitley, "The Judicial Collegium: Issues, Controversies, and the Road Ahead", in Arghya Sengupta and Ritwika Sharma (eds), *Appointment of Judges to the Supreme Court of India: Transparency, Accountability, and Independence* (Oxford University Press, 2018), pp. 45–55.

5. *Special Reference No. 1 of 1998, Re*, (1998) 7 SCC 739.

four senior-most judges for Supreme Court appointments, and the CJI with his two senior-most colleagues for high court appointments. It also required consultation with the senior-most Supreme Court judge familiar with the high court from which a prospective appointee originated (in the case of Supreme Court appointments) or to which the candidate was being considered (for high court appointments).

Both judgments grounded their reading of Articles 124 and 217 in the principle of judicial independence—a core constitutional objective that, they held, would be compromised if the executive enjoyed primacy. The rulings set out different collegium compositions for appointments to the Supreme Court, to the high courts, and for transfers between high courts. Yet across all categories, they decisively affirmed that the collegium would have the final say: the government could raise objections, but if the collegium unanimously reiterated its recommendation, the appointment had to be made.

The collegium process was described by a retired Supreme Court judge and a former member of the collegium as "one of the best kept secrets in the country".[6] Jaitley said:

> The Constitution envisages an important role for the executive. It is a part of the democratic accountability. Past experiences perhaps weighed with the court in diluting the role of the executive in judicial appointments. The executive can give inputs, it can even refer a recommendation back with relevant inputs for reconsideration but is eventually bound by the recommendations. This is contrary to the text of the Constitution.[7]

Jaitley believed that an independent and fearless judiciary was necessary to ensure the its independence and freedom from external pressures and favoured

---

6. Arun Jaitley, "The Judicial Collegium: Issues, Controversies, and the Road Ahead", in Arghya Sengupta and Ritwika Sharma (eds), *Appointment of Judges to the Supreme Court of India: Transparency, Accountability, and Independence* (Oxford University Press, 2018), pp. 45–55.

7. Arun Jaitley, "Recollecting an Important Chapter of History—Judicial Appointments", accessed 24 August 2025, https://www.arunjaitley.com/recollecting-an-important-chapter-of-history-judicial-appointments/.

the judiciary's extensive power to review executive decisions and legislative actions. He believed in maintaining a balance of power between the judiciary, the legislature, and the executive. He shared his experience from the time he was the law minister in the Vajpayee government. He recalled that a particular candidate was recommended as a judge by the collegium to the Madras High Court.

> The recommendation was returned by the central government because of adverse inputs. Despite such inputs, the recommendation was reiterated. In the second round, President A.P.J. Abdul Kalam returned the recommendation giving detailed reasons. The President was overruled by the collegium and the recommendation was reiterated for a second time. The nominee was appointed as an additional judge. His performance as a judge raised many eyebrows confirming the government inputs and the President's concerns. He was not confirmed as a permanent judge. In another case, the central government raised serious security concerns about a candidate recommended for judgeship in the Jammu and Kashmir High Court. The concerns were overruled and he was confirmed as a judge. A series of orders passed by him in a sensitive case in the High Court helped the cause of separatists. Equally crucially, the presence of the executive also grants democratic legitimacy to the appointments process due to the accountability of the executive to the citizens of the country. This is why the world over, as well as in the debates in our Constituent Assembly, appointment of judges is considered a core executive function.[8]

Jaitley favoured a comprehensive approach to judicial reforms, including the establishment of clear criteria for judicial appointments and addressing the issue of post-retirement appointments for judges. He also raised concerns

---

8. Arun Jaitley, "The Judicial Collegium: Issues, Controversies, and the Road Ahead", in Arghya Sengupta and Ritwika Sharma (eds), *Appointment of Judges to the Supreme Court of India: Transparency, Accountability, and Independence* (Oxford University Press, 2018), pp. 45–55.

about increasing judicial activism and its impact on the separation of powers. He emphasised the importance of judicial restraint and the need for the judiciary to focus on its core functions.[9] During his speech as the Leader of the Opposition on the impeachment of Justice Soumitra Sen of the Calcutta High Court in August 2011, Jaitley said that the process of appointments of judges had to be revisited. Emphatically arguing in favour of revisiting the appointments process, he observed:

> Originally, when the Constitution was framed, we had a system where judges were appointed by the Executive Government in consultation with the Chief Justice of India. Ordinarily, the government would be bound by the Chief Justice's advice. In 1993, that system got changed by a judicial interpretation and the advice of the Chief Justice of India was binding on the Executive Government. That is the position today. Today, even though the government is a part of the consultation process, it can refer back the case once, but effectively, our experience has been, this was the experience when the NDA government was in power, this is the experience of the present government, that we are living in a system where judges appoint judges. The government, at best, has only a very marginal say. There is no other process by which there is any kind of a participation in the process of appointment of judges.
>
> The best in this country are not willing to become Judges. We have to seriously consider why. We should seriously consider a system which is being debated about setting up a National Judicial Commission. The National Judicial Commission must have judges. It must have the participation of the executive. It can also have participation of the people selected by a collegium of some eminent citizens. It can't only remain the domain of the judges. Therefore, public interest has to be protected in the matter of appointment of competent judges, in the matter of appointment of judges who are men of integrity, men of scholarship. Not only this, the criteria for appointment today does

---

9. Arun Jaitley in Parliament: Fight Against Terror Is a Battle—India Cannot Afford to Lose", Bharatiya Janata Party, available at https://www.bjp.org/files/books-monographs/arun-jaitley-fight-against-terrorism.pdf.

> not exist. Is it today the discretion of the collegium? Collegium is also a system of sharing the spoils. When the High Courts recommend, members of the collegium share the spoils. This is an impression which close observers have. Therefore, the discretion whether the collegium system continues or we have a National Judicial Commission must also be now statutorily regulated so that arbitrariness can be avoided. ... Therefore, we need ... a system where this should be seriously reviewed.[10]

★

In the year 2014, after the NDA formed the government, the two Houses of Parliament and twenty legislative assemblies passed the Constitution (99th Amendment) Bill, 2014, which established the National Judicial Appointments Commission (NJAC). The National Judicial Appointments Commission Act, 2014 (NJAC Act), which contained the procedure to be followed by the NJAC in recommending appointments to the President of India, was also enacted.

The Constitution (99th Amendment) Bill, 2014, sought to replace the twenty-two-year-old collegium system, where judges appoint judges. This, Parliament expressed, impinged on the concepts of separation of powers and the basic structure of the Constitution. The bill received Presidential assent on 31 December 2014, upon which it became the Constitution (99th Amendment) Act, 2014. Article 124-A was inserted, which provided for the establishment of a six-member NJAC comprising the CJI; two senior-most judges of the Supreme Court; the Union minister for law and justice; two eminent persons nominated jointly by the prime minister, the CJI and the Leader of the Opposition in the Lok Sabha.[11]

---

10. "Arun Jaitley in Parliament: Fight Against Terror Is a Battle—India Cannot Afford to Lose", Bharatiya Janata Party, available at https://www.bjp.org/files/books-monographs/arun-jaitley-fight-against-terrorism.pdf.

11. Notification dated 31 December 2014, Ministry of Law and Justice, accessed 28 September 2025, https://prsindia.org/files/bills_acts/acts_parliament/2014/the-constitution-(99th-amendment)-act,-2014.pdf.

Thus, the judicial component, which prior to the 99th Amendment had primacy, was reduced to half its strength in the NJAC. The CJI would have equal voting rights as other members, and even though designated as the chairman of the NJAC, the CJI was not vested with a casting vote in the event of a tie. If the CJI and two other senior judges on the NJAC supported the appointment/transfer of an individual, the same could be negatived by any of the other two members, including two eminent persons. Through Article 124-C, the details of the selection process were delegated to parliamentary legislation, in pursuance of which the legislature framed the NJAC Act.[12]

Although Jaitley was not holding the portfolio of law, the government leaned heavily on him and Attorney General Mukul Rohatgi in taking this step. Much before the 99th Amendment, Jaitley openly expressed his support for the National Judicial Commission. He defended the 99th Amendment and highlighted the BJP's consistent support for such a commission, dating back to before 1993. As far back as in 2011, Jaitley had proposed the NJAC and emphasised that separation of powers requires that every institution works in its own spheres. Speaking in Parliament then, he stated every institution has to lay down the lakshman rekha of its own jurisdiction.

> But why is it necessary to lay down lakshman rekha of its own jurisdiction? What happens if one steps into the other's domain? And I must candidly confess that this attempt to encroach upon the lakshman rekha is neither coming from governments of the day in the Centre or the states nor is it coming from the executive or the legislature. Some serious sidestepping is coming from the judicial institution itself. Therefore, we require a certain element of judicial statesmanship; we require a certain legislative vision so that we can maintain this separation of powers. Otherwise, what should be the economic philosophy of India? What should be our economic policy? Whether we go to the post-91 policy of liberalisation or we go to state controls is the matter entirely for the executive. Courts cannot say that

---

12. Gopal Subramanium, "The NJAC Case and Judicial Independence: Conceptual and Contextual Safeguards", in Arghya Sengupta and Ritwika Sharma (Eds.), *Appointment of Judges to the Supreme Court of India: Transparency, Accountability, and Independence* (Oxford University Press, 2018), pp. 168–94.

> this is neoliberalism which is creating problems. Courts cannot have an ideology. The only ideology that courts can have is commitment to the rule of law and what law is made by Parliament', he said in his speech in Parliament.[13]

The NJAC was to be the defining judicial reform of the new NDA government that had swept into power in 2014. However, even before it could start functioning, petitions to strike it down had been filed in the Supreme Court. Both the 99th Amendment and the NJAC were challenged. In the summer of 2015, over a period of thirty-two days, the Supreme Court of India heard arguments in *Supreme Court Advocates-on-Record Association and others vs Union of India and others* (NJAC Case).[14]

The government argued for several days as to why the matter must be referred to a larger bench. This argument was made so that Supreme Court Advocates-on-Record Association vs Union of India[15] (Second Judges' Case) could be reconsidered and its ambiguities resolved. This is the second judgment in what are known as the three "Judges' Cases" in the Indian Supreme Court's jurisprudence. This request was, however, denied. The court continued hearing the matter through its summer vacation. On 15 July 2015, the hearings concluded and the court reserved judgment. Soon after, the Supreme Court of India, by a majority opinion, struck down the 99th Constitution Amendment.

Jaitley was disappointed with the verdict. In his first comments on the Supreme Court's striking down of the NJAC, Jaitley asserted that Indian democracy cannot be "a tyranny of the unelected".[16] He argued that the court

---

13. "Arun Jaitley in Parliament: Fight Against Terror Is a Battle—India Cannot Afford to Lose", Bharatiya Janata Party, available at https://www.bjp.org/files/books-monographs/arun-jaitley-fight-against-terrorism.pdf.

14. "Introduction", in Arghya Sengupta and Ritwika Sharma (eds), *Appointment of Judges to the Supreme Court of India: Transparency, Accountability, and Independence* (Oxford University Press, 2018), pp. xiii–xxiv.

15. *SP Gupta vs Union of India*, 1981 Supp SCC 87 is known as the *First Judges' Case*, and *Special Reference No. 1 of 1998, Re*, (1998) 7 SCC 739 is known as the *Third Judges' Case*.

16. Arun Jaitley, "The NJAC Judgement—An Alternative View", accessed 24 August 2025, https://www.facebook.com/ArunJaitley/posts/the-njac-judgement-an-alternative-viewthe-supreme-court-of-india-by-a-majority-o/418492815005939/.

had overstepped its bounds by attempting to re-legislate and rewrite the law, effectively arrogating legislative powers. Later, he expressed his views on the judgment in a Facebook post[17] on 18 October 2015, which he clarified as his "personal views". He wrote:

> Having read the opinion of the five Hon'ble Judges, a few issues arise in my mind. The key rationale behind the majority opinion appears to be that the independence of the judiciary is an essential ingredient of the basic structure of the Constitution. This is unquestionably a correct proposition. Having stated this, the majority transgresses into an erroneous logic. It argues that the presence of a law minister in the commission and the appointment of two eminent persons in the commission by a group, which will, besides Chief Justice of India, comprise the Prime Minister and the Leader of the Opposition, will constitute political involvement in the judicial appointments. Judges appointed on this basis may feel grateful to the politicians. Political persons would be obviously guided by their political interest. The judges warn of "adverse" consequences if politicians were a part of the appointments process. Hence protection of the judiciary from political persons was essential. This is the key reason on which the constitution amendment, unanimously passed by both the Houses of Parliament and the State Legislature, has been struck down.[18]

He said that the judgment ignored the larger constitutional structure of India. Unquestionably independence of the judiciary is a part of the basic structure of the Constitution. It needs to be preserved. But the judgment ignored the fact that there are several other features of the Constitution which comprise the basic structure. The most important basic structure of the Indian Constitution is parliamentary democracy. The next important basic structure of the Indian Constitution is an elected government which represents the will of the sovereign. In parliamentary democracy the prime minister is the most important accountable institution. The Leader of the Opposition is an essential

17. Ibid.

18. Ibid.

aspect of that basic structure representing the alternative voice in Parliament. The law minister represents a key basic structure of the Constitution; the Council of Ministers is accountable to Parliament.

All these institutions, parliamentary sovereignty, an elected government, a prime minister, a Leader of Opposition, and a law minister are a part of the Constitution's basic structure. They represent the will of the people. The majority opinion was understandably concerned with one basic structure—independence of the judiciary—but rubbished all other basic structures by referring to them as "politicians" and passing the judgment on a rationale that India's democracy has to be saved from its elected representatives. The judgment upheld the primacy of one basic structure but diminished five other basic structures of the Constitution.

A constitutional court, while interpreting the Constitution, had to base the judgment on constitutional principles. There is no constitutional principle that democracy and its institutions have to be saved from elected representatives. "Are not institutions like the Election Commission and the CAG credible enough even though they are appointed by elected Governments?" Jaitley said. He argued that democracy would be jeopardised if the authority of elected representatives were diminished. He emphasised that strengthening judicial independence does not necessitate undermining parliamentary sovereignty.

Jaitley faulted the five-judge bench's judgment as based on "erroneous logic" that the independence of the judiciary would be compromised because of political involvement. He criticised the "political bashing" in the judgment and asserted that history has demonstrated that the judiciary is not the sole guardian of democracy. He pointed out that politicians had spearheaded the fight to defend democracy during the Emergency of 1975–77, a period when the Supreme Court, according to Jaitley, had faltered. "If ... there are dangers of emergency, there is no presumption that only the Supreme Court can save it," Jaitley wrote in his Facebook post. At the same time, "There is no principle in democracy anywhere in the world that institutions of democracy are to be saved from the elected."

As someone who had spent more years in court than in Parliament, Jaitley felt constrained to speak out for Indian democracy. He emphasised that as someone who was equally concerned about the independence of the judiciary and the sovereignty of India's Parliament, he believed that the two could and must coexist. Independence of the judiciary was an important basic structure of the Constitution. To strengthen it, one does not have to weaken parliamentary sovereignty which is not only an essential basic structure but is the soul of Indian democracy. He said that while the Supreme Court's opinion was final, it is not infallible.

A year later, Jaitley wrote that a harmonious balance could be struck in an appointing body if it comprises a few judges and, at the same time, has some participation from the executive as well as from members of the public (akin to the eminent persons on the NJAC). The presence of judicial members was essential so as to prevent the kind of situation which existed at the time of the Emergency. The executive branch made serious inroads into judicial independence, and appointments were tainted by executive interference. Judicial members on the appointing authority would act as a buffer against any such executive interference in appointments in the future, as was sought to be done by the NJAC.

However, at the same time, executive participation in the appointing body cannot be wished away, or worse still, startlingly held unconstitutional (as in the NJAC Case). The executive performs the important function of providing information on the antecedents of potential appointees. Lastly, the presence of members of the public, or lay persons, would ensure that citizens who are the ultimate consumers of justice also have a voice in the judicial appointments process. Several countries across the world have opened their judicial appointments processes to participation from the citizens. There is no reason, except the country's own hubris and a frog-in-the-well attitude, as to why India should continue its antiquated, opaque, and semi-feudal practices, keeping its own citizens out of key decision-making functions.[19]

The process of judicial appointments in India is at the cusp of major developments and reform. Even though the NJAC as an appointing body did not see the light of day, the principled changes that it sought to usher in can still be embraced. The collegium system, as formulated by the judgments in the Second and Third Judges' Cases, has been mired in controversy for manifold

19. Arun Jaitley, "The Judicial Collegium: Issues, Controversies, and the Road Ahead", in Arghya Sengupta and Ritwika Sharma (eds), *Appointment of Judges to the Supreme Court of India: Transparency, Accountability, and Independence* (Oxford University Press, 2018), pp. 45–55.

reasons. It is time that the collegium system opens itself to real reform if it has to deliver the judges that India deserves.[20]

Jaitley has gone but the search for a mechanism for appointments that acts as a check against pressures from the government and from within the judiciary must continue if the Indian higher judiciary is to become truly independent.

Jaitley did not favour judges accepting appointments after retirement. As he eloquently observed:

> I have always believed that we must seriously consider this larger issue of almost every retiring judge, barring a few honourable exceptions, holding a belief that he is entitled to a job after retirement. Jobs have been provided in certain statutes; they are created by certain judicial orders. Therefore, search for a job on the eve of retirement begins, as a result of which there is a serious doubt which is raised that retirement eve judgments at times get influenced by the desire to get a job after retirement. Therefore, I think when there is a Bill pending with regard to increasing the retirement age from 62 to 65 in the case of High Court Judges, we should correspondingly think of increasing the strength of judges, even increasing the facilities, remuneration and pension available, but putting a stop to this practice of everybody being entitled to a job after retirement. The desire for a job after retirement is now becoming a serious threat to judicial independence.
>
> Lastly, Sir, it is just a brief comment. I have said in the very beginning that the separation of powers is one of the basic features of our Constitution. At times it's argued that the separation of powers is threatened because governments of the day don't want an independent judiciary. They want to influence the independence of the judiciary. So the theories like committed judges, judges with the social philosophy were all propounded at one point in time. Those are now ideas of the past.[21]

---

20. Ibid.

21. "Arun Jaitley in Parliament: Fight Against Terror Is a Battle—India Cannot Afford to Lose", Bharatiya Janata Party, available at https://www.bjp.org/files/books-monographs/arun-jaitley-fight-against-terrorism.pdf.

Index

C

D

H

I

J

K

L

M

N

O

P

Q

R

S

T

U

V

W

Y

Author's Note

Political observers are often better suited to writing a political biography. Their experience and knowledge qualify them to write about a political person, and their style of reportage makes complex personalities comprehensible to the reader. Furthermore, writing someone's personal biography requires an intimate, long-standing acquaintance with the subject.

I am neither a journalist nor a political observer. Nor did I have the privilege of knowing Shri Arun Jaitley personally enough to gain insights necessary to write his personal biography. My association with him was primarily professional. First, as a young lawyer in awe of an outstanding lawyer with a razor-sharp legal mind, and later, as an admirer of the statesman who ushered path-breaking reforms through many responsibilities.

Yet, despite lacking these qualifications, I undertook the challenging task of navigating the vast landscape of Shri Jaitley's remarkable life. My determination stemmed from a single objective: the story of this extraordinary man had to be told. It is a story meant for the youth of this country and for all who have grown disillusioned with politics, to remind them that there are leaders who stand apart. They should know of this many-sided figure: a legal luminary whose arguments could move the highest courts; one of India's most articulate and influential voices, who elevated public discourse whether or not one agreed with him; a political strategist with friends across party lines and an unparalleled sense of the nation's mood; a visionary finance minister who guided the economy through global turbulence; and an orator capable of untangling the most complex issues with striking clarity. And behind these public roles stood a man of immense warmth, sparkling wit, and steadfast loyalty.

Shri Arun Jaitley was a great reformist, politician and jurist. With his death, an era of refined leadership defined by consensus, humour, charm, wit, vision, intelligence and humility came to an end. His death has left a vacuum in current politics which will be difficult to fill. To paraphrase Shri Jaitley's friend Ashok Malik: When Thomas Jefferson took over from Benjamin Franklin as the American diplomatic representative (ambassador, in today's terms) to France, an acquaintance in Paris is supposed to have asked him, "Have you replaced Ben Franklin?" Jefferson, it is said, shook his head: "No one can replace him. I have only succeeded him." Shri Arun Jaitley's passing evokes a similar sentiment. Capturing this formidable public figure and the compassionate private individual has been my central endeavour in this book.

This book is the culmination of years of research, of nights spent wrestling with history and memory. As I said I am neither a journalist nor a political observer. I am an author who writes non-fiction and fiction books. Both genres require meticulous research and analysis. Writing the biography, particularly of a statesman, requires deep study of the political conditions of his age; the state of the country and also of the society in which he was born and grew up. The character and nature of such person is deeply affected by the events and experiences around him that shape his juvenile mind into a genius. I have studied the vast body of literature including the work left behind by Shri Jaitley himself—his speeches, articles, and interviews, many fragmented, only a few organized. I stand indebted to the countless writers, political analysists, journalists whose works illuminated my path, shaping my understanding of Shri Jaitley and his times even as I wove it with my own understanding of the man. Though I have acknowledged them in my notes, I seek forgiveness for any omissions—for every name left unsaid, every voice uncredited. Also, in a mammoth task such as this, there are bound to be overlaps between chapters as it is often impossible to separate the jurist from the politician and the reformist. So, even at the risk of some repetition, some aspects find mention across chapters.

This book would not have been possible without the insights and recollections of those I interviewed—Shri Jaitley's friends, lawyers, bureaucrats and admirers. Everyone I spoke to had an Arun Jaitley story to tell, all fond memories. Their stories of his legal acumen, his backroom political manoeuvres, his love for food and cricket, and his steadfast friendship brought depth and colour to the historical record. I offer my sincere thanks to them.

Of the many reforms he championed, I was involved in a few of the legal ones, primarily in insolvency and debt recovery laws, from the time I was barely thirty. In a way, I was a beneficiary of his mentorship. Yet, I have not allowed my deep admiration to compromise objectivity or the integrity of this narrative.

My gratitude extends to the team at Om Books International, particularly my editor, Shantanu Ray Chaudhuri, with whom this is my fifth book. The meticulous fact-checking by freelance copy editor A.R. Lakhshmitha was indispensable in ensuring this account's accuracy and integrity. My heartfelt thanks to her. Any shortcomings in this narrative are mine alone.

My family—my wife, Asha, and my children, Dev and Siya—have observed me reading and writing relentlessly, whether case pleadings or literature. Their respect and understanding of my passions, within and beyond the law, have kept me going. I also thank my associates and colleagues in my law chamber for their patience and skill in managing case briefings during my long hours of research and writing.

Shri Arun Jaitley's life was a masterclass in the art of the possible. It is my earnest hope that this book serves not only as a record of his monumental contributions but also as an inspiration, reminding us of the power of intellect, the importance of civility in public discourse, and the enduring value of a well-lived life. I hope this book does justice to his great legacy within its limited pages, elicits optimism in politics, and encourages the youth to follow the path of Shri Arun Jaitley in politics, law, and governance.